Words and Pictures

Lessons in Children's Literature and Literacies

Nina Mikkelsen
Indiana University of Pennsylvania

Boston Burr Ridge, IL Dubuque, IA Madison, WI New York San Francisco St. Louis
Bangkok Bogotá Caracas Lisbon London Madrid
Mexico City Milan New Delhi Seoul Singapore Sydney Taipei Toronto

McGraw-Hill Higher Education

A Division of The **McGraw-Hill** *Companies*

WORDS AND PICTURES: LESSONS IN CHILDREN'S LITERATURE AND LITERACIES

This book is printed on acid-free paper.

1 2 3 4 5 6 7 8 9 0 QPF/QPF 0 9 8 7 6 5 4 3 2 1 0

ISBN 0–697–39357–7

Editorial director: *Jane E. Vaicunas*
Sponsoring editor: *Beth Kaufman*
Developmental editor: *Cara Harvey*
Marketing manager: *Daniel M. Loch*
Project manager: *Mary Lee Harms*
Production supervisor: *Sandy Ludovissy*
Coordinator of freelance design: *Rick Noel*
Senior photo research coordinator: *Lori Hancock*
Senior supplement coordinator: *David A. Welsh*
Compositor: *Shepherd, Inc.*
Typeface: *10/12 Times Roman*
Printer: *Quebecor Printing Book Group/Fairfield, PA*

Cover designer: *Mary Sailer*
Cover art: From *PRETEND YOU'RE A CAT* by Jean Marzollo, pictures by Jerry Pinkney.

Library of Congress Cataloging-in-Publication Data

Mikkelsen, Nina.
Words and pictures : lessons in children's literature and literacies / Nina Mikkelsen.—1st ed.
p. cm.
Includes bibliographical references (p. 462) and index.
ISBN 0–697–39357–7
1. Children's literature—Study and teaching (Elementary)
2. Children—Books and reading. 3. Literature based approach in education. I. Title.
LB1575.M55 2000
372.64—dc21 99–24055
CIP

www.mhhe.com

About the Author

Nina Mikkelsen, author of *Words and Pictures: Lessons in Children's Literature and Literacies,* received her Ph.D. in English from Florida State University. She has completed postdoctoral work in children's literature and literacy at Ohio State University with Charlotte Huck and at Columbia University Teachers College with Lucy Calkins; and at Columbia University School of Library Science, she studied children's literature with Brian Alderson and Roger Sutton. Mikkelsen has taught at universities in Florida, North Carolina, and Pennsylvania in both the English and Elementary Education departments. She is presently teaching at Indiana University of Pennsylvania. She has taught students in the elementary and middle grades in the areas of literature and literacy connections, writing process, and storymaking, and she has instructed college students in children's literature, reading methods, the teaching of writing, college writing, and humanities literature. Her research interests include the cultural contexts of children's literature, multicultural/cross-cultural/multiethnic literature, children's storymaking processes, children's responses to literature, literacy through literature as a classroom teaching approach, and portfolio assessment in the literature class. She has published articles and essays in *Language Arts, The Reading Teacher, New Advocate, English Journal, Children's Literature Association Quarterly, Journal of Youth Services in Libraries, African American Review, Touchstones II,* and *Canadian Children's Literature.* She is also the author of *Virginia Hamilton* (Twayne, 1994), *Susan Cooper* (Twayne, 1998), and *Discussion Guide to Novels of Virginia Hamilton* (Scholastic, 1999).

About the Author

Brief Contents

Part One
LITERATURE AND SOCIETY: CULTURAL CONTEXTS

Part Two
READERS AND WRITERS: CREATIVE PROCESSES

Part Three
CHILDREN AND ADULTS: LEARNING AND TEACHING

Contents

Part Two
READERS AND WRITERS: CREATIVE PROCESSES

Part Three
CHILDREN AND ADULTS: LEARNING AND TEACHING

Preface

Words and Pictures: Lessons in Children's Literature and Literacies is a textbook for preservice or in-service elementary and middle school teachers who are participating in literature-based college classrooms. The "real" books/whole books movement has changed classrooms at all levels. Students reading a wide variety of children's books in their entirety, rather than excerpts in anthologies, need more time for *experiencing* children's literature. At the same time, they need some way to build understandings about this vast assortment of materials, as well as to enrich their reading.

Many special areas are converging upon and shaping the world of children's books now: social contexts (cultural, historical, and political); the authoring process; mediation techniques; literature and literacy approaches for classroom teaching; the classroom book collection; multicultural concerns; and reader response practices. Teachers need a wealth of information as they begin orchestrating their own literature and literacy programs for integrated and interdisciplinary uses. Prospective teachers cannot begin too soon to learn about children's books in all their diversity and versatility.

Words and Pictures focuses on each of these important areas. At the same time, it encourages—and allows—students to read the *real* books; it is not so consuming that it squeezes out time for exploring the books themselves. On the other hand, *Words and Pictures* is extensive enough to give students an expansive view of the world of children's books and their effects on classroom teaching. Students need to read more of these books, but to read them with an understanding of how they fit in to classroom reading instruction.

Taking as it does a broad view of children's literature, *Words and Pictures* can be used as a core text for classes in children's literature and for integrated literature and literacy classes. It can also be used as a supplementary text for reading and language arts classes focusing on literature-based reading and writing programs. In addition, it can be used in upper-level courses that focus on special topics in literature and literacy.

This book has a threefold purpose: to discuss the *conceptual* base of children's literature (the books themselves), the *experiential* base of literature (adult and child authors), and the *practice* of teaching with children's literature (the classroom setting). Thus, the "Words" of the title *Words and Pictures* are the words of children's book authors, teachers, and prospective teachers, critics, and the children themselves—the real insiders. The "Pictures" of the title refer to reprinted illustrations from children's books and descriptions of children, teachers, and the learning process that weave through the book generally.

The three-part purpose corresponds to a three-part structure. Part 1 begins by taking readers right into the world of children's books *now,* with a look at children in three classroom settings examining and responding to three very different kinds of children's books: a picture book, a children's novel, and a collection of folk tales. It continues by taking readers back into earlier times to see how the modern world of children's books came to be—especially how it came to be organized around different genres with different themes, conventions, criticism, and awards.

The section, as a unit, thus presents information about the history, themes, genres, conventions, and important examples of children's literature. Discussion of each of these areas continues throughout the text. Each is an integral part of the literacy process and the classroom, but each also works in combination with the others against the backdrop of the sociocultural context. To separate these areas for examination, at least for any length of time, is impossible both in life and in literature study.

When readers explore the children's book world from a number of different vantage points, looking at elements such as genre, theme, and conventions, they are better prepared—and even eager—to learn about how writers create literature and how readers respond to it. Thus, they are ready for Part 2 of this book.

Part 2 emphasizes the many ways that authors use to create stories and the many ways readers—both adults and children—respond to them in talk and storytelling of their own. This section takes readers behind the scenes to see more about the inner workings of books—or the way the human mind works when it conceives—or receives—literature for children. Students will learn about the many ways readers take on texts, or how they read and write in generative, personal/empathetic, sociocultural, literary, narrative, aesthetic, and critical ways. Students who learn how literature comes to life for both readers and writers are better prepared—and again, more eager—to help bring literature to life in the classroom. At this point, they are ready for Part 3 of this book.

Part 3 focuses on literature-based classroom practices: teaching reading and writing and encouraging storymaking with children's books; defining the purposes for literature-based teaching; and engaging in collaborative planning, teaching, and assessment. This section takes readers right into the classroom, where children's books thread through so many aspects of the instructional program these days. Prospective teachers who learn how teachers use children's books in the classroom are better able—and more eager—to create literature and literacy classrooms of their own.

Each of the three parts and the individual chapters in them include *Investigations.* These activities invite readers to reflect on and *apply* the knowledge they are gaining in productive and creative ways with actual children's books—and, in many instances, with actual children. If prospective teachers

- participate as members of literature study groups—or "circles",
- respond to literature in journals,
- share literature with children and elicit their responses,
- start building classroom book collections of their own,
- tell and write stories and poems,
- explore their own heritage and identity in creative ventures, and
- create literature portfolios and engage in self-assessment procedures,

they are much better prepared—and more likely—to work with children to assist them in these practices.

If students have thought about literary history, themes, genres, and conventions in integrated, interdisciplinary ways—or in terms of social and cultural contexts—they will be better able to teach in interdisciplinary ways. If prospective teachers are to break the cycle of compartmentalized thinking that keeps the real world and the classroom world so artificially separated, they must read with an interdisciplinary viewpoint and learn to integrate not just the "core" curriculum areas—history, science, math, and the fine arts—with literature, but also the smaller components of real-life learning and the curriculum. They must see that literary genres permeate every aspect of literature, that genre is a convention, and that conventions permeate every aspect, also. They must see that history is occurring *now,* as they make it, and that literary themes pervade this history. They must see that new themes, conventions, and genres emerge all the time, and they must comprehend how writers and readers bring them about.

Nearly every chapter contains discussions of multicultural literature, an important new genre, subject category, or literacy within children's literature. Prospective teachers will see that the literature of diversity weaves through all eras, themes, genres, and conventions, and they will be better prepared—and more likely—to emphasize it in their own classrooms in the future.

Part 1, Literature and Society: Cultural Contexts, begins with Chapter 1, which focuses on the "conversation" between authors and readers (adults and children) through the generations. Throughout the various historical eras, so many new ways of writing and illustrating books for children have emerged that we might wonder what kinds of personal, social, and cultural worlds authors and illustrators have been making and how these story worlds combine to produce the larger, cohesive world of children's literature.

Chapter 2 describes books and literary genres that have endured, as it asks, What is a children's book, and how does such a book emerge from the cultural context of its own time and place? What are the important themes of children's literature?

Chapter 3 looks at the way genres are constructed and how the award-winning books of a culture, reflecting as they do society's interests at particular times, produce a many-faceted picture of genre for readers.

Chapter 4 investigates how ideas about gender, class, and ethnicity affect what writers and illustrators do, as they adopt and innovate from the traditional practices of others.

Chapter 5 asks, What makes a children's book good in terms of adult values? What causes the adult "gatekeepers" to decide that one particular picture book is better than another? How do adults decide what books they will share with children and what books they will invite children to choose for themselves? How do adults decide what books they will ignore or suppress?

Lists of children's books appear at the end of chapters 1 through 5 to illuminate genres, concepts, themes, and ideas that arise in these chapters.

Part 2, Readers and Writers: Creative Processes begins with Chapter 6, which investigates how authors (writers and illustrators) produce books for children. What is the nature of the creative process, and what are its sources? How do writers find ideas and reshape them into imaginary worlds? How does learning more about these processes deepen the reader's understanding of children's books themselves?

Chapter 7 explores the creative process further, asking, What can we learn about the more specific worlds of underrepresented ethnicities? How do writers and artists produce authentic multicultural literature?

Chapter 8 asks, How do texts teach? How do readers take in these texts, and how do child readers respond to literature? How is reading a children's book different for children and adults—or is it?

Part 3, Children and Adults: Learning and Teaching begins with Chapter 9, which describes how adults teach reading using children's books and how many different literacies intersect when they do. It goes on to describe how adults teach reading, writing, and storymaking in connected ways—and in ways that connect with literature—or how children learn about *literacy* through literature.

Chapter 10 asks, Why do we teach with children's books throughout the classroom day, across the curriculum, and within the language and literacy program? What do children learn when we do?

Chapter 11 poses yet more questions: How do we help students develop as readers and writers? How can we plan for and assess their competencies, understandings, and use of the literature and literacy process? How do collaborative practices shape our planning, teaching, and assessment procedures?

Five appendices complete the book. The first lists multicultural children's books, categorized by theme and subject. The second lists winners of important awards in the field of children's literature; including the Caldecott, Newbery, Coretta Scott King and Pura Belpre Awards in the United States; the Kate Greenaway and Carnegie Awards in Britain; the Hans Christian Andersen Award (worldwide); the Laura Ingalls Wilder Award (United States), and the Phoenix Award (international). The third appendix discusses resources in the field of children's literature: organizations, conferences, book clubs, publications (journals, magazines, references works, media materials), and websites. The fourth records an interview with an elementary teacher, who tells about how she implemented a literature-based program in her classroom and how she selects children's books for classroom use. The fifth and final appendix describes a literature and literacies portfolio for children's literature classes, with samples of preservice teachers' work.

Four types of boxed features accompany the text. They serve as important literature and literacy experiences for learners, who can use them to take a wider, deeper, or a behind-the-scenes look at the field of children's literature.

The first contains inscriptions from Lewis Carroll's *Alice's Adventures in Wonderland.* These quoted passages introduce each chapter and also introduce readers to this classic by letting it teach a little about each of the concepts and topics under discussion.

The second type of box simply contains information to augment the text.

The third (*A Closer Look*) provides a closer—or deeper—look at a book, an author or illustrator, a concept, or an issue.

And the fourth type provides ideas—called *Investigations*—for student projects and activities, allowing students to apply their learning with real books and real children.

A teacher's guide—*Wonderland of Children's Literature*—provides a detailed outline of the book and suggestions for presenting the material and for using an integrated approach in a literature and literacies college classroom.

Nina Mikkelsen
Indiana University of Pennsylvania

Acknowledgments

I wish to thank the following individuals for their help from the beginning, when this manuscript was merely an idea, throughout the entire process of writing. First, my gratitude goes to Sue Alt of Brown & Benchmark, who worked with the manuscript in its earliest stages and who encouraged me in my plan and helped it grow, and to the McGraw-Hill editors, Beth Kaufman and Cara Harvey, who continued to encourage my plan and who offered many useful suggestions and clear and comprehensive directions along the way. Next come the copyeditor, Anne Caylor Cody, the project manager, Mary Lee Harms, the designers, Mary Sailer and Rick Noel, and the photo researcher, Shirley M. Lanners. Finally, the reviewers whose words guided so many of my revisions and who have helped in so many ways to make this book what it is:

John D. Beach, University of Nebraska at Omaha
Julia De Carlo, C.W. Post-Long Island University
Walter Prentice, University of Wisconsin-Superior
Wendy C. Kasten, Kent State University
Anita Price Davis, Converse College
Carol Fuhler, Northern Arizona University
Lucien L. Agosta, California State University
Kathryn E. Loncar, University of Missouri-Kansas City
Lynn Carol Wake, Concordia University
Marjorie R. Hancock, Kansas State University
Paul Dale Hauser, Kirkwood Community College
Vicki Olson, Augsburg College

I also wish to thank my students and colleagues at Indiana University of Pennsylvania, who have contributed so much to my learning. First, the students in my children's literature and literacy classes, too many to count or name. The ideas and writing products of Tara Burford, Sandra Fairman, Melissa Felix, David Larson, Amy Scripps, and Vincent Mikkelsen II appear in this book. I also thank Bernadette Cole-Slaughter, Department of Professional Studies, who helped with my research on Black History Month, and Rachael Fordyce, Dean of Humanities and Social Sciences from 1988 to 1992, who opened the doors to Twayne Publishers, leading to my first book, *Virginia Hamilton* (1994).

Coming to know Virginia Hamilton during the writing of that book—and long after—has contributed to my knowledge of and commitment to multicultural literature, a prominent theme in this textbook. Many thanks to both Virginia Hamilton, Yellow Springs, Ohio, and to Susan Cooper, Fairfield, Connecticut, the subject of my second book, for helping me to see so much more clearly the way children's authors work, think, and create. My thanks also to Sheila Miller, Librarian, East Pike Elementary School, Indiana, Pennsylvania, for inviting Arnold Adoff, from Yellow Springs, Ohio, to teach poetry to her students and for taping his presentations, parts of which appear in this book.

Colleagues in other times and places have been crucially important to my learning. My graduate children's literature classes with Charlotte Huck, Ohio State University, produced a lifelong quest to know more about this field and to emphasize—and honor—children's responses to literature in my work. A summer institute with Lucy Calkins, Teachers College, Columbia University, led me to explore connections among reading, writing, and children's literature, to create literature and literacy workshops with children, and to write about these ventures. Perry Nodelman, of the University of Winnipeg, published many of my first articles in *The Children's Literature Association Quarterly,* when he was the editor, 1983–1989. David Dillon of McGill University, Montreal, editor of *Language Arts* from 1983 to 1991, published much of my earliest teacher-researcher work. His editorials in *Language Arts* caused me to see with new eyes many important aspects of the literature and literacy field.

Most recently, Elizabeth Keyser of Hollins University, co-editor, with Victor Watson, Homerton College, England, of *The Cambridge Guide to Children's Literature;* Dianne Johnson-Feelings, University of South Carolina, guest editor of *African American Review*, 1998; and John Mason of Scholastic, have encouraged me to write more in the area of multicultural literature, increasing my knowledge and producing more and better information for this book.

Above all, I thank members of my family for their constant help and support before, during, and after the writing of this book. My husband, Vincent Mikkelsen, Department of Professional Studies in Education, Indiana University of Pennsylvania, and co-author of the Instructors's Manual and Test Bank for this book, makes all my work possible. At all times and places, he is there for me as listener, consultant, and computer wizard. My son, Vinny, an art and history major at IUP, who enrolled in my Children's Literature class in 1990, led me into the field of children's literature by devouring children's books from infancy on, and he and his brother Mark have kept me riveted there ever since.

My sister, Sonya, the Sara of this book, has invited me into her first- and second-grade classrooms many times to try out new ideas, read children's books, and elicit children's responses. The teacher Dawn of Chapter 11 is a composite picture of my sister, the elementary teacher, and me, the teacher-researcher. My father and mother always read aloud to us and never stopped telling stories. For years, I played more than I read, and I thank them for being patient about that.

A Note from the Author

Inscriptions to *Alice in Wonderland* that appear at the beginnings of chapters are taken from Lewis Carroll's *Alice's Adventures in Wonderland,* illustrations by Anthony Browne (New York: Knopf, 1988; rpt. 1865), pp.1 (chapter 1); 1–2 (chapter 2); 2 (chapter 3); 5–7 (chapter 4); 22–23 (chapter 5); 20 (chapter 6); 30–31 (chapter 7); 97–98 (chapter 8); 90 (chapter 9); 61 (chapter 10), and 116–117 (chapter 11).

References pertaining to scholarly and professional materials for each chapter follow the appendices, at the end of the book. Details of publication for children's books are cited within the narrative or in the lists at the ends of chapters 1 through 5.

All the names of students and teachers, except those whose names appear in the Acknowledgments or in previously published works, have been changed to protect their privacy.

I am especially pleased by the picture that Beth, Cara, and I chose for the cover of this book. And I thank Jerry Pinkney for granting permission for use of his work. His picture of the child-as-honeybee leads us magically into the world of children's literature, a place where words and pictures pollinate children's lives and children fly—on their own wings—into many wonderlands of their own.

Picture Credits

Cover

From *Pretend You're a Cat* (Dial, 1990) by Jean Marzollo; illustrated by Jerry Pinkney; edited by Phyllis Fogelman (front cover). Used by permission of Dial.

Chapter 1

From *Comet's Nine Lives* by Jan Brett. Copyright © 1996 by Jan Brett. Used by permission of G.P. Putnam's Sons, a division of Penguin Putnam, Inc.

From *The Cybil War* by Betsy Byars. Copyright © 1981 by Betsy Byars; Illustrations Copyright © 1981 by The Viking Press Inc. Used by permission of Viking Penguin, a division of Penguin Putnam Inc.

Illustrations by Barry Moser from *A Ring of Tricksters: Animal Tales from America, The West Indies, Africa* by Virginia Hamilton. Published by The Blue Sky Press, an imprint of Scholastic Inc. Copyright © 1997 by Barry Moser. Reprinted by permission of Scholastic Inc.

From Caxton's version of *Aesop's Fables*, 1484.

From The Horn Book, Inc., 56 Roland St., Suite 200, Boston, MA 02129.

Walter Crane. *"Beauty and the Beast,"* from *Walter Crane's Toy Books*, London: G. Routledge & Sons [187-], color wood engraving. Print Collection, Miriam and Ira D. Wallach Division of Art, Prints and Photographs, The New York Public Library, Astor, Lenox and Tilden Foundations.

Kate Greenaway. *"School's Over,"* from *Under the Window; Pictures and Rhymes for Children*, London: G. Routledge & Sons [1878], color wood engraving. Print Collection, Miriam and Ira D. Wallach Division of Art, Prints and Photographs, The New York Public Library, Astor, Lenox and Tilden Foundations.

Randolph Caldecott. *"Hey Diddle Diddle,"* from *R. Caldecott's Collection of Pictures and Songs,* London: G. Routledge, 188-, colored engraving. Print Collection, Miriam and Ira D. Wallach Division of Art, Prints and Photographs, The New York Public Library, Astor, Lenox and Tilden Foundations.

Cruikshank, George. *George Cruikshank's Fairy Library,* London, 1853-65?, illus. opp. p. 20 (Arents S1151). Arents Collections, The New York Public Library, Astor, Lenox and Tilden Foundations.

Hoffmann-Donner, Heinrich. *The English Struwwelpeter,* Leipzig, 1848, illustration (Spencer German 1848). Spencer Collection, The New York Public Library, Astor, Lenox and Tilden Foundations.

Harris, Joel Chandler. *Uncle Remus, His Songs and His Sayings,* with 112 illustrations by A. B. Frost: D. Appleton & Co., 1895, illustration p. 47 (HAER). General Research Division, The New York Public Library, Astor, Lenox and Tilden Foundations.

1997 National Children's Book Week Poster © 1997 by Peter Sís. Poster was commissioned by The Children's Book Council (CBC) and was reprinted by permission of the artist and the CBC. www.cbcbooks.org .

Chapter 2

Sir John Tenniel. *Alice's Adventures in Wonderland* by Lewis Carroll, London: Macmillan & Co., 1868. Wood engraving. Print Collection, Miriam and Ira D. Wallach Division of Art, Prints and Photographs, The New York Public Library, Astor, Lenox and Tilden Foundations.

Dodgson, Charles. *Alice's Adventures in Wonderland* by Lewis Carroll [pseud.] with forty-two illustrations by John Tenniel, New York: D. Appelton & Co., 1866, illustration (*KL). Rare Books Division, The New York Public Library, Astor, Lenox and Tilden Foundations.

Illustration from *The Tale of Peter Rabbit* by Beatix Potter. Copyright © Frederick Warne & Co., 1902, 1987. Reproduced by kind permission of Frederick Warne & Co.

From *Charlotte's Web* by E.B. White, illustrations by Garth Williams. Illustrations copyright renewed © 1980 by Garth Williams. Used by permission of HarperCollins Publishers.

From *Anne Frank: The Diary of a Young Girl* Jacket cover by Anne Frank. Copyright 1967. Used by permission of Doubleday, a division of Random House, Inc.

Chapter 3

Caldecott, Randolph. *R. Caldecott's Collection of Pictures and Songs,* London, 188–, illustration: *"Sing a Song of Sixpence"* (MEM). Print Collection, Miriam and Ira D. Wallach Division of Art, Prints and Photographs, The New York Public Library, Astor, Lenox and Tilden Foundations.

From *The Snowy Day* by Ezra Jack Keats. Copyright © 1962 by Ezra Jack Keats, renewed © 1990 by Martin Pope, Executor. Used by permission of Viking Penguin, a division of Penguin Putnam Inc.

From *Owl Moon* by Jane Yolen. Copyright © 1988 by Jane Yolen, text. Illustrated by John Schoenherr. Copyright © 1988 by John Schoenherr. Used by permission of Philomel Books, a division of Penguin Putnam Inc.

From *Drummer Hoff* adapted by Barbara Emberley, illustrated by Ed Emberly. Copyright © 1967 Edward R. Emberley and Barbara Emberley. Reprinted with the permission of Simon & Schuster Books for Young readers, an imprint of Simon & Schuster Children's Publishing Division.

From *Madeline's Rescue* by Ludwig Bemelmans. Copyright 1951, 1953 by Ludwig Bemelmans, renewed © 1979, 1981 by Madeline Bemelmans and Barbara Marciano. Used by permission of Viking Penguin, a division of Penguin Putnam Inc.

From *The Little House* by Virginia Lee Burton. Copyright © 1942 by Virginia Lee Demetrios, renewed 1969 by George Demetrios. Reprinted by permission of Houghton Mifflin Company. All rights reserved.

From *Make Way for Ducklings* by Robert McCloskey. Copyright 1941, renewed © 1969 by Robert McCloskey. Used by permission of Viking Penguin, a division of Penguin Putnam Inc.

From *The Little Island* by Golden MacDonald, Leonard Weisgard, illustrator. Copyright 1946 by Doubleday, a division of Bantam Doubleday Dell Publishing Group, Inc. Used by permission of Doubleday, a division of Random House, Inc.

From *Sylvester and the Magic Pebble* by William Steig. Copyright © 1969 William Steig. Reprinted with the permission of Simon & Schuster Books for Young Readers, an imprint of Simon & Schuster Children's Publishing Division.

From *Cinderella* or *The Little Glass Slipper* by Marcia Brown. Copyright 1954 Marcia Brown; copyright renewed © 1982 Marcia Brown. Reprinted with the permission of Atheneum Books for Young Readers, an imprint of Simon & Schuster Children's Publishing Division.

From *Arrow to the Sun* by Gerald McDermott. Copyright © 1974 by Gerald McDermott. Used by permission of Viking Penguin, a division of Penguin Putnam Inc.

From *A Little Pretty Pocket-Book,* Worchester, Mass., printed by Isaiah Thomas, 1787, p. 89 (*"Nothing's for Certain as Death"*) (*KD 1787). Rare Books Division, The New York Public Library, Astor, Lenox and Tilden Foundations.

From *Little House in the Big Woods* by Laura Ingalls Wilder, Garth Williams, illustrator. Pictures copyright © 1953 by Garth Williams, renewed 1981 by Garth Williams. Used by permission of HarperCollins Publishers.

From *Millions of Cats* by Wanda Gag. Copyright 1928 by Wanda Gag, renewed © 1956 by Robert Janssen. Used by permission of Coward-McCann, Inc., a division of Penguin Putnam Inc.

From *A Visit to William Blake's Inn* by Nancy Williard, illustrations copyright © 1981 by Alice Provensen and Martin Provensen, reproduced by permission of Harcourt, Inc.

Chapter 4

From *Goldilocks and the Three Bears* by James Marshall. Copyright © 1988 by James Marshall. Used by permission of Dial Book for Young Readers, a division of Penguin Putnam Inc.

From *Roller Skates* by Ruth Sawyer. Illustrated by Valenti Angelo. Cover illustrated by Cheryl Harness. Copyright 1936 by Ruth Sawyer Durand, renewed © 1964 by Ruth Sawyer Durand. Used by permission of Viking Penguin, a division of Penguin Putnam Inc.

From *Puss in Boots* by Charles Perrault, illustrated by Fred Marcellino, translated by Malcolm Arthur. Translation copyright © 1990 by Farrar, Straus & Giroux, Inc. Illustrations copyright © 1990 by Fred Marcellino. Reprinted by permission of Farrar, Straus & Giroux, Inc.

From *Tar Beach* by Faith Ringgold. Copyright © 1991 by Faith Ringgold. Reprinted by permission of Crown Publishers, Inc.

Illustration by Floyd Cooper from *Jaguarundi* by Virginia Hamilton. Published by The Blue Sky Press, an imprint of Scholastic Inc. Copyright © 1995 by Floyd Cooper. Reprinted by permission of Scholastic Inc.

Two illustrations from *Brother to the Wind* by Mildred Pitts Walter. Illustrations by Diane and Leo Dillon. Illustrations Copyright © 1985 Diane and Leo Dillon. By permission of Lothrop, Lee Shepard Books, a division of William Morrow Company, Inc.

From *The Story of the Milky Way* by Joseph Bruchac and Gayle Ross, Virginia A. Stroud, paintings. Copyright © 1995 by Virginia A. Stroud, paintings. Used by permission of Dial Books for Young Readers, a division of Penguin Putnam Inc.

From *Aunt Harriet's Underground Railroad in the Sky* by Faith Ringgold. Copyright © 1992 by Faith Ringgold. Reprinted by permission of Crown Publishers, Inc.

Chapter 5

From *The Nightingale* by Hans Christian Andersen, illustrated by Lisbeth Zwerger. Copyright © 1984, Neugebauer Press. Copyright © 1988, English text, Picture Book Studio. Reprinted with the permission of Simon & Schuster Books for Young Readers, an imprint of Simon & Schuster Children's Publishing Division.

From *Swamp Angel* by Anne Isaacs, illustrated by Paul O. Zelinsky. Copyright © 1994 by Paul O. Zelinsky, illustrations. Used by permission of Dutton, a division of Penguin Putnam Inc.

From *Caps for Sale* by Esphyr Slobodkina. Used by permission of HarperCollins Publishers.

From *Madeline* by Ludwig Bemelmans. Copyright 1939 by Ludwig Bemelmans, renewed © 1967 by Madeline Bemelmans and Barbara Bemelmans Marciano. Used by permission of Viking Penguin, a division of Penguin Putnam Inc.

Illustration by Kevin Henkes from his *Chester's Way*. Copyright © 1988 by Kevin Henkes. By permission of Greenwillow Books, a division of William Morrow Company, Inc.

From *The Diary of Latoya Hunter* by Latoya Hunter. Cover photo by Jill LeVince. Copyright © 1992 by Latoya Hunter. Reprinted by permission of Crown Publishers, Inc.

Chapter 6

Illustration by Kevin Henkes from his *Chester's Way*. Copyright © 1988 by Kevin Henkes. By permission of Greenwillow Books, a division of William Morrow Company, Inc.

From *Mr. McMouse* by Leo Lionni. Copyright © 1992 by Leo Lionni. Reprinted by permission of Alfred A. Knopf, Inc.

From *Timothy Goes to School* by Rosemary Wells. Copyright © 1981 by Rosemary Wells. Used by permission of Dial Books for Young Readers, a division of Penguin Putnam Inc.

From *Song of the Trees* by Mildred D. Taylor, pictures by Jerry Pinkney. Copyright © 1975 by Jerry Pinkney, pictures. Used by permission of Dial Books for Young Readers, a division of Penguin Putnam Inc.

From *Very Last First Time* text copyright © 1985 by Jan Andrews, illustrations copyright © 1985 by Ian Wallace. A Groundwood Book. Reprinted with permission of Margaret K. Elderberry Books, an imprint of Simon & Schuster Children's Publishing Division.

Jacket illustration by James McMullan from *Jericho* by Janet Hickman. Jacket illustration Copyright © 1994 by James McMullan. By permission of Greenwillow Books, a division of William Morrow Company, Inc.

From *Sweet Whispers, Brother Rush* by Virginia Hamilton, Philomel, 1982. Copyright © Leo and Diane Dillon.

Chapter 7

From *Pocahontas* by Edgar and Ingri d'Aulaire. Copyright 1946 by Doubleday, a division of Bantam Doubleday Dell Publishing Group, Inc. Used by permission of Random House Children's Books, a division of Random House, Inc.

Cover illustration from *All the Colors of the Race* by Arnold Adoff. Illustrated by John Steptoe. Illustration Copyright © 1982 by John Steptoe. By permission of Lothrop, Lee & Shepard Books, a division of William Morrow & Company, Inc., with the approval of the Estate of John Steptoe.

From *Moja Means One: Swahili Counting Book* by Muriel Feelings. Copyright © 1971 by Muriel Feelings. Used by permission of Dial Books for Young Readers, a division of Penguin Putnam Inc.

From *Grandfather's Journey* by Allen Say. Copyright © 1993 by Allen Say. Reprinted by permission of Houghton Mifflin Company. All rights reserved.

From *The Green Man* written and illustrated by Gail E. Haley, Charles Scribner's Sons, Publishers. Copyright © 1979 by Gail E. Haley.

From *Jack and the Bean Tree* by Gail Haley. Copyright © 1986 by Gail E. Haley. Reprinted by permission of Crown Publishers, Inc.

Chapter 8

From *The Fables of Aesop*, designed and drawn on the wood by Charles H. Bennett, London: W. Kent & Co., [1857], illustration: *"The Wolf and the Crane"* (ZBME). General Research Division, The New York Public Library, Astor, Lenox and Tilden Foundations.

From *Tico and the Golden Wings* by Leo Lionni. Copyright © 1964 and renewed 1992 by Leo Lionni. Reprinted by permission of Pantheon Books, a division of Random House, Inc.

From *Frederick* by Leo Lionni. Copyright © 1967 and renewed 1995 by Leo Lionni. Reprinted by permission of Pantheon Books, a division of Random House, Inc.

Chapter 9

From *Alexander and the Wind-Up Mouse* by Leo Lionni. Copyright © 1969 and renewed 1998 by Leo Lionni. Reprinted by permission of Alfred A. Knopf, Inc.

From *Alexander and the Wind-Up Mouse* by Leo Lionni. Copyright © 1969 and renewed 1998 by Leo Lionni. Reprinted by permission of Alfred A. Knopf, Inc.

Chapter 10

From *The Very Hungry Caterpillar* by Eric Carle. Copyright © 1969 by Eric Carle. Used by permission of Philomel Books, a division of Penguin Putnam Inc.

From *Anno's Counting Book* by Mitsumasa Anno. Copyright © 1986. Used by permission of HarperCollins Publishers.

From *The Patchwork Quilt* by Valerie Flournoy, pictures by Jerry Pinkney. Copyright © 1985 by Jerry Pinkney, illustrations. Used by permission of Dial Books for Young Readers, a division of Penguin Putnam Inc.

Chapter 11

From *Annie and the Wild Animals* Copyright © 1985 by Jan Brett. Reprinted by permission of Houghton Mifflin Company. All rights reserved.

From *Rapunzel* by Paul O. Zelinsky. Copyright © 1997 by Paul O. Zelinsky. Used by permission of Dutton Children's Books, a division of Penguin Putnam Inc.

From *When Cats Dream* by Dav Pilkey. Copyright © 1992 by Dav Pilkey. Reprinted by permission of the publisher, Orchard Books, New York.

Appendix 5

From *Goodnight Moon* by Margaret Wise Brown, pictures by Clement Hurd. Illustrations copyright renewed 1975 by Edith T. Hurd, Clement Hurd, John Thacher Hurd, and George Hellyer, as trustees of the Edith and Clement 1982 Trust. Used by permission of HarperCollins Publishers.

From "Fat Fox" by Vincent Mikkelsen, II. Printed by permission of the author. All rights reserved.

PART ONE

Literature and Society: Cultural Contexts

Chapter 1

The World of Children's Books: Then and Now

Topics in this chapter:

- Stepping into the children's book world
- Children's literature and the concept of "childhood"
- Children's literature: A brief history
- Growth and change in children's literature

ALL in the golden afternoon
Full leisurely we glide . . .
While little hands make vain pretence
Our wanderings to guide . . .

. . . The dream-child moving through a land
Of wonders wild and new,
In friendly chat with bird or beast—
And half believe it true . . .

Thus grew the tale of Wonderland:
Thus slowly one by one,
Its quaint events were hammered out—. . .
Pluck'd in a far-off land.

***Poem-epigraph to* Alice's Adventures in Wonderland**
By Lewis Carroll, 1865

Enter any classroom these days, and you are likely to find children's books "starring" in some important role. On this particular day, Lisa has left her campus to visit an elementary school, where she will engage in a literature and literacy experience. She will visit three classrooms, and you will "shadow" her to find out more about what a children's book is and what the world of children's books looks like. Such a brief visit cannot tell everything; it can provide only a glimpse of the huge and inviting subject of how children relate to books. But even a short visit can reveal a sphere of interest that has been growing and changing for centuries in all parts of the world.

STEPPING INTO THE CHILDREN'S BOOK WORLD

Lisa will visit three classrooms this day. The first is a first grade class, where the students are just forming their literature study groups. Lisa joins four children who are clustered together on the floor, examining picture books for their chosen theme of the month—"Making New Friends." Each time the children find a book that they decide fits this theme, they bring the book back to Nikki's table, where she, as theme leader for the week, is collecting the books. Today's find is a book Jon brought from home, one he discovered last night when he and his mother made a trip to the library. The children sit together examining the book, with Jon telling the story his mother read to him the night before. But the other children are active, too, "reading" pictures—and counting.

The book, Lisa soon discovers, is Jan Brett's *Comet's Nine Lives* (Putnam, 1996), the story of a cat that seems destined to lose all nine lives one summer as he meanders on Nantucket Island. "One summer day Comet stopped in a garden to nibble some tasty-looking foxgloves," Lisa reads to herself over Nikki's shoulder. "First they made him feel woozy. Then he fell into a deep sleep." Jon turns the page to show Comet lying with one eye closed. A silvery cat-spirit with angel wings is floating up to the sky, clutching its tummy in agony. "*Oops!*" reads Jon. "You see, he's just lost the first of his nine lives!"

The children become very involved with the colorful, richly detailed scenes. They see Comet in a bookstore buried under a pile of books (he has "turned the page on life number two"). Then they see him caught in a storm at sea and losing his third life. Later, he topples out of a tree into a tuba on the fourth of July (life four is now gone). He nearly drowns in a strawberry milkshake the next day (life five). Still later, he bounces from a bike basket (life six), runs into a flying shoe (life seven), and ends up in a hurricane (life eight)—all before he washes ashore at the doorway of the lighthouse cat (on the brink of his last life).

The children also enjoy the scenes painted on the borders of these pages, which show the wordless picture-story of a lighthouse keeper, which will eventually weave into the main story. The lighthouse keeper has been, from the beginning, advertising for a friend for his cat. Now, at the end of the book, Comet becomes that friend. At the lighthouse, he finds himself *home* at last. He has one life left "as the fall days turn into winter." But he is so content, he might just stay out of trouble "for the rest of his life."

Comet's dangerous—and comical—adventures have drawn the children in easily. They have enjoyed predicting all the mishaps and laughing as their predictions were confirmed—or contradicted. (Comet is a very childlike cat.) The book is about making new friends, so it settles easily into the pile the children have collected for their theme. They also decide to show the book to classmates who are collecting books about dogs, because, as Jon points out, all of the characters except for Comet and the lighthouse cat are dogs. Unlike the cats, the dogs talk, wear human clothing, and act as people on Nantucket Island do. (They buy books, work on boats, play musical instruments, play in the sand, keep lighthouses, and sometimes lose their tempers with the childlike cats.) Comet thinks human thoughts that enter the story in italicized lines: "*Maybe I should find myself a home.*" But he simply "meows" when he meets the lighthouse cat, because they are both cats and they speak the same "language." Thus, the humanlike cats differ from the dogs, who assume human roles. Why? A closer look at the cover pictures helps us to see more.

A Closer Look
. . . On the Outside

Covers of picture books may signal what is to come, lead readers into the story, or take them back out of the story, by placing a finishing touch on things. The cover of *Comet's Nine Lives* does all of these.

Like many recent picture books, this book has pictures on both front and back covers. In fact, if we place the book open and face down, the cover forms a panoramic picture of two framed "windows" that look out on a beach.

On the left side (the back cover) is a scene involving four dog characters: a father dog watches as his two puppies play in the sand, all of them wearing swimsuits. Behind them is the lighthouse keeper (a dog in a sailor suit) and the lighthouse cat.

On the right side of the scene (the front cover), Comet stands facing the reader but farther down the beach. His eight spirit-lives are flying up to the sky, as they will during the story. Each spirit is linked to the next, and each carries something connected to the event that caused Comet to lose *that* life. Spirit One carries a sprig of the foxglove plant that made him sick; Spirit Two is reading a book that fell on Comet; Spirit Three is wrapped in the innertube that carried Comet back to shore—and so on, up to the last life.

Both scenes foreshadow what is to come, and both lead children naturally into the story. The second scene also puts a finishing touch on the story, or an additional (final) scene to the entire book. Taken together, these two pictures provide a window into what the book will be about—and on a deeper level, if we look closely, what the scene might *really* be saying.

Brett draws Comet and the lighthouse cat realistically; they wear no clothing of any kind. In addition, their fur is painted in bright colors, in contrast to the silvery angel-cats that float over Comet's head, whose wings tell us what they are and where they are going. So this pair of pictures implies a great deal about the "deep" structure of the story. The back cover shows a sunny day at the beach, a day full of life. The front cover shows another sunny day, another day at the beach, but beneath the surface, it is a day about death. Comet is in a very perilous position, with only one life left. He must be *very* careful now.

Children "reading" these cover pictures will see *children*—themselves—in the dog characters (children play in the sand and wear swimsuits). They will see *cats* in the cat characters. The cats are *like* children or humans in some ways (children are adventuresome and curious like Comet; children get into trouble; people play havoc with their lives, as Comet does). But although Comet is *like* a child here, Jan Brett saves him from being seen as a child—and thus *saves* him for children—by keeping him a cat. Pets die, and children know that; they live with that fact. Children die, too, but keeping the cat a cat and humanizing the dog characters helps to distance these somber facts. Children can then face Comet's peril as directly as he faces his readers in this picture—and laugh about his adventures, rather than grieve for him.

From *Comet's Nine Lives* (Putnam, 1996) by Jan Brett.

Later in the morning, Lisa visits a fifth grade room. Here, children also are involved in literature study groups, but in this classroom, they are reading clusters of books by particular authors. Lisa settles in with Terry's group, one that is "specializing" this month in Betsy Byars's books. They all read books by Byars on their own each week; then they discuss these books in relation to special questions they create.

Terry, as group leader for the week, previously took a vote on which Byars book the group would begin reading. Jed had read *The Cybil War* (Penguin 1981; reissued as a Puffin paperback, 1990) and recommended it as a book that was easy

From *The Cybil War* (Penguin, 1990) by Betsy Byars.

to get into and funny. So the children decided to read half the book for their group meeting today and to start with the question, "When did you *really* know you were into the book?" Terry says she knew she was "into the story" on page 23, when she read about Simon and Tony walking home from school and Simon thinking about being friends with Tony.

Simon, the main character, is also a fifth grader, as Lisa discovers after taking a quick look at the back cover. "When Cybil Ackerman crosses her eyes at Simon for the first time," the jacket blurb reads, "he knows he's in love. But Simon's best friend, Tony, is too, and he'll stop at nothing to wreck Simon's chances of winning her! Tony tells Simon that Cybil's legs are like popsicle sticks—and then he tells Cybil that Simon said it. When Simon realizes what Tony is up to, the war is on. Only Cybil can decide the outcome. Will she choose Tony or Simon?"

The Cybil War is a children's novel, in contrast to a picture book such as *Comet's Nine Lives.* Byars's book does have eleven illustrations scattered throughout the text, as Lisa notices when she leafs through the book. It is 126 pages long and is divided into fifteen chapters of five to eight pages each. Pages placed before and after the story give additional information.

Terry shares again, reading the part that drew her into the book: "Simon walked beside him [Tony] in silence. His long friendship with Tony, which had brought him such pleasure in the early grades, seemed this year to be bringing him only discomfort. He walked more slowly." This part, Terry explains, reminds her of something that happened to her once, too. Natalie says she was drawn into the book from the very first page, when Simon's class voted on who would be Mr. Indigestion in the class play, and Simon lost the part to Cybil. Everyone laughs remembering the opening scene, and Jed says, "Wait till you see what happens when they put on the play!"

Jed adds, "I know when I was into the book, *really* into it. It was when Simon jabbed Tony in the ribs. But I was into it from the first page, too, when they voted on the play." Angel says she started paying attention on page 23 too, but in the part where Tony told funny stories about his mother telling lies.

Soon the children are focusing on the stories they think are the funniest and why. Terry asks what question they want to think about for the next group meeting, and they decide to continue discussing funny stories, asking "What was the funniest part of the book for you?" Natalie suggests that later they can vote on which Betsy Byars book is the funniest of all—and which is the most serious. A serious Byars book still has funny parts, she adds, like the one she read called *Good-bye, Chicken Little* (Harper, 1979). The children start to describe the different Byars books they have read, but Lisa must leave for her last classroom visit.

In a third grade setting this time, Lisa finds the teacher just beginning a read-aloud time to introduce a new unit on folk tales. The book is *A Ring of Tricksters: Animal Tales from America, the West Indies, and Africa,* by Virginia Hamilton (Scholastic, 1997), with illustrations by Barry Moser. The entire class is clustered around the teacher, who sits on the floor with them. They are examining the cover picture of a large, green alligator with a wide, toothy mouth, who is about to grab a tempting spider-meal.

The teacher begins with a short introduction to the book, telling the children about tricksters around the world. At she speaks, she leafs through the book, showing them the pictures. Lisa, alongside the children, sees luminous portraits of

A Closer Look

. . . On the Inside

The Cybil War begins with a **blurb-page** similar to the one on the back cover. A passage from pages 15–16 (chapter 2) describes Simon remembering the day in second grade when he fell in love with Cybil Ackerman. Following is another paragraph that sums up the major conflict in the story and also helps to explain the title: Tony Angotti, Simon's best friend and the "world's best liar," is Simon's rival for Cybil: "Tony's up to something sneaky, Simon's determined not to get tricked—and Cybil's learning how much fun being in the middle of their war can be."

The **half-title page** is next, containing the words *The Cybil War.* On the following page is a **list** of Betsy Byars books. The **title page** appears next; it repeats the title and provides the illustrator's and publisher's names (Gail Owens and Puffin Books).

Publication data appears on the back side of the title page (the **Copyright page**). These data include addresses of the "parent" publishers (Penguin Books) around the world, followed by the original date of publication (1981) and the publication date of this paperback edition (1990). This page also features a brief summary of the book ("Simon learns some hard lessons about good and bad friendships when his good friend Tony's stories involve him in some very troublesome and complicated situations.") Following the summary, the Library of Congress lists both a subject and a literature category—or genre—for the book. The subject is *Friendship;* the genre category is *Fiction.* The print type is also given, enabling children to find it on their own computers: Times Roman. Finally, this page states that republishing this work in any form without consent of the publishers is illegal under copyright laws that prevent the author's work from being reprinted with no profits going to her. On the facing page is the list of **chapter titles,** which leads on succeeding pages into the **story text** itself, accompanied at times by **illustrations.**

At the end of the book is an **About The Author page** that introduces readers to Betsy Byars: her birthplace, the college she attended, her place of residence, number of children, awards, hobbies and pastimes.

All of this information encases a story meant primarily for the child's reading pleasure. But it shows a great deal about children's books in a *cultural* context. The story summary and quoted material at the beginning are useful for those deciding whether to read the book and for those who might want more information as they begin reading. The list of Betsy Byars books and the About the Author note provide information children might need if they have questions about the author and her work.

Summaries, quotes, and blurbs are marketing devices that publishers use to attract reader attention, but because they are so commonplace these days, they have become *conventions* (customary practices) associated with book production. Other more traditional conventions relate to book format: examples include title and half-title pages and publication data.

The copyright page establishes the book as an artifact and the author and illustrator as artists, a position valued in this culture and era (no one can steal this material without legal ramifications). The fact that this book is available in so many other cultures (the Penguin group extends around the world in English-speaking countries) tells us how large the children's book world has become. Stories that once traveled around the world in the oral tradition now reach children in faraway places through print.

The copyright page also teaches children useful meaning-making strategies. If children learn how to "read" this page (an important and often neglected aspect of **print literacy**), they discover more about genre categories, how others envision the story's subject, and how others summarize it. Their own classification of subject and summary might be significantly different (and equally valid), but seeing another perspective gives them a standard for comparison.

Children who understand print conventions of all kinds operate more independently in the children's book world.

From *A Ring of Tricksters* (Scholastic, 1997) by Virginia Hamilton, illustrated by Barry Moser (front and back covers).

Bruh Rabbit, Old Mister Turtle, Anansi Spider, and Cunnie Rabbit (actually a tiny African deer—only eighteen inches long!). The teacher points out that each of these animals will play tricks on Bruh Gator, grisly Leopard, Sima Tiger, and Big Elephant in these stories. She tells them that the small, cunning, and humanlike animals in these stories taught Africans and slaves of the Plantation Era how to help themselves when they were up against bigger and stronger animals or people.

Later, she tells the children, after they read a few of these stories, they will take out the globe and trace the migration of these trickster tales. They will see how the stories traveled from Africa to America with the slaves who were taken to plantations in the South and in the Caribbean Islands. Later, she adds, the stories traveled back to Africa once again, when some of the freed slaves returned home, taking with them trickster tales they would tell in both the old and new ways. The stories truly formed a *ring* of tricksters, the teacher says.

"This is a book about trickster animals crossing the ocean," she explains "and the circle they made when they crossed back and forth from Africa to the New World and back again." She begins with the best-known animal trickster, "Bruh Rabbit." She asks the children to think about what makes him so famous. "What is he like? How does he manage to win? He is small and not very strong," she points out, "so what is his secret weapon?"

The children are eager to hear the first story, Lisa notices, after they see a comical alligator standing on his hind legs fiddling, a little green hat perched on his head. "Oh, yes! Oh, My!" the teacher begins reading. "Buh Rabby is a cotton-tail, for true! And played a trick on rough-skin Bruh Gator one time. They call Bruh Gator the fiddler." '*Fiddle-faddle fiddle-dee-dum.*' "He's the music man. He plays at the dances for the gator girls and boys. He hollers the calls" (page 15). She launches into the rhyme of the dance call, and the children listen intently as the story unfolds.

When the story ends, the children want to go immediately to the next one, so the teacher begins naming the tricksters in other tales to see which animals they want to hear about—a buzzard and wren; a cat, rat, and fox trio; or a wolf and rabbit? Just one more from this section today, she says, and then tomorrow they will look at the West Indian spider stories. The children cannot decide between the huge fox trickster—again, in a little green hat—raging at the cat and rat, or the big buzzard—in silk top hat—with the saucy bird on his back.

Aesthetic versus Efferent Stances in the Teaching of Literature

Louise Rosenblatt distinguishes between two ways of teaching literature, each falling at some point on a continuum. At one end of the spectrum is the *aesthetic experience* readers have, naturally and spontaneously, when they become lost—or fully absorbed—in literature. This literature might be fiction stories that they hear at read-aloud time or that they read independently. As they listen or read, they form mental images about characters, settings, and plots; they think, feel, see, and hear, through the characters and *with* them. They are actively and personally involved or engaged in the story as a "lived-through" experience. The literature they encounter might also be nonfiction. They might select informational books on the basis of a particular interest or curiosity and then become deeply engaged in their reading on a topic that fascinates them.

At the other end of the spectrum is what Rosenblatt calls *efferent* (fact-based, fact-driven) reading. In this type of reading, adults often direct or guide reading instruction (identifying main ideas, drawing conclusions, making inferences, and understanding vocabulary) before students have had a chance to experience fiction in personal, imaginative, feeling-based ways. In directive—or "guided"—reading instruction, adults might break up a story into short units and then ask students to identify main ideas, draw conclusions, and make inferences. Or they might ask students to study the words they will later encounter in the story, rather than allowing students to sort out word meanings from the story's context. In this approach, students are less likely to engage with literature in personal, imaginative, feeling-based ways; they simply view literature as a means to an end—to develop so-called "thinking" or "reasoning" skills or to learn new words.

When adults take an efferent stance in teaching literature, they call upon students to extract factual information from a story as the primary goal of their reading. Students must identify certain features of the story that an authority figure (a critic, a textbook publisher, or the teacher) uses to test their understanding of the story. The authority figure decides the readers should read the story in a certain way. Before students have a chance to develop their own natural and spontaneous responses to the story, they must engage in exercises and activities to ensure they are reading in the "correct" way.

In Rosenblatt's view, readers must have a chance to develop their own natural and spontaneous responses to literature. Their own meaning-making experiences, she believes, will evoke highly individual "transactions" with text. These transactions lead readers to find aesthetic pleasure in literature. Says Rosenblatt (1983): "The literary work is not primarily a document . . . It is not simply a mirror of, or a report on, life. It is not a homily setting forth moral or philosophic or religious precepts. As a work of art, it offers a special kind of experience. It is a mode of living. The poem, the play, the story, is thus an extension, an amplification, of life itself."

Between these two stances lie a great stretch of possibilities for helping children build meaning-making competencies. Choosing wisely on the continuum means, in Rosenblatt's view, not requiring students to reason *about* literature until *after* they have lived *through* the story alongside the characters—standing in their shoes, peering over their shoulders, getting inside their skins, feeling as they felt, and *knowing* how it felt to be in that particular situation.

Sources: Louise Rosenblatt, Literature as Exploration, Fourth ed. (New York: Modern Language Association, 1983): 278; also Rosenblatt, "Literature—S. O. S.!" Language Arts 68(1991): 444–48.

Lisa must leave, just as Melody begs to hear both stories. Today Lisa has seen children experiencing the pleasures of new and old books. These reading events have been what literary theorist Louise Rosenblatt calls *aesthetic* in nature: Children enter the character's lives, thoughts, and feelings, living through their experiences with them. The reading sessions have also been somewhat interpretive in nature. In each instance, the teacher utilized a classroom procedure—literature study groups or read-aloud time—to strengthen children's meaning-making strategies as they enjoyed the literature.

Today Lisa has also seen more about what a children's book is, in particular, the way it captures the essence of child culture. In the book the first graders chose, she caught a glimpse of what it means to be growing up and getting in trouble, escaping with your life at times, and then finding a friend just like you. In the book the fifth graders chose, she saw children dealing with their friendship problems in clever and resourceful ways. With the third graders, she met animal characters that have been entertaining children for centuries, and she learned how these characters dealt with trouble of all kinds.

As she joined the children's audience, Lisa learned more about how children respond to books and more about the books themselves.

CHILDREN'S LITERATURE AND THE CONCEPT OF "CHILDHOOD"

Consider that a little over a century ago, there was no such thing as a *children's* book, at least as we know it today. Of course there have always been children, and from the beginning, all over the world, these children heard—and reveled in—songs and stories. Later, they followed pictorial stories in cave paintings, sand sketches, clay etchings, and stained glass windows. Eventually the printing press—and peddlers on the street—brought them the printed word in real books.

Throughout the centuries, however, most children did not experience what we think of as *childhood,* a carefree, happy time when children can grow leisurely into adulthood, as the French scholar, Philippe Aries (1960) explains in *Centuries of Childhood.* Aries studied European children from the tenth to the nineteenth century, poring over paintings and religious tracts and reviewing educational practices. He noticed that children of the working classes often became miniature adults as soon as they were strong enough to hold tools or carry loads—or tall enough to reach machine handles.

Keith Thomas (1989), who studied children from the sixteenth to the nineteenth century, took a different view. Children, he said, were very much a "separate society with its own system of order and classification, its own perceptions and values." Thomas asserted that children were "daily to be seen playing in the streets, shouting, swearing, throwing stones, and abusing passersby." Thomas helps us see the dawn of children's literature, occurring several hundred years ago, at a time when the human life span was considerably shorter, when most adults were illiterate, and when few reading materials were available.

When stories, poems, and pictures did emerge in print, children often found in them rules of behavior rather than humor or fun-filled adventures. This was true throughout the European continent, and more particularly in England, where so many "chapters" of our own American story take place and where the Puritan religious sect dominated the cultural landscape in the late 1600s and afterward. By the beginning of the nineteenth century, as Canadian educator and cultural theorist Lissa Paul (1998) notes, "European colonial authority" [dominated] "much of Africa, Asia and India . . . Maps of the world were coloured predominantly pink to illustrate British influence on large tracts of land. The order of colonial author (white people ruling countries which were home to people of colour) was repeated in European domestic order (husbands in charge, wives and children positioned as subordinates)."

Along with Puritan beliefs came fear and distrust of leisure time activities and a similar distrust of fiction and imaginative literature. Puritan thinking, for the most part, censored folk and fairy tales. These stories showed the adventures of animal or human characters; they were filled with supernatural adversaries or helpers, magic, and heroes and heroines engaged in quests to overcome evil. Folk and fairy tales entertained and informed children about values and traditions of their cultures, but in doing so, they often revealed murderous impulses, violent acts, greedy motives, and deceitful habits; the "lesson" being that what it took to survive in this world was dishonest and bloodthirsty behavior.

An early pictorial form for children appeared in Germany in 1658, when Czech theologian and educator John Comenius designed a set of labeled pictures, the *Orbis Pictus,* to give children a view of the entire world—nature, humanity, and religion—with no concessions to innocence. Comensius included pictures and words featuring death, war, and all manner of destruction. The *Orbis Pictus,* says children's literature historian David Lewis (1995), was "a cross between a Latin primer and an illustrated encyclopaedia" and is sometimes described as the first children's picture book. At this time, children often learned to read from small wooden blocks shaped like books. Adults either carved the ABCs, prayers, fables, and biblical passages into the wood, or they wrote religious verses and ABCs on paper that they attached to the wood, then covered with a tough, sheathlike material they called *horn,* producing a *hornbook.*

From *Aesop's Fables.* Woodcut and type for Caxton's version in 1484.

ranne in to the foreſt / And whanne the wyld beeſtes ſawe hym come/they were ſo ferdfull that they alle beganne to flee/ For they wend/ that it had be the lyon/ And the mayſter of the aſſe ſerched and ſought his aſſe in euery place al aboute And as he had ſought longe/he thought that he wold go in to the foreſt for to ſee yf his aſſe were there/ And as ſoone as

Puritans wanted children to learn early about godly ways. Life on earth was short; if you believed strongly in Heaven and Hell, and if your child might die from any number of dreaded diseases, you cared desperately that the child would have every hope of entering Heaven. Earthly fun won in the end, however. Stories seeped into homes through family storytelling and into the streets through peddlers (or *chapmen*) selling small books and pamphlets. These *chapbooks* contained ballads, poems, adventure stories, folk and fairy tales, as well as the ever-present religious tracts and printed sermons.

Chapbooks were similar to the mass-marketed picture books children still see today. The word *chap* comes from Old English *ceap,* meaning "trade," and from Middle English *ceap,* meaning "sale" or "bargain (similar to our word *cheap*)." These books were poorly written with a one-size-fits-all concept of illustration. Printers used the same woodcuts over and over again in different books in the absence of a large-scale publishing industry with regulations and copyright laws. They also printed the books on a poor grade of paper—and on just one sheet of paper, in fact, "so that three quick folds produced a tiny booklet of sixteen pages,

A facsimile of a colonial hornbook.

usually no more than ten centimetres by six" (Lewis, 1995). Many had no cover at all, which may help to explain why so few survived.

The lack of stiff covers on these earliest "paperbacks" had a practical purpose: The peddler, as Iona and Peter Opie (1955) explain, wanted no unnecessary weight on his back. But cheaply made or not, children loved these books, just as twentieth-century children have loved the inexpensive Little Golden Books that first appeared in the 1940s. This emotional attachment also helps to explain why chapbooks did not survive. Children simply read them to "death."

Puritans tolerated the adventure story more easily than the fairy tale. Adventure stories combined exciting and improbable events with down-to-earth everyday life. A young man might leave home to seek his fortune but soon face battles, murder, and shipwrecks, all of which would test his mental and physical abilities. In the 1700s, children were fascinated by these adventure stories for adults.

John Bunyan's *Pilgrim's Progress* (1678) was filled with travel adventures that, for younger readers, crowded out the tale's religious symbolism. Bunyan's story was the adventure story supreme, with its hero setting off for the Celestial City (Heaven) and meeting dragons, monsters, and giants on the way. Other books for adults such as Daniel Defoe's *Robinson Crusoe* (1720), filled with survival lore, and Jonathan Swift's more intellectual but equally entertaining *Gulliver's Travels* (1726), with its whimsical characters and humorous events, were also available to children in condensed and watered-down chapbook versions.

Poetry and make-believe stories provided additional avenues out of the heavy-handed Puritan themes that filled literature for children in these early years. In 1789, William Blake produced one of the first poetry books children could understand, a collection titled *Songs of Innocence.* Blake illustrated the book with his own engravings, and soon the process of engraving was providing a new way to produce pictures for children, one that John Tenniel would use for Lewis Carroll's *Alice's Adventures in Wonderland* in 1865. Blake's books were to pass on into the adult world of books, yet *Alice* has continued to be shared and enjoyed by children. What accounts for this difference in audience? Was it that Carroll wrote his story for one special child, the ten-year-old Alice Liddell? Or that *Alice's Adventures in Wonderland* fits more easily the definition of a children's book? If so, what is that definition?

English critic John Townsend says that *Alice's Adventures in Wonderland*—at least "as far as the child readers were concerned—had the sole aim of giving pleasure". Blake's poetry, although accessible to children, had a much heavier tone. Consider one of Blake's most famous poems in *Songs of Innocence,* "The Lamb":

> Little Lamb, who made thee?
> Does thou know who made thee?
> Gave thee life, & bid thee feed
> By the stream & o'er the mead;
> Gave thee clothing of delight,
> Softest clothing, wooly, bright;
> Gave thee such a tender voice,
> Making all the vales rejoice?
> Little Lamb, who made thee?
> Dost thou know who made thee? (page 85)

It is not surprising that children would later have more fun with the rhyme that Alice recites:

How doth the little crocodile
    Improve his shining tail,
And pour the waters of the Nile
    On every golden scale!

How cheerfully he seems to grin,
    How neatly spreads his claws,
And welcomes little fishes in,
    With gently smiling jaws! (page 11)

Carroll's talent for wordplay and nonsense might account for the popularity of *Alice's Adventures in Wonderland* with children. That he *chose* to write for them in this intentionally playful style is probably a better explanation. "Before there could be children's books," Townsend says, "there had to be children"—children, that is, "who were accepted as beings with their own particular needs and interests, not merely as miniature men and women." This idea of a book written especially to give pleasure to children—*in terms of the child's own preoccupations*—is a good place to start in defining the term "children's literature."

When did the idea that children might read for pleasure take hold? In the beginning, as we have seen, the Puritan movement was highly influential in producing a *moral* construct for children's reading. Children heard or read stories for their personal salvation or for the development of their moral capabilities. Books taught children how to live so that, if they died, their souls would be saved.

In the mid-1700s, literature for children became much more a *social* construct. Books were written to transmit social values. Adults wanted children to learn about life on earth—how to survive, thrive, and even enjoy reading. Books also become more fun to read, because authors produced suspenseful plots, nonsense verse, and humorous wordplay.

By the late 1800s, a *literary* construct was also emerging for children's books. Books that could finally be called *children's* books could now be called children's *literature* as well. Artistic language filled the stories, as did insightful ideas, empathetic characters, exciting, thought-provoking plots; and evocative scenes. Authors such as Lewis Carroll took great pains with their craft so that children would grow up understanding implicitly what good literature meant. Authors such as Beatrix Potter followed easily in Carroll's footsteps, paying a great deal of attention to the way their books were produced. The smallest details merited their attention, and it was not long before the public was to become equally discriminating.

By the mid-1900s, a burgeoning interest in children's book awards was emerging around the world, especially in America, where social and literary traditions were helping to ease children's literature into a *critical* tradition. Editors, reviewers, critics, librarians, teachers, and parents all worked to see that children received what adults considered the best possible literature. Let us look at these social, literary, and critical traditions in more detail.

CHILDREN'S LITERATURE: A BRIEF HISTORY

Before 1800

Children in the late 1600s, like children today, loved animals and excitement. Thus they loved beast fables—stories in which animals converse and engage in the same conflicts and jealousies as humans. The most famous producer of fables was a Greek storyteller, Aesop, who lived around 600 B.C. and supposedly wrote the little stories that we now call "Aesop's fables." Another talented fable writer was Jean de la Fontaine, who lived in seventeenth-century France and produced his fables in verse form.

Fables, with their strong narrative drive, ease of understanding, and lessons about human behavior, satisfied the adult's concern that children receive strong moral teaching, rather than mere entertainment. Aesop's fables arrived on English shores in translated form in 1484. By Puritan times, they were the most obvious example of what we would today call children's literature, although these concise, understated little stories were orginally the literary "property" of adults. Consider the elevated style of Aesop's "The Tortoise and the Hare," one of the most popular fables in children's picture books now:

> A tortoise and a hare started to dispute which of them was the swifter, and before separating they made an appointment for a certain time and place to settle the matter. The hare had such confidence in its natural fleetness that it did not trouble about the race, but lay down by the wayside and went to sleep. The tortoise, acutely conscious of its slow movements, padded along without ever stopping until it passed the sleeping hare and won the race.
>
> *A naturally gifted man, through lack of application, is often beaten by a plodder.*
>
> — (Handford, 1954, page 66)

Bible stories were a literary staple for children; alongside them, adults produced original stories to show children the dangers of dying before they were cleansed of all sin. Parents in an age of high infant mortality wanted to know that their children would be saved from eternal damnation, and children wanted to believe they would go to heaven. Adults saw books as a good way to instruct children in how to escape the devil's clutches; thus, the "message" of the book was all-important. Literary expression—wit, humor, and well-defined characters—were of little or no consequence. Exposing children to death and disaster was the important point. Children needed to behave properly to keep their souls safe, and adults often created child characters as angels converting others in deathbed scenes.

By the mid-1700s, adults were becoming a little wiser in guiding children. English philosopher John Locke theorized in *Thoughts Concerning Education* (1693) that children were blank slates on whose innocent "pages" life wrote a "text." Because children were not innately evil, they could be influenced to behave wisely, Locke felt, rather than flogged and frightened into goodness. What especially concerned Locke was that children had no edifying books that were also entertaining, no books they would *want* to read, no books they would learn to read because they liked poring over them repeatedly—nothing except Aesop's fables.

On the heels of Locke came the French philosopher Jean-Jacques Rousseau, who in a teaching treatise for adults, *Emile* (1762), advocated bringing up children in more natural ways. Give children no moral advice until age fifteen, he said; bring them up in the country, where they could explore the woods, climb trees, and have ample time to grow into adult ways of seeing and thinking; give them a *childhood,* in other words. Children were soon to have new books to accompany these new ideas.

In 1729, a promising English printer had published a popular version of Charles Perrault's *History or Tales of Past Times Told by Mother Goose,* originally published in France in 1697. Perrault's book is not to be confused with the Mother Goose books filled with rhymes that young children still recite. His collection was filled with stories from the oral tradition—"Cinderella," "Red Riding Hood," "Bluebeard," "Puss in Boots"—that he shaped into polished pieces of literature. When English children later read the book in a bilingual edition, the stories fulfilled a useful social purpose (children could learn to read in two languages). Because Perrault was such a graceful writer, these children were also exposed to *literature* rather than the hack writing of chapbooks.

Perrault's title soon adorned a number of "Mother Goose" collections that flowered in the seventeenth and eighteenth centuries. Although his book was filled with fairy tales rather than nursery rhymes, the name eventually came to mean any book filled with songs, jingles, lullabies, games, alphabet and number verses, riddles, and ballads from the oral tradition, told by an old bird-lady. Her storytelling talents and ancient wisdom delivered favorite stories and rhymes, just as the stork supposedly brought babies; thus her name. Illustrators often picture Mother Goose, as folklore scholar Marina Warner (1994) notes, "in her bird shape, with glasses perched on her beak" presiding over the entire tradition of the earliest children's books. In actual fact, it was John Newbery who was doing the presiding.

By 1743, Newbery had emerged as a London publisher who wanted to give children literature they cared about. He was well aware of the natural delight children took in the cheap little books filled with adventures stories, folk tales, and nursery rhymes that peddlers sold in the streets, and he saw a way to use their love of words and pictures in his own business interests. In 1744, Newbery published *A Little Pretty Pocket Book,* filled with rhymes, fables, and proverbs and illustrated with simple woodcut engravings, all designed to teach children how to live as social, rather than just moral, beings. Now children would want to turn the page and go on reading, and their parents would want to buy more of his books.

At this time, an engraving industry was thriving, and soon children had hand-colored and printed paper to cover the three-by-two-inch books that publishers like Newbery designed for small hands. And they had pictures made from wood cuts and copper plate engravings. By the time Newbery died in 1767, he was running such a profitable business that 128 engraving firms were producing work for him.

What Is Wood Engraving?

Thomas Bewick developed a long and involved method of wood engraving. He began by slicing a block of wood from the boxwood tree into squares of several inches. (The boxwood has a trunk only twelve inches in diameter, so the blocks could never be cut in very large squares.) Then he polished the end grain of the wood to a high luster. Next, he used a pencil or pen to make a design on the whitened surface, then cut away the wood around it, leaving a raised design. At this point, he could add more design details on the raised space, if desired; for example, engravers often produced a sculpted feeling with cross-hatched lines. Finally, Bewick coated the wood block with ink and placed paper over the inked block to produce a picture.

Source: Susan Meyer, A Treasury of the Great Children's Book Illustrators (New York: Abrams, 1983).

INVESTIGATIONS: Books before 1800

You can learn better what a children's book is if you examine books of different authors and different eras and then compare them century by century. Read a book published before 1800 to gain a sense of this time period and a better sense of children's literature as a whole. Consider the following list when making your selection:

1484 *Aesop's Fables.* Many modern editions, even picture book versions, are available.

1678 *Pilgrim's Progress* by John Bunyan. Discover why Alcott's heroines like this book; there is even a modern edition now.

1719 *Robinson Crusoe* by Daniel Defoe. This definitive survival story spawned so many imitations that a tradition of "Robinsonades" was born.

1726 *Gulliver's Travels* by Jonathan Swift. Read to discover why children chose this book for pleasure reading.

1729 *Tales of Past Times; Told by Mother Goose* by Charles Perrault, translated into English. Perrault's tales are literary versions of famous folk tales such as "Cinderella," "Little Red Riding Hood," and "Puss in Boots." But the name "Mother Goose" was important for what it later came to signify: nursery rhymes supposedly told by an old, goose-lady. John Newbery presumably published these rhymes in a collection, *Mother Goose's Melody,* around 1765 (no records remain). His firm may also have published a later edition in 1780. The rhymes are notable for their humor, inventive language, and wordplay, as well as for the fanciful situations eighteenth-century readers associated with real people and events.

Many modern versions of *Mother Goose* are available, including those by Blanche Fisher Wright, Tomie de Paola, Arnold Lobel, Raymond Briggs, Alice and Martin Provenson, and Rosemary Wells, each with its own loyal fans. Iona and Peter Opie's *The Oxford Nursery Rhymes Books* (Oxford Press, 1955), which contain reproductions of chapbook nursery rhymes, will help you see the rhymes as children in the 1790s actually saw them. You will also see the woodcut engravings that accompanied the rhymes; some are reprints of the master of woodcuts, Thomas Bewick. *The Annotated Mother Goose* by William Baring-Gould (Bramhall House, 1962) provides copious footnotes, explaining many hidden social and political meanings in the rhymes.

1789 *Songs of Innocence* by William Blake. Read one of the first important poetry collections for children and compare it with the poetry children later "took" for their own.

1800–1900

By the 1850s, three illustrators—Walter Crane, Kate Greenaway, and Randolph Caldecott—were changing the children's publishing world. Crane produced rich compositions, filled with bold colors and heavily detailed backgrounds, for the many fairy tales, legends, and myths he illustrated. He also illustrated alphabet books that helped children just learning to read.

Kate Greenaway produced limpid verses describing children's pastimes and delights. Greenaway revealed what children of her time valued—a new bonnet, the end of the school term, going fishing. She illustrated her verses with idyllic, pastoral—and pastel—scenes filled with the costumed figures (females in long, flowing gowns and wide bonnets, carrying floral bouquets) that became her trademark.

From *Beauty and the Beast* (1874), illustrated by Walter Crane.

From *Under the Window* (1879) by Kate Greenaway.

Randolph Caldecott produced highly active scenes that extended the texts of nursery rhymes, songs, and familiar stories of English folklore. His illustrated storybooks signaled the beginning of the picture book industry that would emerge full-bloom half a century later, as artists increasingly relied on pictures to carry the story line. Their pictures, like Caldecott's, would fill in gaps of text and interpret the words of the stories. Words and pictures would become so interlaced, it would be impossible to determine whether a story were being told through one or the other; each would be equally important.

From *Hey Diddle Diddle* (1882), illustrated by Randolph Caldecott.

One reason picture book artists began to flourish was because of the efforts of a printer, Edmund Evans, who hired Caldecott, Greenaway, and Crane. By the 1850s, Evans had begun printing in more than one color with oil-based inks, and this innovation—plus his cultivation of equally innovative artists—produced an illustrated book, a distinctive form in its own right. Children's fiction was also breaking off Puritan shackles.

Writers such as Maria Edgeworth revealed a talent for portraying the language of real children and even injecting a little humor into their realistic stories. At the same time, Edgeworth had very practical notions about children's needs. In her story, "The Purple Jar," published in her book *The Parent's Assistant* (1796), Rosamond gives up the shoes she needs for the purple jar she wants and soon she is sadder but wiser for her choice. Her shoes wear out; the jar, as Edgeworth is quick to note, is useless. Edgeworth also objected to fairy tales on the grounds that they did not produce useful learning. Children tended to be naughty; thus, they needed to be guided in social responsibility, an attitude to which Lewis Carroll and Beatrix Potter would later give a nod—and a wink.

All this time, fairy tales were making their way onto children's bookshelves, the result of so many translated versions now available. Stories from *The Arabian Nights Entertainments,* a collection that appeared in Arabia in the mid-1500s, were translated into French during the 1600s. Charles Perrault's collection of French fairy tales arrived in England, in 1729. The Grimm Brothers' collection of German folk tales arrived in England in 1823, a century later.

Jacob and Wilhelm Grimm took liberties with the stories they collected from the oral tradition; they omitted—or substituted—details they thought might be objectionable in their own cultural setting. They also blended similar versions for economy, artistic balance and structure, and vibrancy of language. Thus, the imaginative pleasure of their stories far outstripped didactic instruction of the tales, and the literary style of their work, although different from Perrault's, was equally interesting. Stories in both collections have precision of detail, mood-stirring scenes, and engaging characters. Consider the way each writer begins the story of Cinderella. Here is the opening of Charles Perrault's "Cinderella or The Little Glass Slipper" (1697) from Iona and Peter Opie's *The Classic Fairy Tales* (Oxford, 1974), translated by Robert Samber, 1729:

> There was once upon a time, a gentleman who married for his second wife the proudest and most haughty woman that ever was known. She had been a widow, and had by her former husband two daughters of her own humour, who were exactly like her in all things. He had also by a former wife a young daughter, but of an unparalleled goodness and sweetness of temper, which she took from her mother, who was the best creature in the world.
>
> No sooner were the ceremonies of the wedding over, but the mother-in-law began to display her ill humour; she could not bear the good qualities of this pretty girl; and the less, because they made her own daughters so much the more hated and despised. She employed her in the meanest work of the house, she cleaned the dishes and stands, and rubbed Madam's chamber, and those of the young Madams her daughters; she lay on the top of the house in a garret, upon a wretched straw bed, while her sisters lay in fine rooms, with floors all inlaid, upon beds of the newest fashion, and where they had looking-glasses so large, that they might see themselves at their full length, from head to foot. The poor girl bore all patiently, and dared not tell her father who would have scolded her; for his wife governed him entirely. (page 161)

Now compare the opening of the Grimm Brothers' "Cinderella" from *The Complete Grimm's Fairy Tales.* (Pantheon, 1944), translated by Margaret Hunt, 1944:

> The wife of a rich man fell sick, and as she felt that her end was drawing near, she called her only daughter to her bedside and said: 'Dear child, be good and pious, and then the good God will always protect you, and I will look down on you from heaven and be near you.' Thereupon she closed her eyes and departed. Every day the maiden went out to her mother's grave and wept, and she remained pious and good. When winter came the snow spread a white sheet over the grave, and by the time the spring sun had drawn it off again, the man had taken another wife.
>
> The woman had brought with her into the house two daughters, who were beautiful and fair of face, but vile and black of heart. Now began a bad time for the poor stepchild. "Is the stupid goose to set in the parlor with us?" they said . . . They took her pretty clothes away from her, put an old grey bedgown on her, and gave her wooden shoes. "Just look at the proud princess, how decked out she is!" they cried, and laughed, and led her into the kitchen. There she had to do hard work from morning till night, get up before daybreak, carry water, light fires, cook and wash . . . In the evening when she had worked till she was weary she had no bed to go to, but had to sleep by the hearth in the cinders. And as on that account she always looked dusty and dirty, they called her Cinderella. (page 121)

Edward Cruikshank illustrated the Grimms' collection in 1853. His etchings reveal energy, humor, and liveliness of gesture and facial expression, all of which appealed to children's love of action and of boisterous human and animal behavior. Soon after, other artists would add their own interpretations to folk tales, signaling the tradition of illustrated folk and fairy tale books to come.

More fun for children was soon on the way with two books, Heinrich Hoffmann-Donner's *Struwwelpeter* (Slovenly or Shock-Headed Peter, 1845), an import from Germany that arrived in England in 1848, and Edward Lear's *A Book of Nonsense* (1846). Hoffmann-Donner, a physician with talents in both writing and drawing, managed to produce highly memorable pictures and comical, cautionary tales. In cautionary stories, adults warn children not to do certain things (in this case, play with matches, suck their thumbs, or refuse to eat). Children see the dire consequences that follow when the young characters ignore the warnings:

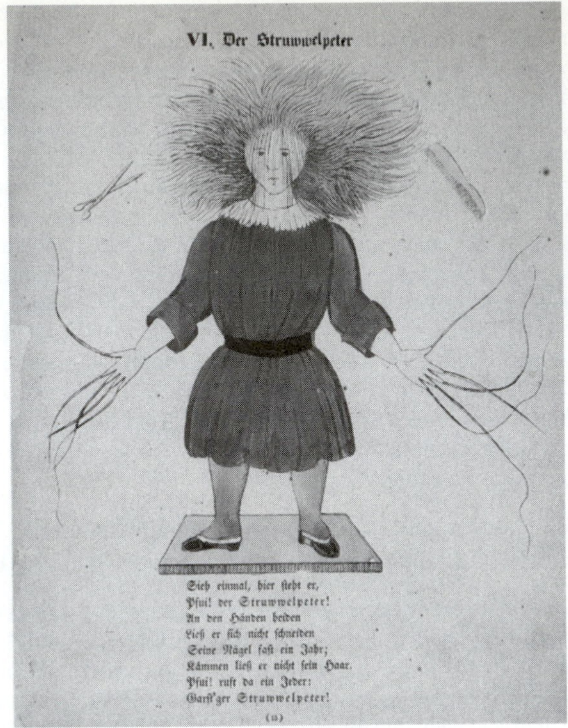

From *Struwwelpeter* (Slovenly Peter) (1845) by Heinrich Hoffmann-Donner.

> Just look at him! There he stands, With his nasty hair and hands.
> See! His nails are never cut; They are grim'd as black as soot;
> And the sloven, I declare, Never once has comb'd his hair;
> Any thing to me is sweeter Than to see Shock-headed Peter (McTigue, page 74).

Lear, a technical artist or draftsman for the London Zoological Society, had studied animals for so long—and with such intensity—that they permeated his imagination, reemerging in very realistic animal drawings but very unrealistic and comic verses. Here is the beginning of *The Scroobious Pip* (Harper, 1968, illustrated by Nancy Burkert), a long verse about an imaginary animal that Lear wrote in 1868 but never completed nor published during his lifetime:

> The Scroobious Pip went out one day
> When the grass was green and the sky was gray.
> Then all the beasts in the world came round
> When the Scroobious Pip sat down on the ground.
>   The cat and the dog and the kangaroo,
>   The sheep and the cow and the guinea pig too,
>   The wolf he howled, the horse he neighed,
>   The little pig squeaked, and the donkey brayed,
>   And when the lion began to roar
>   There never was heard such a noise before.
>   And every beast he stood on the tip
>   Of his toes to look at the Scroobious Pip.

From *Grimm's Fairy Tales* (1853) by Jacob and Wilhelm Grimm, illustrated by Edward Cruikshank.

At last they said to the fox, "By far
You're the wisest beast. You know you are!
Go close to the Scroobious Pip and say,
Tell us all about yourself we pray—
For as yet we can't make out in the least
If you're fish or insect, or bird or beast."
The Scroobious Pip looked vaguely round
And sang these words with a rumbling sound,
"Chippetty flip! Flippetty chip!
My only name is the Scroobious Pip!"

The idea for nonsense poetry grows out of the oral tradition—especially nursery rhymes and folk songs. In Lear's artful crafting of the form, a long verse-story, rooted in an absurd situation, moves quickly into a fresh and appealing fantasy world—and one that is never sentimental, never didactic.

In the same year that Lear's book appeared (1846), Hans Christian Andersen's first collection of literary fairy tales was translated from the Danish for English children. Unlike the Grimm brothers, who were collecting folk tales and reworking them into finished literary pieces that merely echoed the folk tradition, Andersen was a literary artist from the outset. He created and shaped his own stories, although they were often inspired by tales such as those from the *Arabian Nights Entertainments* he had read or those he heard from a local peasant woman in his hometown of Odense.

Andersen's voice is what makes his stories unique. Notice the richness of language, the clarity of detail, and the conversational asides that produce a natural narrative flow in this opening passage of "The Nightingale" (1843), one of his most popular stories (from *Hans Andersen's Fairy Tales,* Penguin, 1981, translated by Naomi Lewis):

> You know, of course, that in China the Emperor is a Chinaman, and all the people around him are Chinese too. This story happened many years ago, but that's exactly why you should hear it now, before it is forgotten.
>
> The Emperor's palace was the finest in the world, entirely made of the rarest porcelain—absolutely beyond price, but so fragile and delicate that you had to take the greatest care when you moved about. The palace garden was full of marvellous flowers, never seen anywhere else; the loveliest of all had little silver bells tied to them—tinkle, tinkle—to make sure that nobody passed without noticing.
>
> Yes, everything in the Emperor's garden was wonderfully planned, and it stretched so far that even the gardener had no idea where it ended. If you kept on walking you find yourself in a most beautiful forest with towering trees and very deep lakes. This forest went right down to the sea, which was blue and deep; great ships could sail right in under the high branches of the trees. In these branches lived a nightingale, which sang so sweetly that even the poor fisherman, with all his cares, would stop while casting his nets each night, to listen. (page 77)

Andersen's work, like that of Lear's, moves the children's book into a distinctive literary sphere of its own. Andersen's careful crafting of his stories, in particular his attention to style and narrative design, placed a new emphasis on the story for the story's sake. Neither Andersen nor Lear was concerned with teaching children morals. Whether characters were good or bad was not the issue; what mattered was whether the story worked to produce aesthetic pleasure for children.

We can see Andersen's careful attention to craft and Lear's mischievous talent for nonsense reemerging two decades later in a book by Lewis Carroll. Carroll wrote the book soon after he told a story for a child in Oxford, England. Carroll's child character, Alice, feels herself in constant danger in this story, and her precarious condition might explain why children have always enjoyed the book. The story also successfully mixes rhyme, nonsense poetry, natural conversation, impossibility, surrealistic fantasy, improvisation, absurdity, mischief, wit, and a strong female child character who stands up to the illogic, oppression, and hypocrisy of the adult world. All of these elements draw children into the story.

Carroll's plot and stylistic treatment set the book apart. Refusing to play by the rules himself, just as his character ultimately refuses to take orders from a pack of playing cards, he redefined the children's book as capable of making its own laws, conventions, themes, subjects, and style. The language itself—playful, witty, fanciful—marked this kind of book as especially different. Yet it was, like the best examples of adult literature, filled with literary strengths such as storytelling power, empathetic, richly delineated characters, and evocative scenes. In addition, his language evoked emotional resonance, had a clearly conceived design and structure, and displayed originality of ideas. Carroll financed *Alice's Adventures in Wonderland* himself to insure the highest-quality printing techniques and artwork. Children deserved the best, Carroll thought; they could become as enthusiastic about good books as poor ones, if only they were exposed to the best.

When *Alice's Adventures in Wonderland* crossed the ocean to America, Americans had for some time been using English books, English influences, and books from the European continent translated into English. At the same time, Americans were also producing literature of their own. James Fenimore Cooper's series, *The Leatherstocking Tales* (1812–1841), set in the forests near Lake Otsego, New York, was filled with romantic visions of a disappearing "Eden" in America. Washington Irving wrote "Rip Van Winkle" and "The Legend of Sleepy Hollow" (1819), stories set in his native region of Tarrytown, New York. Nathaniel Hawthorne retold Greek legends for children in *A Wonder Book* (1852) and *Tanglewood Tales* (1853).

Louisa May Alcott wrote a family novel—*Little Women*—during the same decade that *Alice's Adventures in Wonderland* was published in England (1868).

INVESTIGATIONS: Books from 1800 to 1900

Read a book published between 1800 and 1900 to gain a sense of the books that helped children's literature come into its own. Consider the following list in making your selection:

1806 *The Butterfly's Ball* by William Roscoe. Read this early verse-story, in which animals dress up and have fun, to see one of the earliest children's books with no instructive moral intent.

1822 *A Visit from St. Nicholas* by Clement Moore, the American versifier. Available in many modern picture book editions, this "Night Before Christmas" poem is a story children continue to read and love.

1823 *Grimm's Fairy Tales,* collected by Jacob and Wilhelm Grimm. Compare these stories with fairy tales written by Charles Perrault (1697) and Hans Christian Andersen (1846), and by Joseph Jacob's English and Celtic folk tale collections (1890 and 1894).

1843 *A Christmas Carol* by Charles Dickens. Revisit Scrooge, Tiny Tim, and the Ghost of Christmas Past.

1846 *The Book of Nonsense* by Edward Lear; *Fairy Tales* by Hans Christian Andersen; and *Slovenly Peter* by Heinrich Hoffmann-Donner. A lucky year for children; read and enjoy.

1865 *Hans Brinker* by Mary Mapes Dodge. An American writer set her story in Holland, and many American children have loved Holland ever since.

1876 *Tom Sawyer* by Samuel Langhorne Clemens (Mark Twain). Here is language from the master, plus humor and classic regional realism.

1877 *Black Beauty* by Anna Sewell. Read about life from the horse's perspective and learn what it feels like to be oppressed.

1881 *Pinocchio* by Carlo Collodi. Here is the Italian classic that inspired Walt Disney's Magic Island.

1882 *Treasure Island* by Robert Louis Stevenson. Read the most famous adventure story of its day, and perhaps in this day too (although you will find few females in this story). *The Adventures of Robin Hood* by Howard Pyle. Pyle's words and pictures are important for depicting the hero many children love.

1883 *Heidi* by Johanna Spiri. This novel heralded a new age of realism and was a strong influence on Frances Burnett's *The Secret Garden.*

1889 *The Blue Fairy Book* by Andrew Lang. Read this first collection by the English folklorist, or any of the different "colored" books that he later produced. See how many familiar stories from your own childhood you can find.

1894 *The Jungle Book* by Rudyard Kipling. Discover the original of the Disney adaptation.

Set primarily in Boston, with several chapters describing the American characters abroad, it became immensely popular in England, as would Mark Twain's humorous and subtly satirical adventure stories, *Tom Sawyer* (1876) and *Huckleberry Finn* (1884). Although Twain wrote the books for the American public generally, *Tom Sawyer* became a children's book and *Huckleberry Finn* found its way into the adult canon or honored—and often hotly contested—American classics. (Twain's character's names—such as Injun Joe and Nigger Jim—although they reflect the vernacular of the day in the American White South, do not always meet the approval of multicultural America in the present day.) Both books were important for producing a realistic picture of small town life on the Mississippi River during the days of slavery.

The slavery era was also the focus of Joel Chandler Harris's *Uncle Remus: His Songs and Sayings* (1880). This book needed "translation" for many readers on both sides of the Atlantic because of the heavy Black Southern dialect that Harris created for his narrator, a slave living on a Georgia plantation. But the subtle and humorous illustrations by A. B. Frost needed no translation, and they have continued to delight children on both sides of the Atlantic.

X.

MR. TERRAPIN APPEARS UPON THE SCENE.

"MISS SALLY'S" little boy again occupying the anxious position of auditor, Uncle Remus took the shovel and "put de noses er de chunks tergedder," as he expressed it, and then began:

"One day, atter Sis Cow done run pas' 'er own hadder trying' fer ter ketch 'im, Brer Rabbit tuck'n

'low dat he wuz gwineter drap in en see Miss Meadows en de gals, en he got out his piece er lookin'-glass en

From *Uncle Remus: His Songs and Sayings* (1880) by Joel Chandler Harris, Illustrated by A.B. Frost.

Meanwhile, in England, Robert Louis Stevenson was producing two adventure novels, *Treasure Island* (1883) and *Kidnapped* (1886). These two stories would grant him an important place in children's literature. Between these two novels, in 1885, Stevenson wrote poetry in *A Child's Garden of Verse.* In this era, utilizing one's talents to the fullest meant achieving fame among adults. Lewis Carroll, Robert Louis Stevenson, and Rudyard Kipling, author of *The Jungle Books* (1894–95) and *The Just So Stories* (1902), all wrote for a dual audience.

In 1889, Andrew Lang produced *The Blue Fairy Book,* a collection of folk tales from around the world, and he followed it with eleven more volumes. By 1897, Lang's Red, Yellow, and Pink Fairy books were in print, with more on the way. He included stories from the Grimm and Perrault collections, the Arabian Nights tales, and Hans Christian Andersen's books, plus many more. As the 1800s drew to a close, children could at last take books like *The Blue Fairy Book* for granted, and children's literature as a literary genre—based on the child's perspective and preoccupations as distinct from the adult's—had taken root.

1900–1960

Victorian adults began to conceive of childhood as a separate state and children as basically good or innocent, carryovers from John Locke's earlier "blank-slate" conception of human nature and Rousseau's idea of the natural child. Victorians valued children for their clear-sightedness and for their perception of the *essence* of things—their view influenced by the eighteenth-century English Romantic poet William Wordsworth. Members of the pragmatic middle class also expected children to adhere to "correct" manners and morals. Carroll's Alice is quite concerned that she do the proper, the considerate, the "right" thing.

Democratic ideals prevailed in novels like Frances Hodgson Burnett's *Little Lord Fauntleroy* (1885) and *A Little Princess* (1905). Behavior rather than birth made the little boy a "gentleman" and the little girl a "princess." Some children's books were also designed to teach a more liberal perspective on moral standards. Authors viewed entertainment as a value in itself, and that may be why so many adults today testify to the pleasure they once took in reading Burnett's *A Secret Garden* (1911). Books like *Alice's Adventures in Wonderland, Treasure Island,* and *A Secret Garden* had empathetic characters, exciting plots, and thought-provoking ideas. *Alice's Adventures in Wonderland* also had nonsense rhymes and wordplay.

During the Edwardian Period, the reign of Edward VII in England (1901–10), trends of the Victorian Period (1837–1901) continued with books like Kenneth Grahame's *The Wind in the Willows* (1905), with original illustrations by Ernest Shepherd, and L. M. Montgomery's *Anne of Green Gables* (1908). Grahame's childlike animals live in a pastoral paradise, eating grand feasts on the river, sleeping in cozy little forest places, boating, visiting friends, and indulging themselves in playful pastimes. Montgomery's innocent, lovable Anne Shirley is gifted with problem-solving abilities and resourcefulness, necessary qualities as adults fade in and out of the story.

Childhood is such an important time in these novels that some characters, like Peter in J. M. Barrie's Play, *Peter Pan* (1904), simply cannot give it up. Barrie's play was later adapted in story form (1911) and has since been adapted for stage, screen, and many illustrated books. Childhood innocence is such a recurrent theme that many authors place their child characters into a garden setting, suggesting the Biblical Garden of Eden before evil entered the world.

Beatrix Potter's *The Tale of Peter Rabbit* (Warne, 1905) is an exception: Peter's father met his fate in Mr. McGregor's garden and was made into a pie. Although the book is, of course, make-believe, it presents a more realistic picture of the world than most children's stories of this era. But the vision of a pristine, ideal world is alive and well in Burnett's secret garden, Grahame's Wild Wood, and A. A. Milne's Hundred-Acre Wood, home of *Winnie the Pooh* (Dutton, 1926).

In the 1930s and 1940s, children were facing a different world, with childhood becoming the training period for adult tasks and independence. Children's books in America became vehicles for developing traditional frontier values such as self-reliance, generosity, friendship, imagination, and integrity, as we see in Laura Ingalls Wilder's Little House books (Harper, 1932–43) about pioneer life for a family with four daughters. Traditions and ideals of the mainstream culture continued to hold sway into the 1950s and after, including the tradition inaugurated by Lewis Carroll—of adult writers and illustrators putting their strongest artistic talents to work for children.

In this era, prestigious members of the adult literary establishment authored some of the best children's books, including *Charlotte's Web* (Harper, 1950) by prominent *New Yorker* essayist E. B. White. Some of these authors were Oxford dons like J. R. R. Tolkien, who published *The Hobbit* in 1938 (Houghton Mifflin) and C. S. Lewis, author of the Narnia series (Macmillan, 1950–56). Lewis defended a good children's book as the best possible *literature,* thus heightening the status of such writing.

Susan Cooper, a student of Tolkien and Lewis at Oxford, made her debut on the children's literature stage in the late 1960s with her *Dark is Rising* sequence (Simon & Schuster, 1966–77). She not only followed in her mentors' literary footsteps, producing a sequence of quest fantasies, but she defined a children's book writer, as they did, as one who did not write *intentionally* for children; she wrote, she said, for herself and the child she once was. Because that child remained with her still, she did not think continuously about what children would like or what adults would consider good for them. She knew already; she *was* that child.

Cooper knew something else, too. As a child living through the London Blitz, she had experienced the horror of seeing a neighbor's house bombed and a friend killed when his house was bombed. She lived each day with the fear of going down into the family bomb shelter at night, not knowing what she would see afterward—or whether she would be alive to see anything. She wrote about this in *Dawn of Fear* (Harcourt, 1970), an autobiographical novel that changed the look of children's literature considerably. The question was, could a book like *Dawn of Fear* even be called *children's* literature? By the end of the book, the child characters seemed to have permanently lost their innocence. Each day they passed the place their friend used to live—to see only the gate now standing.

A new world began to emerge with the close of World War II, a confusing, chaotic, fragmented, postmodernist time. Americans and Europeans were confronting evil run amuck during the Holocaust and facing a new monster they had let loose—the atomic bomb. In the midst of this adult uncertainty, picture book authors such as Robert McCloskey and Ezra Jack Keats, and Dr. Seuss show us the American literary "garden" at its best *before* the "fall": their characters were neither alienated, troubled, uncertain, nor anxious, except in universal, commonplace ways. McCloskey wrote of duck "parents" trying to find a safe place in the city to bring up their newly born children in *Make Way for Ducklings* (Viking, 1941) and of a little girl coping with losing a tooth in *One Morning in Maine* (Viking, 1952). Keats depicted a child discovering that a treasured snowball, saved in a snowsuit pocket, could melt in *The Snowy Day*

INVESTIGATIONS: Books from 1900 to 1960

Examine several children's books from the early to mid-1900s. See what makes these books different from those that preceded and followed them. Consider the following books:

1900 *The Wizard of Oz* by L. Frank Baum. Read the book often called the first American fairy tale; then view the film. Try to discover what was cut, rearranged, or emphasized differently in the movie version.

1903 *Johnny Crow's Garden* by Leslie Brooke. This illustrated story book introduces us to some of the most charming picture book animals, even to this day. Pigs are Brooke's strong suit.

1908 *The Wind in the Willows* by Kenneth Grahame. This is perhaps the most famous animal fantasy novel of all time. These animals, engaged in human pastimes, are both human personality types and noble heroes, displaying both courage and gentleness.

Anne of Green Gables by L. M. Montgomery. In this adventure story, the orphan child Anne softens the hard heart of an older person.

1920 *The Brownies Book,* edited by W. E. B. Du Bois and others. Monthly magazine for African-American children and their parents, published in the years 1920 and 1921. The twenty-four issues were filled with stories, folk tales, poetry, biographies of famous black Americans, photography, and artwork. Available now as *The Best of the Brownies Book* (Oxford University Press, 1995), edited by Dianne Johnson-Feelings.

1928 *Millions of Cats* by Wanda Gág. Often cited as the first American picture book. Compelling artwork—in black and write—aligned with a rhythmical, patterned story that never loses its appeal for children.

1932 *Little House in the Big Woods* by Laura Ingalls Wilder. The first book of the series that Wilder, at age 65, wrote about her childhood in an American pioneer family of the 1870s.

1938 *The Hobbit* by J. R. R. Tolkien. Discover high fantasy (the author creates a "secondary" world and tells the story with eloquent language, serious purpose, and stately mood).

1947 *Goodnight Moon* by Margaret Wise Brown. Perhaps the most reassuring picture book for the youngest listeners.

1950 *Pippi Longstocking* by Astrid Lindgren. This book takes the fun of exaggerated fantasy and the theme of the child as outsider and blends them into a tall tale starring one of the most adventuresome, most liberated females we are likely to see in a children's book.

The Lion, the Witch, and the Wardrobe by C. S. Lewis. Read the first book in this series about children who step into a different world to become royalty in a place filled with conflicts of good and evil, fantasy creatures, and humanlike animals.

1951 *Ramona the Pest* by Beverly Cleary. Everyone's favorite kindergartner.

1957 *The Cat in the Hat* by Dr. Seuss. Rhymed fun with a famous mischief maker.

1961 *A Snowy Day* by Ezra Jack Keats. The first Caldecott picture book with a black child as main character. This book is also an artistic achievement in words and collage-style pictures: Peter wears a bright red snowsuit, plays in the white snow all day long, returns home to think and dream about his adventures, and finally wakes up to another snowy day.

1962 *A WrinkLe in Time* by Madeleine L'Engle. In this time travel fantasy, children journey to a futuristic, evil fantasy planet to rescue their father.

(Viking, 1962). Dr. Seuss revealed children coming to terms with their naughtiness in *The Cat in The Hat* (Beginner Books, 1957).

Characters, themes, and subjects at this time focused upon children growing up in an ordered, serene world, rather than a troublesome, hectic existence. But the 1960s brought an end to the certainty that police, parents, or another snowy day could bring children reassurance. In this era of rapidly changing social conditions, children began to take on adult problems and earlier age, as Canadian critic Sheila Egoff reminded members of the American Library Association in 1979.

The 1960s produced more working mothers (and more latchkey children), the emergence of television, new demands for openness and frankness about sex and violence, the Viet Nam conflict, and increased social unrest and defiance of authority.

Egoff's talk, entitled "Beyond the Garden Wall," emphasized that children no longer appeared to be special, innocent, or different from adults; childhood as an idealized state was swiftly disappearing. Not since the Middle Ages, she said, had children been so immersed in the adult world.

1960–1980

In the face of rapidly changing social conditions, writers began producing books for previously underrepresented special interest groups: member of various ethnic groups, handicapped children, adopted children. At this time the "problem" novel emerged with it focused on drugs, child abuse, and absentee parents. The term bibliotherapy (the use of books to help children resolve or cope with such problems) arose at this time too. The child who identified with a particular character supposedly underwent the same trauma as the child character and could find the same resolution. The young reader supposedly gained insights that could be used for resolving personal conflicts.

Judy Blume was especially adept at writing problem novels—which child readers of the 1970s and 1980s flocked to—but not because she was trying to be a therapist. Blume was simply telling the kind of story she wanted to tell, and she had a particular talent for telling it, with empathetic insight and humor. The books differed from earlier books, however, signaling important changes not only in the culture itself but also in children's reading habits. First, Blume's stories focused on particular problems emergent adolescent children might face—getting a first bra or a first period, enduring a pesty younger sibling, being overweight, surviving their parent's divorce. Her books were also shorter than earlier children's novels had been, with more dialogue, fewer details, less description, and fewer well-developed characters. They had special appeal for a generation of children who were growing up watching television rather than reading novels.

The traditional novel was filled with long, gracefully phrased sentences, richness of characterization and setting, and a stable narrative perspective that filled the work with voice and authority. Blume's fiction had a thin literary style as an individual child told his or her own story, in place of the adult sees-all, knows-all narrator of earlier novels by Louisa May Alcott, Frances Burnett, and E. B. White. The characters in Blume's books often seemed problem-types—the rejected, victimized, or troubled child—and the traditional happy ending sometimes became instead ironic. Neither comedy nor tragedy prevailed; the picture was simply one of frustrated hopes, often the opposite of what children expected or wished. A small ray of hope nearly always seeped into the endings of these books, but the picture was still bleaker than in earlier novels.

In this era of the problem novel, Betsy Byars was producing fiction more accessible and timely than the work of writers like Frances Burnett, but "heavier" in theme and literary style than the novels of Judy Blume. Byars's work, like Blume's, frames an era when social upheaval was filtering into children's books—more mothers were entering the work force, adults were increasingly self-absorbed, and Baby Boomers were adopting more chaotic, less family-oriented lifestyles. Her major strength, like Blume's, is *emotional resonance.* But Byars achieves this quality in a different way—by allowing readers to enter children's minds and observe the way they work through their problems. In Byars's books, the adults—rather than the children—are self-absorbed. Like many literary children of this era, her characters have adult responsibilities foisted upon them before they are ready; thus, they often lose a sense of childhood.

Even in *The Cybil War,* an otherwise humorous, lively book, Simon Newton shoulders the burden of a childlike father who has run way from home to "find" himself. But Byars never lets an adult problem crowd out or overwhelm the children's preoccupations. Caught in events beyond their understanding or control, children like Simon make the best of things by simply coming to terms with their lives. Like Simon, they move on, but they do so in ways their literary predecessors would not have considered. The old fairy tales presented a similar you-play-the-hand-that-is-dealt-you perspective, but the result was that child heroes had glorious adventures, idealistic perspectives, and resounding triumphs. Such bold moves and high-spirited actions are missing from more recent books. A grim world faced children in the 1960s and beyond, one more grim than any Grimm tale.

In the face of these social realities, picture books have, for the past three decades, become increasingly experimental, with thematic complexities and sophisticated artistry that have entirely changed their look. When Maurice Sendak began producing his picture book trilogy in the early 1960s, he included few anthropomorphic animals or objects like those in Margery Bianco Williams' *The Velveteen Rabbit* (Doubleday, 1922) or Virginia Burton's *The Little House* (Houghton Mifflin, 1942). The child's world, in Sendak's view, involved pain and distress on an everyday basis, as he would show in *Where the Wild Things Are* (1963), *In the Night Kitchen* (1970), and *Outside Over There* (1981), all published by Harper and Row. Sendak's child characters had only one way to deal with inner turmoil, fear, anger, and jealousy. They turned inward for imaginative solutions.

More books in this stream of psychic distress followed over the next decades. Alongside Sendak's works would soon appear intriguing, artistic, multidimensional, surrealistic picture books by Anthony Browne, Allen Say, Peter Sis, Colin Thompson, Chris Van Allsburg, David Wiesner, and the team of Arthur Yorinks and Richard Egielski. Adult and children's literature began to merge in themes and

INVESTIGATIONS: Books from 1960 to 1980

Examine books by Judy Blume, Betsy Byars, and Maurice Sendak to see how the literature of the post-1960s era differs from earlier twentieth-century children's books.

style to the extent that the traditional world of children's literature, filled with warmth, wonder, and sentiment, appeared to be permanently in eclipse.

As English educator and literary critic Jane Doonan (1994) noted in relation to Sendak's most controversial and adultlike book, *We Are All in the Dumps with Jack and Guy* (HarperCollins, 1994): "Once upon a time the old stories were for every one of those gathered round the fire to take and make what they could from them, but in recent days such stories have come to be seen as belonging only to childhood. Conversely, picture books used to be the property of children but may now take a form to which adults as well can respond in many different ways" (page 166).

Psychic turmoil and adultlike themes is one trend we see in children's books produced in recent decades. Three others are multiethnic literature, active female protagonists, and innovative postmodernist picture books and novels. The recent push for authenticity in multiethnic literature and a surge of interest in strong females reflect modern cultural values. New experiments in pictorial forms and a focus on the grim realities of the real world also reflect a society groping to deal with change.

1980 and Beyond

The need for multiethnic books emerged in the mid-1960s when educator Nancy Larrick, in "The All White World of Children's Books," brought to public awareness the fact that few children's books had black children as leading characters. The greater visibility of black Americans during the civil rights movement provided an impetus for federal funding of multicultural programs in schools and libraries. Consequently, publishers began looking for books about urban life, black leaders, and African-American children. White writers seized the opportunity to produce them; thus, ironically, the old cycle continued. White perspectives on children of color were the ones children saw in their books.

A few members of underrepresented ethnic cultures did manage to catch the eye of mainstream publishers prior to the 1960s. By 1932, the talented team of Arna Bontemps and Langston Hughes had produced *Popo and Fifina* (Macmillan; illustrations by E. Sims Campbell; now available from Oxford University Press). Writers for older children such as Lorenze Graham and Jessie Jackson were producing authentic stories about African-American children in the 1930s and 1940s. Jackson's *Call Me Charley* (Harper, 1945) is an important piece of historical fiction today, as is Graham's *South Town* (Follett, 1958).

By 1945, Jade Snow Wong had published *Fifth Chinese Daughter* (reissued by University of Washington Press, 1989), a much-talked-about book today in ethnic feminist literature circles. Wong focuses on growing up Chinese American in a white supremacist, American world, and also growing up female in a male-dominated, Chinese home. Wong's book is fictionalized autobiography, since it details her life. But Wong uses a narrator to tell the story, rather than telling it in the first person.

It was not until the 1970s that Hispanic and Native American writers came to mainstream attention. Nicholasa Mohr produced a collection of short stories about growing up Puerto Rican in New York City, *El Bronx Remembered* (1973;

reissued by Arte Publico Press, 1989). Mohr's still popular *Felita* (Dial, 1979) and the sequel *Going Home* (Dial, 1986) tell of a nine-year-old girl's life in a large, extended family in the same neighborhood setting as Mohr's earlier book. In *Going Home,* Felita visits her family's native Puerto Rico. Natachee Scott Momaday, mother of the prominent Native American novelist N. Scott Momaday, produced *Owl in the Cedar Tree* in 1975 (University of Nebraska Press), a novel for younger readers about growing up Native American when American values and Navajo customs collide.

The Council on Interracial Books for children formed in 1966 to counter the publishers' claim that no ethnic authors were interested in writing for children—and that they had to continue to hire mainstream white writers. Walter Dean Myers was one of the writers the Council solicited to write about growing up African American (in Myers's case, in Harlem).

As Myers explained in 1986, he had faced painful images of black people in the books he read as a child. The caricatures in *Little Black Sambo,* the supposedly comical black maid in the Bobbsey Twins series, Robinson Crusoe's "savage" sidekick, Friday, and slow-witted Eradicate Sampson in the Tom Swift books populated children's literature at the time. Most of all, Myers remembered "the overwhelming *absence* of blacks in most books." Later, reading Langston Hughes's work, Myers learned that being a black writer meant "understanding the nuances of values, of religion, of dreams. It meant capturing the subtle rhythms of language and movement and weaving it all, the sound and the gesture, the sweat and the prayers, and the recognizable fabric of black life" (page 50).

In the 1970s, many other African-American writers were authoring books alongside Myers. Novelists such as Virginia Hamilton, Sharon Bell Mathis, and Mildred Taylor; poets such as Eloise Greenfield and Lucille Clifton; and picture book artists such as Leo Dillon, Tom Feelings, and John Steptoe were producing books not just for black children but for *all* children, hoping to extinguish caricatures and stereotypes. These writers had only a short-lived time for rejoicing.

Libraries began suffering severe cutbacks during the Nixon and Ford Administrations of the 1970s. By 1984, African-American concerns were no longer a "hot" political topic, and one half of the 900 children's books about the black experience of the 1970s were out of print. Only one in every hundred published books reflected a black child's life at that point. But in the 1990s, the pendulum began swinging back toward multiculturalism.

At this time, educators, librarians, and booksellers began paying more attention to African-American history. In 1926, African-American historian Carter G. Woodson had initiated a week-long black history celebration during February, the month of Lincoln's birthday. In 1976, Negro History Week became Black History *Month.* By the late 1980s and early 1990s, Black History Month was becoming fixed in the public mind as a time—a *month's* time in February—to talk about the African-American contribution to American history. Media events, library and bookstores displays, and school functions and programs continued to reflect this new emphasis throughout the 1990s.

Another reason for the revived interest in multicultural children's literature was the 1982 installation of an official American Library Association medal—the

Coretta Scott King Award—for distinguished books by African-American authors and illustrators. Above all, an explosion in the number of extraordinary new talents in writing and illustrating among African Americans promoted the resurgence of books for and about black children. In the last decade, Joyce Hansen, Patricia and Frederick McKissick, Jerry Pinkney, James Ransome, Faith Ringgold, Eleanora Tate, and Joyce Carol Thomas joined Leo and Diane Dillon, Tom Feelings, Eloise Greenfield, Virginia Hamilton, Walter Myers, John Steptoe, and Mildred Taylor to tell their stories with artistic integrity and literary strength. John Steptoe died in the 1980s, leaving a rich legacy of multicultural children's picture books. (See more on Black History and Culture in Appendix 1.)

African-American authors are not the only talented writers and illustrators of children's books today. Sook Nyul Choi, Allen Say, and Laurence Yep write about growing up Asian and Asian American. Joseph Bruchac, Michael Dorris, Gail Ross, and Virginia Driving Hawk Sneve tell children about growing up Native American. Carmen Lomas Garza, Pat Mora, and Gary Soto have written about children, like themselves, who are Hispanic American. And in 1996, the American Library Association established a new award for Latino authors and illustrators, the Pura Belpre Award. (See Appendix 1 for detailed listings of books by multicultural writers and illustrators.)

Among these multiethnic authors, novelists including Choi, Hamilton, Tate, Taylor, and Yep have produced strong female characters who are gifted in imagination and in their problem-solving capabilities, and who often persist in the face of nearly insurmountable physical, emotional, or social obstacles. Unafraid to take risks and outspoken, these active females display courage during the most trying times as they search for identity and a sense of belonging. Other resourceful females spring out of the works of Karen Cushman, Elaine Konigsburg, Janet Lunn, Katherine Paterson, and Cynthia Voigt.

Nonfiction and picture book writers also feature strong female subjects in their works. Russell Freedman produced a photo-biography of the famous social activist and American First Lady Eleanor Roosevelt in 1993. African American picture book artist Faith Ringgold depicted strong females in *Tar Beach* (Crown, 1991), *Aunt Harriet's Underground Railroad in the Sky,* (Crown, 1992), and *Dinner at Aunt Connie's House* (Crown, 1993). Charlotte Huck and Anita Lobel created an ingenious Cinderella in *Princess Furball* (Greenwillow, 1989).

In England, Ann Jungman and Russell Ayto produced *Cinderella and the Hot Air Balloon* (Frances Lincoln, 1992), a modern retelling of the earlier Cinderella story, with a character who likes "to climb trees, ride horses bareback, skate on thin ice, and run barefoot" and who refuses to go to the ball. Instead, the ball—and the Prince—come to her. Later, Cinderella and the Prince, who hates dancing and likes "skating on thin ice" as much as she does escape everyone by flying off in a hot-air balloon. Jungman's is a *postmodernist* picture book. Many such books call up characters from older stories and produce playful imitations, or parodies, of them. Readers who remember the original Cinderella as oppressed, tearful, and limited in power, will appreciate this new young woman who thinks, speaks, and acts very much for herself.

Not all postmodern children's books are parodies of original texts. Some, like Janet and Allan Ahlberg's *The Jolly Postman* (Little, Brown, 1986), call up characters from older stories and place them in new situations or settings, or among characters from other stories; and they do so simply for the intertextual fun of it. In *The Jolly Postman,* a postman delivers letters to characters from different folk tales—the Three Bears, the Wicked Witch of "Hansel and Gretel," the Giant of "Jack and the Beanstalk," a now-married Cinderella living at the Palace, the Big Bad Wolf at Grandma's cottage, and Goldilocks.

Extra fun for children comes from the pop-up features: envelopes opening out of the book pages are filled with the actual letters, cards, and notes the postman is delivering, so that the reader shares the excitement of getting a letter. Fun for adults arises out of the way the letters cast a wry look at life in modern times: mail order companies, publishing houses, and travel agents pitch their products and services, and greedy lawyers try to drum up business. Litigious lawyers and affluent royals are all immersed in a print-flooded, literacy-soaked world that children can enter easily. Children are the newest members in this world of literature and literacy, and the fun for them arises from pulling out and peeping at other people's letters.

Literary critic and educator Geoff Moss describes the difference between modernist and postmodernist thinking as one of stance. Modernists, according to Moss, ask " 'How can I interpret this world of which I am a part?' " Postmodernists, on the other hand, ask " 'What is a world? What kinds of worlds are there?' " Whereas modernists are concerned with how they can represent life as closely as possible to reality, postmodernists are trying to define reality in an increasingly confusing world—or to redefine reality.

Modernists like Ezra Jack Keats, Robert McCloskey, and Betsy Byars, writing several decades before Jungman and the Ahlbergs, kept the child's world intact, because they saw the world as intact. They could resolve contradictions because the problems they saw were resolvable. Thus, their stories moved in circular plot patterns to "mend" fractured relationships, concepts, and experiences.

In these stories, the child was happily engaged in a unified world, discovering a snowy day, learning to whistle, or creating a neighborhood pet show (Keats) or losing a tooth (McCloskey). Then, something happened that was puzzling or traumatic—experiencing a hurricane (McCloskey) or losing an uncle, a father, or a younger brother (Byars)—and that unified world collapsed. Ultimately, however, the child was able to put things back together in one piece, arriving at a deeper understanding about the way the world works.

Postmodern authors find themselves in a less resilient, less "fixable" world, where problems are not easily solved, traumas are *severely* traumatic, and contradictions are at times simply not resolvable. Often they break the conventions of unity, balance, and resolution, to focus on *how* people tell stories, rather than to tell stories of their own. Many of their books show how both the story-world and the real world are put together, rather than how to fix that world when it falls apart. These writers peep beneath the surfaces of words, pictures, stories, and story-lives to explore what happens when readers step into stories or when life becomes shaky. They move things around to make better sense of them; often, they can only describe the shakiness, of a fractured world.

Two postmodernist picture book artists, Jon Sciezka and Lane Smith, produced *The True Story of the 3 Little Pigs* (Viking, 1989), *The Stinky Cheese Man and Other Fairly Stupid Tales* (Viking, 1992), and *Squids Will Be Squids* (Viking, 1998). In the first, A. Wolf tells his own side of the now-famous incident of the three pigs, seeking to obtain a little sympathy and understanding. In the second, characters from traditional folk tales come to life outside their usual story frameworks and step into one another's stories. In the third, the authors focus on fables, bringing them to life in new and zany ways. In each book, they bounce one story off another to produce innovative new versions—more intertextual fun.

Novels for older children reveal what Hazel Rochman (1998) has called a "recent dark trend" that may have begun with Sendak's picture book *We Are All in the Dumps with Jack and Guy* in 1993, which focuses on the plight of the homeless, from the child's perspective. By the late 1990s, children's fiction was becoming excruciatingly painful even for adults to read; yet adults granted these "dark" books the highest awards and the highest marks in reviews.

Consider Brock Cole's National Book Award winner, *The Facts Speak for Themselves* (Front Street, 1997). In this book, thirteen-year-old Linda has a mother who conceives babies without thought and then saddles Linda with caring for them. Linda's mother has numerous live-in boyfriends and an employer who uses Linda for sex. But Linda accepts her life for what it is and what she can gain from it, because, as *Horn Book* reviewer Patty Campbell says, Linda's "dreadful life has taught her to cope with events as they happen without wasting energy on feelings or trying to make sense of things" (page 678).

Linda is not a passive victim, Campbell adds. She has a "strong sense of order and decency, and she simply gets on with her life by doing what she must." But her matter-of-fact acceptance of events "makes them almost—for an eerie, off-guard moment—appear to the reader as ordinary and normal." Linda's tone of voice *is* matter-of-fact, and the straightforward style of the book increases its mood of acceptance. There is no authorial or narrative commentary to steer the reader in any direction but Linda's; readers must view the book as they will—bizarre, troubling, tragic, ironic, or simply the way things are. What do children do with trauma? Deal with it.

Consider also Karen Hesse's Newbery winner *Out of the Dust* (Scholastic, 1997), a story of the grim realities of the Depression era in Oklahoma. Drought, death, and a bad accident strike the narrator, a fourteen-year-old female named Billie Jo Kelby. But even younger heroines like Rayona Taylor of Michael Dorris's *The Window* (Hyperion, 1997) face—and deal with—grim realities these days. Rayona's mother is in a detox program; Rayona herself has been in two foster care situations that did not work out, and she learns about a mixed-race background that she previously knew nothing about. But her wisdom and humor pull her through all her adversities.

Neglect, abuse, and disturbing "truths" about life in the late twentieth century are all part of Anne Fine's *The Tulip Touch* (Little, Brown, 1997). Twice winner of the Carnegie Medal (Britain's counterpart to the American Newbery Award), Fine is also the author of *Alias Madame Doubtfire* (1990), the YA book that spawned the movie *Mrs. Doubtfire* in America. Fine's humor cuts through the bleak social undertones of these books.

But in the late 1990s, we are no longer looking at so-called problem novels. Problems have become so commonplace, we see them as the essence of contemporary life: one horror story after another, dark, dangerous, and frightening—yet also filled with human goodness and, when we can find it, humor. Says reviewer Hazel Rochman about *The Tulip Touch:*

> This book is better than the movie [*Doubtfire*]: farce, yes, and hilarious one-liners, but also hurt and anger and unexpected kindness. In all her fiction Fine writes funny, furious quarrel scenes . . . This time Fine isn't funny at all; she is part of the current dark trend in children's fiction, but the headlong action here moves with such thrilling intensity that readers will rush to the end and then go back and back to think about the disturbing truth. 'Who cares?' is a question Fine makes us ask, even as she reveals how close we are to the edge. (page 26)

"Children's literature, like any form of literature, will inevitably build on, toy with, and perhaps even destroy conventional forms as it develops," says Moss. What we should expect, along with growth in this field, then, is change.

INVESTIGATIONS: Books after 1980

Read a children's book of the last two decades (1980–99) and compare it to books published in the previous two decades (1960–80). Consider mood, style, story events, values and behaviors of characters, and realities facing children in today's world.

GROWTH AND CHANGE IN CHILDREN'S LITERATURE

In 1919, two important figures in the children's book world decided that each year in November, Americans should celebrate children's books in some important way. As Barbara Bader (1997), tells the story in *Horn Book Magazine,* Franklin Mathiews, Chief Librarian of the Boy Scouts, and Frederic Melcher, secretary of the American Booksellers Association and newly appointed co-editor of *Publishers Weekly,* hatched a plan for an annual children's book celebration.

Both men were enthusiasts of children's books. Mathiews had no use for boys' reading materials at this time, and Melcher would, two years later, donate the medal for the first Newbery Award, a yearly prize for the most distinguished contribution to children's literature. (Thirteen years later, he would also create the Caldecott Award for distinguished work in picture book art.) Together, Mathiews and Melcher were able to garner more attention for children's books and to lift the critical standards applied to them. From that day to this, members of the American

Book Week Poster, illustrated by Peter Sis, 1997

publishing establishment, along with librarians, teachers, and parents, have been honoring Newbery and Caldecott Medalists each February with the announcement of new award winners and celebrating Children's Book Week each year in November. At the core of Children's Book Week is the distinguished poster art that illustrators have created for this annual event since 1919.

These poster-pictures, collected by Leonard Marcus for his book *75 Years of Children's Book Week Posters,* depict the trends, visual styles, political issues, social values, and cultural beliefs reflected in children's books throughout twentieth-century America. They also reveal lapses and oversights: no black child appeared in any poster until 1944, and no African-American artist was invited to produce a poster until 1994.

Using Marcus's introductory chapter of the book as a starting point to map milestone events, we can create a literary "chronology" to better understand the social and cultural forces that have shaped the history of children's books in this century. We will also see the many perspectives—those of librarians, editors, publishers, authors, illustrators, parents, teachers, community and government leaders, and especially children—that converge in this many-faceted, interdisciplinary field.

As the twentieth century draws to a close, children's literature, no matter how we define the term, seems here to stay. The way this concept has reinvented itself in different eras makes it particularly interesting, as the next chapter—which focuses on different genres and themes of children's books—shows.

The Century in Review

Landmarks in the History of American Children's Books, 1900 to the Present

1900–1910	Many urban children living in poverty. Public libraries set up reading rooms for young people. Adults believe literature exerts a moral influence (good books are thought to build character).
1912–15	Boy Scouts leaders advocate annual book week to celebrate children's books. Books for American children are primarily European imports or taken from children's magazines like Scribner's *St. Nicholas.*
1918–19	Frederic Melcher, editor of *Publisher's Weekly,* and Anne Carroll Moore of the New York Public Library organize a Book Week Committee of publishers and booksellers. First slogan is "More Books in the Home." Macmillan publishers sets up a separate department to publish children's books; they are followed by Dutton, Harper, and Doubleday. Women editors head each department.
1921	Frederic Melcher initiates idea—and funding—for a Newbery Medal, a national prize for high-quality children's books to be awarded annually by members of the American Library Association.
1924	*Horn Book Magazine* published in Boston (first American journal specializing in articles and reviews of children's literature). Children's bookstores begin to open in major American cities.
1932	Publishers in Great Depression strive to create cheerful, patriotic mood. Biographies of George Washington, Abraham Lincoln, and Harriet Tubman published, along with Laura Ingalls Wilder's *Little House in the Big Woods.*
1935	American economy improves. More emphasis on books meant to stimulate children's imaginations (slogan for Book Week is "Reading for Fun."
1937	Frederick Melcher creates annual award for illustration, named for nineteenth-century illustrator Randolph Caldecott, to be given by American Library Association.
1936–42	Explosion of talent in American picture books: Munro Leaf and Robert Lawson's *The Story of Ferdinand,* Ludwig Bemelman's *Madeline,* Edgar Parin d'Aulaire's *Abraham Lincoln;* Virginia Burton's *Mike Mulligan and His Steam Shovel,* Robert McCloskey's *Make Way for Ducklings,* H. A. Rey's *Curious George,* Margaret Wise Brown and Clement Hurd's *The Runaway Bunny.*
1943	War industry is helpful for children's books (Book Week slogan is "Build the Future with Books"). Materials in short supply for bikes and toys; Americans turn to books. More nursery schools for mothers working in war industry means more picture books for children. Fifty book companies now publishing children's books. Simon & Schuster inaugurates new imprint—Golden Books—sold for 25 cents.
1944	Canadian born artist Nedda Walker produces first poster with a multicultural cast (children of African and Asian descent appear alongside children of European and Euro-American ancestry).
1946–56	Postwar "baby boom" increases publication of picture books. Book week posters are now produced by artists specializing in children's books: William Pene du Bois, Roger Duvoisin, Garth Williams, Maud and Miska Petersham, Edgar Parin and Ingri D'Aulaire, Marcia Brown.
1955–57	Rudolf Flesch accuses American schools of failing to teach reading skills in *Why Johnny Can't Read.* Random House publishes Dr. Seuss's *The Cat in the Hat* (children can now *enjoy* a story while learning to read). Harper publishes an I Can Read series featuring Else Minarik's *Little Bear,* illustrated by Maurice Sendak.
1958–65	Supreme Court decision of 1954 brings desegregation to schools in the South by 1959. Americans awaken to the lack of books featuring children of African heritage. Two more book posters (by Adrienne Adams, 1963, and Ezra Jack Keats, 1965) include African-American children. First Caldecott award to feature a black child is Ezra Jack Keats's *The Snowy Day,* 1963.

1965–69	President Johnson's initiatives produce large sums of money for school libraries, which prompts the publication of more children's books. Ellen Raskin depicts first Hispanic child for Book Week Poster, 1968. Inauguration of *Sesame Street* (PBS).
1973–75	Nixon administration begins dismantling federal funding for children's books. Library cutbacks cause publishers to produce paperbacks tailored to younger readers' interests. "Problem" novels about divorce, sex, and drugs emerge.
1975–80	Baby Boomers begin buying children's books for their children. More children's bookstores open. More teachers use children's books in the classroom. More children's books published. More variety in children's books (board books for babies, pop-up books, multicultural books). More books feature African-American children.
1970–80	Explosion of talent in book poster art by children's book illustrators: Mercer Mayer, Arnold Lobel, William Steig, Margot Zemach, James Marshall, Richard Scarry, Uri Shulevitz, Anita Lobel, Laurent de Brunhoff, Rosemary Wells, and Trina Hyman.
1982	American Library Association institutes annual award for distinguished children's books by African-American writers and illustrators (Coretta Scott King Award).
1980–89	Book Week posters designed by Tomie DePaola, Chris Van Allsburg, Stephen Kellogg, Richard Egielski, Trina Schart Hyman, and Wendy Watson, all prominent children's book artists. Sales in children's book publishing reach $475 million.
1990–2000	More books reveal African-American children's experiences. More bilingual books available to children. New levels of sophistication in picture books; artistic styles reflect surrealism, popular culture, filmmaking. Ed Young is first Asian-American artist to illustrate a Book Week poster (1990). Jerry Pinkney is first African-American artist to illustrate Book Week poster (1994). Sales in children's book publishing top $1 billion.

CHILDREN'S LITERATURE

Illustrated Classics

African-American Folktales: Brer Rabbit Stories

HAMILTON, VIRGINIA. *The People Could Fly: American Black Folktales.* Illustrated by Leo and Diane Dillon. New York: Knopf, 1985.

———. *Her Stories.* Illustrated by Leo and Diane Dillon. New York: Scholastic, 1995.

———. *A Ring of Tricksters.* Illustrated by Barry Moser. New York: Scholastic, 1997.

HARRIS, JOEL CHANDLER. *Uncle Remus.* Illustrated by A. B. Frost. New York: Schocken Books, 1965 (rpt. 1880).

LESTER, JULIUS. *The Tales of Uncle Remus.* Illustrated by Jerry Pinkney. New York: Dial, 1987.

———. *More Tales of Uncle Remus.* Illustrated by Jerry Pinkney. New York: Dial, 1988.

———. *The Last Tales of Uncle Remus.* Illustrated by Jerry Pinkney. New York: Dial, 1994.

PARKS, VAN DYKE, AND JONES, MALCOLM (ADAPTERS). *Jump! The Adventures of Brer Rabbit* by Joel Chandler Harris. Illustrated by Barry Moser. San Diego: Harcourt Brace, 1986.

———. *Jump Again!* More Adventures of Brer Rabbit. Illustrated by Barry Moser. San Diego: Harcourt Brace, 1987.

Hans Christian Andersen

ANDERSEN, HANS CHRISTIAN. *Fairy Tales.* Illustrated by Arthur Rackham. London: Harrap, 1985 (rpt. 1932).

———. *The Snow Queen.* Adapted by Naomi Lewis. Illustrated by Errol Le Cain. New York: Viking Penguin, 1979.

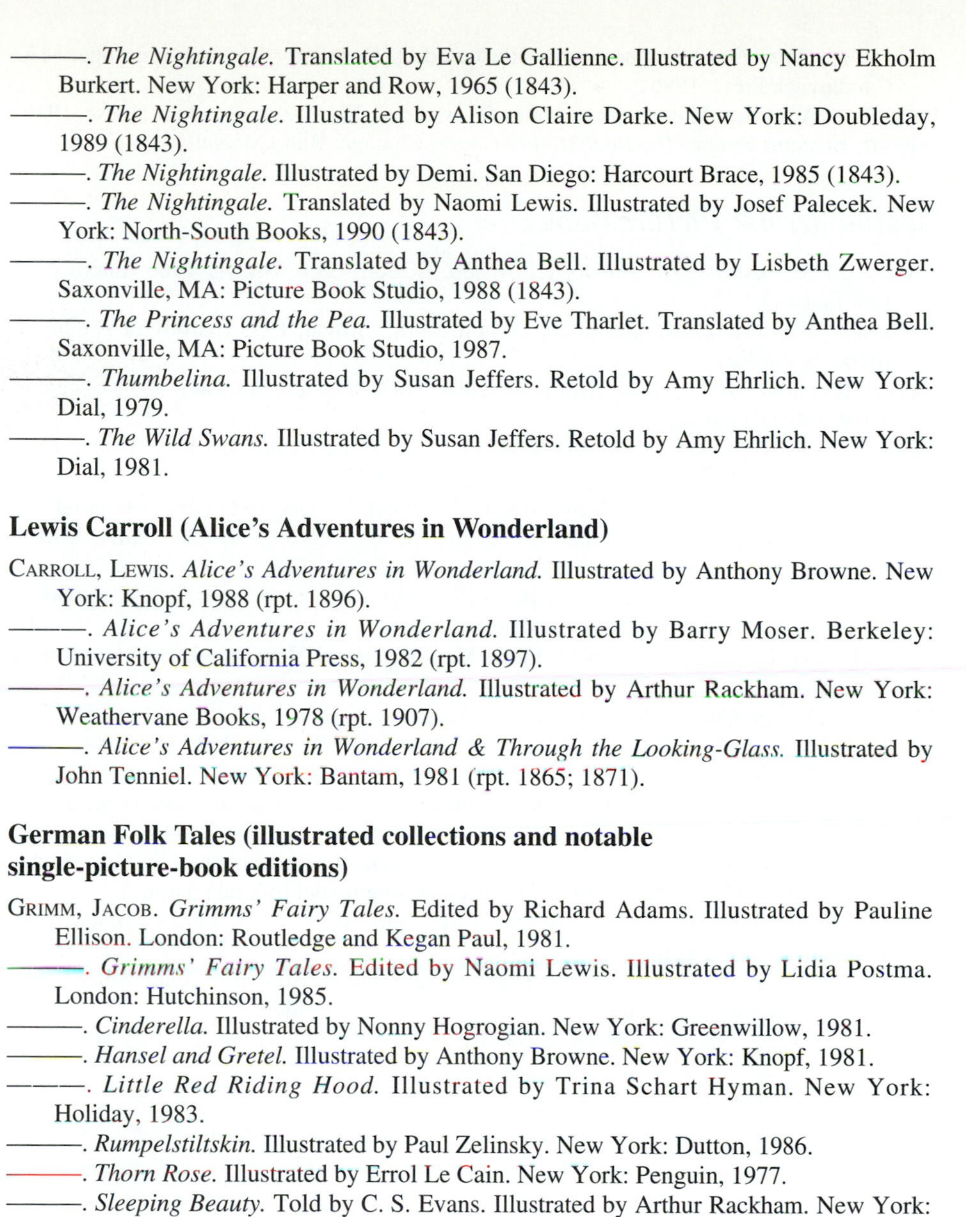

———. *The Nightingale.* Translated by Eva Le Gallienne. Illustrated by Nancy Ekholm Burkert. New York: Harper and Row, 1965 (1843).

———. *The Nightingale.* Illustrated by Alison Claire Darke. New York: Doubleday, 1989 (1843).

———. *The Nightingale.* Illustrated by Demi. San Diego: Harcourt Brace, 1985 (1843).

———. *The Nightingale.* Translated by Naomi Lewis. Illustrated by Josef Palecek. New York: North-South Books, 1990 (1843).

———. *The Nightingale.* Translated by Anthea Bell. Illustrated by Lisbeth Zwerger. Saxonville, MA: Picture Book Studio, 1988 (1843).

———. *The Princess and the Pea.* Illustrated by Eve Tharlet. Translated by Anthea Bell. Saxonville, MA: Picture Book Studio, 1987.

———. *Thumbelina.* Illustrated by Susan Jeffers. Retold by Amy Ehrlich. New York: Dial, 1979.

———. *The Wild Swans.* Illustrated by Susan Jeffers. Retold by Amy Ehrlich. New York: Dial, 1981.

Lewis Carroll (Alice's Adventures in Wonderland)

CARROLL, LEWIS. *Alice's Adventures in Wonderland.* Illustrated by Anthony Browne. New York: Knopf, 1988 (rpt. 1896).

———. *Alice's Adventures in Wonderland.* Illustrated by Barry Moser. Berkeley: University of California Press, 1982 (rpt. 1897).

———. *Alice's Adventures in Wonderland.* Illustrated by Arthur Rackham. New York: Weathervane Books, 1978 (rpt. 1907).

———. *Alice's Adventures in Wonderland & Through the Looking-Glass.* Illustrated by John Tenniel. New York: Bantam, 1981 (rpt. 1865; 1871).

German Folk Tales (illustrated collections and notable single-picture-book editions)

GRIMM, JACOB. *Grimms' Fairy Tales.* Edited by Richard Adams. Illustrated by Pauline Ellison. London: Routledge and Kegan Paul, 1981.

———. *Grimms' Fairy Tales.* Edited by Naomi Lewis. Illustrated by Lidia Postma. London: Hutchinson, 1985.

———. *Cinderella.* Illustrated by Nonny Hogrogian. New York: Greenwillow, 1981.

———. *Hansel and Gretel.* Illustrated by Anthony Browne. New York: Knopf, 1981.

———. *Little Red Riding Hood.* Illustrated by Trina Schart Hyman. New York: Holiday, 1983.

———. *Rumpelstiltskin.* Illustrated by Paul Zelinsky. New York: Dutton, 1986.

———. *Thorn Rose.* Illustrated by Errol Le Cain. New York: Penguin, 1977.

———. *Sleeping Beauty.* Told by C. S. Evans. Illustrated by Arthur Rackham. New York: Dover, 1971 (rpt. Heinemann, 1920).

———. *Snow White* and the Seven Dwarfs. Illustrated by Wanda Gäg. New York: Coward-McCann, 1938.

Mother Goose

BAYLEY, NICOLA. *Nicola Bayley's Book of Nursery Rhymes.* New York: Knopf, 1975.

BRIGGS, RAYMOND. *The Mother Goose Treasury.* London: Hamish Hamilton, 1966.

CALDECOTT, RANDOLPH. *Sing A Song of Sixpence.* New York: Barron's, 1988 (1880).

DEPAOLA, TOMIE. *Mother Goose.* New York: Putnam, 1985.

EDENS, COOPER. *The Glorious Mother Goose.* New York: Atheneum, 1988.

LOBEL, ARNOLD. *The Random House Book of Mother Goose.* New York: Random House, 1986.

OPIE, IONA AND PETER. *A Nursery Companion.* Oxford, England: Oxford University Press, 1980.

———. *My Very First Mother Goose.* Illustrated by Rosemary Wells. Cambridge, MA: Candlewick Press, 1996.

PROVENSEN, ALICE AND MARTIN. *The Mother Goose Book.* New York: Random House, 1976.

WRIGHT, BLANCHE FISHER. *The Real Mother Goose.* Chicago: Rand McNally, 1916.

Postmodernist Picture Books

AHLBERG, JANET AND ALLAN. *The Jolly Postman.* Boston: Little Brown, 1986 (intertextual folk fantasy).

BREATHED, BERKELEY. *Goodnight Opus.* Boston: Little, Brown, 1993 (parody of children's literature classic).

BRIGGS, RAYMOND. *Jim and the Beanstalk.* New York: Coward, McCann & Geoghegan, 1970 (folk tale parody).

BROWNE, ANTHONY, ARTIST AND RETELLER. *Hansel and Gretel by the Brothers Grimm.* New York: Knopf, 1981 (folk tale parody, surrealistic style).

COLE, BABETTE. *Prince Cinders:* New York: G. P. Putnam's Sons, 1987 (folk tale parody).

INNOCENTI, ROBERTO, ARTIST AND RETELLER. *Cinderella* by Charles Perrault. Mankato, MN: Creative Education, 1983 (folk tale update; surrealistic style).

JUNGMAN, ANN. *Cinderella and the Hot Air Balloon.* Illustrations by Russell Ayto. London: Frances Lincoln, 1992 (folk tale update; parody).

MARK, JAN. *Haddock.* Illustrations by Fiona Moodie. Hemel Hempstead, England: Simon & Schuster, 1994 (parody).

MEDDAUGH, SUSAN. *Cinderella's Rat.* Boston: Houghton Mifflin, 1997 (folk tale parody).

NYGREN, TORD. *The Red Thread.* Stockholm and New York: R & S Books, 1987 (surrealistic style).

SCIESZKA, JON. *The Frog Prince Continued.* Paintings by Steve Johnson. New York: Viking Penguin, 1992 (folk tale parody).

———. *The Stinky Cheese Man and Other Fairly Stupid Tales.* Illustrated by Lane Smith. New York: Viking Penguin, 1992 (metafiction, intertexual folk tale parody).

———. *Squids Will Be Squids.* Illustrated by Lane Smith. New York: Viking, 1998 (metafiction, fable parody).

———. *The True Story of the 3 Little Pigs!* by A. Wolf. Illustrated by Lane Smith. New York: Viking Kestrel, 1989 (metafiction, nursery tale parody).

STANDLEY, DIANE. *Rumpelstiltskin's Daughter.* New York: Morrow, 1997 (folk tale parody).

Chapter 2

Genre and Theme in Children's Books

Topics in This Chapter:

- Children's books in the "real" world
- Genres in children's literature
- Themes in children's literature

Alice was beginning to get very tired of sitting by her sister on the bank, and of having nothing to do: once or twice she had peeped into the book her sister was reading, but it had no pictures or conversations in it, 'and what is the use of a book,' thought Alice, 'without pictures or conversation?'

So she was considering in her own mind (as well as she could, for the hot day made her feel very sleepy and stupid) whether the pleasure of making a daisy-chain could be worth the trouble of getting up and picking the daisies, when suddenly a White Rabbit with pink eyes ran close by her.

There was nothing so very remarkable in that; nor did Alice think it so very much out of the way to hear the Rabbit say to itself, 'Oh dear! I shall be too late!' (when she thought it over afterwards, it occurred to her that she ought to have wondered at this, but at the time it all seemed quite natural); but when the Rabbit actually took a watch out of its waistcoat-pocket, and looked at it, and then hurried on, Alice started to her feet, for it flashed across her mind that she had never before seen a rabbit with either a waistcoat-pocket or a watch to take out of it, and burning with curiosity, she ran across the field after it, and fortunately was just in time to see it pop down a large rabbit-hole under the hedge.

In another moment down went Alice after it, never once considering how in the world she was to get out again.

"Down the Rabbit-Hole" in Alice's Adventures in Wonderland, 1865
—Lewis Carroll

We have been examining the world of children's literature through the ages and exploring what makes a book a *children's* book. In this chapter, we will take a deeper look at this question as we examine the ways children's books can be classified according to genre—form, purpose, and subject matter—or theme.

Children's books come in all different types, depending on their form, purpose, or content. We call these different types of books **genres.** The word *genre* comes from Old French and means a distinctive kind (type, class, or variety) of composition in art or literature.

We begin noticing **form** as soon as we pick up a book, from earliest childhood on. First we notice—as Alice did—whether a book has pictures or conversations; later, we notice whether words dominate pictures and if so, whether the words are highly patterned, as in poetry. We begin noticing **purpose** almost as early. We ask whether a story really could have happened (whether the author was reporting a *nonfiction* story or imagining a *fiction* story). We notice **content,** too, as soon as we have heard a few folk tales and legends and know that some stories have heroes, witches, or tricksters. We see that some books, like mysteries or science fiction, are about a particular subject—solving a mystery, or science in a future world. This subject or idea we call **theme.** We notice themes in literature as we think about the places where stories take place, the characters and their fates, and the reiteration of similar ideas running through many books. Thus, genre and theme often merge or are closely connected.

When we notice kinds of books, or genres, and ideas in books, or themes, we can begin to categorize or organize literature so that we are not coping with a jumble of books in the library, the bookstore, the classroom, or on the living room floor. We can place similar books into a group to make better sense of literature—and better sense of the world that literature represents or suggests.

CHILDREN'S BOOKS IN THE "REAL" WORLD

Enter any mass market bookstore these days and you will find shelved around the walls fiction of every kind—popular fiction, classics, mystery, romance, fantasy. On center aisles and shelves, you will find many nonfiction categories: biography, history, psychology, travel, self-help, cooking, religion, and animal care, to name a few. Along with these categories, you will see sections for poetry and perhaps even multicultural or multiethnic books. And set off to one side of the store, you will find the children's section, filled for the most part with picture books and fiction (usually paperback editions) arranged by age. In smaller areas of this section, you will find nonfiction works for children: biography, information, history, and science books. You will also find folk tales, poetry, and classics in hardcover editions that are sometimes labeled "gift books." The store might have a section for multicultural children's books.

At the public library, the children's section will be similar, except that hardcover editions will far outnumber paperbacks, and you may see a section displaying Newbery and Caldecott award winners. What do all these divisions or sections in bookstores and libraries mean? Simply this: We usually organize, study, or use books according to categories; in *children's* literature, the categories usually include fiction, nonfiction, poetry, folklore, and picture books as *genres.*

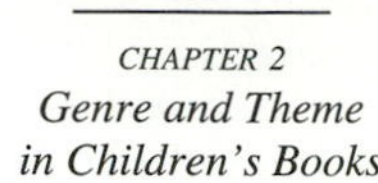

From *Alice's Adventures in Wonderland* (1865) by Lewis Carroll.

We often describe our interests in terms of these literary genres—Regina writes poetry, Ray loves ghost stories; Reggie is a science fiction fan. But most readers—and children are no exception—have diverse tastes and preoccupations. They may be reading biographies alongside travel books or novels, or poetry alongside fairy tales, in different places or at different times of the day. We may have no reason to think consciously about book categories unless we are searching for books in stores and libraries. But we must know about genres because they account for the way the world organizes literature.

Libraries and bookstores are built around these categories. Customers use them to find books although they might do so more or less unconsciously. Publishers use them to market books. Editor's and reviewers organize their columns around genres. Award committees make choices in terms of them. As readers, we negotiate texts of all kinds through genre categories. They help us know what to expect as we thread our way through books. If we know nothing about a particular genre, and we suddenly encounter that kind of book in our reading, we may find ourselves taking a wrong turn when we begin sorting out a story. We might become so confused that we reject the work completely.

Suppose we begin reading *Alice's Adventures in Wonderland.* In the beginning, everything seems logical and understandable (Alice is reading quietly with her sister on a riverbank). Suddenly, Alice encounters a talking rabbit—a very formal rabbit, with waistcoat and pocketwatch—and follows him down a rabbit hole, shrinking and expanding as she falls. She seems frightened, and we say, "This book is just too crazy. Rabbits don't talk; they don't wear coats and carry pocketwatches; girls don't follow rabbits down rabbit holes; children don't shrink and expand. Why would anyone write such foolishness?!"

But of course we would not say that, would we? For years now, we have been reading books in which animals talk and stories suddenly shift from absolute realism to the most impossible circumstances. Even as preschoolers, we would have had no problem accepting a talking rabbit. By that time, we had heard nursery rhymes, folk tales, and picture books filled with elements of fantasy. So we know what to expect, and we move easily into the story.

Expectations about genre underlie many of our literary responses, and we begin forming those expectations from the very first time we hear, see, or read literature. One story teaches us how to interpret the next; the more we read, and the more we enjoy variety in our reading, the better we become at reading. Exposure to literary genres helps us to recognize genres, and knowledge about genres helps us to become skillful readers. The more books we read from different genres, the better prepared we are to appreciate a practice that most inventive authors use—*genre blending.*

If as children we were steeped in both folk tales and picture books, it was not difficult to step into folk tale picture books. Once we had read several folk tale picture books, it was not difficult to step into illustrated folk tale collections. Once steeped in illustrated books, it was not difficult to step into novels—realistic or fantasy—with perhaps only a few illustrations in the entire story, or no illustrations except for the cover picture. But what happens if we take one step beyond these well-defined categories?

Suppose we find ourselves reading fiction that blends realism and fantasy? What if we begin reading a book like *Charlotte's Web* by E. B. White and see a child in a very realistic situation, begging her father to save a pig's life? Later, we see her watching the pig, safe now in his new home in the barn. Still later, we see her listening as the pig reveals he is a very humanlike animal that talks, frets, and loves life as much as the child believed he must.

Are we totally disoriented by this time? Do we throw up our hands in horror or pitch the book across the room? No, we have met these categories before in our reading; we might even have met them blended in some form, as they are here, and we are prepared for them. Even if we have never read anything previously except supermarket picture books and series books, White enables us to glide so smoothly from one genre to another, we scarcely notice the moment we leave the real world and cross over into fantasy. It has simply happened, and as a result of this experience—as a result of our exposure to this blending of realism and animal fantasy—we are much better prepared to take on more complex genre forms the next time we encounter them. With *time fantasy,* a thematic genre, we must not only be able to glide back and forth between real and fantasy worlds, alongside the characters; we must also be able to operate in both worlds at once—and on two different time planes.

Children's books have their own rules, customs, and conventions, a self-generating logic that can shift from book to book. The categories that form around children's books remain fairly stable from era to era, from culture to culture. But innovative, one-of-a-kind books and authors do come along from time to time to upset our neat, compartmentalized system of organization; then we must do a little rearranging—on our bookshelves and in our thinking. One of the best ways to become acquainted with children's books from the perspective of literary genres is to visit the places where these unique books are situated.

We might enter the library and pull from the shelves every book that one of our favorite authors has written. Taking some time to study these books, we can note whether an author always works in a particular genre, as Leo Lionni always produces animal fantasy picture books, or produces books in many different genres and genre blendings, as do Janet and Allen Ahlberg, Susan Cooper, Virginia Hamilton, and Laurence Yep.

There are five major kinds of books or literary genres: fiction, nonfiction, poetry, folk literature, and pictorial forms. Within these five major groups are many subcategories. **Fiction** refers to imagined stories that seem real. We can subdivide the fiction genre into fantasy and realism. Fantasy involves a magical, supernatural, nonsensical, or wildly exaggerated vision of other (impossible) worlds. Realism involves the possible—and probable—events of everyday life in the present or the past. **Nonfiction** refers to factual stories or accounts; these are narratives or reports that can be verified as actual—rather than imagined—occurrences. We can subdivide nonfiction into history, biography, and science. (For more on children's fiction and nonfiction, see the end of Chapter Three.)

Poetry refers to literary forms with expressive, stirring language and rhythmical patterns. Poetry can be subdivided into song, rhyme, verse, ballads, lyrics, and narrative forms. **Folk literature** refers to materials arising from oral tradition. This type of literature can be subdivided into legend, myths, fables, folk tales, and fairy tales. Finally, **pictorial forms** are works in which illustrations are either crucial or highly important. Picture books, picture storybooks, and illustrated books are the subdivisions in this category. (For more on children's picture books, poetry, and folk literature, see the end of the next chapter.)

We will better understand the various kinds of children's books if we study books that exemplify these genre categories. In this chapter, we will examine seven books that have given children pleasure for many years; these books appear in the order they appeared in print. *Alice's Adventures in Wonderland* (1865) by Lewis Carroll is the first, followed by *Little Women* (1868–69) by Louisa May Alcott, *Peter Rabbit* (1905) by Beatrix Potter, *A Little Princess* (1905) by Frances Hodgson Burnett, *Charlotte's Web* (1952) by E. B. White, *The Diary of Anne Frank* (1952) by Anne Frank, and *Where the Wild Things Are* (1963) by Maurice Sendak.

In terms of literary genres, *Alice's Adventures in Wonderland* and *Charlotte's Web* are both fantasies, whereas *Little Women* is realistic fiction. *A Little Princess*

INVESTIGATIONS: Favorite Authors and Their Genres

Go to the library and pull from the shelves every book that one of your favorite authors has written. Study these books and try to see whether the author always works in one particular genre. Leo Lionni always produces picture books filled with talking animals; Ezra Jack Keats nearly always produces picture books about urban children. On the other hand, the author may produce books in many different genres. John Burningham produces picture books that sometimes feature talking animals and are sometimes filled with real-life situations; Beverly Cleary writes stories about mice riding motorcycles and children riding bikes and stories in which these mice and children meet. Still other authors may produce many innovative genre blendings. Janet and Allen Ahlberg weave modern characters into old, familiar folk tales; Laurence Yep weaves old Chinese folk tales into his modern stories about Chinese immigrants in America. Virginia Hamilton places a ghost on an urban street. What does your favorite author do?

is realism with elements of fairy tale woven into it. *The Diary of Anne Frank* is autobiography (nonfiction). *Peter Rabbit* is a picture storybook (Potter's pictures *supplement* and *extend* her words), and *Where the Wild Things Are* is a picture book (Sendak's pictures *complete* his words; words *complete* his pictures).

We will consider these seven books as a text set—a small cluster of books, linked in any number of ways, for classroom use. We saw text sets in use when we shadowed Lisa in her visits to three classrooms in chapter 1. First graders were collecting books for the theme "Making New Friends," and fifth graders were reading a set of Betsy Byars books. Text sets are very popular with teachers who set up literature study groups.

Books in the text set we are examining are linked by a common theme that runs through many children's books: **the "outside" child.** This theme focuses on a child who feels isolated, rejected, lonely or strange, or who is simply unusually curious and sets off to explore. The child might reject her home, might have been taken involuntarily from her original home, or might simply be fascinated by something in the world outside her original home.

In a second home, this child is both an unwanted insider and an unwanted outsider. There is usually a fantasy aspect to the story, a dream, a dreamlike scene, or a fantasy place; or the story might be a fantasy from beginning to end. In the end,

More about Text Sets . . .

Harste and Short (1988) define a text set as "Two or more texts that have similar characteristics, such as similar themes, text types [genres], topics, and so on" (page 358). Readers understand books differently, say these educators, when they read two or more rather than one book alone. Learning means making connections—connections between a book and our past experiences, and between our experiences with different books.

Text sets also give students a great deal to talk about. They can compare and contrast related books. Harste and Short describe two different ways teachers use text sets in classrooms: they may have all students read the same set of books, or they may let students choose different books from the set. With the first method, students identify the most important similarities and differences among the books. Then they produce creative extensions to the books (drama, artwork, writing). With the second method, each student reads one or two of the books from the set; then students share what they learned from different texts. They ask questions, discuss similarities and differences among books, and devise categories for the connections they are making. As students hear about other books, they often decide to read one another's books, or decide to read one particular book. The group may decide then how it will share its set of books with other groups or with class as a whole.

The teacher's role is to gather the books for the text sets and explain to students how the procedure works. Initially, groups deal with three to four books at a time. Later they might browse through twenty-five books as a set, selecting those they wish to read or discuss. (Materials such as maps and newspapers can also become part of the set.) Students might write in journals or logs, then share their written responses.

Text sets may include different versions of the same folk tale; stories with the same general theme, genre, subject, or cultural setting; books including the same characters (series books); books by the same author or illustrator; or the same folk tale illustrated by different artists. (See the end-of-chapter booklists and Appendix I for more text sets, or books arranged by genre, story version, reading level, subject, or theme.)

Source: Jerome Harste and Kathy Short, with Carolyn Burke, *Creating Classrooms for Authors* (Portsmouth, NH: Heinemann, 1988), pp. 358–365.

the child leaves the second home and goes either to a new place or back to the original home (the home-adventure-home pattern), where both the place and the child are changed. The place seems different to the child; the child *feels* different too. Thus, this story reflects the child's emotional growth. In the case of "Goldilocks and the Three Bears," the child flees a frightening situation and returns home, having learned a little something—or a lot—about manners and about intruding on others.

Of course, many themes run through children's literature. The outside child theme is merely one possibility to consider, as we move through the "book talks" we will discuss in this chapter. Another way to think about these books is in terms of *literary patterns* that reveal the themes we see forming as we read—and reread. Repeated words, phrases, actions, or ideas in the work provide clues to meaning. Still other ways to think about the books are in terms of *literary strengths* of the different authors and *classic* status. (What has enabled these books to survive for so many years?)

Reading to see genre and theme involves a special way of reading that differs from the browsing, scanning, and skimming we often use on a first reading. In the beginning, readers think primarily about the feelings and ideas the words and pictures call forth. They live through the story, forming mental images about characters, settings, and actions on a personal level. They become involved in the pleasure of empathizing with characters and turning the pages to see what happens next. Readers often discover more about their early responses to literature if they keep journals, writing down what they are feeling and thinking about the piece as they read.

Later, readers might reexamine literature to strengthen their *interpretive* pleasure—or to produce stronger meaning. At this point, they begin to notice literary patterns, authorial strengths, and authorial choices. They might ask themselves questions: What patterns do I see forming here? What words, phrases, actions, and ideas do I see repeated or emphasized? What do these patterns cause me to see about the story? Readers will also engage in creative ventures of their own as they ask, What story or poem do I want to produce after reading this one?

In the book talks that follow, we will focus on interpretive categories such as those listed in the box called "A Closer Look . . . Interpretive Reading." Each of these seven books focuses on an outside child, and each fits a different genre category, as we will soon see.

INVESTIGATIONS: The Reading Journal

One good way to discover more about children's literature is to write about it; writing is itself a meaning-making process. One thought causes another to unfold; soon, you are creating new ideas as you respond to the ideas of others (the author, the characters, other readers). You might write about any of these seven books during your reading—or afterward—to stimulate the meaning-making process. As you write, ask yourself questions such as:

- What am I noticing?
- What puzzles me?
- What do I expect to happen as the story unfolds?
- What is surprising?
- What does the story—or poem—cause me to think about, wonder about, or imagine?
- How do the comments and observations of others cause me to see more—or to see differently?

A Closer Look
Interpretive Reading

Reading for interpretive pleasure means reading (and writing) to investigate patterns of meaning. Patterns emerge in the

- LITERARY CHOICES the author has made;
- AUTHORIAL VALUES as they weave through the story, subtly or more directly;
- SUBJECT MATTER (the ideas).

Interpretive pleasure also emerges as readers

- sort out what they think are the LITERARY STRENGTHS of the author or the work
- notice the author's STYLE (word choices, arrangements of phrases, lines or passages)
- revisit the work with CREATIVE EXTENSIONS.

Literary choices

1. **Characters:** Who are the memorable ones to you—and why?
2. **Plot:** What are the important "threads" of story?
3. **Names:** Did names tell you anything about the characters, such as the way they feel about themselves or how others feel about them? Did a name signify something special—or defining—about a person in the story?
4. **Setting.** When does the story take place? Where? Is the time and place a crucial part of the story? If the story happened during another time in history or in another place, how would this change the story—or would it?
5. **Narrative Design:** What kept happening in the story? What did you keep seeing? What was repeated?
6. **Genre:** How would you classify this work? Fiction? Nonfiction? Poetry? Folk Literature? Picture book? Illustrated Story? Some subcategory of these such as Nonfiction/ Autobiography? Some blending of these such as Picture Storybook?
7. **Themes:** What were the BIG issues and ideas in the story?
8. **Conflicts:** What tensions were there in the story—inside characters' minds or between characters?
9. **Title:** What meaning did you make of the title in terms of the entire story? How did the title help to focus the story for you, or did it?

Values

What cultural or social values did you see emerging in the story, either from the author's perspective or your own? What personal values of the author did you see?

Subject matter

Ideas: What did the book leave you wondering? What new thoughts emerged for you as you read—and afterward? What questions would you like to ask the author? What questions would you like to ask others who have read the book?

Literary strengths

What is the major strength of the author—or the book?

- Storytelling power?
- Empathetic characters?
- Depth of character?
- Narrative design?
- Original ideas?
- Experiments in language?
- An ear for dialogue or natural language patterns (people conversing or thinking)?
- A talent for humor?
- Emotional resonance?
- Evocative scenes? (A special sense of place?)
- Classic status? What do you think has caused this book to remain popular through the years? Why do you think this book appealed to children in its own time? Is its appeal fading or in any way tarnished now? What do you think is the possibility for this book surviving another generation—or longer?

Style

What phrases, lines, or passages were memorable ones for you? What were some special or favorite words?

Creative extensions

Becoming an author: What stories would you like to tell or write after reading this one? What ideas did the work give you for producing a poem, a play, a drawing, a film?

Experimenting with language: What would you want to jot down to remember, after reading this book? A new word? A word used in a new way? A joke? A rhyme? A way of seeing the world differently?

INVESTIGATIONS: Reading for Aesthetic and Interpretive Pleasure

In this chapter, you will be reading seven children's books for **aesthetic** pleasure—to enter the characters' lives, thoughts, and feelings and to live through their experiences with them. You might also jot down responses in your literature journal, chatting with others about the books and reading the book talks that follow, as you go along—or afterward. Later you might reread some of the books for **interpretive** pleasure—to strengthen your meaning-making strategies. Think about patterns you see in the stories; literary elements such as plot, conflict, characters, and setting; authorial strengths; authorial choices; and creative extensions you might like to try to respond further to the books.

The book talks begin with *Alice's Adventures in Wonderland.* Lewis Carroll's book was one of the first children's books to produce both pleasure for children and a one-of-a-kind literary experience, and it continues to do so when adults take the time to share it with children today.

GENRES IN CHILDREN'S LITERATURE

Fiction: Fantasy

***Alice's Adventures in Wonderland* (1865) by Lewis Carroll (Charles Lutwidge Dodgson)**

As the story opens, Alice sits on a riverbank watching her sister read a book that has neither pictures nor conversations in it. What good is such a book? Alice wonders sleepily, when suddenly she sees a white rabbit hurry by. The rabbit takes a watch out of his waistcoat pocket and frets that he is late. Down a rabbit hole he goes, and Alice, bored with her book, follows him.

Expanding and shrinking, as she falls down the deep hole, Alice makes her way to a magical underground world, where she meets strange, irritating, and puzzling creatures—the Cheshire Cat, the Mad Hatter, and the Queen of Hearts, to name just a few. They try her patience, boss her, confuse her, meddle with her, and finally cause her to explode in anger and frustration.

Alice is famous for her courage; she is not frightened to break the strongest taboo of the child's world—talking back to adults in protest, telling some of them at last that they are nothing but a pack of cards (which, in this case, is true). But a plot summary cannot do justice to the clever conversations, the odd twists and turns of plot, and the strange "logic" of the illogical world Lewis Carroll depicts.

The book, says English educator and critic Fred Inglis, is a novel "amazingly packed" with characters and poetry. It is "deeply soaked in the rhythms and inflections of the verses and masters (most obviously [William] Wordsworth), which he seeks to parody. There can hardly be a better introduction to poetry. . . . If you celebrate courtesy *and* courage, calm good sense *and* dauntlessness, grace *and* candour, you can hardly do better than Alice" (page 107).

Alice is also the prototypical outside child in children's literature. As cultural historian Julia Briggs notes, Alice is one who "refuses to become an object, who

Fantasy and the Storymaker's Art

J. R. R. Tolkien's theories about fantasy shed light on Carroll's *Alice's Adventures in Wonderland.* What really happens "when the story-maker's art is good," Tolkien says, "is that the story-maker proves a successful 'subcreator.' He makes a Secondary World which your mind can enter. Inside it, what he realizes is 'true': it accords with the laws of that world. You therefore believe it, while you are, as it were, inside" (1965, page 37).

Lewis Carroll makes two Secondary Worlds—one for readers and one for Alice. The reader's Secondary World is the story itself; Alice's Secondary World is her dream. While she is dreaming, Alice accepts the dream as reality, just as we believe in our dreams while immersed in them. As readers watch Alice, they therefore believe in her "reality," too. Neither Alice nor the reader discovers Wonderland is a dream until Alice awakens at the end. But because Alice is dreaming, she is also creating her own Secondary World—she is a story-maker too. What, for Tolkien, does this way of story-making entail?

"Fantasy," says Tolkien, involves "the making or glimpsing of Other-worlds." He goes on to explain, "The human mind is capable of forming mental images of things not actually present. . . . The mental power of image-making is . . . called Imagination." Imagination means the "perception of the image, the grasp of its implications, and the control, which are necessary to a successful expression"; they "may vary in vividness and strength." Alice's image-making arises from her subconscious, which in turn controls what happens in her dream—or controls her imagination, in a circular process.

Fantasy, says Tolkien, "is a natural human activity" that does not blunt nor destroy reason. On the contrary, he adds, the "keener and the clearer is the reason, the better fantasy will it make . . . for creative Fantasy is founded upon the hard recognition that things are so in the world . . . on a recognition of fact . . . so upon logic was founded the nonsense that displays itself in the tales and rhymes of Lewis Carroll."

Source: J. R. R. Tolkien, *Tree and Leaf* (Boston: Houghton Mifflin, 1965), pp. 37–55.

won't be intimidated by the constant stream of orders and instructions she receives, and who remains firmly in command of herself. However small she becomes physically—at one stage she is smaller than a mushroom—her spirit is undiminished" (page 240). It may be Alice's spirit in the face of such a bewildering world that has endowed the book with its appeal through the years, and Carroll's chosen genre, fantasy, achieves the perfect fit for Alice's conflict.

Fantasy, whether it is embedded in a Mother Goose rhyme or a science fiction novel, takes the reader to another world, a world filled with magical "realities" that bring the reader a fresh, imaginative vision of what is or what could be. The characters may begin in the other (magical) world, or they may visit it while living in this one. In either case, fantasy reveals truths we may not have seen or noticed before and helps us to uncover some mystery of human nature or some new view of the actual world. Fantasy means the suspension of the possible as we know it (physical laws or human abilities). When we embrace fantasy, we embrace the supernatural, the make-believe, extrasensory, nonsensical, or illogical.

In *Alice's Adventures in Wonderland,* Carroll utilizes the literary device of a dream to explain how his young character passes into a wildly impossible fantasy world. Alice wakes at the end of the story to discover that everything she saw and did in Wonderland was a dream. But because she was the one doing the dreaming, we know that *her* wishes and *her* fears are what set this world in motion, kept it going, and finally brought it to a halt. Alice "wakes up" to the callous, insensitive, and hypocritical adults who attempted to control her in the dream world and are perhaps doing the same in her real world, too.

From *Alice's Adventures in Wonderland* (1865) by Lewis Carroll.

Thus, there are two fantasies here—the author's story of Alice, and the story Alice dreams for herself. Carroll created both of these fantasies, but when he chooses to have Alice dream a story for herself, he also chooses to have her achieve something important of her own. She does the fantasizing; she becomes the storyteller or "writer" of her own experience. In a sense, Alice is not simply controlled by the author who is telling her story; she acts upon the world herself—dreaming her own sense of the ways things are.

John Tenniel's illustrations, which accompanied the original publication of the book, are the perfect complement to Carroll's text. Tenniel had little understanding of the technical process of engraving, but he had a superb imagination. He produced pencil drawings on tracing paper that he then transferred to the wooden block. The engraver, Joseph Swain, took it from there, making Tenniel's precise and delicate lines thicker for the famous pictures we still enjoy today. Many artists have attempted to interpret Carroll's story for themselves, but it is Tenniel's work that remains the standard by which all others are judged.

Fiction: Realism

Little Women (1868–69) by Louisa May Alcott

Louisa May Alcott's story begins on Christmas Eve as the four March sisters, ages twelve to sixteen, talk together about this year's Christmas with no presents. Their father is away at war—the American Civil War of the 1860s—and Marmee, their mother, is devising ways to help them all through a hard Boston winter. The story continues by tracing each sister's life story, up through the time of Jo's marriage.

The plot line is fairly thin for a book so rich in characters and scenes. Oldest sister Meg has just decided to marry. Next door neighbor Laurie (short for Lawrence) falls in love with Jo; Jo is one year younger than Meg and, readers may assume, will soon follow Meg to the altar. But a great deal happens before it emerges that Jo's and Laurie's marriage is not to be. In the meantime, Amy, the youngest sister, goes abroad to pursue her interest in art, and Jo, who desires to become a fiction writer, joins her one year later. One sister remains at home—gentle Beth. Eventually, Beth's weak heart fails, and her sisters mourn her death. Jo eventually realizes her dream of becoming a writer, with the help of Professor Bhaer, an older man who critiques her work. In the end, Amy marries Laurie, and Jo marries the professor.

Little Women is the story of a family in nineteenth-century America. It focuses on the March family and on how each member nurtures and supports the others. The four sisters must suppress boisterous tendencies in favor of patience and self-sacrifice, and the choices they make must fall within the constrictions facing women in the nineteenth century. Meg chooses marriage. Beth accepts with good grace her poor health and later her imminent death, making family, music, and home life the joys in her life. Amy prefers travel, society, and the arts, but later she realizes she has limited talents for painting and chooses a marriage and social life. Jo continues to write, finally taking a job in New York where she meets her future husband.

The book also focuses especially on Jo, the outside child of this family, the one who strikes out to be what girls of her day did not become—career women. Jo wants to be a writer from the beginning; she shows talent and fortitude for such a career. Later she leaves home and family to assume this role. It is perhaps disappointing for female readers today that Alcott did not allow Jo to complete her quest to become a writer, as Alcott herself did. Even though Alcott never married and even though she became the famous writer Jo aspires to be, the customs of Alcott's time prevail in the book. Jo marries and takes on the rearing of her husband's sons from a former marriage—leaving little time for writing and little need for financial independence.

The book is a bundle of intersecting genres, depending on where we stand in history when we classify it. In its own day, the story was called domestic fiction or a family novel. Its opposite was adventure fiction, in which a nondomesticated male went out into the world to make his fortune. In this gender-based world, males read—and wrote—adventure novels, in which few female cast members appeared, and females read—and wrote—domestic fiction, or family stories in which traditional female roles dominated. In this day, we simply categorize the book as realistic fiction, literature in which social context, social background, and social observation reflect real life and are all-important to the story.

The book falls into several subgenres as well: the feminist quest novel, the female *bildungsroman,* or novel of emerging self; and the female coming-of-age story. Four heroines search for a role in life, as well as for understanding, friendship, and love (the quest). As in any *bildungsroman;* the education and growing wisdom of a young person plays a central role; in this case, four young girls—with Jo as principal "learner"—are growing into knowledge of self and society, through reading, writing, travel, social and family relationships, and finally through work inside and outside the home. These qualities also fit the coming-of-age theme.

All of these types of fiction help us see why the book has maintained its popularity: they all depend on character delineation. So richly drawn is the picture Alcott creates of her characters, they rise above any fixed place or time. As film critic Caryn James says, from among these four sisters is a favorite for nearly any female reader. James quotes notable feminist Carolyn Heilbrun, who found Jo the most memorable character: " 'Jo was a miracle,' a role model for 'girls dreaming beyond the confines of a constricted family destiny' "(page 3). James remembers that her best friends from childhood wanted to be like Beth, and that she bore a strong resemblance to "responsible Meg." But, she adds, "the character you long to be is never the one you most resemble." The "pampered princess of *Little Women* is Amy," she says. "That's what I liked about her" (page 17).

Realistic Fiction with Fairy Tale Motifs

A Little Princess (1905) by Frances Hodgson Burnett

Twenty years after Louisa Alcott produced *Little Women,* Frances Burnett published a long short story or novelette entitled *Sara Crewe* (1888). Fourteen years later, Burnett rewrote the story as a play, and an editor who saw it encouraged her to rewrite it as a full-scale novel. *A Little Princess* (available today in many different editions) was the result.

In its own day, Burnett's books appealed to audiences of all ages. Children's and adult literature at this time blended easily with one another as *family reading.* Many children today would probably choose the shorter version, and they can still do so; *Sara Crewe* remains in print (Scholastic; Apple paperback, n.d.). But each book offers something important of its own. *Sara Crewe* gives children a fast-paced, action-filled story. *A Little Princess* gives them a large, interesting cast and a strongly delineated character—Sara, an imaginative child who rises above her troubles by pretending she is a princess.

Both versions focus on the child Sara Crewe, who was born in India and then came to England with her father when she turned seven, her mother having died earlier. Sara's father buys her beautiful clothes and a doll, nearly as large as she is, that she names Emily. Then her father leaves her in London, a student in Miss Minchin's select girl's school, and returns to India. When he later dies of jungle fever, supposedly in a penniless state, Miss Minchin turns Sara into a servant girl, an unwanted "outsider" who must live in the attic, wear rags, go hungry, and never see her beloved storybooks. One day a man comes searching for Sara; he wants to return the fortune her father had unknowingly made from investments before he died. When she goes to live with this friend of her father's, Sara finds a home at last. She also finds a place in high social standing, one where a real princess might reside.

At all times, in rags or riches, Sara has behaved like a true princess by giving to the poor and facing her troubles with courage and determination. Her concept of a princess supports the entire story. What is a princess, in Burnett's view? It is a person who is strong enough to rise above self-indulgent emotional outbursts, who never answers her enemies and always holds her rage inside. Self-control and self-discipline are the primary traits of a princess, as Sara sees it. But there is a great deal more.

Self-control also means self-sacrifice, social responsibility, or in this case generosity. When Sara finds a silver piece in the street one day, enough to buy four buns at the bakery, she asks the shopkeeper if the money is hers. Impressed with Sara's honesty, the shopkeeper gives Sara six buns. But even as hungry as Sara is, she remembers that a true princess always shares her wealth, and she gives five of the buns to a homeless child sitting on the curb.

Another trait of a princess is inner strength arising from inner resources. This strength Sara finds in her storytelling talents. When she is stripped of her possessions, her status as favorite pupil in the classroom, her "fair weather" friends, and her father, she still has one thing that never fails her—a rich imagination. Sara's stories—those she tells herself for consolation and strength and those she tells others to amuse, console, and teach them—help her and others to survive. Using her imagination, she nurtures and strengthens her storytelling powers, her empathy for others, and her ability to see what needs to be done in the world.

But Sara's work as a self-made princess neither begins nor ends with imagination. Just as she puts her imagination to work, envisioning the power that she as a child, and especially as a poor child, does not have, her imagination puts *her* to work, helping her to see what she can do for others, despite her constricted life. She gives buns to the homeless girl who is starving; she tells stories to her classmate who cannot read; she helps the scullery maid see beyond the class differences that keep her oppressed. She also smiles at the Indian man-servant next door and speaks to him in his native language when she senses he is lonely.

Never does Sara's life seem boring to readers, no matter how drab and hopeless it becomes. *A Little Princess* has a strong, suspenseful plot and richly empathetic characters, and the book has survived with readers because of Burnett's storytelling power. In either *Sara Crewe* or *A Little Princess,* the plot drives the story. Without digressions or didactic comments, says notable critic Margery Fisher, "the account of Sara's fortunes drives simply and steadily on, showing how a child with a warm heart, the example of a soldier father, and a strong personal imagination deals with a shocking reversal of fortune, which, for most eleven-year-old girls, could have led to bitterness or despair"(page 45).

Also as Fisher notes, the story contains strong irony: the reader knows before Sara does about her reversal of fortune. Sara is a rare character in children's fiction, "a likeable good child," neither a prig, in her goodness, nor a misunderstood—and unlikeable—child like Burnett's Mary Lennox of *The Secret Garden.*

The genre—or genre-blending—of *A Little Princess* also contributes to its popularity. The book, at first glance, is surely realism or realistic fiction. Readers are so firmly grounded in details of setting, characters, situations, and events, they feel they are standing at Sara's shoulder, walking through Sara's long-ago London and living through her troubles with her. But this is a very different realism from that of *Little Women.* Both Alcott and Burnett provide a wealth of description and natural dialogue. But here, from the beginning, the romantic twists of Sara's destiny drive the action. First she has everything; then she has nothing; finally she has a great deal more than she had before, although the loss of her father is permanent. This rags-to-riches, fairy tale plot reveals the wish-fulfillment aspects of any Cinderella story: the high-born child reduced to servant status who finds herself at last—through hard work, goodness of spirit, and good luck—restored to a high place.

INVESTIGATIONS: Favorite Books from Childhood

Caryn James wrote about her childhood memories of *Little Women,* just as Lynne Sharon Schwartz and Madeleine L'Engle wrote about *A Little Princess.* Choose a children's book that you remember reading as a child and write about it as they did, exploring what made the book special to you and what might have made it special to others through the years. Share your book, your memories, and your ideas with others.

Says children's author Madeleine L'Engle, remembering the book from childhood, "there is an amazing mixture of realism with romanticism in this book, and how I loved the romanticism when I was a child, especially when the Indian Lascar sneaks into Sara's room at night and transforms it into a place of beauty and comfort, providing warm food and clothes as well as pretty wall hangings and objets d'art" (page xi).

On the other hand, it may be something about the character herself that keeps the book going. Sara is brave and strong, and most readers do not think they could endure her struggles as graciously or as long as she did. As novelist Lynne Sharon Schwartz has said, "More than its romantic fantasies of royalty and luxury and fine clothes . . . the glamour of integrity is ageless." *Honor,* and *dignity,* and *character* are other words Schwartz uses to describe the quality that helps Sara endure hardship "without giving way to rage or self-pity or despair" (page 230).

What the book gives us in Sara, says Schwartz, is the conviction that "a child, even at the earliest age, is a 'distinct little individual,' with opinions and tastes, like and dislikes" (page 225). It also gives us the knowledge that "we truly are who we feel ourselves to be" and that "we can trust this inner certainty regardless of how others perceive us, or what they wish us to become" (page 224). Such inner strength enables Sara to stand up to Miss Minchin, and this "inner might," adds Schwartz, is what made the book so compelling to her at age nine.

Pictorial Forms: Picture Storybook

The Tale of Peter Rabbit (Warne, 1905) By Beatrix Potter

With Burnett's *A Little Princess,* we enter the realm of literature as a social construction. Children (and adults also) could read the book primarily for entertainment, amusement, escape, or pleasure. At the same time, they receive subtle but solid instruction in how to live their lives: keep a stiff upper lip, don't indulge in self-pity, remember your social responsibility toward those less fortunate. If we are not careful, we might see Beatrix Potter's animal stories as cut of the same cloth, when in fact Potter takes the opposite approach. She tells a good story, yes; but if we look carefully, we find a very different lesson from the one we see at first glance.

We all, no doubt, remember the story. Peter Rabbit's mother tells Peter not to go into Mr. McGregor's garden (his father had an "accident" there; he was caught by Mr. McGregor, and Mrs. McGregor baked him in pie). But Peter goes anyway and has quite an adventure. Chased by Mr. McGregor, he barely escapes. Not only does he lose his clothes, he misses the milk and blackberries that his better-behaved sisters have for their supper. He is dosed instead on camomile tea to combat the effects of gorging in the garden—or to teach him a lesson about rash behavior. The last page shows us the female bunnies feasting on bread and blackberries. Peter is all but forgotten; our last glimpse of him is a few pages back, where he lies in a heap, sound asleep, as his mother gazes calmly (and lovingly) down at him.

What is the lesson? That blackberries for supper are better than the thrills of the chase? That keeping your coat on is more important than having the adventure of your life? Or something else? Consider the pictures, which tell a very different story from the words. We know from the beginning what is going to happen. As the rabbit siblings start off for the fields with a warning not to go into the garden,

From *Peter Rabbit* (Warne, 1905) by Beatrix Potter.

Peter is already turning in the opposite direction—away from Mother Rabbit and his sisters, who are reaching for the blackberry basket. Peter's mother knows where he is headed. In the next frame, she pulls Peter back to fasten his top coat button, and so tight is her grasp that his head snaps back. She is strangling him with rules and warnings, and as soon as he is out of sight, we know, he will throw caution to the wind.

But far from the cautionary tale that it purports to be, this story is a comical but risky adventure from beginning to end. It is also a deadly serious one because the stakes are so high. Peter's father really did get baked in a pie, and so will Peter if he is not careful—or at least luckier than his father. Yet we know that as soon as Peter learns about his father, he will have to follow the father's model as a risk taker. Peter is "very naughty," the narrator tells us, and he runs "straight away" to the garden to squeeze "under the gate!" The exclamation point tells us the narrator is as caught up in the risk taking as Peter is and will be cheering for him all the way. Peter's hindquarters are hard pressed by the gate, and as he pushes up under it in his new jacket, his glance, already darting toward the vegetables, provides the next comic touch.

In the next picture, Peter is nibbling bright red-gold radishes in this garden paradise. So powerful is the image, the words do very little to compete with it: "First he ate some lettuces and some French beans," we read, "and then he ate some radishes." And there is nothing in the words about the pert red robin that watches Peter and flits in and out of the remaining pages (a bright red "thread" that pulls us through the story—and through Peter's adventure). The robin stands back watching from the corner of its eye as Peter faces us, patting his middle after the garden feast and "feeling rather sick." But he is not sick enough to forego the parsley he spies—another humorous touch. Then the robin stares at Peter's little shoe, lost among the cabbages after Peter, startled by Mr. McGregor, rushes "all over the garden."

Next we see Peter upside down, entangled by one of his brass buttons in a gooseberry net, looking more stunned than "dreadfully frightened," as the words say. On the next pages, Potter tells us that Peter "gave himself up for lost, and shed big tears," but it is not a pathetic rabbit, we see in the picture simply a very plump, furry one, his coat nearly torn off, as three plump sparrows implore him to "exert himself." And he does. In the next scene, Peter leaps up, a sieve balanced ominously over his head, as the sparrows fly up, too, and the coat is left behind. Peter has shrugged off all conventions now—rules, clothes, even tears. In the need to save himself, he reverts entirely to instinct, jumping into a watering can in the tool-shed and producing, unfortunately, a sneeze (another comic touch) that sends Mr. McGregor after him "in no time." (All we see are two tiny ears sticking out of the huge green can.)

Peter wins by being himself—a rabbit jumping out windows and upsetting plants. Mr. McGregor, exhausted with the chase, gives up and goes back to his work. Peter trembles, thrilled as well as frightened by the chase. Damp and disoriented, he wanders about, "lippity—lippity." Frustration and a few fears set in when he finds a locked door in the wall, and a mouse who does not answer when Peter calls for help. (Do children ever encounter locked doors? Do they ever find themselves lost? If so, who is Peter, really, a rabbit—or a boy?)

Finally, Peter meets a white cat, but he is a little hesitant to go near her. Now he is *all* rabbit, having learned from his cousin, little Benjamin Bunny, what cats do to rabbits. (Or is he? Who have cousins anyway—rabbits or boy?) From where Peter perches in a wheelbarrow, he spies the gate, and beyond it, Mr. McGregor is hoeing onions. In another turn of the plot, Mr. McGregor catches sight of Peter, but Peter knows how fast he is now and does not care. Soon Peter *Rabbit* has slipped under the gate and is safe outside in the woods.

If there is any lesson here, it is not the one Mother Rabbit tries to teach Peter; it is instead that doing what comes naturally leads us both into and out of trouble. If we follow our impulses and are vigilant, keep our wits about us and exert ourselves, we will find ways to outsmart our oppressors. All of this Peter easily does, once he throws off his blue coat and scampers off like a rabbit.

English critic Humphrey Carpenter describes Peter as "the little fellow, the folk tale hero who has nothing but his courage and his wits, struggling against an opponent of far superior physical strength." Peter, he adds, is "a familiar figure from the Victorian moral tale, the disobedient child." In this case, he is a "burglar" who has "daringly got into the giant's lair" and "rewarded himself with the treasure," then "escaped through his own exertions" (pages 286–87). Characters in Maria Edgeworth's eighteenth-century stories, he reminds us, were always being implored to exert themselves and raise themselves out of slovenly ways. Thus, Potter, a century later, is having a little fun.

As Carpenter points out, Potter is surely a "rebel, albeit a covert one, demonstrating the rewards of nonconformity, and exhorting her young readers to question the social system into which they found themselves born," rather than "decorously instructing her nieces and child-friends in acceptable social behavior" (page 279). Or as Fred Inglis puts it: "Beatrix Potter sets down, in the thoroughly settled farmlands, gardens, and villages of Westmorland [England], the colour and variety of Victorian society, its firm structures, its strong base in home and family, its disobedient heroes, its polite little girls, its rich patterns of gentility and roguery. Young readers can best begin there: She includes so much of the great abstractions—history, morality, class, work—and gives them her special vividness, in both words and water-colour" (page 110).

Potter's words and pictures together produce the kind of illustrated story that began with Randolph Caldecott. Caldecott's special way of illustrating nursery rhymes allowed the pictures to tell a great deal more than the text did. Later, in Maurice Sendak's work, pictures tell even more of the story. Potter's words do the greater share of the telling, but words are certainly not the whole story. The text does not tell about the robin. It does not tell just how constricting Mother Rabbit's hold is on Peter's collar, nor how happily unfettered Peter looks as he lies sleeping that night on the "soft sand" of the rabbit hole.

In the scene where the little shoe is lost amongst the cabbages. Pictures support and explain the text. But pictures also *complete* the texts, in a later scene where Peter's coat is now worn by "a scare crow to frighten the blackbirds" as the robin perches nearby. In fact, the robin is standing on the wooden frame that holds the coat, as if to protect Peter once again. And Peter's little shoes tilt happily up, creating a mood of reassurance and hope. Peter is safe, the pictures seem to imply; losing his clothes (his human identity) and reverting to "rabbithood" has saved him. In a later scene, Peter sleeps peacefully, unencumbered by hierarchies, constrictions, rules, or roles. He is just a rabbit sleeping after a hard day's "work" in the garden.

Potter's pictures thus illuminate her text, filling gaps of meaning. The simple tilt of Peter's shoes tells us worlds about the fun of breaking rules, being naughty, getting into mischief, and doing what for children or rabbits is the "right"—or natural—thing to do. But why does Potter make Peter a rabbit? And why does she, at the same time, make Peter a person in human clothes? Why is he both rabbit and child?

A child can relate to a rabbit. Both are small and powerless. At the same time, animals can do things children sometimes cannot do, such as hide in a watering can or run back to their own homes when humans frighten them. Children can also relate to human behaviors: risk taking, curiosity, disobedience, discipline, overeating and then feeling sick, losing clothes, crying. Children can sympathize with Peter when Mr. McGregor chases him; yet they can distance their fears about him getting caught (Peter is not *really* a child). They can experience satisfaction when Peter escapes, and have fun—alongside him—when he takes risks as a disobedient child. They can be subject to discipline but still feel loved (both children and rabbits have mothers).

Perhaps this rabbit-child configuration is one reason why *The Tale of Peter Rabbit* has remained so popular over the years. But Potter's strong sense of dramatic scene is equally important. Her animals are not just animals dressed as humans or humans in animal disguise. They are real animals feeling a range and depth of human emotions, and child readers have always been able to invest their own emotions easily in heroes like Peter Rabbit.

Language and artistic expertise also add to *Peter Rabbit's* appeal. Potter uses sound melodiously to convey meaning, as with the sieve that Mr. McGregor "intended to pop upon the top" of Peter. Her balanced phrasings exhibit precision, elegance, and economy. She conveys both emotions and meanings in her pictures, as when Peter is proportionately large when he eats alone in safety, but small when he encounters Mr. McGregor. She places Peter against a painted backdrop when he is trapped, constricted, or hidden; she removes the backdrop when he is running from Mr. McGregor's rake. Through the use of blank, white space, she increases the tension.

Potter's books, unlike most published previously and many that came afterward, had covers that helped describe the story. Peter, the famous *out*sider rabbit-child, is scurrying across the cover, taking us right *into* the story, where he will remain the outsider to the very end. (On the last page, as we see, Peter is noticeably absent!)

Genre-Blending: Fantasy and Realism

Charlotte's Web **(Harper, 1952) by E. B. White**

Garth Williams illustrated E. B. White's novel some years after he had begun illustrating Laura Ingalls Wilder's Little House books. For Wilder's books, he produced soft pencil sketches; for *Charlotte's Web,* he made pen and ink drawings. And it is difficult to imagine any other kind of picture for this book, so perfectly matched is William's artistic style to the fantasy genre. The thin, wavering, highly distinct line illuminates mood and characters as no other medium would have done.

In White's story, Fern, a farmer's daughter, fights to save a newborn pig, the runt of the litter, that is about to be killed. Fern makes the pig her pet, naming him Wilbur. As he grows, she begins visiting him in the barn, where she hears the animals talking and telling their stories. So in this genre-blending of realism and fantasy, readers discover a set of "inner" stories, growing out of the narrator's overarching story of Fern's friendship with Wilbur and her desire to save his life.

The first of these inner stories involves Wilbur and the animals in the barn. Soon this story grows into one about Charlotte the spider and how she helps Wilbur to survive, despite her own short life span. Her noble, heroic deed of spinning

From *Charlotte's Web* (Harper, 1952) by Garth Williams.

words about him—"some pig," "terrific," and "humble"—shows children what humans are put on earth to do—help others by exercising their various talents. Later comes the story of the county fair; Charlotte saves Wilbur's life with her clever trick, and then she dies. Fern is distanced now as the animals take over the main story. As the fair ends, Wilbur takes Charlotte's place, greeting and befriending Charlotte's offspring after her death; just as Charlotte had befriended—and saved—him. Life goes on, Wilbur learns, and he goes on living with good friends and good memories of his best friend, Charlotte.

The skillful way White merges real and fantasy worlds is the genius of the book. Growth, a puzzling and therefore *magical* concept to children, is a major theme. Growth means life, but life inevitably leads to death—an equally puzzling idea, and a central part of the book, too. Wilbur's death, or the possibility of it, floats ghostlike around the fringes of the inner stories, from beginning to end. By keeping Wilbur a "child" throughout the book and giving him an adult mother figure (Charlotte), White keeps the child alive and allows the adult to die. Ultimately the book turns into a story about accepting and celebrating life—all the good sights and sounds and smells of it. Life beams joyfully out of the barn setting, where so much animal life abounds and so much of the story takes place.

The barn is the place where Fern, the outsider in this animal world, sits patiently watching Wilbur. She is so in tune with her pet that she hears him speaking, and we hear him speaking through her. We recognize the book as fantasy (natural laws are for the moment suspended) when we hear Wilbur and his animal friends speaking. We enter this fantasy world the night Charlotte sings Wilbur to sleep. After the song ends, Fern goes home, and the fantasy is launched. Fern might have been imagining Wilbur's story into existence or watching a magical world that really does exists—at least for her. In either event, she is "tuned in" to the animal world, and by imagining it so clearly and completely, she becomes an important insider in it.

At the county fair, Fern goes off with her friend, Henry Fussy, and Wilbur and Charlotte are left to work out Wilbur's life-and-death problems alone. Fern tunes

From *Charlotte's Web* (1952) by E. B. White, illustrated by Garth Williams

out or stops imagining, but her ability to see (or imagine) Wilbur as real—and therefore able to stand on his own now, independent of her—helps produce the solution to the original problem: how to save the pig's life. In the barn, Fern has begun hearing Wilbur's story; like a spider, she has been spinning it. Now the story can go spinning off on its own, just as stories and characters do take on lives of their own, once authors stand back to let them evolve naturally.

Eventually those at the fair hear Wilbur's story, when Charlotte takes over as storyteller. They read Charlotte's words about Wilbur, the ones she spins into her web. They believe her words, and Wilbur's life is saved—in the book-world. In the real world, readers enter the fantasy and believe White's characters are *real* because Charlotte the fantasy spider has, like the good fairy, or fairy godmother, saved Wilbur, before she goes on to die, as animals and humans *do* die.

Within a realistic framework, White makes his fantasy believable, and seamless. He and Fern save Wilbur the only way they can, by telling and writing a story. "You shall not die," Charlotte tells Wilbur (page 51). How will he be saved? he wonders. Readers soon learn that he will be immortalized with words. Writing will save him, both in the story-world, and in the real world of readers. Stories live on, even though people and animals die.

White helps Fern—and child readers—understand the world better as he reveals that death is a natural part of life. Someday Wilbur will die of old age, of course, but for now, he is safe. The realistic but whimsical line drawings capture the lighter, fantasy mood that White frames with a darker realism. The author eases children into the facts of life that Fern must face.

One of White's biographers, John Griffith, calls *Charlotte's Web* an "original hybrid of the old-fashioned, realistic story of life on the farm, the talking-animal story, the fairy tale of the innocent saved from death by a magic helper, and playful satire on gullibility and advertising" (page 6). It is also a children's book that marks the end of an era. Before this time, the 1950s, a monocultural perspective dominated the children's book world. In the following decade, the postwar, postmodern era began, and diversity or multiculturalism began to color literature for children. Editors, writers, and critics all began asking questions like which children have we been excluding as major players on the children's book stage? Who—or what—defines a major player now? The white, middle class, mainstream American child like Fern? Or someone else? Who are the insiders? Who are the outsiders?

Nonfiction: Autobiography

***Anne Frank: The Diary of a Young Girl* (Doubleday, 1952) by Anne Frank (1929–45)**

Written in a brief span of time, 1942–44, Anne Frank's diary was first published in 1947, two years after Anne's death, as *Het Achterhuis* (*The House Behind* or *The Secret Annexe*). Five years later, the book was translated from Dutch into English, and the world learned what it meant to be young, in love with life, and then suddenly torn away from home, friends, and freedom—and finally from life itself.

What does a thirteen-year-old girl do, confined in a small space at the back of a house in Holland, when to set foot outside the door means certain imprisonment or annihilation? What do eight people do for two years during the Nazi occupation, when they have only one another as companions? They think a lot, as Anne shows us. They read and write (friends brought them books and newspapers). They argue;

From *Anne Frank: The Diary of a Young Girl* (Doubleday, 1952) by Anne Frank.

they laugh; they even fall in love (Anne received her first kiss in the Secret Annexe). They have birthdays and receive presents. They hear stories and construct a family tree. They think about nature and life a great deal. They listen to the radio. Anne is excited as she thinks about going back to school. She knows as much about war, politics, and current events as anyone out in the world, she writes.

The genre here is, of course, nonfiction, but the diary has a fictional format. Anne constructs a character, Kitty, a friend she addresses as she writes. Thus the reader "becomes" for the moment Kitty, and is addressed as a friend. The book is also a survival story; it reflects a young woman coping with the unexpected, danger, life-and-death issues, and risk taking. It causes us to ask as we read, How would *I* cope? What would *I* do in Anne's place? How would *I* feel? Melissa, a student in a children's literature class, says it well:

> I can remember when I was in seventh grade and I read *The Diary of Anne Frank.* I felt close to Anne; her diary was her friend, which she named Kitty, and I came to know Anne (and Kitty). They were my friends too. Anne started to write a diary because she wanted to tell someone everything that she thought, imagined, and dreamed of, but she couldn't do so. In her situation of hiding out from the Nazis for two years, she lived in constant fear and isolation. I was able to relate to Anne because she was a girl close to my own age and in many ways like me. She had a wonderful family and home, as well as friends and relatives; yet at thirteen she felt alone in the world. I remember having the same feelings.
>
> I remember as I continued reading Anne's diary, I felt that things could never be as bad for me as what she lived through, and I really admired her for her strength and courage to endure until the very end. I remember how I used to

> imagine what I would do if I were in her place. It was scary even to think such a thought. Her book really made me realize a lot about myself and about the world.
>
> It allowed me to enter another country and imagine the impact war could have. It allowed me to learn a lot about love, strength, courage, pain, but most of all about the will and spirit to continue to live. Not least of all, it allowed me to explore the world through another person's mind, when she was just my age. It's important for children to be exposed to a story actually written by a child. The child reading the story and the child who wrote it have something in common. They are both children.

Anne's diary is truly *children's* literature, because it is a child-authored work. It is also children's *literature,* because it is written so gracefully and is so filled with insight and sensitivity. Anne wanted to be a writer, an important criterion for successful writing at any age; and she certainly *was* a writer. "Anyone who doesn't write doesn't know how wonderful it is," says Anne. "I must have something besides a husband and children, something that I can devote myself to! I want to go on living even after my death! And therefore I am grateful to God for giving me this gift, this possibility of developing myself and of writing, of expressing all that is in me. I can shake off everything if I write; my sorrows disappear, my courage is reborn . . . I can recapture everything when I write, my thoughts, my ideals, and my fantasies" (pages 177–78).

Anne was producing fiction at this time, too. Her fiction was published later as *Anne Frank's Tales from the Secret Annexe.* But her autobiographical writing has earned her the immortality she wished for, largely because the diary is so much more than autobiography. It is, as social activist and First Lady Eleanor Roosevelt said in the introduction, "one of the wisest and most moving commentaries on war and its impact on human beings that I have ever read . . . [it] made me intimately and shockingly aware of war's greatest evil—the degradation of the human spirit . . . At the same time, Anne's diary makes poignantly clear the ultimate shining nobility of that spirit" (page vii).

As Mrs. Roosevelt notes, Anne's warmth, wit, and intelligence sustained her—and they sustain us now. The diary "tells us much about ourselves and [causes us to feel] how close we all are to Anne's experience, how very much involved we are in her short life and in the entire world" (page vii). Thus, at least one thing may cause the child-authored book to survive—the spirit of the child him or herself. Readers experience Anne's individual needs, interests, and preoccupations at the same time that Anne, the child writer, does.

Anne's story has brought readers in all parts of the world together as perhaps no other book of the postwar era has done. Over ten million copies have now been printed in at least forty different languages, revealing that child culture knows no national borders, no race, ethnic, class, nor gender distinctions. Anne was the hated outsider of her own time and place, when Nazi rulers were overrunning Europe. But she has since that time become a well-loved insider in millions of readers' lives. The hope that fills Anne's last entries, when D-Day has just come and gone, is the same emotion readers experience reading the book, even though they know, as Anne did not, the postscript to the story.

A few weeks after Anne wrote her last lines, the Nazis invaded the Secret Annex. Fortunately for the world, they did not see the diary lying on the floor among a pile of other things. Anne and the diary were separated at this point. She died some months later in a prison camp, without the solace of being able to write. The diary lives on.

Pictorial Forms: Picture Book

Where the Wild Things Are (Harper, 1963) by Maurice Sendak

With Sendak's modern classic, we arrive at the picture book form and a book that broke with conventions completely. No child before this had been quite as iconoclastic as Max, the boy who conquers his adult oppressors in a most resourceful way—through his own imagination. Sendak produces a naughty child who needs no instruction, no didacticism, no moral teaching, no lessons to deal with the feelings bursting onto the pages. Max is a child powerful enough to solve his own problem. What is that problem? Actually, it is very similar to that of *The Tale of Peter Rabbit.*

Max is the consummate outside child, voyaging off to learn more about the world and rebelling against the constrictions that hold him back. Like Peter, he breaks the rules—not life-or-death rules, but those that children understand perhaps even better. He risks parental wrath by putting a hole in the wall, tormenting the dog, wrecking havoc on domestic sanity, and he is sent to his room, a place that leaves him very much on the outside—isolated, excluded, and confined.

Max has gone beyond the bounds of the acceptable, so he is sent beyond the bounds of the place where acceptable people can be. But he suffers no remorse, no pain, no authorial teaching. He gets mad—and gets even—by creating a place where he has the power to tame himself, or the monster within. He creates his own lesson, teaching himself how to get around constrictive rules: Don't hammer nails, don't chase the dog, don't act like a monster, don't be rowdy. BE STILL!—and imagine.

Max creates his own monsters, spurred on by the monster-picture he has drawn earlier, the one tacked to the wall in an opening scene of the book. Then he tames these monsters, frightening them with his "magic" trick of staring them down. They make him king, and he celebrates with a wild rumpus as grand as Peter's chase through Mr. McGregor's garden. So grand it is that it chases away the borders that have been so tightly encasing him in every scene.

Dark blue backgrounds fill the pages as the rumpus begins. A full moon bursts out overhead, replacing the three-quarter moon that hung over Max's head when he found himself alone in his room, hatching his plan—giggling at the thought of it—then sailing off in a "private boat" to "where the wild things are."

The rumpus continues until dawn, as the monsters hoist Max to their shoulders and carry him about until night returns once more and he stops the action of his own little play by sending the Wild Things off to bed without *their* supper. Turnabout is fair play, but having power is not as much fun as he imagined. He is lonely and hungry and missing home. So home he goes, where the adults rule and he must give up being king of "where the wild things are."

It is not easy to go, the wild things love him so (and he so loves being wild). But he says no. He sails back home under a fuzzy full moon, revealing the break with fantasy; reality is about to set in. He lands in his "very own room" where supper, "still hot," sits waiting under the same open window. There are "openings" for us; we simply have to see they are there, the pictures show. And the moon, now solid, still, and full, hangs lower in a star-filled sky. The fantasy will remain with Max in the real world, and he has grown just a little larger on the page now, signifying his inner growth.

The complementary relationship between words and pictures is stronger at this point, sixty years after Potter produced *Peter Rabbit.* Sendak refined the economics of picture-telling beyond what children's book artists before him had achieved, and that feat, plus the subject matter and execution of these evocative scenes, may account for the popularity of the book. We do not learn from the words that Max is wearing a werewolf costume as he plays monster; we merely *see* the suit. The words do not tell us that Max was playing king under a tent in his room, as he hammered the nails. We are not even told he was hammering nails or that this is the same tent under which he later sits, crowned as king, in the land of the Wild Things.

The words do not tell us that Max drew a monster picture and then assumed the monster role in his play world. We simply have pictorial clues that show us more each time we revisit the book. We are not told that the monsters on the title page foretell the inner world Max will bring into play (or that they are his parents), but we begin to sense these ideas as we move through the book. We are not told that all of these monsters are humans drawn from Max's rule-filled world, but we sense that, too.

The words do at times repeat what the pictures tell us. They say the Wild Things have yellow eyes, and they do. They say the monsters were frightened of Max, and their gestures show that they *are* frightened. They say that Max's supper was waiting for him, and it is. Sendak lets the words and pictures speak for themselves, and sometimes the words say the exact opposite of what we see—thus, we really see two stories instead of one.

We hear the world *terrible* a great deal in this book; yet the Wild Things are really toylike and comical figures that are afraid of Max's power. Thus, they do all the silly and counterproductive things that children may see adults doing, when their well-ordered, well-defined adult existence is threatened. They gnash and roar; they clutch and grip children—or they ignore them. Adults also do a few things that Max may wish his parents would do more often: they play with him, loving a wild rumpus as much as he does.

Powerful emotions like anger are frightening to both adults and children when they play on the feelings of the other. Sendak resolves Max's threatening feelings through humor and inventiveness, a feat that has kept this book popular among readers of all ages for the past three decades. By the time it reached its twenty-fifth anniversary, *Where the Wild Things Are* had sold over a million hardcover copies and over two million copies in paperback. It had been exported to countries as far away as South Africa, Japan, and Denmark. Initially, however, no one would have predicted any of this.

So many adults were accustomed to conventional books that taught lessons in less obscure ways, they missed the lesson of this one (look carefully at these pictures,

INVESTIGATIONS: Producing Your Own Book Talk

Creating text sets is a valuable way to learn about themes, genres, and literary patterns in children's books. Try compiling another text set of your own. Choose another book by each of these authors, such as Lewis Carroll's *Through the Looking Glass,* Frances Hodgson Burnett's *The Secret Garden,* Beatrix Potter's *Benjamin Bunny,* E. B. White's *Stuart Little,* Anne Frank's *Tales from the Secret Annexe,* and Maurice Sendak's *In the Night Kitchen.* (Instead of another book by Alcott, you might wish to read a book with male characters such as Robert Louis Stevenson's *Treasure Island* to see what the boy's adventure story of this era was like.)

After reading these books, choose one you particularly like; then compose your own book talk, telling listeners what happens in the book and describing the literary patterns, especially genre and theme. If you think the outsider theme is important in the book, explain how it threads through the book. Share your book talk with others.

Sendak seems to be saying, and think deeply about these words). They saw the words *terrible* and *wild;* they saw pictures of teeth and claws, and they decided the book was too frightening for children. Fortunately, children were able to reassure adults before they could permanently censor Max and his Wild Things.

A generation later, the book is still going strong; few children's books have superceded it in popularity, critical attention, and sales. In fact, Max's story helps us to see better what a children's book is. The outsider theme it illuminates so well has been, from the beginning, a central theme of children's literature, no matter what era, genre, or author.

THEMES IN CHILDREN'S LITERATURE

Consider the way that the **child as outsider** theme threads through so many children's books, often in the same five ways:

1. At some point in the story, a child feels isolated, rejected, different, uninvited, excluded, or ignored, or the child is a stranger in his or her original home or favored place. Why? Growth is causing the child to become a threat to others, and usually these others are adults: parents, stepparents, neighbors, townspeople, or rulers of the land. The child may be too curious, like Goldilocks; too inquisitive, like Alice; too destructive, like Max; too rebellious, like Peter Rabbit; too beautiful, like Snow White or Cinderella; too poor, like Sara in *A Little Princess;* or too different, like Jo March, Peter Rabbit, or Anne Frank and her Jewish family. So the child becomes rebel, "villain," captive, exile, or victim.
2. At some point in the story, the child rejects the home or the favored place. Why? Growth is causing the child to feel threatened. So the child goes to a second home—an intermediate stage that signals the growth process—as when Fern visits the barn. Leaving home to explore the outside world, the child is often rejected as different also, and so he or she eventually returns home, as Peter Rabbit and Max do. Or the child or young adult returns home to conform to the prevailing customs (Alcott's Jo marries in spite of her quest for a writing career). This home-adventure-home cycle emerges in many children's books. In some cases, the adventure takes place only in the child's mind: Instead of returning home, the child might wake in the same place from a dream, after having journeyed away from that place in the dream, as Alice does. Or the child might walk away into a new place as if released from a dream, as Fern does when she drifts away to the country fair and seems to forget the barn. Finally, the child might go to a new and better home, as Snow White, Cinderella, and Sara, a modern day Cinderella figure, do. We might argue that *The Diary of Anne Frank* is not really a children's book because it does not have a happy ending. We know the real-life tragic ending, and this knowledge causes us to feel the pain and irony of Anne's "hope." She does not return home; she dies in a concentration camp. But the diary itself ends with Anne's own hope to return home and to grow up like any child.
3. At some point in the story, the child voyages out to explore the world, faces rejection or conflict in the world, and carries on in spite of it. The child might flee, as Goldilocks does; the child might create a second home, in order to

think things through, as Max does; or the child might make the best of things, as Sara does, by pretending, inventing a persona, telling stories to comfort others, or doing good deeds. In other words, the child sees an alternate behavior and takes on a new role, finding a place to fit in. (Fern does this when she first goes to the barn to listen to, or spin out, Wilbur's story, and when she later goes to the fair and becomes involved with Henry Fussy.) At the same time, the child models for others his or her old role (curious, like Goldilocks, or disturbing and creative, like Max), a behavior that changes the child—or others—as he or she learns the new role. The child leaves the original home in order to reenter it changed—or having changed others. The child creates new life, on the child's own terms, while out in the world.

4. At some point in the story, a fantasy dream sequence may take place, or the entire story may be a fantasy. Within realistic fiction, there may be a dream or dreamlike place that enables the character to construct an alternate reality; Katherine Paterson's *Bridge to Terabithia* (Crowell, 1977) is a good example. This "reality" often appears as a house or edifice that either expands, breaks down, shrinks, disappears, or is vacated by the child character (the growth metaphor). Baby Bear's bed collapses, as do the walls of Max's room. Cinderella's pumpkin coach materializes, then disappears. Sara's attic room is transformed. Alice's "Drink me" discovery causes her to expand and shrink. Peter's clothing is cast off. Fern's barn is left behind. Snow White's glass coffin is cast aside.
5. At some point in the story, often at the end, the child leaves the second home and goes to a different place, as Sara does. This place might be the original home, but it seems different now, or the child has changed, as Peter Rabbit has, as he lies asleep after his great adventure. Because of these changes, the child "fits" better in the home setting, as we see from the look of relief on Max's face.

Themes other than the outside child thread through *Where the Wild Things Are,* of course. There is the *angry child* theme, as Sendak has described it (the child finding ways to circumvent constriction and boredom), the *child as inventor,* the *child in the family,* and the *magic journey,* to name just a few. But the outsider theme stands out in this story, as in many children's books. This may be because as Nina Bawden, author of *The Outside Child* (Puffin, 1989) has said: "It is possible that outside children are in fact inherently more interesting. People on their own, up against it, in some kind of crisis, are much more intriguing than people for whom life is straightforward and easy. You want to see how they make out" (page 694).

The outsider theme speaks "across all sorts of barriers—race, country, sex, age" (Bawden, page 694), and it tells us more about what a children's book is, because so many children's books show strong evidence of it. Consider the many other themes of

INVESTIGATIONS: The Outsider Theme

We have focused on the outsider or outside child theme in children's books, an important thread running through stories from *Alice's Adventures in Wonderland* to Nina Bawden's *The Outside Child.* Read to discover more instances of this theme in children's literature and write about your discoveries in your journal.

children's literature in stories that have outside children as major characters. There is the **abandoned or rejected child,** a theme in the Grimm brothers' "Hansel and Gretel" and in the old English folk tale *Babes in the Woods,* illustrated by Randolph Caldecott (rpt. Hutchinson, 1988). We also see it in recent children's fiction like Cynthia Voigt's *Homecoming* (Scribner, 1981) and Nina Bawden's *The Outside Child.* The oldest story about a rejected child is probably "Cinderella."

All Cinderella stories contain examples of the **working child** as outsider. In the "lost slipper" variants, the girl is kept in the kitchen or near the hearth fire so long, she is covered with ashes and dirt; hence her various names: Ash-girl, Little Cinders, Cinderella. In the "rejecting father" and "hated marriage" variants, she leaves home (is cast out or escapes) to earn her way as a kitchen servant. In the "magic doll" variant, she works hard for Baba Yaga.

But working children do not stop with Cinderella. Karen Cushman shows us the child put to work early in the medieval period in *The Midwife's Apprentice* (Clarion, 1995). Joan Aiken shows us children in Victorian England working in *Midnight Is A Place* (Penguin, 1974). And Katherine Paterson recounts the story of a child working in the New England mills during the same historical period in *Lyddie* (Dutton, 1991).

Working children are sometimes immigrants, as in Laurence Yep's *Dragon's Gate* (Harper, 1993), and **immigrant children** are often outsiders. We see them in Jean Little's *Listen for the Singing* (Dutton, 1977), the story of a German child whose family moves to Canada; in Shelley Tanaka and Ron Berg's *Michi's New Year* (Peter Martin of Toronto, 1980), about a Japanese child whose family has settled in Canada; in Laurence Yep's Asian-American fiction, *Dragonwings* (Harper, 1975), *The Star Fisher* (Penguin, 1991), and *Thief of Hearts* (Harper, 1995); in Joyce Hansen's *Home Boy* (Clarion, 1982) in Latoya Hunter's *The Diary of Latoya Hunter* (Vintage, 1992), about a Caribbean child who moves to New York City, and in *Marianthe's Story* (Greenwillow, 1998) by Aliki about a Greek child in America.

Ethnic children, whether immigrants or native-born Americans, are often outsiders in the American mainstream culture. We see these children in Laurence Yep's *Thief of Hearts* (Harper, 1995), about an Asian-American child; in Virginia Hamilton's *Plain City* (Scholastic, 1993), about a mixed-race child; in Arlene Hirschfelder and Beverly Singer's collection, *Rising Voices: Writings of Young Native Americans* (Ballantine, 1992); in Gary Soto's *Taking Sides* (Harcourt, 1991), about a Mexican-American child; in Mitali Perkins's *The Sunita Experiment* (Little, Brown, 1993), about an East Indian-American child; in Barbara Cohen's *Molly's Pilgrim* (Morrow, 1983), about a Jewish-American child who is also an immigrant, and in Allen Say's *Allison* (Houghton Mifflin, 1998, about a Japanese child who has been adopted by an American couple.

Children with special talents are yet another type of outsider. We see them in Alcott's ***Little Women,*** L. M. Montgomery's ***Anne of Green Gables*** (1908), and Louise Fitzhugh's ***Harriet the Spy*** (Harper, 1964), each focusing on girls who want to be writers. We meet other such children in Noel Streatfield's *Ballet Shoes* (1936) and Laurence Yep's *Ribbons* (Putnam, 1996), each focusing on girls who want to be dancers. **Strong females** of all kinds are often outsiders.

Lost, displaced or dislocated children are most especially outsiders. Good examples of this category include Anne Holm's *I am David* (Harcourt, 1965) and Sook Nyul Choi's *Year of Impossible Goodbyes* (Houghton, 1991). These

We find Cinderella stories told and retold in cultures around the world, from earliest times to the present. Five of the most popular variants in North America are: lost slipper, rejecting father, hated marriage, magic doll, and ugly sister. Among these, the *lost slipper* variant is the most familiar.

In these stories, the female (usually a poor stepchild) meets and charms a prince or high ruler at a ball. He pursues her, and she runs away, losing a slipper on the way. He searches for the one girl whose foot will fit the slipper (she is the one with the tiniest feet, a sign of beauty in many cultures through the years). When he finds her, he identifies her as the one he will marry. The outcast, outside child thus becomes the highest-ranked insider: a princess or queen. Sometimes the usual pattern of outsider *female* is reversed, producing a Cinder-lad story, as in "The Princess on the Glass Hill" recorded in Peter Asbjornsen and Jorgen Moe's *Norwegian Folk Tales* (Pantheon, 1982). Then the test for identity is different: Cinder-lad must possess a horse sturdy and sure-footed enough to ride up a glass hill.

Lost slippers come in all materials and colors. The glass shoe is perhaps the most familiar to American children, so popular has been the Disney film version of *Cinderella* (see *Walt Disney's Cinderella,* Western Publishing, 1986) based on the 1697 Perrault version called *Cendrillon.* Ann Laurence has produced a modern translation of Perrault's stories, *Tales from Perrault* (Oxford University Press, 1988), and many picture book artists have retold Perrault's Cinderella (see Marcia Brown's *Cinderella,* Scribner's, 1954; Errol Le Cain's *Cinderella,* Bradbury, 1973; and Susan Jeffers's *Cinderella,* Dial, 1985, retold by Amy Ehrlich).

The golden, cloth, metal, or leather slipper has been very popular too. The oldest written version of the Cinderella story features a golden slipper and comes from ninth-century China (see Ai-Ling Louie's *Yeh-Shen,* illustrated by Ed Young, Philomel, 1982). Darrell Lum's *The Golden Slipper: A Vietnamese Legend,* illustrated by Makiko Nagano (Troll, 1994) provides another Asian version.

From the oral traditions of Russia and Germany, we also have golden shoes in Aleksandr Afanas'ev's *Russian Fairy Tales* (Random House, 1973) and in the Grimm Brothers' nineteenth-century collection (see *The Complete Fairy Tales of the Brothers Grimm,* translated by Jack Zipes, Bantam, 1987). The Grimm version is available in many picture book versions today; see *Aschenputtel,* illustrated by Bernadette (North-South, 1977); and *Cinderella,* illustrated by Nonny Hogrogian (Greenwillow, 1981).

In warmer climates, the slipper is sometimes described as a golden sandal (see Rebecca Hickox's recent picture book retelling, *The Golden Sandal: A Middle Eastern Cinderella Story,* illustrated by Will Hillenbrand, Holiday, 1998; and Shirley Climo's *The Egyptian Cinderella,* illustrated by Ruth Heller, Harper, 1989).

In a Celtic version, "Fair, Brown, and Trembling," the shoe is green to represent Ireland (see Joseph Jacobs' *Celtic Fairy Tales,* illustrated by Victor Ambrus, Bodley Head, 1986). Richard Chase has recorded an Appalachian version, "Ashpet," in *Grandfather Tales* (Houghton Mifflin, 1948), in which the girl wears a red shoe. Recently, Robert San Souci has uncovered an a French Creole version of the Perrault tale in which the Cinderella figure wears tropical pink slippers. (See *Cendrillon: A Caribbean Cinderella* with pictures by Brian Pinkney, Simon, 1998.)

In the *rejecting father* variant, three daughters compete for a father's love and the youngest is sorely tested for her honesty and self-sacrifice, as in Shakespeare's "King Lear." For an Appalachian version of this theme, see "Like Meat Loves Salt" in Richard Chase's *Grandfather Tales.* Picture book versions include William Hooks's *Moss Gown,* illustrated by Donald Carrick (Clarion, 1987), from the American South; Margot Tomes's *Tattercoats* (Putnam, 1989), a story retold earlier by Joseph Jacobs in his collections from the British Isles; Andrew Peters's *Salt is Sweeter Than Gold,* illustrated by Zdenka Kabatova-Taborska (Barefoot Books, 1994), a Czech story; and Nina Jaffe's *The Way Meat Loves Salt: A Cinderella Tale from the Jewish Tradition,* illustrated by Louise August (Holt, 1998), a story set in Poland.

In the *hated marriage* variant, a girl is running from a male oppressor who intends to marry her themes—children with special talents and children of displacement—are closely connected to the **child alone,** as we see in Frances Burnett's *A Little Princess* (Sara is both a talented storyteller and a dislocated child). Scott O'Dell's *Island of the Blue Dolphins* (Houghton, 1960), Anne Holm's *I Am David,* and Astrid Lindgren's *Pippi Longstocking* (Viking, 1950) add to this category. The children in these stories have unusual self-reliance or strength (inner or outer) but are isolated or dislocated.

The **child in the family** is sometimes an outsider among his or her own siblings because of divergent needs, interests, or preoccupations, as in Alcott's *Little Women.* Or the child might be experiencing feelings of anger, frustration, or hostility within the family, as in Sendak's *Where the Wild Things Are* or Hiawyn Oram and Satoshi Kitamura's *Angry Arthur* (Puffin, 1984). The child might be coming to terms with a special-but-different heritage from others in the family, as is Buhlaire Sims in Virginia Hamilton's *Plain City* (Scholastic, 1993). Discovering that her father's mother is white is a shocking experience for this child, who is growing up in an otherwise monocultural African-American family.

Children might have different physical traits or capabilities from others in their families, as in Hans Christian Andersen's "The Little Mermaid." Or they might be growing and changing: the **ugly-duckling-into-swan** theme stretches from Hans Christian Andersen's "The Ugly Duckling" to L. M. Montgomery's *Anne of Green Gables* and Betsy Byars's *Summer of the Swans* (Viking, 1970).

Cinderella in Children's Literature (continued)

against her will, molest her, or engage in an incestuous relationship with her. The girl escapes through a disguise (if she wears animal fur, she can wander through the forest more easily and safely). She finds a castle and a job as a servant; she bakes a cake for the Prince (or makes a soup) into which she drops a ring that later identifies her as the one he will love—and marry. (See Richard Chase's "Catskins" in *Grandfather Tales,* Virginia Hamilton's "Catskinella" in *Her Stories: African American Folktales, Fairy Tales, and True Tales,* illustrated by Leo and Diane Dillon, Scholastic, 1995; and Charlotte Huck's *Princess Furball,* illustrated by Anita Lobel, Greenwillow, 1989, based on a Grimm tale called "Thousand Furs.")

The *magic doll* variant comes to us from Russian stories, in which the child's doll (a present from her dying mother) provides magical help when her wicked stepmother and stepsisters send her to visit the witch, Baba Yaga. Aleksandr Afanas'ev records "Vasilisa the Beautiful" in *Russian Fairy Tales.* Elizabeth Winthrop retells the same story in *Vasilissa the Beautiful,* illustrationed by Alexander Koshkin (Harper, 1991); see also Virginia Hamilton's "Baba Yaga, the Terrible" in *The Dark Way,* illustrated by Lambert Davis (Harcourt, 1990).

The *ugly sister* variant arises frequently in African-American and Native-American stories. But we also see it in European stories like Grimm's "Aschenputtel," in which a kind sister wins the prize (a prince or diamonds and fine dresses) because of her kind, faithful, and obedient ways, while her sisters (or stepsisters) are greedy, demanding, thoughtless, or cruel. Terry Berger's "Baboon Skins," in *Black Fairy Tales,* illustrated by David White (Atheneum, 1969), comes from Swaziland, and John Steptoe's *Mufaro's Beautiful Daughters* (Lothrop, 1987) from Kaffir, Zimbabwe. Two ugly sister stories from the American South are Virginia Hamilton's "Good Blanche, Bad Rose, and the Talking Eggs," in *Her Stories,* illustrated by Leo and Diane Dillon (Scholastic, 1995), and Robert San Souci's *The Talking Eggs,* illustrated by Jerry Pinkney (Dial, 1989). From the Algonquin Indians comes Martin Rafe's *The Rough-Face Girl,* illustrated by David Shannon (Scholastic, 1992).

Children often have childhood fears (fear of the dark, fear of being deserted, fear of sibling displacement), and a story can help them resolve their fears by demonstrating how a fearful character copes. The **fearful child** theme emerges subtly in Margaret Wise Brown's classics of reassurance, *Goodnight Moon* (Harper, 1947; illustrations by Clement Hurd) and *The Runaway Bunny* (Harper, 1942; illustrations by Clement Hurd). Young characters struggling with their first ventures away from home and finding inventive solutions to problems produce humorous and empathetic experiences for child readers. The **precocious child** theme is well represented in Beverly Cleary's Ramona stories, including *Ramona the Pest* (Morrow, 1968) and *Ramona the Brave* (Morrow, 1975).

The child away from home also introduces the theme of the **traveling child,** seen in realistic fiction from Frances Burnett's *Little Lord Fauntleroy* (1886; rpt. Puffin, 1981) to Gary Soto's *Pacific Crossing* (Harcourt, 1992). We also see this theme in fantasy novels such as E. Nesbit's *The Story of the Amulet* (1906; rpt. Puffin, 1959)—where it intersects with the theme of the **magical journey**—and in time travel stories such as Madeleine L'Engle's *A Wrinkle in Time* (Farrar, 1962).

Above all, children are themselves outsiders in the adult world. Adults guide, limit, determine, and often constrict everything that children do—or wish to do—from the moment they first breathe. Similarly, children's literature is the outsider in the world of adult books. The outsider status of children's literature is, in fact, what causes endless discussions focusing on the question, What is a children's book? Because of the dual audience for children's books (adults select, evaluate, and mediate books for children; children clamor for or resist the books they choose), the role of the adult in children's books is pivotal in defining what makes a work a *children's* book. Sometimes the adult-child dynamic also tells us a great deal about the era in which the book appeared.

In the beginning, adults taught and children learned morals, manners, social behaviors, and expectations for class and gender. Lewis Carroll was one of the first authors, if not the first, to allow his child character to face down her adult oppressors. Nineteenth-century children's authors went on to present children as the "doers" of the story, with adults often taking a back seat. The adults were either absent or unimportant, as in Edith Nesbit's work; supportive and exemplary, as in Louisa Alcott's fiction; or self-absorbed and oppressive, as in Frances Burnett's novels.

More recently, adult characters in children's books have run the gamut between absent and ineffectual, as in books by Maurice Sendak; Astrid Lindgren, and E. B. White, or present to provide support, guidance, or friendship when necessary, as in

INVESTIGATIONS: Tracing a Theme through History

Read a children's book that fits one of the themes mentioned in this section to see how the theme works as the "big idea" of the story, drawing you in and keeping everything—characters, conflicts, and actions—connected. Then make a study of one of these themes, tracing it through history to see how the theme has grown and changed in the hands of writers in different times and places. For the theme of the **magical journey,** as an example, you could study fantasies such as *Alice's Adventures in Wonderland; The Story of the Amulet; The Wizard of Oz; The Lion, the Witch, and the Wardrobe; and Where the Wild Things Are. For the theme of* ***Strong females,*** *see end of chapter list.*

books by Betsy Byars, Elaine Konigsburg, Beverly Cleary, and Susan Cooper. Ethnic authors often provide a much stronger cast of adult characters; family members (from the nuclear or extended family) and adults in the community play an important part in the child's world from beginning to end in many of their stories. Most often, however, children's authors place children very much outside the adult world.

Nina Bawden, who writes fiction for both adults and children, has thought deeply about the differences between the two audiences, and she has produced some interesting answers to this question, What is a *children's* book? The "important difference between writing for adults and writing for children," says Bawden, "is not style or subject matter, though those things come into it, but the point of view you're looking from" (page 4). She goes on to describe what separates children from adults. Children are "singularly helpless," she says. "In real life they can't make anything happen. All they can do is stand by and watch"(page 8). The "central fact of a child's life is that everything that happens to her depends on the uncertain whims of the adults" (page 11).

Adults in children's literature, Bawden remembers from her own childhood reading, never seemed to be the "uncertain, awkward, quirky, *dangerous* creatures" she knew them to be (page 8). Children have their own awareness of right and wrong, she points out. As a child, she often felt herself to be "very bad and wicked." But children in the books she read as a child "never seemed to have the kind of dark, angry feelings" that she worried about (page 9).

So the children's book must not only omit what the child cannot yet comprehend, it must show children what a child can—and does—see. It must look at life from the child's own perspective, limited as that viewpoint might be. It must concentrate on the child's feelings, the child's interpretations of life events. It must look through the child's own lens at the child's world, holding an "honest mirror" up to that world and telling children what they want to know.

Bawden remembers the kind of books she enjoyed most as a child. Like many children, she preferred adventure stories—and not simply for the excitement. "In adventure stories [children] can see themselves taking part in the action and not only that; they can also test themselves, measure themselves against the characters in the book. Would *they* be brave in such a situation, or would they run away? Would they be honest, or would they lie?"(page 8). In the next chapter, we will be thinking more about genres or different kinds of books as we continue to explore the ever-changing—and often mystifying—concept of *children's literature.*

CHILDREN'S LITERATURE

Realistic Fiction: Contemporary

Picture Books

Ackerman, Karen. *Song and Dance Man.* Illustrated by Stephen Gammell. New York: Knopf, 1988.

Bateson-Hill, Margaret. *Shota and the Star Quilt.* Illustrated by Christine Fowler. New York: Zero to Ten Limited, 1998.

Bunting, Eve. *Smoky Night.* Illustrated by David Diaz. New York: Harcourt Brace, 1994.

———. *The Wall.* Illustrated by Ronald Himler. New York: Clarion, 1990.

Cooney, Barbara. *Island Boy.* New York: Viking Penguin, 1988.

———. *Hattie and the Wild Waves.* New York: Viking Penguin, 1990.

———. *Miss Rumphius.* New York: Viking Penguin, 1982.

DE PAOLA, TOMIE. *Nana Upstairs & Nana Downstairs.* New York: Putnam's, 1973.

FOX, MEM. *Wilfrid Gordon Mcdonald Partridge.* Illustrated by Julie Vivas. New York: Viking Penguin/Puffin, 1987.

GREENFIELD, ELOISE. *Grandpa's Face.* Illustrated by Floyd Cooper. New York: Philomel, 1988.

HALL, DONALD. *Ox-Cart Man.* Illustrated by Barbara Cooney. New York: Viking, 1979.

HOFFMAN, MARY. *Amazing Grace.* Illustrated by Caroline Binch. New York: Dial, 1991.

HUGHES, SHIRLEY. *Dogger.* New York: Lothrop, 1977.

JUKES, MAVIS. *I'll See You in My Dreams.* Illustrated by Stacey Schutt. New York: Knopf, 1993.

KEATS, EZRA JACK. *The Snowy Day.* New York: Viking, 1962.

———. *Whistle for Willie.* New York: Viking, 1964.

MCCLOSKEY, ROBERT. *Blueberries for Sal.* New York: Viking, 1948.

———. *Make Way for Ducklings.* New York: Viking, 1941.

———. *One Morning in Maine.* New York: Viking, 1952.

———. *Time of Wonder.* New York: Viking, 1957.

MCCULLY, EMILY ARNOLD. *Mirette on the High Wire.* New York: Putnam and Grosset Book Group, 1992.

MACLACHLAN, PATRICIA. *Through Grandpa's Eyes.* Illustrated by Deborah Kogan Ray. New York: Harper and Row, 1980.

MILLER, ARTHUR. *Jane's Blanket.* Illustrated by Emily A. McCully. New York: Viking, 1953.

MITCHELL, RITA PHILLIPS. *Hue Boy.* London: Victor Gollancz, 1992.

MORA, PAT. *Thomas and the Library Lady.* Illustrated by Raul Colon. New York: Knopf, 1997.

PILKEY, DAV. *The Paperboy.* New York: Scholastic, 1997.

RATHMANN, PAGGY. *Ruby the Copycat.* New York: Scholastic, 1991.

RICE, EVE. *New Blue Shoes.* New York: Macmillan, 1975.

WALLACE, IAN. *Morgan the Magnificent.* Toronto: Doublas & McIntyre, 1987.

YOLEN, JANE. *Owl Moon.* Illustrated by John Schoenherr. New York: Philomel, 1987.

Fiction

BAWDEN, NINA. *The Outside Child.* New York: Penguin, 1991.

BLUME, JUDY. *Here's to You, Rachel Robinson.* New York: Franklin Watts, 1993.

BOND, NANCY. *Truth to Tell.* New York: Macmillan, 1994.

BYARS, BETSY. *The Cartoonist.* New York: Viking Penguin, 1978.

CLEARY, BEVERLY. *Dear Mr. Henshaw.* New York: William Morrow, 1983.

———. *Ramona the Pest.* New York: William Morrow, 1968.

FITZHUGH, LOUISE. *Harriet the Spy.* New York: Harper, 1964.

FOX, PAULA. *Western Wind.* New York: Orchard Books, 1993.

HAMILTON, VIRGINIA. *Bluish.* New York: Scholastic, 1999.

———. *Cousins.* New York: Philomel, 1990.

———. *Second Cousins.* New York: Scholastic, 1998.

HANSEN, JOYCE. *The Gift-Giver.* New York: Clarion Books, 1980.

HICKMAN, JANET. *Jericho.* New York: Morrow, 1994.

HURWITZ, JOHANNA. *The Adventures of Ali Baba Bernstein.* New York: William Morrow, 1985.

KONIGSBURG, E. L. *The View from Saturday.* New York: Atheneum, 1996.

LOWRY, LOIS. *Anastasia Krupnik.* Boston: Houghton Mifflin, 1979.

MOWAT, FARLEY. *Owls In the Familly.* Boston: Little, Brown, 1962.

Paterson, Katherine. *Parks Quest.* New York: Penguin, 1988.
Smucker, Barbara. *Amish Adventure.* New York: Viking Penguin, 1984.
Soto, Gary. *Taking Sides.* New York: Harcourt, 1991.
Tate, Eleanora. *Thank you, Dr. Martin Luther King, Jr.!* New York: Franklin Watts, 1990.
Yep, Laurence. *The Cook's Family.* New York: G. P. Putnam's Sons, 1998.
Yumoto, Kazumi. *The Friends.* New York: Farrar Strans at Groux, 1996.

Realistic Fiction: Historical

Picture Books

Bartone, Elisa. *Peppe the Lamplighter.* Illustrated by Ted Lewin. New York: Lothrop, 1993.
Cohen, Barbara. *Molly's Pilgrim.* Illustrated by Michael Deraney. New York: William Morrow, 1983.
Cooney, Barbara. *Hattie and the Wild Waves.* New York: Viking Penguin, 1990.
———. *Island Boy.* New York: Viking Penguin, 1988.
———. *Only Opal: The Diary of a Young Girl.* New York: Scholastic, 1994.
Fitzgerald, Elizabeth. *Chita's Christmas Tree.* Illustrated by Floyd Cooper. New York: Macmillan, 1989.
Haley, Gail E. *Jack Jouett's Ride.* New York: Viking, 1973.
Hall, Donald. *Ox-Cart Man.* Illustrated by Barbara Cooney. New York: Viking, 1978.
Hamilton, Virginia. *The Bells of Christmas.* Illustrated by Lambert Davis. New York: Harcourt, 1989.
Hest, Amy. *When Jessie Came Across the Sea.* Illustrated by P. J. Lynch. Cambridge, MA: Candlewick, 1997.
Hopkinson, Deborah. *Sweet Clara and the Freedom Quilt.* Illustrated by James Ransome. New York: Knopf, 1993.
Howard, Elizabeth Fitzgerald. *Chita's Christmas Tree.* Illustrated by Floyd Cooper. New York: Macmillan, 1989.
Johnson, Tony. *The Wagon.* Illustrated by James Ransome. New York: Tambourine, 1996.
Lasky, Kathryn. *She's Wearing a Dead Bird on Her Head!* Illustrated by David Catrow. New York: Hyperion, 1995.
Levinson, Riki. *Watch the Stars Come out.* Illustrated by Diane Goode. New York: Dutton, 1985.
Little, Lessie Jones. *Children of Long Ago.* Illustrated by Jan Spivey Gilchrist. New York: Philomel, 1988.
Say, Allen. *The Bicycle Man.* Boston: Houghton Mifflin, 1982.
Turner, Ann. *Nettie's Trip South.* Illustrated by Ronald Himler. New York: Macmillan, 1987.
Winter, Jeanette. *Klara's New World.* New York: Knopf, 1992.
Yarbrough, Camille. *Cornrows.* Illustrated by Carole Byard. New York: Coward, 1979.

Fiction

Avi. *The True Confessions of Charlotte Doyle.* New York: Orchard, 1990.
Bawden, Nina. *Carrie's War.* New York: Lippincott, 1973.
Brink, Carol Ryrie. *Caddie Woodlawn.* New York: Macmillan, 1935.
Choi, Sook Nyul. *Year of Impossible Goodbyes.* Boston: Houghton Mifflin, 1991.
Curtis, Christopher Paul. *The Watsons Go to Birmingham—1963.* New York: Delacorte, 1995.
Cushman, Karen. *Catherine, Called Birdy.* New York: Clarion, 1994.

———. *The Midwife's Apprentice.* New York: Clarion, 1995.
FOX, PAULA. *The Slave Dancer.* Scarsdale, NY: Bradbury Press, 1973.
GIFF, PATRICIA REILLY. *Lily's Crossing.* New York: Delacorte Press, 1996.
HESSE, KAREN. *Letters from Rifka.* New York: Holt, 1993.
———. *Out of the Dust.* New York: Scholastic, 1999.
HUNTER, MOLLIE. *The Thirteenth Member.* London: Hamish Hamilton, 1971.
LASKY, KATHRYN. *The Night Journey.* New York: Frederick Warne, 1981.
LEVITIN, SONIA. *Journey to America.* New York: Atheneum, 1970.
LITTLE, JEAN. *Listen for the Singing.* Toronto: Clarke, Irwin, 1977.
LOWRY, LOIS. *Number the Stars.* Boston: Houghton Mifflin, 1989.
MACLACHLAN, PATRICIA. *Sarah, Plain and Tall.* New York: Harper, 1985.
O'DELL, SCOTT. *Sing Down the Moon.* Boston: Houghton Mifflin, 1970.
PATERSON, KATHERINE. *Lyddie.* New York: Dutton, 1991.
PETRY, ANN. *Tituba of Salem Village.* New York: HarperCollins, 1964.
ROBINET, HARRIETTA GILLEM. *Washington City is Burning.* New York: Atheneum, 1996.
SAWYER, RUTH. *Roller Skates.* New York: Viking Penguin, 1936.
SMUCKER, BARBARA. *Days of Terror.* Toronto: Clarke, Irwin, 1979.
SPEARE, ELIZABETH GEORGE. *The Witch of Blackbird Pond.* Boston: Houghton Mifflin, 1958.
TAYLOR, MILDRED. *The Friendship/The Gold Cadillac.* New York: Dial, 1989.
———. *The Road to Memphis.* New York: Dial, 1990.
———. *Roll of Thunder, Hear My Cry.* New York: Dial, 1976.
———. *Song of the Trees.* New York: Dial, 1975.
WALSH, JILL PATON. *A Parcel of Patterns.* London: Kestrel, 1983.
WILDER, LAURA INGALLS. *Little House in the Big Woods.* Illustrated by Garth Williams. New York: Harper, 1932.
———. *Little Town on the Prairie.* Illustrated by Garth Williams. New York: Harper, 1941.
YEP, LAURENCE. *Dragon's Gate.* New York: HarperCollins, 1993.
YOLEN, JANE. *The Devil's Arithmetic.* New York: Viking Penguin, 1988.

Nonfiction

General Reference: Books about Art

BANG, MOLLY. *Picture This: Perception and Composition.* Boston: Little, Brown, 1991.
BJORK, CHRISTINA. *Linnea in Monet's Garden.* Translated by Joan Sandin; Illustrated by Lena Anderson. New York: Farrar Straus and Giroux, 1987.
BLIZZARD, GLADYS. *Come Look With Me: Enjoying Art with Children.* New York: Lickle, 1996.
———. *Come Look With Me: World of Play.* Charlottesville, VA: Thomasson-Grant, 1993.
CESERANI, GIAN PAOLO. *Grand Constructions.* Illustrations by Piero Ventura. New York: Putnam, 1983.
EMBERLY, ED. *Drawing Book of Animals.* New York: Scholastic, 1970.
KENNET, FRANCES, AND TERRY MEASHAM. *Looking at Paintings.* Illustrated by Malcolm Livingston. New York: Van Nostrand Reinhold, 1978.
MACAGY, DOUGLAS AND ELIZABETH. *Going for a Walk with a Line.* Garden City, NY: Doubleday, 1959.
ROALF, PEGGY. *Looking at Paintings: Cats.* New York: Hyperion, 1992.
VENTURA, PIERO. *Houses.* Boston: Houghton Mifflin, 1993.

History

COOPER, ILENE. *The Dead Sea Scrolls.* Illustrated by John Thompson. New York: Morrow, 1997.
FABER, DORIS. *The Amish.* Illustrated by Michael Erkel. New York: Doubleday, 1991.
FREEDMAN, RUSSELL. *Buffalo Hunt.* New York: Holiday House, 1988.

———. *Children of the Wild West.* New York: Clarion, 1983.
———. *Immigrant Kids.* New York: Dutton, 1980.
———. *Kids at Work: Lewis Hine and the Crusade Against Child Labor.* New York: Clarion, 1994.
GOODALL, JOHN S. *The Story a Castle.* New York: McElderry Books, 1986.
HAMILTON, VIRGINIA. *Anthony Burns.* New York: Knopf, 1988. (Runaway slave in Boston.)
———. *Many Thousand Gone.* Illustrated by Leo and Diane Dillon. New York: Knopf, 1993.
HAMPTON, WILBORN. *Kennedy Assassinated! The World Mourns: A Reporter's Story.* Cambridge, MA: Candlewick, 1997.
KING, DR. MARTIN LUTHER. *I Have A Dream.* Illustrated by Fifteen Corceta Scott King Award Artists. New York: Scholastic, 1997.
LASKER, JOE. *Merrily Ever After.* New York: Viking, 1976. (Life in the medieval period.)
LEVINE, ELLEN. *If You Traveled on the Underground Railroad.* Illustrated by Richard Williams. New York: Scholastic, 1988.
LYONS, MARY. *Letters from a Slave Girl: The Story of Harriet Jacobs.* New York: Simon & Schuster, 1992.
MACAULAY, DAVID. *Castle.* Boston: Houghton Mifflin, 1977.
———. *Cathedral.* Boston: Houghton Mifflin, 1973.
———. *City.* Boston: Houghton Mifflin, 1974.
———. *Pyramid.* Boston: Houghton Mifflin, 1975.
MELTZER, MILTON. *The Hispanic Americans.* New York: Crowell, 1982.
MOCHIZUKI, KEN. *Passage to Freedom: The Sugihara Story.* Illustrated by Dom Lee. New York: Lee & Low, 1997. (Japanese consul saves Jewish people during the Holocaust.)
PAUL, ANN WHITFORD. *Eight Hands Round: A Patchwork Alphabet.* Illustrated by Jeanette Winter. New York: HarperCollins, 1991. (ABC book for older readers; life in early America.)
SHERROW, VICTORIA. *The Iroquois Indians.* New York: Chelsea House, 1992.
STANLEY, JERRY. *Digger: The Tragic Fate of the California Indians from the Missions to the Gold Rush.* New York: Crown, 1997.
VERGES, GLORIA AND ORIOL. *Journey Through History: Prehistory to Egypt.* Illustrated by Maria Rius. New York: Barron's Educational Series, 1988.
———. *Journey Through History: The Middle Ages.* Illustrated by Maria Rius. New York: Barron's Educational Series, 1988.
———. *Journey Through History: The Renaissance.* Illustrated by Garme Peris. New York: Barron's Educational Series, 1988.
———. *Journey Through History: Modern Times.* Illustrated by Maria Rius. New York: Barron's Educational Series, 1988.
VOYAGES OF DISCOVERY (SCHOLASTIC). *The History of Making Books.* New York: Scholastic, 1996.

Science

BAKER, JEANNIE. *Where the Forest Meets the Sea.* New York: Scholastic, 1987.
COLE, JOANNA. *The Magic School Bus Inside the Earth.* Illustrated by Bruce Degen. New York: Scholastic, 1987.
COLLARD, SNEED. *Animal Deeds.* Boston: Houghton Mifflin, 1997.
DEMAURO, LISA. *Bats.* New York: Dell, 1990.
DORRIS, ARTHUR. *A Tree is Growing.* New York: Scholastic, 1997.
FRADIN, DENNIS. *The Planet Hunters: The Search for Other Worlds.* New York: Margaret McElderry/Simon & Schuster, 1997.
GILETTE, LYNETT. *Dinosaur Ghosts: The Mystery of Coelopyhsis.* Illustrated by Douglas Henderson. New York: Dial, 1997.

GRAHAM, ADA AND FRANK. *Bears in the Wild.* Illustrated by D. D. Tyler. New York: Delacorte, 1981.

———. *Whale Watch.* Illustrated by D. D. Tyler. New York: Delacorte, 1978.

LAUBER, PATRICIA. *Journey to the Planets.* New York, Crown, 1982.

———. *Volcano: The Eruption and Healing of Mount St. Helens.* New York: Bradbury Press, 1986.

LING, MARY, AND MARY ATKINSON. *The Snake Book.* Photographs by Frank Greenaway and Dave King. New York: DK Publishing, 1997.

LURIE, ALISON. *The Heavenly Zoo: Legends and Tales of the Stars.* Pictures by Monika Beisner. New York: Farrar, 1979.

MICUCCI, CHARLES. *The Life and Times of the Honeybee.* Boston: Houghton Mifflin, 1995.

PATENT, DOROTHY HINSHAW. *Grey Wolf, Red Wolf.* Photographs by William Munoz. New York: Clarion, 1990.

PATTERSON, FRANCINE. *Koko's Kitten.* Photographs by Rohald Cohn. New York: Scholastic, 1985. (Gorilla's story.)

PFEFFER, WENDY. *A Log's Life.* New York: Simon & Schuster, 1997.

PRINGLE, LAURENCE. *An Extraordinary Life: the Story of a Monarch Butterfly.* New York: Orchard, 1997.

SATTLER, HELEN RONEY. *Our Patchwork Planet.* Illustrated by Giulo Maestro. New York: Lothrop, 1995.

SIMON, SEYMOUR. *Comets, Meteors, and Asteroids.* New York: Morrow, 1994.

———. *Galaxies.* New York: Morrow, 1988.

TRESSELT, ALVIN. *Hide and Seek Fog.* Illustrated by Roger Duvoisin. New York: Lothrop, 1965. (Mood piece about the weather; picture book classic.)

WALLACE, KAREN. *Think of an Eel.* Illustrated by Mike Bostock. Cambridge MA: Candlewick, 1993.

WICK, WALTER. *A Drop of Water.* New York: Scholastic, 1997.

WILDSMITH, BRIAN. *Squirrels.* Oxford, England: Oxford University Press, 1974.

ZOLOTOW, CHARLOTTE, *The Storm Book.* Illustrated by Margaret Bloy Graham. New York: Harper, 1952. (Mood piece about the weather; also a picture book classic.)

Biography

BRUCE, HARRY. *Maud: The Life of L. M. Montgomery.* New York: Bantam, 1992.

BRUCHAC, JOSEPH. *A Boy Called Slow: The True Story of Sitting Bull.* Illustrated by Rocco Baviera. New York: Philomel, 1994.

BURNS, BREE. *Harriet Tubman.* New York: Chelsea House, 1992.

CESERANI, GIAN PAOLO. *Marco Polo.* Illustrated by Piero Ventura. New York: G. P. Putnam's Sons, 1982.

COX, CLINTON. *Fiery Vision: The Life and Death of John Brown.* New York: Scholastic, 1997.

D'AULAIRE, INGRI, AND EDGAR PARIN. *Benjamin Franklin.* New York: Doubleday, 1950.

DAVIS, ANITA AND HALL, ED Y. *Harriet Quimby: America's First Lady of the Air.* Spartanburg, SC: Honoribus Press, 1998.

FREEDMAN, RUSSELL. *Eleanor Roosevelt.* New York: Clarion, 1993.

———. *Lincoln: A Photobiography.* New York: Clarion Books, 1987.

FRITZ, JEAN. *The Double Life of Pocahontas.* Illustrated by Ed Young. New York: Viking Penguin, 1983.

———. *What's the Big Idea, Ben Franklin?* Illustrated by Margot Tomes. New York: Coward, 1982.

———. *Where Do You Think You're Going, Christopher Columbus?* Illustrated by Margot Tomes. Putnam, 1980.

———. *Why Don't You Get a Horse, Sam Adams?* Illustrated by Trina Schart Hyman. New York: Coward, 1982.

———. *You Want Women to Vote, Lizzie Stanton?* Illustrated by Dyanne Disalvo-Ryan. New York: Putnam, 1995.

GIBLIN, JAMES CROSS. *Charles A. Lindbergh: A Human Hero.* New York: Clarion, 1997.

GREENFIELD, ELOISE. *Mary McLeod Bethune.* Illustrated by Jerry Pinkney. New York: HarperCollins, 1977.

HAMILTON, VIRGINIA. *Paul Robeson, the Life and Times of a Free Black Man.* New York: Harper, 1974.

HEARNE, BETSY. *Seven Brave Women.* Illustrated by Bethanne Andersen. New York: Greenwillow, 1997.

HURWITZ, JOHANNA. *Anne Frank: Life in Hiding.* New York: Jewish Publication Society, 1988.

KREMENTZ, JILL. *A Very Young Actress.* (Lauren Gaffney) New York: Knopf, 1991.

LEWIS, MARGUERITE. *Illustrator Randolph Caldecott* The Children's Hagerstown, Maryland: Alleyside Press, 1992.

LYONS, MARY. *Catching the Fire: Philip Simmons, Blacksmith.* Boston: Houghton Mifflin, 1997.

MARTIN, JACQUELINE BRIGGS. *Snowflake Bentley.* Illustrated by Mary Azarian. Boston: Houghton Mifflin 1998.

MCGOVERN, ANN. *Runaway Slave: The Story of Harriet Tubman.* New York: Scholastic, 1965.

PETRY, ANN. *Harriet Tubman: Conductor on the Underground Railroad.* New York: Crowell, 1955.

PROVENSEN, ALIVE AND MARTIN. *The Glorious Flight.* New York: Viking, 1983.

ROWLAND, DELLA. *The Story of Sacajawea: Guide to Lewis and Clark.* Illustrated by Richard Leonard. New York: Parachute Press, 1989.

SCHROEDER, ALAN. *Minty, A Story of Young Harriet Tubman.* Illustrated by Jerry Pinkney New York: Dial, 1996.

SHERROW, VICTORIA. *Phillis Wheatley, Poet.* New York: Chelsea House, 1992.

STERLING, DOROTHY. *Freedom Train: The Story of Harriet Tubman.* New York: Doubleday, 1954.

TURNER, ROBYN MONTANA. *Faith Ringgold.* Boston: Little, Brown, 1993.

WINTER, JONAH. *Diego.* Illustrated by Jeannette Winter. New York: Knopf, 1991.

YODER, JOSEPH W. *Rosanna of the Amish.* Scottdale, PA: Herald Press, 1973.

Autobiography

CLEARY, BEVERLY. *A Girl From Yamhill.* New York: William Morrow, 1988.

DAHL, ROALD. *Boy.* New York: Farrar, 1984.

EHRLICH, AMY, EDITOR. *When I Was Your Age: Original Stories About Growing Up by Mary Pope Osborne, Laurence Yep, James Howe, Katherine Paterson, Walter Dean Myers, Susan Cooper, Nicholasa Mohr, Reeve Lindbergh, Avi, and Francesca Lia Block.* Cambridge, MA: Candlewick, 1996.

FILIPOVIC, ZLATA. *Zlata's Diary: A Child's Life in Sarajevo.* New York: Viking Penguin, 1994.

FRANK, ANNE. *Anne Frank: The Diary of a Young Girl.* New York: Doubleday, 1967.

FRITZ, JEAN. *Homesick: My Own Story.* Illustrated by Margot Tomes. New York: G. P. Putnam's Sons, 1982.

HAUTZIG, ESTHER. *The Endless Steppe.* New York: Harper, 1968.

HIRSCHFELDER, ARLENE, AND BEVERLY SINGER. *Rising Voices: Writings of Young Native Americans.* New York: Ballantine Books, 1993.

LESTER, JULIUS. *To Be A Slave.* Illustrated by Tom Feelings. New York: Dial, 1968.

LITTLE, JEAN. *Little By Little: A Writer's Education.* Markham, Ontario: Penguin Books Canada, 1987.

LOWRY, LOIS. *Anastasia Krupnik.* Boston: Houghton Mifflin, 1979.

———. *Looking Back: A Book of Memories.* Boston: Houghton, 1998.

NAYLOR, PHYLLIS REYNOLDS. *How I Came to Be a Writer.* New York: Macmillan, 1987.

NICKENS, BESSIE. *Walking the Log; Memories of a Southern Childhood.* New York: Rizzoli, 199.
POLACCO, PATRICIA. *Firetalking.* Photographs by Lawrence Migtale. Katonah, NY: Owen, 1994.
SPINELLI, JERRY. *Crash.* New York: Knopf, 1996.
RYLANT, CYNTHIA. *But I'll Be Back Again.* New York: Orchard Books, 1989.
SPINELLI, JERRY. *Knots in my Yo-Yo String: The Autobiography of a kid.* New York: Knopf 1998
WHITELEY, OPAL. *Only Opal: The Diary of a Young Girl.* Illustrated by Barbara Cooney. New York: Scholastic, 1994 (picture book).

Fantasy

Animal Fantasy (unless otherwise noted, the books listed are picture books)

AUCH, MARY JANE. *Peeping Beauty.* New York: Holiday House, 1993.
BROWN, MARGARET WISE. *Goodnight Moon.* Illustrated by Clement Hurd. New York: Harper, 1947.
———. *The Runaway Bunny.* Illustrated by Clement Hurd. New York: Harper, 1942.
DE BRUNHOFF, JEAN. *The Story of Babar the Little Elephant.* London: Methuen, 1934.
FOX, MEM. *Koala Lou.* Illustrated by Pamela Lofts. New York: Harcourt, 1988.
———. *Possum Magic.* Illustrated by Julie Vivas. New York: Harcourt, 1983.
GRAHAME, KENNETH. *Wind in the Willows.* London: Metheun, 1908 (novel).
LAWSON, ROBERT. *Rabbit Hill.* New York: Viking, 1944 (novel).
LEAF, MUNRO. *The Story of Ferdinand.* Illustrated by Robert Lawson. New York: Viking, 1938.
LIONNI, LEO. *Fish is Fish.* New York: Pantheon, 1970.
———. *Mr. McMouse.* New York: Knopf, 1992.
O'BRIEN, ROBERT. *Mrs. Frisby and the Rats of NIMH.* New York: Atheneum, 1971 (novel).
POTTER, BEATRIX. *The Pie and the Patty Pan.* New York: Frederick Warne, 1905.
———. *The Tale of Benjamin Bunny.* New York: Frederick Warne, 1905.
———. *The Tale of Mrs. Tiggy-Winkle.* New York: Frederick Warne, 1905.
———. *The Tale of Peter Rabbit.* New York: Frederick Warne, 1905.
———. *The Tale of Two Bad Mice.* New York: Frederick Warne, 1904.
———. *The Tailor of Gloucester.* New York: Frederick Warne, 1903.
STEIG, WILLIAM. *Abel's Island.* New York: Farrar, 1976 (novel).
———. *Brave Irene.* New York: Farrar, 1986.
———. *Sylvester and the Magic Pebble.* New York: Simon & Schuster, 1986.
WELLS, ROSEMARY. *Max's Dragon Shirt.* New York: Dial, 1991.

Toys and Objects

ALEXANDER, MARTHA. *I'll Protect You from the Jungle Beasts.* New York: Dial, 1973 (wordless picture book).
ANDERSEN, HANS CHRISTIAN. *The Steadfast Tin Soldier.* Illustrated by Rachel Isadora. New York: Philomel, 1996
AYRES, BECK HICKOX. *Matreshka.* Illustrated by Alexi Natchev. New York: Delacorte, 1992 (picture book involving the legendary Russian nesting doll and the Baba Yaga figure).
BANKS, LYNNE REID. *The Indian in the Cupboard.* New York: Doubleday, 1990 (novel).
BURTON, VIRGINIA. *The Little House.* Boston: Houghton Mifflin, 1942 (picture book).
CONRAD, PAM. *The Tub People.* Illustrations by Richard Egielski. New York: Harper, 1985 (picture book).
INGPEN, ROBERT. *The Idle Bear.* London: Blackie and Son, 1986 (picture book).

LIONNI, LEO. *Alexander and the Wind-Up Mouse.* New York: Knopf, 1969 (picture book involving the Russian nesting doll, *matrioska* in the illustrations).
MILNE, A. A. *Winnie-the-Pooh.* Illustrations by Ernest H. Shepard. New York: Dutton, 1926 (novel).
ORAN, HIAWYN. *Baby Yaga and the Wise Doll.* Illustrated by Ruth Brown. New York: Dutton, 1998 (picture book).
SLEATOR, WILLIAM. *Among the Dolls.* Illustrations by Trina Schart Hyman. New York: (picture storybook).
WAHL, JAN. *Humphrey's Bear.* Illustrated by William Joyce. New York: Holt, 1987 (picture book).
WINTHROP, ELIZABETH. *The Castle in the Attic.* New York: Holiday, 1985 (novel).
WILLIAMS, MARGERY. *The Velveteen Rabbit.* Illustrated by William Nicholson. New York: Doubleday, 1958.

Humans and Talking Animals

BURNINGHAM, JOHN. *Mr Gumpy's Outing.* London: Jonathan Cape, 1970 (picture book).
CLEARY, BEVERLY. *The Mouse and the Motorcycle.* Illustrated by Louis Darling. New York: Morrow, 1965 (novel).
DAHL, ROALD. *James and the Giant Peach.* Illustrated by Nancy Ekholm Burkert. New York, Knopf, 1961 (novel).
MCKISSACK, PATRICIA. *Nettie Jo's Friends.* Illustrated by Scott Cook. New York: Knopf, 1989 (picture book).
SELDEN, GEORGE. *The Cricket in Times Square.* Illustrated by Garth Williams. New York: Farrar, 1960 (novel).
WHITE, E. B. *Charlotte's Web.* Illustrated by Garth Williams. New York: Harper, 1952 (novel).
WILLIAMS, MARGERY. *The Velveteen Rabbit.* Illustrated by William Nicholson. New York: Doubleday, 1958 (picture storybook).
YORINKS, ARTHUR. *Hey, Al.* Illustrations by Richard Egielski. New York: Farrar, 1986 (picture book).

Humans in Magical Situations

AGEE, JON. *The Incredible Painting of Felix Clousseau.* New York: Farrar, 1988 (picture book).
BABBITT, NATALIE. *Tuck Everlasting.* New York: Farrar, 1975 (novel).
———. *The Eyes of the Amaryllis.* New York: Farrar, 1977 (novel).
DAHL, ROALD. *Charlie and the Chocolate Factory.* New York: Knopf, 1954 (novel).
HAMILTON, VIRGINIA. *Drylongso.* Illustrated by Jerry Pinkney. New York: Harcourt Brace, 1992 (picture storybook).
LANGTON, JANE. *The Diamond in the Window.* New York: Harper and Row, 1962.
———. *The Fledgling.* New York: Harper and Row, 1980 (novel).
MCKISSACK, PATRICIA. *Mirandy and Brother Wind.* Illustrated by Jerry Pinkney. New York: Knopf, 1988 (picture book).
NESBIT, E. *The Enchanted Castle* (1907). New York: Puffin, 1979 (novel).
———. *Five Children and It* (1902). New York: Dell, 1986 (novel).
———. *The Story of the Amulet* (1906). New York: Puffin, 1959 (novel).
RINGGOLD, FAITH. *Aunt Harriet's Underground Railroad in the Sky.* New York: Crown, 1992 (picture book).
———. *Tar Beach.* New York: Crown, 1991 (picture book).
SHULEVITZ, URI: *Snow.* New York: Farrar Straus Giroux, 1998.
SIS, PETER. *The Three Golden Keys.* New York: Doubleday, 1994 (picture book).
TRAVERS, P. L. *Mary Poppins.* New York: Harcourt Brace Jovanovich, 1934 (novel).
WALTER, MILDRED PITTS. *Brother To the Wind.* Illustrated by Diane and Leo Dillon. New York: Lothrop, 1985 (picture storybook).

WIESNER, DAVID. *Tuesday.* New York: Clarion, 1991 (picture book).
YORICKS, ARTHUR. *Hey, Al.* Illustrations by Richard Egielski. New York: Farrar, 1986 (picture book).
———. *Louis the Fish.* Illustrations by Richard Egielski. New York: Farrar, 1980 (picture book).

Tall Tale Fantasy

ISAACS, ANNE. *Swamp Angel.* Illustrated by Paul Zelinsky. New York: Dutton, 1994.
LINDGREN, ASTRID. *Pippi Longstocking.* New York: Viking, 1950.
MCKISSACK, PATRICIA. *A Million Fish . . . More or Less.* Illustrated by Dena Schutzer. New York: Knopf, 1992 (picture book).
SEUSS, DR. *The 500 Hats of Bartholomew Cubbins.* New York: Random, 1938 (picture book).

Dream/Daydream Fantasy

BAUM, L. FRANK. *The Wonderful Wizard of Oz.* Illustrated by W. W. Denslow. Chicago: George Hill, 1900 (novel).
CARROLL, LEWIS. *Alice's Adventures in Wonderland.* Illustrated by Arthur Rackham. New York: Crown, 1978, rpt. 1907, 1865 (novel).
GREENFIELD, ELOISE. *Africa Dream.* Illustrated by Carole Byard. New York: John Day, 1977 (picture book).
LIVELY, PENELOPE. *The House in Norham Gardens* (1974). London: Puffin, 1986 (novel).
SENDAK, MAURICE. *In the Night Kitchen.* New York: Harper and Row, 1970 (picture book).
———. *Outside Over There.* New York: Harper and Row, 1981 (picture book).
———. *Where the Wild Things Are.* New York: Harper and Row, 1963 (picture book).

Fantasy of a Secondary World/High Fantasy (Story set in a "high" kingdom that the author has invented; hero aspires to rule this kingdom, or he or she must find a way to navigate through it.)

ALEXANDER, LLOYD. *The Book of Three.* New York: Holt, 1964 (novel; first of a five-part series).
LEGUIN, URSULA. *A Wizard of Earthsea.* New York: Parnassas Press, 1968 (novel; first of a four-part series, including *The Tombs of Atuan, The Farthest Shore,* and *Tehanu*).
LEWIS, C. S. *The Lion, the Witch and the Wardrobe.* New York: Macmillan, 1950 (novel; first of a seven-part series).
PULLMAN, PHILIP. *The Golden Compass.* New York: Knopf, 1996 (novel; first of the trilogy: "His Dark Materials").
———. *The Subtle Knife.* New York: Knopf, 1998 (novel; second of the trilogy "His Dark Materials").
TOLKIEN, J. R. R. *The Hobbit.* New York: Ballantine Books, 1965, rpt. 1937 (novel).

Folk Fantasy (Modern characters meet figures from folklore, or the entire story is set in a folk tale or a mythic world.)

AIKEN, JOAN. *The Moon's Revenge.* Illustrated by Alan Lee. New York: Knopf, 1987 (picture book).
BABBITT, NATALIE. *The Search for Delicious.* New York: Farrar, 1969 (novel).
FURLONG, MONICA. *Wise Child.* New York: Knopf, 1987 (novel).
HALEY, GAIL. *The Green Man.* New York: Charles Scribner's Sons, 1979 (picture book).
HUNTER, MOLLIE. *A Stranger Came Ashore.* New York: Harper, 1975 (novel).
MARK, JAN. *Haddock.* Illustrations by Fiona Moodie. London: Simon & Schuster, 1994 (picture book).
MCGRAW, ELOISE. *The Moorchild.* New York: Simon & Schuster, 1996 (novel).

SENDAK, MAURICE. *Outside Over There.* New York: Harper, 1981 (picture book).
WRIGHTSON, PATRICIA. *A Little Fear.* New York: Atheneum, 1985 (novel).
———. *The Nargun and the Stars.* New York: Macmillan, 1974 (novel).

Time Fantasy (Legendary: Characters travel back in time and meet figures from myth or legend, or figures from mythic/legendary time travel to the present to encounter present-day children.)

BOND, NANCY. *A String in the Harp.* New York: Atheneum, 1981 (novel).
COOPER, SUSAN. *The Boggart.* New York: Macmillan, 1993 (novel).
———. *The Boggart and the Monster.* New York: Simon & Schuster, 1997 (novel).
———. *The Dark is Rising.* New York: Atheneum, 1973 (novel).
———. *The Greenwitch.* New York: Macmillan, 1974 (novel).
———. *The Grey King.* New York: Macmillan, 1975 (novel).
———. *Matthew's Dragon.* Illustrated by [Joseph] A. Smith. New York: Macmillan, 1991 (picture book).
———. *Silver in the Tree.* New York: Atheneum, 1977 (novel).
GARNER, ALAN. *Elidor.* London: HarperCollins, 1965 (novel).
———. *The Moon of Gomrath* (1963). London: HarperCollins, 1972 (novel).
———. *The Owl Service* (1967). New York: Ballantine, 1981 (novel).
———. *The Weirdstone of Brisingamen* (1960). New York: Ballantine, 1981 (novel).
HAMILTON, VIRGINIA. *The Magical Adventures of Pretty Pearl.* New York: Harper, 1983 (novel; also a blending of history and legendary time fantasy).
LIVELY, PENELOPE. *The Ghost of Thomas Kempe.* New York: Dutton, 1973 (novel, blending of legendary and historical time fantasy).
———. *The Whispering Knights* (1971). London: Mammoth, 1995 (novel and blending of legendary and historical time fantasy).
MAYNE, WILLIAM. *Cradlefasts.* London: Hodder, 1995 (novel).
———. *Earthfasts.* New York: Dutton, 1967 (novel).
WESTALL, ROBERT. *The Wind Eye* (1976). New York: Macmillan, 1994 (novel).
WRIGHTSON, PATRICIA. *Balyet.* New York: Macmillan, 1989 (novel).

Time Fantasy (Historical: Characters travel back in time to meet figures from the past.)

BOND, NANCY. *Another Shore.* New York: Atheneum, 1988 (novel).
BOSTON, L. M. *The Children of Green Knowe.* New York: Harcourt, 1982, rpt. 1955 (novel).
CAMERON, ELEANOR. *Beyond Silence* (novel).
———. *The Court of the Stone Children.* New York: Norton, 1968 (novel).
FARMER, PENELOPE. *Charlotte Sometimes.* London: The Bodley, 1969 (novel).
KING-SMITH, DICK. *Lady Daisy.* London: Penguin, 1992 (novel).
LIVELY, PENELOPE. *Astercote* (1970). London: Mammoth, 1996 (novel).
———. *A Stitch in Time* (1976). London: Mammoth, 1994 (novel).
———. *The Driftway* (1972). London: Mammoth, 1993 (novel).
———. *The House in Norham Gardens* (1974). London: Puffin, 1986 (novel).
LUNN, JANET. *The Root Cellar.* New York: Scribner's, 1981 (novel).
NESBIT, EDITH. *The Story of the Amulet* (1906). New York: Puffin, 1959 (novel, blending of historical and legendary time fantasy).
PARK, RUTH. *Playing Beatie Bow.* New York: Atheneum, 1982 (novel).
PEARCE, PHILIPPA. *Tom's Midnight Garden.* New York: Harper, 1986, rpt. 1958 (novel).
RINGGOLD, FAITH. *Aunt Harriet's Underground Railroad in the Sky.* New York: Crown, 1992 (picture book).

SAUER, JULIA. *Fog Magic.* New York: Viking, 1943 (novel).
WALSH, JILL PATON. *A Chance Child.* New York: Farrar, 1991, rpt. 1978 (novel).
YOLEN, JANE. *The Devil's Arithmetic.* New York: Viking Penguin, 1988 (novel).

Futuristic Fantasy

L'ENGLE, MADELEINE. *A Wrinkle in Time.* New York: Farrar, 1962 (novel).
———. *Wind in the Door.* New York: Farrar, 1973 (novel).
———. *A Swiftly Tilting Planet.* New York: Farrar, 1978 (novel).
LOWRY, LOIS. *The Giver.* Boston: Houghton Mifflin, 1993 (novel).
MAHY, MARGARET. *Aliens in the Family.* New York: Scholastic, 1985 (novel).
WALSH, JILL PATON. *The Green Book.* New York: Farrar, 1982 (novel).

Fiction and Nonfiction with Strong Females

ALCOTT, LOUISA MAY. *Little Women.* 1968–69.
BABBITT, NATALIE. *Tuck Everlasting.* New York: Farrar, 1975.
BURNETT, FRANCES HODGSON. *A Little Princess.* 1905.
CARROLL, LEWIS. *Alice's Adventures in Wonderland.* 1865.
CHOI, SOOK NYUL. *Year of Impossible Goodbyes.* Boston: Houghton Mifflin, 1991.
COOPER, SUSAN. *Greenwitch.* New York: Macmillan, 1974.
CUSHMAN, KAREN. *The Ballad of Lucy Whipple.* New York: Clarion, 1996.
———. *The Midwife's Apprentice.* Boston: Houghton Mifflin, 1995.
FITZHUGH, LOUISE. *Harriet the Spy.* New York: Harper, 1965.
FRANK, ANNE. *The Diary of Anne Frank.* New York: Doubleday, 1952.
FREEDMAN, RUSSELL. *Eleanor Roosevelt.* New York: Scholastic, 1993.
HAMILTON, VIRGINA. *Arilla Sun Down.* New York: Scholastic, 1995 (rpt. 1976).
———. *Bluish.* New York: Scholastic, 1999.
———. *Justice and Her Brothers, Dustland, The Gathering (The Justice Trilogy.)* New York: Greenwillow, 1980–81.
———. *Zeely.* New York: Macmillian, 1967.
HAUTZIG, ESTHER. *The Endless Steppe.* New York: Harper, 1968.
HANSEN, JOYCE. *I Thought My Soul Would Rise and Fly.* New York: Scholastic, 1997.
ISSACS, ANNE. *Swamp Angel.* Illustrated by Paul Zelinsky. New York: Dutton, 1994.
JIANG, JI LI. *Red Scarf Girl.* New York: HarperCollins, 1997.
KONIGSBURG, E. L. *T-Backs, T-Shirts, Coat and Suit.* New York: Atheneum, 1995.
L'ENGLE, MADELEINE. *A Wrinkle in Time.* New York: Farrar, 1962.
LINDGREN, ASTRID. *Pippi Longstocking.* New York: Viking, 1950.
LOWRY, LOIS. *Number the Stars.* Boston: Houghton Mifflin, 1989.
LUNN, JANET. *The Root Celler.* New York: Scribner's, 1983.
LYONS, MARY. *Letter from a Slave Girl.* New York: Simon & Schustesr, 1992.
O'DELL, SCOTT. *Island of the Blue Dolphins.* Boston: Houghton Mifflin, 1960.
PATERSON, KATHERINE. *Lyddie.* New York: Penguin, 1991.
PETRY, ANN. *Harriet Tubman.* New York: Harper, 1964.
———. *Tituba of Salem Village.* New York: Harper, 1964.
RINGGOLD, FAITH. *Aunt Harriet's Underground Railroad.* New York: Crown, 1992.
———. *Dinner at Aunt Connie's House.* New York: Hyperion, 1993.
———. *Tar Beach.* New York: Crown, 1991.
SAN SOUCI, ROBERT. *Fa Mulan.* Illustrated by Joan and Mou-Sien Tseng. New York: Hyperion Books, 1998.
SPEARE, ELIZABETH GEORGE. *The Witch of Blackbird Pond.* Boston: Houghton Mifflin, 1953.

Chapter 3

More About Genre

Topics in This Chapter:

- Genre as a social construct
- Caldecott and Newbery books
- Studying genre with Caldecott books
- Studying genre with Newbery books
- Reflections on genre as literary concept and social construct

"Well, I've tried to say 'How doth the little busy bee,' but it all came different!" Alice replied in a very melancholy voice.

"Repeat, 'You are old, Father William,' " said the Caterpillar.

Alice folded her hands, and began:

" 'You are old, Father William,' the young man said,
'And your hair has become very white;
And yet you incessantly stand on your head—
Do you think, at your age, it is right?'

"Down the Rabbit-Hole" in Alice's Adventures in Wonderland, 1865
—Lewis Carroll

We have been looking at the practical side of genre, or the traditional *literary* aspect—literature as an art form. This side gives us a mental "roadmap" for making sense of literature. But there is another side too, a social and cultural side we often overlook. We also need to know about genre in relation to the human condition—the *humanities* side of literature. The formation of genres is rooted in social contexts, networks of social relationships and cultural values. If we neglect this other side of genre, we know less about ourselves, others, and the world.

GENRE AS A SOCIAL CONSTRUCT

Why do we as readers value one kind of book over another? Why do we pick up *Alice's Adventures in Wonderland* or *Charlotte's Web* in the first place? Why, in fact, do we value literature? Why do we browse in bookstores? What is Shawn doing in the library, and why is he heading for the fiction section? Why does Josh like mysteries? Why does Reggie choose science fiction? Why does Regina write poetry? And why is Lewis Carroll's Alice trying to recite "How doth the busy bee?" Preference for a particular genre, like preferences for particular books or authors, may relate to gender, class, culture, schooling, nationality, family traditions, time and place in history, or personal experiences. It can be interesting to track down the reasons behind our preferences.

For any reader's—or writer's—preference in genre, we might ask, What leads to this interest? And if many readers or writers are preoccupied by works of a particular genre, we might ask, What is producing this interest? On the other hand, if writers are producing works that are similar in nature but do not seem to fit any existing genre category, we might ask, What is driving the production of this new form? Why, for example, do we hear the term *multicultural literature* so often these days? Why do book catalogs and bookstores have sections labeled *multicultural books* when, just a few years ago, there were none? Are multicultural books a new genre, a new way of writing or reading, or perhaps a new social or cultural need?

If new or different kinds of books are suddenly appearing in a particular culture, then knowing about them might tell us something about that culture. What are the culture's values, priorities, and preoccupations? How does the culture organize reality, as opposed to how it lived and thought before? If so many multicultural books are produced that the local bookstore sets up a special section for them, we might conclude that the culture is, at this time, valuing diversity. If multicultural books become so plentiful that librarians and booksellers give them a special place on the shelves, we might conclude that culture—human activity—is shaping literature and that the culture values multicultural books. Such activity also reveals that genre is a social construct; genres do not categorize and name themselves. Members of the culture decide how books fit into different categories; they define these categories; and they redefine them, making new spaces and new labels for them, when new genres emerge.

Booksellers, librarians, teachers, and parents all think about genre as a literary concept a great deal of the time, although they might not do so with any conscious awareness. They might notice a particular genre that is popular with children—pop-up books or wordless picture books—and then collect this particular kind of books for displays, book talks, teaching units, or family reading. This is the *literary* side of genre. But there is also a *social* side.

INVESTIGATIONS: Exploring Genre Preferences

What kinds of books do you like reading best? Realistic fiction? Fantasy? Nonfiction? Poetry? Folk tales? Try to decide why you like a particular genre. Maybe it began in childhood, with a particular book. Consider how you might have been cultural, socially, and personally "constructed" as a reader. Readers, like writers, constantly experience the cultural and social worlds that weave in and out of their personal lives. Start by trying to decide what might have caused you to like certain kinds of books. Did an older brother or sister like a particular kind of book, and that was a model for you? Did you have a teacher who read aloud certain books, such as Beverly Cleary's chapter books about Ramona, Ellen Tebbits, and Henry Huggins. Did you like that kind of book and begin choosing it for yourself? Or perhaps you are drawn to the artwork in certain books. Try to remember yourself as a child reader. If you cannot remember, interview members of your family to see what kinds of books you read as a child.

If members of a culture—booksellers or customers, librarians or readers, teachers or students, parents or children—discover many examples of pop-up books, they might start thinking about whether pop-ups are a new kind of book. They might even designate this kind of book as a new genre. A little exploring in a secondhand bookshop might lead them to see the evolution of the pop-up as a children's book "toy." They might discover that the pop-up book is not really new, that it was popular during the Victorian period, although at that time it was called the "movable" book.

Why do children have such a fascination with pop-ups? they might begin asking themselves. Why have these books been so popular for such a long time now? Are they as popular with adults as with children? With a quick glance at library reference shelves, they might discover that pop-ups, at least in America, have not fared particularly well among prominent award committees. No pop-up book has ever won the prestigious Caldecott Medal, for example. Wordless books have done better. Two wordless picture books have won the Caldecott Medal, *Noah's Ark* by Peter Spier (Doubleday, 1977) in 1978 and *Tuesday* by David Wiesner (Clarion, 1991) in 1992; and *The Grey Lady and the Strawberry Snatcher* by Molly Bang (Four Winds, 1980) won a Caldecott Honor Award in 1981.

One of the best ways to understand children's books in a social context is to examine the medals or prizes that members of a culture present to their most valued children's writers and artists. A look at prizing in children's literature tells us a great deal about the needs, interests, and preoccupations of adults at particular times in history. Adults choose books based on their

- preferences for different genres,
- interest in encouraging children to read particular genres,
- definitions of different genres,
- openness to new ways of seeing—or defining—a particular genre, and
- openness to genre blendings and new genres as valid—and valued—art forms.

A look at award-winning books also tells us more about genre in both a literary and a social context. Awards selectors must think about traditional genre classifications as they group books for examination and discussion. They must search for the best examples of these genre categories. So they must think about what makes a children's book good—the best of its kind artistically. But they also make decisions, on a less conscious level, based on their own interests, preferences, and openness to new views.

For the remainder of this chapter, we will do the same; we will take a deeper look at genre as a literary concept and a social construct, drawing our examples from Caldecott and Newbery winners. We will not examine every award-winning book from the beginning to the present. (For a full listing of these and other prominent awards in this field, see Appendix II.) We will merely notice books—picture books, fiction, nonfiction, folklore, and poetry—that have remained interesting and important through the years because of their artistry and their socially constructed features.

CALDECOTT AND NEWBERY BOOKS

Each year in January, the Association for Library Service to Children, a division of the American Library Association, announces the winners of the most distinguished children's books published during the preceding year in the United States. The most distinguished picture book wins the Caldecott Award, named in honor of the famous nineteenth-century illustrator, Randolph Caldecott. The most distinguished contribution to literature for children wins the Newbery Award, named in honor of the famous eighteenth-century bookseller, John Newbery. Several honor awards (runners up to the winners) are also announced in each category. *Horn Book Magazine* publishes a list of these recipients in its May-June issue; it publishes the acceptance speeches in its July-August issue, after the presentations of the medals at the ALA summer conference. The ALA journal, *Youth Services in Libraries,* also publishes these speeches in its summer issue.

The Caldecott and Newbery Awards are the most prestigious awards for children's books in the United States; winners of these awards are therefore the most accessible and familiar for American readers. We will use these awards as a reference point for learning more about genre as both a literary concept and a social

Selection Criteria for Caldecott and Newbery Awards

The American Library Association presents the Caldecott Award each year for the most distinguished *picture book* for children and the Newbery Award for the most distinguished contribution to *literature* for children published in the United States during the preceding year by an American citizen or permanent resident.

A *picture book,* by ALA definition, provides the child with a visual experience. It has a story line, theme, or concept developed through a series of pictures. Criteria for a "distinguished" picture book include excellence in

- execution of artistic technique;
- visual interpretation of the work;
- illustrative style; and
- visual delineation of plot, setting, mood, theme, or characters.

Literature for children, by definition, is fiction, nonfiction, or poetry written for a potential audience of children through age fourteen. The book must respect children's abilities and level of understanding. Criteria for "distinguished" literature for children include excellence in

- thematic interpretation;
- presentation of information (clear, accurate, and well-organized);
- character delineation;
- stylistic techniques.

Notice that children are considered a *potential* rather than a *primary* audience for Newbery books; the award-winning books are often read by a wide audience of interested adults as well as by children. The Newbery books are really for everyone.

Because *excellence* is such a relative term, the Caldecott and Newbery Committees, each composed of fifteen members, must meet a number of times to discuss and vote on the books. Throughout the year, committee members review lists of books, make suggestions about books to one another, and receive more suggestions from ALA members who do not serve on the committee.

Committee members draw up individual lists of nominations, along with reasons for their choices. These written lists and reasons are circulated before open discussion and balloting begins. On the first ballot, members vote for three books they have ranked with points. The winning book needs eight points for a first-place ranking. Balloting continues until a winner emerges. After this time, the committee names the Honor books (books with the next highest number of votes).

Sources: "Caldecott Award" and "Newbery Award," (Chicago: ALA, Association for Library Service to Children, 1987; materials disseminated by ALA, 1998).
Bette J. Peltola, "Choosing the Newbery and Caldecott Winners." Chicago: ALA, 1979; article disseminated by ALA, 1998.

construct. First we will examine picture books, and the many genres this form encompasses, through the lens of the Caldecott Award. Then we will examine children's books of all kinds through the lens of the Newbery Award.

STUDYING GENRE WITH CALDECOTT BOOKS

It is no coincidence that American librarians chose to name America's most important picture book award for Randolph Caldecott. "Caldecott's work heralds the beginning of the modern picture book," says Maurice Sendak, himself the winner of the Caldecott Medal in 1964 and the author-illustrator of two Caldecott Honor books in 1971 and 1982. Caldecott "devised an ingenious juxtaposition of picture and word, a counterpoint that never happened before. Words are left out—but the picture says it. Pictures are left out—but the word says it. In short, it is the invention of the picture book" (page 21).

Children experiencing picture books today see a constantly evolving form that includes every possible kind of book. But if we try to classify the long list of Caldecott winners from 1938 to the present in terms of traditional literary genres, we find that, like Caldecott himself, the illustrators of these inventive books often leap over, under, and around the usual categories. Even at the beginning, when categories seemed fairly stable, creative artists were playing with conventions and bending the rules. Or perhaps it was just the opposite: The artists who caught the jurists' attention—and went on to win the coveted medals—were the few who saw life, and the categories of genre, just a little differently.

Consider Berta and Elmer Hader's Caldecott winner *The Big Snow* (Macmillan, 1948), which seems to be animal fantasy, because the animals speak. What do they talk about? Things of concern to animals: seasonal changes, the weather, habits of food gathering, hibernation patterns. But they are not dressed in human clothing like Beatrix Potter's animals. These animals, therefore, are more realistic than fantasy animals (real animals do communicate, although humans are not privy to their means of communication).

At this time—the 1940s—most artists were producing books about actual human characters in probable situations—or traditional *realism*—and these books were also winning the Caldecott.

Realism

Among earlier Caldecott books, *White Snow Bright Snow* (Lothrop, 1947) by Alvin Tresselt, winning pictures by Roger Duvoisin, shows recognizable human problems, struggles, and adventures. An entire village or town prepares for a snowstorm. The children play; the postman slips and falls. The police officer's wife checks the medicine cabinet for cough mixture. Eventually winter turns into spring, and the rabbits at last come hopping our of their burrows. The book is, in fact, so recognizable, so ordinary, we wonder how it can be a Caldecott book; but then we remember that in 1947, Americans just two years past Hitler, Hiroshima, and the Holocaust would have celebrated the common cold, children playing in the snow, and a spring day—and celebrated it with realistic words and pictures.

Among later Caldecott books, Ezra Jack Keats's *The Snowy Day* (Viking, 1963) shows a little boy waking to discover it is snowing and venturing out to explore this

A Closer Look

Randolph Caldecott's Sing a Song of Sixpence

Randolph Caldecott was a nineteenth-century creator of "picture-stories" who often took a nursery rhyme or folk tale and illustrated it by telling—or showing—several intersecting stories at once. One was the main story itself; the others were stories he, as illustrator, imagined alongside the main story. Caldecott framed the text and his own illustrations of the main story with little wordless picture-stories of his own. Thus, he was able to produce a richer and more complete story than the rhyme itself told. The strong, active lines of his drawings nearly always created a sense of drama in the scene as well, and their lively movement produced humorous effects.

In *Sing a Song of Sixpence* (Barron's, 1988), originally published in England in 1880, we see just how Caldecott's talents worked to make something entirely new. He took a Mother Goose rhyme and placed one line of text on one side of the page and a large colored scene to illustrate it on the other side. Then, underneath the line of text, he produced another picture—a smaller, pen-and-ink line drawing of another scene that springs from the same line of text. In the opening of this book, we thus have the first line: "Sing a song of sixpence, A pocket full of rye" accompanied by two scenes. The large painted picture on the facing page shows an old lady holding up a sixpence, illustrating the first half of the line. The smaller drawing shows an old man emptying grain from his pocket as three children gather around the table top to watch, illustrating the second half of the line.

In addition, Caldecott tells another story through the pen-and-ink drawings. This story runs parallel to the main story and puts both human interest and suspense into the rhyme. A tall, handsome soldier happens along by the castle, and he strikes up a courtship with the King and Queen's maid, who is hanging clothes out in the garden. The soldier also appears before this, when the Queen is in the parlor eating bread and honey and the King is in his counting house, counting out his money. (Caldecott pictures the King and Queen as a young girl and boy, revealing that a *children's* book industry—and audience—is in full bloom by this time in the late nineteenth century.)

As the little King is counting, we see across the page in two small drawings, a jolly, fat man running. He leads a small group, among whom is a tall, strutting soldier. They stop at the counting house door, where they gather to peep at the boy-king counting. The effect is an early motion picture (two stills), the result of Caldecott's genius with line. Wisely, he chose pen and ink rather than total color throughout: the black and white drawings enable us to see more clearly the way line works to reveal both running movement and comic gesture. The jolly fat man walks at a fast clip, pointing; the others rush forward after him. The soldier labors under a heavy gun, just keeping pace.

Two pages over, we see more of the tall, strutting soldier. Across from the large, full-color picture of the maid hanging clothes, the soldier comes marching down the road in another little black and white scene. In the next color illustration, placed this time on the left side of the page spread, the maid is holding a baby blackbird for the young King and Queen to see. Across from this painting, on the right side, is a pen-and-ink drawing of a large blackbird perched on a branch, cawing loudly. (Is the mother bird afraid her baby will be made into another pie?) The words come next in this pen-and-ink scene: "When down came a blackbird and snipped off her nose." Below these words is the second part of the drawing: a picture of the maid, standing below the bird, grasping her nose.

Turning the page, we see the final scene—another line drawing—and the last line of the rhyme, "But then there came a little wren and popped it on again." The drawing is larger than usual, to show us the soldier embracing the maid as the little wren performs the required nose job.

And there is more. Turning back through the pages for a second, even closer look, we see the little Queen eating bread and honey. Behind her, hanging on the parlor walls are other Caldecott paintings, including a scene from *Babes in the Woods.* On the door of the toy cabinet in this same room is his painting of Red Riding Hood and the wolf. Taken together, these paintings show us what children in Caldecott's day read.

In a Caldecott book, words and pictures dance together to the tune of intricate—and innovative—meaning-making. It is his genius that inspires picture book artists—and selectors of the Caldecott Awards—today, as they go about their work.

From *Sing a Song of Sixpence* (Barron's Educational Series, 1988; original 1880), illustrated by Randolph Caldecott.

From *Sing a Song of Sixpence* (Barron's Educational Series, 1988; original 1880), illustrated by Randolph Caldecott.

new world. Collage designs give texture to the realism, but color carries the day: Peter, a black child, walks out into an all-white world wearing an elfin-red snowsuit. An all-white publishing world during the dawning Civil Rights era noticed a symbolic pictorial moment and pronounced the book an award winner. Artistic merit has kept the book alive ever since. Words and pictures mesh easily—and melodiously—as on the page that says, "Down fell the snow—plop!—on top of Peter's head," and we see in the pictures Peter's red peaked hat dripping with snow. Peter—with one eye open and one eye closed—looks up in surprise before turning to walk on, his footprints trailing him up the white, wordless page.

Jane Yolen's more recent Caldecott book *Owl Moon,* winning pictures by John Schoenherr (Philomel, 1987), also explores and celebrates nature. On a winter night, a father and his young daughter go searching for an owl, and the sensitive rendering of scene produces both verbal and visual poetry. Yolen's child tells her story in the familiar and dramatic first person: "It was late one winter night, long past my bedtime, when Pa and I went owling." From high above the cold, still scene, we see the tiny humans setting out on their adventure.

We can easily classify books like *The Snowy Day* and *Owl Moon* as traditional realism, but many Caldecott winners, like Barbara Emberly's *Drummer Hoff,* winning pictures by Ed Emberly (Prentice Hall, 1967), are less easily labeled.

From *The Snowy Day* (Viking, 1963) by Ezra Jack Keats.

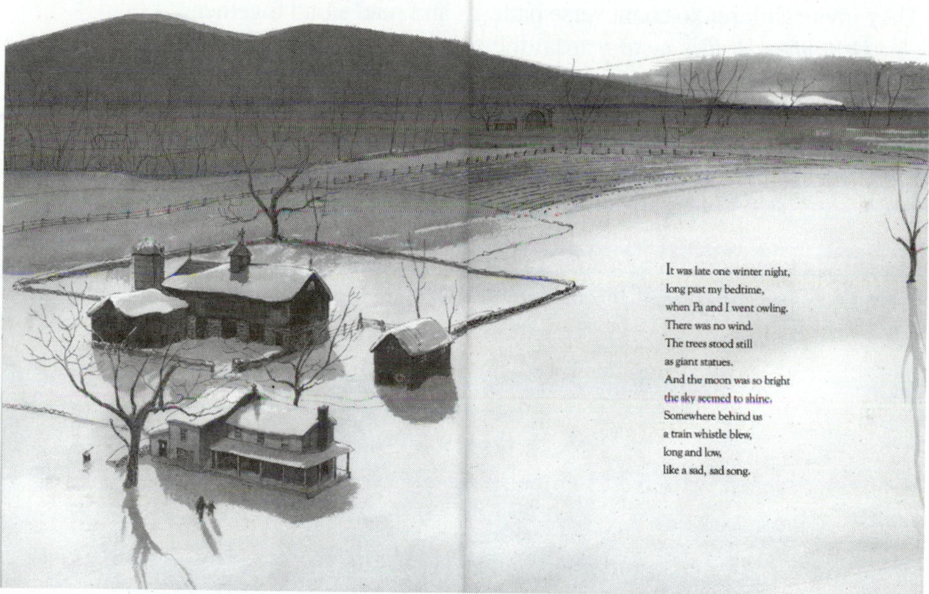

From *Owl Moon* (Philomel, 1987) by Jane Yolen, illustrated by John Schoenherr.

Genre Blendings

Drummer Hoff is an example of a **cumulative tale,** a patterned story from folk tradition in which each segment of the tale introduces a new character who joins in on a long chain of linked events. The verse pattern works to keep the cumulative order planted firmly in our minds, just as it needed to be for storytellers of centuries past, who depended on memory rather than print. In this case, the lead character, Drummer Hoff, gives his signal for the cannon blast (he "fired it off"). So despite the fact that "Private Parriage brought the carriage," "Corporal Farrell brought the barrel," "Sergeant Chowder brought the powder," and even "General Border gave the order," it is Drummer Hoff who actually fires the ultimate shot.

Child readers have no difficulty slipping into the musical drummer boy's "shoes," as they chant the rhyming couplets. But where would this book, with its colorful sequence of dynamic woodcuts, fit on library shelves? Is this a picture book, a poetry book, or an illustrated folk tale? It is all of the above; this book is a hybrid, a cumulative tale that is better told for being in verse, a folk story that is more memorable, arranged as it is in a cumulative verse pattern. Best of all, the cumulative verse pattern explodes into brilliant colors and designs, producing a powerful picture book.

Another category into which this book might be placed is the **interactive book**—one that invites reader participation. (Although it should not be confused with CD-ROM programs, also called "interactive," the *interactive picture book* has a similar participatory function.) In *Drummer Hoff,* the verse pattern—or chant—elicits children's verbal engagement, as it does with nonsense poetry and Mother Goose rhymes. Some interactive books invite children to count; others (ABC books) invite them to guess words linked to letters; still others (wordless picture books) invite them to tell stories about the pictures; whereas pop-up books, game books, and "scratch-and-sniff" books invite engagement in sensory experiences. The "big books" that many elementary teachers now use in reading classes are also interactive books. They invite children to chant verse patterns and read aloud together.

Drummer Hoff is a story from the oral tradition, and like many folk stories, it is marked by magical happenings in a long-ago time. At the end of the story, flowers bloom "magically" out of the chaos and violence of war. "KAHBAHBLOOM" shouts the cannon blast from a fire-splashed (blood-soaked) page. Then the final scene bursts into view: a rusted carriage and barrel now laid to rest in a bed of spider webs, birds' nests, brilliant emerald leaves, and bright yellow flowers. Life

From *Drummer Hoff* (Prentice Hall, 1967) by Barbara Emberly, illustrated by Ed Emberly.

Award-Winning Interactive Books by Janet and Allan Ahlberg

In England, the companion award to the Caldecott is the Kate Greenaway Award, presented each year by the British Library Association for the most distinguished illustrations for a children's book published in the United Kingdom during the preceding year. The 1979 Kate Greenaway winner was *Each Peach Pear Plum* (Penguin, 1979), by Allan Ahlberg, with winning illustrations by Janet Ahlberg.

The Ahlbergs' inventive picture books have achieved great popularity in America. Three types of interactive picture books emerge in this inventive book: the patterned picture book, the story-game, and the intertextual story.

Each Peach Pear Plum is first of all a **patterned picture book,** a form very useful for reading instruction. The book is available in a big book edition (Scholastic-Tab, 1989). Every opening of this book has a picture on one side of the page that completes the idea the words express, and the words in this case are arranged as a verse-text. The pictures help children sort out words and story meanings, and the interlocking pattern of words and pictures helps children learn the words of the text.

This book is also a **story-game** of I-Spy: The verse statements about the pictures stimulate readers to respond to the narrator's unspoken invitation to play a game. Words on one side of a page: "Each Peach Pear Plum / I spy Tom Thumb" send readers across the page to a picture of a tree, where they spy a small boy—Tom Thumb—hidden in the branches. The boy is reading a book of nursery tales like this one, filled—as this book is—with folk characters like Mother Hubbard, Cinderella, the Three Bears, Jack and Jill, and others. So the story-game deepens; child readers play I-Spy with the boy's book, too.

As the story unfolds, Tom Thumb becomes entangled with the folk characters, producing an **intertextual story.** *Intertextual* means that different stories—or characters from these stories—are blended together. In this case, characters from different nursery tales mingle with one another to produce a new story. Finally the embedded characters all emerge on the same page at the end, settling down to a feast of plum pie. Other intertextual books by the Ahlbergs are *The Jolly Postman* (Little, Brown, 1986), which had sold over a million copies in hardcover by 1990, *The Jolly Christmas Postman* (Little, Brown, 1991), which won the Kate Greenaway Award in 1992, and *The Jolly Pocket Postman* (Little, Brown, 1995). All of the Ahlbergs' Postman books are also **pop-up books.**

In *The Jolly Postman,* letters—and many other written forms—pop out of envelopes attached into the book pages. These letters are waiting for the child reader to pull out and enjoy, alongside the words and pictures that tell about the jolly, bike-riding postman who comes from "over the hills and far away" to deliver letters to The Three Bears, the Wicked Witch in the woods, Jack's giant at Beanstalk Gardens, Cinderella at the palace, B. B. Wolf, and Goldilocks at Banbury Cross.

Goldilocks writes a friendly letter to the bear family, actually an *invitation* to her birthday party. Gobgoblin Supplies, a business firm, sends an *advertising brochure* to the witch, and Jack sends a *postcard* to the giant. Harold Meeny, an attorney, writes a *business letter* to Mr. Wolf—a legal form, warning him against harassing Miss Riding-Hood. Goldilocks receives a *birthday card.* Pied Piper Press sends the *announcement* of a new children's book to Cinderella (*The Story of a Fairytale Princess* by Janet and Allan Ahlberg), along with a complimentary copy of the book, a tiny paperback Cinderella story that pops out of another envelope pocket. This book is the story of the Princess's life, similar to the many stories about Princess Diana that were starting to emerge at this time, soon after the wedding of Prince Charles and Lady Diana in 1981.

In *The Jolly Christmas Postman,* the Ahlbergs recreate some very old toy pop-up books of the Victorian era: a *Christmas Card story,* a *board game,* and a *jigsaw puzzle.* In *The Jolly Pocket Postman,* the now-familiar postman meets famous characters from different children's literature classics: Lewis Carroll's Alice, Hans Christian Andersen's Little Tin Soldier, Potter's Peter Rabbit, and L. Frank Baum's Dorothy from *The Wizard of Oz.* The Gingerbread Boy, the Bad Wolf, the Three Bears and Goldilocks, and Little Miss Muffet also appear. Allan Ahlberg was a classroom teacher for ten years before he became a full-time writer. Before that time, he was a postman.

blooms in this green place that Emberly created for children in 1967, and Caldecott jurists, who each night faced TV footage of rising death tolls in Viet Nam, rewarded him with their medal.

Ludwig Bemelmans' *Madeline's Rescue* (Viking, 1953) reveals verse couplets used for a quite different purpose than those in *Drummer Hoff.* Humor, improbability, incongruity, exaggeration, and surprise all mark Bemelman's story as an example of **whimsy,** a category a breath away from fantasy. If a story setting breaks free of reality, the genre does actually become fantasy. In Bemelmans' book, the setting is the Paris of the real world, rather than any created mythical kingdom or otherworldly place. But the mood is fanciful and humorous. So to call the book realistic fiction, as we normally would, fails to describe it accurately.

The story is that of a found, lost, and then found again dog that twelve little girls discover in the old Parisian convent where they live. The dog saves the life of the heroine, the mischievous, adventuresome, irrepressible Madeline, then disappears. Unpredictability is a common trait of humorous, whimsical stories. In this case the dog finally turns up, giving birth to twelve puppies (one for each little girl), a delightful surprise for all.

From *Madeline's Rescue* (Viking, 1953) by Ludwig Bemelman.

Until the day she slipped and fell.

Bemelmans actually wrote six Madeline books over a twenty-two-year period (1939–61). They have been published in a collection, *Mad About Madeline* (Viking, 1993), and a recent film, *Madeline* (Tri Star Pictures, 1998), is based on Bemelmans' character. Similar books could also be categorized as whimsy, like the Pippi Longstocking books written by Astrid Lindgren in the same decade, the 1950s. Lindgren's books, like Bemelmans' are part fantasy, part realism.

Another Caldecott winner, James Thurber's *Many Moons,* winning pictures by Louis Slobodkin (Harcourt, 1943), blends fantasy with folk tale. A little princess wants the moon, and no one can grant her wish—not the King, not the Lord High Chamberlain, not the Court Jester, not the Royal Wizard, not the Royal Mathematician. So she must solve the problem herself—and she does. But this is not really a story from the oral tradition. Thurber has merely created his story-text in the folk style: "Once upon a time, in a kingdom by the sea, there lived a little Princess named Lenore," the story begins. The pictures, filled with dreamlike shapes, tilting structures and objects, wispy wavering lines, blue, pink, and yellow (nursery) colors, emphasize the unreality of a fairy tale world.

Hybrid forms like *Many Moons* can be quite useful in the classroom, where teachers often need books to fulfill many purposes. Thurber's book works well for pleasure reading (individualized reading or read-aloud story time); it also has a strong problem-solution story pattern. For literature study groups and text sets, the thematic possibilities are rich indeed: The story features an inquisitive, problem-solving female, an impossible wish that comes true, clever (as opposed to helpless and weepy) females, and stories about the moon. In terms of curriculum needs, *Many Moons* serves as a model for students to follow in writing fantasy with a folk tale setting. It is also particularly useful for critical thinking; teachers can invite children to become partners in puzzling out the book's genre classification.

Shimmering as it does between fantasy and folk tale, a book like Thurber's is also useful for relating literature study to "real" purposes. Children can wear the librarian's or the bookseller's hat and decide where they would shelve this book in the classroom bookcase. Wearing the teacher's hat, they can help decide how to use the book for classroom activities. One activity might involve sending children to find more books that fuse folk tale and fantasy. They might discover Maurice Sendak's *Outside Over There* (Harper, 1981), a Caldecott Honor Book written forty years after *Many Moons* was published and a century after Caldecott published *Sing a Song of Sixpence.*

Sendak's inspiration for *Outside Over There* was a Grimm brothers folk tale, "The Elves," but he did not retell the Grimm tale; he merely borrowed certain details and the general idea of a human child stolen by fairies. His book also fits the category of **literary fairy tale,** in which an author reworks a story from the oral tradition, as Hans Christian Andersen and Charles Perrault embroidered upon folk tales they heard as children.

In Sendak's book, a little girl named Ida spends an exciting day flying to the goblin caves and rescuing her baby sister, who had been stolen by the goblin-elves. She carries the baby home safely, passing Mozart in his tiny Austrian summerhouse, merrily playing his harpsicord. Ida might be imagining these goblins, as her sideways, faraway glance often suggests. Or they might be supernatural creatures that many people in Ida's eighteenth-century world accepted as real. In either case, we are in the realm of fantasy, or more specifically, **folk fantasy,** a genre blending in which humans mingle with gnomes, elves, goblins, brownies, boggarts, ghosts, spirits, or dragons—creatures that folk did once claim to see. Documenting their presence, however, was as difficult as producing a photograph of the Loch Ness monster or an extraterrestrial visitor these days.

Sendak's earlier Caldecott winner, *Where the Wild Things Are* (Harper, 1963), was a fantasy—pure and simple—rather than either folk fantasy or literary fairy tale. Max's monsters, part animal, part human—humorous, whimsical, boisterous, and above all, magical—are not tied to folklore. They are creatures he sees (but has clearly invented) as he travels—in his imagination—to the land of the Wild Things. Perhaps the reason they have seized the imaginations of so many readers is that they are so unique—and so unclassifiable.

Fantasy

Two of the earliest Caldecott fantasies are Virginia Burton's *The Little House* (Houghton Mifflin, 1942) and Robert McCloskey's *Make Way for Ducklings* (Viking, 1941). Each book presents talking objects or animals (a humanized house and a family of Mallard ducks) against the backdrop of a realistic human setting. Because each book was written over fifty years ago, and each emphasized the social context of an earlier day, the stories contain echoes of history for today's children. On the other hand, we might simply describe them as realistic family stories projected onto animals and houses.

Burton's Little House dreams of the days when she was surrounded by country life. "Planted" as she was then in a field of daisies and apple trees, she saw the sun by day and the moon and stars by night. Gone are the days when horse and carriage traveled past her door and she was curious about life in the big city. Now, a century later, the city has come to *her.* There came a day, when the steam shovel came along, digging a bigger road; soon after came trucks, cars, an even bigger road, more houses, city lights, trolley cars, and so much smoke, dust, and smog that she can no longer even distinguish the seasons.

From *The Little House* (Houghton Mifflin, 1942) by Virginia Burton.

In the Fall,
when the days grew shorter
and the nights colder,
she watched the first frost
turn the leaves to bright yellow
and orange and red.
She watched the harvest gathered
and the apples picked.
She watched the children
going back to school.
10

Sad and lonely, the Little House sits above the subway and below the skyscrapers—dirty, shabby, and deserted—until the granddaughter of her original owner discovers her and moves her back to the country where she is once again "lived in and taken care of." Summary cannot do justice to Burton's intricate patterning of words and pictures, the way she uses color to show the seasonal changes and urban/rural contrasts, and swirling lines in both pictures and word arrangements to reveal the unfolding of time and the circle of life.

Unlike Burton's Little House, McCloskey's ducks are not just dreaming of a new place to live. They are searching in earnest because baby ducks are on the way and the city seems a safer place than the country—or at least, safe from duck-eating foxes. The pond in the Boston Public Gardens seems just the right place for this duck family, except for the human children who come barreling through on bikes. The bank of the Charles River pleases them more. These ducks talk; the ducklings, once hatched, have rhyming ducklike names (Jack, Lack, Mack, Pack, and Quack). But a walk to the Public Gardens puts friendly Michael the policeman, the Boston police force, and the ducks to the test. *Make Way for Ducklings* is clearly fantasy (real ducklings do not dabble in phonics), but because people like Michael the policeman also enter the story as characters, it is not a typical *animal* fantasy.

Two more Caldecott books that *seem* to be animal fantasies are Golden MacDonald's *The Little Island,* pictures by Leonard Weisgard (Doubleday, 1946), and William Steig's *Sylvester and the Magic Pebble* (Simon & Schuster, 1969). *The Little Island* reveals a talking cat and fish and an island that actually speaks, too. What the cat and the little island talk about, however, puts us into another realm: *information* about what an island really is, part of the land since "all land is one land under the sea," says the fish. The cat's eyes shine with the "secret" of what it hears. Later, when the cat exits the island along with the people picnicking, the narrator tells us more about the island. Night comes, the bat flies around, a storm blows through, autumn comes and goes, winter arrives, snow falls, years pass.

From *Make Way for Ducklings* (Viking, 1941) by Robert McCloskey.

From *The Little Island* (Doubleday, 1946) by Golden MacDonald, illustrated by Leonard Weisgard.

How good it feels to be the little Island, which is both a "part of the world and a world of its own."

The Little Island shows children a great deal about the natural world, but to call it nonfiction or a nature information book ignores the obvious: the fictional story plays the largest role here. The language patterns are certainly poetic, but poetry is not the major emphasis either. Fantasy is what shapes the book, but what marks the book as fantasy is not so much the cat and fish conversations as it is the cartoon-style Halloween cat with luminous azure eyes looming over the jade green fish it captures. The cat will not let the fish go unless the fish can tell it how an island can be part of the land. Thus the childlike cat assumes a powerful position—both visually and verbally—over the adultlike fish, producing similar feelings of power for the child reader.

Taken together, the scientific information, the poetic mood, and the fantasy story produce a special kind of book, one very worthwhile for teachers to know. Children learning science concepts through fantasy discover new ways of seeing the world. When the fish tells the cat about how the island is part of the land, the cat sees how the cat itself is part of the world, too. And when children read about how the island and the cat are both part of the world, and yet each is also a world of its own, they make the same connection about themselves—that they are "as little as big is big." All things are relative, and all are connected to the living world.

In **nature fantasies** like this, magical events occur against a realistic backdrop. Animals speak, children discover themselves mirrored in the animals' discoveries, and the natural world comes to life in words and pictures.

William Steig's *Sylvester and the Magic Pebble,* on the other hand, is pure **animal fantasy.** The story world here certainly breaks from the real world, at least as we know it. Animals (in this story, donkeys and others) live, dress, talk, and behave like people. They have names and addresses, as humans do. "Sylvester Duncan lived with his mother and father at Acorn Road in Oatsdale," the story begins. They also have hobbies, as people do—Sylvester collects pebbles of unusual shape and color. In fact, it is a pebble that sets the magic of the story in motion.

One day in the rain, as he is studying one of his pebbles, Sylvester wishes that the rain would stop, and immediately it does! Soon he guesses—correctly—that this is a magic pebble. He can hardly believe his luck; now he and his parents can have anything. Then, as "luck" would have it, Sylvester sees a lion and panics. He wishes to be what he loves best—the biggest pebble possible—a rock. Unfortunately, Sylvester is no longer holding the magic pebble after he makes his wish. It lies beside him on the ground. So when he gets his wish—when he becomes a rock—he has no way to reverse the magic and wish himself back into a donkey again. His only hope, as he sits as a rock, day after day, month after month, season after season, is that someone might find the pebble and wish him back to his original self. An impossible hope, it seems, or one based entirely on chance or luck; no one knows where he is or that the pebble has magical powers.

We could call this a modern folk tale or fable—and in some ways, it is. It includes the inevitable magic object and the folk hero who succeeds, through luck and good intentions, in gaining what he wants. Sylvester, because of his courage and patience, his rocklike endurance, night and day all through fall, winter, and spring, is an obvious hero. In fact, it is patience that wins the day for him. Like so many folk tale heroes, he is passive ("stone-dumb") and can only wait for the answer to come from some magical outside agent.

His "fairy godmother" in this case turns out to be just that—his own mother—who one spring day sits down on the Sylvester-rock, warming it and waking him from his winter sleep. His father is equally important; he finds the red pebble, remembers how Sylvester would have loved it, and then—unknown to Sylvester—he places it up on the rock. Finally, as his parents sit by this very rock having their lunch, his mother wishes that Sylvester could be with them. Unfortunately, she is not holding the pebble; Sylvester is "holding" it himself. He *is* the rock, and the pebble is on top of him. But because he does not know he now controls his own fate, he can only hear the sadness in his mother's voice and respond with a true and natural wish to be himself once again. And in less than an instant, he is.

Like any **fable,** this story allows us to observe human behavior through animal characters in order to learn about the social values of a particular society. We learn that good fortune often comes to us for no apparent reason, just as the magic pebble originally came to Sylvester. When the lion arrives and Sylvester makes his near-fatal wish, we see that good luck can be followed by bad, also for no apparent reason. We also see it is human nature to become preoccupied by certain things at times—rocks, gems, money, or in this case, pebbles—and to make stupid wishes because of our obsessions. In the end, Sylvester's father decides wisely to put the magic pebble in an iron safe "for now." They have all they could want (each other), so why wish for more?

What is interesting about the way words and pictures work together in this story is that all the time Sylvester is inside the rock (almost the entire book), we do not see him. But as we make our way through the book, watching his parents search for him, watching the seasons change all around the rock, we actually do

From *The Magic Pebble* (Simon & Schuster, 1969) by William Steig.

"see" him. We never lose sight of him imaginatively, his plight is so strong for us. When we do see him once again at the end, tearfully embracing his mother, his father gleefully dancing in the foreground, it is not shock or surprise we feel, simply the natural unfolding of something right.

What do readers take as an insight from this fantasy-fable-picture book? What social values seep through the words and pictures? When we are loved, the story may be saying, and when we respond with love, we have all we need. To forget or lose sight of this, only for an instant, means that we lose ourselves. Only in accepting ourselves—wishing simply to be ourselves—are we ever "found." This focus on heroes searching and finding a personal and cultural identity is also a crucial part of folk literature, myths, legends, folk tales, or fables, of many cultures.

Often a folk hero or heroine is, like Sylvester, trapped, hidden, or "lost" in a mistaken identity, and a "recognition" scene causes the story to end happily, as it does here. Proving one's identity is the point of many tales from the oral tradition. Discovery of identity, or being discovered as oneself—recognizing one's own *true* identity, as in the Cinderella story—becomes linked to one disagreeable task after another before members of the hero's (or heroine's) society sees the person as who he or she really is.

Folk Literature

Two Caldecott books of the "folk" category have the journey to selfhood as their primary focus: *Cinderella,* Marcia Brown's graceful and delicate retelling of

The next night the two sisters were off again to the ball, and so was Cinderella, but this time even more splendidly dressed than before. The prince never left her side. All evening he paid her charming compliments. The young miss found this so far from boring that she forgot her godmother's warning. She was horrified to hear the first stroke of midnight before she thought it could be eleven o'clock. She rose and fled as lightly as a doe. The prince followed her, but he could not overtake her. In her haste, Cinderella dropped one of her glass slippers. The prince gathered it up with the greatest care.

Cinderella reached home all out of breath, with neither coach nor footmen, and in rags. Nothing was left of her finery but one little slipper, the mate to the one she had lost.

The guards at the palace gate were questioned. Had they seen a princess leave? No, they had seen no one but a young woman in rags, and she looked more like a peasant girl than a fine young lady.

From *Cinderella or the Little Glass Slipper* (Antheneum Books for Young Readers, 1954) by Marcia Brown.

Charles Perrault's version of the old tale (Macmillan, 1954), and *Arrow to the Sun,* Gerald McDermott's vibrant rendering of a Pueblo story (Viking, 1974), which blends myth, legend, and folk tale.

In Brown's retelling of the Cinderella story, we see the usual motifs of **fairy tale:** magical objects and agents, indefinite time and place, powerful enchantments and transformations. In addition, we see the usual motifs of Cinderella tales through the ages: a ball where hopeful maidens congregate, a royal male figure selecting his consort, and a magical shoe test to identify the "right" maiden, the one with the tiniest foot.

Brown also includes the particular motifs of Perrault's version (glass shoes, fairy godmother, pumpkin coach) that Walt Disney used for his film (although Disney added characters and emphases of his own). Brown's fragile, eloquent drawings are particularly important in the light, airy, but powerful sweep of line that emphasizes Cinderella's flight from the ball—and in establishing the fairylike mood. The story of Cinderella, however, is a very old one, from the oral or folk tradition. In a ninth-century Chinese version, the heroine is called Yeh-Shen. In a seventeenth-century Italian version, she is called Zezolla, and in the nineteenth-century Grimm version she is known as Aschenputtel. All of these literary versions began as simple **folk tales,** handed down from teller to teller; sometimes they were recreated as **fairy tales** or **literary fairy tales.**

McDermott's study of the male hero's quest is equally impressive because of the bold, colorful patterns of geometric design symbolizing the three-tiered Pueblo world. The humans are Corn Planter, Pot Maker, and Arrow Maker. Far above is the boy's father, the Lord of the Sun, who has impregnated the boy's mother through a shaft of sunlight that entered her pueblo. Connecting the upper and lower worlds is the rising Sun/Son. Nature forms a stylized backdrop for the boy's journey to discover his identity, to meet the tests of manhood, and to assume his role of cultural leader, once he is recognized for the person he truly is. The boy (who is given no name) travels to his father as an arrow that Arrow Maker fits to

A Closer Look

Fairy Tales and Folk Tales

The terms *fairy tale* and *folk tale* should not really be used interchangeably; they have different meanings. A folk tale is a story from the oral tradition that might include magical elements such as supernatural characters, though it might not. It might be a story collected from a teller and rewritten, as the Grimm brothers often blended or recast stories they heard. A fairy tale, on the other hand, is a literary creation, in which authors draw on elements of folk tales to rework old stories in new or different ways.

Although Charles Perrault was responsible for writing and inspiring others to write folk tales, the use of the words *fairy tale,* say cultural historians Iona and Peter Opie, probably originated with a writer of Charles Perrault's day, Madame d'Aulnoy. She published a volume of her written stories, *Contes des Fees,* or *Tales of the Fairies,* in 1698. The word *literary* often precedes the words *fairy tale* to indicate that the teller *wrote* the story, with conscious attention to literary style and form. The word *fairy* refers to a broad range of magical happenings in the story. These stories did not always feature actual fairies, although many people still believed in fairies in the 1700s, when d'Aulnoy was writing. "Fairy" tales did often include talking animals, enchantments, and other supernatural aspects.

Characters in folk or fairy tales are either noticeably good or notoriously bad at the beginning, and they stay that way. They experience neither growth nor development of character. They often have names to describe their basic traits; Cinderella is forced to work in the kitchen near the cooking fire, as a servant-girl; her proximity to cinders and ashes gives her her name.

Folk and fairy tales both focus primarily on plot (action or situation) rather than characters. They exhibit very little depth of character. Often they focus on romances in royal families, they are set in a vague long-ago time and place, and their background details provide a clear picture of social customs and the values in the teller's own setting. We hear about dresses embroidered with diamonds and pearls in some stories, about hair waved and rippled nearly to the ground in others. We hear about ambassadors who are sent to do a king's bidding and their strong loyalty and obedience to the king, causing them to do almost anything to ensure the king's will and safety. A strong desire for immortality reigns on the part of king and commoner alike. People value possessions—jewels, gowns, horses, swords, kingdoms, and gold—and physical traits such as tiny feet and golden hair, and the point of many of these stories is that these values can become obsessive.

In d'Aulnoy's day, members of her audience valued courage and faithfulness on the part of their heroes and heroines, as we can see from the stories. Men took on tasks at the king's bidding (or to fulfill a female's wish) despite risks, hazards, loss of fortune or life, and they often did so impulsively; this "romantic" behavior was the accepted—and unquestioned—order of things. Women did the same when it came to marriage and childbirth. Thus the popularity of this genre, then and now or the popularity of romance fiction for centuries.

Humans still face danger, change, risk, their own impulsiveness, enemies who plot against them for their own self-aggrandizement (as Cinderella's sisters did), selfish "loved ones" who ask the impossible (as Cinderella's stepmother did), and power structures that allow little concern for individual lives or preferences (Cinderella is chosen; she does not do the choosing).

Characters in these stories, whether folk or fairy tales, are people with whom readers can feel close ties. They renew the hope that a magical "presence" could intervene in their behalf, if they exhibited the same caring impulses of many folk heroes and heroines.

Source: Iona and Peter Opie, *The Classic Fairy Tales* (New York: Oxford University Press, 1974).

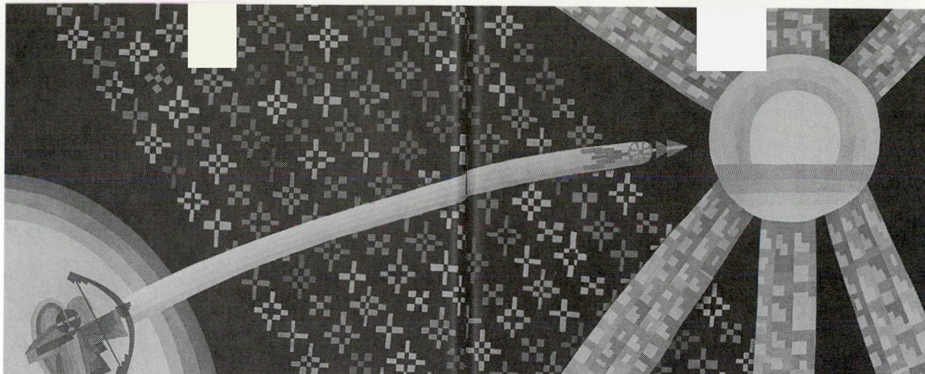

From *Arrow to the Sun* (Viking, 1974) by Gerald McDermott.

his bow. In one dynamic, brilliantly colored, double-page spread, the boy soars between human (Arrow Maker) and god (the Sun) to begin his tests of courage.

This is not a story of gaining courage; the boy already has the traits he needs for these tasks as the story begins. He simply has to demonstrate his gifts to prove who he is—and how he knows his identity. We are in the realm of **legend** here, the story of a hero who endures and achieves despite the suspicion or distrust of others. In this story, other boys of the village mock the boy for having no father, and their taunts awaken him to his quest. He must search for the father who will identify him and give him his rightful place in the community.

This story also places us in the realm of **myth,** a story that explains, through imaginative thinking, how the world, its people, or its animals were created or came to be in some distant time and place. Once he has passed his father's tests for manhood, the boy returns from the Kiva of Lightning, walking a rainbow, as warriors in Native American tales often passed from earth to the Sky World. Then, once again as an arrow, he returns to the human world, bringing his father's spirit with him. The story thus explains how the Sun came to Earth.

Myth and legend embody powerful, intricate, and complex ideas for young readers. It is puzzling that we do not see more examples of the folklore category among Newbery winners, for example, books like Virginia Hamilton's *In the Beginning: Creation Stories from Around the World* (Harcourt, 1988). Hamilton's book attained Newbery Honor status in 1989 for its text, although the illustrations by Barry Moser were equally impressive. The Newbery award does not concentrate exclusively on picture books, as the Caldecott does; neither does it exclude picture books from consideration. In the next section, we will examine genre through the lens of Newbery award winners.

STUDYING GENRE WITH NEWBERY BOOKS

The Newbery Medal was instituted sixteen years before the Caldecott, in 1922; so it is not surprising that the award was named for a man whose interest in pictures was equal to his interest in words. John Newbery was an eighteenth-century English

A Little Pretty
POCKET-BOOK,
Intended for the
INSTRUCTION and AMUSEMENT
OF
LITTLE MASTER *TOMMY*,
AND
PRETTY MISS *POLLY*.
With Two Letters from
JACK the GIANT-KILLER;
AS ALSO
A BALL and PINCUSHION;
The Use of which will infallibly make *Tommy*
a good Boy, and *Polly* a good Girl.

To which is added,
A LITTLE SONG-BOOK,
BEING
A *New Attempt* to teach Children the Use of
the *English Alphabet*, by Way of Diversion.

LONDON:
Printed for J. NEWBERY, at the *Bible and Sun*
in St. *Paul's Church-Yard*. 1767.
[Price Six-pence bound.]

From *A Little Pretty Pocketbook* (1744).

publisher who invented a new way of producing children's books, one designed to appeal to children's interests, not merely advance their moral training. In *A Little Pretty Pocketbook* (1744), one of the first, if not the first, *real* children's books, we find pictures in plentiful supply, as well as stories, games, rhymes, fables, proverbs, poems, and even letters "written" to children by folk tale characters.

Newbery was first of all a businessman; he recognized a promising money-making venture as well as large book chains like Waldenbooks and Barnes & Noble do today. So it may seem strange that the Newbery Award is not called the Aesop, the Charles Perrault, the John Carroll, or the Louisa May Alcott Award. But naming an award for a particular author would have focused attention on the genre in which that author worked (fables, fairy tales, fantasy, or realism), thus tending to limit the award to books of that genre. Just as naming an award for Randolph Caldecott revealed one form (the picture book) at its best, naming an award for a bookseller showcased the *many* distinguished genres of children's literature.

If we separate the long list of Newbery awards (1922–present) into the five traditional genre categories, we discover that **realism** accounts for by far the greatest number, with over fifty-three titles (contemporary and historical realism are equally balanced). **Fantasy** follows with thirteen titles, then **nonfiction** with seven. Finally, **folk literature** and **poetry** are tied with two titles each. Interestingly, many of these titles are actually blendings of various genres; for example, the 1998 winner, Karen Hesse's *Out of the Dust* (Scholastic), is an interesting blending of historical fiction and poetry. The first-person narrator tells the story of life in Oklahoma during the Depression, when drought, death, and a tragic accident all strike the heroine one year—and she tells it in rhythmic free verse.

One of the 1998 Newbery Honor books is another innovative blending. Gail Carson Levine's novel *Ella Enchanted* (Harper) blends fantasy and folk tale (the Cinderella story) with realistic touches of modern feminist thinking.

Realism, Biography, and History

Clearly, our culture values realism in children's books for older readers (among Caldecott winners, realism and folk literature have equal numbers of winners). In one decade, the 1950s, the ratio of realism to fantasy books among Newbery winners was 10:0. The American culture either nurtures a strong talent for producing realism, a strong inclination to produce it, or both. (Among British imports we see the opposite—a strong talent and inclination for producing fantasy books: magical, quest, time travel.)

Among earlier Newbery books, Carol Ryrie Brink's *Caddie Woodlawn* (Macmillan, 1935) is remembered for its adventurous and spirited heroine. Caddie, who lives during the American frontier days, is based on the Brink's own grandmother. The book is therefore a genre blending of realism, biography, and historical fiction, similar to the Little House books Laura Ingalls Wilder wrote, beginning with *Little House in the Big Woods* in 1932. Five of Wilder's books were Newbery Honor Books of the late 1930s and early 1940s: *On the Banks of Plum Creek* (Harper, 1937), *By the Shores of Silver Lake* (Harper, 1939), *The Long Winter* (Harper, 1940), *Little Town on the Prairie* (Harper, 1941), and *These Happy Golden Years* (Harper, 1943).

The Little House books recreate Wilder's childhood in an American pioneer family from her preschool years to her marriage in 1885—and beyond. Most obviously, they are **historical fiction.** Wilder remembered names, places, dates, and happenings with precise clarity: the foods; the household tasks; the holidays and presents; the stories her father told (tall tales filled with realistic detail and comic spirit) to amuse, instruct, entertain, and console his family; the animals that roamed the woods beside their various homes in Wisconsin, Kansas, Minnesota, and the Dakota Territory; the perils and hardships; the sleigh bells and Christmas stockings; Pa's fiddling; Ma's knitting; the firelight of the little log cabin; the adventure of it all. As Garth Williams, the illustrator of these books, said, "Laura saw the world through rosy glass . . . the beauty of everything simple" (page 7).

In many ways, Wilder's books are also **nonfiction,** in particular **autobiography.** Laura paints a comprehensive portrait of her family: herself, her sisters, and her parents, Charles and Caroline Ingalls, a loving, perfectly matched couple, each self-actualizing and autonomous, yet always working in tandem. Laura's parents were anxious at times, but also hopeful and courageous, always making things safe and right for their children—Laura and her sisters, Mary and Carrie.

The books are, in addition, survival stories, a thematic genre. Laura's life was filled with blizzards, prairie fires, drought, illness, cyclones, floods, near starvation, sacrifices—but never boredom, and never mean-spirited behavior. What we see above all else is a family's resourcefulness and determination, what has come to be known as the American pioneer spirit. Newbery jurists living through World War II valued the visibility of this spirit in the children's book world.

From *Little House in the Big Woods* (Harper, 1932) by Laura Ingalls Wilder, Illustrated by Garth Williams.

Caddie Woodlawn's dilemma (would she escape the constricting, well-defined roles for females of her day, or would she become socialized into them?) and Laura Wilder's narrative talents have overshadowed another important female among earlier Newbery Honor characters, Greta Addington from Julia Sauer's *Fog Magic* (Viking, 1943).

Realism and Fantasy Blended: The Time Travel Book

Sauer's book illustrates one of the most interesting genres of children's literature, and one that children's authors often cultivate—the **time travel fantasy,** a unique blend of realism and fantasy. Sometimes called the "time slip" story, this kind of fantasy explores both historical and legendary time. Children in the present travel back into other times and places to encounter real or legendary people; in other stories, legendary or historical figures from the past move forward in time to mingle with modern children. Characters may also travel into the future—into a world in which life is much different from the life we know. But when characters enter the future, the genre usually becomes **science fiction** or **science fantasy.**

Time fantasy has a particular *form;* parallel stories of past and present (or future and present) run alongside one another throughout the book. This type of fantasy also has a particular *structure* similar in some ways to that of folklore stories. The hero or heroine feels "called" to some other time or dimension, fulfills a personal, social, or cultural "quest" and then returns home. Time fantasy also has a particular *subject* (time) and explores a particular set of *questions:* Can we exist on more than one time plane at once? (Can we live in two different "worlds" at once?) What advantages does this dual existence have? Are children more successful in crossing worlds of time? Finally, time fantasy has a particular *theme:* the child's unique ability to exist in two dimensions and to believe and act in them both.

In *Fog Magic,* eleven-year-old Greta, sensitive, adventuresome, and inquisitive, wanders through the fog in her village in Nova Scotia and enters a time in the past—the late 1800s—when nearby Blue Cove was filled with houses. There she meets a new friend, Retha, and Retha's cat, Princess. Greta has the "gift" of being able to see people from another time, but because she will soon be turning twelve, her time in the fog-world of the past is passing quickly.

In many time fantasies, the ability to "see" or pass into other dimensions of time, or to engage in magical travel between then and now, belongs only to the child and ends when childhood ends. Children in these stories believe in magic and can cross time planes more easily than adults. If fantasy lies at the heart of children's literature as its most inventive and exuberant genre, then time fantasy surely lies somewhere close to the heart of fantasy as its most thought-provoking form.

Historical Fiction and Coming-of-Age Novels

In the 1950s, Elizabeth George Speare produced another unique blending for the field of children's literature: historical fiction and the female coming-of-age novel. Set in the Puritan era in America, *The Witch of Blackbird Pond* (Houghton Mifflin, 1958) focuses on Kit Tyler, who leaves her home in Barbados to come to Connecticut in 1687. There she befriends an elderly, eccentric, and harmless Quaker woman thought to be a witch. Independent, spirited, and creative, Kit does not succumb to conventional ways of thinking or behaving, even when her loyalties

INVESTIGATIONS: Exploring an Unfamiliar Genre

Find a genre category that is unfamiliar to you. Look for examples of notable books in this category and start reading. Maybe you know nothing about *science fantasy,* a category of books that bridges the "space" between fantasy and science fiction, and you want to learn something about it.

Consider reading Madeleine L'Engle's *A Wrinkle in Time* (Farrar, 1962), Newbery winner for 1963. In this book, Meg Murray, her brother Charles Wallace, and their friend Calvin travel through time to a new planet, Camazotz, in search of the Murray children's father. Mr. Murray is a scientist who has been taken captive by a totalitarian government. On Camazotz, Charles Wallace is brainwashed and held captive, too, but Meg is ultimately able to free them all through the power of her love for them.

As an alternative, read a more recent example of science fiction, like Lois Lowry's *The Giver* (Houghton Mifflin, 1993), Newbery winner for 1994. A thought-provoking page-turner, Lowry's book, like many Newbery winners, stirred up controversy regarding certain features of the future world it describes. Most complaints focused on the practices and customs of this society; some adults thought they might be too disturbing for children or too far removed from traditional values and religious beliefs. For example, Lowry concocts a child-bearing experiment in her story in which some women are assigned the role of birthmothers. Their job is to incubate artificially conceived embryos. Some elderly people, as well as weak, unhealthy, or troublesome infants, are "released" whenever those in power deem it "necessary" for the welfare of the group (calculated murder becomes standard operating procedure). Efficiency, responsibility, and cooperation replace love as a bond in families.

and freethinking habits cause her to be persecuted as a witch. In the end, when she is set free, Kit chooses as her mate not the conventional and affluent farmer who has chosen her, but an enterprising sailor as spirited as she.

The **coming-of-age novel** has been an important fictional genre in children's literature since Louisa May Alcott wrote *Little Women.* But the process of coming of age, especially for girls, has been evolving or changing through the decades. In Alcott's day, the question was whether a girl would marry or pursue a career. In the 1930s and 1940s, the genre focused on how the female character could find her "place" in the conventional social scheme without forsaking spirited fun for more sedate "female" activities, as in *Caddie Woodlawn.*

These days, **female coming-of-age fiction** involves any number of ideas: friendship, romance, dreams of the future, sacrifices, social and cultural roles, separation from parents, and escape from constricting gender roles through creative works or social action. Speare's *The Witch of Blackbird Pond* was well ahead of its time; it explored all these areas with sensitivity and inventiveness.

More recently, Karen Cushman, a Newbery Honor medalist for *Catherine, Called Birdy* (Harper, 1994) and a Newbery winner for *The Midwife's Apprentice* (Clarion, 1995), has written about lively, insightful females coming of age in the Middle Ages. Catherine faces, as Caddie Woodlawn did, a mother intent upon turning her daughter into a conventional female; she must also, like Kit Tyler, deal with oppressive social customs and practices. Still, Catherine grows into adulthood with spirit and strong imaginative capability.

Male coming-of-age Newbery books emerged in the 1970s with two novels by Virginia Hamilton. *The Planet of Junior Brown* (Macmillan, 1971), a Newbery Honor book, is the story of two friends living in New York City. One is struggling with an absentee father, an incredible musical talent, and mental illness; the other is homeless. *M. C. Higgins the Great* (Macmillan, 1974) is the story of two friends living in the rural Midwest. One struggles with the results of a strip mining problem; the other, a boy of mixed race, faces prejudice that others have about his identity. The first book by an African American to win the Newbery Award, *M. C. Higgins the Great* is important historically, culturally, and artistically.

Realism, History, and Multicultural Literature

The Story of the Negro (Knopf, 1948), a nonfiction book by Arna Bontemps, was the first book by an African American to win a Newbery Honor Award. In 1970, William Armstrong's *Sounder* (Harper, 1969) was the first novel about African Americans to win the Newbery. But Armstrong was not African American, as Hamilton was. It is Hamilton's books that have continued to resonate with those who regard authenticity (literature written by insiders of a particular cultural group) as an indispensable feature of *distinguished* literature for children.

M. C. Higgins the Great is the story of an Appalachian African-American family living in the path of a slag heap. This precarious situation produces severe distress for the young male character, who cannot rouse his family to action. Filled with realistic details of place—the border of Kentucky and southeastern Ohio—the book focuses on a forty-eight-hour period during which M. C. struggles with the peril of the soil heap, his father's prejudice toward his mixed-race friend, his mother's undiscovered singing talents, and a girl who fascinates but continues to reject him.

Since the book portrays the history and traditions of two very different African-American families, it can also be classified as **multicultural literature**, a new genre we are recognizing—or defining—these days. Multicultural literature centers around subject matter: the social realities of a particular ethnic or racial group, or of two or more such groups as they interact. In the late 1970s, another Newbery book by an African American fit this category, Mildred Taylor's *Roll of Thunder, Hear My Cry* (Dial, 1976). This book's genre was historical fiction; the novel was set in Mississippi in the 1930s.

Walter Dean Myers has won Newbery Honor status twice for his multicultural novels, *Scorpions* (Harper, 1988) and *Somewhere in the Darkness* (Scholastic, 1992). Both books focus on growing up African American, written from an insider's perspective. In 1993, another African-American writer, Patricia McKissack, won Newbery Honor status for *The Dark-Thirty: Southern Tales of the Supernatural* (Knopf, 1992). This book contained African-American ghost stories framed by authorial commentary about the tales.

In 1994, Laurence Yep received a Newbery Honor award for *Dragon's Gate* (Harper, 1993), the story of a Chinese immigrant in 1867 who struggles through rough times in the Sierra Nevada as he helps build the transcontinental railroad. Yep had previously won Newbery Honor status for *Dragonwings* (Harper, 1975), the story of Chinese immigrants in early twentieth-century San Francisco. Yep's novels blend historical fiction, male coming-of-age stories, multicultural themes, and Asian folklore.

In 1996, two more African-American writers won Newbery Honor Awards. Carol Fenner wrote *Yolanda's Genius* (McElderry, 1995), a realistic novel about a

ALA Awards Honoring Insider Writers

Each year, the American Library Association presents the Coretta Scott King Award to African-American authors and illustrators who have made outstanding contributions to African-American children's literature published in the United States during the preceding year. The purpose of this award is to encourage artistic expression that focuses on the African-American experience through biographical, historical, or fictional treatments. The winning books must have a clear plot, well-delineated characters who grow and develop during the story, accuracy of details, a writing style suitable to a child audience, and high-quality illustrations.

The Pura Belpre Award is presented every two years to outstanding children's books published in the United States or Puerto Rico and written in Spanish, English, or bilingual format by established residents of the United States or Puerto Rico. The purpose of the award is to "portray, affirm, and celebrate the Latino cultural experience." *Latino* is defined as the culture of the Spanish-speaking hemisphere. Both text and illustrations must present positive, accurate, authentic portrayals of Latino culture, and they must speak from the insider's voice. In addition, they must reveal excellence of presentation in plot, setting, character delineation, artistic technique, and appropriateness for the child audience.

The major difference between insider and mainstream awards is that insiders must write and illustrate the books that win insider awards; these awards value authenticity in depicting the insider culture. Insider award committees are also more likely to have a majority of insiders casting votes for the awards; thus, knowledge about the beliefs, traditions, and values of the insider culture is strong among the voting members. Mainstream awards may depict an insider culture, but the authors of these books—and those voting for the awards—do not have to be insiders; in fact, the winning books sometimes evoke controversy later when some readers question whether they present an accurate picture of the insider culture.

family in inner-city Chicago, and Christopher Paul Curtis produced *The Watsons Go to Birmingham—1963* (Delacorte, 1995), a work of historical fiction.

Like picture books, multicultural literature encompasses all genres, traditions, and pictorial forms, and it has spawned many inventive narrative techniques and two new American Library Association Awards: the Coretta Scott King and the Pura Belpre Awards.

The 1997 Newbery winner, Elaine Konigsburg's *The View from Saturday* (Atheneum, 1996), is particularly inventive in its multicultural themes. The author brings together—as friends—the members of a sixth grade academic "bowl" team called "The Souls"; within this group is nearly every possible contender for multicultural status in America. Noah Gerchom is a child of Jewish-American heritage, Konigsburg's own ethnic background. Nadia Diamondstein, half Jewish, half Protestant, is a child of divorce who visits her grandfather in Florida and ends up helping to save the endangered turtles there. Ethan Potter is the child of rural farmers in central New York State, where the novel—and the bowl competition—take place. Julian Singh is a child of East Indian heritage. Eva Marie Olinski, the children's teacher, is disabled as the result of an automobile accident.

Each of these individuals is linked to the others in a wide web of relationships and concerns. They are friends; two are related by their grandparents' marriage; they are teammates; and they are kind and caring human beings—*souls*—who come together as members of an extended or surrogate "family." At a time when many special interest groups—the disabled, the elderly, environmentalists—and many cultural groups—monocultural, cross-cultural, polycultural, and multiethnic—are all contending for multicultural status, the book becomes both a warm, humorous send-up of political correctness and a serious validation of multicultural concerns.

Konigsburg had previously won, in the same year, both a Newbery Award for *From the Mixed-Up Files of Mrs. Basil E. Frankweiler* (Athenium, 1967) and a Newbery Honor Award, for *Jennifer, Hecate, Macbeth, William McKinley, and Me, Elizabeth* (Atheneum, 1967). Both books are realistic novels. The Newbery Honor book has, in addition, a multicultural emphasis: Jennifer, who is black, and Elizabeth, who is white, are best friends. Both books are mysteries.

Realism, Mystery, and Adventure

From the Mixed-Up Files of Mrs. Basil E. Frankweiler is the story of sixth-grader Claudia and her younger brother, who run away from home to live at the Metropolitan Museum of Art. Once there, they discover a statue whose origin is a mystery to everyone except the original owner, Mrs. Frankweiler, who helps Claudia through a labyrinth of clues to the eventual answer. In one sense, the book fits the category of **detective story,** because the reader receives the clues alongside the detective (Claudia). In another sense, the novel is more like a traditional **mystery,** because no criminal is involved.

Konigsberg brings special qualities to the children's mystery novel: sensitive and perceptive characters, a well-constructed plot, a witty and sophisticated literary style, and originality. The story is filled with insights about growing up, or simply *growing* at any age. (Mrs. Frankweiler is eighty-two—and still learning). Konigsberg's book is not just mystery, however. It is also an **adventure story,** a fictional form that usually describes a book filled with physical action, exciting turns of plot, and chilling, suspenseful scenes.

The adventure in this novel is more in the psychic than the physical realm. Similar to the novels Nina Bawden writes and remembers liking as a child—because she could compare herself to the child characters for qualities like bravery and honesty—Konigsberg's novel is one in which a young-reader could identify with Claudia, who faces a challenging and exciting task: She must solve a mystery—and do it largely alone. In doing so, Claudia achieves something important in terms of social action. Because of its setting, a famous art museum, the story also focuses on the visual arts, a category often less visible among Newbery winners.

Pictorial Forms

No picture book has ever won the Newbery award, although many illustrated books have won Newbery Honor Awards. The first important American picture book, *Millions of Cats* by Wanda Gäg (Coward-McCann, 1928), was a Newbery Honor book for 1929. The book blends folk tale motifs in an intricately patterned design of words and pictures. The story is patterned, too. A very old man and woman are lonely, and they wish for a cat. The old man sets out and finds a hill covered with cats:

> Cats here, cats there,
> Cats and kittens everywhere,
> Hundreds of cats,
> Thousands of cats,
> Millions and billions and trillions of cats.

From *Millions of Cats* (Coward, McCann, 1928) by Wanda Gäg.

Everywhere he looks, he sees another cat "so pretty he could not bear to leave it, and before he knew it, he had chosen them all." His wife wants to let the cats decide which one the couple will keep—which is the prettiest one—a decision that leads to the grandest cat fight ever. One not-so-pretty cat wins the coveted spot in the couples' home because it never thought itself pretty and thus stayed out of the fight. The old man and woman bathe and brush and feed the cat. Later, the old man (who had seen hundreds of cats, millions and billions of cats—and so ought to know) declares it the "most beautiful cat in the world." Intriguing questions remain. Does the cat grow beautiful because it is cared for and loved? Does the couple see it as pretty because it is theirs? Gäg's *ABC Bunny* (Coward-McCann, 1933), a **concept** picture book and one of the first ABC books, was also a Newbery Honor book four years later.

Ludwig Bemelmans' *The Golden Basket* (Viking, 1936) was a **picture storybook** about two little English girls visiting the quaint Belgium city of Bruges. The book, featuring a cameo appearance by Madeline, was an Honor book in 1937. A picture storybook is a richly illustrated story, longer than a picture book but shorter than a novel, in which the words carry the story, but the pictures nevertheless play an important role. (Beatrix Potter's animal fantasies fit this category also, as we have seen.) Later, in 1977 and 1983, William Steig produced two picture storybooks for the Honor lists, *Abel's Island* (Farrar, 1976) and *Dr. DeSoto* (Farrar, 1982). Both are animal fantasies, and *Abel's Island* is also a survival story: a very literate Edwardian mouse finds himself stranded on an island.

Arnold Lobel's animal fantasy *Frog and Toad Together* (Harper, 1972) was a Newbery Honor book in 1973. In terms of genre, it is a **chapter book,** a fictional form in which loosely related episodes are connected by a main character, group of characters, or a subject, much like a collection of short stories in which one person is the main character. In this book, the Frog and Toad characters share the limelight equally. Together they are the "glue" holding the episodes together.

Holling Clancy Holling's *Seabird* (Houghton, 1948) is a **nonfiction picture storybook** about whaling and clipper ships. It won Newbery Honor status in 1949. Patricia Lauber's *Volcano: The Eruption and Healing of Mount St. Helens* (Bradbury, 1986), an **illustrated nonfiction science book,** was an Honor book in 1987. (The illustrations are colorful and artistic photographs.)

An interesting situation emerged in 1982 when Nancy Willard's *A Visit to William Blake's Inn: Poems for Innocent and Experienced Travelers* (Harcourt, 1981) won both the Newbery Award for words and Caldecott Honor status for the pictures by Alice and Martin Provensen. The most significant genre category for the book, however, is **poetry.** Williard's book is composed of theme-centered poems about life at an imaginary inn run by eighteenth-century poet William Blake, author of *Songs of Innocence* in 1789.

Willard produces a pun or play on the words *inn* and *innocence,* when she sets her story in an inn. The poet himself is in charge, as we see in the first poem, "William Blake's Inn for Innocent and Experienced Travelers":

> This inn belongs to William Blake
> and many are the beasts he's tamed

From *A Visit to William Blake's Inn: Poems for Innocent and Experienced Travelers* (Harcourt, 1981) by Nancy Willard, illustrated by Alice and Martin Provensen.

and many are the stars he's named
and many those who stop and take
their joyful rest with William Blake.

Two mighty dragons brew and bake
and many are the loaves they've burned
and many are the spits they've turned
and many those who stop and break
their joyful bread with William Blake.

Two patient angels wash and shake
his featherbed, and far away
snow falls like feathers. That's the day
good children run outside and make
snowmen to honor William Blake.

Poetry blends with fantasy (magical impossibility, talking flowers and animals, whimsy, nonsense, innocence as fun), and the illustrations are equally fanciful. But even though the illustrations are of Caldecott caliber, the poems could stand alone, so many rich details fill the lines. Thus, the book is less a picture book than an **illustrated poetry book.** Words supercede pictures.

Another clear-cut example of an illustrated poetry book is Paul Fleischman's *Joyful Noise* (Harper, 1988), illustrations by Eric Beddows, which won the Newbery Award in 1989. The pictures *support* rather than *complete* the text.

Of course, the text of a poem should produce such clear, precise, and important *word-pictures* that very little additional visual stimulus is necessary—or at least no stimulus will overshadow the words. *Joyful Noise* was composed for reading aloud in two voices, an intriguing idea and one especially useful for choral reading activities. Fleischman's collection, like Willard's, is theme-centered. In this case, the poems are about insects, but the poet's primary purpose is certainly not to convey scientific information.

Near the end of this same decade, the 1980s, Russell Freedman's *Lincoln: A Photobiography* (Clarion, 1987) won the Newbery. Nonfiction **photobiography** is another intriguing pictorial form. **Biography** focuses on a famous or important person in order to transmit information about a topic of interest, and Freedman's book concentrates on many topics of interest to children. Readers learn about Lincoln as a child and a young man, as well as about slavery, the Civil War, and Lincoln's assassination. But it is the photographs that carry the story. Readers viewing these pictures come closer to an intriguing, crucial figure in American history—one who, like so many historical figures, has seemed distant, elusive, and unreal.

Photography not only exposes children to an important art medium, one that they themselves might handle with success; in this case, it might inspire them to produce their own biographies of parents, grandparents, friends, or pets, or even to write their own autobiographies. In addition, if children were to create photobiographies, they would accept genre blendings as true genres. The unconventional genres of our childhood often become so familiar to us as time passes that, before we know it, they become customary and usual aspects of our reading lives.

INVESTIGATIONS: Exploring More Genres

We have been examining many kinds of children's books through the lens of Caldecott and Newbery books. Choose a category that you would like to explore further and read the children's books described in this chapter that exemplify this category. Perhaps *whimsy* intrigues you; if so, examine books in Ludwig Bemelmans' Madeline series. Or read Thurber's *Many Moons*. Or go beyond Caldecott and Newbery books to explore Astrid Lindgren's *Pippi Longstocking* (Viking, 1950). Can you find any books published after the 1950s that could fit this category? Has whimsy disappeared in the postmodern era?

Perhaps you are more interested in pictorial forms. Many famous illustrators grace the Newbery list; you might want to explore Newbery books with inventive illustrations. Garth Williams illustrated the Little House books by Laura Ingalls Wilder and also illustrated *Charlotte's Web,* which won Honor status in 1953, and *The Cricket in Times Square* (Farrar, 1950), an Honor book in 1961. William Pène du Bois, who is famous for his artwork as well as his story writing, illustrated his own Newbery winner of 1948, *The Twenty-One Balloons* (Viking, 1947). Meindert DeJong's Newbery winner, *The Wheel on the School* (Harper, 1954), and his Newbery Honor book, *The House of Sixty Fathers* (Harper, 1956), were both illustrated by America's premier children's book illustrator, Maurice Sendak. Sendak also illustrated Randall Jarrell's *The Animal Family* (Pantheon, 1965), a Newbery Honor book for 1966.

REFLECTIONS ON GENRE AS LITERARY CONCEPT AND SOCIAL CONSTRUCT

When we examine books by Caldecott and Newbery winners, we see many ways that social and cultural values drive the plot, conflict, setting, theme, and character delineation in books. At the same time, children's books include nearly any genre imaginable, and several genres may intersect in one book. Children's fantasy, pictorial forms, and genre blends are unique contributions that children's literature gives to the wider world of literature, so inventive and distinguished are the works produced in terms of these areas.

Pictorial forms—picture books, picture storybooks, and illustrated books—form a foundation for many or all other genres of children's literature. (For more on pictorial forms, see the end of this chapter.) All reading begins with the youngest child, who needs pictures to maintain interest in the story or text, and the interest in pictorial forms continues with readers of all ages, whether they want and expect picture books or intriguing cover art for a novel.

Picture books come in all genres:

- **Folk literature** (nursery rhymes, fables, folk tales, legends, myths);
- **Fantasy** (talking animals/toys/houses; magical stories; humans in alternative worlds);
- **Realism** (contemporary and historical fiction, mystery, adventure stories);
- **Poetry** (narrative, lyric, nonsense);
- **Nonfiction** (information/concept books, biography, autobiography, history, science).

Picture books also come in many genre blendings. Genre is a very fluid concept; not only do genres go forth and multiply, but picture book artists work in all styles, media, and formats. Picture books both tell and complete stories; the interdependence between words and pictures defines this form. In many ways, pictures give children their first chance to "read" the world and their first opportunity to behave as real readers.

Pictorial forms—picture books, picture storybooks, and illustrated books—are the mainstay of children's literature. They fuse the oral tradition of words, wordplay, verse, lullaby, nursery rhyme—and stories of all kinds—with the visual tradition of color, line, shape, and texture, all of which have been part of the child's world since birth.

Pictures stimulate reading, writing, talking, storytelling, counting, laughter, word play, and rhyming. One of the most important categories of picture books is the interactive book that invites the child to participate in the word or picture patterns. In this category we find ABC books, counting books and cumulative tales, Mother Goose rhymes, pop-up books and those providing tactile experiences, humorous books, nonsense rhymes, game books, and books with wordless scenes or entire wordless stories.

Inventive authors for children often break away from established genre categories. Very few creative artists, writers, or, for that matter, readers, hold to fixed notions and compartmentalized thinking. Their creativity depends on breaking out of previously "fixed" categories. Authors who win the most prestigious awards are often the most unconventional.

In the next chapter, we will take a deeper look at literary and social conventions and the ways inventive artists and writers break these conventions to produce change and growth in children's books.

CHILDREN'S LITERATURE

Picture Books

Interactive Picture Books

ABC Books

ANNO. *Anno's Alphabet.* New York: Harper and Row, 1975.
AZARIAN, MARY. *A Farmer's Alphabet.* Boston: David R. Godine, 1981.
GÄG, WANDA. *The ABC Bunny.* New York: Coward, McCann, & Geoghegan, 1933.
JOHNSON, STEVEN. *Alphabet City.* New York: Viking, 1995.
PROVENSEN, ALICE AND MARTIN. *A Peaceable Kingdom.* New York: Viking, 1978.

Counting Books

ANNO. *Anno's Counting Book.* New York: Thomas Y. Crowell, 1977.
FEELINGS, MURIEL AND TOM. *Moja Means One.* New York: Dial, 1971.
YOLEN, J., AND ZALBEN, JANE. *An Invitation to the Butterfly Ball.* New York: Parents' Magazine Press, 1976.

Cumulative Books

EMBERLEY, ED. *Drummer Hoff.* Englewood Cliffs, NJ: Prentice-Hall: 1967.
HUTCHINS, PAT. *Good-Night, Owl!* New York: Macmillan, 1972.
———. *The Surprise Party.* London: The Bodley Head, 1970.

Humorous Books

BARRETT, JUDI AND RON. *Cloudy with a Chance of Meatballs.* New York: Macmillan, 1978.
HOWE, JAMES, AND HOBAN, LILLIAN. *The Day the Teacher Went Bananas.* New York: E. P. Dutton, 1984.
MAHY, MARGARET, AND KELLOGG, STEVEN. *The Boy Who Was Followed Home.* New York: Dial, 1975.
MARSHALL, JAMES. *George and Martha.* Boston: Houghton Mifflin, 1974.
SHANNON, DAVID. *No David!* New York: Scholastic, 1998.
SLOBODKINA, ESPHYR. *Caps for Sale.* New York: Harper and Row, 1940.

Tactile/Sensory/Sound Books

BENNETT, JILL, AND SHARRATT, NICK. *Noisy Poems.* Oxford, England: Oxford University Press, 1987.
CARLE, ERIC. *The Grouchy Ladybug.* New York: HarperCollins, 1977.
———. *Have You Seen My Cat?* New York: Scholastic, 1991.
———. *The Very Busy Spider.* New York: Philomel, 1984.
———. *The Very Hungry Caterpillar.* New York: World Publishing Company, 1969.
———. *The Very Quiet Cricket.* New York: Philomel, 1990.
HOBAN, TANA. *Take Another Look.* New York: Greenwillow, 1981.

Patterned Books (Words or Pictures)

HUTCHINS, PAT. *Rosie's Walk.* New York: Viking, 1970.
———. *Titch.* New York: Viking, 1971.
———. *You'll Soon Grow Into Them, Titch.* New York: Greenwillow, 1983.

Patterned Books (Wordplay/Verse)

KRAUSS, RUTH, AND SENDAK, MAURICE. *A Hole Is to Dig.* New York: Harper and Row, 1953.

———. *A Very Special House.* New York: Harper and Row, 1953.

———. *Open House for Butterflies.* New York: Harper and Row, 1960.

LEE, DENNIS, AND WIJNGAARD, JUAN. *Jelly Belly.* Toronto: Macmillan, 1983.

ROSEN, MICHAEL, AND STEELE, SUSANNA. *Inky Pinky Ponky: Collected Playground Rhymes.* Illustrated by Dan Jones. London: Picture Lions, 1990.

ROSEN, MICHAEL. *We're Going on a Bear Hunt.* Illustrated by Helen Oxenbury. New York: Macmillan, 1989.

SEUSS, DR. *The Cat in the Hat.* Boston: Houghton Mifflin, 1957.

WATSON, CLYDE AND WENDY. *Father Fox's Pennyrhymes.* New York: Thomas Crowell, 1971.

Wordless Picture Books

ANNO. *Anno's Britain.* New York: Philomel, 1982.

BRIGGS, RAYMOND. *The Snowman.* New York: Random House, 1978.

GOODALL, JOHN. *Puss in Boots.* New York: Macmillan, 1990.

———. *The Story of a Castle.* New York: Macmillan, 1986.

MCCULLY, EMILY. *Picnic.* New York: Harper, 1984.

SPIER, PETER. *Dreams.* New York: Doubleday, 1986.

———. *Rain.* New York: Doubleday, 1982.

Poetry Picture Books and Illustrated Collections

ADOFF, ARNOLD. *Chocolate Dreams.* Illustrated by Turi MacCombie. New York: Lothrop, Lee & Shepard, 1989 (innovative word patterns/configurations).

———. *Sports Pages.* Illustrated by Steve Kuzma. New York: Harper, 1986.

BRUCHAC, JOSEPH, AND LONDON, JONATHAN. *Thirteen Moons on Turtle's Back: A Native American Year of Moons.* Illustrated by Thomas Locker. New York: Philomel, 1992.

FEELINGS, TOM, ANTHOLOGIST AND ARTIST. *Soul Looks Back in Wonder.* New York: Dial, 1993 (African-American ethnicity, lyric voices; thirteen distinguished poets focus on African-American history and aesthetics).

GERRARD, ROY. *Sir Cedric.* New York: Farrar, Straus and Giroux, 1984 (narrative form).

GREENFIELD, ELOISE. *Honey, I Love and Other Love Poems.* Illustrated by Diane and Leo Dillon. New York: Thomas Y. Crowell, 1978 (African-American ethnicity, lyric form).

———. *Nathaniel Talking.* Illustrated by Jan Spivey Gilchrist. New York: Black Butterfly Children's Books, 1988 (African-American ethnicity, reflective mood).

———. *Night on Neighborhood Street.* Illustrated by Jan Spivey Gilchrist. New York: Dial, 1991 (African-American ethnicity, reflective mood).

HUCK, CHARLOTTE. *Secret Places.* Illustrated by Lindsay George. New York: Greenwillow, 1993 (lyric form).

LEAR, EDWARD. *The Scroobious Pip.* Illustrated by Nancy Ekholm Burkert. New York: Harper, 1968 (nonsense form).

LITTLE, LESSIE JONES. *Children of Long Ago.* Illustrated by Jan Spivey Gilchrist. New York: Philomel, 1988 (African-American ethnicity, historial era).

MORA, PAT. *This Big Sky.* New York: Scholastic 1998 (Mexican American and Native American life in the Southwest; animals, nature, people; writing poetry; lyric and narrative voices)

MYERS, WALTER DEAN. *Harlem.* Illustrated by Christopher Myers. New York: Scholastic, 1997 (African-American ethnicity, lyric voices).

NIKOLA-LISA, W. *Night Is Coming.* Illustrated by Jamichael Henterly. New York: Dutton, 1991 (reflective, sensitive mood).

O'NEILL, MARY. *Hailstones and Halibut Bones.* Illustrated by John Wallner. New York: Doubleday, 1989 (rprt. 1961) (reflective mood; lyric poetry).

PLATH, SYLVIA. *The Bed Book.* Illustrated by Emily Arnold McCully. New York: Harper, 1976 (nonsense, humor, lyrical form).

POMERANTZ, CHARLOTTE. *The Tamarindo Puppy and Other Poems.* Illustrated by Byron Barton. New York: Mulberry Books, 1980 (Hispanic ethnicity).

PRELUTSKY, JACK. *The Random House Book of Poetry for Children.* Illustrated by Arnold Lobel. New York: Random House, 1983 (variety of forms, moods, cultures).

———. *The Terrible Tiger.* Illustrated by Arnold Lobel. New York: Macmillan, 1970 (narrative form).

RYLANT, CYNTHIA. *When I Was Young in the Mountains.* Illustrated by Diane Goode. New York: E. P. Dutton, 1982 (nostalgic mood, lyrical prose).

SILVERSTEIN, SHEL. *A Light in the Attic.* New York: HarperCollins, 1981 (nonsense verse).

SILVERSTEIN, SHEL. *Where the Sidewalk Ends.* New York: HarperCollins, 1974 (nonsense form, humor).

THOMAS, JOYCE CAROL. *Brown Honey in Broomwheat Tea.* Illustrated by Floyd Cooper. New York: HarperCollins, 1993 (African-American ethnicity and focus; sensitive, quiet mood; lyric voice).

———. *Gingergread Days.* Illustrated by Floyd Cooper. New York: HarperCollins, 1995 (African-American ethnicity and focus; sensitive, quiet mood; lyric voice).

VIORST, JUDITH. *If I Were in Charge of the World.* Illustrated by Lynne Cherry. New York: Macmillan, 1981 (humorous form, sensitive mood).

WILLARD, NANCY. *A Visit To William Blake's Inn.* Illustrated by Alice and Martin Provensen. New York: Harcourt, 1981 (historical background, lyric form).

ZOLOTOW, CHARLOTTE. *River Winding.* Illustrated by Kazue Mizumura. New York: Thomas Y. Crowell, 1978 (sensitive, quiet mood; lyric voice).

Folklore Picture Books and Collections

Fables

BENNETT, CHARLES H., ILLUSTRATOR. *Aesop's Fables.* London: Bracken Books, 1986.

HOLDER, HEIDI. *Aesop's Fables.* New York: Macmillan, 1981.

SOPKO, EUGEN, ILLUSTRATOR. *Aesop's The Miller, His Son and Their Donkey.* London: North-South Books, 1981.

ZWERGER, LISBETH, ILLUSTRATOR. *Aesop's Fables.* Saxonville, MA: Picture Book Studio, 1989.

African-American Folk Tales

HAMILTON, VIRGINIA. *Her Stories.* New York: Scholastic, 1995.

———. *The People Could Fly.* Illustrated by Leo and Diane Dillon. New York: Knopf, 1985.

———. *A Ring of Tricksters.* Illustrated by Barry Moser. New York: Scholastic, 1997.

LESTER, JULIUS. *Black Folktales.* Illustrated by Tom Feelings. New York: Grove Press, 1969.

MCKISSACK, PATRICIA. *The Dark-Thirty: Southern Tales of the Supernatural.* Illustrated by Brian Pinkney. New York: Knopf, 1992.

SANFIELD, STEVE. *The Adventures of High John the Conqueror.* Illustrated by John Ward. New York: Dell, 1989.

Appalachian Folk Tales

CHASE, RICHARD. *Grandfather Tales: American-English Folk Tales Selected and Edited by Richard Chase.* Illustrated by Berkeley Williams, Jr. Boston: Houghton Mifflin, 1948.

HALEY, GAIL. *Jack and the Bean Tree.* New York: Crown, 1986.

———. *Jack and the Fire Dragon.* New York: Crown, 1988.

Asian Folk Tales

AI-LING LOUIE, RETELLER. *Yeh-Shen: A Cinderella Story from China.* Illustrated by Ed Young. New York: Philomel, 1982.

FOREMAN, MICHAEL. *Monkey and the Three Wizards.* Translated by Peter Harris. Scarsdale, NY: Bradbury Press, 1976.

MOSEL, ARLENE. *The Funny Little Woman.* Illustrations by Blair Lent. New York: E. P. Dutton, 1972.

PATERSON, KATHERINE. *The Tale of the Mandarin Ducks.* Illustrations by Leo and Diane Dillon. New York: Dutton, 1990.

ROBERTS, MOSS, TRANSLATOR AND EDITOR. *Chinese Fairy Tales and Fantasies.* New York: Pantheon, 1979.

YAGAWA, SUMIKO. *The Crane Wife.* Translated by Katherine Paterson; Illustrated by Suekichi Akaba. New York: Morrow, 1981.

YEP, LAURENCE. *The Rainbow People.* Illustrated by David Wiesner. New York: Harper Collins, 1989.

YOUNG, ED. *Lon Po Po: A Red Riding Hood Story from China.* New York: Scholastic, 1989.

British Folk Tales

BRIGGS, KATHERINE. *Abbey Lubbers, Banshees and Boggarts.* Illustrated by Yvonne Gilbert. New York: Pantheon, 1979.

———. *British Folktales.* London: Routledge, 1977.

DE LA MARE, WALTER, RETELLER. *Molly Whuppie.* Illustrated by Errol Le Cain. London: Faber and Faber, 1983.

GALDONE, PAUL, RETELLER AND ILLUSTRATOR. *The Three Little Pigs.* New York: Clarion, 1970.

JACOBS, JOSEPH, COLLECTOR. *Celtic Fairy Tales.* Illustrated by Victor Ambrus. London: The Bodley Head, 1970.

———. *Tattercoats.* Illustrated by Margot Tomes. New York: G. P. Putnam's Sons, 1989.

SCIESZKA, JON. *The True Story of the 3 Little Pigs!* Illustrated by Lane Smith. New York: Viking Kestrel, 1989 (postmodernist picture book; folk tale rewrite).

"The Three Bears" in Story Collections

BRIGGS, KATHERINE. "The Three Bears" by Joseph Cundall in *British Folktales.* New York: Pantheon, 1970. (Originally published in Cundall's *A Treasury of Pleasure Books for Young People,* 1856; visitor to the bears' house is a little girl called Silver Locks.)

JACOBS, JOSEPHS. "The Story of the Three Bears," in *English Fairy Tales* (1890). New York: Puffin, 1968. (Replicates a version of the story attributed to Robert Southey and originally published in *The Doctor,* 1837, then again in 1890. Visitor to the bears' house is a little old woman.)

———. "Scrapfoot" in *More English Fairy Tales* (1894). New York: Puffin, 1968. (Visitor to the bears' house is a fox. Early version from the worldwide Bear and Fox animal tales.)

OPIE, IONA AND PETER. "The Story of the Three Bears" in *The Classic Fairy Tales.* New York: Oxford University Press, 1974. (Text taken from Robert Southey's *The Doctor,* 1837; visitor is a little old woman. Visitor becomes a little girl called Golden Hair in *Aunt Friendly's Nursery Book,* 1868.)

Modern "Three Bears" Picture Books (visitor to the Bears' house is a little girl, Goldilocks)

BRETT, JAN. *Goldilocks and the Three Bears.* New York: Dodd, Mead, 1987.

CAULEY, LORINDA. *Goldilocks and the Three Bears.* New York: Putnam's, 1981.

GALDONE, PAUL. *The Three Bears.* New York: Scholastic, 1972.

MARSHALL, JAMES. *Goldilocks and the Three Bears.* New York: Dial, 1988.

ROJANKOVSKY, F. *The Three Bears.* Racine, WS: Western Publishing, 1948.
ROSS, TONY. *Goldilocks and the Three Bears.* London: Andersen Press, 1976.
TURKLE, BRINTON. *Deep in the Forest.* New York: Dutton, 1976.
WATTS, BERNADETTE. *Goldilocks and the Three Bears.* North-South Books, 1988.

Native-American Folk Tales

BRUCHAC, JOSEPH. *Flying with the Eagle, Racing the Great Bear: Stories from Native North America.* New York: BridgeWater Books, 1993.
———. *The Girl Who Married the Moon: Tales from Native North America.* New York: BridgeWater Books, 1994.
HARRIS, CHRISTIE. *The Trouble with Princesses.* Toronto: McClelland and Stewart, 1980.

Worldwide Folk Tales (different versions, retellings, and illustrators of famous tales)

Cinderella (lost slipper variant—glass slipper of Perrault's *Cendrillon,* 1697, or gold, silver, or cloth slippers or sandals)

BROWN, MARCIA, TRANSLATOR AND ILLUSTRATOR. *Cinderella.* New York: Scribner's, 1954 (glass).
CLIMO, SHIRLEY. *The Egyptian Cinderella.* Illustrated by Ruth Heller. New York: Harper, 1989 (golden sandal).
GALDONE, PAUL, ILLUSTRATOR. *Cinderella.* New York: McGraw-Hill, 1978 (glass).
HOGROGIAN, NONNY, ILLUSTRATOR. *Cinderella* (from the Brothers Grimm). New York: Greenwillow, 1981 (silver slipper).
INNOCENTI, ROBERTO. *Cinderella.* Mankato, MN: Creative Education, 1983 (glass).
KARLIN, BARBARA. *Cinderella.* Illustrated by James Marshall. Boston: Little, Brown, 1989 (glass).
LE CAIN, ERROL. *Cinderella.* Scarsdale, NY: Bradbury, 1973 (glass).
LOUIE, AI-LING, RETELLER. *Yeh-Shen: A Cinderella Story from China.* Illustrated by Ed Young. New York: Philomel, 1982 (golden slipper).
SAN SOUCI, ROBERT, ADAPTER. *Cendrillon: A Caribbean Cinderella.* Illustrated by Brian Pinkney. New York: Simon, 1998 (pink cloth slipper).

Red Riding Hood (based on variants from different parts of the world)

BROTHERS GRIMM. *Little Red Cap.* Translated by Elizabeth Crawford. Illustrated by Lisbeth Zwerger. Natick, MA: Picture Book Studio, 1983 (German).
GOODALL, JOHN. *Little Red Riding Hood.* New York: Macmillan, 1988 (German).
HAMILTON, VIRGINIA. "A Wolf and Little Daughter" in *The People Could Fly.* Illustrated by Leo and Diane Dillon. New York: Knopf, 1985 (African American).
HYMAN, TRINA SCHART, RETELLER AND ILLUSTRATOR. *Little Red Riding Hood, by the Brothers Grimm.* New York: Holiday House, 1983 (German).
MARSHALL, JAMES, RETELLER AND ILLUSTRATOR. *Red Riding Hood.* New York: Dial, 1987 (German).
ROSS, TONY, RETELLER AND ILLUSTRATOR. *Little Red Riding Hood.* New York: Penguin, 1978 (modern recreation).
YOUNG, ED. *Lon Po Po: A Red Riding Hood Story from China.* New York: Scholastic, 1989 (China).

Snow White

CALVINO, ITALO, COLLECTOR AND RETELLER. "Bella Venezia" in *Italian Folktales.* Translated by George Martin. New York: Harcourt, 1980.
GÄG, WANDA. *Snow White and the Seven Dwarfs.* New York: Coward-McCann, 1938.
GRIMM, JACOB. *Snow-White and the Seven Dwarfs.* Translated by Randall Jarrell. Illustrated by Nancy Ekholm Burkert. New York: Farrar, Straus and Giroux, 1972 (German).

———. *Snow White and the Seven Dwarfs.* Illustrated by Wanda Gäg. New York: Coward-McCann, 1938.

———. *Snow White.* Translated by Paul Heins. Illustrated by Trina Schart Hyman. Boston: Little, Brown, 1974 (German).

———. *Snow White.* Illustrated by Bernadette Watts. London: North-South Books, 1983 (German).

PUSHKIN, A. *The Tale of the Dead Princess and the Seven Knights.* Translated from the Russian by Peter Tempest. Illustrated by V. Konashevich. Moscow: Raduga Publishers, 1984 (Russian).

Legends

BIERHORST, JOHN. *The Ring in the Prairie: A Shawnee Legend.* Illustrated by Leo and Diane Dillon. New York: Dial, 1970.

DOMINIC, GLORIA. *First Woman and the Strawberry; A Cherokee Legend.* Illustrated by Charles Reasoner. New York, Troll, 1998.

FRITZ, JEAN. *The Good Giants and the Bad Pukwudgies.* Illustrated by Tomie de Paola. New York: Putnam, 1982 (Wampanoag Indians, Massachusetts).

HALEY, GAIL. *The Green Man.* New York: Charles Scribner's Sons, 1979 (British Isles).

HODGES, MARGARET. *Saint George and the Dragon.* Illustrated by Trina Schart Hyman. Boston: Little, Brown, 1984 (British Isles).

KEEPING, CHARLES. *Beowulf.* Illustrated by Kevin Crossley-Holland. Oxford, England: Oxford University Press, 1982 (British).

LEE, JEANNE. *The Song of Mulan.* Arden NC: FrontStreet, 1995.

LESTER, JULIUS. *John Henry.* Illustrated by Jerry Pinkney. New York: Dial, 1994 (African American).

MILES, BERNARD. *Robin Hood: His Life and Legend.* Illustrated by Victor Ambrus. New York: Hamlyn, 1979.

OSBORNE, MARY POPE. *Mermaid Tales from Around the World.* Illustrated by Troy Howell. New York: Scholastic, 1993.

PYLE, HOWARD. *The Merry Adventures of Robin Hood.* New York: New American Library/Signet, 1986 (rpt. 1883).

———. *The Story of King Arthur and His Knights.* New York: New American Library/Signet, 1986 (rpt. 1903).

SAN SOUCI, ROBERT. *Fa Mulan; The Story of a Woman Warrior.* Illustrated by Jean and Mou-sien Tseng. New York: Hyperion, 1998.

SPIER, PETER. *The Legend of New Amsterdam.* New York: Doubleday, 1979.

STEPTOE, JOHN. *The Story of Jumping Mouse.* New York: Mulberry Books, 1984 (Great Plains Indians).

Myths

AARDEMA, VERNA. *Why Mosquitoes Buzz in People's Ears.* Illustrations by Leo and Diane Dillon. New York: Dial, 1975 (African).

D'AULAIRE, INGRI AND EDGAR. *D'Aulaires' Book of Greek Myths.* Garden City, NY: Doubleday, 1962.

———. *D'Aulaires' Norse Gods and Giants.* Garden City, NY: Doubleday, 1967.

ERDOES, RICHARD, AND ORTIZ, ALFONSO. *American Indian Myths and Legends.* New York: Pantheon, 1984.

GOBLE, PAUL. *Star Boy.* New York: Macmillan, 1983 (Native American).

HAMILTON, VIRGINIA. *In the Beginning: Creation Stories from Around the World.* Illustrated by Barry Moser. New York: Harcourt, 1988.

MCDERMOTT, GERALD. *Arrow to the Sun: A Pueblo Indian Tale.* New York: Viking, 1974.

MARRIOTT, ALICE, AND RACHLIN, CAROL. *American Indian Mythology.* New York: Crown, 1968.

Biblical Stories

Noah's Ark (different illustrators)

DELESSERT, ETIENNE. *The Endless Party.* Oxford, England: Oxford University Press, 1980.

ELBORN, ANDREW, AND GANTSCHEV, IVAN. *Noah and the Ark and the Animals.* Natick, MA: Picture Book Studio, 1984.

SPIER, PETER. *Noah's Ark.* Garden City, NY: Doubleday, 1977.

WILDSMITH, BRIAN. *Professor Noah's Spaceship.* Oxford, England: Oxford University Press, 1980.

Literary Fairy Tales

ANDERSEN, HANS CHRISTIAN. *Hans Andersen's Fairy Tales.* Translated by Naomi Lewis. Illustrated by Philip Gough. New York: Viking Penguin, 1981 (story collection).

HALEY, GAIL. *Birdsong.* New York: Crown, 1984 (picture book).

———. *Go Away, Stay Away.* New York: Charles Scribner's Sons, 1977 (picture book).

HAMILTON, VIRGINIA. *The All Jahdu Storybook.* Illustrated by Barry Moser. San Diego: Harcourt Brace, 1991 (story collection).

LEVINE, GAIL CARSON. *Ella Enchanted.* New York: HarperCollins, 1997 (novel).

MAYER, MARIANNA, RETELLER. *Beauty and the Beast.* Illustrated by Mercer Mayer. New York: Macmillan, 1978 (picture book).

MCKINLEY, ROBIN. *Beauty.* New York: Harper and Row, 1978 (novel).

PERRAULT, CHARLES. *Tales from Perrault.* Translated by Ann Lawrence. New York: Oxford University Press, 1988.

TAN, AMY. *The Chinese Siamese Cat.* Illustrated by Gretchen Schields. New York: Macmillan, 1994 (picture book).

YOLEN, JANE. *The Hundredth Dove and Other Tales.* Illustrated by David Palladini. New York: Crowell, 1977 (story collection).

———. *The Moon Ribbon and Other Tales.* Illustrated by David Palladini. New York: Crowell, 1976 (story collection).

Chapter 4

Exploring Conventional and Unconventional Books

Topics in This Chapter:

- Life and literary conventions
- Traditional literary practices
- Conventions and social attitudes
- Nontraditional literary structures, styles, and subjects
- Multicultural literature: Themes and inscribing processes

"What sort of people live about here?"
"In that direction," the Cat said, waving its right paw round, "lives a Hatter; and in that direction," waving the other paw, "lives a March Hare. Visit either you like: they're both mad."
"But I don't want to go among mad people," Alice remarked.
"Oh, you can't help that," said the Cat, "we're all mad here. I'm mad, you're mad."
"How do you know I'm mad?" said Alice.
"You must be," said the cat, "or you wouldn't have come here."

"Pig and Pepper" in Alice's Adventures in Wonderland, 1865
—Lewis Carroll

We have been discussing genre as both a literary concept and a social construction. By examining Caldecott and Newbery Awards, we saw how books can be placed into various genre categories, at least from the reader's point of view. Now we want to focus more closely on books that elude categories and labels because award-winning authors and illustrators are so inventive—and at times so controversial as a result of their inventiveness. First, we will examine the concept of *conventions* as it relates to the world of children's books and to life.

LIFE AND LITERARY CONVENTIONS

The word *convention* might seem unfamiliar at first glance, but we face conventions everywhere. Each time we must make a decision about behavior, dress, or speech "codes," we are dealing with habits or practices that have turned into customs or traditions. When these practices become something we do unthinkingly, because it is expected—and because breaking with these practices would disrupt the "normal" scheme of things—we call them *conventions*. Should we wear just anything to a fancy restaurant, talk in the library, leave a tip—or leave nothing, shrug off—or speak out against—sexual harassment or ethnic slurs? What are the rules we choose to follow, the practices we deem acceptable? Where have we decided to draw the lines—or to cross them even if it seems "mad" to do so?

Life conventions flow easily into the literary world. In the 1940s and 1950s, movies could show a male and female in bed only if the girl kept one foot on the floor, as the song "Girl Meets Boy" from Andrew Lloyd Webber's musical *Sunset Blvd.* tells us. Other "ground rules" for screenwriters, according to Joe and Betty in this play, were that good guys don't break the law, no one mentions a Communist, and you can't take a black friend out for dinner. All of these rules were based upon the "life rules" Americans (or at least some Americans) were living by in this era.

The "fallen" woman always came to death or destruction in the adult fictional world of centuries past. Thus, in children's books, Little Red Riding Hood was told to stay on the beaten path; when she did not—in Perrault's version of 1697—the wolf consumed her. Later, in the Grimm version of 1812–22, this convention reversed itself: A woodcutter who skinned the wolf saved Red Riding Hood. Our culture continues to prefer the Grimm version, revealing the desire to protect children from predatory behavior.

Today we are also more tolerant of challenging or freethinking females. In earlier days, even healthy curiosity met with a stern lesson against trespassing, being nosy, or prying. This convention (punishing females who had bad manners) propelled the old English story, "Goldilocks and the Three Bears," into popularity and kept it alive for many years.

Various tellers, including the prominent English poet Robert Southey in 1837, recorded the Goldilocks story in different ways or with different characters as the intruder. First it was a fox who wandered into the three bears' house; then it was an old, silver-haired lady; later, a little silver-haired girl; and finally, the now-famous Goldilocks. In each version, the trespasser performed the same actions: tasted the porridge, tried out the chairs and beds, then ran away when the bears returned to howl their complaints and frighten the stranger away.

In earliest stories, the bears were male—not the best situation for a trespassing female child. Later they became a bear *family.* Thus, the story functioned first as a cautionary tale for female listeners. Later, it served as a vehicle for correcting the child's bad—intrusive—manners. In either case, the lesson was that incautious or overly curious females must eventually run for their lives.

Conventions die hard; in fact, most of the time, they do not die—they linger on. Eventually they may fade away, or people may question and debate them. Finally, if no one takes them seriously, we see them spoofed in cartoons and jokes. James Marshall produces a humorous reversal of the Goldilocks tale. In his *Goldilocks and the Three Bears* (Dial, 1988), a Caldecott Honor book, he draws a

From *Goldilocks and the Three Bears* (Dial, 1988) by James Marshall.

stuffy, Victorian bear family who must endure the intrusion of a plump, self-assured, and jovial little girl. This Goldilocks is "one of those naughty little girls who do exactly as they please," says Marshall, with a wink instead of a shudder. He sends her off into a forest filled with thumb-tacked signs: "Danger!" "Very Risky!" "Turn Back"; "Go the Other Way"; "Not a Good Idea."

At the bears' house, Goldilocks gags on Papa Bear's hot cereal: " 'Patooie!' cried Goldilocks. And she spat it out." Kicking back in Baby Bear's chair, she gorges on porridge before breaking his rocker and borrowing his bed. A shivering Goldilocks wakes up to three very cold stares and goes tumbling out the window, never to return. Marshall's Goldilocks is irrepressible and irreverent at the beginning; dazed and glum at the end. However, we know she will recover; if she does not visit the bears again, we can well imagine her getting into mischief elsewhere.

In a postmodern world filled with multiple perspectives about moral and social codes, the idea of stay-on-the-path rules may seem hopelessly out of date. Even the word *convention* may seem a bit dry and dusty to us now, bringing to mind pictures of long-ago children in Kate Greenaway dresses and Little Lord Fauntleroy suits.

But knowing the conventions is still important. It is the unconventional, mind-expanding books that win awards and gain more exposure in classrooms and libraries. So authors must be familiar with accepted practices—or conventions—if they are to flaunt, subvert, or overturn them. Readers must be familiar with them, too, if they are to appreciate the innovative techniques authors use. We will be taking a close look at conventions to learn more about how writers either accept or dismiss them as they produce the notable and often iconoclastic books of their times.

Surprise is a key word to understanding conventions. Popular books of the moment often give us what we expect; even more popular books in the long run (the ones that have staying power) give us the unpredictable. They jolt us into seeing more, seeing differently, or seeing what we did not expect. But if the jolt is *too* far from the familiar (too different, too unconventional), the book may suffer at the hands of protective (or overprotective) adults. Time has to elapse before a book with such strikingly new ideas reaches the child audience.

Many of Maurice Sendak's books fall into this ahead-of-their-time category. Some critics deem Sendak's very unconventional books too complex, too frightening, too risky, too revealing, or even too depressing for the child audience. Whereas breaking conventions may mean producing an inventive, award-winning book, it can also mean controversy, even censorship. Battles arising from changing conventions trigger major issues in the field of children's literature, and Sendak's books have supplied grist for many of the major controversies of the past three decades.

Should children meet large, ugly, perhaps even scary creatures in children's books (*Where the Wild Things Are,* Harper, 1963)? Should they see frontal nudity of a male child in children's books (*In the Night Kitchen,* Harper, 1970)? Should disassociated, complex, symbolic images appear in a children's book (*Outside Over There,* Harper, 1981)? What about complex, symbolic images *plus* a child's death *plus* images of the Holocaust in a picture book that will reach younger children (*Dear Mili,* Farrar, 1988)? And what about a mixture of AIDS, Auschwitz, same-sex adoption, universal greed, and children as victims in a children's picture book? Is this too much to "dump" on children (*We Are All in the Dumps with Jack and Guy,* Harper, 1993)?

Adults who consult children before dismissing Sendak's books are often pleasantly surprised. English critic and educator Jane Doonan (1994) says that children ages ten to fourteen were not disturbed by *We Are All in the Dumps:*

> [They] have drawn upon what they have seen on television . . . about kids in Rio de Janeiro living in boxes, about famine victims in Ethiopia and Somalia, and have strung webs between rye, dough, bread, money, aid to the Third World, AIDS, a hungry black child, and cardboard cities. They interpret the smoke as deadly air pollution, which of course it is. In general terms Sendak is not showing them anything they don't already know about (page 167).

In this chapter, we will examine the widely accepted literary practices first. Next, we will examine conventions that arise from social structures of gender, class, and culture. Then we will examine literary structures, styles, and subjects of books as they break away from conventional molds. Finally, we will examine one important subject in children's books these days—multiculturalism.

INVESTIGATIONS: Exploring Maurice Sendak's Unconventional Books

Make a study of Maurice Sendak's picture books. First read them yourself and jot down your responses. See if you find them too controversial for children. Then share some of these books with children to learn about what *they* see. Discover what children can teach you about children's books.

Writers and artists often rely on accepted practices and devices that audiences have learned to expect; this allows readers to become involved in the story more quickly and easily. The difference between conventional and unconventional authors is that one includes a great deal that readers already know and understand—and sticks to that—and the other plays with the familiar to produce ideas that are unusual, unfamiliar, unique, and sometimes even threatening to what readers know and understand. Unconventional books are often mind stretching because they enable readers to see in new ways—even if readers find the new views complex or frightening.

In this section, we will look at the traditional practices as a foundation for the more nontraditional. We will begin with the simplest devices to detect in stories—names, settings, and genres. Then we will examine one of the most important devices in terms of literacy learning—the child-as-reader convention.

Literary Devices: Names

Naming a character to represent a particular trait has always been a useful literary device. In 1789, Isaiah Thomas named his miserly character in *The Juvenile Biographer* Master Simon Lovepenny and his bookworm, Jemmy Studious. In the next century, Charles Dickens used this device extensively (Scrooge in *The Christmas Carol* is a particularly famous miser), and Beatrix Potter adopted the same convention. Consider the names she chose for her characters—Jemima Puddleduck, Mrs. Tiggy-Winkle, Timmy Tiptoes, and the Flopsy Bunnies, to name a few—and the way they produce sharp mental images of characters.

Names are a quick and easy way to fill out the "picture" for readers, and creative writers use this device to produce deeper insight into characters, setting, plot, and theme. Why does Susan Cooper name her strong, young questing character Will in the *Dark is Rising* sequence (Atheneum, 1966–77)? Why does Virginia Hamilton name her strong, female quest figure Justice in the Dustland trilogy (Greenwillow, 1981)? Consider how much will power Cooper's character must have to fulfill his quest. Consider how often Hamilton's character is called upon to exert leadership and to weigh right and wrong in her mission.

INVESTIGATIONS: Exploring the Naming Convention

The literary device of naming characters is fascinating to study. Try to discover whether names denote special character traits in the children's books you are reading. Make a list of your findings and share your insights with others.

Literary Devices: Settings

Placing characters in settings that evoke ready-made responses is another literary device writers and artists often use. Victorian writers for adults often set orphans in large, gothic mansions on the moors or in rat-infested attics of London townhouses to create a mood of terror, pity, or suspense, and we see Frances Burnett adopting this same convention in both *A Secret Garden* and *A Little Princess.* Ghost stories also feature old, creepy, creaking houses as a device to create spine-chilling scenes. Some houses, however, are unforgettable as the author builds an entire story around them. Consider Virginia Hamilton's *The House of Dies Drear* (Macmillan, 1968). In this story, a large house in Ohio, once an Underground Railroad "station," has long, dark tunnels and walls that move and open up to disclose passages where slaves once hid.

C. S. Lewis's Narnia books and Susan Cooper's *Dark is Rising* sequence use the device of a magical passageway that allows children to move in and out of mythic times and places. In the Narnia stories, the children pass into a world peopled with fawns, witches, and dwarves. In Cooper's *Over Sea, Under Stone* (Harcourt, 1966), the child characters explore an old house on the seacoast of Cornwall and find a magical map from King Arthur's day behind an old-fashioned wardrobe (a free-standing closet). In the later books in Cooper's sequence, the children enter older, mythic worlds through enchanted doors carved in rocky hills and mountains.

Both of these writers use these conventional devices of setting to ease child readers into what has become a conventional plot pattern for some books: A character passes between his or her own time and place and past or future worlds. Usually these child characters—or time travelers—mingle with people or creatures of myth, legend, or history to solve problems and mysteries of the past or to have important adventures in enchanted worlds.

Literary Devices: Genres

English children's novelist Edith Nesbit first used the literary device of time travel in *The Story of the Amulet* (1906). Eventually this device became so popular with writers that a new genre—the time slip fantasy—began to flourish. Now we find examples of the device (and the genre based on this device) everywhere. From Canada comes Janet Lunn's Civil War time fantasy, *The Root Cellar* (Penguin, 1981). From the United States come Nancy Bond's *A String in the Harp* (Atheneum, 1976), a legendary time fantasy set in Wales; Eleanor Cameron's *The Court of the Stone Children* (Penguin, 1973), a historical time fantasy set in present-day California and in France during the Revolution; Virginia Hamilton's *Justice and Her Brothers, Dustland,* and *The Gathering* (Greenwillow, 1981), mythic time fantasies involving interplanetary travel; and Jane Yolen's *The Devil's Arithmetic* (Penguin, 1988), a historical time fantasy about the Holocaust. From Australia comes Ruth Park's *Playing Beatie Bow* (Penguin, 1980), which shifts back to Victorian days in Sydney,

INVESTIGATIONS: Exploring Time Travel Fantasy

Explore a time fantasy from the list in this section. Try to determine what makes this genre so popular among writers of many different times and places. Why have British writers been so attracted to this genre? Were they more aware of layers of historical and legendary time for their characters to explore? Read some American time fantasies and investigate how authors in the New World find ways for their characters to travel in time.

and Patricia Wrightson's inventive blendings of time and folk fantasy in *The Nargun and the Stars* (Macmillan, 1974) and *Balyet* (Macmillan, 1989).

From England there are too many examples to count. Philippa Pearce's *Tom's Midnight Garden* (Oxford, 1958) is one of the most famous, having won the Carnegie Award (England's "twin" to the Newbery). C. S. Lewis's mythic worlds and Susan Cooper's legendary time-shifts are even better known. But many of England's most distinguished children's authors—Alan Garner, L. M. Boston, Penelope Farmer, Penelope Lively, William Mayne, and Jill Paton Walsh—have created intriguing time fantasies; and Dick King-Smith produced an inventive genre blend of talking-doll story and time fantasy in *Lady Daisy* (Viking, 1992).

Sometimes literary practices form the basis for new genres. Humanized animals in Aesop's fables set the stage for Joel Chandler Harris and Beatrix Potter to create their own famous animal fantasies featuring Brer Rabbit and Peter Rabbit. The convention of humanized toys arose in similar ways. In 1846, an English writer named R. H. Horne produced a talking doll as a memorable character for a book entitled *Memoirs of a London Doll;* today the talking-doll fantasy story is a staple of children's literature. Humanized animal toys, for example, A. A. Milne's *Winnie the Pooh* (1926), have also become a popular and effective device for enticing children into books.

Authors also invite young readers into books by creating stories in which child characters are strongly immersed in the literacy process as readers, writers, or storytellers. Living through the book experience with these characters, readers become engaged in literacy processes as well. Of course, children's authors do not usually set out with any intent to indoctrinate children about reading or writing. Their interest in connecting literature to literacy seems to emerge naturally; often they were deeply engaged readers and writers as children, and as adults, they create stories that reflect these literacy experiences.

The Child-as-Reader Convention

Authors using the child-as-reader (or literacy in literature) convention may not realize that their fictional children stand in a long line of characters learning and growing as they move toward adulthood. In England, such books were called Apprenticeship Novels; in Germany, they were categorized as a *Bildungsroman.* (*Bild* means portrait; *ung* means development, growth, or education; *roman* means novel.) When the young person was an artist or writer, the form was called a *Kunstlerroman* (*Kunst* means art.) More recently, in America, these books have been called coming-of-age novels.

Whatever the time or place, the story focuses on the development of a young person. Traditionally such stories focused on a character—usually a male—who was learning about the world, and a great deal of this learning came from reading.

Nineteenth-Century Readers and Writers

Literature has always provided a fundamental way for adolescent and young adult characters to think about the world, but in the nineteenth century, before the advent of film and television, reading and literature were especially important. Learning about the world through literature was the major theme of many nineteenth-century novels, and this convention, in which a young person was immersed in books, eventually dribbled down into children's books. Louisa Alcott often used the child-as-reader (and writer) convention, Jo is an aspiring writer, and she and her sisters are also readers; they are quite familiar with John Bunyan's *Pilgrim's Progress* (1678), and Jo is reading Charlotte Yonge's *The Heir of Redcliffe* (1853), an English novel that crossed the ocean in Alcott's day. Frances Burnett used this convention too; both Mary Lennox of *The Secret Garden* and Sara Crewe are avid readers. Sara is also an accomplished storyteller.

Ruth Sawyer, a famous storyteller in her own day, used the child-as-reader convention in her 1937 Newbery winner, *Roller Skates* (Penguin, 1936). This autobiographical novel is set in the same era as Burnett's *A Little Princess,* the 1890s, but it takes place in Sawyer's own New York City. Sawyer, as narrator, tells the story of ten-year-old Lucinda, and Lucinda's diary entries appear at the end of each chapter. Side by side, the narrator's and the child writer's voices tell the story. We see from a distance what happened in great detail, and we also see (up close through her diary entries) how Lucinda felt about it all. Sawyer, as narrator, tells us about the books Lucinda is unpacking when her parents have gone away for a trip, leaving her with friends:

> She smoothed her copy of [Nathaniel Hawthorne's] *Tanglewood Tales* with a gold Pegasus riding over a crimson cover; she patted [Charles Kingley's] *Water Babies,* without pictures and a feckless binding that matched *The King of the Golden River* [by John Ruskin] and *Plutarch's Lives.* There was Hans Christian Andersen, with a frontispiece of Little Ida and her flowers [from "The Snow Queen"]. Every story Andersen had written was in the book; and Lucinda had read them all since her tenth birthday. Next came *Alice in Wonderland.* Secretly Lucinda laid her own claim to the adventures, so many times had she followed the White Rabbit down the hole, swum the pool of Alice's tears, read the labels and drunk from the two bottles, been invited by the Queen of Hearts to play croquet, with a flamingo for a mallet. Beside Alice, on the shelf, went *The Peterkin Papers* [by Lucretia Hales]

From *Roller Skates* (Penguin, 1936/1986) by Ruth Sawyer. Cover illustrations by Cheryl Harness.

> and next to that her beloved *Uncle Remus* [by Joel Chandler Harris], *Hans Brinker* [by Mary Mapes Dodge], *Jan of the Windmill* [by Juliana Horatia Ewing], *Robin Hood* [by Howard Pyle] and *Swiss Family Robinson* [by J. D. Wyss] . . . The last book she opened at random, as from long habit. It didn't matter where her fingers found a place in the story of Diamond, it was sure to catch her up and carry her off with him to the back of the North Wind [a reference to George Macdonald's *At the Back of the North Wind,* 1871]. (pages 20–21)

Sawyer presents an important survey of the books an upper-middle-class child might have read at the turn of the century. That night, when Lucinda writes in her diary, she does not mention any of the books Sawyer remembers so fondly. She merely says, "Being an orphan makes you feel elegant—like being Dick Whittington. Only I have no cat; and no bells rang for me when I rode up in Mr. Gilligan's Handsome Cab" (page 24). Her natural reference to this English folk story, "Dick Whittington and his Cat," reveals how reading fits so naturally into her life.

INVESTIGATIONS: Retracing the Nineteenth-Century Child Reader's Steps

Collect and examine some of the books Ruth Sawyer read as a child (or that her ten-year-old character Lucinda read). Step into Lucinda's shoes and discover what a late nineteenth-century, upper-middle-class child read.

Literate Animal Characters

Thirty-five years after Sawyer wrote her book, Robert O'Brien produced another Newbery winner, *Mrs. Frisby and the Rats of NIMH* (Atheneum, 1971), an animal fantasy that introduces rats who have taught themselves to read and write. The rats of NIMH (National Institute of Mental Health) escape a laboratory where they have been quartered for experimental reasons and where an electric floor shocks their feet if they leave their cages. As part of the experimental research, the rats have received injections to increase their intelligence to human proportions. When they escape, they find an uninhabited mansion with a book-lined study, and they begin to read and write, as Nicodemus the rat tells Mrs. Frisby, their mouse neighbor.

Eventually they must leave the estate, but when they do, the rats know much more than when they arrived: "The reading we did!" says Nicodemus, as they prepare to leave. "We knew very little about the world, you see, and we were curious" (page 159). They had learned about astronomy, biology, mathematics, music, art, and poetry. But what they liked best was history, which gave them ideas about how to live. Reading about rats, they discovered they were hated for stealing and valued for participating in scientific experiments.

Learning that, at one point in history, rats had organized themselves into admirable civilizations, the rats of NIMH decide to renew this promising side of their heritage. They make plans to begin all over again as admirable—and respectable—animals in a secluded area called Thorn Valley. Because they now see the futility of a life made too easy by stealing, they have advanced well ahead of humans, morally.

Along with reading, storytelling takes an important place in their literacy. After the rats leave the mansion, Mrs. Frisby tells her children the story Nicodemus has told her. The mice children learn how stories produce legends, history, and legendary heroes—like Justin, who has died in the rats' exodus, saving his rat-friend, Brutus.

Cross-Cultural Readers and Writers

Four years after O'Brien published his book, Laurence Yep produced *Dragonwings* (Harper, 1975), a Newbery Honor book. Yep's story is set in 1903, which presents an intriguing cross-cultural version of the child-as-reader convention. Moon Shadow, a Chinese immigrant in California, wrestles with several problems: the prejudice of his peers, a father obsessed with flying a rickety, home-made plane, and the rigors of learning a new language. Befriended by his neighbor, Miss Whitlaw, and her niece Robin, Moon Shadow soon learns English and teaches his new American friends a great deal, too.

Telling his friends stories his father has told him about dragons, Moon Shadow broadens their vision beyond the Euro-American literary tradition, which teaches that all dragons are evil. (In Chinese lore, dragons are both good and bad, he explains to them, and they can be huge—or as tiny as ants.) Later, Robin introduces Moon Shadow to her favorite author, E. Nesbit. Robin's aunt encourages Moon Shadow to write short paragraphs about dragons that she and Robin proofread together. He then composes longer stories about the dragons near his village back in China, "of their feuds and wars, of the love affairs between men and dragon maidens (who would take human form) and of the friendships that had helped" him (page 129).

Eventually, he tells them stories of his homeland—of "the waters of the Pearl River: thick and milky and colored a reddish yellow like the color of sunset distilled from the air," of a "stately junk, tottering its way upstream, slatted sails rising to meet the wind" (page 129). Miss Whitlaw is such an intent listener that Moon Shadow is convinced she was a Tang Woman in a former life. But the reader sees *why* she listens: Moon Shadow—and Lawrence Yep—are eloquent storytellers.

Another cross-cultural child-as-reader appears in *The Sunita Experiment* (Little, Brown, 1993) by Mitali Perkins. Sunita (like the author, Perkins) has East Indian grandparents, and she hears wonderful stories of her grandfather's childhood in India and of the courtship for his arranged marriage that she retells in her journal at school. Sunita is an emerging writer who imagines herself the heroine of a teen romance each time she sees or thinks about her boyfriend, Michael. One of her favorite books is Frances Hodgson Burnett's *The Secret Garden;* her favorite film is *Casablanca* (1942). Her teacher, Mr. Riley, helps her to become a better reader of both.

INVESTIGATIONS: The Child-as-Reader Convention

Collect and examine books that portray child characters as readers, writers, poets, and storytellers. Consider how the child's literacy process contributes to his or her emotional, social, and intellectual growth and how it is central to the important themes in the book. Then write about this subject in your journal, and share your impressions with others. To get started, see the end of this chapter for more books related to the child-as-reader convention.

After spending a week at school identifying cultural stereotypes in movies and videos, Sunita begins asking, "Didn't Sam [the black piano player in *Casablanca*] have a life of his own? Why did he have to call her [the white female character] Miss Ilsa when she just called him Sam? Where was Casablanca anyway? Wasn't it in Africa? Why were there no black Africans in the entire movie?" (pages 98–99). Even before Mr. Riley begins discussing classic children's books, Sunita frowns as she reads the passage in which Burnett's child character, Mary Lennox, reveals overt bigotry toward the natives of India. Soon Sunita is reading against the grain of Burnett's text as a critically conscious reader.

Class, culture, and ethnicity intersect in this unconventional, mind-stretching book. We see an old classic in new ways—through the eyes of a child with a diverse cultural background. At the same time, we see a child become more consciously aware of literature and the literacy process. Portraying a child character as a resistant reader and writer—one who is questioning the author's conscious or unconscious literary choices—Mitali Perkins helps child readers see how *they* can choose to be unconventional members of the wider literary world, too.

CONVENTIONS AND SOCIAL ATTITUDES

Conventional writers and artists often reflect what society—or what they as members of society—agrees to tolerate in regard to gender, class, or cultural differences. Unconventional writers and artists often question or resist prevailing social attitudes—and this resistance often emerges in subtle ways in their work.

Gender and Culture

Shirley Ernst (1995) studied Newbery and Caldecott books of the 1990s to see if current books were presenting images of girls taking chances, making important decisions, and taking charge of their own destinies—or if girls appeared to be supportive, nonassertive nurturers, depending on men for guidance and protection. She found a predominance of active male characters who exhibited problem-solving abilities. What were the female characters like?

In the four Newbery books Ernst examined, three male characters did not accept things the way they were; they took action to change things. The one female

INVESTIGATIONS: Reading for Cultural Inequities

Choose several books you have read, admired, and never questioned, just as Mitali Perkins's character Sunita never questioned the film *Casablanca* or Frances Burnett's *The Secret Garden* before Mr. Riley taught her to read critically. Reread these books, asking yourself if you can detect inequities of gender or class, or bigotry arising from ethnic or racial differences. If such examples occur, ask if the sexist, elitist, or bigoted character's feelings represent the author's own ideas, or if the author is simply using the character to make a point about sexism, classism, or racism. Do other characters challenge the character's bigoted words or actions, or do they let the bigotry go unrefuted? Write about this subject in your journal, and share your impressions with others.

protagonist, Summer in Cynthia Rylant's *Missing May* (Orchard, 1992), was "a follower" (page 73) who allowed others to make her decisions. Rosemary, the only important female child in Lowry's *The Giver* (Houghton, 1993) was, in the end, not up to the task of leadership. The majority of the Newbery Honor books also featured boys who were adventuresome, resourceful, and courageous.

The Caldecott books showed similar patterns. In Emily McCully's *Mirette on the High Wire* (Putnam, 1992), the female character (Mirette) was brave and persevering, but her bravery was important only because she helped a fearful male adult character successfully use *his* talents. Of the thirteen Caldecott Honor books, only two focused on female characters at all.

If we believe that children's books help to introduce readers to their future social roles, these facts will trouble us. Newbery and Caldecott books gain the attention and respect of critics, librarians, teachers, and parents; the values these books exhibit are often the ones society approves. Unless award-winning books are highly unconventional—as they sometimes are—the conventions they support are society's most ingrained values. These literary conventions can easily become *life models* for female readers, so child readers need to see books in which female characters find new ways to escape constricting life conventions.

Educator Susan Lehr discusses the problems both male and female writers still face as they try to decide "where women fit in" (page 202). When she began looking for strong images of female characters in children's books from earlier literature, she found many, but there was always a downside. George MacDonald's *The Princess and the Goblin* (1972) features a female of Victorian times who could enter a world of danger and solve problems, says Lehr, but who remains a princess on a pedestal. C. S. Lewis's *The Lion, the Witch and the Wardrobe* (1950) shows us a "strong, feisty, intelligent" female, but she is "forbidden to hold a sword in battle. She knew her place as a woman. Hers were the healing gifts" (page 199).

Madeleine L'Engle's *A Wrinkle in Time* (1962), the first in a three-part series, reveals a strong female; but by the end of the series, she has become "a domestic woman [a traditional wife], much more vulnerable and less willing to engage in battles" (page 200). This also happens with Jo of *Little Women* (1968) and Caddie of *Caddie Woodlawn* (1935).

Lloyd Alexander, in *The Castle of Llyr* (1966) and other books of the Prydain series, creates a feisty female, but one who is "stuck in a place with limited options"; Taran, the male character, fights the real battles. Susan Cooper's *Greenwitch* (1974) shows us Jane, the only female of the four children, "who completes the quest successfully," but the boys are the active, risk-taking participants of the adventure (pages 200–201).

From one perspective, authors have an opportunity to present strong females who are not sitting on pedestals, not merely healers, not retiring to blissful domesticity, not held back from the real battles, not deprived of physical adventures. From another perspective, writers might not be focusing on or even thinking about gender roles when they set out to tell a story. They are simply telling a story, not setting a political agenda.

Can we blame a writer who chooses to tell the story that is simply bubbling up from her mind? Can we blame the writer who is balancing a great many aspects of the story if she fails to focus on just one particular aspect—on gender? Are there times when writers have opportunities to portray strong females, and other times when they are obliged to be true to their personal imaginings? Where do we draw the lines, as we select—and critique—books, so that female children, growing into their own social roles, are not held back?

One solution is to study more closely what we are rewarding in children's books and to point out the lapses, as Ernst and Lehr are doing, so that child readers have different personal visions to draw from when they produce their own stories for the next generation. Another solution is for adult readers to tell writers what they themselves liked as children and what they find worthwhile in today's offerings. Lehr singles out Lloyd Alexander's *The Llyrian Adventure* (Dutton, 1986) as having a strong female child with no gender-related constrictions.

Deborah Stevenson (1997), assistant editor of *The Bulletin of the Center for Children's Books,* finds a new way to classify unconventional heroines. Alcott's Jo, she says, capitulated to the "Rules" in the end, as did Caddie Woodlawn. In fact, Stevenson describes a "Caddie Woodlawn syndrome, where girls' energy is really an adorable and completely safe sauciness" (page 657). She finds this syndrome alive and well today in recent books such as Karen Cushman's *Catherine, Called Birdy* (1994). Catherine is at first both "feisty" and "spunky," says Stevenson, two words readers use to describe heroines with the courage to "to be fierce in a world that understands they can be nothing of the kind" (page 657). (Later, Catherine also bends to the rules.) In these stories, "plucky" girls have limited power; they can be as feisty as they want because "ultimately it means nothing" Stevenson says (page 658). This pluckiness threatens no one; it leaves the status quo very much intact.

What we need, Stevenson says, are heroines who go beyond feistiness to "challenge the rules" (page 659). She cites Louise Fitzhugh's *Harriet the Spy* (Harper, 1964), in which the title character must learn to lie; Suzane Fisher Staples's *Shabanu* (Knopf, 1989) and *Haveli* (Knopf, 1993), in which the heroine knows the rules she lives under and breaks them; Kyoko Mori's *Shizuko's Daughter* (Ballantine, 1993), in which the protagonist acknowledges the limitations she lives with, but refuses to give in to them; and Cynthia Voigt's *Bad Girls* (Scholastic, 1996), featuring two fifth-grade girls who "won't let other people's limits stop them"; they "rewrite the Rules" (page 659). Mikey and Margalo are never cowed by consequences; they are intelligent, skillful manipulators of the classroom social world. Willful and powerful, they present us with new pictures of female children, throwing off the "plucky" and "spunky" shackles of the past.

INVESTIGATIONS: Strong Females in Children's Books

Study recent children's books to discover examples of strong females. See how many you can find that Ernst and Lehr might have missed. What about females of African-American, Hispanic, Native American, and Asian American heritage? What about Virginia Hamilton's Justice Douglass in *Justice and Her Brothers* (Greenwillow, 1980), *Dustland* (Greenwillow, 1980), and *The Gathering* (Greenwillow, 1981), or Lawrence Yep's Cassia in *The Serpent's Children* (Harper, 1984) and *Mountain Light* (Harper, 1985)? What about Velma Wallis's Bird Girl of *Bird Girl and the Man Who Followed the Sun* (Harper, 1997) or Nicholasa Mohr's Felita in *Going Home* (Dial, 1986)? Do any or all of these characters seem strong, active, and resourceful?

Still another solution is to look at old feminist questions in new ways. Is doing what the boys do the best we can ask of female characters? Consider the Lady of Susan Cooper's *Dark is Rising* sequence or Justice Douglass of Virginia Hamilton's Dustland trilogy. Each of these females is different, yet equal, and each does make a difference. Both Cooper and Hamilton work with conventional images, yet bend the conventions to help readers see things in new ways.

The Lady of Cooper's *Dark is Rising* sequence demonstrates both fragility and strength. Justice is strong, adventuresome, and assertive when she needs to be; at the same time she is nurturing, and her caring spirit is what keeps the Dustland mission going, just as the caring spirit of Cooper's Jane keeps the quest for the Light going. Neither the Lady, Jane, nor Justice merely does "what the boys do." Each does things *her* way, revealing a strong but nurturing and original female who gives females choices. Consider also Laurence Yep's books, filled with strong but nurturing females of all ages who face not only gender constrictions but also, and even more often, constrictions of class, race, and ethnicity.

Gender, Class, and Culture

Life conventions that limit people to constricting roles of class, race, or gender arise from habitual practices that members of a society deem acceptable. We find them filling the pages of children's books, whether they are popular series books or Newbery winners. Often if an award-winning book succeeds in the gender category, it falls in another.

Consider the previously mentioned *Roller Skates* by Ruth Sawyer. In this book, the female child is breaking the constricting social-conventions of her day, rather than upholding them. Lucinda, from an old upper-class New York family, befriends various lower- and middle-class people when her parents leave for a trip to Italy. A true "democrat," she treats these people as equals, which means risking her upper-class "respectability," at least in the eyes of her pretentious and snobbish relatives. In this egalitarian cast, we see what multicultural literature looked like in 1936—or more accurately, what it looked like a generation before, when Sawyer was Lucinda's age.

Lucinda encounters an Italian immigrant family; two Irishmen—Mr. Gilligan, a hansom cab driver, and patrolman M'Gonegal; a Jewish theater family, the Solomans; an Irish storyteller, Johanna; a poor Polish violinist and his daughter, Trinket; and the Asian Princess Zayda. Only the black servant eludes this democratization process. "Black Sarah" (no last name) gives Lucinda frosted cupcakes, but never really enters the story to reveal any problems Lucinda can help solve.

Although paternalistic adult males and nurturing adult females protect and at times literally "save" Lucinda, she is the one who sees problems and sets out to remedy them. She masterminds a plot to get patrolman M'Gonegal to save her friend Tony Coppino from the bullies who are stealing fruit from his father's grocery stand. She knows that Trinket Browdowski, the violinist's daughter, will die without medical attention, so she arranges for her physician, Doctor Hitchcock, to attend the child. And when she discovers the corpse of Princess Zayda, she never flinches; she knows she must get help, and she does.

Equally important to the value of the book is that Sawyer is recounting the facts of her own life and era. Lucinda's story is an *authentic portrait* of life as it was in the social world of Sawyer's childhood, even though the book's portrayal of the rigid conventions of class and culture were not Sawyer's values. The book shows a child acting against gender and class constraints. Because Sawyer was an insider in that world—a female and a member of an elitist class of "old" New York society—her book helps children today better see a world that has long since vanished.

Some authors, like Sawyer, exploit life conventions of gender, class, and culture to produce innovative books for their own time and authentic historical portraits for our time, also. Other authors exploit stylistic conventions to produce "breakaway" books that might become classics of the future.

NONTRADITIONAL LITERARY STRUCTURES, STYLES, AND SUBJECTS

One of the most interesting and thought-provoking illustrated picture books of recent times is Fred Marcellino's *Puss in Boots* (Farrar, 1990, translated by Malcolm Arthur), a Caldecott Honor book for 1991. This book demonstrates the way an unconventional artist plays with conventions of literary structure to produce an innovative book.

Literary Structures

Marcellino is a master at using facial expression and gesture to convey character traits. His cat is *all* child, and the adults in this old tale take a pale and lazy backseat as he bosses them about and outsmarts them at every turn. Humor—or the fun of watching the "have-nots" win—overshadows the fact that the youngest son is a scamp who follows the cat in his trickster antics, no questions asked. In other words, both the cat "child" and the youngest son have fun at the expense of the adults.

Other aspects of the story show how the author has "kidnapped" an old tale and cleverly reworked it for children. Marcellino capitalizes on the ogre segment of Perrault's story. Like any good artist, he keeps the childlike cat in a position of power at all times. Even when the ogre is glaring ominously down at the cat, the cat is looking over its shoulder *at us,* as if to say, with a shrug, "What are *you* making of this fellow?" Even when the ogre, transformed into a ferocious lion, appears to be pouncing on something at the left side of the page, the cat is bouncing up to the window on the far right, making his getaway in tiny, high-heeled boots that whisk him up and out of the fray.

At the end of the adventure, the youngest son does not return home, as occurs in the usual circular structural pattern of children's books. (The hero usually leaves home, has an adventure, and then returns home.) Instead, he spirals up in wealth and power into the ogre's residence—and stays there. The cat has tricked the ogre into turning himself into a mouse he can gobble up. With the ogre out of the way, the cat—in this clever reversal of fortune—becomes the great lord of the manor, with his portrait hanging on the castle wall. In plumed hat, fringed cape, and magical high-heeled boots, he is the child playing the distinguished gentleman. He has even given up chasing mice—except once in a while, just for fun.

From *Puss in Boots* (Farrar, 1990) by Fred Marcellino.

Pictorial Elements

Jane Doonan speaks of two "pictorial styles" in which picture book artists work: "linear" and "painterly" (page 87). In the first, artists produce a strongly defined outline; in the second, they emphasize tonal modeling, textured surfaces, and color.

Conventions of style arise from the pictorial elements of **line, color, shape, texture,** and **scale.** We speak of a *network* of linear rhythms, a *scheme* of colors and of light and dark contrasts, an *arrangement* of shapes and surface characteristics, and an *order* of small- and large-scale patterns. (page 14). Out of these networks, schemes, arrangements, and orders, arise conventions and conventionalized *meanings*.

The "quality of the outline" is most important for conveying meaning, says Doonan (page 44). Lines have a character and life of their own: "wiry, nervous, bold, rapid, confident, sinuous" (page 86). "A major recurring image" made by lines, colors, or shapes reveals a dominant *theme* of the picture (page 46). The "density of objects," or whether there is cluttered or open space, affects the *mood* and *pace* of the story (page 56).

Finally, a picture will have a "viewpoint," or a way to establish the reader's vantage point and attitude about the story (page 89). A low viewpoint (we stand below the scene) gives elevated importance to the subject of the picture. A higher viewpoint (we stand some distance above the scene) gives elevated importance to the reader or observer. Multiple viewpoints (we see a panoramic sweep across a scene) cause the reader's gaze to travel—or to wander about freely.

Source: Jane Doonan, *Looking at Pictures in Picture Books* (South Woodchester, England: Thimble Press, 1993).

Often in folk tales, the main character is an adultlike child—or a childlike adult—who becomes a trickster figure in animal disguise. (Anansi the spider of African and Caribbean tales; Brer Rabbit, the famous trickster of both African and African-American stories; and Monkey of Chinese lore all come to mind.) When this animal persona emerges, the "magic" of the trickster is likely to be at its most powerful for the child reader, because the oppressed underdog in our world is often a child. In *Puss in Boots,* the cat-trickster is having fun playing the child, and child readers have fun playing the trickster. At the same time, Marcellino plays with conventions of pictorial style.

Literary Styles

Marcellino exploits the stylistic conventions of visual perspective to explore one important meaning of the story: the cat-child is playfully working to outstrip the rich. The reader is often placed high above the scene, and the distance, plus the height, gives elevated importance to the observer. We watch the comedy of the cat subverting life conventions and threatening the status quo. This "cat-and-mouse" game provides a comic subplot of power plays, as when the cat tricks the ogre into becoming a mouse, then pounces on him.

The story begins with the reader at a lower vantage point. We look up at the scene of the miller's son, the mill, and the people; as our glance wanders farther up, we see the cat perched on a ledge, looking down at everything. Who is the important one here? Right now, it is these elegant characters. Several of the most dramatic scenes place us at this lower vantage point, thus emphasizing the lion's importance. The ogre stares at the cat—and at us—and the lion-ogre terrorizes the cat, who scrambles quickly up to the roof.

Yet because Marcellino is playing with conventions, we do not tremble with fear. Instead, we laugh at the lion's paws arched daintily in midair because the cat is safely out of the way, at the opposite side of the room. Or we cheer for the cat that never jumps out of its boots, even when it is scrambling for its life. The last picture produces a comedy of small- and large-scale patterning. The mice, staring at the cat's portrait above their heads, see the cat encumbered with layers and layers of finery. The implied "moral" as the story ends: Wealth and pomposity weigh heavily in cat-and-mouse games.

Some authors and artists work in a *surrealistic* style to produce random images and events that suggest a character's inner feelings, dreams, or psychic life.

INVESTIGATIONS: Artistic Designs

Choose an illustrated version (or a folk tale picture book) of a familiar folk tale such as "Cinderella," "The Three Bears," or "Snow White," and study its pictorial style. Or compare different picture book versions of a literary fairy tale such as Hans Christian Andersen's "The Nightingale," and study the pictorial styles of each illustrator. Consider elements of line, color, shape, texture, scale, and viewpoint, and decide how each of these aspects contributes to your meaning-making for the story. Can you see the artists playing with conventions—overturning them, expanding upon them, breaking away from the usual way of doing things?

Puss became a great lord and gave up chasing mice, except just once in a while, for the fun of it.

From *Puss in Boots* (Farrar, 1990) by Fred Marcellino.

(For more on surrealistic children's books, see end of this chapter.) Some go beyond surrealism to produce *magical realism.* Faith Ringgold often does both. In her stories of African-American children, random images and events of the character's fantasy life often grow out of an external reality, as when her child characters take flight to escape constricting social conditions.

In Faith Ringgold's world, historical happenings and levitating figures appear equally real—and are more meaningful because of their intermingling. *Tar Beach* (Crown, 1991) is a Caldecott Honor book, a winner of the Coretta Scott King Award for illustration, and a *New York Times* Best Illustrated Book. In this story, eight-year-old Cassie Lightfoot lies on the roof of her apartment building in 1939; at the same time, her spirit flies over the George Washington Bridge. Flying, says Cassie, takes you somewhere "you can't get to another way." It means claiming something as your own that is beautiful and has ties to you through family history. Cassie's father helped build the bridge, but he is prevented from joining the union because he is black; so Cassie also wishes to "claim" the union building—to fly over it and give it to her father.

As an ethnic feminist, Ringgold often focuses on females as culture-bearers. A painter and soft sculpture artist, she created this children's picture book from an

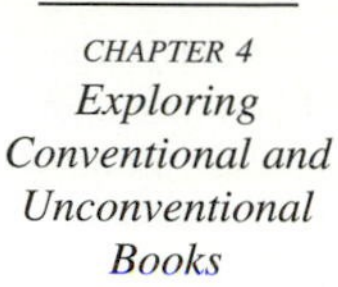

From *Tar Beach* (Crown, 1991) by Faith Ringgold.

African-American quilt. Across the top and bottom borders, she printed the words of her story about a flying child in tiny letters—art as story; story as art. The picture book reverses the quilt pattern: Tiny quilt squares, reproduced from Ringgold's earlier story-quilt, outline the text and pictures (acrylics on canvas).

The art style is an inventive blending of the *linear* (heavy, bold lines) and the *painterly* (brilliant, dark colors). Both of these traditions emphasize Ringgold's theme for this story: the stability of Cassie's African-American family. Through good and bad times, Cassie's parents provide security, laughter, and love for Cassie and her younger brother, Be Be. The wandering visual viewpoint allows readers to travel with Cassie through the pages. Sometimes we are looking up at a scene, which elevates the importance of the characters, as when the story opens and we look up to see Cassie flying overhead. In the next scene, we see her flying over her brother, who is lying on the roof of the family's apartment building as the other family members sit talking. Cassie's *power*—her ability to fly—is a *female* power too; she—not her brother—is the one overhead.

At this point, we view Cassie sleeping below, and *we* become the important ones; we are watching her dream and journey through her family history. Later we are still positioned above the scene, but we move alongside Cassie as she flies over the scene in her dream/wish memory vision. So we look down with Cassie to see her mother sleeping under a vibrant red, green, and yellow African quilt pattern. Now Cassie assumes adult importance: She is watching over her sleeping mother. And child readers assume this importance alongside her.

Tar Beach represents a genre blending, another way authors and artists have of enlarging and deepening the child's literary powers, or of freeing the child to think

From *Tar Beach* (Crown, 1991) by Faith Ringgold.

in multiple perspectives. It is impossible to separate realism and fantasy in Ringgold's books, so many scenes of magical realism occur. The book is a mix of autobiography, realism, fantasy, American history and culture, family history, and mythic folk legend. The flying-slave story of African-American folklore forms the cultural wellspring for Cassie's inspired visions of flight.

Floyd Cooper's illustrations for *Jaguarundi* by Virginia Hamilton (Scholastic, 1995) produce another inventive genre blending. *Jaguarundi* is part fantasy—a story in the African tradition of talking animals—and part informational book. The subject is endangered animals, and the glossary of endangered animals at the end of the book provides a catalog of pictures with accompanying descriptions of appearances, personalities, habitats, and eating patterns. Most especially, *Jaguarundi* is a rainforest science book.

Rundi Jaguarundi, one of the big cats, is fleeing the rain forest. Like the slaves who escaped on the Underground Railroad, he hopes to find a Northern place where he will be safe from hunters, hunting dogs, traps, settlers, cleared land, and depleted forests. One by one, other endangered animals appear to tell

From *Jaguarundi* (Scholastic, 1995) by Virginia Hamilton, illustrated by Floyd Cooper.

their stories of displacement. Dressed in muted, realistic colors, and moving in soft, sinuous lines, they add a vibrant sense of touch to this folk-information fantasy. Working in the painterly tradition, Cooper expands upon the convention of texture to bring readers closer to his subject. (See the end of this chapter for more on genre blendings.)

Literary Subjects

Books that blend fiction and nonfiction, as *Jaguarundi* does, cause us to define the term *genre* just a little differently. Such books cluster together because of their subject matter rather than because of their form. *Jaguarundi* is about endangered animals, of course, but such a category is too specific to denote a literary genre. The book resonates with references to both African life and culture and African-American history, and it also shows how creatures of different colors or backgrounds learn to respect one another's ways of thinking and living.

We might call *Jaguarundi* a **multicultural** book, a literary category that has been becoming more genre-like recently, perhaps because of the political and social implications of the term *multicultural.* Understanding ethnic and racial differences may help avoid or resolve ethnic quarrels and conflicts. "Over the last generation," says critical theorist Reed Dasenbrock (1987), "there has been such an explosion in writing from a global range of cultures that, arguably, multicultural literature dominates literature in English today" (page 10).

"Multicultural literature," say Cai and Bishop (1994), "is a concept in search of a definition" (page 57). Does it mean books that focus on children of color, or on groups that differ in some way from the dominant group—in language, traditions, values, or behaviors? Are these children members of one different culture or of different cultures worldwide? Or does it mean books that focus on children from all ethnic or regional *strands* in a dominant culture? Could it mean immigrant children of all origins—Polish, Jewish, East Indian, Asian, Hispanic, African-Caribbean, and Appalachian (Scotch-Irish) children, as well as indigenous (Native American) and slave-descended (African-American) children?

Does it also include groups united by some trait other than ethnicity (disabled or handicapped children, children growing up with same-sex parents, or homeless children)?

Is it literature *about* the people of a particular culture (written by anyone—insiders or outsiders)? Or is it literature *by* the people of the culture? Which counts—being an outsider with an interest in a particular group, or being an insider who has personal memories of growing up in the group and has experienced outsiders' prejudices? In either case, should the multicultural book be free from stereotypes and inaccurate details? Or should a deeper authenticity concern us? Do the outsider's views overshadow the insider's traditions and world view?

Are multicultural books classified on the basis of political perspective? In other words, are they a type of literature that many people think will help children of underrepresented groups see themselves as part of the general cultural fabric and help children of the dominant culture celebrate diversity? Or are multicultural books classified on the basis of literary conventions: a particular structure, style, or subject? (Are they defined by a multicultural *aesthetic?*)

There are no easy answers to these questions, but ideas do seem to be emerging, not only from critics and researchers, but also from children's authors. Virginia Hamilton (1992) uses the term *parallel cultures* to designate multiethnic communities as different from—but *equal* to—the dominant American cultural "community." By *multiethnic,* Hamilton means such underrepresented, and often unassimilated, groups as African-American, Asian-American, Native American, and Hispanic-American literature. But as the mother of bicultural children (African-American and Russian-Jewish-American), Hamilton has managed to break away from the usual definition of *multicultural.* In *Plain City* (Scholastic 1994), she creates twelve-year-old Buhlaire, a coming-of-age female of mixed-race heritage. Her mother's family is African-American; her father's mother is white, and the novel explores how the child comes to terms with her newly discovered bicultural identity.

MULTICULTURAL LITERATURE: THEMES AND INSCRIBING PROCESSES

One important theme in multicultural books is the search for ethnic identity. Members of parallel cultures engage in this search when the dominant culture tends to overwhelm and absorb cultural differences. Children who are members of more than one ethnic or racial group are certainly *multi*cultural. And the child of bicultural or multiethnic heritage searching for cultural identity is certainly a valid theme of children's literature, although few writers have explored it. But many themes or emphases must be recognized in the broad, inventive category of **multicultural** books:

- Growing up in a parallel culture in America/North America (Growing up African American, Asian American, Hispanic American, or Native American)
- Growing up in a polyethnic/polycultural family
- Growing up between two cultures
- Growing up in a parallel culture worldwide
- Crossing cultures: Immigrant / emigrant / refugee experiences
- Crossing cultures: Traveler's experiences
- Struggling with cultural and historical inequities
- History and culture:
    - African-American experiences
    - Asian-American experiences
    - Hispanic-American experiences
    - Native-American experiences
- Preserving heritage: Continuity of family and culture

A book like Hamilton's *Plain City* fits two of these categories. Buhlaire's nuclear family is monocultural African American, rather than polycultural. (Her biracial father is rarely present in her life.) But because the major conflict centers around her awakening to a mixed-race identity, she is **growing up African American** (growing up in a parallel culture in American/North America) and, at the same time, **growing up between two cultures.**

Laurence Yep has written many books about **growing up Asian American;** two of the most recent—and the most timely—are *Thief of Hearts* (Harper, 1995) and *Ribbons* (Putnam, 1996). In the first, Stacy, a second-generation Chinese-American girl, finds herself rejecting a first-generation Chinese-American classmate who needs her understanding and has a great deal to teach her about heritage and identity. In the second book, second-generation Chinese-American Robin both learns from and teaches her Chinese grandmother, newly arrived in the United States and certainly a challenge to Robin's entire family.

Gary Soto has written many books about **growing up Mexican American;** two of the most recent are his novel, *Taking Sides* (Harcourt, 1991), and his picture book, *Too Many Tamales* (Putnam's, 1993; illustrations by Ed Martinez). In the first, eighth-grader Lincoln Mendoza has recently moved from the barrio to the suburbs of San Francisco, and the challenges of adjusting to new friends, a new basketball team, and divided loyalties between "brown" and "white" produce serious but surmountable conflicts. In the second book, Maria is part of a large, loving Mexican-American family. Watching her mother make tamales at Christmastime, Maria suddenly decides to try on her mother's diamond ring, and the ring slips into the *mesa.* Where is the ring? Maria's mother decides to teach her daughter a little lesson and slips the ring back on her finger without saying a word. When four children try out all the tamales, hoping to bite into the ring, they end up eating too many tamales and shedding a few tears before everyone can share in the laughter.

Joseph Bruchac has written many books about **growing up Native American.** One of the most timely is *Fox Song* (Philomel, 1993; illustrated by Paul Morin), a picture storybook. Jamie remembers the special times she and Grama Bowman shared—peeling birch bark to make baskets, hunting for fox tracks, and singing the Abenaki welcoming song to the sun—before her grandmother died.

In *Black is brown is tan* (Harper, 1971; illustrations by Emily Arnold McCully), Arnold Adoff shows children—like his own children, Leigh and Jaime—growing up with an African-American mother and a Euro-American/Jewish-American father. Readers "hear" idioms and familiar expressions from the different family members; they learn about ethnic foods and how to prepare them. Stories, songs, and musical instruments are part of the story, too. Adoff emphasizes that the traditions of both sides of the children's family are important; experiencing these traditions alongside the children in the story helps readers understand what it means to **grow up polyethnic.** The children in this family are engaged in the usual mealtime, bedtime, and other family experiences, but the family members are individuals of particular ethnicities, and their differences count.

Sharon Dennis Wyeth has also written about growing up in a polyethnic family in *The World of Daughter McGuire* (Delacorte, 1994). In this realistic novel, eleven-year-old Daughter—of African, Italian, Irish, Jewish, and Russian extraction—explores her multifaceted American heritage when her absentee father returns home and helps her deal with the identity conflicts she faces as a multiethnic child.

Rafik Schami has written about **growing up in a parallel culture worldwide** in *A Hand Full of Stars* (Penguin, 1990). This realistic novel is about a young boy in Syria, who helps to change his culture through his writing abilities. Schami uses the child-as-writer convention to create a child who makes a difference.

In this same category, African-American educator Mildred Pitts Walter has created an innovative picture storybook, *Brother to the Wind* (Lothrop, 1985; illustrations by Leo and Diane Dillon). In this story, the wind is a female with magical powers of her own, and Emeke is an African boy who wants to fly. The wind calls

INVESTIGATIONS: Diversity Within Ethnicities

It is easy to think of a particular ethnicity in terms of commonalities. We might assume all members of this group think alike, speak alike, have the same interests and political viewpoints, the same abilities, and the same lifestyles. We might think they all live in the same area or region, the same kind of neighborhood, the same type of house. We often forget that members of ethnic groups are individuals, with unique preoccupations, experiences, and and perspectives. They travel; they settle in different places; they form values and traditions; they also adapt and change.

Try to discover a new book from each of the four parallel cultures, and read it to see if you can find *diversity* within a particular ethnic group. Notice the characters' regional backgrounds, their language patterns, their values, behaviors, interests, abilities, and talents. Consider Virginia Hamilton's *Second Cousins* (Scholastic, 1998), in which children in a large, extended African-American family come together from different areas of the United States for a family reunion in the midwest. Consider also Joseph Bruchac and Jonathan London's *Thirteen Moons on Turtle's Back* (Philomel, 1992), illustrations by Thomas Locker, a collection of poems from different Native American tribes including Cherokee, Cree, Sioux, Huran, Micmac, and Northern Cheyenne, each of which celebrates a moon (a month) of the year.

Emeke her brother, and when she helps him to fly with colors that glow like the wind, she becomes his sister and he becomes "Brother to the Wind."

Walter traveled to Nigeria in 1977 as a delegate to the Black and African Festival of the Arts in Lagos, and she wrote this story based on what she learned about African beliefs, traditions, customs, and folklore. Walter blends the flying African character that emerges in so many African American folk tales, such as Hamilton's *The People Could Fly* (Knopf, 1986), with the African folk tradition of talking animals. The story appeals to children anywhere, however. With its focus on trusting yourself—and others—if you are to make your wishes come true, it is particularly well-suited for children who want to achieve something special—but also want their peers to accept them.

In this story, the wind and the animals help Emeke in his quest. The animals teach him to follow his dreams, even when his friends ridicule him for daring to fly like a bird. Good Snake shows him how to make a kite from the bark of a baobab tree and three large bamboo poles, and when he does at last fly, his friends—impressed with his daring—are there to cheer him.

Karen Hesse has written about the child **crossing cultures as immigrant, refugee, and traveler** in *Letters from Rifka* (Holt, 1992). Rifka, in the early twentieth century, travels from Russia to Poland to Belgium, where she is, for a time, separated from her family. Then she sets off again, and the focus shifts to the experiences of a refugee—and later, an immigrant.

Joyce Hansen wrote about **struggling with cultural and historical inequities** in *Out From This Place* (Walker, 1988). In this story, ex-slave children in South Carolina after the Civil War struggle with loneliness, hard physical toil, injustice, brutality, even murder of their loved ones.

From *Brother to the Wind* (Lothrop, 1985) by Mildred Pitts Walter, illustrated by Leo and Diane Dillon.

Then softly as the flutter of a bird's wing came a whisper: "My brother." Emeke trembled with the excitement that comes with dancing. Be still and listen, he told himself. Again the whisper: "My brother." That is the right wind! He felt light with happiness.

The rest of the night, Emeke slept without dreaming.

The morning of the festival came with the sound of many drums. The air was heavy with excitement. Today I will fly, Emeke thought when he awoke.

Emeke walked with his family to the center of the village. His friends gathered around him, excited about the games and races to be held at the festival.

"I will fly today," Emeke said matter-of-factly. "Look up and you will see me."

"Then look down," Ndumu said. "Oooh, no more Emeke! He is splattered like a bird's egg." Ndumu fell to the ground, arms and legs spread. All the boys bent with laughter.

"I will fly. You will see," Emeke said.

When the center of the village was overrun with people, Emeke slipped away with his kite and rock. He hurried up the mountain to meet Good Snake.

Often themes of **history and culture** intersect closely with the themes of growing up in a particular ethnicity and struggling with cultural inequities or celebrating customs and lifestyles, as we see in *Children of Promise: African-American Literature and Art for Young People* (Abrams, 1991). In an anthology of historical memoirs, narrative accounts, letters, speeches, poetry, songs, and paintings, Charles Sullivan, who edited this collection, presents a stunning visual experience of African-American history from 1761 to the present day.

In the picture book category, we find historical fiction like Elizabeth Fitzgerald Howard's *Chita's Christmas Tree* (Macmillan, 1989; illustrations by Floyd Cooper), set in Baltimore a century ago. Patricia McKissack's book, *The Dark-Thirty: Southern Tales of the Supernatural* (Knopf, 1992; illustrations by Brian Pinkney) reproduces folk tales. Her collection, springing out of African-American history and the ghost tale tradition, was a Newbery Honor book for 1993. More cultural folk tales, this time representing Asian-American history and culture, appear in Laurence Yep's *The Rainbow People* (Harper, 1989).

Nearly all of Joseph Bruchac's work in Native American literature fits the category of history and culture. He has collected—and retold—coming-of-age stories in *Flying with the Eagle, Racing the Great Bear: Stories from Native North America* (BridgeWater Books, 1993) and in *The Girl Who Married the Moon* (BridgeWater, 1994), written collaboratively with Gayle Ross. Ross was also his writing partner for the folk tale picture book *The Story of the Milky Way: A Cherokee Tale* (Dial, 1995; pictures by Virginia Stroud), a creation tale about a giant spirit dog that the people drive into the sky to save their cornmeal from being stolen.

Stroud created particularly striking—and authentic—artwork for this story. She decided to set the scenes in the early 1800s, before the forced removal of Cherokees from the southeastern United States in the late 1830s (the famous Trail of Tears), as she explains in an illustrator's note. At this time the Cherokee people were still living in the Smoky Mountains, where they had adopted some non-Indian forms of clothing but still wore other, more traditional forms like the turkey-feather cape that Beloved Woman wears in this story.

Authentic artwork is often the mainstay of the history and culture category, as we see in Carmen Lomas Garza's *Family Pictures: Cuadros de Familia* (Children's Book Press, 1990). In this autobiographical picture book, Garza reveals her experiences growing up Mexican American near Kingsville, Texas. The book is a bilingual celebration of customs that might someday disappear in the face of cultural assimilation. Thus, Garza's story is particularly important for creating—and helping readers to see—an American history of multicultural experiences. Telling readers about how she acted out the Christmas story for "Las Posadas," made tamales, picked nopal cactus that her grandmother would cook for breakfast, hit the piñata at her sixth birthday party, remembered the *curandera* healing her neighbor when she had the flu, and dreamed of someday becoming an artist, Garza both *celebrates* and *preserves* an earlier day in Mexican-American life.

At times, children are not simply growing up in a parallel culture, discovering heritage, living a cultural identity, or even telling about it later to celebrate it. They are instead engaged in preserving heritage, as Garza does. The impulse to save an experience by telling about it in words and pictures might result from cultural *conflict,* as well as from the desire to keep and share cultural memories. A sudden collision with familial, historical, or cultural traditions might cause writers to question

From *The Story of the Milky Way: A Cherokee Tale* (Dial, 1995) by Joseph Bruchac and Gayle Ross, illustrated by Virginia Stroud.

whether they will keep or give up their cultural identity, as Laurence Yep depicted in *Dragonwings* (Harper and Row, 1975) and *The Star Fisher* (Penguin, 1991).

In books of this category, **preserving heritage and the continuity of family and culture,** *multiculturalism* is built into the texture of the book itself—and into its focus, emphasis, subject matter and theme—because characters are trying to make sense of multicultural conflicts and misunderstandings. Often sorting out the cultural worlds in these stories is a particularly difficult challenge for readers if they are not insiders of the group depicted. As Reed Way Dasenbroch notes, multi-ethnic authors *inscribe* readers into texts in various ways (page 17).

Children's authors have intriguing—and inventive—ways of inscribing readers. In *Dragonwings* and *The Star Fisher,* Laurence Yep reverses the usual convention of placing foreign words in italics. He places all the *English* conversations of his Asian-American characters in italics, and he places everything else in conventional print. Thus, Yep invents a bilingual mode of presentation that elevates the Asian language in importance, because it places the monocultural reader in the bicultural character's shoes. At first, Yep's use of italics is disorienting, as he likely intends it to be. Thus, readers discover how confusing it can be to "step" into a different culture.

In *The Moon Lady* (Macmillan, 1991; illustrations by Gretchen Shields), Amy Tan produces continuity of culture through two conventions of ethnic storytellers, the literary device of the frame-story and the cultural tradition of the

Great-Mother-as-Storyteller. As the story begins, Nai-nai and her three granddaughters are talking about secret wishes in a scene that leads readers into the main story.

As the little girls settle down to listen to their grandmother's story, Nai-nai describes the Chinese moon festival of her childhood and her own secret wish at that time. As a child, Nai-nai (then called Ying-ying) became separated from members of her family at the festival and spent a scary—but adventuresome—afternoon trying to find her way back. She discovered her family and a stronger sense of self when she found the courage to shout her "secret" wish. But in doing so, she had to break an important tradition in her culture: Always keep your wishes to yourself; to tell them or to ask openly for a wish is to be selfish.

Ying-ying was able to break this taboo because of her discovery that the "Moon Lady" of the festival was really an ugly old man in disguise. She was shocked by this display of adult deception, and her feelings about tradition were shattered, along with her innocence. Once the spell was broken, she made up her mind to save herself by shouting her secret wish—to be found. Making a wish no longer seemed selfish to her. As Nai-nai tells her granddaughters in the last scene, she discovered that the best wishes are those you decide for yourself.

Telling stories has, for centuries, served as a way to transmit cultural values and traditions. Children learned from stories how to live and what was expected of them. Once stories entered a *literary* tradition, writers often placed the teller into the text to make the storytelling event visible. Today, in a media-oriented culture, writers often try to give readers a more immediate experience: they discard the frame, leaving the teller out of the tale. Tan could have simply produced a story about the child Ying-ying.

But if she had removed the frame, she would have erased the special role—or tradition—of the Great Mother, in which the grandmother as clan storyteller transmits personal and cultural memories. Amy Tan has taken a time-honored convention of the oral tradition and brought it to life for children by producing two new or unconventional genres: the **multicultural book** and the **frame-story picture book.** Thus, children of the dominant culture, alongside those of Asian background, can share in a narrative convention that might have been lost.

One of the most mind-stretching, nonconventional multicultural books of the 1990s is Faith Ringgold's *Aunt Harriet's Underground Railroad in the Sky* (Crown, 1992). Ringgold brings back Cassie and Be Be once again. But this time

INVESTIGATIONS: Ethnic Storytelling: Frame Stories and the Great Mother Tradition

Explore other frame-story picture books and picture storybooks that incorporate the Great Mother tradition. Joseph Bruchac chooses the grandmother as clan storyteller to frame the Native American poetry of *The Earth Under Sky Bear's Feet* (Philomel, 1995; illustrations by Thomas Locker). Fittingly, the Iroquois grandmother is telling her granddaughter about Sky Bear, a great she-bear, who travels the sky seeing and hearing much of what happens on earth. In Bruchac's *Thirteen Moons on Turtle's Back,* written with Jonathan London (Philomel, 1992; illustrations by Thomas Locker), the clan teller whose story frames the poems is an Abenaki elder and grandfather.

both children fly, not just to claim a cultural place in the present world but to recover a time and a place in their cultural history, when the Underground Railroad was "running." The subject now is *flight*—not flying. Harriet Tubman is the children's guide for this picture book that blends four themes of multicultural literature: growing up in a parallel culture, struggling with cultural and historical inequities, history and culture, and preserving heritage.

In one of the few picture books to explore historical time fantasy, Ringgold's children discover "an old ramshackled train in the sky." When Be Be jumps aboard and Cassie fears that her brother may be lost forever, Harriet Tubman suddenly appears to comfort Cassie with stories of slavery days and to encourage her to follow Be Be on foot. The best way for Cassie—and for child readers—to learn more about their American and African-American heritage, implies Ringgold, is to reinvent themselves as slaves. Cassie begins her travels, following the instructions Harriet gives her. On route, she finds notes and keepsakes Be Be has left behind, which gives her hope; and Harriet continues to serve as magic helper, teaching Cassie—and the reader—what it was like and how it felt to take this "train."

As the story reaches its climax, the steam-vapor of Niagara Falls forms a soft blanket that lifts Cassie up and over the bridge to Canada. There she finds Harriet and Be Be, a real slave child now who carries a baby "brother," Freedom, tied to his back. In the waterfall scene, flowing, vertical lines lead the reader's viewpoint downward. At the same time, splashes of horizontal white brush strokes push the viewpoint into the next scene, where Harriet and Be Be float horizontally under a cloud "cover" of African-American female slaves dressed in white. The real conductors of the Railroad, Ringgold says in an endnote, were "white sympathizers, freeborn Negroes, and escaped-slaves, many of whom were women."

At first glance, this book seems to have too much story-text and too many genres for the picture book form. Perhaps it would have worked better as a novel or a wordless picture book, we may decide. But the more closely we look at the book and the more times we examine it, the more it begins to make sense. The book requires our patience; it makes us revise our expectations about genre. It also makes us think more about Dasenbroch's definition of multicultural literature. Such literature, he says, "offers us above all an experience . . . in which not everything is likely to

From *Aunt Harriet's Underground Railroad in the Sky* (Crown, 1992) by Faith Ringgold.

be wholly understood by every reader" because it is mirroring the misunderstandings that arise in the multicultural situations it depicts (page 12).

Ultimately, we may realize that for Ringgold to produce an authentic multicultural experience for readers, she must propel them as quickly into this traumatic time in the past as she has propelled Cassie and Be Be. Readers must feel as disoriented as these children felt. Ringgold's choice of *magical realism*—another genre that gets poured into the story "cauldron" here—was perhaps the only way to convey this jarring moment in the past. In this particular blend of realism and fantasy, the artist and the child characters respond to cataclysmic events by imagining visions that emerge magically as actual occurrences in everyday life. What would otherwise be a realistic story is blended with both folk tale and fantasy, and the story-theme takes on larger-than-life dimensions.

Multicultural literature is one of the richest veins of children's literature. (For more on multicultural children's books, see Appendix I.) Its ability to break away from, play with, and expand conventions promises to help children become more perceptive about ethnic literature and ethnicities—because insiders of various parallel cultures tell their own stories. Yet a question arises: Should we separate books about various ethnic groups from other genres and place them in a category of their own?

On the one hand, books by Yep, Ringgold, Hesse, and Hamilton really are a part of the genre of realistic books, and to separate them from historical fiction or other realistic books seems illogical. Placing them in the multicultural category simply emphasizes the Anglo-American culture as dominant and supports the practice of segregation. On the other hand, placing these books in the fiction category runs the risk of leaving them overshadowed, ignored, or underrated, especially if readers fail to do the necessary "work" to appreciate them. Does keeping these artists in a separate multicultural category promote equality—or discourage it?

Such questions lead us to think about the canon of children's books: what is selected and what is swept aside; what is reviewed, analyzed, awarded, and what is not; what receives our praise or our blame. We will focus on all of these considerations in the next chapter.

CHILDREN'S LITERATURE

Literacies in Literature (children as readers, writers, poets, storytellers, and artists)

Children (or animal characters) as Readers

Alcott, Louisa May. *Little Women* (1868). New York: New American Library, 1983 (novel: realism).

Breathed, Berkeley. *Goodnight, Opus.* Boston: Little, Brown, 1993 (postmodernist picture book).

Burnett, Frances Hodgson. *The Secret Garden* (1911). New York: Bantam, 1987 (realistic novel).

Cleary, Beverly. *Emily's Runaway Imagination.* New York: Morrow, 1961 (chapter book; realistic fiction).

———. *Mitch and Amy.* New York: Morrow, 1967 (chapter book; realistic fiction).

———. *Ramona the Pest.* New York: Morrow, 1968 (chapter book; realistic fiction).

———. *Ramona Quimby, Age 8.* New York: Morrow, 1981 (chapter book; realistic fiction).

COOPER, SUSAN. *The Dark is Rising.* New York: Atheneum, 1973 (fantasy novel).

———. *Matthew's Dragon.* Illustrated by Joseph A. Smith. New York: Macmillan, 1991 (fantasy picture book).

———. *Over Sea, Under Stone.* Illustrated by Margery Gill. New York: Harcourt, 1966 (realistic novel).

HAMILTON, VIRGINIA. *The House of Dies Drear.* New York: Macmillan, 1968 (novel: realistic fiction).

HAUTZIG, ESTHER. *A Gift for Mama.* Illustrated by Donna Diamond. New York: Viking, 1981 (chapter book; realistic fiction).

HOFFMAN, MARY. *Amazing Grace.* Illustrated by Caroline Binch. New York: Dial, 1991. (picture book; realism).

HOPKINSON, DEBORAH. *Sweet Clara and the Freedom Quilt.* Illustrated by James Ransome New York: Knopf, 1993 (picture book; historical fiction).

HURWITZ, JOHANNA. *The Adventures of Ali Baba Bernstein.* New York: Scholastic, 1985 (chapter book; realistic fiction).

MILLER, WILLIAM. *Richard Wright and the Library Card.* Illustrated by Gregory Christie. New York: Lee & Low, 1997 (picture book; realism).

MORA, PAT. *Tomas and the Library Lady.* Illustrated by Raul Colon. New York: Knopf, 1997 (picture book; realism).

NESBIT, EDITH. *The Story of the Treasure Seekers* (1899). New York: Puffin, 1958 (novel: realism).

O'BRIEN, ROBERT. *Mrs. Frisby and the Rats of NIMH.* New York: Atheneum, 1971 (animal fantasy novel).

PATERSON, KATHERINE. *Park's Quest.* New York: Dutton, 1988 (realistic novel).

PERKINS, MITALI. *The Sunita Experiment.* Boston: Little, Brown, 1993 (realistic novel).

SAWYER, RUTH. *Roller Skates* (1936). New York: Puffin, 1986 (novel: realistic fiction).

SPEARE, ELIZABETH GEORGE. *The Sign of the Beaver.* Boston: Houghton Mifflin, 1983 (novel).

STEIG, WILLIAM. *Abel's Island.* New York: Farrar, 1976 (illustrated novel; animal fantasy).

VIORST, JUDITH. *Rosie and Michael.* Illustrated by Lorna Tomei. New York: Macmillan, 1974 (verse picture book).

WALTER, MILDRED PITTS. *Justin and the Best Biscuits in the World.* Illustrated by Catherine Stock. New York: Lothrop, 1986 (picture storybook; realism).

WIESNER, DAVID. *Free Fall.* New York: Lothrop, Lee & Shepard, 1988 (fantasy picture book; wordless).

YEP, LAURENCE. *Dragonwings.* New York: Harper, 1975 (novel: historical fiction).

Children as Writers

AYRES, KATHERINE. *Family Tree.* New York: Delacorte, 1996 (novel; realistic fiction).

BROWN, MARC. *Arthur Writes a Story.* New York: Little, Brown, 1996 (picture book, realism).

CLEARY, BEVERLY. *Dear Mr. Henshaw.* Illustrated by Paul Zelinsky. New York: Morrow, 1983 (novel, realistic fiction).

———. *Ellen Tebbits.* Illustrated by Louis Darling. New York: Morrow, 1951 (chapter book, realistic fiction).

———. *Strider.* Illustrated by Paul Zelinsky. New York: Morrow, 1991 (novel, realistic fiction; sequel to *Dear Mr. Henshaw*).

COONEY, BARBARA. *Only Opal: The Diary of a Young Girl.* New York: Philomel, 1994 (picture book; diary).

DEJONG, MEINDERT. *The Wheel on the School.* Illustrations by Maurice Sendak. New York: Harper, 1954 (novel: realism).

EHRLICH, AMY, EDITOR. *When I Was Your Age: Original Stories About Growing Up.* Cambridge MA: Candlewick Press, 1996 (short stories by children's authors; autobiographical fiction and notes about the authors' growth into writers).

FARMER, PENELOPE. *Charlotte Sometimes.* New York: Bantam, 1987 (novel; time fantasy).

FILIPOVIC, ZLATA. *Zlata's Diary: A Child's Life in Sarajevo.* New York: Viking, 1994 (autobiography).

FITZHUGH, LOUISE. *Harriet the Spy.* New York: Harper and Row, 1964 (novel; realism).

FRANK, ANNE. *Anne Frank: The Diary of a Young Girl.* New York: Doubleday, 1967 (diary, autobiography).

———. *Anne Frank's Tales from the Secret Annex.* New York: Doubleday, 1983 (original stories and essays by Anne Frank).

GREENFIELD, ELOISE. *Sister.* New York: HarperCollins, 1974 (novel; realistic fiction).

GUY, ROSA. *The Ups and Downs of Carl Davis III.* New York: Delacorte, 1989 (novel; realistic fiction).

HAMILTON, VIRGINIA. *Arilla Sun Down* (1976). New York: Scholastic, 1995 (novel: realism and psychic realism).

———. *Bluish.* New York: Scholastic, 1999 (novel: realism)

HANSEN, JOYCE. *I Thought My Soul Would Rise and Fly: The Reconstruction Era Diary of Patsy.* New York: Scholastic, 1997 (novel: historical fiction).

HUNTER, LATOYA. *The Diary of Latoya Hunter: My First Year in Junior High.* New York: Crown, 1992 (autobiography).

HUNTER, MOLLIE. *A Sound of Chariots.* New York: Harper, 1972 (novel; realism).

———. *The Dragonfly Years.* London: Hamish Hamilton, 1983 (novel; realism).

———. *Out From This Place.* New York: Walker, 1988 (historical fiction).

KEATS, EZRA. *A Letter to Amy.* New York: Harper & Row, 1968 (picture book).

LOWRY, LOIS. *Anastasia Krupnik.* Boston: Houghton Mifflin, 1981 (novel: realistic fiction).

LYONS, MARY. *Letters from a Slave Girl: The Story of Harriet Jacobs.* New York: Simon & Schuster, 1992 (novel: biographical fiction).

MCKISSICK, PATRICIA. *A Picture of Freedom: The Diary of Clotee, A Slave Girl, Belmont Plantation, 1859.* New York: Scholastic, 1997 (novel: historical fiction).

NYE, NAOMI SHIHAB. *Habib:* New York: Simon and Schuster, 1997 (realistic fiction).

SCHAMI, RAFIK. *A Handful of Stars.* New York: Penguin, 1990 (novel; realism).

SCHOTTER, RONI. *Nothing Ever Happens on 90th Street.* Illustrated by Kyrsten Brooker. New York: Orchard, 1997 (picture book; realism/psychic realism).

STINE, R. L. *Goosebumps: The Blob That Ate Everyone.* New York: Scholastic, 1997 (horror fiction).

WILLIAMS, VERA. *Stringbean's Trip to the Shining Sea.* New York: Scholastic, 1988 (picture book; realistic fiction).

———. *Three Days on a River in a Red Canoe.* New York: Morrow, 1981 (picture book; realistic fiction).

Children (and animal characters) as Poets

ADOFF, ARNOLD. *Love Letters.* Illustrated by Lisa Desimini. New York: Scholastic, 1997 (poetry).

GREENFIELD, ELOISE. *Honey, I Love.* Illustrated by Diane and Leo Dillon. New York: Crowell, 1972 (poetry).

———. *Nathaniel Talking.* Illustrated by Jan Spivey Gilchrist. New York: Black Butterfly, 1988 (poetry).

HIRSCHFELDER, ARLENE, AND SINGER, BEVERLY, EDITORS. *Rising Voices: Writings of Young Native Americans.* New York: Ballantine, 1993 (collection of children's original writing).

JARRELL, RANDALL. *The Bat-Poet.* Illustrated by Maurice Sendak. New York: Macmillan, 1963 (picture storybook; animal fantasy).

L'ENGLE, MADELEINE. *A Ring of Endless Light.* New York: Farrar, 1981 (novel; realism).

———. *Troubling a Star.* New York: Farrar, 1994 (novel; realism).

LIONNI, LEO. *Frederick.* New York: Pantheon, 1967 (picture book; animal fantasy).
THOMAS, JOYCE CAROL. *Brown Honey in Broomwheat Tea.* Illustrated by Floyd Cooper. New York: HarperCollins, 1993.

Children as Storytellers

ALCOTT, LOUISA MAY. *Little Women* (1868). New York: New American Library, 1983 (novel; realism).
BURNETT, FRANCES HODGSON. *A Little Princess* (1905). New York: Penguin, 1990 (novel; realism).
CREECH, SHARON. *Walk Two Moons.* New York: Harper, 1994 (novel; realism).
HAMILTON, VIRGINIA. *The Magical Adventures of Pretty Pearl.* New York: Harper, 1983 (historical and legendary time fantasy).
———. *M. C. Higgins the Great.* New York: Macmillan, 1974 (novel; realism).
———. *The Mystery of Drear House.* New York: Macmillan, 1987 (novel; realism).
———. *Zeely.* New York: Macmillan, 1967 (novel; realism).
JOHNSON, ANGELA. *Tell Me A Story, Mama.* Illustrated by David Soman. New York: Orchard, 1989 (picture book; realism).
LASKY, KATHRYN. *The Night Journey.* New York: Frederick Warne, 1981 (novel; realism).
LINDGREN, ASTRID. *Pippi Longstocking.* New York: Viking, 1950 (novel; tall tale fantasy).
MCKISSACK, PATRICIA. *A Million Fish . . . More or Less.* Illustrated by Dena Schutzer. New York: Knopf, 1992 (picture book; tall tale).
MONTGOMERY, L. M. *The Story Girl* (1911). New York: Signet, 1991 (novel; realism).
POMERANTZ, CHARLOTTE. *The Chalk Doll.* Illustrated by Frane Lessac. New York: Lippincott, 1989 (picture book; realism).

Children (or Animals) as Artists

ALIKI [BRANDENBERG]. *Marianthe's Story:Painted Words: Spoken Memories.* New York: Greenwillow, 1998 (picture storybook; realistic fiction).
ARMSTRONG, ROBB. *Drew and the Bub Daddy Showdown.* New York: HarperCollins, 1996 (illustrated chapter book; realism).
BANG, MOLLY. *Tye May and the Magic Brush.* New York: Greenwillow, 1981 (picture story book, fantasy).
BYARS, BETSY. *The Cartoonist.* New York: Viking, 1978 (novel, realism).
COHEN, MIRIAM. *No Good in Art.* Illustrated by Lillian Hoban. New York: Greenwillow, 1980 (picture book; realism).
COONEY, BARBARA. *Hattie and the Wild Waves.* New York: Viking, 1990 (picture book; realism.
———. *Miss Rumphius.* New York: Viking, 1982 (picture book; realism).
DE PAOLA, TOMIE. *The Art Lesson.* New York: Putnam's, 1989 (picture book; realism).
DUBOIS, WILLIAM. *Lion.* New York: Viking, 1974 (picture storybook; animal fantasy).
FOX, PAULA. *Village by the Sea.* New York: Orchard, 1988 (novel; realism).
HURD, THACHER. *Art Dog.* New York: HarperCollins, 1996 (picture book; animal fantasy).
ISADORA, RACHEL. *Willaby.* New York: Macmillan, 1977 (picture book; realism).
LEVINE, ARTHUR. *The Boy Who Drew Cats.* New York: Dial, 1993 (picture book; fantasy).
LIONNI, LEO. *Matthew's Dream.* New York: Knopf, 1991 (picture book; animal fantasy).
MORRISON, TAYLOR. *Antonio's Apprenticeship.* New York: Holiday House, 1996 (picture book, realism).
PATERSON, KATHERINE. *Bridge to Terabithia.* New York: Crowell, 1977 (novel; realism).
SAY, ALLEN. *Emma's Rug.* Boston: Houghton Mifflin, 1996 (picture book; realism).
SCHWARTZ, AMY. *Begin at the Beginning.* New York: Harper, 1983 (picture book; realism).
WILLIAMS, VERA. *Cherries and Cherry Pits.* New York: Greenwillow, 1986 (picture book; realism).

Genre Blendings

Beskow, Elsa. *Pelle's New Suit.* New York: Harper, 1989 (realistic fiction, historical fiction, science, history, picture book).

Bruchac, Joseph, and London, Jonathan. *Thirteen Moons on Turtle's Back: A Native American Year of Moons.* Illustrated by Thomas Locker. New York: Philomel, 1992 (poetry, Native American historical experience, Native American folklore, science, picture book).

Burningham, John. *Hey! Get Off Our Train.* New York: Crown, 1989 (picture book, realism, fantasy, dream fantasy, animal-human fantasy, science).

———. *Time to Get Out of the Bath, Shirley.* New York: Crowell, 1978 (picture book, realism, fantasy, daydream fantasy, folklore, medieval romance/adventure, time fantasy, parallel worlds).

Carle, Eric. *The Very Hungry Caterpillar.* New York: Philomel, 1987 (rpt. 1969) (interactive picture book—counting, tactile experience; science, fantasy).

Crews, Donald. *Freight Train.* New York: Greenwillow, 1978 (picture book; concept book—colors, motion, information, language).

D'Aulaire, Ingri and Edgar Parin. *D'Aulaires' Trolls.* Garden City, NY: Doubleday, 1972 (picture book, history, fantasy, legend, folklore).

Hamilton, Virginia. *Drylongso.* Illustrated by Jerry Pinkney. New York: Harcourt Brace, 1992 (realism, mythic fantasy, African-American folklore, science, picture book).

———. *Jaguarundi.* New York: Scholastic, 1995 (picture book, science, African-American history, fantasy, African-American folklore, information).

———. *The Magical Adventures of Pretty Pearl.* (New York: Harper and Row, 1983 (fantasy, African-American folklore, history, African-American history, magical realism).

———. *Many Thousand Gone: African Americans from Slavery to Freedom.* Illustrated by Leo and Diane Dillon. New York: Knopf, 1993 (biography, history, African-American history; illustrated stories).

———. *The People Could Fly: American Black Folktales.* Illustrated by Leo and Diane Dillon. New York: Knopf, 1985 (history, African-American history and folklore, fantasy, slave narrative, illustrated folk tales).

———. *Sweet Whispers, Brother Rush.* New York: Philomel, 1982 (fantasy, realism, African-American history and folklore, time fantasy).

Hirschfelder, Arlene, and Singer, Beverly, editors. *Rising Voices: Writings of Young Native Americans.* New York: Ivy Books, 1992 (history, Native American history, poetry, autobiography).

Hoberman, Mary Ann. *A House Is a House for Me.* Illustrated by Betty Fraser. New York: Viking, 1978 (poetry, science, picture book, information).

Issacs, Anne. *Swamp Angel.* New York: Dutton, 1994 (picture book, tall tale fantasy, invented legend of female giant).

Jarrell, Randall. *The Bat-Poet.* Illustrated by Maurice Sendak. New York: Macmillan, 1964 (fantasy, animal fantasy, poetry, illustrated story).

Kroll, Virginia. *Masai and I.* Illustrated by Nancy Carpenter. New York: Four Winds Press, 1992 (realism, daydream fantasy, information, geography, science, information).

McGowen, Tom. *Encyclopedia of Legendary Creatures.* Illustrated by Victor Ambrus. Chicago: Rand McNally, 1981 (history, information, folklore).

Musgrove, Margaret. *Ashanti to Zulu.* Illustrated by Leo and Diane Dillon, New York: Dial, 1976 (picture book, history, geography, ABC book, information, language, African heritage).

Ringgold, Faith. *Aunt Harriet's Underground Railroad in the Sky.* New York: Crown, 1992 (African-American history, fantasy, picture book, history, magical realism).

———. *Tar Beach.* New York: Crown, 1991 (fantasy, realism, history, multicultural, art, autobiography, and magical realism).

SHELDON, DYAN. *The Whales' Song.* Illustrated by Gary Blythe. New York: Dial, 1991 (picture book, realistic fiction, fantasy, legend, science).

SPIER, PETER. *The Legend of New Amsterdam.* New York: Doubleday, 1979 (history, legend, picture book).

TATE, ELEANORA. *Retold African Myths.* Logan, IA: Perfection Learning, 1993 (myth, African folklore, history, information).

WALSH, JILL PATON. *The Green Book.* New York: Farrar, 1982 (science fiction, fantasy, metafiction, science).

WIESNER, DAVID. *Free Fall.* New York: Lothrop, 1988 (dream fantasy, wordless, picture book, legend).

WILLIAMS, VERA. *Three Days on a River in a Red Canoe.* New York: Greenwillow, 1981 (fiction, nonfiction, science, information, picture book).

WILLIAMS, VERA AND JENNIFER. *Stringbean's Trip to the Shining Sea.* New York: Scholastic, 1988 (realistic picture book, travelogue, diary, autobiography).

YEP, LAURENCE. *Dragonwings.* New York: Harper: and Row, 1975 (fiction, historical fiction; nonfiction; Asian-American history, biography; fantasy, Asian folklore).

Surrealistic Picture Books

BROWNE, ANTHONY. *Alice's Adventures in Wonderland by Lewis Carroll.* New York: Knopf, 1988.

———. *Bear Goes to Town.* London: Hamish Hamilton, 1982.

———. *Changes.* New York: Knopf, 1990.

———. *Piggybook.* New York: Knopf, 1990.

———. *The Visitors Who Came to Stay.* London: Hamish Hamilton, 1984.

CLEMENT, CLAUDE. *The Painter and the Wild Swans.* Illustrated by Frederic Clement. New York: Dial, 1986.

DELAMARE, DAVID. *Cinderella.* New York: Green Tiger Press, 1994.

LEVINE, ARTHUR A. *The Boy Who Drew Cats.* Illustrated by Frederic Clement. New York: Dial, 1993.

ORAM, HIAWYN. *Angry Arthur.* Illustrated by Satoshi Kitamura. New York: Viking Penguin, 1984.

PILKEY, DAV. *When Cats Dream.* New York: Orchard Books, 1992.

SENDAK, MAURICE. *Outside Over There.* New York: Harper, 1981.

SIS, PETER. *The Three Golden Keys.* New York: Doubleday, 1994.

THOMPSON, COLIN. *Looking For Atlantis.* New York: Knopf, 1993.

VAN ALLSBURG, CHRIS. *Jumanji.* Boston: Houghton Mifflin, 1981.

WAHL, JAN. *Humphrey's Bear.* Illustrated by William Joyce. New York: Holt, 1987.

WIESNER, DAVID. *Free Fall.* New York: Lothrop, 1988.

———. *Tuesday.* New York: Clarion Books, 1991.

YORINKS, ARTHUR. *It Happened in Pinsk.* Illustrated by Richard Egielski. New York: Farrar, 1983.

———. *Louis the Fish.* Illustrated by Richard Egielski. New York: Farrar, 1980.

Chapter 5

How Readers Select and Evaluate Children's Books

Topics in this chapter:

- The concept of a literary "canon"
- Literary criteria and the selection of children's books
- Critical analysis of children's books
- Personal, social, and cultural values of authors and readers
- Issues of authenticity
- Censorship issues
- Issues of elitism

. . . when they had been running half an hour or so, and were quite dry again, the Dodo suddenly called out, "The race is over!" and they all crowded round it, panting, and asking,"But who has won?"

This question the Dodo could not answer without a great deal of thought, and it sat for a long time with one finger pressed upon its forehead (the position in which you usually see Shakespeare, in the pictures of him), while the rest waited in silence. At last the Dodo said, "Everybody has won, and all must have prizes."

"But who is to give the prizes?" quite a chorus of voices asked.

"Why she, of course," said the Dodo, pointing to Alice with one finger; and the whole party at once crowded round her, calling out in a confused way, "Prizes! Prizes!"

Alice had no idea what to do, and in despair she put her hand in her pocket, and pulled out a box of comfits (luckily the salt water had not got into it), and handed them round as prizes. There were exactly one a-piece all round.

"A Caucus-Race and a Long Tale" in Alice's Adventures in Wonderland, 1865
—Lewis Carroll

We have discussed how authors who question or resist established social values often produce unconventional, award-winning children's books. In this chapter, we will examine how adult readers (reviewers, critics, award selectors, teachers, librarians, booksellers, editors, publishers, and parents) receive, recognize, appraise, and award these mind-stretching works.

In any discussion of selection and evaluation, we must consider the concept of authoritative lists of recommended books—and why evaluators and critics recommend them. In the field of literature, the word *canon* usually describes an influential list of books or works considered "classic" or "sacred." The term comes from the Greek word *kanon,* meaning "rule," and the later Latin word *canon,* meaning a line by which to measure something—a rule or model.

THE CONCEPT OF A LITERARY "CANON"

The word *canon* has become synonymous with culturally valued books or classics, the books readers have handed down through the years—and even centuries—as important and valued works. But such an "official" list is by no means set in stone. As literary theorist Wendell Harris says, "Literary canons have always implicitly allowed for at least the possibility of adding new or revalued works" (page 111), and the same is true for children's literature.

Alice Jordan's *Horn Book* list on classics, for example, was certainly not a permanent one. Paul Heins, who succeeded her thirty years later as compiler of the list, dropped Walter Scott's *Ivanhoe* to make room on his list of 113 books for newer works such as E. B. White's *Charlotte's Web.* Heins also considered Frances Burnett's *The Secret Garden* and J. R. R. Tolkien's *The Hobbit* important enough to add to the list, and he decided to remove pictorial forms such as Beatrix Potter's *The Tale of Peter Rabbit* and Wanda Gäg's *Millions of Cats,* placing them on a separate list.

What causes books to land on such prestigious lists? Heins describes *recommended* books as "some of the best ever written for, or adopted by, children" (page 11). But what makes a children's book *good*—or the *best* ever written? Myles McDowell (1973) says that a "good children's book makes complex experience available to its readers; a good adult book draws attention to the inescapable complexity of experience" (page 143). Margaret Meek (1997) echoes the same sentiment when she describes works that "make children wise by letting them explore the big issues of life on a scale adapted to their understanding" (page 102).

Alice Jordan speaks of the "charm of style," "simplicity," and "sincerity" (page 4) of a good children's book, which provide a "foundation for the growth of discriminating literary taste" (page 9). English educator Fred Inglis says that good children's books "try to tell children how to live together better, in both present and future" and they "seek to portray as many people as they can, and to make as many people as possible recognize themselves as being portrayed" (page 228). According to Inglis, social, cultural, and personal values, rather than any *intrinsic* properties of a book, are what keep it interesting through the years. Jordan is looking at literature as an *art;* Inglis is looking at it as a *humanity.*

Social, cultural, personal, and aesthetic values thus determine whether a children's book finds an audience in its own day, and whether it survives over a great

Defining a Classic

Literary critic and novelist Italo Calvino has defined classics as books "treasured by those who have read and loved them" (books that have strongly influenced readers). Classics are also books that never finish saying what they have to say, says Calvino. Every "rereading of a classic is as much a voyage of discovery as the first reading." (We change with every reading; therefore, the reading changes. The times and places where readers live change, too.)

English critic and long-time reviewer of children's books Margery Fisher describes a children's classic as "layered and expandable, available to different ages in different ways," a book that offers "universal truths, universal values, to one generation after another, impermeable to the erosion of Time." Some books, she adds, become classics "by common consent"; modern classics we can only predict, although common consent is at work here, too.

Writing for *Horn Book Magazine* in 1947, children's book specialist Alice Jordan defined a classic as a book that has "weathered one generation and is accepted in the next." It is also a book that inspires "warm affection" from children and is intensely imaginative, in Jordan's opinion. Her list included, among others:

Alice in Wonderland (Lewis Carroll)
Robinson Crusoe (Daniel Defoe)
Pilgrim's Progress (John Bunyan)
Andersen's Fairy Tales (Hans Christian Andersen)
A Child's Garden of Verses (Robert Louis Stevenson)
Mother Goose (Kate Greenaway)
Nonsense Books (Edward Lear)
Tom Sawyer and *Huckleberry Finn* (Mark Twain)
Merry Adventures of Robin Hood and *Story of King Arthur* (Howard Pyle)
Swiss Family Robinson (J. D. Wyss)
Tom Brown's School Days (Thomas Hughes)
The Arabian Nights
At the Back of the North Wind and *The Princess and the Goblin* (George MacDonald)
The King of the Golden River (John Ruskin)
The Wonder Book and *Tanglewood Tales* (Nathaniel Hawthorne)
Hans Brinker (Mary Mapes Dodge)
Little Women (Louisa May Alcott)
Heidi (Johanna Spyri)
Grimm's Fairy Tales (Brothers Grimm)
Pinocchio (Carlo Collodi)
The Wonderful Adventures of Nils (Selma Lagerloff)
Mary Poppins (Pamela Travers)
The Wind in the Willows (Kenneth Grahame)

Children's literature specialists John Griffith and Charles Frey have more recently produced a shorter list of classics. They include **folk and fairy tales** from the collections of Charles Perrault and Mme. de Beaumont (France), the Brothers Grimm (Germany), Hans Christian Andersen (Denmark), Peter Asbjornsen and Jorgen Moe (Norway), and Joseph Jacobs (British Isles); **verse** by Edward Lear; **verse** and **fantasy** by Lewis Carroll; **verse** and **adventure stories** by Robert Louis Stevenson; **fiction** by Charles Dickens *(A Christmas Carol),* John Ruskin *(The King of the Golden River),* Carlo Collodi *(The Adventures of Pinocchio),* Louisa May Alcott *(Little Women),* Mark Twain *(The Adventures of Tom Sawyer),* L. Frank Baum *(The Wonderful Wizard of Oz),* Kenneth Grahame *(The Wind in the Willows),* Rudyard Kipling *(The Jungle Books),* Laura Ingalls Wilder (the Little House series), and C. S. Lewis (the Narnia series); and **illustrated works** by Randolph Caldecott, Kate Greenaway, and Beatrix Potter.

Sources: Italo Calvino, *The Uses of Literature* (New York: Harcourt Brace, 1986), 126–127.
Margery Fisher, *Classics for Children & Young People* (Stroud, England: Thimble Press, 1986), 1.
John Griffith and Charles Frey, *Classics of Children's Literature* (New York: Prentice Hall, 1995).
Alice Jordan, *Children's Classics* (Boston: The Horn Book, 1947), 4–8.

stretch of time. If many different people decide the books on a list, different kinds of lists—or different "canons"—arise. The lists we usually associate with quality children's books are similar to those Alice Jordan and Paul Heins compiled, the ones designating the "classics," or bestowing literary awards.

Books winning the most prestigious awards often go on to become modern classics or members of the "official" canon. We tend to think these are the books we must know about, so that we can help children to know them, too. Children's book writers and illustrators are therefore overjoyed—and overwhelmed—when they win such an award. Consider the opening words of Paul Zelinsky's Caldecott Medal acceptance speech in 1998, when his picture book *Rapunzel* (Dutton, 1997) won this coveted award:

> I have a confession to make: this is a moment I have staged in my imagination, any number of times, when I've needed cheering up. I stand at a podium in a vast room. Surrounding me, a festive crowd fills a sea of round tables and disappears off into the misty distance. The image of this transcendent scene, I'm embarrassed to say, has lulled me to sleep during troubled times that accompanied more than one book. (page 432)

Zelinsky ends his speech with equally joyous words: "I think that nothing in the world is comparable to this" (page 441). Reception into the canon brings recognition, monetary reward, respect from one's peers, and strong feelings of validation and self-worth. Zelinsky's words are therefore not surprising, coming as they do from a dedicated artist. But consider the books that win no awards. Booksellers and librarians pore over descriptive listings of books in the publishers' catalogs in order to make their purchasing decisions. Few are award winners. Also consider the lists that teachers make for text sets or that parents place on their children's gift lists. Each of these "lists"—based on awards, sales, teaching methods, or purchasing—involves different values, different priorities, different ways to measure or rank books.

In this chapter, we will be looking first at the **critical** canon and how it intersects with the **selective** and **personal** canons. Then we will look at both the selective and personal canons in terms of cultural and personal values.

INVESTIGATIONS: Taking a Deeper Look at a Classic

From either of the lists in the box "Defining a Classic," choose a classic that you have never read, and read it now. Then write about the book in your journal. List important traits you think might have made the book a classic. Tell whether you think the book deserves classic status now.

INVESTIGATIONS: How Do Books Become Classics?

Consider how a children's book might achieve classic status in a culture. Do children love the book, or do adults want—or expect—children to love the book as *they* did (thus, the book is handed down from one generation to the next)? Or does the book have strong literary strength (intrinsic worth)? On the other hand, perhaps the book reflects the social values of the author's day. Construct your own theory and write about it, using books that you consider classics to support your arguments.

The critical canon causes us to focus on the literary strength or artistic integrity of children's books. Often we utilize literary criteria to rank books or designate them as significant, taking notice of awards, reviewers' notices, and critical attention. Yet literary criteria are not the only tools we can use to rank books. When children's books attract social and cultural attention because of conflicting ideologies among readers, they often gain unexpected significance—as we will see later in this chapter.

Different Canons, Different Rules

Wendell Harris has described a number of "canons" at work in the literary world. We can see six canons operating in the children's book world: the **potential, accessible, selective, critical, personal, official,** and **pedagogical** canons.

A **potential** canon would include all books ever written. Large libraries include many of the books published in a particular culture, but no one has ever compiled a list of every book published anywhere, and no one could, even if all of them had been translated. Children's literature is, of necessity, culture-bound in many ways. Children are therefore limited to books theoretically *accessible* to them, or to

- books published in their native language, or in translation, in their native land;
- books purchased by libraries (public and school) for public use;
- books purchased by bookstores; and
- books purchased by family members.

These are the components of the **accessible** canon—the books potentially available to a reader.

The books that publishing companies actually decide to print and that librarians and booksellers actually decide to purchase make up the **selective** canon. Editors accept certain books for publication (they *select* from the many manuscripts submitted) and print these books for readers. Publishers also *select* certain books from other countries and acquire the rights to publish them in this country. Reviewers *select* some of these published books and recommend them to booksellers, librarians, teachers, and parents. Librarians *select* and purchase some of these books for their shelves, and teachers *select* some of the books on the shelves for classroom use. Children pull certain books from library and bookstore shelves as their own *selections.* The question is, *which* books do editors, reviewers, and readers select?

The key word in selection is *values.* Editors' values cause them to select certain books for publication. Publishers' values cause them to translate certain foreign books for publication. Readers—critics, reviewers, librarians, teachers, parents, and children—choose books they value and recommend them to others.

When adults closely read books and, in Harris's words, "see unexpected significance and intriguing modes of argument" (page 112), they compile a **critical** canon. The critical canon is also rooted in values, and values are rooted in personal feelings and experiences. The **personal** canon—the list of books readers love and recommend to others—intersects at times with the critical canon. The critical canon in many ways is the **official** canon—the books we think we *must* read to be well-educated. The most discriminating "judges" have deemed them important.

Pedagogical canons grow out of what is "commonly taught" at different levels, in different eras, in different places, says Harris (page 115). Thus do canon "wars" arise: People disagree about which books we should read or teach and about which books should be added to the canon. Pedagogical canons are much more strongly entrenched at the secondary level; works such as *Macbeth, Huckleberry Finn,* and *To Kill a Mockingbird* often seem fixed in curricular stone. At the elementary level, popular writers such as Judy Blume and Roald Dahl often mix easily with Newbery and Caldecott winners.

Source: Wendell Harris, "Canonicity," *PMLA* 106 (January, 1991): 110–121.

LITERARY CRITERIA AND THE SELECTION OF CHILDREN'S BOOKS

When critics speak of the "strength" of a literary piece, they usually point to qualities such as depth of character, evocative scenes, artistic use of language, and distinctive narrative design or structure. For many adults, a *good* book must have strong artistic integrity. These adults want children to read books that will help them become *discriminating* readers. The best books, from this perspective, are those with high literary standards. But critics decide upon literary standards based on their personal values—values not only concerning what makes a children's book good, but what makes a book a *children's* book.

Literary and Artistic Merit

The primary purpose of the **selective** canon, as we have seen, is to inform us about currently available books through descriptive lists, whereas the purpose of the **critical** canon is to set standards or tell us why certain books belong on those lists. John Townsend combines the two functions in *Written for Children,* a survey of children's fiction, poetry, and picture books, and he has specific ideas about why these books have literary merit.

For Robert Louis Stevenson's *Treasure Island* (1883), Townsend cites reader engagement: The book "has swept nearly all readers away" since it first appeared (page 45). He also cites "creation of a world of the author's own that carries absolute conviction," "vividly drawn characters," and "total liberation from didacticism" (pages 44–46). Thus, Townsend expresses his own personal value: Children's literature should be read for pleasure, not for instruction.

Writing about Frances Burnett's *The Secret Garden* (1911), Townsend cites a character struggling to achieve heroic status and the books "rich texture" rather than

Criteria for Literary Elements in Children's Books

Characters

- Child character struggles to achieve heroic status
- Child character achieves something *real* (inner-directed behavior), *important* (the child places something into the world that was not there before), and *adultlike* (the child is self-reliant)

Setting

- Created world carries conviction
- Story has a strong sense of place
- Setting achieves an enduring place in time

Point of View / Child's Perspective

- Aim or purpose of the book is pleasure (versus didacticism)
- Child's eye is at the center of the story
- Treatment of the child is sincere; we see real (versus idealized or sentimentalized) lives of real children

Style / Language

- Characters are vividly drawn
- Writing is precise and clear
- Story is full, rich, and straightforward

Source: John Rowe Townsend, *Written for Children* (New York: Harper, 1992).

one-dimensional story line. He also sees a child's "real, important, adult-level achievement." The children in the story are self-reliant, constructive, and inner-directed, and they cooperate to make something (the garden) (pages 65–66).

Critiquing Alison Uttley's *A Traveller in Time* (1939), Townsend finds a "profound and loving sense of place" and "the endurance of that place in time" (page 139). To *Charlotte's Web* (1952), he credits a "straightforward story that is astonishingly full and rich" (page 215). Consequently, as he discusses a great number of books, he establishes criteria for four literary elements: characters, setting, point of view, and literary style.

Townsend also helps us see what to look for in different genres. In **poetry,** he searches for language "full of colour and flavour, offering brief intense experiences" (page 301), as he sees in Grace Nichols' poems. In **picture books,** he looks for strongly detailed illustrations that children can pore over and explore, as he notices in Janet and Allen Ahlberg's *The Jolly Postman* (1986). He also seeks words and pictures "full of life and movement and ideas" (page 160), as he finds in Ludwig Bemelman's *Madeline* (1939). And Townsend looks for "ingenious development of original and truly visual ideas" (page 161), as he finds in books by Dr. Seuss.

In **contemporary fiction,** Townsend mentions the "tackling of tough subjects" (page 269); he sees this in Katherine Paterson's work. He notes "sympathy that never becomes sentimental" (page 253), which he finds in Nina Bawden's fiction. He also looks for a "profound sense of [the author's] involvement [with the main character]" (page 247), as he notices in Mollie Hunter's books.

In **historical fiction,** Townsend searches for the writer's ability to bring the past to "pulsing life" and "to make a historical story comprehensible and attractive to the younger readers" (pages 178–79), traits he feels are characteristic of Rosemary Sutcliff's many novels. In **fantasy,** he notices "memorable people" "a mysterious sense of time"

Criteria for Literary Genres in Children's Books

Poetry

- Brief, intense experiences of different voices
- Unpretentious verses about children's everyday experiences

Picture Books

- Strongly detailed illustrations children can pore over and explore
- Pictures completely integrated with words
- Words and pictures full of life, movement, and ideas
- Truly original visual ideas, coupled with ingenuity

Contemporary Realistic Fiction

- Tackling of tough subjects
- Sympathetic rather than sentimental treatment of subject
- Depth of feeling arising from author's emotional involvement with characters or subject

Historical Fiction

- Past brought to life vividly
- Past made comprehensible and attractive to young readers

Fantasy

- Action and setting real enough to make an impact on readers
- Memorable characters
- Mysterious sense of time and place
- Well-constructed, well-designed work

Source: John Rowe Townsend, *Written for Children* (New York: Harper, 1992).

and place, and a "perfectly constructed and proportional work" (pages 235–36), all of which he finds in Philippa Pearce's *Tom's Midnight Garden* (1958).

We might argue that some of these criteria are so subjective, they offer us little practical good as a model. The character one person would designate as "memorable" might differ significantly from another person's designation, and people might have very different views of what constitutes a "sentimental" treatment. Yet Townsend's ideas about books and genres give us an important reference point for making our own judgments; critics help us to see with new eyes.

Of course, Townsend is not the only reviewer defining literary criteria for us. Experienced readers everywhere and in all eras tend to rank authors. In children's literature, reviews and criticism help readers select the "best" books. The many committees that sponsor awards, prizes, and medals for artistic integrity also help define the criteria for "good" or the "best" children's literature.

Consider the Orbis Pictus Award, given by the National Council of Teachers of English each year since 1990, for outstanding *nonfiction* for children—a category Townsend's study does not include. These books must be designed to share information, and they may be biography, historical fiction, folklore, or poetry. Four selection criteria are at stake: accuracy, organization, design, and style.

Selection Criteria for the Orbis Pictus Award

What constitutes "excellence" in nonfiction? The National Council of Teachers of English named their award for a nonfiction book by Johannes Amos Comenius published in 1657. His work, *Orbis Pictus—The World in Pictures* may be the first book actually planned for a child audience. Comenius, a Czech theologian, produced a book about the world (*Orbis Pictus* means The World Pictured). It contained a text and labeled woodcut engravings that depicted the natural world, everyday life, a religious view of life, and learning itself.

Nonfiction designated as "outstanding" by NCTE members must be **accurate.** The book's facts should be up-to-date and comprehensive, and fact and theory should be in balance. Authentic details are important, and the point of view must reveal scope and variety. Authors should be qualified to take on the chosen subject, and they must avoid stereotypes.

Winning books must also be **organized** logically, with a clear sequence of events or ideas and clear connections. The **design** of the book should attract readers; readability is also important. Pictures must complete words, and the placement of pictures must work well with media, format, and print type. The writing **style** needs to stimulate the child reader's curiosity and maintain reader interest. The author's enthusiasm for the content is crucial; his or her language should be both rich and appropriate for the subject matter. Because these award-winning books will be used in K–8 classrooms, they should encourage thinking and additional reading. They must also be timely and present a model of strong nonfiction writing. Winners must also have been published in the United States during the preceding year.

Orbis Pictus winners have included *The Great Little Madison* by Jean Fritz (Putnam, 1990); *Franklin Delano Roosevelt* by Russell Freedman (Clarion, 1991); *Flight: The Journey of Charles Lindbergh* by Robert Burleigh and Mike Wimmer (Philomel, 1992), *Children of the Dust Bowl* by Jerry Stanley (Crown, 1993); *Across America on an Emigrant Train* by Jim Murphy (Clarion, 1994); *Safari Beneath the Sea* by Diane Swanson (Sierra Club, 1995); *The Great Fire* by Jim Murphy (Scholastic, 1996); *Leonardo da Vinci* by Diane Stanley (Morrow, 1997); and *An Extraordinary Life: The Story of a Monarch Butterfly* by Laurence Pringle, illustrated by Bob Marstall (Orchard 1998), and *Shipwreck at the Bottom of the World* by Jennifer Armstrong (Crown, 1998).

Source: "The NCTE Orbis Pictus Award" (Urbana, IL: NCTE, 1999).

Prizes

Every other year, the International Board on Books for Young People (IBBY) brings together publishers, librarians, educators, authors, and illustrators of children's books to promote high standards for children's books around the world, share ideas, exhibit children's books, and grant awards. Their prize for the entire body of an author's work (words or pictures) is the Hans Christian Andersen Award. In 1990, the IBBY Conference was held in the United States, with the award for writing going to Tormod Haugen from Norway and the award for illustration going to Lisbeth Zwerger from Austria.

Remarks by Ana Maria Machado, President of the Hans Christian Andersen Jury, help us understand more about literary and artistic merit in children's books. They also help us to see the accessible canon at work, because jurists of this international award must often seek help from translators. Juries for this prestigious award examine books from around the world for a year's time. Then the eight-member group, all from different cultural backgrounds, meet to share opinions and decide who produced the best children's books from all over the world.

Prior to meeting in person, the jurists write to one another as they build a framework for criteria. Then when they convene, they share their judgments of each author they've selected during a first round of discussion. Debates arise; then voting begins, with jurists submitting the names of half the nominees for elimination purposes. Discussions continue on the narrowed list; then the committee takes the next vote. On and on they go, as do the Newbery and Caldecott committees, until they narrow the list to one writer and one illustrator.

In the 1990 awards, Machado, a painter, children's book writer, children's bookstore owner, professor at the University of Rio de Janeiro, news editor, and literary critic, described the winners in terms of their perceived aesthetic strengths. The jurists decided Lisbeth Zwerger is "able to give a poetical depth to everyday objects and characters"; her "characters are always individuals," her "sense of colour" has "an unexpected mixture of humor and poetry, with a dancelike movement in her characters." Zwerger "makes her own style," Machado adds, managing "to create in each illustration a work of art in itself" (pages 64–65).

Machado begins describing Tormod Haugen by describing strengths for any finalist. He has "masterly craftsmanship," she says, "in building stories, in developing characters, in deepening situations little by little, using a meaningful detail in one paragraph, suggesting a certain mood in another, choosing the perfect point of view, creating a very personal rhythm in his prose." She goes on to describe what makes Haugen's work particularly special—or one of the best writers for children and young people all over the world. Haugen "opens new paths to children's literature." He has the power to tell a moving story; he goes deeply "into suffering and pains that may haunt the soul of a child in a world full of problems that cannot be fully understood or completely solved." He also has the "power to create a world, something that could not be suspected to exist before and whose absence cannot be imagined afterwards" (page 66).

In Haugen's world, the child's "most intimate and individual fears and pains, the most personal hopes and dreams, become common experiences, so well are they expressed." He reveals the "darkest corners of a person's soul . . . in a magic mirror and, by doing so, help[s] [them] to grow and see things more clearly." His child characters

From *The Nightingale* (Picture Book Studio, 1984) by Hans Christian Andersen, illustrated by Lisbeth Zwerger.

"find the necessary strength to fight nightmares made of real problems and symbolic monsters, and to finally overcome them with their own resources" (page 66).

Haugen's acceptance speech further illuminates Machado's words. He notes that the "worst thing that can happen to a child when it disappoints the expectations of a grown-up is to be punished by being thrown out. And there the child has to stand outside the door in the feeling of cold darkness, knocking on the door to be let in. And the door does not open until the grown-up finds it suitable . . . It is as if we adults forget that our lives are based on childhood—that childhood is the main place from which we communicate with ourselves . . . and get essential information about ourselves as whole human beings" (page 73).

Haugen's special subject, "the emotional life of children threatened by uncomprehending adults," is one that he crafts with "fantastic devices and poetic sensitivity," Machado notes (page 68). These qualities we see in Haugen's *Keeping Secrets,* translated by David Jacobs and illustrated by Donna Diamond (New York: HarperCollins, 1994), as he describes his child character, Nina:

> That terrible time.
> She was six years old and ran away from home.
> She didn't remember why any more. The rest she would never forget:

Night came, and darkness.
She cried and was alone.
A policeman found her and took her home.
The lights in the window were good.
The door was safe.
But Eva [her mother] was crying, and Martin [her father] was standing
white and stern behind her chair . . .
'How could you do this to us?
How could you frighten us so!'
She was punished. She had to go to bed without a
comforting word or supper or a warm hand against her cheek. (pages 4–5)

Each year in England, the journal *Signal Approaches to Children's Books* presents an award for poetry published in Britain during the previous year. At times, it also publishes articles in which award selectors describe the selection process for this award. In the May 1993 issue, three selectors discussed their choices for the 1992 award. Diana Hendry expressed the need for poets to develop "voices that could speak to children" (page 71). The winner was Jackie Kay's *Two's Company* (London: Blackie, 1991), and Hendry voted for Kay because of her feeling that Kay's voice was a new one "rough and raw at the edges . . . but possessing a lot of energy in its newness and above all addressing children in their own tongue, which is not (if you eavesdrop on them) the tongue of adults" (pages 71–72).

Said Hendry, "My need, in poetry, is for less story and more silent space. It is the silent spaces that allow me to apply both my own imagination and experiences to the words on the page . . . For me, a poem is a structure in words that allows the equivalent of light—a kind of timeless time—to pass through it." She added that she loved "the mystery left intact" in a poem, so that "we are left free to apply our own personal experiences to [it]" (pages 73–74).

Another selector, Stephen Bicknell, added that Kay "had more to say" than the other contenders: "I felt that she not only wanted to communicate but that she *needed* to communicate, and the communication happened so effectively because she possessed her own style and used it with passion." Bicknell valued the way Kay cared "passionately about the people in her life and the world we live in." Passion, fun, social realism, vivid imagination of childhood, and the theme of

The Laura Ingalls Wilder Award

In America, a "twin" to the Hans Christian Andersen Award is the Laura Ingalls Wilder Award: It also encompasses the entire body of an author or illustrator's work. Every three years, the American Library Association presents an award to a children's author who has made a substantial and lasting contribution to the field, occupies an important place in literature for American children, has been read and continues to be read by children, and produces literature of artistic merit. In addition, the author's body of work must provide a leading example of a particular genre or establish a new genre or new trends in the field. Winners include Laura Ingalls Wilder, Clara Judson, Ruth Sawyer, E. B. White, Beverly Cleary, Dr. Seuss, Maurice Sendak, Jean Fritz, Elizabeth Speare, Marcia Brown, Virginia Hamilton, and Russell Freedman.

Source: "Laura Ingalls Wilder Awards" (Chicago: ALA, 1978; materials distributed 1998).

love's strength against the forces of hate and oppression are the qualities that make Kay's book feel "authentic" (page 80).

"The voices in poems," wrote Jennifer Wilson, a third selector, "are what makes them specific; the keys to understanding and the music in the words . . . and each 'hearing' of an individual voice brings more understanding of the subtleties of meaning in the words." *Voice* means "expressing opinions, making ourselves heard." The poet's voice "may harmonize with a reader's own voice"; or it may "provoke discord or introduce new tones." The best poems, "are about keenly felt experience, carefully and economically expressed in a variety of poetic forms . . . Adults don't read poetry to see themselves in a plain glass mirror, but to find resonance of their experience in other worlds, and children need the same" (pages 87–89).

Wilson called Kay's *Two's Company* "intensely personal poetry" about having hurt feelings, being a different color, speaking with a different accent, being envied, feeling anger, frustration, and defiance. "Alive and kicking," it was "well-suited to dramatic delivery," as we see in "Big Brother's Big Catch" (pages 89–90):

> On the tiny rowing boat my brother disgusted me
> hammering his great catch with a massive mallet
> almost maliciously, his eyes glinted when ages
> later the bloody fish started to jump again. (page 90)

Each November, the *New York Times* chooses what it considers the ten best illustrated children's books of the year. The judges are listed, but not their criteria. However, if we turn to reviews of the winning books, often published in the same issue, we can see what is noteworthy about these books.

Reviews of Children's Books

The *New York Times Book Review* publishes reviews of children's books every two to three weeks. Twice yearly, in May and November, it publishes a special section

The NCTE Poetry Award

In America, a "twin" to the Signal Poetry Award is the NCTE Award for Excellence in Poetry for Children. Every three years, the National Council of Teachers of English recognizes and fosters distinguished children's poetry by awarding a living American poet for the entire body of his or her work. The award encourages publishers to publish poetry and teachers to use it in the classroom.

The criteria for selection include literary merit, the poet's contribution to the field, evolution of the poet's work, and the appeal of the poet's work to children. A poem has literary merit if the poet is able to "excite the reader's imagination with keen perceptions and sharp images" and "touch the reader's emotions." Authenticity of the poet's voice is another criterion; the poet must have technical and artistic expertise and produce a variety of poetic styles and expressions. The poet's style must also be evolving; the poet must take risks in order to grow. Children must be excited by this author's work, which should stir "fresh insights and feelings."

Winners include David McCord (1977), Aileen Fisher (1978), Karla Kuskin (1979), Myra Cohn Livingston (1980), Eve Merriam (1981), John Ciardi (1982), Lillian Moore (1985), Arnold Adoff (1988), Valerie Worth (1991), Barbara Juster Esbensen (1994), and Eloise Greenfield (1997).

Source: "The NCTE Award for Excellence in Poetry for Children" (Urbana, IL: NCTE, 1998).

From *Swanp Angel* (Dutton, 1994) by Anne Isaacs, illustrated by Paul Zelinsky.

devoted to children's books. In 1994, two of the *Times'* best illustrated books were *Swamp Angel* by Anne Isaacs, illustrated by Paul Zelinsky (Dutton), and *The Three Golden Keys* by Peter Sis (Doubleday). Jack Zipes, who has written a great deal about feminist revisions of folk tales, wrote the review of *Swamp Angel.* Patricia Hampl, who has written a memoir about Prague, the setting of Sis's book, wrote the review of *The Three Golden Keys.* Both reviewers focus on these books in terms of their own special interests.

Zipes notes the way Anne Isaacs has reversed many conventions of traditional legends in this picture book, featuring a brave female who takes on a mammoth bear that threatens the Tennessee folk. He points out the "dry, tongue-in-cheek style" and the "stunning primitive and burlesque-style oil paintings done on wood veneers" that make the book "one of the most intriguing and hilarious tall tales to be published in recent years." Describing Angel as "savvy" and "strong," Zipes says there are "very few tall tales about extraordinary women in American folklore." And "this comic rendition about a "gifted, powerful and helpful woman is in all ways superb" (page 30).

Hampl notes the fantasy premise of Peter Sis's book. In this autobiographical fantasy, Sis returns to Prague in a hot-air balloon in an attempt to recover his personal past. But to do so, he must first find the "communal past" of this Czech setting of his childhood. As he unearths scenes of his childhood home, Sis revisits three ancient figures: a mythic Prince, the legendary Golem of Jewish folklore, and a fifteenth-century artist who made an astronomical clock for Prague.

Sis produces a unique portrayal of the dream state as he transforms memory into myth, says Hampl. The reviewer sees the strength of the book as its artwork. She points out the buildings that are "just slightly human—dour with debonair mustaches, gates sporting decorative nose rings" and the three "great padlocks" that close Sis out of his past, "his deepest world." She notices that the "facelike windows of the house [of his childhood] have a ghostly vacancy." She notes the "sentient" streets," with the "lamplight pooling in lost corners" (page 34).

Most especially, Hampl brings to our attention Sis's depiction of the "grand Strahov Library" and the librarian with his "leather-bound book-spine nose, his open encyclopedia of hair and his tidy goatee of trimmed pages, the tomes of his hands holding . . . books and maps and open pages." Sis, she notes, has produced a book that "even his magical Strahov librarian would clasp to his heart—or maybe *make* his heart" (page 34).

The book is a rarity—a time-travel fantasy in picture book form—but because of its dark and brooding mood, it may be too conceptually sophisticated for children to clasp to their own hearts. As Hampl says, Sis created "a book not only for his child, but for the adult she will one day be" and "one an adult will keep reaching for" (page 34).

Reviewing at its best gives us a brief look at what a book is about, its literary strengths, and the qualities that make it unique in terms of artistic integrity, ideas, and authenticity. Reviewers help us to see what we might otherwise miss, and, like critics, they must be perceptive readers. Unlike critics, however, as Patricia Wrightson (1986) notes, reviewers function as "consenting" readers, "free to enter the story, to fly or float with it, to respond to it directly without the screen of awareness, and even to work with it unconsciously." Such "participation" is what stories are made for, in her opinion (pages 180–81).

Critics approach stories differently, Wrightson explains. They are searching for values and drawing conclusions, trying to establish what in particular a writer has to contribute to the literary world. To do so, she says, the critic must break the reader's "truest link" with the work, the emotional "chain" that binds the reader to the story. Stepping back to examine this chain and to assess its links, the critic comes to "know the source of its power," unlike the reader, who "must only consent" (pages 178–80).

The major role of reviewers, then, is to help readers sort through the huge piles of newly published books (the **potential** canon) and to weed out the weaker "vessels"—those lacking the emotional power to draw readers into the story. The job of the critic is to take a deeper and longer look at a new work, to salvage an old and perhaps forgotten one, or to take a book apart like a watch, as Wrightson says, to "test its power" (page 181). But what causes critics to proclaim a book worthy of close inspection? What makes them decide a book is worth salvaging? In the next section, we will try to answer this question.

CRITICAL ANALYSIS OF CHILDREN'S BOOKS

What exerts the strongest influence on critics of children's literature? Aesthetic standards? Historical, social, and cultural contexts? Personal experiences? Literary theories? Interdisciplinary perspectives? The child's perspective? What *should* exert the strongest influence? And in what ways do children to enter the critical picture?

The Critic, The Child Audience, and the Implied Child Reader

Barbara Bader is presently critic at large for *Horn Book Magazine.* But in 1976, she produced *American Picturebooks from Noah's Ark to the Beast Within,* a classic reference work in children's literature and the first historical study of American picture books. Bader came to her task well-prepared; she had been an art historian, a children's librarian, and a reviewer of children's books. The focus in her book is the picture book as an art form, in the context of social and cultural history and in relation to her knowledge of the child audience. Her aim is to examine books, both the popular successes and the prize winners, for their artistic integrity and for the way they tell children about themselves or the way they illuminate the child's own feelings.

Consider how Bader discusses a book very popular with children through the years, but nearly impossible to analyze—Esphyr Slobodkina's *Caps For Sale* (Harper, 1940). The book works—and works especially well with children, who love the comic situation—but what more can we say, especially when to analyze humor is often to destroy it? Bader finds a way.

She begins by discussing the book in some detail. A peddler, wearing the stack of caps he is trying to sell, takes a walk in the country and falls asleep under a tree. Waking, he discovers that monkeys playing in the tree have stolen all the caps except his own. They will not give back the caps, so in frustration, he throws down his own cap, and the monkeys—in imitation—do the same. The peddler then retrieves his caps and walks back into town.

Bader quotes lines from the text to reveal the narrative patterns, to describe the writer's strategies for dramatizing the peddler's frustration, and to emphasize the comic aspects of his behavior—for example, the way he walks to keep the caps poised on his head.

Next she discusses the book in terms of her experience with child readers, especially the way children love to mimic the peddler as he lashes out at the monkeys and the monkeys "talk back": "Tsz, tsz, tsz." Then she attempts to unravel the book to explain why it gives pleasure to children. It is an old tale, Bader begins. (Slobodkina, an abstract artist, emigrated to America from Russia in 1928, bringing the story with her.) But the artist has, in Bader's words, "stripped" the tale down "to plot-scheme, suspense, patterned language and repetition" and into a "great comic situation." If we wanted to produce the "ideal picture-story by rote," she adds, "this would be a model to follow" (page 235).

Then Bader delves into the way pictures work to "make" the story mean something—or mean something comical to children. Slobodkina used cut-out colored paper because she thought she could produce a simpler line with scissors than with pen. Color layout, as it meshes with text, is equally important, as Bader explains:

> The pictures are important, partly because they are extraordinarily good—meticulous in the manner of the modern primitives, colored an odd memorable mustard, red, and robin's-egg blue; and partly because the text and the layout play to them. One need only look at the peddler napping, note his checked trousers, tight collar, mustache, tie; the different solid trees in the back to right and left, the gnarled outspread branches above, studded with single leaves, each in its way genus *tree;* the red tulip-form flowers, genus *flower;* and capping all, the pillar of caps—to

From *Caps for Sale* (Harper, 1940)
by Esphyr Slobodkina.

> appreciate the difference between simplicity and inspired simplification. And one has only to turn the page to the sun smiling down on a single flower on a curve of the world, a corner of the globe, while the text reads "He slept for a long time," to understand contrast and harmony. (page 235)

Bader teaches us to see what makes the book succeed—or in this case, how it fuses the serious purpose adults seem to crave in books for children with the light touch that actually draws children in. She also teaches us more about what a picture book is. The picture layout tells how the story is being told; thus, it becomes part of the story. Color, size, and direction change as the story unfolds. At the same time, the pictures show what the story is about: man in nature, man versus nature, and man acting according to his own nature.

The peddler steals away from his work to enjoy *nature,* but he encounters a problem. The monkeys—in nature—want to enjoy *culture* (the humanmade caps). How does the man solve the problem? He simply *acts* and *reacts,* according to human nature, and the rest follows naturally. The monkeys follow his lead and—presto—he has his caps back. Then back to civilization he goes to sell his wares, and as he goes, he calls out the same words that began the book: "Caps! Caps for sale! Fifty cents a cap!"

Everything is simple, clear-cut, and proportioned for a child's comprehension, amusement, and understanding; and that is what makes this picture book good.

The Critic and the Remembered Child

Roger Sale's experience as a professor of literature, a parent, a child reader, and an adult reader all inspired him to create one of the first book-length critical examinations of children's books in *Fairy Tales and After* (1978). Sale's perspective was that of a person simply "wanting to write about very good books." Literary analysis of children's books was, as he said at that time, still in an embryonic state: "Many people see no need for criticism of children's literature, since for them criticism is mostly explication, and children's literature demands little explicating" (pages 2–3).

Yet, if the definition of literature is "that it gives profit and delight," Sale reasoned, children's literature had every reason to be considered *literature.* He discovered his own adult delight in this field when he read the Oz books (by L. Frank Baum) to his children and when then reread them again ten years later (thirty years after he heard them as a child). At this time, he knew "that something so persistently profitable and delightful had to be accounted for" (page 3).

Sale's aim in this book is to discover what effect the early love of children's books had on his later reading and to discuss strengths and weaknesses of several children's books that inspired "imaginative sympathy" (page 5). He opens this study of children's classics, including *Alice in Wonderland, Peter Rabbit,* and *Charlotte's Web,* with discussions of several books from his own childhood reading, including Dr. Seuss's *The 500 Hats of Bartholomew Cubbins* (1938) and Jean de Brunhoff's *The Travels of Babar* (1934).

Sale tells us that Dr. Seuss's book gave him a "residual sense of wonder and possibility" and the knowledge that when we confront the "angry kings and cavernous castles" of our later lives, we go on being ourselves. All we need we already have, Sale explains, just as Bartholomew Cubbins had all he really needed each time he took off another hat. As readers, we trust there will be no hat beyond the five hundredth, as the title foretells, but not because we have an explanation. We do not know why the hats stop appearing any more than we know why they appeared in the first place. The fun is in the mystery, the magic, and the control the reader has in knowing that all will end happily. Thus, the magic will always be present (the mystery will never be unraveled).

The magic of Jean de Brunhoff's Babar story lies in the pictures. Sale remembers staring at them as he stared at no other book; he found somberness in the words but playfulness in the pictures. Thus, as a child he realized that you can fight a dragon by staring it down, "since even the most shocking moments will last no longer than the most satisfying ones: both take no longer than two facing pages" (page 14). The "essential message of the text" for Sale as a child, then, was simply what he gained from the pictures.

"It is no accident," he adds, that "my happiest moments of reading aloud to my children were with the Babar books. I could watch the child stare at the pictures, solemn but never frightened, amused but never laughing, and derive my own pleasure from the way the apparently skimpy text released us both into enjoying the pictures. De Brunhoff allies child and adult so that each can arrive at the same place by a somewhat different route" (page 15).

With Seuss, Sale realizes, his pleasure as an adult replicated his childhood feelings. With de Brunhoff, he sees more now, but the reading pleasure—then and now—does not conflict with his new understanding. Both writers show him the pleasure of accepting "the actual and possible in the midst of magic, confusion, loss, and lostness" (page 19). Accept the unfathomable, and you will somehow survive it (Dr. Seuss); accept the bad because it is as short-lived as the good that precedes or follows it (Jean de Brunhoff). Acceptance is potential power for the child, says Sale. The theme Sale extracts from his childhood reading is the one he most often searches for and chooses in adult writers. Thus, he concludes, childhood reading is highly important for influencing adult tastes and understanding.

The Critic, the Child Reader, and the Child Character

In her introduction to *Mad About Madeline: The Complete Tales of Ludwig Bemelmans* (Viking, 1993), novelist, essayist, and parent Anna Quindlen begins by telling how her three children loved the Madeline books. They emulated Madeline, quoted her words, and imitated her actions. What accounts for this affection? Madeline's *attitude,* Quindlen says. Madeline is "utterly fearless and sure of herself, small in stature but large in moxie."

Quindlen discusses the "gutsy girls" she remembers reading about as a child, especially those like Anne Shirley (of *Anne of Green Gables*) and Jo March (of *Little Women*), who were "outspoken, smart, strong, and just a bit disobedient." Then she talks about storybook heroines for younger readers—and the compliant princesses of fairy tales. "When I think of Madeline grown up," says Quindlen, "I think of her as the French Minister of Culture or the owner of a stupendous couture house, sending her children off to Miss Clavel to be educated."

What accounts for Madeline's confidence? Quindlen's answer is "structure." Madeline's fearlessness is "set within a backdrop of utter safety . . . Miss Clavel is concerned but competent, and life is safe within 'the old house in Paris that was covered with vines.'" In this Parisian boarding school, where the nun forms the girls into "two straight lines," the children, says Quindlen, "march predictably through life, with Madeline the admired wild card."

Quindlen goes on to discuss Ludwig Bemelmans' artwork and why it appeals to children. Children, too, draw faces with dot eyes and u-shaped mouths, and they scribble. But Bemelmans' simplicity is deceptive, she adds, drawing our attention to the scene of Madeline standing on the bed, showing her appendectomy scar to the others as a "rendering of carriage-as-character" worthy of a portrait by Holbein. Then she quotes from her eldest child, who said approvingly of Bemelmans, "He colors outside the lines."

INVESTIGATIONS: Introducing a Book to Readers

Study an older children's book to see what makes it appealing to child readers. Consider the book's literary standards and the child's interests and preoccupations, as remembered from your own childhood or observed in children now. Assume that this book will be printed in a new edition and that you have been chosen to write an introduction to it. The book might be any classic that has attained a valued place in the personal canon of many families. Your job is to analyze why it has attained this popularity.

But the biggest surprise by far—
on her stomach
was a scar!

From *Mad about Madeline* (Viking, 1953)
by Ludwig Bemelman.

Quindlen concludes this introductory essay by saying that some children's authors express what they think children should be like or what they think children will like. Others "understand that children prize both security and adventure, both bad behavior and conformity, both connections and independence." *Madeline* charms because of its rhyme and meter, she says, its "vivid illustrations and engaging situations." But it endures, she adds, because it epitomizes what children "fear, what they desire, and what they hope to be in the person of one little girl. A risk taker. An adventurer."

The values children or adults hold and the way these values seep into literature bring us to the next category for selecting and evaluating children's books: the social and cultural attention readers give books, especially when the books disturb cherished beliefs.

PERSONAL, SOCIAL, AND CULTURAL VALUES OF AUTHORS AND READERS

English educator Peter Hollindale discusses three ways that social, political, and moral beliefs—or ideologies—embed themselves in writers' and readers' minds. First, an author may be consciously transmitting *personal* values, and readers may consciously pick up on them. Second, writers and readers might hold shared *social* values or assumptions on an unconscious, unexamined level (in other words, members of a society might share similar values that they rarely notice or think about). Third, writers and readers may share entire *cultural* worlds (everyone in the culture—or nearly everyone—shares the same values), and then uncovering such beliefs becomes nearly impossible.

Identifying Ideologies

An author's personal ideology is sometimes quite "conscious, deliberate, and in some measure 'pointed' " Hollindale says, (page 11). This is what he calls the first level of ideological content.

Personal Values

An author may weave political and social ideas, consciously or at least semi-consciously, into his or her story. Burnett's stoic Sara in *A Little Princess* comes to mind. We know from the character's behavior, speech, and inner thoughts what Burnett's own feelings, ideas, and social principles are. Burnett might have been aware of these feelings. Because her ideology closely matched that of the culture in which she was writing, readers saw and accepted her ideas, too.

In Tormod Haugen's words, quoted earlier, we see the conscious belief that sending children to their rooms (excluding them) is counterproductive. Haugen expresses his ideology very clearly. On the other hand, Sendak's Max, in *Where the Wild Things Are,* is angry when he is sent to his room, but gets even by imagining something productive for his psychic well-being. Sendak sends no pointed "message" to readers about child-rearing practices, as Haugen does. Instead, Sendak's message seems to be that children have inner resources for coping. If Sendak has any negative feelings about excluding children that are spilling over from his childhood experiences, they are at least more deeply buried than are Haugen's and would therefore fall into Hollindale's second set of ideological values.

Shared Social Values

An author's ideology might be entirely passive, Hollindale tells us, or based on the "individual writer's unexamined assumptions" about many different beliefs (page 12). We might wonder, for example, why Max's mother sends him to his room, rather than outside to play. Or we might wonder why Sendak writes so many stories about children who are angry, frustrated, or excluded from their parents' attention.

We might also wonder why so many female writers of children's books continue to create female characters who are not as self-actualizing as their male characters. The reason may be that female writers are just learning to question the values of the patriarchal culture they live in. "Unexamined, passive values," says Hollindale, "are widely *shared* values." We cannot underestimate the power that unconscious ideologies play in reinforcing status quo values, he says (page 13).

Many readers would consider a book embedded with widely shared values about passive females—no matter how disappointing to feminists—a *good* book. Sometimes, however, as Hollindale points out, our consciously expressed beliefs and our unconcious, unexamined values can be at odds with one another. Consider Elaine Konigsburg's Newbery Honor book, *Jennifer, Hecate, Macbeth, William*

McKinley, and Me, Elizabeth (Atheneum, 1967). In this story, the author quite pointedly advanced the value of interracial friendships. Yet at the same time, she wrote a scene in which the black family is growing a watermelon.

Konigsburg's conscious ideology was well-intentioned, but as a member of a strongly segregated culture of the 1960s, she may have internalized negative or stereotyped images that many white Americans shared at this time. Widely shared values are, however, different from totally shared values; with the latter, we move into a third set of ideological values.

Shared Cultural Worlds

Many times, the passive or unconscious norm of the text reflects the norms of the culture itself. Readers in our culture do not question in Sendak's *Where the Wild Things Are,* the child-rearing practice of sending a child to his room. This practice is simply the "norm." Yet readers from a foreign culture without such a norm might find the book puzzling or even repugnant.

Of course, many so-called norms fail to satisfy all members of a culture, and the larger and more culturally diverse the culture, the more fluid and changing will be the norms. As Hollindale explains, "Writers for children are transmitters not of themselves uniquely, but of the worlds they share" (page 15). Even in America, children's writers of different eras often reveal culturally shared perspectives, whether they are writing about the oppression of black Americans in the 1930s, fear of communism in the 1950s, or the push for multiculturalism in the 1990s. Thus, the valued books of one culture or one era will differ significantly from those of another.

It is important to be able to uncover personal ideologies embedded in books; then we are better able to understand the ideologies that are socially and culturally constructed.

Uncovering Ideologies

We can study children's books to uncover the three ideological levels that Hollindale describes:

- Conscious transmission of the author's personal values
- Unconscious transmission of the author's unexamined assumptions
- Unconscious transmission of the culture's widely—or totally—shared norms

One way to search for ideologies is to look closely at the main character of a story. Consider what that person does or stands for in contrast to other characters, especially those painted in less heroic terms. Sometimes, of course, a troubled, flawed, or conflicted main character grows to become more heroic. Then we must examine how the character works through a conflict to see more clues to the writer's values.

Mary Lennox in Burnett's *The Secret Garden* becomes more admirable as the story progresses; Sara Crewe in Burnett's *A Little Princess* is admirable throughout. But it is not difficult to detect Burnett's values in either book; she never hides her belief in the importance of a healthy interest in others, in contrast to dangerous self-absorption.

Beatrix Potter's ideologies are less obvious. The overt "message" of *Peter Rabbit* is the one Mother Rabbit so pointedly sends: Peter is very naughty and his sisters are very good. Children should obey their parents. But if we look more deeply beneath the surface, we see that Potter finds Peter's mischief-making, disobedience, and risk-taking amusing and admirable. At the same time, the story reveals widely shared values about gender roles in Potter's day. Peter is disobedient, his sisters are *good;* Peter has fun, his sisters miss out; he has choices, and takes risks, they don't.

So another way to uncover ideologies, is to consider what the characters in the story do, and why. Does Peter Rabbit act as he does because he is a boy? (Boys are adventuresome; boys are disobedient; boys get dirty; boys lose things; "boys will be boys.") Do his sisters act as they do because they are girls? (Girls are good, nice, clean, tidy, obedient, ladylike—at least by Victorian standards.) Do Mr. McGregor's actions reveal he is old and cranky or that he is simply trying to preserve his garden? Do Mother Rabbit's words and actions show she is a strict Victorian-style disciplinarian or that she is simply a mother like any other (sensible, protective, loving, forgiving, worrisome)? In other words, what unexamined assumptions or shared cultural values do authors and readers bring to the written page? What pointed "messages" do they send and receive?

Peter Rabbit seems simple enough to sort out, but what happens when we read a children's novel like Kenneth Grahame's *The Wind in the Willows* or J. R. R. Tolkien's *The Hobbit?* Each of these books features few or no female characters. When an author excludes females, we can assume the author has little interest in or concern for females. But this absence might also tell us that very few people in the author's culture had any concern for females.

When an author produces a negative character, we can also learn a great deal about the author's social, political, and moral beliefs, especially if the "bad" character's motives are never explored. If the cards are stacked against the wicked witch, the evil stepmother or stepsisters, or the big, bad wolf, as in so many folk tales, we can look at that character's beliefs, values, and feelings to discover more about the author's unexamined assumptions. What characters the author likes or does not like tells us a great deal about the author's culture.

If an author consistently ignores or stereotypes a particular group of people, we also learn a great deal about that person's ideology or the ideologies of his or her culture. Before the 1960s, children's authors often treated African Americans, Native Americans, and immigrants—particularly Asians and Hispanics—in their stories with little or no respect, if they portrayed them at all. When members of these groups did appear in children's books, the authors were often outsiders rather than insiders of the ethnic culture, and this outsider condition reduced the chances for a fully authentic portrait. The outsiders had not lived the experiences they were trying to depict.

Three sociocultural issues that Hollindale touches on but does not emphasize are **Authenticity, Censorship,** and **Elitism.** These issues raise the following questions:

- Who should write for the members of a particular ethnicity, race, or cultural group, insiders or outsiders? Who produces the most authentic literature? (Authenticity)
- When do tensions among conflicting ideologies cause the suppression of literature? (Censorship)
- Do children, females, members of ethnic groups, and members of the working class "count" for us in literature? Or do only the award-winning books count? How do members of the elite in terms of age, gender, class, and culture affect children's books? (Elitism)

ISSUES OF AUTHENTICITY

In the March/April 1993 issue of *Horn Book Magazine,* editor Anita Silvey took a strong stand in favor of insiders producing literature for their own cultures, and her editorial set off a barrage of controversy. Silvey began by pointing out that this is not a new idea; it had created a stir as far back as the late 1960s. White writers were then producing most of the books about children of color—at least, the few books there were—and members of the black community were beginning to speak out against this practice.

Silvey reminded readers that some take the side of "artistic freedom and license" (page 132). An artist, they say, should be able to *imagine* what it is like to grow up as a member of a particular cultural or ethnic group—if they so choose. Silvey also described those who feel that when outsiders write about insider cultures, their stories are not valid. She went on to differentiate between universal books—those about "any child, at any time"—and literature that is culturally specific, that reflects the nuances of "behavior, speech, and patterns of life of a particular culture" (page 132). In the first category, we find books like Ezra Jack Keats's *A Snowy Day;* in the second category, stories such as those Mildred Taylor writes. Universal literature need not be written by insiders, Silvey said, but culturally specific literature should be.

The problem with this reasoning, some might say, is that there is no such thing as a "universal" child; children are too diverse to be gathered under the "universal" label. Even if playing in the snow is something all children love to do, would they all make snow angels? Or is this an activity children from certain places would more specifically know and choose to do? Do we tend to define *universal* by our own notions of what is usual and customary? Of course, Keats's Peter is African American (a child of African descent living in America); therefore he makes snow angels just as any other American child might do.

In a sense, then, the term *universal* has little or no meaning once we understand that, even within a culture as all-encompassing as the American one, children come from many heritages and homelands. They have qualities and traits in common; they also have individual, social, and cultural differences, and authors need to consider these differences if they wish to produce realistic portraits. Have outsiders of ethnic groups been able to do the job well? So many stereotypes, negative images, illogical aspects of plot and characterization, and lapses in credibility run rampant in so many children's books featuring ethnic children that the answer is far from a clear-cut "yes."

Silvey did say that writers produce better books when they draw from what they know best or when they see their child characters from the inside: "Getting in touch with the memories, feelings, places, and sensations of [their own] childhood can remain a lifelong quest for those seeking to create genuine books for children . . . We know that writers create best the landscape that they know—in their minds or in their hearts" (page 133). Silvey also reminded readers that because outsiders had been telling the insiders' stories, insider writers were not getting a chance to tell their own stories.

Silvey mentioned writers such as Virginia Hamilton, Walter Dean Myers, Mildred Taylor, and Jerry Pinkney from the African-American culture who emerged in the 1960s and 1970s to become "brilliant re-creators of the African-American experience." She predicted that, given another thirty years, we will look back and reap the harvest from the ethnic writers of today, if we encourage them to find their own voices and sing their "varied carols" (page 133).

Silvey took a courageous stand: The best books, the books deserving canon status, she argued, are those in which writers go "to the source of their own emotional experiences" (page 132). But not everyone agrees. Personal authenticity in children's books may at this time be a consciously voiced value in our culture, but it has by no means become a totally shared value. We can see this when we consider the letters—on both sides of the question—that poured into *Horn Book* after Silvey's article was published.

In the July/August 1993 issue, Marc Aronson, an editor at Holt publishers, wrote to express disagreement with Silvey. Aronson stated that we are all too culturally mixed these days to be truly monocultural. "We are not our ethnicity," he wrote; "our ethnicity does not determine the scope of our imagination; and, in modern America, it is very difficult to say where one ethnic group ends and another begins" (page 390).

Aronson felt that people are shaped and influenced by one another's cultures, and he reminded us of mixed neighborhoods that bring people of different ethnicities together and of mixed marriages that enable individuals from different classes, races, genders, regions, dialects, languages, customs, and religious faiths to produce "blended" offspring. Is culture defined more by one factor than another? he asked. The proof is in historical fiction, he asserted, a genre in which all writers must mix research with imagination. "All of us can go to the library," he said, and "those with literary talent can use their studies to create art. Can life experience make an author better able to imagine the past? Maybe," he admitted, but not always (page 391).

The main concern for Aronson and for other editors who must select stories for publication is literary talent, which they define as originality of ideas and an accomplished literary style. Experience might supply the backdrop on which a writer's imagination can work, said Aronson, but without imaginative spark, the work will never ignite reader interest. In other words, a writer's heritage, though important, brings with it no guarantee of writing talent. But what constitutes talent? Yet another literary critic tried to answer that question.

Robin Denniston, an English publisher, wrote that same year (1993) in *Signal:* "Do they [editors of children's books] look for qualities of imagination, of historical authenticity, of good writing, of . . . sympathetic identification? Yes, they do. But apart from this, and to my mind more importantly, they rely on their own enjoyment and appreciation of the script they are reading" (page 50). Enter the **personal** canon.

Many editors, it would seem, are stirred by stories that do not meet high standards of authenticity. But because of their inability to recognize inaccuracies, they accept for publication stories with literary strength even if these stories might still promote negative images of an insider culture the authors know nothing about, or even if the stories depict the author's personal values, beliefs, and traditions, rather than those of the insider culture. The editors deem the books *good,* but good for whom?

One solution to this problem would be for publishers to employ members of various cultures and ethnicities to read manuscripts, checking for both authenticity *and* literary talent. Another solution would be for editors of magazines, journals, and newspapers to hire insiders to review stories in which children of color appear. These insiders could then use their knowledge to weed out inauthentic books before the books went on to flood library bookshelves, win awards, and crowd out more authentic books.

When Christopher Paul Curtis, author of *The Watsons Go to Birmingham—1963* (Delacorte, 1995), reviewed three new children's books about African-American families for the *New York Times* (22 June 1997), he was able to tell readers which of the books had false notes and which "rang true." Said Curtis: Valerie Wesley's *Freedom's Gifts* (Simon & Schuster, 1997) "takes off running and never slows"; it charts "beautifully" the friendship of June and Lillie. On the other hand, according to Curtis, Scott Russell Sanders's *A Place Called Freedom* (Atheneum, 1997) "stumbles" by glossing over the "horrors and difficulties faced by newly freed slaves." Even worse, Jane Resh Thomas's *Celebration!* (Hyperion, 1997) "brushes uncomfortably close to stereotypes," with a character who is either "basketball-obsessed" or dreaming of becoming a tap dancer.

None of these three authors—Wesley, Sanders, and Thomas—is new to the scene of children's publishing; each has produced several books. Valerie Wesley seems to be an insider to the African-American culture; the other two writers, at least from Curtis's discussion, appear to be outsiders. Interestingly, established writers—outsiders or insiders—especially those with large followings, often assert the right to write about any group on the basis of artistic freedom. In the September/October 1993 issue of *Horn Book,* white author Mary Stoltz, who has written about black children, defended the power of imagination as equal to insider knowledge. African-American writers Virginia Hamilton and Walter Dean Myers have made the same argument.

Another solution would be for editors to examine manuscripts very carefully when outsiders are writing about other cultures. Outsider writers might well produce accurate details about clothing, housing, food, climate, plants and animals—the *surface* structure of authenticity. But they tend to blend these surface details with their own world view, their own understandings about nature and human behavior or about the way the world works. In doing so, they may unintentionally coopt the insiders' ideas, beliefs, and traditions—the *deep* structure of authenticity.

Checklists are one way to determine the authenticity of a text, but doing nothing more than checking for misrepresentations still allows inauthentic books—books with superficial or inaccurate portrayals of ethnic *traditions*—to pass into children's hands and minds. Checklists need to reflect both surface and deep structures of authenticity. Children's self-esteem can be damaged when their culture is ignored or portrayed in negative ways. Giving children of the dominant culture a false picture about other cultural groups is especially problematic. Ignorance breeds ignorance through the decades.

The March/April 1995 issue of *Horn Book* was devoted entirely to the subject of authenticity. Hazel Rochman argued that the outsider-insider battle had gone too far: "What about those who say that an American can never write about Japan, that men can't write about women, that Chinese Ed Young cannot illustrate African-American folklore, or that the African-American writer Virginia Hamilton cannot retell the story of the Russian witch Baba Yaga? In fact, some take if further," she added. "Only Indians can really judge books about Indians, Jews about

Jews. And further still, you get the extreme, whites should read about whites, Latinos about Latinos, locking us into smaller and tighter boxes" (page 150).

Katherine Paterson's comments in the January/February 1991 issue of *Horn Book* revealed another problem. Said Paterson, "I have heard teachers and librarians say that they don't buy Mildred Taylor or Virginia Hamilton or Walter Dean Myers for their libraries because they don't have any African-American children in their schools" (page 35). She went on to say,

Checking for Authenticity

African-American Stories

- Inclusion of cultural traditions, rituals, and celebrations, as central to family life
- Attention focused on a variety of social groups, classes, and experiences in many settings
- Variety of language patterns and dialects (regional, class-based, and invented)
- Extended families as central feature of culture, including many different individuals within them
- Exploration of a variety of topics and themes within many genres and art styles
- Self-actualizing children and adults (white "saviors" are not the major problem solvers)
- Exploration of integral female contribution to social structure

Asian-American Stories

- Attention focused on a variety of national and cultural groups in many settings
- Attention focused on a variety of different social groups within these settings
- Depiction of different body sizes, shapes, and features of different Asian-Pacific groups
- Exploration of a variety of different interests, occupations, and talents
- Exploration of a variety of different personality constructs
- Exploration of a variety of different philosophies, sensibilities, and character traits
- Self-actualizing children and adults (white "saviors" are not the major problem solvers)
- Exploration of integral female contribution to social structure

Hispanic-American Stories

- Exploration of a range of Latino "voices" (from different social classes, educational backgrounds)
- Portrayal of realistic, as opposed to idealized, sentimental, or exotic, experiences
- Self-energized, rather than victimized, children and adults
- Portrayal of adults in the community as strong, supportive influences
- Attention focused on extended, close-knit, supportive families
- Sensitivity to the importance of education (oral and literary traditions) as a cultural value
- Self-actualizing children and adults (white "saviors" are not the major problem solvers)
- Exploration of integral female contribution to social structure

Native-American Stories

- Depiction of a variety of different clothing styles and materials
- Portrayal of a variety of everyday experiences in both past and present
- Variety of natural language patterns
- Names reflecting traditions, beliefs, and actual naming practices of various eras
- Art styles reflecting a variety of different groups and their traditions
- Behaviors, actions, and character traits reflecting values and traditions of the group
- Self-actualizing children and adults (white "saviors" are not the major problem solvers)
- Exploration of integral female contribution to social structure

Source: Elaine Aoki, Rosalinda Barrera, Violet Harris, Donnarae MacCann, and Sonia Nieto, *Teaching Multicultural Literature in Grades K–8*. Edited by Violet Harris (Norwood, MA: Christopher Gordon, 1993).

> That's about the worst reason I can think of for not buying these books. Every child deserves the chance to hear those authors' stories. In a school review of *Come Sing, Jimmy Jo* [one of Paterson's children's books], the librarian said that the children in her upper-class suburban school would not be interested in the story of a country singer from Appalachia. With this kind of reasoning, a whole generation of children will grow up who sneer at persons who are different from themselves. (page 36)

Paterson's comments also reveal the fine line between book selection and censorship, when those who select books reduce readers to one viewpoint or way of seeing the world.

INVESTIGATIONS: Insiders versus Outsiders

Read two children's books, each focusing on growing up in a parallel American culture, one written by an insider and the other by an outsider. Compare the books for authenticity and depth of realistic detail about setting, characters, social conflicts, and cultural traditions. Try to decide where you stand on the insider-outsider issue. Should books about ethnic children be written about members of that group, or by anyone who wishes to do so?

CENSORSHIP ISSUES

When we think of the word *censorship,* we might conjure up visions of huge flames leaping from piles of books that powerful people in churches, schools, or society in general have decreed are unfit for our children. We might remember certain books pulled—or gently retrieved—from our hands until age and experience had caught up with curiosity and the thirst for knowledge. We might have heard about or witnessed book battles in the classroom or public library, or we might have seen a favorite teacher fired for selecting a particular book. Should books like *Little Black Sambo* remain on the shelves? Do Judy Blume's books contain too much explicit sex? Should Katherine Paterson use the words "dammit" and "hell" in a children's book (*The Great Gilly Hopkins;* Harper, 1978)?

Prohibition, suppression, and *persecution* are three words that lead us directly into the forest of censorship issues. Book bans often result from restrictions on free speech, free thinking, and open discussions about politics, religion, sexual practices, or language use. "Literature," says Italo Calvino (1986), "is one of a society's instruments of self-awareness—certainly not the only one, but nonetheless an essential instrument, because its origins are connected with the origins of various types of knowledge, various codes, various forms of critical thought" (page 97).

"Criticalness," adds Canadian educator David Dillon, involves "piercing or dismantling the conventional meanings that have been given to us and that we've operated upon. It helps us to peel away myths we've accepted uncritically, to try to see our reality more clearly, with new eyes, and to *act* on the basis of this new awareness in order to transform our world" (1988, page 536). At the same time, "criticalness" makes the critical thinker—writer, reader, educator, or social activist—especially vulnerable.

To those who are preserving the status quo—editors, publishers, reviewers, parents, teachers, school administrators, religious leaders, or government officials—a critical thinker may be dangerous. "I've often wondered," continues Dillon, "if a measuring rod of how critically we're teaching is how much trouble we get into—how much danger we experience of being shunned, reprimanded, fired, even deported? Is critical literacy actually a dangerous thing? Does it take courage to teach it?" (page 536).

Consider Sara, a second-grade teacher who one year finds herself dealing with the concerns of a parent-tutor, the mother of one of her seven-year-old students. After listening to children read a biography of sharpshooter Annie Oakley (*Little Sure Shot: The Story of Annie Oakley* by Stephanie Spinner; illustrations by Jose Miralles; Random House, 1993), the parent tells Sara she does not want her daughter seeing a gun-toting female as a model, "a hero-figure." On another day, she voices her objections to *Chester's Way* by Kevin Henkes (Greenwillow, 1988), an animal fantasy about three mice friends called Chester, Wilson, and Lilly. "I don't want my daughter reading this book," she says. "These mice [Chester and Wilson] are *too* close and there is a sleepover" at Lilly's house.

Regarding the first book, Sara explains to this parent that Oakley was an expert target shooter by vocation and talent, but that if the parent does not wish for her daughter to read the book, she has many other books to choose from.

Sara is for the moment dumbfounded by the parent's remark about *Chester's Way;* she tells her that the book is part of the class collection, and not required reading, and the parent accepts Sara's reasoning with no further complaint. (See Appendix IV for an interview with Sara about selecting books for classroom use, teaching with children's books, and dealing with censorship.)

After school Sara pores over the book to examine the mixed-gender sleepover, wondering how problematic it might be. (Chester and Wilson spend the night at Lilly's

From *Chester's Way* (Greenwillow, 1988) by Kevin Henkes.

Chester and Wilson and Lilly, Lilly and Wilson and Chester. That's the way it was.

house, where they discover that Lilly has her own nightlight and that peanut butter and jam on toast tastes better with strawberries, cheerios, and mandarin orange slices.) "But these are mice!" Sara says to herself. "This is a *mouse* sleepover."

Logic and rationality are often missing in censorship battles. Some parents go far beyond this parent's behavior, demanding that *all* children in a classroom be "protected" from literature they find objectionable. Sometimes they make even demands in classrooms in which they have no children. As taxpayers or concerned citizens, they take it upon themselves to control every student's reading, imagining that *their* way of seeing the world is the right way.

This parent's complaint, however puzzling, is important because it gives us a glimpse of what motivates censorship cases, especially in regard to children's books. Educator and literary critic Hamida Bosmajian cites fears about human differences as the factor, on the deepest level, that motivates censors. Some of the differences she cites involve "ethnicity, sexual orientation and mores, and religious practices and scientific (as distinct from technological) exploration" (page 316).

On the one hand, she says, there is the "fear of developing the imagination through fantasy books, which are accused of returning us to paganism, and fear of values clarification as well as critical thinking skills as a means of knowing . . . because both are possible challenges to authority." She also mentions "hypersensitivity to language and usage and the neglect of viewing texts in contexts" (page 316), as we see in protests against Katherine Paterson's books.

Taken together, we see censorship issues rising out of

- fear of difference;
- fear of fantasy;
- fear of clarifying values and critical thinking;
- hypersensitivity to language; and
- failure to read words and passages in context.

In Sara's situation, the parent interprets the close friendship of Henkes's mice characters as a sexual relationship; she does not take a closer look at their friendship within the context of the entire book. If she did, she might see an innocent story about learning to be yourself and learning to accept differences in others. In addition, she does not seem to see the value of *fantasy* in educating her daughter's imagination. Chester, Wilson, Lilly, and Victor are humanized child-mice, all with contrasting and comical personalities. Henkes's book is a rich animal fable, and like all fables, it mirrors what it is like to be human—with human foibles, interests, and talents.

Literary theorist Michael Holquist traces the complexity of censorship battles back to the Roman institution of the censor, a high public official who had two roles: He registered the people for tax purposes—a political role designed to distinguish insiders from outsiders in Rome—and he oversaw public morals—an instructive, cultural role. The moral role was instrumental in forming a "community of values" (page 14). Censors were chosen for their ability to fill in interpretative gaps in many different kinds of texts. They decided what a text was saying—and their decision was law, even though others might have reached a different conclusion. It is the "undecidability of language," Holquist says, that enables the censor to read between the lines and create one particular meaning over another. Censorship is essentially a strategy to control difficult-to-determine meanings—or to control the way people think.

Censors do not explore the many ways we can read a text, as Holquist reminds us. They do not celebrate multiple perspectives. They do not try to keep the "play of language . . . gaping" so that new interpretations can continue "to flow" (page 21). Instead, they work to "seal up" or close gaps of meaning they find in texts. They reduce the variety and complexity of a text to a single meaning just as the "moral" ending of a fable fixes the meaning and interpretation of the story with an obvious, direct statement. Thus, censors suppress the interpretive freedom of readers. Fear of interpretive freedom is, according to Holquist, "the essence of all censorship. Censors view a text as something that can be "read in only one way" (pages 21–22).

The classroom can and must, Holquist states, serve as a "protected zone" in which texts can be "freely interrogated" (page 23). Does Sara's parent-censor leave Sara with such a possibility? Perhaps, for other children; but not for her own daughter. She does at least cause us to ponder some solutions for censorship problems. The problem in this case is that the parent wants to keep her daughter shielded from seeing a female shooting a gun. But Sara could talk about all the *ideas* that stream out of the Annie Oakley book without ever asking this parent's child to open the book. She could encourage classroom talk about

- female roles,
- the use and misuse of weapons,
- the need to learn about self defense,
- the sport of target shooting, and
- Annie Oakley's life and times.

This parent-censor does what educational researcher Patrick Shannon (1989) says censors do: They exclude alternative points of view, seeing just one side of an issue or distorting reality so much that only one position seems workable. But consider the discussions teachers might initiate with children after censors leave their classrooms—or better still, consider what might happen if they invited protesters to stay and listen and share their ideas. Teachers can find many ways to deal constructively with complaints, even though at the outset, the censor's remark may cause bewilderment or dismay.

Consider this mother's complaint about *Chester's Way* and what it causes us to realize: that the book itself is—in a way—about censorship. The parent makes an effort to influence Sara's behavior; she complains about the book. She believes her way of reading it is the *right* way. Now consider the title of this book and the first line: "Chester had his own way of doing things." This signals the censor's basic stance—close-mindedness. Chester has one way of thinking, acting, and doing things. He always does things the same way (in fact, the word *always* is repeated four times in the first two pages).

What can teachers like Sara do in the face of would-be parent-censors? Would it help if Sara organized a literature study group for parents, so that multiple perspectives could emerge and this mother could become a more openly interpretive reader? Consider the story that Canadian teacher educators Dennis Sumara, Brent Davis, and Dolores Van Der Wey (1998) tell about their experiences with Lois Lowry's Newbery winner, *The Giver* (Houghton Mifflin, 1993). When they realized that the fifth- and sixth-grade teachers they were working with felt too uneasy about the controversial topics of sex and violence in the book to assign it in their classes, they decided to invite parents to participate in their discussions. A dozen parents joined the group, and lively—and divergent—interpretive readings followed. Instead of censoring the book, the parents insisted it be taught because of the social relevance of Lowry's ideas.

Another possibility is that classroom teachers can work with their students to open up texts, so that when these students become parents, they can function as open-minded readers. Fighting against censorship, says educator Alleen Pace Nilsen, means "more than amassing intellectual arguments to use with today's censors. It includes working with young readers to keep them from becoming tomorrow's censors" (page 312).

A Closer Look
Chester's Way by Kevin Henkes

As *Chester's Way* begins, we learn all about Chester—what he always did, always ate, always carried around with him. Chester is a creature of habit. What is more, Chester's best friend Wilson does just what Chester does, which explains why they are such good friends, a twosome no one can tell apart. No alternative perspective intrudes here. There is just one way, one point of view, one approach to things, all gaps closed, all variety sealed up—total consensus.

Of course, in their self-absorbed complacency, in their limiting *sameness,* Chester and Wilson do not realize how firmly entrenched they are in their safe, predictable habits: peanut butter and jam sandwiches, sunscreen at the pool, an umbrella in the rain, two mittens on a string, double-knotted shoes, no sliding headfirst on the baseball lot, no swinging at the first pitch.

Then along comes Lilly in her red cowboy boots, with her "fifty disguises" and her squirt gun. She pierces the conventional meaning of their lives, peeling away the myths they have accepted so uncritically. Lilly is a new idea, and they quickly attempt to stamp her out. They refuse to take her phone calls. They cross to the other side of the street and hide behind trees when she appears. They try to avoid her entirely, until the day Lilly—in her cat disguise—saves them from the big boys.

Now Lilly opens up their safe, sheltered lives; they cannot restrict themselves to just one way of seeing any more. When they let her in the door, she teaches them to make stars and flowers and bells out of their diagonally cut sandwiches. At her sleepover, they discover common fears (they all have nightlights) and obvious differences that, blended together in the give and take of friendship, would produce a well-rounded mouse-child.

Lilly tempts them to add strawberries to their peanut butter and jam on toast. They teach her the safety of hand signals; she shows them how to pop wheelies. Soon Lilly, Wilson, and Chester become a *threesome* no one can tell apart. They share the same umbrella, wear sunscreen together, rake leaves, and never throw snowballs. But they do everything boisterously now.

The problem is that this new social fusion—this new trio of friends—soon produces the same "mono-focal" vision as before: "Chester and Wilson and Lilly, Lilly and Wilson and Chester. That's the way it was." Or the way it was until the last page, "when Victor moved into the neighborhood." Just in time, Victor leaps ominously over the page, bringing along new life, new possibilities for learning.

The last picture (on the back cover) shows the four mouse children on a seesaw. Chester and Lilly snuggle happily together on the lower end; Wilson and Victor sit together on the upper end. Wilson grips the board to keep his balance. Victor, with arms outstretched and legs sailing into the air, holds aloft a slice of watermelon.

Chester's Way has a spiraling story pattern or movement. Two mice are close friends; then a third mouse—the outsider mouse—invades their space, opening new possibilities for seeing the world. Now three mice are close friends; then a fourth mouse—another outsider—leaps into the picture, opening even more possibilities and more new ways of seeing. At the end, four mice are close friends. Will a fifth mouse—still another outsider mouse—enter and change the picture? Perhaps. This spiraling story pattern helps us to see that diversity is necessary, even crucial, for enriching our lives.

Teacher Jennifer Rossuck has written about how she explores censorship with her high school students, and her ideas are easy to adapt for use with elementary students. Rossuck asks students to read a book that at some time has been banned and identify passages that censors might target. She then asks students to express their personal reactions to these passages. Students later choose books that have faced censorship battles, such as Shel Silverstein's *A Light in the Attic* (Harper, 1981) and *Where the Sidewalk Ends* (Harper, 1974) and various books by Judy Blume. The students record lines and passages that might be problematic for some readers and define the literary purpose they think each passage serves.

During this exploration, Rossuck's students learn never to isolate just one objectionable word, sentence, scene, or passage of a work; instead, they consider the entire work as a whole. They invite adults who object to the books into the classroom to discuss their concerns. Then they try to restore the objectors' confidence in the books by recounting their own experiences with the works. (Reading a Shel Silverstein poem about breaking dishes did not cause the students to go out and break dishes.)

The effectiveness of Rossuck's approach is largely dependent on whether we think children have a right to select and interpret their own reading materials. How much does the child's voice count? From the censor's point of view, a realistic answer might be, very little. In the world of children's books, adults usually write, illustrate, edit, publish, market, review, analyze, award, select, teach, and sometimes even censor, books that supposedly belong to children.

INVESTIGATIONS: Censorship and Ideology

Katherine Paterson tells the story of walking past a bookstore window and seeing a selection of about three dozen books. They were arranged under a sign reading: "Some people consider these books dangerous". One of the books was her own novel, *Bridge to Terabithia* (Crowell, 1997); another was P. L. Travers's *Mary Poppins* (Harcourt Brace, 1934). Anne Frank's diary was displayed, too, along with many books for adults. Even the Bible was included. Paterson says she was never able to discover why her book had been censored. Read *Bridge to Terabithia,* and try to find out what might have disturbed someone. Or read *Mary Poppins,* and try to uncover the ideologies of readers at work as censors.

Source: Katherine Paterson, "Tale of a Reluctant Dragon," *New Advocate* 2 (Winter, 1989): 1–8.

ISSUES OF ELITISM

In Sara's classroom, children keep journals and write stories, and they share these stories and exhibit them alongside regular children's books. The children are treated as authors themselves, even though they know that they are not as famous as Kevin Henkes. But what about the world outside the classroom, the adult worlds of publishing, writing, reviewing, book selling, book borrowing, parenting—and teaching? Do adults give adequate recognition to children's written responses to literature? Are children's works a part of any canon—selective, critical, or personal? Or do adult responses hold sway at all times?

Do children's reading choices count as much as the adult critic's choices? Obviously not. But perhaps we should pay more attention to children's reactions;

consider the story Elaine Moss tells about her own daughter, Alison. Moss, a prominent children's book reviewer in England, calls her story "The 'Peppermint' Lesson."

"Don't go looking round the bookshops for *Peppermint*" (Merrigold Press, 1950), says Moss. The creator of this undistinguished book, Moss tells us, is Dorothy Grider. The book is one of the American mass-market books, like *The Pokey Little Puppy,* that made its way to England when Moss's daughter was a child. The book sold for twenty-five cents, but to Alison it was, and still is, "pure gold" (page 141).

At the time Alison discovered the book, Moss herself was reviewing classic picture books from one of the more prestigious publishing houses. Her daughter would never have seen the book if a relative had not given it to her. The story, as Moss explains, is about a kitten nobody wants—at least not until a little girl with no kitten and no money discovers Peppermint in a candy store, and the owner gives the kitten to her. Home goes Peppermint to be lovingly bathed and combed, to win first prize in a pet show, and to live happily every after with the little girl.

What accounts for Alison's love of this "watered-down, vulgarized *Ugly Duckling* story"? Says Moss: "Alison is an adopted child; her hair is pale straw, her eyes are blue; she was taken home, like Peppermint, to be loved and cared for and treasured. It was a matter of identification not just for the duration of the story but at a deep, warm comforting and enduring level" (page 142).

The book taught Moss an invaluable lesson, she recalls: "The artistically worthless book—hack-written and poorly illustrated—may, if its emotional content is sound, hold a message of supreme significance for a particular child. If it does, it will be more important to that child's development than all the Kate Greenaway [or Caldecott] Medal-winning books put together. For a book by itself is nothing . . . one can only assess its value by the light it brings to a child's eye" (page 142).

Do we make a mistake, then, assessing books for children in adultlike ways—according to artistic merit? Is the adult's literary and artistic taste more important than the child's self-concept? Are children capable of discerning the "best" for themselves, in accordance with their own emotional needs? What is the primary value of a book from the child's point of view?

"Children tend to declare particular books as their 'favorites' on the basis of how much pleasure and enjoyment they get from the stories and illustrations," says educational researcher Patricia Cianciolo. "Responses to these books usually focus on the feelings, sensations, and sensory images children experience when they read the stories and look at the illustrations" (page 27). Rarely are children concerned about or even aware of artistic merit as adults define it, she continues. Not that children cannot learn about literary criteria, so that they do notice artistic styles; it is simply that their needs and preoccupations, and thus their preferences, lie elsewhere. What about adult preoccupations? Do we need to reexamine them in the light of Moss's discovery, more carefully-considering children's needs?

Because they noticed the bifurcation between children's needs and adult preoccupations, members of the International Reading Association and the Children's Book Council began in 1969 to construct a canon, a list of children's books, based on children's choices, for the classroom teacher to use. Every summer, publishers send carefully chosen children's books from their current lists to teams of K–8 educators. The teams work with several thousand children; 10,000 children throughout the United States responded to over 700 books in 1997. The children read and vote on the books; then, in October, *The Reading Teacher,* the IRA journal for elementary and middle school teachers, publishes a list of children's favorites. (See the end of this chapter for more on the Children's Choices list.)

A CLOSER LOOK

A Closer Look: Peppermint and the "Canon"

When adults refer to the concept of a literary canon, they often call it *the* canon, as if there were only one official list of appropriate books for students. When they wish to add other books to expand the **official** canon, they try to establish the aesthetic qualities of the "nominated" book. (Is this book well-written? Are the illustrations dynamic or unique?) They may also try to establish some cultural *need* for the book. (Is this book about a strong female? Is this book about a Native American child who is solving her own problems?) Or they might try to show the book has both qualities—it fills a cultural need *and* has artistic strength. In other words, they imagine a fixed list of books that children *should* read.

But no such "perfect" list actually exists; there are simply too many different people selecting the books, and they all have too many individual preferences to be very consistent in their choices. Even for such a supposedly unimportant book as *Peppermint,* we can imagine a number of different canons converging on the book. Thus, we see how a canon is a social construct; personal, social, and cultural ideologies produce these "privileged" lists.

Starting with the **potential** canon (all books—those written anywhere, any time), we would expect to find *Peppermint* in places such as supermarkets, children's bookcases, attics, and yard sales. Because it is a mass-produced, mass-marketed, inexpensive, read-to-death and then discarded book, we would *not* expect to see it in libraries. Thus, we would not be likely to find it in the **accessible** canon.

The book's only hope of long-term survival is the publisher's willingness to reissue it in response to popular demand. *Peppermint* is, in fact, still available in supermarkets, through Merrigold Press, as of 1997. Whether it continues to be available to children only those who develop other canons can decide.

One such canon is the **selective** one. Will parents continue to choose this book for their children? Will children continue to enjoy it? Another canon is the **critical** canon. Distinguished critic Elaine Moss *does* find unexpected significance in the book. Other critics might have similar reactions if they looked at the book *from the child's perspective.* In other words, the qualities critics presently value in children's books (aesthetic qualities or the fulfillment of social and cultural need) would have to change. Children's own values would have to take precedence.

To discover what children value, adults would need to study children's responses to a variety of books, watching to see how personal feelings affect a child's deep engagement with books. Moss indicates that a book's emotional content may be its primary value for the child reader. Thus, the **personal** canons of a variety of child readers come into play. Do these canons ever intersect with the **pedagogical** canon—or could they?

Could a book like *Peppermint* be included in a text set focused on pets or cats? Could teachers invite children to bring favorite books from home, no matter how tattered or threadbare, no matter how undistinguished from a literary standpoint? Could teachers bring in their favorite childhood books? Adults would have to consider what *really* matters: children enjoying reading, engaging in a great deal of reading, and becoming lifelong readers, or children learning about the highest artistic standards, and becoming *discriminating* readers? With the one, we develop an entire culture of *readers;* with the other, we develop an entire culture of readers who recognize—and expect—only the *best.*

Yet how will we define *best,* once we have heard the story of Alison Moss and her experience with *Peppermint?* Is the best book the one adults select as Book of the Year? Or is it one that readers of any age find important, special, and necessary at a particular moment in their lives? Australian children's writer Patricia Wrightson chooses the latter, opining that " 'Whatever book speaks most directly and deeply to you, is for you the Book of the Year' " (Saxby, page 181).

The Children's Choices list shows us the **selective** and **accessible** canons at work. If children select their own books, they can tell us what they are able to understand and enjoy, and we then know better what they enjoy and *need,* in terms of emotional content. We learn even more about children's feelings and ideas when the entries include the words of actual children telling us what they liked about the books. As One child said, referring to Harry Allard's *The Stupids Die* (Houghton, 1981), "I like everything about this book: Funny things happen, the names of the characters are neat, the cartoon illustrations are colorful and good fun. I like the Stupids!" (*Reading Teacher,* October 1982, page 74).

Another child said of *Jumanji* (Houghton, 1981), Chris Van Allsburg's Caldecott Medal winner for 1982: "I hope the person who wrote this book writes more like it. The story kept me in suspense all the way!" (*Reading Teacher,* October 1982, page 76). Some reviewers also describe children's responses, as in this review of Arnold and Anita Lobel's *On Market Street* (Greenwillow, 1981):

> In this distinctively different alphabet book, a little boy strolls the length of Market Street to see what he can buy for a friend. Kindergarten children enjoyed identifying all the things they would buy for friends. The outstanding illustrations were warmly admired by older readers. (*Reading Teacher,* October 1982, page 74)

At the same time, the Children's Choices list has its faults. The annotations from the 1997 list included only four examples that reflected children's responses. The notes did not directly quote any children; they contained few (if any) references to what children thought about the books or did with them. The citations described a little about the books or about what children appeared to like (rhymes, humor, suspense, intriguing pictures, animals, stories about friends), but this is no substitute for hearing from the children themselves.

In addition, the Children's Choices list at times reveals adult elitism at work. Adults first select the books children choose from, and, as educator Julie Jensen noted in 1983 (over a decade after the list was in place), no child-authored books appear on the list. "Clearly a rich literature for classroom reading or hearing is escaping notice," she said (page 13). Should children's writing count? If so, why doesn't it? she asks. The low number of child-authored books available is the most obvious answer.

"Given the number of juvenile trade books published annually," says Jensen, "the proportion of titles which include children's writing is clearly miniscule" (page 13). But children, she adds, clearly enjoy peer creation, and teachers can encourage children to write and publish work for their own classroom library

INVESTIGATIONS: Children's Choices

Consult any October issue of *The Reading Teacher* to discover what books made the Children's Choices list for the previous year. Then collect several books from this list and read them to children. Note the children's responses; begin a file that describes each book and the children's reactions to it. Also, keep a file of the Children's Choices listings for recent years; seek out the books that seem to elicit interesting and insightful responses from children. Finally, add new books to your list as you discover more books that children enjoy.

shelves. She recommends that students create scrolls and accordian books, along with more formally bound creations, as well as classroom newspapers, advertisements, letters, diaries, and picture books.

Mainstream and alternative presses do publish some children's work, although not as frequently as children's magazines such as *Cricket.* In 1992, Vintage Books published *The Diary of Latoya Hunter,* written by Latoya herself, a child born in 1978 in St. Ann, Jamaica, who moved to the Bronx in New York City in 1986. She was attending P.S. 94 as a sixth grader when her teacher noticed her strong writing talent.

As her editor at Vintage, Richard Marek, tells the story, he saw a *New York Times* article about Latoya's class. In the article, Latoya's teacher spoke of exceptional students in the class, including Latoya. The teacher's remarks interested Marek. He contacted the teacher, asking if Latoya could keep a diary of her school year the following year and submit it to his company for possible publication.

Latoya and her parents met with Marek and his assistant, and Marek commissioned her to do some sample work, which turned out very well. Latoya signed a book contract, and "the diary was born" (page vii). The diary covers a ten-month span of time when Latoya was in seventh grade and every word of the diary is hers. The editors corrected spelling and asked her to expand certain passages and ideas, but changed nothing else. The result is a rich—and authentic—portrait of Latoya's life in an American inner city, her cross-cultural immigrant experience, and the school and home experience of an emergent adolescent female in the early 1990s.

In addition, the diary "paints" interesting portraits of Latoya's siblings and parents adjusting to life in America. At one point, Latoya takes a trip back to Jamaica to explore her family roots. She also tells the story of her newborn nephew and of her first love. The book ends as twelve-year-old Latoya turns thirteen. Throughout the diary, not only do child readers hear a child's voice as author, but Latoya's voice

From *The Diary of Lotoya Hunter* (Vintage, 1992) by Latoya Hunter.

as a multiethnic child. As an African-Caribbean immigrant, Latoya Hunter has a great deal to tell us about one of the most rapidly growing cultures in America these days, when so many Caribbean people are immigrating to this country.

In 1996, Bruce Hucko, a teacher, artist, and photographer working with Navajo children in connection with the Utah Arts Council, produced *A Rainbow At Night: The World in Words and Pictures by Navajo Children* for Chronicle Books, a small press based in San Francisco. The book is not only an exciting new venture for eliciting and recording children's artwork and stories; it also is important because it declares that children of a parallel culture count. Hucko's photography is especially effective, as are his introductions to each piece, in which he tells about Navajo traditions and how they influence children's creative processes. In addition, following each child's contribution are suggestions for creating artwork or writing that connects to Navajo traditions.

The book begins with Stephanie Manybeads, age eleven, who has produced a vibrant red, yellow, and blue watercolor entitled "Sunrise Girl." Hucko introduces the picture, saying that Navajos believe that "every part of nature is related to them like family" (page 4). Each day, he tells us, they rise to "face the east and say, 'Good Morning, Father Sun.'" They greet an old tree or an animal of knowledge, such as the horned toad, in the same way. They might describe plants and animals as "cousin," "sister," or "brother," just as Stephanie has greeted the sun as her "friend." Her picture of the sun reveals a girl with long hair, and the watercolors painted on wet paper produce the effect of long, layered hair and a fringe of bangs, just as Stephanie has.

Stephanie's words about her painting appear as a poem, a fitting complement to the striking colors of the picture, so lively is the writing style:

> Her name is Sunrise girl.
> She is fresh.
> Her vivid colors are shining her reflection on the ocean in the morning.
> Her hair is like an orange in the sun, red as a cherry squished.
> Her face is yellow as lemon that has sat in the hottest sun
> for a week
> Her reflection is vivid.
> The ocean is blue as blueberries.
> She awakes to light the day.

In italics below Stephanie's words are Hucko's words, telling children to think of the sun or moon or some part of nature they might want to bring into their family; then to paint this object so that it fills up the paper. "How will you greet it?" he asks.

Children's poetry and stories also fill *Rising Voices: Writings of Young Native Americans* (Scribner's 1992), another book that demonstrates that literature of the nondominant culture counts—and is sorely needed. In this case, readers learn about the bitter struggle for identity many native children faced when they were forced to attend boarding schools in the late 1800s, and they lost contact with both family life and cultural traditions. Many of the pieces focus on contemporary children, however. Editors Arlene Hirschfelder and Beverly Singer combed published materials, including children's work and classroom projects, across the nation to produce this rich tapestry of children's ideas.

Child-authored materials like these are important for all children. In the next two chapters, we will examine closely the creative processes children's authors use

INVESTIGATIONS: Investigations: Determining Literary Strength in Children's Books

Consider the critical standards listed for the children's literature genres that follow. Then choose a children's book from one or each of these genres and decide whether it meets these standards. You might want to include a child-authored book among your choices. You might also want to include the child's perspective along with other selection criteria. Think back to Elaine Moss's story about *Peppermint* and consider whether "children's strong response to emotional content" is a criterion you would like to add to each of the genre categories.

Poetry

- Strong rhythmical pattern
- Vivid imagery
- Multiple meanings
- Evocative tone
- Compelling mood
- Humor or quiet sensitivity
- Close match between subject and children's experiences

Fiction

- Lively, realistic, imaginative characters
- Diverse cast of believable characters
- Nonracist / nonclassist / nonsexist characters
- Creative problem solving by characters
- Suspenseful plot with dramatic scenes
- Richly detailed or memorable setting
- Significance of subject matter
- Authentic narrator's voice
- Graceful, artistic, accessible writing style

Nonfiction

- Balanced point of view on narrator's part
- Author's high regard for facts and theories
- Respect for animal and human life
- Challenging problems and concepts clearly explained
- Well-detailed text and pictures
- Technical drawings or clearly defined photographs or imaginative paintings
- Copious research for background material
- Clear and accessible writing style
- Close match between subject and children's interests

Folk Literature

- Retelling that retains the spirit of the original story
- Close match between language and values or beliefs of the culture represented
- Illustrations that recreate the mood, setting, and theme of the text
- Gender balance, if stories are part of a collection
- Cultural diversity in characters, if stories are part of a collection
- Lively, accessible storytelling style
- Resonance of child's experiences in story-world
- Compelling and engaging characters
- Stirring language patterns and story design

Picture Books

- Richly interpretive text and pictures
- Curious, active, inventive child character in a powerful position at crucial moments of the story
- Simple but well-developed plot, with one dominant thread running throughout
- Creative child character engaged in problem solving
- Sequence of actions building to a surprise resolution, insight, or revelation
- Nonsexist/nonclassist/nonracist characters and solutions
- Lively, graceful, accessible writing style
- Pictures that match the mood, tone, meaning or spirit of the words
- Close match of characters' and child readers' experiences

and try to step into this process alongside the authors. Then, when we enter the classroom, we should be better able to help children engage in the authoring process. If we value child-authored materials, we must discover ways to elicit and celebrate them in children's classrooms.

CHILDREN'S LITERATURE

Children's Choices for 1997 (All books published in 1996. Unless otherwise noted, author is also the illustrator. Annotations follow the citation unless title explains itself.)

Beginning Readers

BROOKS, ALAN. *Frogs Jump: A Counting Book.* Illustrated by Steven Kellogg. New York: Scholastic, 1996.

CHWAST, SEYMOUR. *Mr. Merlin and the Turtle.* New York: Greenwillow, 1996. Tactile book; Mr. Merlin transforms his turtle into many different animals—hidden under flaps.

DECESARE, ANGELO. *Anthony the Perfect Monster.* New York: Random House, 1996. Learning to be yourself.

ERNST, LISA CAMPBELL. *The Letters Are Lost.* New York: Viking, 1996. Alphabet blocks with missing letters connect to objects, promoting understanding of letter-sound relationships (ABC book).

FAULKNER, KEITH. *The Wide-Mouthed Frog: A Pop-Up Book.* New York: Dial, 1996. Frogs demonstrate the food chain.

GROSSMAN, BILL. *My Little Sister Ate One Hare.* Illustrated by Kevin Hawkes. New York: Crown, 1996. Cumulative story that rhymes (counting book).

HARDY, TAD. *Lost Cat.* Illustrated by David Goldin. Boston: Houghton Mifflin, 1996. Rhyming story about child whose cat is lost and found by disgruntled adult; bright colors.

HOWARD, ARTHUR. *When I was Five.* New York: Harcourt Brace, 1996. Jeremy—at 6—has changed, but his best friend remains the same.

HUBBARD, PATRICIA. *My Crayons Talk.* Illustrated by G. Brian Karas. New York: Holt 1996. Crayons speak in rhymes filled with action words; colorful pictures.

HUDDLESTON, RUTH, AND MADGWICK, WENDY *Time for Bed.* Illustrated by Tony Linsell. Brookfield, CT: Millbrook, 1996. Tactile book; Benny Bear puts his birthday friends to bed.

LONDON, JONATHAN. *Froggy Goes to School.* Illustrated by Frank Remkiewicz. New York: Viking, 1996. Froggy worries about the first day of school.

MCNAUGHTON, COLIN. *Boo!* New York: Harcourt, 1996. Preston likes to scare people; his father is annoyed.

PAXTON, TOM. *The Marvelous Toy.* Illustrated by Elizabeth Sayles New York: Morrow, 1996. Toy is passed down through the generations.

PFISTER, MARCUS. *The Rainbow Fish Board Book.* London: North-South, 1996. Rainbow Fish decides to share its shiny scales to make friends; compare Leo Lionni's story of Tico.

RYAN, PAM MUNOZ AND PALLOTTA, JERRY. *The Crayon Counting Book.* Illustrated by Frank Mazzola, Jr. Watertown MA: Charlesbridge, 1996. Rhymed counting book with vivid color.

STOCKE, JANET MORGAN. *Minerva Louise at School.* New York: Dutton, 1996. Hen in a schoolroom.

STRICKLAND, PAUL. *Dinosaur Stomp! A Monster Pop-Up.* New York: Dutton, 1996. A dinosaur goes to a dance.

TILDES, PHYLLIS LIMBACHER. *Animals: Black and White.* Watertown MA: Charlesbridge, 1996. Riddles about animals with pictures that elicit predictions.

WALSH, MELANIE. *Do Pigs Have Stripes?* Boston: Houghton Mifflin, 1996. Q-A format; animal traits.

YEKATI, NIKI. *Bears at the Beach: Counting 10 to 20.* Brookfield CT: Millbrook, 1996.

Young Readers

BROWN, MARC. *Arthur Writes a Story.* New York: Little Brown, 1996. Arthur sticks to his own story idea, despite the sometimes overwhelming pressure of his classmates' suggestions.

DADEY, DEBBIE, AND JONES, MARCIA THORNTON. *Mrs. Jeepers Is Missing!* Illustrated by John Steven Gurney. New York: Scholastic, 1996. Is this third-grade teacher really a vampire?

DEFELICE, CYNTHIA. *Casey in the Bath.* Illustrated by Chris Demarest. New York: Farrar, 1996. Fun at bath time with a new kind of soap.

DEGEN, BRUCE. *Sailaway Home.* New York: Scholastic, 1996. Adventures of a traveling pig; in rhyme.

DE GROAT, DIANE. *Roses Are Pink, Your Feet Really Stink.* New York: Morrow, 1996. It's Valentine's Day, and Gilbert makes new friends.

ELSTE, JOAN. *True Blue.* Illustrated by DyAnne DiSalvo-Ryan. New York: Grosset & Dunlap, 1996. Suspense in a chapter book about friendship and a hunting dog named Blue.

GERARD, ROY. *Wagons West!* New York: Farrar, 1996. Rhyming story of Buckskin Dan. Compare other rhyming stories by Gerrard; always well-illustrated.

GRINDLEY, SALLY. *Peter's Place.* Illustrated by Michael Foreman. New York: Harcourt Brace, 1996. An oil spill occurs on a beautiful watercolor landscape; Peter tells us how he loves the wildlife there.

HAGUE, MICHAEL. *The Perfect Present.* New York: Morrow, 1996. A toy comes to life.

HEINZ, BRIAN. *The Monsters' Test.* Illustrated by Sal Murdocca. Brookfield CT: Millbrook, 1996. Who is the scariest monster on a Halloween Trick-or-Treat night?

HENKES, KEVIN. *Lilly's Purple Plastic Purse.* New York: Greenwillow, 1996. Lilly's new purse is a sensation in the classroom, but her teacher is not amused. See other funny mice stories by Henkes.

HOFF, SYD. *Danny and the Dinosaur Go to Camp.* New York: HarperCollins, 1996. Fitting in at summer camp.

HURD, THACHER. *Art Dog.* New York: HarperCollins, 1996. Arthur Dog, an artist, guards the museum and helps solve the crime others think he has committed.

JEWELL, NANCY. *Silly Times with Two Silly Trolls.* Illustrated by Lisa Thiesing. New York: Harper Collins, 1996. Simple text and funny pictures teach time and direction.

KEILLOR, GARRISON. *The Old Man Who Loved Cheese.* Illustrated by Anne Wilsdorf. New York: Little, Brown, 1996. Rhyming text about Wallace who loves smelly cheese.

LEVY, ELIZABETH. *Cleo and the Coyote.* Illustrated by Diana Bryer. New York: HarperCollins, 1996. A dog, Cleo, tells the story of meeting a coyote in the desert. The theme is the sense of belonging.

MACDONALD, AMY. *Cousin Ruth's Tooth.* Illustrated by Marjorie Priceman. Boston: Houghton Mifflin, 1996. Humorous rhymes about finding a lost tooth.

MCKEE, DAVID. *Elmer and Wilbur.* New York: Lothrop, Lee & Shepard, 1996. Ventriloquist elephants in unusual colors.

MELMED, LAURA KRAUSS. *The Marvelous Market on Mermaid.* Illustrated by Maryann Kovalski. New York: Lothrop, Lee & Shepard, 1996. Funny rhymes in a story about Grandma's store.

NOVAK, MATT. *Newt.* New York: HarperCollins, 1996. A salamander learns about friendship.

O'BRIEN, JOHN. *Mother Hubbard's Christmas.* Honesdate PA: Boyds Mills, 1996.

PARK, BARBARA. *Junie B. Jones and That Meanie Jim's Birthday.* Illustrated by Denise Brunkus. New York: Random House, 1996. A kindergartner is not invited to the birthday party.

POWELL, POLLY. *Just Dessert.* New York: Harcourt Brace, 1996. Imaginary characters, favorite desserts, and a surprise ending.

RAY, MARY LYN. *Mud.* Illustrated by Lauren Stringer. New York: Harcourt Brace, 1996. Winter moves into spring with many muddy things to do.

ROOT, PHYLLIS. *Mrs. Potters Pig.* Illustrated by Russell Ayto. Cambridge MA: Candlewick, 1996. Humor in a barnyard setting.

SANDVED, KJELL B. *The Butterfly Alphabet.* New York: Scholastic, 1996. ABC book featuring poems and photographs of butterflies with alphabet letters in their wing patterns.

SELZER, ERIC. *4 Pups and a Worm.* New York: Random House, 1996. Whimsy, nonsense rhymes, memorable pictures.

SIMON, FRANCESCA. *Spider School.* Illustrated by Peta Coplans. New York: Dial, 1996. Fear of a new school stimulates Kate's fantasy about a classroom with a gorilla for a teacher.

———. *The Topsy-Turvies.* Illustrated by Keren Ludlow. New York: Dial, 1996. Family that does everything backwards saves the day when things go wrong for a neighbor.

SLYDER, INGRID. *The Fabulous Flying Fandinis.* New York: Cobblehill, 1996. Bobby learns to like people who are different.

TESTA, MARIA. *Nine Candles.* Illustrated by Amanda Schaffer. Minneapolis: Carolrhoda, 1996. Raymond, at age seven, has a mother in prison, but in two years they will be together again.

WHITE, LINDA. *Too Many Pumpkins.* Illustrated by Megan Lloyd. New York: Holiday House, 1996.

WILLIAMS, ARLENE. *Dragon Soup.* Illustrated by Sally Smith. HJ Kramre/Starseed, 1996. Clever female, Tonlu, helps settle a dragon conflict and pay her father's debt.

WOOD, AUDREY. *Bright and Early Thursday Evening: A Tangled Tale.* Illustrated by Don Wood. New York: Harcourt Brace, 1996. Pictures reveal a place midway between real life and dreams.

YACCARINO, DAN. *If I Had a Robot.* New York: Viking, 1996. Problem solving about unlikable tasks.

YEE, WONG HERBERT. *Mrs. Brown Went to Town.* Boston: Houghton Mifflin, 1996. Rhymes about farm animals and memorable pictures.

Intermediate Readers

ARMSTRONG, ROBB. *Drew and the Bub Daddy Showdown.* New York: HarperCollins, 1996. Drew draws cartoons and comic book stories, which brings him friends and money.

BYARS, BETSY. *Tornado.* Illustrated by Doron Ben-Ami. New York: HarperCollins, 1996. Farmhand tells childhood stories as family waits out a tornado in this easy-to-read chapter book.

CLARKE, GILLIAN, EDITOR. *The Whispering Room: Haunted Poems.* Illustrated by Justin Todd. New York: Kingfisher, 1996. Scary poems effectively composed and illustrated.

CLEARY, BRIAN. *Give Me Back My Schubert.* Illustrated by Rick Dupre. Minneapolis: Lerner, 1996. Verse tale of a child's attempt to escape music lessons; information about music and play.

CROWTHER, ROBERT: *Robert Crowther's Pop-Up Oympics: Amazing Facts and Record Breakers.* Cambridge, MA: Candlewick, 1996.

DAHL, ROALD. *James and the Giant Peach.* Adapted from the film by Karey Kirkpatrick. Illustrated by Lane Smith. Burbank CA: Disney, 1996. Dahl wrote the book; Disney made a movie of it; now Kirkpatrick turns the movie into a picture book. Full circle for this amazing story.

DAKOS, KALLI. *The Goof Who Invented Homework, and Other School Poems.* Illustrated by Denise Brunkus. New York: Dial, 1996. Poems about school; humor; memorable pictures.

FRIEDRICH, ELIZABETH. *Leah's Pony.* Illustrated by Michael Garland. Honesdale PA: Boyds Mills, 1996. Leah must sell her pony to save the farm during the Great Depression.

HADDON, MARK. *The Sea of Tranquillity.* Illustrated by Christian Birmingham. New York: Harcourt, 1996. Author remembers astronauts first walking on the moon during his childhood.

HARRISON, DAVID. *A Thousand Cousins: Poems of Family Life.* Illustrated by Betsy Lewin. Honesdale PA: Boyds Mills, 1996. Cartoon art; humor; poetry.

HECKMAN, PHILIP. *Waking Upside Down.* Illustrated by Dwight Been. New York: Atheneum, 1996. Morton wakes to find he can defy gravity.

HOPKINS, LEE BENNETT, EDITOR. *Opening Days: Sports Poems.* Illustrated by Scott Medlock. New York: Harcourt Brace, 1996.

JENKINS, MARTIN. *Fly traps! Plants that Bite Back.* Illustrated by David Parkins. Cambridge MA: Candlewick, 1996. Narrative information book about carnivorous plant life.

KNAPP, RON. *Mummies.* Springfield NJ: Enslow, 1996. Much information about mummies in Pompeii, their individual stories, and the ways scientists uncover ancient cultures.

LANGSEN, RICHARD. *When Someone in the Family Drinks Too Much.* Illustrated by Nicole Rubel. New York: Dial, 1996. Easy-to-read information book.

LESSEM, DON. *Utahraptor: The Deadliest Dinosaur.* Illustrated by Donna Braginetz. Minneapolis: Carolrhoda, 1996. Information book; color photographs.

LONG, JAN FREEMAN, ADAPTER. *The Bee and the Dream: A Japanese Tale.* Illustrated by Kaoru Ono. New York: Dutton, 1996. Dream adventure filled with exciting events and resolving in a happy ending.

LORBIECKI, MARYBETH. *Just One Flick of a Finger.* Illustrated by David Diaz. New York: Dial, 1996. Guns won't make a man of him, a teen male tells us in rap and rhyme. Memorable pictures.

LOWRY, LOIS. *See You Around. Sam!* Illustrated by Diane de Groat. Boston: Houghton Mifflin, 1996. Sam wants to run away to Alaska after his mother says he can't wear his vampire fangs.

The Magic School Bus Blows Its Top: A Book About Volcanoes. Based-on the series by Joanna Cole. Illustrated by Bruce Degen. New York: Scholastic, 1996.

MICKLETHWAITE, LUCY, EDITOR. *I Spy A Freight Train: Transportation in Art.* New York: Greenwillow, 1996. Interactive picture book; children play the I-Spy game to detect different kinds of transportation; many different art styles and eras displayed.

PILKEY, DAV. *God Bless the Gargoyles.* New York: Harcourt Brace, 1996. Rhyming story about gargoyles.

SAVAGE, JEFF. *Drag Racing.* Parsippany NJ: Crestwood House, 1996. Photo illustrations about a sport children might enjoy learning more about.

SILVERSTEIN, SHEL. *Falling Up.* New York: HarperCollins 1996. Poems and drawings by the master of modern nonsense rhymes.

Advanced Readers

ANDERSON, JOAN. *Batboy: An Inside Look at Spring Training.* Photographs by Matthew Cavanaugh. New York: Lodestar, 1996.

BOHLMEIJER, ARNO, AUTHOR AND TRANSLATOR. *Something Very Sorry.* Boston: Houghton Mifflin, 1996. Story of a family dealing with their mother's death in auto accident.

BYARS, BETSY. *Dead Letter: A Herculeah Jones Mystery.* New York: Viking, 1996.

COHEN, DANIEL. *Werewolves.* New York: Cobblehill/Dutton, 1996. Information and stories about werewolves.

FLETCHER, RALPH. *Buried Alive: The Elements of Love.* Photographs by Andrew Moore. New York: Atheneum, 1996. Free verse poetry.

GERINGER, LAURA. *Hercules the Strong Man.* New York: Scholastic, 1996. Greek myth in comic book mode.

GERINGER, LAURA. *Ulysses the Soldier King.* New York: Scholastic, 1996. Chapter book depicting the life of the famous hero of Greek myth.

GLENN, MEL. *Who Killed Mr. Chippendale? A Mystery in Poems.* New York: Lodestar, 1996. High school teacher is shot; free-form poetry explores the act as students and teachers speak.

KEHRET, PEG. *Earthquake Terror.* New York: Cobblehill/Dutton, 1996. Suspenseful story of Jonathan and his sister trying to survive an earthquake.

PEDERSEN, TED. *True Fright: Trapped Beneath the Ice!* New York: Tor, 1996. True horror stories.

PIPE, JIM. *In the Footsteps of the Werewolf.* Illustrated by McRae Books Agency. Brookfield CT: Copper Beech/Milbrook, 1996. Fact and fiction about werewolves.

SATEREN, SHELLEY SWANSON. *The Humane Societies: A Voice for the Animals.* Parsippany NJ: Dillon, 1996.

SAVAGE, JEFF. *Monster Trucks.* Parsippany NJ: Crestwood House, 1996. Photos illustrate this book about monster truck racing.

———. *Supercross Motorcycle Racing.* Parsippany NJ: Crestwood House, 1996. History of supercross racing and stories of champions.

SMITH, ROLAND. *Journey of the Red Wolf.* New York: Cobblehill/Dutton, 1996. Informational book about red wolves.

SPINELLI, JERRY. *Crash.* New York: Knopf, 1996. School bully deals with friends and grandfather's illness.

VAN LEEUWEN, JEAN. *Blue Sky, Butterfly.* New York: Dial, 1996. Grandmother helps with child's struggle through her parent's divorce.

WRIGHT, DAVID. *Arthur Ashe: Breaking the Color Barrier in Tennis.* Springfield NJ: Enslow, 1996. Biography of the famous African-American tennis player who died of AIDS.

PART TWO

Readers and Writers: Creative Processes

Chapter 6

Why—and How—Authors Produce Books for Children

Topics in This Chapter:

- The nature of the creative process
- Creating picture books
- Creating fiction
- Creating poetry

> *"What is a Caucus-race?" said Alice; not that she much wanted to know, but the Dodo had paused as if it thought that somebody ought to speak, and no one else seemed inclined to say anything.*
>
> *"Why," said the Dodo, "the best way to explain it is to do it." (And, as you might like to try the thing yourself some winter day, I will tell you how the Dodo managed it.)*
>
> ***"A Caucus-Race and A Long Tale" in Alice's Adventures in Wonderland, 1865***
> **—Lewis Carroll**

In the last chapter, we investigated what makes a children's book good in terms of critical standards as well as personal, social, and cultural values. In this chapter, we will examine how a children's book comes into existence and how it evolves. And why are we stopping to investigate the creative process? Because, as the Dodo says, the best way to understand how something "works" is to engage in it—whether it is running a race or authoring a book. We will begin by looking at a small group of children's book authors to see how they view the creative process, or why they write for children. We might even discover that they do not consciously write for children—that they are not even thinking of children—as they begin.

THE NATURE OF THE CREATIVE PROCESS

Some children's authors simply write, and then find by chance that their work fits the children's audience. **Susan Cooper** (1976) tells about writing her first children's book, *Over Sea, Under Stone* (Harcourt, 1966). She saw a notice for a contest sponsored by the publishers of the Victorian children's writer, E. Nesbit. The sponsors wanted a family adventure story, so she invented three children and a "rather vague plot of villainy and hidden treasure":

> And then a funny thing began to happen. A lot of unexpected ideas jumped in and took over from the original intention, and before I quite realised what I was doing, the plot began to change completely. The murmurings of events beyond reality came invading my mind, and suddenly I'd quite forgotten about the E. Nesbit prize and the adventure story. I found I was writing a fantasy, full of images that had haunted me since childhood; things I'd never thought of putting into fiction. . . . After that I stopped trying to tell my imagination what to do. I reconciled myself to that pattern in which the author simply writes the book that wants to be written, and lets his publisher tell him what it is when he's finished. So far, my publisher has told me I've written books for children—even once when I was sure the book I'd written was an adult novel. . . . And whether or not I write the books for children, there they sit, on the children's list. Clearly their appeal must be at that end of the seesaw; something in them must draw a greater response from the mind of the child than from the adult. (page 53)

Like Susan Cooper, **Kevin Henkes** (1992) was thinking very little about a child audience as he began his career in children's books. He simply wanted to be an illustrator, and he knew from his junior year of high school that creating picture books would be "the perfect occupation . . . pictures and words—working together" page 39). He began reading picture books and reading books about how to produce work in this genre; then he started making sample picture book layouts, or "dummies." During college, Henkes took his portfolio to New York and began making the rounds of publishers, and Susan Hirschman at Greenwillow quickly snapped up his work.

Fortunately, Henkes's ideas mesh easily with a children's audience, because the emotional content of his work comes from childhood memories—tiny details he saw very clearly, like the outfit he wore the first day of kindergarten. His parents always made things turn out all right, he remembers, and he wants his books to end on that hopeful note: "Something terrible will happen—and then everything will suddenly turn around." He began trying to put a sense of joy into his books, and joy often came in the form of a character. "I love Lilly, more than anything; she's my favorite character," says Henkes (1992). "I had to create Lilly to do the things I couldn't do," he adds, launching into a story of how Lilly's red cowboy boots were once his own (black with red trim) but "much too showy" for him (page 46).

Leo Lionni, author of the four Caldecott Honor books *Inch By Inch* (1960), *Swimmy* (1963), *Frederick* (1967), and *Alexander and the Wind-Up Mouse* (1969), remembers his childhood and the way it influenced his picture book career. Like Cooper, he says he never thinks or worries about his audience.

"When I was a child," says Lionni, "I was a passionate collector of small animals, mostly reptiles. I kept them within the glass walls of terrariums where in a mixture of order and randomness I arranged sand and stones, mosses and ferns, to simulate a natural habitat . . . they were alternative worlds for my contemplation, and of my own creation. They were safe, predictable, stable substitutes for an ever-moving reality. They were my refuge from the hostile and uncertain world that surrounded me" (page 729).

LILLY had her own way of doing things....

From *Chester's Way* (Greenwillow, 1988) by Kevin Henkes.

From *Mr McMouse (*Alfred A Knopf, Inc.: New York, 1992) by Leo Lionni.

As an adult, Lionni discovered that the characters of his stories were the "same little silent actors" of his childhood play and that they had influenced his thematic choices and "the whole intricate game of symbols" running through all his work (page 730). It is the child's world, then, that seems to provide the essential forces that shape the adult imagination and eventually direct the adult's literary style. The child's view is essential, but not a conscious purpose, as many writers and illustrators tell us.

Do authors of children's books ever write for the children's audience knowingly and with full intent from the beginning? Authors of ABC and counting books and of books with controlled vocabulary choices and sentence length would, of course, create books with children as the intended audience. But what about other children's writers?

Elaine Konigsburg (1995) obviously knew she was writing for a children's audience when her own children, each day at lunch time, listened intently to what she had written that morning while they were at school. Konigsburg worried that her children would miss books that included "quarrels among siblings and cross mothers and bathrooms," realistic books in which they would find themselves, as she had never been able to do in the books she read as a child (page 74). So she began to write books in which children could relate to the characters as real children.

Beverly Cleary (1975) expressed a similar need to write children's books that caught her childhood experiences:

INVESTIGATIONS: A Work of Your Own

Consider creating literature yourself as a way into understanding—from the inside—what a children's book is, how it comes to life for its author and continues to evolve until it "speaks" to children.

Begin by asking yourself what story is inside you waiting to get out. What story wants to be told? What picture wants to be drawn? What character wants to come to life? At this point, do not think about an audience or a genre. Instead, let the audience and the genre find or choose you. Do not tell your imagination what to do. Let it tell you where you are headed.

For now, simply concentrate on getting to know your characters and letting them get to know one another. Imagine them, watch them, name them, dream and daydream about them. Let them come back to you from your childhood, as Henkes remembered himself wearing black cowboy boots. Let your characters lead you, as Lilly and her red cowboy boots led Henkes, into a setting, a sequence of actions, a conflict, a story. Or let a particular remembered object, like Lionni's collection of small animals, or a remembered setting, like Cleary's childhood neighborhood, lead you into a story. See what pictures form in your mind. Watch these pictures as if you were watching a mental TV screen. See where they take you.

Try to jot down (or sketch) something about your characters and your story. It does not matter which comes first—words or pictures. Note some details, some lines of dialogue, or some pictures that may be forming in your mind. Then let your ideas sit for a time, as you go about your life. Do not force a story on your characters before they are ready.

When you have a few scenes in your mind (or on paper), when you have a few words or lines or the seed of story, begin thinking about how you will present it. Is this going to be a long text with few if any pictures? A short piece with many pictures? A story? A poem? A picture book? (Remember that the length of a picture book is, at most, 500 words.)

If you do not have answers yet, just keep going. Wade slowly into the work, letting the piece guide you, showing you how it needs to be written or drawn. Let your ideas tell you where to go and what to put down on paper. Later, as you read on in this chapter, you will learn more about writing in different genres, and you can try different approaches.

> In those important years of childhood reading that followed victory over our school readers, we wanted fun, excitement, adventure, magic. Most of all we wanted stories that would make us laugh. . . . I longed for stories about my neighborhood and about my classroom—that place of continuing drama far more interesting to me than the subjects taught. Why didn't authors write books about everyday problems that children could solve by themselves? Why weren't there more stories about children playing? Why couldn't I find more books that would make me laugh? These were the books I was eventually to write. (page 364)

But Cleary still did not write simply for children, as she later explained (1982):

> As I wrote I discovered I had a collaborator, the child within myself—a rather odd, serious little girl, prone to colds, who sat in a child's rocking chair with her feet over the hot air outlet of the furnace, reading for hours, seeking laughter in the pages of books while her mother warned her she would ruin her eyes. That little girl, who has remained with me, prevents me from writing down to children, from poking fun at my characters, and from writing an adult reminiscence about childhood instead of a book to be enjoyed by children. And yet I do not write solely for that child; I am also writing for my adult self. We are collaborators who must agree. The feeling of being two ages at one time is delightful, one that surely must be a source of great pleasure to all writers of books enjoyed by children. (page 558)

With all of these writers' ideas in mind about *why* they write, we will pause now to consider *how* adults produce books for children. Like Konigsburg and Cleary, they might be writing or illustrating children's books to fill a gap in their childhood reading. Like Cooper, they might be putting to rest images that have haunted them since childhood. Or like Henkes and Lionni, they might be pursuing a career in the art of making picture books. In any case, talented adults work hard in the interests of children, whether their conscious purposes—or their unconscious ideas—lead them to do so.

We will begin by looking at picture books, then proceed to children's fiction and poetry. But first, as the Dodo would advise: Consider creating something yourself.

CREATING PICTURE BOOKS

Stories in picture books can be divided into four categories: animal fantasy, human fantasy, folklore, and realism; we will begin with the oldest and most popular of these.

Animal Fantasy

We met the mice characters of Kevin Henkes, in particular Chester and Lilly, in our discussion of censorship. Listen as Henkes tells how he creates his characters:

> More often than not it's a character or a name or a title that comes first. From that point, it may take me a couple of years to write the book. The ideas tend to overlap and slip away and resurface . . . The words always come first. I'll write the story, and that can take anywhere from a week to two months. . . . I write three lines, and that may take three hours. But I'll sit there and just doodle if I have to. Usually I'll have the opening, and I'll know where I want to end up; working on the middle takes the most time. I always read aloud when I write. I read it back to myself over and over—because a good picture book is read over and over. It's got to have a certain rhythm. . . . Because I learn so many things about the story

and the characters throughout the course of a book, it's best for me to develop the story in progression. The character grows and changes, and I want to do something in the art to symbolize the change. (1992, pages 40–42)

Henkes wants the story to be exciting (to have tension); thus, the character must have a problem, he says. But, as he adds, "the only way a book can be real, for me, is to have the character first and then take the story from there." Any other format, such as a planned plot or problem-book, is simply too constricting: "Even though, for instance, Chester is a mouse, I think of him as a real person. There are specific things about him that make him Chester. I didn't think of *Chester's Way* as a book about friendship; I just had Chester in my head. I had him in my head long before I even knew there would be a Lilly" (pages 42–43).

Why is Chester a mouse and not a boy? In Henkes's first four books, he used human characters and a realistic art style. Then humor started creeping into his texts, and he found that drawing animals was a good way to convey humor and that he did not need a real model in his studio in order to draw them. He could sketch more freely from his imagination. First he drew rabbits, discovering he could convey emotion in the way he drew their ears. Then he remembered a favorite cup he had had as a child, with a mouse head and eyes that shifted as the cup moved, and Chester arrived in his mind. "There is a lot I can do with their tails and ears," he says, "and there are so many levels on which I can visually tap the humor. If you have a mouse, jumping for joy, three feet up in the air—in a kind of contorted posture—it looks joyful, but if you try to draw realistically a human child doing the same thing, it looks all wrong"(page 43).

Rosemary Wells confirms Henkes's ideas about the value of animal characters for the artist. Why are her characters raccoons and not people? Animals can do things children would look too cute doing, says Wells, and they can be "superbly funny" in situations where children would simply look slapstick. The artist can dress her animal characters in costumes from an older time, producing a world child readers can "climb right into," with "no color barriers, because animals come in all colors and no one minds" (1990, pages 134–35).

Also, children care deeply about animals. Says Wells, "The characters in a children's book must reach into the heart of the reader on page one. Emotional content is the main reason a child and a parent will go back to a book again and again" (page 130). Wells remembers the idea that came to her for *Timothy Goes to School* (Dial, 1981) and the way the idea echoed both her own grade school years and something that happened to her daughter, Victoria, in her first grade class. A haughty classmate, Melissa, told Victoria that " 'Nobody wears an everyday kilt to the Christmas concert!' " Victoria was devastated (page 132).

Wells turns Victoria into Timothy, a raccoon and a boy, because the story focuses on a quarrel about clothing. Claude greets Timothy's friendly smile with the comment, "Nobody wears a sunsuit on the first day of school." Timothy's mother makes him a wonderful new jacket to wear the next day, but Claude, sporting a new polo shirt, informs Timothy that he isn't supposed to be wearing "party clothes on the second day of school."

"Boys are as sensitive about clothes as girls are," says Wells, "but if you make the lead characters girls in a book about a clothing fight, they come off as bitchy stereotypes. Boys come off funny and very real" (page 135). In the real world, Wells gave her daughter sympathy and a bag of M & M's for her agony, and her own sweet revenge was that Melissa's comment gave her a good idea for a story.

From *Timothy Goes to School* (Dial, 1981) by Rosemary Wells.

How do writers actually produce stories once they have some ideas? Wells speaks of a "writing screen." She sees her stories as projected onto the screen from something like an "unseen space in the cosmos" (page 143). But most writers, reading her words, might wonder how they could "log in" to this wonderful "screen."

Length is sometimes another difficulty for writers. A picture book manuscript is much too long at three-and-a-half single-spaced pages, as Mem Fox, author of *Possum Magic* (Harcourt, 1983), explains: "With very few words, the illustrations reveal much of the action, character, setting, and tone . . . [the] number of words per page has to be limited to the amount of time it takes for a child to absorb the pictures before the page is turned." *Possum Magic* was in good shape with 512 words (two single-spaced typed pages). This short text, Fox adds, must be unforgettable, as "the best words are placed in the best possible order" (pages 146–47).

Like Beatrix Potter, Fox does not shy away from long, difficult words: "Children who are learning to read are perfectly capable of identifying the long words in *Possum Magic,* such as *invisible, miserable,* and *lamington,* because they're important words in the story" (page 147). The American version of Fox's book also provides a glossary of Australian terms—like lamington—at the end of the book.

In another book, *Night Noises* (Harcourt, 1989), Fox was not hesitant to create striking metaphors—"Outside, clouds raced along the sky, playing hide and seek with the moon"—and similes filled with images of sight and sound: "Her hair was as wispy as cobwebs in ceilings. Her bones were as creaky as floorboards at midnight" (page 148). Rich, figurative language like Fox's enriches a child's literacy.

Tips for Developing a Story

Anne Lamott, who writes fiction for adults, advises prospective writers to write about their childhoods in order to recover the childhood gift of noticing things and empathizing with others: "Write about that time in your life when you were so intensely interested in the world, when your powers of observation were at their most acute, when you felt things so deeply. Exploring and understanding your childhood will give you the ability to empathize, and that understanding and empathy will teach you to write with intelligence and insight and compassion" (page 225).

"Don't worry about the plot," she also tells prospective writers. "Plot grows out of character. If you focus on who the people in your story are . . . something is bound to happen . . . Let what [the characters] say or do reveal who they are, and be involved in their lives, and keep asking yourself, Now what happens? The development of relationship creates plot" (page 44–54–55). Plot, she says, is what characters do in spite of anything the writer decides ahead of time or chooses for them to do.

Writers need to find out what their characters care about most in the world, adds Lamott. Then they will discover what's at stake for their characters. "Find a way to express this discovery in action," she says, "and then let your people set about finding or holding onto or defending whatever it is" (page 55). She tells how the creative process works for her:

> I imagine my characters, and let myself daydream about them. A movie begins to play in my head, with emotion pulsing underneath it, and I stare at it in a trancelike state, until words bounce around together and form a sentence. Then I do the menial work of getting it down on paper, because I'm the designated typist, and I'm also the person whose job it is to hold the lantern while the kid does the digging. What is the kid digging for? *The stuff.* Details and clues and images, invention, fresh ideas, an intuitive understanding of people. I tell you, the holder of the lantern doesn't even know what the kid is digging for half the time—but she knows gold when she sees it. Your plot will fall into place as, one day at a time, you listen to your characters carefully, and watch them move around doing and saying things and bumping into each other. You'll see them influence each other's lives, you'll see what they are capable of up and doing, and you'll see them come to various ends. (page 56)

Source: Anne Lamott, *Bird by Bird* (New York: Atheneum, 1994).

INVESTIGATIONS: Animal Fantasy Picture Books

Examine books by Kevin Henkes and Rosemary Wells; then try creating some childlike animal characters in your own story to introduce humor and intensify emotional content. Study the language patterns, the striking metaphors and similes, and the sight and sound imagery of Mem Fox; then try experimenting with language in the story you are writing. See if you can produce a striking metaphor, simile, or image.

Human Fantasy

The most celebrated picture book artist of the post-1960s is **Maurice Sendak.** His work falls within the category of *human fantasy,* a genre (or subgenre) in which natural laws are suspended. Human fantasies might feature some animals, and the animals might talk or do other humanlike things, as in Sendak's *Pierre* (Harper, 1962), but these stories focus mostly on humans who hear the animals talking or see them doing unbelievable things. Humans are the main characters, and they are usually either gifted with extraordinary powers or abilities, or they are dreaming, daydreaming, or imagining magical events. In either case, human impossibilities form the crux of the story.

Sendak has created many fantasies that feature children as the main characters. Yet he does not "set out to do books for children," as he explained to interviewer Jonathan Cott. The books simply capture a children's audience, though Sendak claims he doesn't know why: "I'm an artist who does books that are apparently more appropriate for children than for anyone else, for some odd reason." It may have something to do with the ability he shares with Beverly Cleary to remain in touch with his inner child. "The pleasures I get as an adult," he says, "are heightened by the fact that I experience them as a child at the same time" (Cott, 1983, pages 64–66).

Sendak has described himself as a very difficult child who hated school and was riddled by countless terrors even on the home front—such as those aroused by the vacuum cleaner. However, he loved movies (many of which also terrified him). Relatives scared him, too, and he recollects "dreadful Sundays in Brooklyn when my sister, my brother, and I had to get dressed up for our aunts and uncles" (1988a, page 213). He liked none of them, and he was especially resentful that these relatives were coming to eat the family's food and to pinch his cheek and say, "You look so good, we could eat you up" (1988a, page 214)—an expression he later used in *Where the Wild Things Are.*

When Sendak began creating his books, all of these memories cropped up in his words and pictures. *Outside Over There* (Harper, 1981) is the most personal of his books and his favorite:

> Much of it is based on what scared me when I was little. I remember as a very small child seeing a book about a little girl who is caught in a rainstorm. She's wearing a huge yellow slicker and boots, and the rain comes down harder and harder, and begins to rise and spill into her boots, and that's when I would always stop looking at the book. It scared me too much. I never found out what happened to the little girl. . . . So *Outside Over There* is partly about that fear. It's also about Mozart, because I love Mozart . . . So I was thinking of [Mozart's] *The Magic Flute,* thinking of a little girl in a raincoat and boots, thinking of the end of the eighteenth century. And I was also thinking of my sister, Natalie, who is nine years older than I am and who had to care for me. (1988a, page 209)

Music is essential to Sendak's work: "I feel an intense sympathy between the shape of a musical phrase and that of a drawn line. Sketching to music is a marvelous stimulant to my imagination, and often a piece of music will give me the needed clue to the look and color of a picture" (1988b, page 146). Perhaps music enables Sendak to produce his trademark—the delicate balance of words and pictures.

All of Sendak's work contains a strong rhythmic dialogue between visual and verbal line. The animated sequence of picture book art is, in fact, Sendak's own major contribution to the genre. His ability to produce "moving" pictures might have grown out of a childhood experience he recounts for interviewer Jonathan Cott. "I was convalescing after a long, serious illness," he recalls:

> I was sitting on my grandmother's lap, and I remember the feeling of pleasant drowsiness. It was winter. We sat in front of a window, and my grandmother pulled the shade up and down to amuse me. Every time the shade went up, I was thrilled by the sudden reappearance of the backyard, the falling snow, and my brother and sister busy constructing a sooty snowman. Down came the shade—I waited. Up went the shade—the children had moved, the snowman had grown eyes. I don't remember a single sound. (Cott, page 44).

Yet this balance of words and pictures separates when he begins a book. Everything begins with the words:

> No pictures at all—you just shut the Polaroid off; you don't want to be seduced by pictures because then you begin to write for pictures. Images come in language, language, language: in phrases, in verbal constructs, in poetry, whatever. I've never spent less than two years on the text of one of my picture books, even though each of them is approximately 380 words long. Only when the text is finished—when my editor thinks it's finished—do I begin the pictures. *Then* I put the film in my head. (1990, page 60)

And when Sendak is creating the illustrations for another author's retelling of a folk tale, as he often does, his concepts begin with the teller's words.

Illustrated Folk Tales

Speaking about himself as an illustrator of many Grimm folk tales, Sendak explains to interviewer Charlotte Otten that he has to "burrow" himself into the text "to find the writer in the text, or to find the subtext—the routes to what the author was trying to achieve" (Otten, 1992, page 112). Thus, he found he could not illustrate the words of many writers. Sendak feels a symbiosis must form between writer and illustrator if the words and pictures are to fuse as they do in any good picture book in which the illustrator and writer are the same.

Sendak's early collaborations with writer Ruth Krauss produce the happiest of symbiotic relationships. His pictures of the gleeful jumping boy in *A Very Special House* (Harper, 1953) could not be better matched with the whimsical and funny rhymes Krauss gives the boy to chant:

> I'm bringing home a turtle
> and a rabbit and a giant
> and a little dead mouse
> and a little dead mouse
> —I take it everywheres—
> and some monkeys and some skunkeys
> and a very old lion which . . .
> . . . is eating all the stuffings from the chairs chairs chairs
> They and I are making secrets
> and we're falling over laughing
> and we're running in and out
> —and we hooie hooie hooie—
> then we think we are some chickens
> then we're singing in the opera then
> we're going going going going ooie ooie ooie.

Jon Scieszka is the author of the funny and bizarre folk tale recastings *The True Story of the Three Little Pigs!* (Viking, 1989) and *The Stinky Cheese Man* (Viking,1992), both illustrated by **Lane Smith.** But Smith's art work is so distinctive and it so easily captures the mood, tone, and intention of Scieszka's storytelling, we may forget that two individuals produced in this venture. How does such a seamless collaboration happen?

Smith says that even as a child he loved the "more macabre side of things," and that is why he never tries to tone down what he creates for children—the "definite dark side" of his work (page 64). In fact, he does not consider himself a children's book illustrator, simply an illustrator creating books that children like and that come naturally to him.

Smith's first book emerged from a set of Halloween ABC paintings he had produced that the publisher gave to Eve Merriam; she composed poems to accompany them. He was pleased with his *Halloween ABC* (Demco Media, reprint; 1995), but he says it was banned everywhere as satanic. Then he met Jon Scieszka, a teacher who was, at this time, teaching his classes how to rewrite fairy tales. Scieszka liked the "dark side" of Smith's work, and they teamed up to make what turned into their rewrite of The Three Pigs. They put humorous details in to amuse themselves, but they knew child readers would find the story funny, too.

With both books, but especially *The Stinky Cheese Man,* Scieszka and Smith were "playing with all the conventions and really turning them upside down—taking the classics and deconstructing them." In the first book, the wolf tells his version of the story; in the second, the narrator spoofs several old stories, including Cinderella and Little Red Riding Hood. Scieszka and Smith read early versions of *The Stinky Cheese Man* to children and drew such a positive reaction that they decided to add transitional characters to tie the stories together. The manuscript grew to be 56 pages, twice the size of a regular picture book; but as Smith says, "it works as a whole; and its transitional elements give it a filmlike quality. It has running gaps. It's completely resolved at the end. And it's really fun." The best thing, he adds, is that the book inspires children to reread the classic fairy tales (pages 68—69).

Realistic Picture Books

Jerry Pinkney has illustrated every possible genre of children's picture books. In addition, he has illustrated numerous books of longer fiction, biography, and memoir, such as Mildred Taylor's *Song of the Trees* (Dial, 1975) and Eloise Greenfield's *Mary McLeod Bethune* (Harper, 1977) and *Childtimes* (Harper, 1979). Pinkney's illustrating style is always realistic, a unique blending of photography, pencil sketches, and watercolors or pastels.

In his early work, we see mostly pencil drawings (no full-color pictures); Pinkney's use of photography began with Mildred Taylor's *Song of the Trees,* he says, when he had live models act out the text. At this time, he also began producing pictures of characters looking out at the reader to forge the reader-writer connection.

INVESTIGATIONS: Human Fantasy Picture Books and Illustrated Folk Tales

Examine books by Maurice Sendak. Then:

- Try to recall your childhood angers and fears and the fantasies you created to cope with your feelings. What fantasies do you see blooming on your creative "screen"?
- Try composing a story to music, and see how it affects your composing process. What music would you choose?

Now examine books by Jon Scieszka and Lane Smith. Consider how you might retell an old story, changing it in some way to entertain readers and to add something to the world that was not present before.

Family members—an uncle, nephews, nieces, his wife, even Pinkney himself—have served as models for the Polaroid snapshots he uses as a starting point: "We bring the models into the studio . . . I get people to respond to me and to each other. But I don't just take a photograph and then draw from it. Sometimes I fill in a lot; certainly when there's a male figure, I'm very often that male figure, and that way I can exaggerate the action" (1991, page 176).

Unlike Kevin Henkes, who works from beginning to end on a picture book, Pinkney begins with a scene that makes him feel comfortable; it is usually something from the middle of the book. He works from middle to end and then starts developing the beginning of the book. Like Maurice Sendak, Pinkney wants the book to function as a unit. "I think of all the drawings for a book as one piece of art," he says. "I'm trying to get the reader to turn the page. I'm trying to get him or her to look at the page and then be curious about turning it. So I'm trying to hold you and make you move at the same time . . . I have to give up spelling it all out on a particular page. I have to give up having a piece stand on its own, because I need my work to be a narrative" (pages 178–79).

African-American culture plays a large role in Pinkney's creative process, and the people in his work, he says, "tend to be proud and upright" (page 179). This approach, coupled with the realism rooted in his photographs of himself and other family members, helps to lend power, dignity, and authenticity to his characterizations and settings.

Authenticity is a particular challenge for the outsider illustrating books about an insider culture. When Canadian author-illustrator **Ian Wallace's** (1989) editor

From *Song of the Trees* (Dial, 1985) by Mildred Taylor, illustrated by Jerry Pinkney.

approached him to create the pictures for a story about an Inuit child, Wallace's exposure to the Inuit people, who live in the far Northern area of Canada, was limited to books and television. But author Jan Andrews's words cast a powerful spell over Wallace; the story, *Very Last First Time* (Douglas and McIntyre, 1989), captured not only his imagination but his spirit. Like Sendak, Ian Wallace is an interpretive artist, with a strong belief in the emotional link between teller and illustrator.

"To discover the emotional link of a story," he says, "the illustrator must understand all levels on which the story functions: intellectual, physical, psychological, and spiritual" (page 77). Then the illustrator must discover the appropriate medium, color, perspective, and position of one character to one another. Color and perspective are very important in *Very Last First Time.* Wallace needed two main colors to reflect the two linked worlds that Eva, the Inuit child, discovers as she passes into adulthood when she walks alone on the bottom of the sea one day to gather mussels. So he made the light above-ground world yellow, and the dark underwater ice world purple. Wallace knew that the Inuit people refer to their homeland as the "Land of Purple Twilight," so he also used purple for the end papers.

When Wallace took the pictures to a classroom to show some children his progress, they discovered more in his picture than he, the artist, had seen. They found—to his surprise—that among the images of a wolf, a bear, and a seal, which he had hidden in the underwater ice world, was the image of Eva's mother (actually an optical illusion resulting from the way he had drawn the rocks in a pool of

From *Very Last First Time* (Douglas & McIntyre, 1985) by Jan Andrews, illustrated by Ian Wallace.

Soon her mussel pan was full, so she had time to explore.

water). They interpreted the figure as Eva's mother's spirit, guiding Eva in her search. "Your mother is always with you," they told him (page 80).

Wallace was intrigued by the children's discovery and the fact that their interpretation corresponded closely with Inuit beliefs, even though neither he nor they were Inuit. Wallace likens himself to an Inuit sculptor. "It seems quite natural," he explains, "that at some point my subconscious would take over and incorporate spirit images into the illustrations, in much the same way that when an Inuit sculptor sits down to carve a piece of bone or stone, the sculptor waits for the spirit to emerge. The sculptor does not begin to carve before the spirit presents itself" (page 81).

Later, when the illustrator visited the small Inuit community of Lac La Marte, the Chief introduced himself to Wallace, thanking him for understanding the Inuit spirit world and treating it with respect. Wallace's story shows us that outsiders can succeed in recreating insider stories, perhaps for the reasons he himself describes. The characters who inhabit his books, he says, are those "with whom I can empathize on a personal level." At the same time, they are "universal characters with universal emotions and universal experiences" that he respects "for their dignity of spirit and purpose in life, characters who struggle, who test limits, and who endure . . . [and] go through some kind of change" (page 82).

Wallace hopes that his readers will also undergo change as they finish his books. His first responsibility, he says, is to the story. Therefore, "careful thought, born out of scrupulous research, and realized in words and pictures fundamental to the story" guides his artistry. "Finding the emotional link is the key," he says, "and its discovery will make the search a journey worth taking for both the creator and the reader" (page 82).

CREATING NOVELS

Children's novels can be subdivided into three categories: contemporary realistic fiction, historical fiction, and fantasy. We will begin by examining the creative process as it relates to realism.

INVESTIGATIONS: Realistic Picture Books

Examine books illustrated by Jerry Pinkney; then illustrate your own story with drawings you make from photographs or with the photographs themselves. Place your friends in various scenes as characters in your story, or have someone photograph you. Try to plan your photographs to increase the reader's curiosity and add suspense to the story.

As an alternative, examine books by Ian Wallace; then try telling a story about a culture different from your own, one that you like and respect. Think about what you need to learn about this culture before you get started. What books will you need to read? What members of this culture might you be able to visit and come to know? Think about the cultural beliefs of this group you might want to transmit. What colors or motifs will you include or emphasize? What are you learning about this culture?

Consider letting a group of children see your work in progress, as Wallace did. Let them show you more in your work. Listen closely to their comments. Is there anything they notice that you have not consciously emphasized? Learn from their interpretations what meanings are emerging in your story.

Language and emotional content are what **Elaine Konigsburg** wants readers to take from her books. As she says in an interview (Jones, 1986), "I love words and I love stringing them together to make poetry sounds and also to communicate" (page 183). A writer, she says, "writes out of a certain need to communicate, and often the writing itself helps define that need" (page 178). Konigsburg believes every author has a particular theme, and hers is a child finding his or her sense of identity.

Neither characters nor plot come to this author one before the other; instead, the two appear at the same time: "The plot couldn't happen unless it happened to those people, and unless there were those people, those things wouldn't be happening" (page 182). "I have some characters that are bothering me," Konigsburg says. They begin living in me somewhere, and when I know where they're going and when I know a major incident along the way, I start writing. Somewhere in the course of writing, the characters take over and often begin writing their own dialogue. . . . It's almost as if you're a conduit for what's happening" (page 178).

Like Konigsburg, **Beverly Cleary** produces word pictures that are both insightful and funny. But unlike Konigsburg, who began her career as a mother writing about children growing up near New York City, Cleary found that characters began forming in her mind, when, as a children's librarian in Yakima, Washington, she was meeting children at the circulation desk and telling stories to them at story hour:

> Most vividly of all I remember the group of grubby little boys, nonreaders, who came once a week during school hours, marching in a column of two from nearby St. Joseph's School. . . . I soon learned there was very little in the library the boys wanted to read. 'Where are the books about kids like us?' they wanted to know. Where, indeed. There was only one book I could find about kids like them, kids who parked their earmuffs on the circulation desk in winter and their baseball mitts in summer. That book was *Honk, the Moose* by Phil Strong, a story about some farm boys who found a moose in a livery stable . . . It was funny. (1995, page 236)

Cleary bought herself a portable typewriter and determined to launch her career as a children's book writer. Several years later, as a full-time homemaker with no children in sight yet, she had her entire day to write; all she needed was a story. She remembered her own neighborhood on Hancock Street in Portland, Oregon, when she was the same age as the boys in the library in Yakima. It was a place "where boys teased girls even though they played with them, where boys built scooters out of roller skates and apple boxes, wooden in those days, and where dogs, before the advent of leash laws, followed the children to school" (1995, pages 330–31). Then she remembered a funny story about a family that hid its dog in a box to get it home in the pouring rain because dogs were not allowed on streetcars.

"Aha," Cleary thought, "the germ of a plot just right for little boys" (1995, page 331). But she still did not know how to write the story:

> If, in the 1940s, there had been writer's groups, I probably would have joined one. Fortunately, they did not exist, or if they did, I did not know about them. I believe a writer's work should spring from one person's imagination, unassisted by a group of friends who may be helpful but who also may be of questionable judgment . . . As I sat . . . thinking of the boys from St. Joseph's, my story-hour audiences . . . it occurred to me that even though I was uncertain about writing, I knew how to tell

> a story. What was writing for children but written storytelling? So in my imagination I stood once more before Yakima's story-hour crowd as I typed the first sentence: 'Henry Huggins was in the third grade.' Where Henry's name came from I do not know. It was just there, waiting to be written, but I do know Henry was inspired by the boys on Hancock Street who seemed eager to jump onto the page . . . When I came to the skinny dog who found Henry, I needed a name. We happened to have spareribs waiting in the refrigerator, so I named the dog Spareribs and continued the story, based on the family who took their dog home on a streetcar. I changed the family to one boy, and the streetcar into a bus. Writing without research, bibliography, or footnotes was a pleasure. So was rearranging life. If I needed a character or incident, all I had to do was pull it out of my memory or imagination without searching a card catalog. . . . What freedom! (pages 332–33)

A friend gave Cleary the name of a publisher, and even as she walked back from the post office, more story ideas for Henry were coming to her. The story came back needing more work, though it did have "humor, action, and realism" the editor told her, and boys in particular would enjoy it. Perhaps she could weave several of her stories into a plot, with suspense and climax, and produce a book-length manuscript. Cleary began remembering more incidents; she disciplined herself to write each day. She realized she was writing about only children (since she was herself an only child) and decided to create a sister for Henry's friend Beezus. She overheard a neighbor call out to another child whose name was Ramona. And the rest is history; all the famous and well-loved Beverly Cleary books featuring Ramona Quimby were to follow.

Cleary later became the mother of twins, and her fiction continued to flow steadily through the years. She has produced nearly thirty children's books, won many awards, gained much popularity and attained "a satisfying life of writing" (1995, page 345). Is it always this easy? Obviously not, as **Janet Hickman** tells us in her story of the long road she took to produce *Jericho* (Greenwillow, 1994).

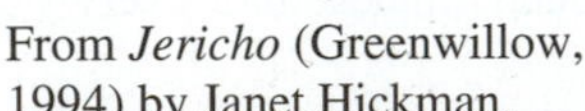

From *Jericho* (Greenwillow, 1994) by Janet Hickman.

Like Cleary, Hickman found that her job, in this case, part-time teaching, gave her little time to write. But one summer, in 1980, when her daughter was thirteen, she and her family found themselves spending every weekend in the town where she had grown up. Her grandmother was dying at age ninety-one, and Hickman learned from her mother more about her grandmother's life at this time. When fall came, she continued to think about her grandmother; she even dreamed about her: "I began to think more and more about what a powerful force she had been in my growing-up years, how loving and proud she had been, and sometimes how very difficult. What could shape such a person, I wondered?" (1996, pages 52–53).

Hickman began making notes about her mother's stories, but midnight was her only time to write, and by then she was half-asleep. What came up on the typed pages was, she says, "more dreamed than planned . . . There on the page was a little girl named Arminda (a name I had seen on a nineteenth-century document), her slightly older sister Lucy, their half-grown sister Delia, and the older brothers—all gathered for supper with their father on an evening not long after their mother's death. After almost a dozen years of fussing and rewriting, that piece stands almost word for word in *Jericho* as first written" (page 53).

Hickman continued to write in chunks of two to four pages from four different viewpoints—grandmother, mother, daughter, and granddaughter—as she told her grandmother's story. Eventually she decided to limit herself to the youngest and oldest members of this quartet, hoping to attract a young adult audience. In the years that elapsed between early and later drafts, her own children grew up and left home, and the writing called her to make sense of her quickly changing life and "the limits to the control we think we have over our own lives" (page 55).

Hickman could now devote one day a week to making a fresh start on this book. Her big writing problem at this point was determining how to integrate the grandmother's past and the granddaughter's present. Listening one day to a radio story read in the past tense, she found the device she needed to pull the two voices together: She would recast the granddaughter's story in the present tense and keep the grandmother's story in the past. The rest of the book came to her quickly, and soon she had a finished manuscript—one that won the 1995 Boston Globe-Horn Book Honor Award for fiction. It was well worth the wait.

In terms of productivity, Cleary and Hickman stand as opposites, revealing that no one way of writing a book works for all authors. Between them is **Phyllis Naylor,** whose long list of published novels makes her like Cleary, but whose reason for writing is similar to Hickman's: "We come to understand ourselves through what we write," Naylor says. "One of the reasons I write—why I need so to write—is because I feel I have so little control over life, certainly over the lives of those close to me. I can't put them in a glass bubble and protect them always. So in my books, I decide what will happen" (1987, page 105).

Writing is a way to become somebody else, Naylor says. She keeps a notebook filled with her story ideas, plots, and characters. When she starts a new book (Naylor is the author of more than fifty books, including the Newbery Award winner for 1992, *Shiloh*), she usually knows how it will begin and end and has some idea about what will happen in the middle:

> Other than these specific guideposts, however, the rest of the plot is usually something of a mystery, as though I am walking through a maze. Sometimes I seem to be leading my characters and other times they are leading me, but if I try

> to make them do something that is not absolutely right for them, the writing becomes laborious and the magic goes out of the page. Then I have to stop, go back, and get in touch with them again . . . But half the fun of writing is to bring out several different sides of a personality and to weave subplots in and around the main plot, tying them together in the end." (page 101)

The book is pointless, Naylor says, "unless the main character changes in some way" (page 100), though he or she need not change for the better. **Nancy Bond,** known for her convincing and meticulous realism even in the the time fantasy genre, has similar feelings. "I have trouble identifying with a completely virtuous character," says Bond, the author of the Newbery Honor book *A String in the Harp* (Atheneum, 1976),

> but one who is in conflict, who is struggling with problems and faults—now there's someone who speaks to me. The most difficult and important task I face when I begin to write a book is getting to know my characters. First I must find names, and then I must begin to define the people behind them. Interestingly enough, one of the best approaches for me is through their flaws and weaknesses. The rough parts offer much better handholds than the smooth ones. The rough parts are almost invariably more interesting as well. If a good character does something good—that's nice but only to be expected. If a weak or a flawed character does something good—or brave or unselfish—that's a story. (1984, page 302).

Nina Bawden would agree. The children in her own books during childhood, as she remembers (1976), "never seemed to have the kind of dark, angry feelings that worried me. They were often naughty in a jolly way, but they were never bad. None of them felt as I did when I was nine years old, no one in the world." These books, she says, omitted the adult world that she knew, never presenting adults "as children really see them . . . Not only were they never beastly to children except in a stereotyped, fairy tale way, but they were never beastly to anyone. They were never the uncertain, awkward, quirky, *dangerous* creatures that I knew adults to be" (pages 8–9).

Discussing her book *The Outside Child* (Penguin, 1989), Bawden, in a 1991 essay, explains that her father remarried when her half-sister was four years old. When Nina was born soon after, her mother accused the half-sister of pushing Nina down the stairs one day, out of jealousy. Soon after this incident, her father sent his first daughter away to live with relatives.

Many years later, Bawden decided to write this story, focusing on what she thought her half-sister's experience might have been. She could not know for sure how her sister had felt; she herself was only nine months old when the event occurred, and as a child she never even knew that her father had been married before. But she imagined it all "fairly accurately," she later learned, when her sister read the book and said the story "seemed true to her, to her memories of how she had thought and felt" (page 691).

Bawden's ability to intuit her sister's feelings may stem from the fact that she herself was evacuated to Wales during World War II. Living in a Welsh mining village among strangers, she learned "what it felt like to be sure no one would want me, because that was how I felt." In *Carrie's War* (Lippincott, 1973), she tells about her period of homelessness and how it aroused in her a deep interest in outside children of all kinds: refugees, victims of abuse, the homeless, the rejected, as well as "awkward children, the ones who don't fit" (page 694).

Elizabeth George Speare teaches us more about how a writer produces characters from another time, but unlike Bawden's, her characters are not autobiographical. Speare (1989) tells of beginning all of her historical novels with the questions, "How must it have seemed to the people who lived through this experience? What choices would I have made in their place?" (page 463). Then she finds the answers by going back into the past and "living" with her characters until their world becomes as real to her as the room in which she is working.

Speare's method for writing historical fiction consists primarily of borrowing characters. She finds an intriguing but little-known character in history, and the story springs to life largely from her imagination. Her first novel, *Calico Captive* (Houghton Mifflin, 1957) sprang from a story written by Susanna Johnson in 1807 about an Indian attack that occurred in 1754.

It was Susanna's younger sister, scarcely mentioned in the story, that Speare began to envision for her own story, because Susanna's sister's life was so full of promise. Says Speare (1995): "I could not forget this girl, and day by day her adventures began to grow in my mind" (page 616). Speare's story remained true to

INVESTIGATIONS: Realistic Fiction

Choose one of the eight authors from the following list and try some of the author's techniques.

1. Examine books by Elaine Konigsburg; then write a story about a child living in a setting similar to your own childhood setting. Begin with characters that bother you in some way: characters who will not leave your thoughts or who drive you to think about them. Think about the ideas they would express, the questions they have, their needs. "Listen" for the characters to begin "writing" their own dialogue and developing their own plot.
2. Examine books by Beverly Cleary; then write a story about a humorous incident from your childhood. Think about a need, a wish, or a small problem the main character might have as your story begins; keep readers in suspense as to how the character will resolve it, and include enough action to make the plot interesting.
3. Examine Janet Hickman's *Jericho;* then think about an elderly person in your family. Try to learn more about this person's youth and later life. Explore ways to shape the person's life into a story, and write it.
4. Examine books by Phyllis Naylor; then think of some names for characters in your story. Do you think of the names first and then let the characters' personalities flow out of the names? Or do you picture what the characters are like and then choose names for them? Write a story about your characters.
5. Examine books by Nancy Bond; then create a main character for an original story. Is your character struggling with a problem or fault? What is your character's flaw or weakness. What happens as a result of your character's flaw? Does the character do something good in spite of this flaw?
6. Examine books by Nina Bawden; then think back to your own childhood and try to recall if you ever felt like an outsider. Did you ever experience rejection, and could you explore this experience in a story? Did you ever observe another child's experience as an outsider? If you tried to imagine that child's experience now, how would you start? Would you need to begin writing the story in order to uncover the rest of the story?
7. Examine books by Elizabeth George Speare; then ask yourself whether you were drawn to any particular ethnic group when you were a child. What assumptions did you hold about this group? Were they romantic or realistic? Read historical narratives written by or about members of this group to find a character who inspires you to flesh out a story. (It might be a minor character who captures your imagination, someone not fully developed, leaving you gaps to fill.)

Susanna's brief narrative, but it expanded to include imaginary people, Indian and French, as she tried to relive the sister's experience. "Slowly, these adventures grew into a book and became *Calico Captive,* and I had discovered the most absorbing and rewarding occupation of my life," she says (page 616).

For her second children's novel, Speare visited the historical town of Wethersfield, Connecticut, and tried to imagine the town three centuries earlier as a busy seaport. At this point, "an imaginary girl began to walk and talk in my mind" she says. The girl was "an outsider, coming this time from the lush and sunny British island of Barbados to the harsh Puritan town where I hoped she would find one only. . . a place for herself, and a love for this narrow hard country" (page 616). The book would become Speare's Newbery winner, *The Witch of Blackbird Pond* (Houghton, 1958).

In each of these novels, Speare wrote about the Native Americans of New England, where she lived and wrote before her recent death; thus, she was often asked if she were Indian, part Indian, or if she had Indian friends. Why did Speare feel such strong identity with Native Americans, she often wondered, when she was not of Native American heritage?

Speare (1989) tells of reading a set of books in childhood, the Deerfoot series. "I have never seen this book since, and I do not recall the adventures it contained, but the life of the Indians in the forest cast over me a spell," she says, "that still echoes like a remembered strain of music." Later she was a Campfire Girl in high school, wearing a beaded headband, an adopted name, and long, fringed gowns. She admits all of this was "pure romance," but she was "enthralled by it" (page 462).

As an adult writer, she needed to trade fantasy for fact: "[M]y concern now was for authenticity," she says, and "the history of the American Indian is not romantic; it is deeply tragic and continues to be so today, and the records are heartbreaking" (page 462). However, there have always been men and women, she adds, "who have stood bravely against danger and injustice and tyranny" (page 464). Speare wanted to show children about the values of human strength, loyalty, and family bonds for overcoming danger and injustice.

Fantasy

When **Virginia Hamilton** began writing *Sweet Whispers, Brother Rush* (Philomel, 1982), she drew on African-American beliefs in the ghost figure that appears in the story. Brother Rush (the ghost) often materializes in the center of a wooden table in a little room; his niece Teresa (Tree) Pratt thinks of this room as her special place. Brother Rush always draws her back into their family past through a small circle of springtime light, a mirrorlike image that he holds in his hand and into which Tree looks to find her family "tree." Whether readers consider the book realism or fantasy depends on whether they believe in ghosts—or whether Hamilton can make them believe that *this* ghost is real.

Hamilton says her concern when she created the story

> was that the reader wouldn't believe in the ghost, Brother Rush . . . I worried whether a reader would be convinced of a circle of springtime in a ghostly hand . . . I almost threw out Rush and his springtime. But whenever I wrote about Tree, whatever she did, Rush was there beside her, whether she was aware of him or not. Whenever I wrote about her, I thought about and saw him. That condition never varied. And, finally, I was convinced that my ghost was right on. First lesson for a

From *Sweet Whispers, Brother Rush* (Philomel, 1982) by Virginia Hamilton, illustrated by Leo and Diane Dillon.

> writer: Trust the primary idea and the developing structure; trust one's instincts . . . Writing fiction means slowing down the mind long enough to allow the hands to type what is seen in one's head. (1984, page 26)

After a number of novels, Hamilton says, she is able "to see very well and interpret" what goes on in her head. She sees and thinks in terms of stories:

> Everything that goes on in me and around me that I perceive as fresh and new lends itself to story-making. I see stories in a series of pictures to which I add words. I change words. I string them together. The pictures move and are animated lots of times, but not all the time. It depends on what the character is doing or feeling, whether or not a great deal of movement takes place . . . I watch the things that go on inside my head, just as some people watch television. I have done that since childhood. Daydreaming out a window, I watched what went on within. It's a strange way to live. Writing, making the book, brings this self-viewing into reality. (1984, page 27)

But Hamilton always begins with characters. "When you write fiction," she says, "you write with a whole character in mind. You don't do parts of the person. You do the whole person at once. I don't know *how* it's done. I do it, but I can break it down only so far. What happens is that you get a whole image, and you find the words to project the image to the reader" (Mikkelsen, 1994, page 401). "I think I create characters and the characters create the society in which they live." She also says:

> Once the characters are defined, they have brought their world with them, and so I have uncovered that world. We don't live in a vacuum; we live in a community. And every character is like that. In a sense it's like a painting. You fill in all this around the person—the history, the time, and the place. It's an amazing process. If you start out and you have this picture, then the problem is finding words to describe what you see . . . *Sweet Whispers* is probably a classic problem-solving

example. When I was a child I saw a ghost. Well, as an adult I know that ghosts don't exist. So there's the conflict: the childhood memory which is absolutely pure and I know it to this day, and the adult knowing that it didn't happen. (Mikkelsen, 1995, page 75)

E. B. White also wrote stories to solve problems and make sense of things, as one of his biographers, Beverly Gherman, tells us. The idea for *Charlotte's Web* came from his feelings about a real pig on his farm in Maine. The pig died one year, despite the fact that White spent many hours trying to save it. In an essay, "Death of a Pig," White (1947) wrote about the troubling situation of raising a pig for food, knowing he would someday kill it, yet later trying desperately to save the pig's life because it had become, in some ways, human. When he began writing *Charlotte's Web,* White was able to further explore these questions.

At the same time, White had encountered a large gray spider in his farm shed and had become intrigued by the way it was spinning its egg sac. He watched as the tiny spiders emerged from the sac, and he began studying books to learn more about spiders, "what they ate, where they lived, how many kinds there were" (Gherman, page 91). Then he began writing. In one of his early drafts, he wrote, "Charlotte was a big gray spider who lived in a doorway. But there is no use talking about Charlotte until we have talked about her close friend—a pig named Wilbur." Later, as one of White's literary biographers, Peter Neumeyer, tells us, he would write: "A barn can have a horse in it, and a barn can have a cow in it . . . but if a barn hasn't got a pig in it, it is hardly worth talking about" (Neumeyer, pages 492–93).

White continued to write different beginnings—about the barn, the spider, or the pig—until he had a new idea. He would feature a little girl named Fern and begin with her question, "Where's Papa going with that ax?" This was the story opening he liked and that eventually emerged in *Charlotte's Web* (Harper, 1952), a book that presented more writing problems than his first children's book, *Stuart Little* (Harper, 1945). The earlier story about a mouse child began easily when White dreamed of "a tiny creature wearing a hat and twirling a cane" (Gherman, page 73).

Pictures always spurred **C. S. Lewis** to write, too. As he wrote to one child, Susan (February 5, 1960): "All I can tell you is that pictures come into my head and I write stories about them. I don't know how or why the pictures come." To another child, Meredith (December 6, 1960), he wrote, "What ' inspires' my books? Really I don't know. Does anyone know where exactly an idea comes from? With me all fiction *begins with* pictures in my head. But where the pictures come from I couldn't say" (1988, pages 92, 95).

What White and Lewis and Hamilton are talking about, when they say their stories begin with pictures, is the subconscious at work. **Susan Cooper** (1996), author of the *Dark is Rising* sequence (Atheneum, 1966–77), *The Boggart* (Macmillan, 1993) and *The Boggart and the Monster* (Simon & Schuster, 1997) explains why fantasy and the subconscious are so linked:

> Writing is one of the loneliest professions in the world because it has to be practiced in this very separate private world, in *here.* Not in the mind; in the imagination. And I think it is possible that the writing of fantasy is the loneliest job of the lot, since you have to go further inside. You have to make so close a connection with the unconscious that the unbiddable door will open and the images fly out, like birds. It's not unlike writing poetry. It makes you superstitious. Most writers indulge in small private rituals to start themselves writing each day. (page 115)

Cooper begins each day by reading the notes she made the day before when she stopped writing. She might wander to her bookshelf and read a favorite piece by another author or play with a shell or ceramic piece. "What I'm doing," she says, "is taking myself out of the world I'm in, and trying to find my way back into the world apart. Once I've managed that, I am inside the book that I'm writing, and am *seeing* it, so vividly that I do not see what I'm actually staring at: the wall, or the typewriter, or the tree outside the window. I suppose it is a variety of trance state" (page 116).

We can never be certain we will reach the imagination, she adds. "We cast spells to find our way into the unconscious mind, and the imagination that lives there, because we know that's the only way to get into a place where magic is made . . . Our readers believe that the process is magical, too. That's why they say to us in that bemused, incredulous, faintly envious way, 'Where do you get your ideas?' . . . [T]hey know that it's a magic garden. They've been there, transported to it while they read the book" (page 117).

CREATING POETRY

"Where do ideas come from?" asks **Jack Prelutsky,** the humorous and popular children's poet. From everywhere, he answers. "They come from everything I have inside. They come from everything I have ever seen or felt or dreamed or read or seen on television or at the movies or remembered or experienced. Things I was told." He is smart enough to carry around a notebook, too. Many authors know they wouldn't remember all their ideas otherwise. Prelutsky equates poetry with the nonverbal arts: "It's a distillation of experience. But most of all it's communication, right up there with sculpture and photography and painting and music" (1990, pages 102–3).

Like Cooper, Prelutsky emphasizes the role the subconscious plays in his writing:

INVESTIGATIONS: Fantasy

Choose one of the following four writers, and try some of his or her techniques.

1. Examine a book by Virginia Hamilton; then as you begin a story of your own, fill in an entire "world" around your characters as you create them. (Describe a community, a time, a family, the history of a particular place). Or try remembering an important childhood experience; then bring the memory to life for readers, so that they believe in the "reality" of it.
2. Examine a book by E. B. White; then experiment with his drafting technique. Make one draft of a story; wait a while, then make another. See if the focus of the story changes. Wait a little longer; then create a third draft. What is happening in your story now? Have new characters arrived? Are you finding new twists to create in your plot?
3. Examine a book by C. S. Lewis; then think about the stories you have been imagining. Where did your ideas come from? How did the ideas emerge for you? Did you "picture" them? Did you "see" them in a dream? Do they relate to questions or dilemmas or problems in your life that you cannot resolve?
4. Examine a book by Susan Cooper; then try getting in touch with your subconscious. Make free associations of your ideas. Jot down ideas as they come to mind, as Henkes doodles or as Cooper engages in rituals as she begins to write. Can you create a story from your ideas?

> Sometimes I just close my eyes and let the muse take over. Most writers will tell you that often they don't tell the poem or the story what to do; the story or the poem tells them what to do. It takes over. And very often, by the time I've finished a poem it doesn't resemble anything I had set out to create. Never be afraid to let your imagination take wing. Sometimes I have a rhyme in mind. It can be something as simple as pig/wig. Sometimes it's just a word . . . Sometimes it's a couplet. A couplet will just come to me, and I'll work in both directions from those two lines. Or it could be a sentence. Or part of a sentence . . . just some vague notion of what I want to say. (page 104)

Also like Cooper, Prelutsky often begins to write by engaging in a ritual. His studio is filled with objects to help him enter his subconscious: wind-up toys, a frog collection, a plastic flower. Sometimes an object—or simply a word like *sneeze*—ends up in his poems. "I've written three or four poems that talk about sneezing: about someone sneezing on a trapeze; about the 'sneezy snoozer,' someone who sneezes and snoozes at the same time; about a man who sneezes seven times, and each sneeze is louder than the previous one, and on the seventh sneeze his head flies off. Those 'eeze' words have always tickled me" (page 108). His poem "Don't Ever Seize a Weasel by the Tail," in *Zoo Dogs* (Greenwillow, 1983), emerged from a visit to the zoo. Later, as he thought about the weasel, he began playing with the word, just having fun with it.

Wordplay, observation, and thinking about childhood experiences are the creative processes that guide Prelutsky's work. "When I was younger," he says, "I was a very insular person; it was hard to get to know me. So I wrote of myself as a turtle hiding inside a shell" (page 110). The more he writes about his childhood, the more he remembers. The memory of a friend who ate a worm and convinced him to do the same inspired the poem, "Willie Ate A Worm," published in *Rolling Harvey Down the Hill* (Greenwillow, 1980). The incident also spawned the comical last line, "I think I'll eat one too."

His mother's warning that the bogeyman would get him if he didn't eat his spinach led Prelutsky to write "The Bogeyman," published in *Nightmares* (Greenwillow, 1976). The poet wrote all the poems for *Nightmares* in the middle of the night:

> In the desolate depths of a perilous place
> the bogeyman lurks, with a snarl on his face.
> Never dare, never dare to approach his dark lair
> for he's waiting . . . just waiting . . . to get you." (page 114)

Prelutsky writes about what is real to children: "When I was a kid," he says in an interview (Vardell, 1991), "I was subjected to poems about hills and daffodils, which is fine, and there's a place for that, but I was not interested in that sort of thing. I wanted to hear poems about other kids like me and about sports, monsters, dinosaurs, outer space, and weird people—silly things. That's what I write about. I really try to stay in touch with the child I used to be" (page 108). A folksinger, he keeps a guitar in his studio, and he finds that setting his lines to music helps his meter. The words come to him before the melodies.

Prelutsky begins a poem working from the notebook he carries with him at all times:

> I transfer many of the notes into the computer and into an idea pod. When the idea pod gets really fat, I start working on it and I take out the ideas that I think will make poems and I start outlining poems on the computer. Then I make a

printout and I work on the printout, sitting in my recliner, and fix things with a pen. Then I go back to the computer and start over. I go back three, four, five, or twenty times. Eventually I have a poem. (page 104)

Award-winning children's poet **Eve Merriam,** also carried a notebook for jotting down words and phrases she did not want to forget. Merriam kept the notebook by her bed and carried it in her purse or pocket each time she left her house, even to go to the post office. She did not always work from it, but the notebook fixed the phrases that came to her, as she told her interviewer in 1989, three years before her death, so "you don't have to carry it around in your head" (Cox, page 141). She did not work with a computer; she had only a manual typewriter for her hunt-and-peck typing style. But Merriam preferred working on paper in longhand: "The pages are very, very messy, and many of them I rewrite and rewrite: I copy one page to another and another, even if I'm just changing a piece of punctuation. And then I get to the point where I put it on a typewriter so I can see what it looks like, and then I do more corrections in longhand" (Cox, page 141). She even wrote lines to illustrate this messy process in "How to Eat a Poem," from *A Sky Full of Poems* (Dell, 1986):

Don't be polite.
Bite in
Pick it up with your fingers and lick the juice that may run down your chin.
It is ready and ripe now whenever you are.

Merriam believed that poetry "is the essence of living," that words "are directly related to the rhythms of one's body," and that you must use the body to develop rhythm. As a child, she loved to jump rope: "That has such a beat to it . . . when I went away to summer camp, I liked games that you could play and anything that particularly had rhythms and rhymes—where you could clap hands. . . . I also had a strong sense of dance, which I think is related to rhythms and poetry" (Cox, pages 140, 142).

Poetry, Merriam said, begins with the gift of a word or line; from that word or line, "things take off." She was always writing "to find out" for herself or to please herself. She explored her word or line on paper until it took shape, but she never knew what shape the poem would take until more lines began to form: "It's more, I suppose, like a painter doing a rough sketch, but really more like a few brush strokes of watercolor." Her children's poems rhymed; poetry is music, Merriam said, and the joy and fun of it comes from reading aloud (Cox, pages 140–41).

The emotional content of the poems was important for Merriam. In "Mean Song," published in *Jamboree: Rhymes for All Times* (Dell, 1984), she made up what she has called "hard, tough words" like "sniggles and podes," "wriggles and grodes." She wanted "to give little children the feeling that they could get just mad as hops and could sound off" (Cox, page 147).

Social issues such as war and racism were also important to Merriam: "The two greatest forms of insanity, to me, have always been war—to kill another human being—or any form of discrimination—to deny somebody something because the way they look is different from you." She intentionally wrote "I Am A Man" (from *I Am A Man,* Doubleday, 1971), after Martin Luther King's murder because she was trying to explain how such a tragedy could happen:

"Strange was the land, strange were its ways:
Two seeking shelter entered inside:
room for them both, yet one was denied.
Two hungry men with money to pay:
one was served food, one turned away . . . (Cox, page 145)

Merriam's voice is the sympathetic outsider voice, observing the racist act inflicted on the African-American child's heritage and identity. It differs significantly from an insider voice like that of **Nikki Giovanni.** Consider Giovanni's "The Drum" and "poem for rodney," from *Spin a Soft Black Song* (Farrar, 1985). In each poem, the child narrator speaks for him or herself:

the drum

daddy says the world is
a drum tight and hard
and i told him
i'm gonna beat
out my own rhythm

poem for rodney
people always ask what
am i going to be
when i grow
up and i always
just think
i'd like to grow
up

In the next chapter, we will take a closer look at insider voices and how they engage in the creative process. As we learn more about multiethnic literature, not only do we begin to celebrate diversity within the larger culture and to discover similarities in all human beings, but we also begin to value the way stories help keep ethnic heritage and identity intact.

Creations: *Poetry*

Examine poetry collections by Prelutsky, Merriam, or Giovanni, or another favorite children's poet such as Shel Silverstein. Notice the subjects, words, phrasing, rhythms, humor, nonsense, and fun that poets produce for children. Notice also how these poets arrange the words on the page (spacing, indented lines, punctuation) and how it reads aloud.

Now try some of the techniques Pretlutsky and Merriam say they use to get started writing poetry. Create a poem (or a group of poems) of your own. You might begin by carrying a small pocket notebook and jotting down ideas, words, and phrases as they come to you. You might continue by arranging some of these words on a page. Try to discover what interests you as you write. Is it emotional content? Is it rhythm and wordplay or humor? Is it a subject of interest to children?

If you have an interest in writing for children, consider sharing your poetry with them. Invite their responses and learn what matters to them.

Chapter 7

Multiethnic Literature and the Storytelling Process

Topics in This Chapter:

- How—and Why—writers and illustrators produce ethnic literature
- Multiethnic fiction
- Multiethnic poetry and stories
- Multiethnic illustrated books and picture books

"It was much pleasanter at home," thought poor Alice, "when one wasn't always growing larger and smaller, and being ordered about by mice and rabbits. I almost wish I hadn't gone down that rabbit-hole—and yet—and yet—it's rather curious, you know, this sort of life! I do wonder what can have happened to me! When I used to read fairy-tales, I fancied that kind of thing never happened, and now here I am in the middle of one! There ought to be a book written about me, that there ought! And when I grow up, I'll write one . . ."

"The Rabbit Sends in a Little Bill," Alice's Adventure's in Wonderland, 1865
—Lewis Carroll

If Carroll's blond, blue-eyed Alice was looking for a book about herself and could not find it in nineteenth-century England, consider what children of darker complexion, non-Anglican religion, or underclass status found in children's books in Alice's day. Was it any different in America a century later when Elaine Konigsburg, a child of Jewish-American heritage, was growing up in rural Pennsylvania? Says Konigsburg:

> I never found the kind of going-home book where I could recognize the heroine as me. I could identify with lots of heroines—with *A Little Princess* say, or with *Mary Poppins*—but I never enjoyed the shock of recognition that going-home

books afford. And I missed them. And just imagine all the African-American children and all the Mexican-American children who missed them for a long, long time after I did" (page 73).

HOW—AND WHY—WRITERS AND ILLUSTRATORS PRODUCE ETHNIC LITERATURE

If present patterns continue, the United States could become the most mixed nation, in multiethnic terms, among technologically developed countries. Fifty years from now, a majority of Americans could be members of what Virginia Hamilton has described as "parallel" cultures—African American, Asian American, Native American, or Hispanic American—present in the "polyethnic, culturally diverse communities of present-day America" (1992, page 6). These communities are different from the currently dominant Euro-American culture, but they are certainly *equal* in human strength, integrity, and spirit, a fact that the term *minority* does not emphasize. In fact, the term *minority* seems almost intended to render ethnic groups as powerless.

The term *parallel culture* surfaced in print in 1986 in a remark by Arnold Adoff. In an essay for the children's literature journal *Lion and the Unicorn,* Adoff said: "If all the parallel cultures and literatures of all the Americas are not presented with force and conviction, then no part of the so-called American children's literature is true; *all* must fall like some house of cards built on partial foundations" (page 10). Writing for the same issue of this journal, Virginia Hamilton (Adoff's wife) described how she created multicultural literature in terms of her own African-American experiences:

> Through character, time and place, I've attempted to portray the essence of a race, its essential community, culture, history and traditions, which I know well, and its relation to the larger American society . . . My books generally have an historical aspect that becomes an integral part of the fictions. A novel taking place in the present will often evoke an atmosphere of former generations. We carry our pasts with us in the present through states of mind, family history and historical fact. (page 15)

Hamilton referred to a statement made by African-American historian Carter Woodson: "If a race has no history, if it has no worthwhile tradition, it becomes a negligible factor in the thought of the world and it stands in danger of being exterminated" (page 16). Whatever art she herself possesses is "a social action in itself," says Hamilton, because "storytelling is not merely a thing of the past, but a continuing cultural imperative." Her stories, she says, "illuminate the triumphs of talking and telling among the people in the present and reveal the connections of this ethnic group to its historical self." In stories, "people have always found ways of keeping their courage, their pride and talent, their imaginative consciousness" (pages 16–17).

In this chapter, we will examine the literature of parallel cultures and how authors and artists create and transmit ethnic heritage—or how they turn their lives into stories. We will begin with fiction, letting Hamilton lead the way; we will continue with poetry, stories, and pictorial forms.

A Closer Look
What Does the Word Multicultural *Mean?*

The term *multicultural* is slippery, encasing many concepts of race, ethnicity, nationality, religion, gender, language, special interests, abilities, or orientations, depending on who is defining the word. Many speakers these days are replacing the concept of "race" with "ethnicity." As African-American social commentator Brent Staples has said, "As early as the 1700s, the clearest fact about slavery was the lightening of its skin. The trend continued until there were almost no blacks of strictly African descent. In this context, race-based identity is problematical at best, and genetically based theories of race and intellectual difference seem absurd." One concept of great importance in any definition of multiculturalism is therefore *social reality.* Different cultures, or different ethnicities within these cultures, have different views of the world. What they do, say, or *are* springs from that world view.

An ethnic group—or, even different clans, tribes, families, or peoples within such a group—has common traditions, a common language, and a common geographical region of origin. Often when we speak of ethnic groups, we are speaking of underrepresented and unassimilated cultures (Native Americans, African Americans, Hispanic Americans, and Asian Americans). Within these groups are both monoethnic and polyethnic people, depending upon how often members of a group have married and procreated outside the culture.

Literature by black Americans, for example, seems at first glance to be monoethnic (one ethnicity serves as the major focus of this group). But "pure" ethnic strains are actually hard to find. So-called monocultural or monoethnic authors frequently mention differences in skin color, signaling the mixes among different groups from the beginning. Slaves from different parts of Africa, for example, formed relationships with Native Americans of many different tribes and clans and with whites who came to America from many different European countries. (Plantation owners often forced black female slaves to procreate; slaves often took refuge with Native American tribes, becoming "Black Indians"; and whites often married Native Americans, either entering the tribe or bringing their spouses into the white culture outside the tribe.) Says Staples: "In fact, the sexual barrier between the races had never really existed."

Multicultural can also mean *cross-cultural;* many children are immigrants, refugees, or dislocated or displaced from the culture of their heritage. *Multicultural* can also apply to children of a dominant culture coming to know about other cultures—and vice versa. In the broadest sense, *multicultural* means people of different heritage, religions, or geographical backgrounds learning to live together or to respect one another's ways of thinking and living. Many authors, whether insiders or outsiders, emphasize cultural pluralism; in their literature, characters transcend cultural boundaries. This focus encourages readers to form communal bonds with those of a different culture (nation, ethnicity, or clan).

In a more specific sense, *multicultural* means people of various cultural backgrounds going about their lives as members of a particular culture. Some might be learning about—or simply *living*—their own cultural traditions. Others might be reflecting on the ethnicity, race, religion, or nationality, which makes them culturally "different" from other groups. Still others might be searching for an identity if they live in a culture that erases or ignores their group patterns and world views—or if their identity is not clearly established within the dominant culture. For example, a polycultural child who is descended from several different ethnicities might not feel strong ties to any one culture.

In any event, multicultural authors emphasize diversity, either among different cultural groups or within a particular group. Their readers see what it means for a child to grow up in a culture or ethnicity or family different from his or her own. They also see what it means to grow up within a society that suppresses or ignores groups that are different, and they see the difficult social realities children may face because of cultural differences. In *The Window* (Hyperion, 1997), Michael Dorris creates eleven-year-old Rayona, whose father is white and whose mother is black and Indian. Rayona is a complex and resilient child in a world that is giving her tough times.

Continued

A Closer Look

What Does the Word Multicultural *Mean? (continued)*

Dorris examined this medley of cultural groups with sensitivity and insight because his own background was a mixture of white and Native American. As more bicultural and polyethnic writers like Dorris begin to explore complexities of heritage, we may learn more about the constantly changing concept of multicultural literature. For the cultures themselves are changing, as more and more intercultural marriages take place and more ethnic groups blend with one another.

Although America is not really a mosaic of separate and easily identified ethnic groups, neither is it becoming a totally blended, nonwhite culture any time soon. As writer Michael Lind asserts, although black-white marriages are on the increase, they still occur much less often than marriages between whites and Hispanics, Asians, or American Indians. It will take ethnic writers like Dorris, Hamilton, and Adoff, who have experienced the social realities of multiculturalism, to write about them. Or it will take writers like Laurence Yep, who know well the present day social realities of bi-culturalism, to reflect those realities in their fiction. Yep's recent novels *Ribbons* (Putnam 1996) and its sequel, *The Cook's Family* (Putnam 1998) feature Robin Lee, the daughter of a Caucasian father and a Chinese-American mother.

Sources: Michael Lind, "The Beige and the Black," *New York Times Magazine,* 16 August 1998: 38–39.
Brent Staples, "The Shifting Meanings of 'Black' and 'White,' " *New York Times,* 15 November 1998, 4:14.

MULTIETHNIC FICTION

How does **Virginia Hamilton** create multiethnic literature that reflects her African-American cultural background? She begins, as she says (1993), with the institution of slavery and the exclusion of family names from official records. Her great-grandmother, the character Sarah in *M. C. Higgins the Great* (Macmillan, 1974), "remains nameless throughout oral accounts, as does her husband, sold away from his wife and son. . . . The boy Levi [Hamilton's grandfather, Levi Perry], never knew her name more than Mother. Or at least, he never spoke it. We suppose that Great-grandmother Perry worked on the Underground [Railroad]. Something happened to her, likely, and she was forever gone. This last is a story I tell myself, to finish her life in my mind. Novelists always have to know the ending. If they do not know it, they make it up" (page 365).

How does Hamilton tell the multicultural child's story? Through layer upon layer of stories (she has written thirty-four children's books—fiction, folk tales, and biography). As she explains:

> There is an overall plot in the books and in the fictions. But beyond the main plot, there may be story after story. Characters tell stories to themselves and to one another. The narrator, me, tells stories about this or that character . . . I think I continue to do what tribal people have in their communities the world over. I weave the history of my tribe in my art, into the fabric of my fiction and nonfiction. (page 375)

Hamilton's use of stories tells us more about the tradition of ethnic storytelling itself:

> I think how I use stories is the way I was taught what the world is like, what my family was like, what was expected of me, what values were. My family and my extended family were storytellers. And I learned about my social order through

> the way they told family tales. I learned about how people lived and what was expected of them. So I think story means to me that everybody has a story, that our lives are stories. And that's how we relate to one another. I realize now that a lot of people don't know anything about telling stories. They don't know that it is a way of carrying on traditions. My family storytelling meant continuing a family history and continuing a family. (Mikkelsen, 1995, page 79)

The family stories that form the scaffolding of Hamilton's fiction also weave through the African-American novels of **Mildred Taylor.** A father and daughter prompted Taylor to produce a fictional saga of the Logan family, which includes seven books (all published by Dial Press) thus far. Nearly all of the stories center on a young girl called Cassie Logan. The most famous of Taylor's books is her 1977 Newbery winner, *Roll of Thunder, Hear My Cry* (1976), a companion volume to the much shorter book, *Song of the Trees* (1975), and to *The Friendship* (1987), and *Mississippi Bridge* (1990). Taylor has also produced two novel-length sequels to *Roll of Thunder—Let the Circle Be Unbroken* (1981) and *The Road to Memphis* (1990)—and a prequel, *The Well* (1995), an illustrated picture storybook about David Logan, Cassie's father, when he was a child.

Taylor uses her father, Wilbert Lee, as the model for Cassie's brother, Stacey, and father, David Logan. Taylor remembers her father as a master storyteller who taught her to question discrimination and to value strong family ties. In her Newbery acceptance speech, she tells of the trips back from Ohio to the "rich farm country of Mississippi" (page 401) where she was born and where relatives gathered and told the stories she would later retell in her children's books:

> At those gatherings there was always time for talk, and when we children had finished all the games we could think to play, we would join the adults, soon becoming enraptured by their talk, for it would often turn to a history which we heard only at home, a history of Black people told through stories . . . And if people believe the book to be biographical, it is because I have tried to distill the essence of Black life, so familiar to most Black families, to make the Logans an embodiment of that spiritual heritage; for, contrary to what the media relate to us, all Black families are not fatherless or disintegrating. Certainly my family was not. (pages 403–4)

In the stories Taylor read in her history books or in the library books she found after school, she saw nothing about the "small and often dangerous triumphs of Black people," nothing about "human pride and survival in a cruelly racist society." There were no black heroes in these books, only the tales of a "docile, subservient people happy with their fate who did little or nothing to shatter the chains that bound them, both before and after slavery." The books about black families were often written by white writers who did not understand the black experience and the "principles upon which Black parents brought up their children and taught them survival" (pages 404–5).

Because Taylor did know this ethnic experience, she felt driven to "paint a truer picture of Black people . . . to show the endurance of the Black world, with strong fathers and concerned mothers . . . [and] happy, loved children" (page 405). She knew she would write these stories, even during her high school years. It was not until much later, however, after she had completed a stint in the Peace Corps and attended graduate school, that Taylor found a way to fulfill her literary quest. One year, an alter ego in the form of "a spunky eight-year-old, innocent, untouched by discrimination, full of pride, and greatly loved" appeared in Taylor's mind.

The child's name was Cassie Logan, "and through her I discovered I now could tell one of the stories I had heard so often as a child" (page 405), Taylor says. Her book *Song of the Trees* (Dial, 1975) was the result. Writing it, she discovered she could incorporate childhood teachings as well as many of the stories she had heard in her family as she grew up. She also found she could weave factual events with her own childhood feelings "to produce a significant tapestry which would portray rural Black southern life in the 1930s" (page 406). If children can relate to the Logans, Taylor says, "perhaps they can better understand and respect themselves and others" (page 408).

Both Taylor and Hamilton refer to themselves as "black" or "Black American," rather than "African American." Says Hamilton, "I've decided I'm not an African American. You can't turn it around. I'm not American African! So I'm American Black. You can turn it around—Black American. To be honest, I would be American Afro-Indian [her mother], Euro-Creole [her father] American. But who's counting?" (personal correspondence with Hamilton, 9/25/98).

Whereas Taylor and Hamilton both had a firm knowledge of their identities as they grew up in large, extended Black American—or American Black—families, **Laurence Yep** was a member of a cross-cultural, Asian-American, second-generation immigrant family. In his autobiography *The Lost Garden* (Julian Messner, 1991), he tells about the conflict he experienced as a child who did not want to be Chinese in America and why this conflict is the focus of many of his novels for children.

Yep's parents were Americans who grew up in Chinatown in San Francisco but who held traditional Chinese values, insisting that their children put their studies above everything else and show deep respect for their teachers. At the same time, Yep was an outsider to Chinatown, since he did not speak Chinese. Whereas his friends were monocultural Asian-American, he saw himself as "a bunch of different pieces that had been dumped together in a box by sheer circumstance" (page 91). Not only was he a second-generation Chinese-American with little knowledge of his parents' native language, but he was also living in a black neighborhood—a monocultural group in which he was the outsider. Thus, Yep became a child too American to fit into Chinatown and too Chinese to fit in elsewhere. He was, as he says, like a Chinese puzzle with the instructions "locked up inside of him—and no way to get at them" (page 70).

He could not escape his heritage, however. His maternal grandmother had, as an immigrant, developed a self-reliant toughness in America, and she transmitted her survival strategies to him early in life. From her, Yep not only learned about himself and his ethnic heritage, but he was able to fill in the pieces of the "puzzle that was himself" (page 54). To find these pieces, he began to keep a file of his family history; later, remembering family stories became his entryway into writing for children.

In high school, Yep began making up stories as a way to solve problems. Through writing, he could reach back into his memories and "stitch them together," trying out different combinations to see which one pleased him most. "I could take these different elements, each of which belonged to something else, and dip them into my imagination, where they were melted down and cast into new shapes so that they became uniquely mine" (page 91).

Yep's first children's book, *Sweetwater* (Harper, 1973), is a science fiction novel that emerged from the memory of his living room as a child. One day, as light rippled over the ceiling, it reminded him of a pool of water. He began to imagine what it would be like if the streets outside were flooded throughout the city of San Francisco. His second book, *Dragonwings* (Harper, 1975) honored his father, who came to America at the age of ten and had a tough time adjusting: "Writing *Dragonwings* was a way of stepping into his shoes," Yep explained (page 92).

In 1977, at the age of twenty-nine, he produced *Child of the Owl* (Harper), a book that reveals Yep coming to grips with his ethnicity. "I wanted to do so in company with my grandmother," he says, "if only in my imagination. I began to write about a Chinese-American girl who has to live with her grandmother in Chinatown. For the first time in her life, the girl has to confront being Chinese" (page 110).

Marie Lee, his grandmother, became the inspiration for characters in four of his children's books: American Casey's grandmother, Paw Paw, in *Child of the Owl;* Cassia, a rebel in nineteenth-century China, who appears as a teenager in *The Serpent's Children* (Harper, 1984) and as a new bride growing into a unique woman who survives struggle and misery to become her own person in *Mountain Light* (Harper, 1985); and American Joan's mother, Mama, in *The Star Fisher* (Morrow, 1991).

Yep composes his stories to music, and many of his characters tell stories to one another to transmit and internalize cultural learning. Sometimes these stories are legends or folk tales, as in *Child of the Owl* and *The Star Fisher;* sometimes they are dream stories, as in *Dragonwings.* Paw Paw's story of the owls, Mama's story of the Star Fisher that Joan tells to her little sister, and Windrider's story of the dragon in *Dragonwings* are all narrative insets, or small, jewellike stories that fit closely into the larger plot, providing both lyrical beauty and thematic insight. These stories help outsider readers understand the insider ethnicity; they also confirm and extend insider readers understanding of their ethnicity, and they help child characters better understand the ethnicity integrated into their lives. The stories become "passages" into adulthood for the child characters.

Michael Dorris has also used inner stories to encourage cultural learning in characters and readers. He stitched three creation stories into the story fabric of *Guests* (Hyperion, 1994), a coming-of-age story of two Algonquin children in early American times. Dorris discussed this book and his creative process in an essay called "Waiting to Listen" (1995) that he wrote not long before his death in 1997. In the essay, he used the knowledge, values, and traditions of his own ethnic heritage to describe the way characters, plots, and ideas often came to him:

> An Inuit hunter is trained to endure bad weather and endless boredom while standing motionless beside a hole in the ice, trusting that dinner will eventually need to come up for a breath of air. There are special waiting songs to sing—spirit songs and inviting songs. The hunter keeps his eyes fixed on a piece of swan's-down suspended in the ice hole; the approach of a seal will create a stir, a rush of air. When the feather hangs still for an interminable stretch of time, doubts are sure to arise. The whole enterprise begins to seem irrational and impossible. And then, in a flash, the swan feather vibrates, there is a swirl, a dark swatch of color, a dazzle of movement. The hunter must be ever vigilant, or the single opportunity passes and may never come again.
>
> A writer waits, too, sitting at a desk in early morning. . . . The spear is a pencil or a ballpoint pen, poised to write . . . when that flicker of unmistakable revelation

bubbles into consciousness. Morning Girl, for instance, became herself and nobody else the split second she said, 'If the day starts before you do, you never catch up. You spend all your time running after what you should have already done, and no matter how much you hurry, you never finish the race in a tie. The day wins.' 'Gotcha!' I said, reaching for the yellow pad. 'Now, tell me more!' (page 699)

How did Dorris find his plots? It helps, he said, to come from a family of accomplished storytellers, including his ninety-eight-year-old Native American

INVESTIGATIONS: *Fiction and Nonfiction*

In this chapter we have read about several authors who have explored a particular ethnic heritage in their stories and essays. Perhaps they have stirred your interest in exploring your own heritage. To get started, consider any of the following suggestions:

1. Research your family history to see where the point of origin was. What gaps are there in family members' knowledge about their family history? Are there any stories you would want to imagine and write about your family to fill in these gaps?
2. What family stories do you remember hearing as a child? Which ones were your favorites? Which ones would you want to retell or to embellish?
3. Consider what is an important tradition, belief, or value of your own particular cultural group, or ethnicity, in relation to the larger American society. Or consider a defining moment in the history of your group. How might you portray your group or some aspect of it in a piece of fiction? How could you cause readers to care about this group, especially about their wishes and dreams—past or present?
4. Read a biography or historical account about some member of your ethnic group or background. If there are gaps in the details, try filling them with imagined scenes of your own. What stories do you find yourself imagining about a character? What stories do you hear the characters telling to other characters?
5. Was there any member of your family who told stories? Were the stories important to your cultural identity? Did the stories teach you about your family's culture? Would any of those stories find a place in your story? (Would you want to retell a family member's story?)
6. Do any cultures "cross" in your background? Have any cultures crossed in the backgrounds of your parents or grandparents? If so, try telling or imagining such a story as either autobiography, biography, or fiction. Make up aspects of the story to fill in gaps or to create scenes, characters, and conflicts as you need to do so.
7. Was there a grandparent in your life who served as a model for you and who helped you to learn more about your heritage and identity by sharing family and cultural stories? If so, consider telling some of these stories. Or create a story that features a strong grandparent figure. You might even imagine a story about this person when he or she was young and living either in a foreign culture, before coming to America, or living as an immigrant child in this country. Consider the value conflicts or the struggle to understand a new culture that this person might face in such a situation.
8. Write a story that contains a smaller story within the larger—main—one. This "inner" story or narrative inset might be a folktale, a legend, or an invented story of your own. An older person might be telling it to a younger one; a child might be telling it to another child. In either case, the storytelling will probably help the listener or reader learn more about the ethnic heritage and identity of the character.
9. Read fiction by Virginia Hamilton, Mildred Taylor, Laurence Yep, or Michael Dorris to see what ethnic values and traditions these authors weave through their books. Do not read merely to extract information about these values; instead focus on the way that African-American, Asian-American, and Native American children are coming to understand better their own values and traditions, as the story unfolds. Read to "shadow" these characters and experience their traditions alongside them.

grandmother whose creations "always assume formal shape" (page 701). From her, he learned to identify beginnings and endings when adapting fiction from life experiences. The most difficult thing for the storyteller is to know where and when to stop telling, Dorris said. The storyteller must also discover the right voice or point of view for the story; this he learned by experimenting. First-person narration allowed him to step into a favorite character; third-person gave him total omniscience. When the right voice emerges, it takes over everything, drowning out the author.

As Dorris wrote *Guests,* he was searching "for the cadence of a Native-American boy living in the northeastern woodlands around the time of the first Thanksgiving" when, at age twelve or thirteen, he must make his vision quest in the wilderness. Dorris believed that a writer is also engaged in a vision quest. The writer finds him or herself "absolutely alone for the first time ever and having, as a result, to listen closely to one's own story, one's own voice, to the structure of one's past and future, without the filter of other people." Like the boy in the forest of *Guests,* he says, writers are guests in the "wondrous world of the might-have-been, the should-have-been, the might-yet-be. We follow the trails presented us without any guarantee of a safe destination," losing the way more often than finding it. "But every now and then, the branches part, a clearing opens, and there we are" (pages 702–3).

Says Anne Lamott, "Think of those times when you've read prose or poetry that is presented in such a way that you have a fleeting sense of being *startled* by beauty or insight, by a glimpse into someone's soul. All of a sudden everything seems to fit together, or at least to have some meaning for a moment. This is our goal as writers, I think; to help others have this sense of . . . wonder, of seeing things anew, things that can catch us off guard, that break in on our small, bordered worlds" (page 100). Her words define well Dorris's poetic prose and the essence of poetry itself.

MULTIETHNIC POETRY AND STORIES

What do Joseph Bruchac, Gary Soto, and Arnold Adoff have in common? Poetry, yes; but in addition, each is either a poet who also writes stories, or a storyteller who also writes poetry. Each is also a pioneer in addressing the needs of an underrepresented group.

Joseph Bruchac, of Abenaki heritage, has over the past decade produced a rich collection of literature for Native American children. His books are especially important, because for years, only members of the dominant culture were writing books about Native children. These writers often held unsympathetic views of Native people; they filled their stories with beliefs and values that came from their own contemporary American majority culture; they took short-cuts in the research process or conducted no research at all. Bruchac's endnotes to his books—and he rarely publishes a book without extensive notes about his research process—testify to the copious research that even insiders undertake to preserve that culture. They also tell us a great deal about Bruchac's creative process, which is guided by Native American traditions and beliefs.

A Closer Look

Native American Literature and Outsider Writers

Educator Donnarae MacCann has discussed the fact that outsider writers often describe Native American societies in negative, inaccurate, and patronizing ways. Fiction cannot achieve a cultural balance, MacCann explains, when the only "good" children in the book are white or Anglo or when the Native American culture is "portrayed in white supremacist terms" (page 144). This imbalance occurs, in Laura Ingalls Wilder's *Little House on the Prairie* (Harper, 1935) and in Lynne Reid Banks's *The Indian in the Cupboard* (Doubleday, 1980), says MacCann.

MacCann points out that in Banks's book, "Little Bear [a plastic toy that comes to life in the child character's magic cupboard] is either violent or childishly petulant . . . The historical culpability of the cowboy and others who invaded Amerind territory is ignored. Native Americans are seen as the primary perpetrators of havoc, even as they defend their own borders" (page 145). According to MacCann, Banks, who is an outsider to Native American culture, has internalized many stereotypes about this group, and nothing in her own cultural experience enables her to avoid them in her writing.

The outsider's responsibility to research story subjects and to take on a new frame of reference (to step into an insider culture with a full understanding of its cultural references) is enormous. Outsiders must produce a balanced picture of the culture they are depicting. They must also concern themselves with the human aspects of the culture, making certain they depict the characters' belief system accurately. Finally, they must supply information—copious details in both words and pictures—rather than misinformation about the culture in their stories.

Another writer whose work concerns MacCann is Jean Fritz, whose historical fiction is nearly always humorous, insightful, and balanced, according to critics, reviewers, and award committees. Yet in *The Double Life of Pocahontas* (Viking, 1983), says MacCann, "Fritz seems interested in contriving a romance rather than shedding light upon her subject." She portrays the English as "mere bunglers" and the Native Americans as "invaders and butchers" (pages 159–60).

If subtle instances of cultural imbalance arise even when well-meaning and talented outsiders like Jean Fritz depict insider cultures, consider the less subtle instances that occur in older but still popular books like Ingri and Edgar Parin d'Aulaire's picture book, *Pocahontas* (Doubleday, 1946). The book is filled with illustrations of strong artistic integrity, vibrant color, stong line, and large- and small-scale patterns that provide lively contrasts and linear rhythms. Yet it is also filled with negative stereotypes; the village chief and his wife are described as "ugly and cruel people" (page 34), and the emotional content of the pictures reflects the emotional coding of the words.

Children—insiders and outsiders both—need stories that reflect the reality of insider kinship patterns, rituals, and cultural traditions. If writers do not portray these subtle areas, children of insider cultures miss the opportunity to learn more about their heritage and ethnic identity, and outsider children lose the opportunity to learn more about other groups—or to learn more about their culture and nation as a whole.

Source: Donnarae MacCann, "Native Americans in Books for the Young," in *Teaching Multicultural Literature in Grades K–8,* edited by Violet Harris (Norwood, MA: Christopher Gordon, 1993, pp. 137–69).

Bruchac's writes about Native American storytelling in the Afterword to *Flying with the Eagle, Racing the Great Bear: Stories from Native North America* (BridgeWater Books, 1993). Just as Michael Dorris speaks of listening closely to one's own story and one's own voice, Bruchac speaks of listening to many voices as he compiled his collection of Wampanoag, Cherokee, Osage, Lakota, and Tlingit traditional tales. One of the voices was that of his friend Swift Eagle, an Abenaki elder. Another was the Apache/Pueblo storyteller who reminded him to listen to the voice of the leaves. Two others included an Abenaki tradition-bearer and a Clan Mother of the Onondaga Nation.

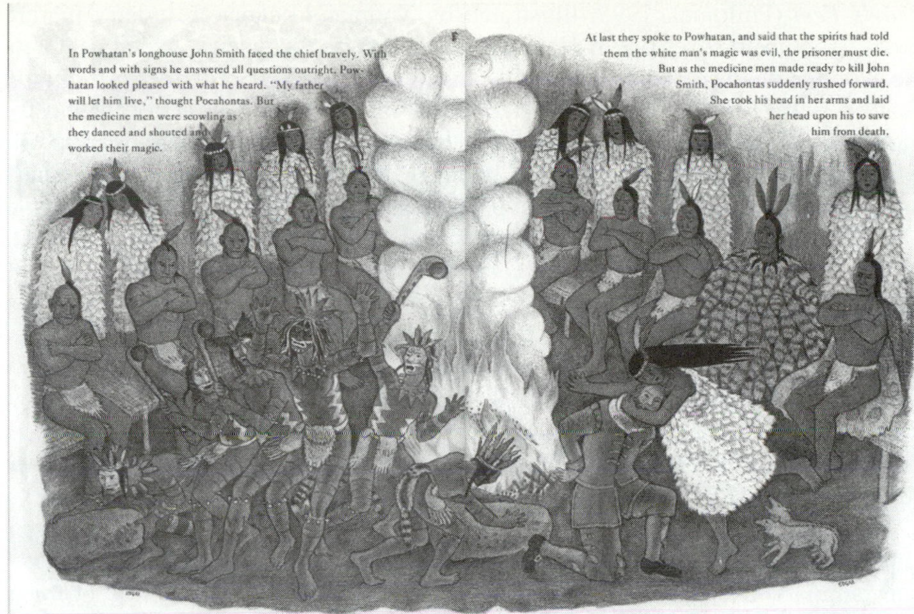

From *Pocahontas* (Doubleday, 1946) by Ingri and Edgar Parin d'Aulaire.

As Bruchac retold these stories, he thought about the name the Clan Mother had given him: The Good Mind. The person with this name, she told him, would "speak with honesty and honor and keep one's thoughts away from selfishness and vanity, especially when speaking on a topic as important as the passage of a boy from childhood into young manhood" (page 127). In the Introduction to the book, Bruchac tells of designing these tales "not only to help the boy find his way to full manhood, but also to help the man remember the boy within himself, so that he can be sympathetic and helpful to the coming generations" (x).

Stories such as these grow with us, he says. He describes the way children's literature works for both child listener and adult teller—and for readers of any ancestry, Native American or otherwise: "We learn about ourselves by understanding others. Our own traditions can be made stronger only when we pay attention to and respect the traditions of people who are different from ourselves" (pages x–xi).

His companion volume to *Flying with the Eagle* is *The Girl Who Married the Moon* (BridgeWater Books, 1994). In this book, Bruchac and coauthor **Gayle Ross** collected stories celebrating the young girl's entrance into womanhood. In the Afterword to this book, Ross tells what she and Joe Bruchac have learned about stories: that they are "living spirits" and that the role of the Native storyteller is "to care for the tales in our keeping." It is her hope, she adds, to have rendered the tales with "the respect they deserve" (page 124). Bruchac reveals his own respect by writing an acknowledgment to each of the tellers whose stories he relates. He seeks permission from each oral teller before including a tale in his books because he believes strongly that certain tellers are "entrusted" with particular tales by their people. A story, again, is a *living* thing.

Bruchac's *Thirteen Moons on Turtle's Back* (Philomel, 1992; written with Jonathan London and illustrated by Thomas Locker) and *The Earth Under Sky*

Bear's Feet (Philomel, 1995; illustrated by Thomas Locker) are poetry picture books. The poetry rises out of Native legends, songs, and stories, which celebrate the wonder of the seasons, the land, and the heavens. In *Thirteen Moons on Turtle's Back,* Bruchac presents thirteen different moon stories (a story-poem for each cycle of the moon) that spring from thirteen different tribal nations from different regions of North America. His intent is "to give a wider sense of the many things Native American people have been taught to notice in this beautiful world . . . [all of] which . . . must be listened to and respected."

In *The Earth Under Sky Bear's Feet,* Bruchac presents twelve narrative poems about the way twelve different tribes have each told about Sky Bear (the Big Dipper). The Mohawk poem that begins the book is one Bruchac tells of hearing in childhood. Three hunters and their dog find the tracks of a giant bear. They follow the tracks that night until they see the bear climb a hill that glitters with snow. Running after the bear, they find themselves high above the earth with the bear "running on through the stars." The poem ends, "Look up now/and you will see her,/circling the sky."

The Winnebago poem in this collection is especially well-suited for children. "In the time when the grass/begins to run green/and the nights grow warm," it begins, animals wake and Sky Bear watches and smiles down on a family of mice. At dusk, when the mice come out, one mouse "reaches up so high that he/thinks he can touch the sky." Then he sings: "On this whole earth, who is there like me? . . . I alone can touch the sky!"

Bruchac includes many different tribal tales in his collections, demonstrating what he says is the Native people's concept of multiculturalism as "*all* people" (1995, page 158). Bruchac notes significant differences among the many Native peoples who inhabited the North American continent before the Norse arrived and five hundred years before Columbus. The most obvious difference was language: More than four hundred different cultural groups and languages were alive and well at that time. These groups had different types of dwellings, different rituals, and different stories.

Bruchac also emphasizes important similarities among these diverse groups—for example, all of these different cultures responded to the ecosystem of the land, and most traveled far, wide, and freely. Hospitality and storytelling were sacred traditions: "People listened to one another's stories, and a storyteller was said to be always welcome in anyone's lodge" (page 159). Multiculturalism, in Native terms, did not divide people; it meant cooperating for survival, listening to one another's stories, and seeing one another as human beings. "Ideas of multiculturalism," says Bruchac, that exclude no group—majority or minority, "can empower all our children" (page 158).

Gary Soto has written poetry, fiction for children in middle grades, and the texts for several picture books. But it is his poetry that he often discusses when he explains his creative process. In the Foreward to his poetry collection *A Fire in My Hands* (Scholastic, 1990), Soto tells of how, as a college student of Mexican-American heritage, he immersed himself in Spanish and Latin American poetry. He particularly liked Pablo Neruda's work because it celebrated "common things like tomatoes, socks, scissors, and artichokes" (page 6).

When he began to write poetry himself, Soto turned to the common experiences of his childhood: "dogs, alleys, my baseball mitt, curbs, and the fruit of the

[San Joaquin] valley, especially the orange" (page 6). Because he also admired poets of the American majority culture who often wrote about home or about places they remembered for important reasons, he decided to write about the place where he grew up in California:

> Some of my poems are stark observations of human violence—burglaries, muggings, fistfights—while others are spare images of nature—the orange groves and vineyards, the Kings River, the bogs, the Sequoias. I fell in love with the valley, both its ugliness and its beauty, and quietly wrote poems about it to share with others. I like to think of my poems as a 'working life,' by which I mean that my poems are about commonplace, everyday things—baseball, an evening walk, a boyhood friendship, first love, fatherhood, a tree, rock 'n' roll, the homeless, dancing. The poems keep alive the small moments which add up to a large moment: life itself. (page 6)

In this volume, Soto explores his Mexican-American identity. In poems like "Black Hair," he tells the story of watching a baseball player, Hector Moreno, who was also Mexican: "I came here because I was Mexican, a stick/Of brown light in love with those/Who could do it—the triple and hard slide,/The gloves eating balls into double plays" (page 9). At the same time, he shares experiences common to all identities. In "Learning to Bargain," he tells about a friend tormenting a cat: "I'm at that window, looking/Onto the street: dusk,/A neighbor kid sharpening/A stick at the curb./. . . When he looks/Up, his eyes dark as flies/I ask about the cat, the one dead/Among the weeds in the alley" (page 11).

Not everything in these narrative poems is true, Soto explains in his endnotes for the book. His friend, he explains, did not kill the cat; he simply threw a brick at it and missed. But he did not like the idea of the boy trying to hurt the cat, so he threatened to tell on the boy. He made the scene in the poem even worse to show "how people start conspiring at a very early age" (page 60).

In an essay called "Dressing Like a Poet," Soto (1997) tells more about his sensitivity to life experiences and certain people and places, and what this concern for others means in terms of poetry writing. He felt particularly concerned for people in pain: "We may see and feel for a worker in the poem, his hands frozen as fish as he scrubs a bumper in a car wash. We may see someone old as our own grandparents, and this may for a moment make us contemplate our own flesh." Those with strong sensitivities never respond with a callous thought or remark, Soto says; instead, they find their hearts pulsing, and then they often begin, as he did, to write poetry.

To generate ideas, he thinks back to his childhood in the early 1960s—the pickle store across the street, the broom factory down the alley, the Sun-Maid Raisin factory a little father away, a ceramic Buddha that sat by the phone in his home. These mental pictures, he says,

> muster up a power inside me, a delicious feeling of memory, imagination, and the willingness to care for the smallest of objects—shards of glass, taps on my shoes, a chicken claw that I worked like a lever, a bicycle part, and an innertube I rolled from one end of the yard to the other. . . . Just as I'm ready to write, it's not unusual for me to close my eyes for a moment and remember the Buddha . . . gold-splotched . . . with a large belly and laughter on his face. (Silvey, 1995, page 614)

Soto begins a poem, doodling a few words or lines, and soon settles in to write. Every line receives a great deal of attention. He changes verbs, reworks line breaks, cuts words; and often, halfway through the poem, he discovers a title that captures the poem. To begin, he simply feels something he wants to share with others. "If you're a poet at heart," he says, "the ache that separates you from others is probably there, the ache that says we have something to say" (Silvey, 1995, page 614).

Arnold Adoff is the author of thirty-two books. Several are anthologies of black American poetry; two are collections of prose by African-American writers; one is a biography of Malcolm X. But most of Adoff's books are poetry picture books, several of which are story-poems, or a sequence of poems that tell a story. Whether he is writing narrative or lyrical poetry, Adoff weaves his words into stories. A former teacher, Adoff is comfortable in classroom settings, and he often conducts poetry workshops with children, explaining his creative process and what it means to be an author—through stories. His first objective is to familiarize children with authors—particularly poets—so that children see artists as people. Then, he believes, they will feel like jumping into the process themselves.

"Home is where my work is," Adoff tells children at East Pike Elementary School in Indiana, Pennsylvania (videotape, 1992). "But my work is back in Yellow Springs, Ohio." At this point, he backs up to tell about himself from the beginning. He was born in 1935 in the Bronx, New York; his Jewish parents came from Russia and were very poor. Living in Greenwich Village in the late 1950s, he met and married Virginia Hamilton, of African-American and Native American heritage, who had come from Yellow Springs to New York to try her luck at writing fiction.

A writer, as Adoff explains to the children, is sometimes self-employed and sometimes unemployed; the only contract he has is the one he receives for each book, and he then earns a percentage for each copy sold. "You go to work," he says, "but you don't leave home." He gets up each morning at 6:00, and by 7:00, he is sitting in his study in a gray sweatsuit writing poetry. For the next six hours, he goes up and down the stairs getting books, newspapers, and magazines from the shelves. "Most of my work as a writer is reading, researching, and rewriting," he explains to the students. "The smallest part of what I do is writing. I begin with writing and then the remainder of my time is spent with these three processes. At the end I have a book that is published."

The rest of his day is spent going to the supermarket, buying a newspaper, going to the library (for more reading and researching), cooking, watching television, and—when he faces a deadline—going back to the word processor that night for more rewriting. A writer is like a carpenter, Adoff says; writing is like planing and sawing to get the manuscript in shape. He begins with a rough sketch, a list of ideas on his yellow legal pad, but it might be a year before this draft becomes the final poem. Adoff might go through as many as nineteen drafts before he has a finished product.

Adoff rolls out the long, cut-and-taped scroll of one of his manuscripts. Ideas for Adoff come from things right in front of him, he explains. "Race, skin color of our family, a twinkie from the planet Twinkie (a reference to a line in his book, *Eats Poems,* Lothrop, 1979), a girl who wants to fly, a dog-friend, chocolate. "I like to take the things that are really close to me, something ordinary, and say, 'What if?' " he says. Adoff keeps a journal. He likes to scribble notes, and he always begins a poem or a book of poems with lists of what he might want to write or read about.

The tone of his poetry ranges from humorous to serious; the style is sometimes narrative, sometimes lyrical. In *Chocolate Dreams* (Lothrop, 1989, illustrated by Turi MacCombie), Adoff says, he is trying to exaggerate and be funny. He warns readers not to lick the pages of this chocolate book; he advises them to bite and chew the delicious *words* on these pages, but not to drip chocolate juice onto the book—or chew the cover.

One of the children in the workshop asks about the way Adoff breaks conventions of capitalization and punctuation. "Sometimes I write books with every line beginning with a capital letter," replies the poet. "Sometimes I write books where there are no capital letters and no punctuation. Some days I might wear a shirt and tie; some days I might wear a turtleneck; some days I might wear a t-shirt. There are as many styles in poetry and in dressing as we can think of. But poets give themselves poetic license. In poetry you can do any style you want. There's a big difference between poetry and prose; in prose you must do the prose style." By "prose style," Adoff means following formal conventions such as capitalizing certain words and using appropriate punctuation in sentences.

Poetry was Adoff's favorite pastime as a child, he tells his audience: "My dream in fourth and fifth grade was to be a published author." The large collection of poetry picture books, arranged around Adoff in this school auditorium as he talks, shows that dreams of becoming a writer do come true when you work at your craft as steadily as he has. Some of his books are about growing up in a bicultural family; some are simply about growing up (sibling rivalry, vacations, sports events, pets, the fun of eating chocolate); others are about growing up with a particular ethnic heritage or growing up polyethnic. No matter what the subject, the shape and structure of Adoff's poetry illuminates it.

Notice how Adoff structures the poem, "Chips. One" from *Chocolate Dreams.* The arrangement of letters and spaces makes rhythm, sound, and meaning—demonstrating the idea of chocolate pieces as separate individuals living in one land, America:

More Than Two Hundred
And Forty Million In
di
vid
u
al
Pieces Of
Chocolate Are Sold
In This C o u n t r y
E v e r y D a y . (page 28)

From the same book comes "Chocolate Dreams. Two," a poem that blends the fun of eating chocolate with the poignant wish of the ethnic child to grow up as a member of the "dominant" culture (fitting in instead of being different). But the subject of color is so subtly introduced, it is possible to read the poem as having no reference to multicultural issues at all. It begins with the phrase "Chocolate Sun"; then the poem turns quickly into a listing of the child's chocolate dreams: a chocolate moon, clouds, and raindrops that sprinkle on a child's head. Next the poem describes everything about the child as chocolate (hair, face, body) while the child runs through chocolate streets and splashes through chocolate puddles and wades across chocolate streams. Then comes the thematic punch line; the chocolate world of the last line brings the poem full circle from the image in the first line, the Chocolate Sun:

Chocolate Streams. I
Must
Swim
Swift
Chocolate Rivers. I
Must
Swim
Some
Unsweetened
Chocolate Sea. I
Dream A
Chocolate World For
Me.

Chocolate World For
Me. (page 9)

Many of Adoff's poems, like "I am making a circle for myself" in *All the Colors of the Race* (Morrow, 1982), illustrated by John Steptoe, focus on the circle of family and the theme of growing up in a bicultural family. It is a situation he knows well, having watched his own children growing up in a bicultural household:

From *All the Colors of the Race* (Morrow, 1982) by Arnold Adoff, illustrations by John Steptoe.

I am making a circle for my self
and

I am placing into that
circle: all who are for me,
and
all that is inside.

If I am only white and Jewish then mama stays
outside.

If I am only black and Protestant
then daddy stays
outside.

But Golda is in the circle. Ben Gurion. Moses.
And Grandpa Jack is
surely
in. (page 13)

The first part of the poem appears on one page. The second part appears on the next page, and Adoff keeps many of the words the same, but he arranges the spacing of the middle stanza differently, beginning with the words "If I am . . . outside," because he wants to show the circle of family first widening, then contracting. As we "hear" the child speaking, we begin thinking about exclusion and inclusion and the way the child's self needs many voices, many experiences, many identities to breathe and grow. Thus, the cultural "circle" brings people into the cultural group, rather than pushing them out:

I am making a circle for my self
and

I am placing into
that circle: all who are for me;
all that is inside
me.

If I am only black and Protestant:
then daddy stays outside.
If I am only white and Jewish:
then mama stays outside.

But Harriet is in the circle. Martin King. Malcolm.
And Great
Grandpa Perry is
surely
in. (page 14)

The poem focuses on the widening identity children can experience when they are encouraged to think beyond labels, categories, and limitations, and how rich the possibilities are if they can learn to see human beings as multidimensional. Adoff's poem, "On my applications" addresses the social issue bicultural and polyethnic children face when they have to choose one ethnicity over another when they identify themselves on forms. What if it were otherwise? the child narrator seems to be asking. What if the world saw me simply as a multifaceted *individual?*

On my applications I can
                    put:
this girl:
        a black,
          white,
Christian,
Jewish,
        young
        woman:
          student,
        musician,
singer,
dancer,
runner   in the middle distance races,

          is willing to help you
          if you take her as she
                    is. (page 22)

If there is a metaphor for his life and work, says Adoff (Chapman, 1985), it is the juggler "balancing symmetrical form, truth, beauty and some new American way!" (page 10).

MULTIETHNIC ILLUSTRATED BOOKS AND PICTURE BOOKS

Perhaps more than any type of writer, picture book authors juggle their skills and ideas as they integrate words and pictures. Some authors—like Tom Feelings, Allen Say, and Gail Haley—also weave cultural traditions through their texts and illustrations.

Tom Feelings has described himself as both a "storyteller in picture form" and "an African who was born in America." His work is "rooted in the culture of Africa and expanded by the experience of being black in America" (page 685). This dual heritage—African and American—affects everything about Feelings's work—including content, form, technique, and subject matter—and causes him to react with strong personal emotion to the social scene in America, particularly to the way social forces affect his ethnic group. His work began during the Civil Rights Movement in 1958, when he was drawing figures and settings in his own Brooklyn community. Focusing on black children, he noticed that the adults, but not the children, had negative images of themselves.

Feelings understood the reasons for this adult perspective; at the same time, he wanted to retrieve the childhood joy and explore it in its original state. So he traveled to Ghana in West Africa, where he worked for several years, experiencing for the first time the feeling of being part of a majority. There Feelings discovered the joy of a free people, and this filled him with strength and conviction. His artwork prospered; his lines became more dancelike, fluid, rhythmic, and flowing; his colors became brighter, "as though they had light radiating from within." This light is what he brought back to America for children.

As Feelings began to illustrate books about Africa, he used a new technique he had discovered—or invented—and that he has been using ever since, one that enabled him to create "warm, light tones and luminous black-and-white contrasts that embellished the theme" (page 690). Feelings placed tissue paper placed over pen-and-ink drawings filled in with water-based white tempera paint. The ink and paint began to run together, creating exciting shapes and forms. Then, while the

INVESTIGATIONS: Poems and Stories

You might want to continue exploring your own heritage by creating poems, stories, and folk tales that reflect it. If so, consider the following suggestions:

1. Collect folk tales from your cultural group and place them into a book. Produce an endnote for each story. Tell where you found the story (the source) and what the story has meant to members of this group of people—and to you.
2. Think about common, everyday objects or traditions from your heritage, your childhood, your neighborhood, or your ethnic group, and consider how you might celebrate these things in a poem.
3. Consider writing a poem or story about a person you feel concern or caring for—an oppressed person, an older person, or someone who causes you to think more deeply about the human condition.
4. Think about your house, your street, or your neighborhood in childhood. Try to create mental pictures of this place. Let the small details take you back into a world that brings words, phrases, and lines of text to your page. Experiment with different arrangements of your words and lines, and substitute different words to give your poem a changed mood or meaning. See what title seems to spring from the poem. Then continue to work with the poem, cutting some words, adding others, and breaking your lines at different places to produce the sounds and sense you want.
5. Think about your heritage and identity. Is it monocultural? Is everyone in your family originally from the same country or culture? Or is it polyethnic? Is your mother's family from one culture and your father's family from another? Or are your grandparents from several different cultures? Write a poem or story in which you focus on family traditions in several different branches of your family. Ask yourself, How do the branches differ? What common threads run through all of them? Or write a poem or story in which you explore diversity—of talents, interests, preferences, values, tastes, styles, abilities, disabilities, opportunities, wishes, dreams, and adventures—in a monocultural family.
6. Write a poem or story in which you let others see you as different from members of your family, your circle of friends, or your classmates. Show yourself more clearly and more completely than you ordinarily would. Consider what details you will need to include, what incidents, what ideas, what images.
7. Read Gary Soto's *Neighborhood Odes* (Harcourt, 1992), which includes twenty-one celebrations of things as simple and universal as his cat, his neighborhood library, fireworks, the yard sprinkler, a wedding, family photographs, and a fruit—the pomegranate—that grows in the San Joaquin Valley in California, where Soto lives. At the same time, he weaves details of his ethnicity, as well as Spanish words like *gato* (cat) and *abuela* (grandmother) into the poems to give them ethnic substance and authenticity. Then write a poem about a subject you select, weaving in details of your cultural or ethnic group in order to personalize it.
8. Read some of Gary Soto's fiction—for example, *Taking Sides* (Harcourt, 1991). Notice the many ways Soto inscribes outsiders into the Hispanic ethnicity in this book, such as including Spanish words as part of the story. Then create a story, real or imagined, in which you introduce readers to your own culture or ethnicity in creative and authentic ways.

From *Moja Means One; Swahili Counting Book* (Dial, 1971) by Muriel Feelings, illustrations by Tom Feelings.

tissue paper was still wet, Feelings painted ink washes into the dark areas, and he painted white tempera mixed with ink into the light sections or over the dark areas, always "trying to capture the right mood" (page 690). Feelings liked the spontaneity and uncertainty of not knowing what would happen when the ink, tissue paper, and paint flowed together. He also liked the way this art technique helped him to search for "a certain emotional mood in the final painting" (page 691). All of these effects helped with the most important thing—telling the story.

Storytelling, as Feelings describes in the Introduction to *The Middle Passage* (Dial, 1995), his widely acclaimed illustrated book for adults, is an "ancient African oral tradition through which the values and history of a people are passed on for the young." His illustrated books, as he said a decade before he produced this one, are "a natural extension of this African oral tradition," or a way to tell stories through art in order to "communicate on a large scale to people young and old" (page 693). The social content of his work is of greatest importance to Feelings. He cannot separate life and art; therefore, he needs to speak about the black child's social situation in this country in his own way.

Feelings's creative process in *Daydreamers* (Dial, 1981) shows how artwork and story fuse in his work. He developed the pictures from drawings he made of black children over a twenty-year time span. He wanted to connect these children in some way, in order to tell a story. He sent the pictures to the African-American poet Eloise Greenfield, who shared the same vision for black children he did, and she pulled all the portraits together with a poem-text for the book. The drawings were, at that point, pen-and-ink and pencil sketches, and Feelings decided to use a dual color scheme to unify the pictures. He chose "a cool blue-black that would make the images recede and a warm sepia that would bring them forward, and sometimes a mixture of both, to reflect the joy and sorrow in black life" and the way that African Americans must "deal with both sides of the coin of all human experience" (page 693).

Pain and struggle are constant companions for many black Americans, Feelings explains, and in his artwork, he wants to show children hope in the face of "sometimes overwhelming, staggering odds" (page 695). Black Americans are always "surrounded by restrictions and limitations," he says. Yet "we improvise in spite of those restrictions. . . . We celebrate life; we can take the pain; we have endured it" (page 695). Black readers therefore do not want their experience presented in just any manner, he explains. It must move, flow, pulsate, glow, and sing, like jazz, a deep heartbeat, or the old spirituals.

Allen Say moved to America from Japan in 1953, at the age of sixteen. But his mother remembers that his artistic talents were evident much earlier—from the time, as a child, that he drew on the walls. At school, Say drew during recess as children stood behind him and watched. It gave him a "kind of power," he says (audiotape interview with Philip Heller, 1992). Say grew up in a generation of children that all wanted to be cartoonists, he explains. He apprenticed himself, when he was twelve years old, to one of the most famous cartoonists in Japan, Noro Shinpei. Shinpei blended historical and modern periods. He was also a surrealist in many ways, and Say's work reflects these art styles.

Once in America, Say attended several art schools before he was drafted during his student years at Berkeley. In the Army, he experimented with photography, becoming a commercial photographer later in his career. Children's books became a sideline for his artistic talent. He did the artwork first and then "somehow," he says, "the story came out, almost by itself. And this is the way I work today" (Heller, 1992). *Tree of Cranes* (Scholastic, 1992) took ten months, as he explains:

> I worked on the art. Then I sat down and wrote the story in three days. It is the story of my mother, who was born in Oakland, California. One Christmas eve, before the war came to the mainland of Japan, my mother was suffering from homesickness. I was sick in bed; I heard noises from the backyard, and it was my mother sawing a tree. She brought it in and decorated it, and told me the story of Christmas. It's a true story; many of my stories are . . . I usually know what the first picture is going to be. And it takes me a long time. With *Tree of Cranes,* the first picture took me a month. And then by the time you're finished with that, it would suggest the second picture. I do them in order from beginning to end. And by the time I'm through with the art, there's the story. . . . I try to write what I know. I'm always trying to remake my childhood experiences in the way that I think should happen. (Heller, 1992)

Say based *The Bicycle Man* (Houghton Mifflin, 1982) on a true story from his childhood. One day two American soldiers, one white and one black, visited his Japanese school, and the black soldier performed tricks on a bicycle, to the delight of the children. It was field day at Say's school and he was a very bad athlete, a slow runner. He remembers: "I had to run and I dreaded it and I was praying there'd be a huge storm or something, and it was a beautiful day. Then these two Americans showed up, and it saved my day, because no one thought of races anymore after that" (Heller, 1992). Also, as he explains to another interviewer, "[I]t was amazing to see this soldier, an African-American man, riding a bicycle in a spectacular way . . . It was one of those extraordinary experiences that happens once or twice in a lifetime" (Marcus, 1991, page 296). Japanese people are very practical about their bike riding, according to Say, never doing acrobatic tricks with their bikes.

Say based his Caldecott winner, *Grandfather's Journey* (Houghton Mifflin, 1993), on both lived—and imagined—experience: the memories of a grandfather he knew only briefly, and of his mother, from whom he was separated when he was ten. When he began work on this book, the only photographs he had were of

He wore European clothes for the first time and began his journey on a steamship. The Pacific Ocean astonished him.

From *Grandfather's Journey* (Houghton Mifflin, 1993) by Allen Say.

himself; the portraits of all the others are imaginary, including the first illustration of the book, which is actually a picture of the author as a young man. "My grandfather was a young man when he left his home in Japan and went to see the world," the book begins (page 4).

The story tells of Say's grandfather's journey to the New World: what he wore, what he saw, what astonished him, what he explored, how he often walked "for days on end" (page 7), where he settled, and how he returned one day to Japan to marry his childhood sweetheart and bring her back to California. They had one child, a daughter, Allen's mother. Then his grandfather thought about his childhood; he remembered his home and the songbirds he had raised, and when his daughter was almost grown, he moved his family back to Japan.

There in Japan, Allen's mother married and gave birth to him. As a child, Allen visited his grandfather and heard stories about California, the place his grandfather could not forget. "So he planned a trip" there. But the war came; bombs fell, destroying the house where his grandfather raised his songbirds. All their lives were scattered now "like leaves in a storm." And his grandfather "never kept another songbird" (pages 25–28).

The last time Allen saw his grandfather, the old man was longing to see California one more time—but this was not to be. When Allen was almost an adult, he decided to go and see California for himself. Coming to love the place that his grandfather loved, he also came to miss the land of his childhood, as his grandfather had missed it, too. "The funny thing is, the moment I am in one country," says Allen, as narrator, "I am homesick for the other." And because of that longing, he has come to know—really *know*—his grandfather now, and he misses him "very much" (pages 31–32).

The last illustration is a framed photograph of Allen Say's grandfather as a young man, a smaller picture of the portrait we saw at the beginning. For this last picture, Say had intended to show the face of an old man, but one day, he tells us,

> I was lying on my studio floor, doing yoga and waiting for inspiration, when I saw pinned on the wall the original rough sketch of the first picture—the one of the young man in a kimono . . . and staring at it made the little hairs on the back of my neck rise. How right it seemed to end the story with the same image that begins the book! My grandfather's story merging with mine, one journey linking with another to form a circle. The endless circle. (page 32)

Gail Haley is the descendant of English settlers in the Appalachian mountains of North Carolina. In one sense, then, she is a member of the dominant Euro-American culture. But in another sense, she is a member of an underrepresented, unassimilated ethnicity—the Appalachian mountain people of the mid-Atlantic states, descendants of the Scotch-Irish-English immigrants who settled there. Like Allen Say, Haley has made a number of journeys back to her ancestral land to learn more about her heritage. But these are not the only journeys she has taken, and all of her trips have given her ideas for her picture books. Haley's first journey took her to school, ten miles away from her Appalachian home in Shuffletown, North Carolina. Later, in the 1960s, she went to college to study art and began experimenting with creative ideas for children's books.

The next journey took Haley to New York and then to the Caribbean, where she fell in love with African-Caribbean stories and designs. When she returned to New York, she began to conduct research in Caribbean and African folklore. "I took a course in African dance," says Haley (1986). "I learned to prepare African food. I haunted museums and private collections of African artifacts. I even befriended a stranded African magic woman who shared our New York apartment for almost a year, imbuing me with her country and culture" (page 120). Later Haley would produce a Caldecott winner, *A Story, A Story* (Atheneum, 1970), the retelling of a Caribbean folk tale.

Living in England from 1973 to 1980, Haley produced *The Post Office Cat* (Scribner's 1976); a Kate Greenaway winner, and *The Green Man* (Scribner's, 1979), her own recreated story about the legendary vegetation god that weaves through so many stories and artifacts in Europe. (Haley is the only person, thus far, to have received both the Caldecott and Greenaway medals.) "I don't find ideas," Haley (1982) has said, "they find me—usually when I'm involved in something else." She found inspiration for *The Green Man* on a pub sign in London: "I was going to lunch, but I stopped in my tracks, unable to take my eyes off the strange leaf-clad figure. He woke some ancient memory in me that was so strong, I had to know more right away" (page 3).

Haley found mythic Celtic "green men" everywhere—over doorways, on buildings, carved into wood. When she found herself dreaming about this haunting

From *The Green Man* (Scribner's, 1979) by Gail Haley.

figure, she began to conduct research in earnest. She found wild men and green men in the stories, myths, and legends of many cultures; they were always linked to spring festivals, animals, fertility rituals, and the hope for plentiful crops. "My story about the green man," says Haley, "is part of the living link between the storytellers of the past and children of today and tomorrow who will find and read the story tucked inside its pages" (page 8).

Soon after publishing *The Green Man,* Haley returned to live and work in Boone, North Carolina, near her hometown of Shuffletown. She has remained in this rural area "of small, one-family farmers, who still plowed with mules, made dresses and pajamas out of feed sacks, made their own dyes and soaps, and wore 'poke bonnets'" like those Queen Anne wore in England (page 8). When Haley was a child, it was her dream to go to Europe and explore the fairy tale world she loved. Now she has come home to learn more about her Appalachian roots, which are, in turn, rooted in the British Isles. And occasionally she returns, in spirit, to those roots to produce another picture book set on English soil. Haley's picture book *Dream Peddler* (Dutton, 1993) is the story of John Chapman, a legendary character from a fifteenth century British folktale that she places in the eighteenth century to show the growth of the printing industry. (In an end note, she provides instructions for producing a chapbook, using the endpapers of her book.)

"My maternal grandparents, though flatlanders, still say *ye* for *you;* 'I reckon,' 'go fetch a pippin for the young 'un,' and various other phrases which are typically English," Haley recalls (page 8). During her stay abroad, Haley grew more and more aware of these British influences. Back home, she soon found herself clogging, as well as making a pilot television show about Appalachian Jack of mountain folk tales, a folk hero who traveled to America with the English settlers. She discovered that Jack and the green man were linked. The bean tree of "Jack and the Beanstalk" suggested growth, fertility, and the hope of a successful crop, just as the Green Man did. Both Jack and the Green Man were tricksters, and each was often "portrayed as a face looking down out of the top of a tree" (page 13).

From *Jack and the Bean Tree* (Crown, 1986) by Gail Haley.

Soon Haley found herself working on several books about the American Jack, two picture books, *Jack and the Bean Tree* (Crown, 1986), *Jack and the Fire Dragon* (Crown, 1988), and *Maintain Jack Tales* (Dutton, 1992), a collection of eight stories plus a mountain version of "Molly Whuppie." In these books, Haley frames the story, in order to produce a traditional storytelling mood and structure. In *Jack and the Bean Tree,* for example, the narrator introduces the storyteller, Poppyseed: "When it comes nightfall in these parts, the mountains settle down to sleep and clouds come to nestle in their laps. . . . Poppyseed's a-telling stories tonight, and you're invited. . . ."

Then Poppyseed picks up the storyline herself: "You all come and set a spell, because I've got a story that's just ripe for the telling. . . ." Haley has described Poppyseed as her own "alterego," a "story dreamer with a tree full of stories growing in her head" (1986, page 119). When Haley travels to present her books, and especially when she is in Appalachia, she dons a costume, produces a mountain dialect, and becomes Poppyseed as she reads her books aloud to audiences. "I no longer even attempt a book unless it is first a tellable story," Haley (1990) says. "Stories help us participate in our own lives because every person is potentially a hero or heroine and can make choices in overcoming the dilemmas of his or her own life" (page 2).

Haley's most recent journey into cultural diversity is a Native American legend arising also from her Appalachian roots, a picture book titled *Two Bad Boys; A Very Old Cherokee Tale* (Dutton 1996). Haley spends at least a year creating each picture book. During this time, she listens to music, imagines the setting, and makes the characters so real in her mind that she can "see" every aspect: "In short, I create an internal hologram of the story that lives three-dimensionally in my mind" (page 10). Then she turns this internal experience into the book itself. Haley's most amazing discovery is that "the internal hologram is somehow transmitted to the mind of the reader . . . Children take the experiential clues that they are given in words and pictures and give them life and form within their own sensory visualization." It sounds "mystical," she

INVESTIGATIONS: Illustrated Books and Picture Books

You might want to continue exploring your own heritage by creating an illustrated story or a picture book. If so, consider trying some of the following techniques that Tom Feelings, Allen Say, and Gail Haley use:

1. Try sketching children and adults in your community; then experiment with a technique that allows you to use different media to capture various moods. Try to make your own personal statement about the social situation and the cultural setting. You might use pen and ink, paint, crayon, or pencil, but you will be using art to help you explore your ideas. (Tom Feelings)
2. Try composing your own family story using photographs of yourself or others. Focus the story on several generations of your family in order to produce a cross-cultural, cross-generational tale. See what connections you discover among family members, especially between yourself and another person, such as a parent, grandparent, or great-grandparent. What might you have in common with someone separated from you in time and space? (Allen Say)
3. Think of journeys you have made and how they increased your multiethnic learning—journeys in your neighborhood, to school, to college, on vacations. What members of other cultures did you meet? What new people, places, stories, artifacts, or foods did you encounter? What new ideas did you discover? What did you find that you would like to know more about? Read, talk about, and think more about this subject; then create a picture, a sequence of pictures, a picture book, or an illustrated story to share your discoveries. (Gail Haley)
4. Explore folk tales that emerge from your own ethnic or cultural group and choose one that connects in some way to your life. Consider recasting the tale in your own words and making your own illustrations for it. Consider also performing the tale for an audience, wearing authentic clothing from an earlier day to strengthen the story mood. (Gail Haley)

adds, but it happens: "I have had enough feedback from children over the years to know that this is true" (page 10).

In the next chapter, we will consider how readers and stories come together to create a literary experience, when, as Haley indicates, authors write stories and child readers infuse them with meaning.

Chapter 8

Authorial Signposts and Reader Response

Topics in This Chapter

- How authors make literary choices
- How readers receive clues to meaning from authorial choices
- The meaning-making process: Texts versus readers

"Stand up and repeat 'Tis the voice of the sluggard,' " said the Gryphon.
"How the creatures order one about, and make one repeat lessons!" thought Alice. "I might as well be at school at once." However, she got up, and began to repeat it, but her head was so full of the Lobster Quadrille, that she hardly knew what she was saying, and the words came very queer indeed:

Tis the voice of the Lobster; I heard him declare,
'You have baked me too brown, I must sugar my hair.'
As a duck with its eyelids, so he with his nose
Trims his belt and his buttons, and turns out his toes. . . .

"That's different from what I used to say when I was a child," said the Gryphon.
"Well, I never heard it before," said the Mock Turtle, "but it sounds uncommon nonsense."
Alice said nothing; she had sat down with her face in her hands, wondering if anything would ever happen in a natural way again.
"I should like to have it explained," said the Mock Turtle.
"She can't explain it," hastily said the Gryphon. "Go on to the next verse."
"But about his toes?" the Mock Turtle persisted. "How could he turn them out with his nose, you know?"
"It's the first position in dancing," Alice said; but was dreadfully puzzled by it all, and longed to change the subject.

"The Lobster Quadrille" in Alice's Adventure's in Wonderland, 1865
—Lewis Carroll

In the last two chapters, we discussed how authors create their books. We tried to get behind the scenes, to hear the authors' actual words and to see how they think. In the chapter following this one, we will be looking at how children reshape literature structures and styles to fit their own ideas as they become readers and writers. In this chapter, as a bridge between what adults do—consciously or unconsciously—to produce children's literature and what children do in response to it, we will examine the "signs" that authors send out to readers, and the way these clues stimulate meaning-making and the reader's engagement with the text.

HOW AUTHORS MAKE LITERARY CHOICES

If we learned anything from the last two chapters, it is that authors rely greatly on the unconscious mind as they write. Literary "signs" often emerge in texts without the author's conscious intention. And authors themselves often have trouble explaining what happens as they create. As we heard Virginia Hamilton say in regard to the way she creates characters, "I don't know *how* it's done. I do it, but I can break it down only so far. What happens is that you get a whole image and you find the words to project the image to the reader" (Mikkelsen, 1994, page 401). Similarly, in *Alice's Adventure's in Wonderland,* Alice simply cannot give the Mock Turtle any explanation for her puzzling recitation process and her recreation of the lines of the poem as she goes along. Her unconscious, her prior experiences, and freely associated images and ideas, cause her to recompose and rearrange words, but she has no inkling why.

The answer is rooted in what we call "reader response." Authors send certain "signs" or "signals" to readers to get across their consciously or unconsciously intended meanings, and readers receive these meanings in highly individual ways.

Even if children were rewarded for remembering every word of a poem, the chances that they would be able to do so in Alice's strange situation are slight indeed. And when we encourage children to respond *freely,* choosing meanings as easily as they might choose friends or favorite desserts, the chances that they will produce convergent responses are even slighter.

Is it simply a happy coincidence, then, when author and reader "connect," or communicate clearly one to the other? Or do readers make meanings that authors themselves never anticipate? And when readers take off on their own interpretive paths, how do authors feel?

Consider what Katherine Paterson (1989a) says about her work: "A book is a cooperative venture. The writer can write a story down, but the book will never be complete until a reader of whatever age takes that book and brings to it his own story. I realize tonight, as I realize every time I speak, that I am addressing an audience that includes many of my coauthors" (page 37).

Think also about what C. S. Lewis says in his correspondence with child readers: "Dear Denise, I am delighted to hear that you liked the Narnian books, and it was nice of you to write and tell me. There *is* a map at the end of some of them in some editions. But why not do one yourself! And why not write stories for yourself to fill up the gaps in Narnian history? I've left you plenty of hints—especially where Lucy and the Unicorn are talking in *The Last Battle.* I feel *I* have done all I can!" (page 104).

Virginia Hamilton also says about the author-reader connection: "I've always said if I didn't have readers, I wouldn't write, because that's the other half of it. Everyone brings to the writing their own set of prejudices, values, whatever. We all see things differently. But there are signposts that you leave along the way so that readers understand a lot of the same things. I remember in one of the folk tales [from *The People Could Fly*], "Little Eight John," I have the mother with a dishrag in her hand, and she sweeps it across the table—and there are crumbs. How many times have I seen my mother take a dishcloth to clean up the table and leave a little trail of crumbs behind! I think that's an experience a lot of people can relate to" (Mikkelsen, 1994, page 401).

Hamilton's words tell us that writers do sometimes try to leave clues for readers to follow or relate to. Thus, at times, authorial choices are intentional; authors even work diligently to achieve a desired effect. At other times, the author's subconscious may be hard at work, spinning out unintended clues. The author's subconscious choices connect with the reader's subconscious and the result is optimum communication.

Writers and readers, then, work *together* to find the meaning in literature—to discover what authors have sent and what readers receive. Younger readers might be affected by a cover picture and drawn into the story by it. Later, they might notice the way words and pictures work together to support one another or the way pictures fill in gaps of text. Older readers will notice the way words produce mental images in texts that have few or no pictures.

More on Authorial Choices . . .

All readers, consciously or unconsciously, respond to authorial choices. To bring the reception process to a more conscious level, we as readers can ask ourselves questions:

- What did the author choose as the major premise of the story?
- What pattern did the author use to develop the plot? Is it linear? Circular? Spiral? Something else?
- Who tells the story: I, as the narrator? He or she, as the narrator? An all-knowing narrator?
- How did the author portray the characters? Are they well-developed? Flat? Highly individualized? Culturally specific? Culturally generic? Stereotypical? Atypical? Typical?
- How did the author arrange words and pictures in relation to one another?
- What color scheme, art style, and art medium did the author choose?
- What did the author repeat in order to emphasize an idea—what details of setting? What words and actions of the characters? What events in the plot?
- What gaps or blank spaces did the author leave for readers to fill in for themselves?
- What clues did the author leave to help readers fill in the gaps?
- What inner stories did the author include to fill out the story line?
- How did the author construct the time scheme? Is the story told in chronological order? Is it told through flashbacks that move the story backward in time? Does the book contain stories-within-the-story, or narrative insets that slow down the action or move it backward or forward?

HOW READERS RECEIVE CLUES TO MEANING FROM AUTHORIAL CHOICES

Authorial Signposts and Reader Response: Picture Books

Novelist Anne Tyler writes of making her first important connection with literature, when she responded to a book read to her in childhood, Virginia Lee Burton's *The Little House* (Houghton Mifflin, 1942). Tyler received *The Little House* on her fourth birthday, but she has never ceased returning to it, she says. The story is "simple enough," as she explains:

> [A] small house sits on a hill among apple trees. The illustrations show two symmetrical windows with their curtains looped back at the sides—like the forehead of a little girl with braids . . . Far away the lights of the city glow, and the Little House sometimes wonders how it would feel to live there. But then the children grow up and leave, and the scenery begins to change. (page 56)

Eventually, the encroaching city sprawl blots out the lights, the Little House's view of the changing seasons, and the stars. The Little House ages; her paint peels. Finally a caring family moves her to the country, where all ends happily for her.

As a child of four, Tyler remembers noticing the "book's tone of voice . . . quiet but rhythmic" and the way it caused those reading aloud to her "to sound hushed and gentle and sad." But she found much more to the book than its writing style. The story had emotional content: The child reader feels comforted, knowing that even though alarming changes invade our lives, "the same kind of change can happen to a Little House—and that the house can weather it . . . Not only that," Tyler adds, "but rescue is possible. Conditions can be reversed. Or at least, partly reversed."

The book spoke to the child Anne of time passing. How did Burton's words and pictures bring this abstract concept to life? Changes came to her as a child in "sudden jolts," she says. At this time, she experienced time unreflectively: "So here was this story that spelled out for me all the successive stages. The sun rises and sets across one entire page, and a whole month of moons wheels across another. The seasons march in order, defined by the length of the days." Just as children find change both exciting and saddening, the Little House " 'missed the field of daisies and the apple trees dancing in the moonlight' " (page 56). The Little House is a child herself. (See Chapter 3, pp. 98–99, for more on *The Little House.*)

When Tyler sees the words of the book now, as an adult, she remembers her mother's voice and recalls her own feeling of sorrow, at age four. The book brought a sudden jolt of insight at that time: "It seems that I'd been presented with

INVESTIGATIONS: Remembering Childhood Books

Try to remember a book you heard or read as a child, one that made a strong impression on you and that you have perhaps revisited through the years, as Anne Tyler revisited *The Little House.* Study the book to see what authorial choices the author made to produce a strongly engaging book. What feelings and insights did the book give you when you were young? What does it reveal to you now?

a snapshot that showed me how the world worked: how the years flowed by and people altered and nothing could ever stay the same. Then the snapshot was taken away. Everything there is to know about time was revealed in that shapshot, and I can almost name it, I very nearly have it in my grasp but then it's gone again, and all that's left is a ragged green book with the binding fallen apart" (page 56).

It is the comfort, the reassurance—the joy—of this insight that has sent Anne Tyler back to this picture book over and over again through the years. Tyler's response to *The Little House*—then and now—testifies to a book's ability to change and yet to remain the same, especially when it is a favorite book from childhood.

The older a book, story, poem, or play, the better the chance it has been a favorite of many different readers in many different eras and the more likely it is to elicit many different interpretations. Consider the fable, one of the oldest literary forms.

Authorial Signposts and Reader Response: The Fable

Fables, whether they come from the Greek storyteller Aesop who lived around 600 B.C., from the seventeenth-century French verse writer Jean de la Fontaine, or from modern picture book authors like Leo Lionni, are simple, concise, and lively stories about human behavior. But humans never actually appear in these stories; they are always disguised as animals.

These animals usually portray two human "types" in conflict with one another, producing a lesson about two different ways of thinking, acting, or being. Thus, they teach something about human values; they make a comment about life as humans know it—and have known it from the time the fable was invented. Some things never change, and human behavior—including manipulation, mischief, and tests of strength and power—is one of them.

The animals in fables, as they depict human personalities, also act according to the dominant traits of their particular animal species (or according to human perceptions of these traits.) In a story such as "The Tortoise and the Hare," the tortoise creeps and the hare bounds speedily along in a race. But they also act according to human traits, with all their foibles, conceits, wit, and wisdom; the hare becomes overconfident, falling asleep by the side of the path, and the tortoise wins, having plugged steadily along from start to finish. In later years, translators and editors added explicit statements at the end of the fable, such as "Slow and steady wins the race." These "morals"—or statements about human behavior—interpret the stories for listeners, thus strengthening the teaching function.

The meaning of any story depends on both the literary choices the teller makes and the way listeners interpret these choices. Tellers adapt materials to fit their own time and place. Listeners do the same. Thus the details of any fable, including its moral statement, vary from teller to teller, era to era, and place to place, just as readers, including translators, interpret the stories differently at different times and in different places.

Says translator S. A. Handford (1954): "We do not know whether Aesop's own versions of any fables were written down by him or by any of his contemporaries; and even supposing that some of them were written, it is very unlikely that they are preserved in the versions that we possess. It is clear that Aesop's name was so closely associated with this kind of story that *any* fable came to be spoken of as a fable of Aesop" (pages xv–xvi).

A popular fable attributed to Aesop—"The Wolf and the Crane" demonstrates the many interpretive voices that help shape meaning. In this story, a trusting heron takes a risk and helps a wolf, but the wily wolf outwits it, and the heron barely escapes with its life. In the following translation that Handford made for the Penguin edition published in 1954, the intended audience is an adult one. Consider the sophisticated language and phrasing of the moral:

> A wolf which had swallowed a bone went about looking for someone to relieve him of it. Meeting a heron, he offered it a fee to remove the bone. The heron put its head down his throat, pulled out the bone and then claimed the promised reward. 'Are you not content, my friend,' said the wolf, 'to have got your head safe and sound out of a wolf's mouth, but you must demand a fee as well?'
> *When one does a bad man a service, the only recompense one can hope for is that he will not add injury to ingratitude.* (page 29)

Jean de la Fontaine (1621–1695) used many of the Aesop fables for his own collections. His intended audience was also adults, but the verse form made his fables attractive to children, though they probably did not absorb much of the wit and subtlety. Notice the way the wolf twists the situation so that the crane—who in this version is a female stork—appears shameless because of her seeming ingratitude. Notice also that La Fontaine leaves the story as a *story,* it entertains and enlightens without the explicit didactic teaching of a moral statement at the end:

> It is wolfish nature to eat greedily,
>   and one of them, a typical glutton,
>   gobbled up a leg of mutton
> so fast that he choked. It seemed that speedily
> his end would come, because the bone had stuck
> deep in his throat. By chance a passing Stork
> noticed Wolf's gurgling (he could not longer speak)
>   and saw that he was choking.
> So, with her sensitive and probing beak
> she fished out the bone. The surgery over, she
> politely asked him for a modest fee.
> 'A fee?' her patient said. 'You must be joking!
>   You would now be dead
> if I had not refrained from biting off your head.
>   Have you no gratitude?
> Take care that never again do I have to see
> a bird with such a shameless attitude. (page 40)

Famous nineteenth-century British illustrator Charles Bennett included this same fable in his collection, *The Fables of Aesop* (Bracken Books, rpt. 1986). In Bennett's version, the crane is male, and the tale emphasizes the Victorian male world of commerce as well as the court system. The words that filter into the translation reveal this emphasis: *property, client, recompense, obstructive matters, throttle, knowing wig,* and *rustling robe.* (In England, court officials always wear powdered wigs and long robes, a long-standing English tradition).

The pictures in Bennett's version take us directly into the values and behaviors of the illustrator's day. His picture shows the vested characters standing before Old Bailey (the Court); the crane hands the wolf a Bill of Costs, and the Wolf takes a combative stance, ready to slug it out. Bennett's intriguing and humorous artwork

From *Aesop's Fables* (Bracken Books 1986, rpt. 1857), drawn by Charles H. Bennett.

appeals to adults and children alike, but the literary style is certainly more suitable for adult readers:

> A ragged-haired, sharp-fanged Wolf, having, through overgorging himself with honest men's property, brought on an uneasy sensation about his throat, which threatened to be fatal, applied to a clever Crane of the long-billed species to help him through his trouble, upon condition of a very considerable reward for the practitioner's pains. The Crane, by skillfully removing certain perilous obstructive matters, brought the Wolf's throat out of danger, and then claimed the fulfillment of his client's promise.
>
> 'What!' said the knavish brute; 'have I not let you go without even the mark of my grip round your own throttle? Be thankful that I have not mangled your lean carcass for you, stripped your head of its knowing wig, and your back of its glossy, rustling robe.' Expect no greater recompense for saving the life of a Wolf. (page 62)

Now suppose we create our own version of this fable, trying to eliminate all explicit details designed to send messages about attitudes or values. We will eliminate references to gender, class, and culture. We will also omit any moral statement at the end, because we want readers to decide or construct the meaning—and the moral—for themselves:

> Once a Wolf found a bone stuck in its throat. It felt such distress that it ran in circles begging for help, even promising a reward to anyone who could loosen the

bone. 'Open your jaw very wide,' said the Crane. Then, putting its long neck down the Wolf's throat, the crane worked the bone loose, and out it flew. But when the Crane asked for its reward, the Wolf only laughed. 'You put yourself inside a Wolf's jaw and lived to tell about it! That should be reward enough for you.'

Our story, like most traditional fables, provides only the bare-bones plot of a story. Nevertheless, it is a story, and this simpler, more neutral, version can help us see how diverse reader response can be.

"The Wolf and the Crane": Reader Responses

Some readers might see the Crane as the main character, or the character they empathize with the most. This would certainly be a natural reaction, since the Crane's life is endangered. Therefore, in constructing a moral statement, readers might speak directly to the Crane: "When someone promises you something, you can't expect more than they're willing to give," or "When you do something for someone else, you shouldn't look for a reward." These readers would be indicating that they thought the Crane needed advice or help in order to learn something from the experience.

Some readers might align themselves so closely with the Crane that they use the plural "we" instead of "you" ("We shouldn't expect a reward for everything we do"), revealing even stronger empathy for this character.

Still others might place themselves in an advisory capacity telling the Crane quite simply what it should learn from its experience. These readers might construct morals such as:

- Virtue is its own reward.
- Sometimes the best reward is the less obvious one (knowing you did a good deed or a good job).
- Don't mess around with a wolf and expect him to be fair.
- A wolf will never be honest.
- Good will shouldn't expect rewards.
- Don't believe everything people tell you.
- Find satisfaction in the simpler rewards of life.
- Don't expect a reward for every good deed.
- Don't count on a desperate man's promises.
- No wolf is good or upright.
- Don't help a wolf.

INVESTIGATIONS: Writing a Fable

Select a fable from Aesop or La Fontaine; then rewrite it for an audience of your own time and place. Be inventive. Use the fable to make a subtle comment about human behavior. Or use your story as a stimulous to social action—to encourage others to think about human behavior you find foolish, comical, or disturbing.

Consider what animals you will use to represent particular human behaviors. Consider what authorial signposts you will set up to convey your intended meanings.

Share your fable with others. If you constructed a moral statement for the fable, keep it to yourself and ask your listeners to share what they think the moral of the fable is. Listen as they describe what they think your fable "means." Did they see your intended meaning? Did they see something new and different that adds to your understanding?

On the other hand, a reader might speak directly to the Wolf, advising "Don't make a promise you're not going to keep." This reader would probably identify the Wolf as the main character. Such a response differs from the others we have described. It could express either what the Crane might have said to the Wolf, had the story continued, or what the Wolf—or anyone—can take as a lesson from the story. Which point of view is the "right" interpretation of the story? The answer is "neither."

This is the crux of what reader response is all about. No one response is correct or incorrect—or even more nearly correct than another. One reader is not "comprehending" while another "misses the point." Instead, readers engage with stories or poems in individual ways, gaining unique pleasures and insights from their literary encounters. Readers share different reactions and help one another to see more. Reader response depends on the reader's interpretation of *nuances*—the little shades of meaning different readers notice.

"The Wolf and the Crane": Different Ways of Reading

As we begin reading a text, we construct meaning in very rudimentary ways; we simply sort out plot and note things that help us to build a framework for understanding—what we might describe as a **generative reading.** The basic question we ask is "What happened?" What happened to the Wolf? What happened to the Crane? What happened at the end? How do we feel?

Asking questions about feelings moves us into another way of reading, a more personal, empathetic role we take on, once we have generated some framework or outline of meaning. Consider the response of one student, Peter, to "The Wolf and the Crane," previously quoted: "Don't help a wolf." (The responses in the previous list really came from fifteen children's literature students—preservice teachers—who were constructing their own meanings for the neutral version of "The Wolf and the Crane.")

"The Wolf is the boss," said Peter. "It could be an animal, like it is here, or a force like a river. Whatever it is, it has all the power. The Crane is the one who does the work and doesn't get any credit for it. People use people. You could write it [the fable] from the point of view of the Wolf. Then it would be more interesting."

When we engage in **personal/empathetic reading,** we begin to have feelings about the characters, their behaviors, and the outcomes of their actions. In this case, most readers would be more likely to sympathize with the Crane than with the Wolf, given its overbearing, unjust, and ungracious behavior. Peter, however, suggests reversing things to try to see through the Wolf's eyes—and thus gain a little insight into *its* side of things.

Personal/empathetic reading causes us to notice certain details in the story that others may not notice—or causes us to notice *different* details. We notice certain details of stories because of our own interests, experiences, and preoccupations. We may even decide that one character (the Wolf or the Crane) is more interesting or important to us or to the story than the other character is, based either on how the author or teller has shaped the story or on how our experiences have shaped us. Whether we identify ourselves with a trickster, such as the wolf in this story, will depend on how appealing the teller makes such a character and on what kinds of personal experiences we have had with power figures, trickster personalities, or people skilled in manipulative behavior.

When Peter sees the Wolf as a boss and the Crane as an underling who does the work and gets no credit, he is engaging in still another kind of reading, something we might call **sociocultural reading.** Peter is examining motivation, based on what he knows about human behavior in the real world. Why did the Wolf behave in such a callous way? Why was the Crane so trusting? One was a power figure, we might say, who assumed control, even to the point of twisting the facts and reneging on its contract. The other was bigger-hearted—or perhaps more naïve, even gullible. The student who wrote the response, "Don't believe everything people tell you," has also moved into sociocultural reading. She implies that the Crane is gullible and overly trusting.

When Peter says, "People use people," he is describing social patterns and behaviors. These patterns help to explain the Wolf's behavior, or why the Wolf made a promise it apparently never intended to keep. This fable, like fables generally, reveals how the world sometimes works, and this sociocultural connection explains why fables have remained popular to this day. Peter's comparison of the Wolf to a force like a river also provides a sociocultural interpretation: Might makes right. Natural forces often bear down on innocent bystanders.

Such conditions—natural and social—have always affected human lives. They give rise to difficult questions, such as What do we do about bloodthirsty creatures—animal or human? Social concerns often arise as we read stories, causing us to see the questions authors and storytellers are exploring. If we ask ourselves, What is this story about? we are engaging in still another way of reading—**literary reading.** We may be puzzling over who the main characters are and what they wanted. Did the Crane want simply to help someone? Did it want a reward? Or both? What is the big idea in the story, the one thread of meaning that weaves through the story fabric and holds it together? If we step back, what do the patterns show? What is the *theme* of this story?

A theme is not to be confused with the moral statement we often find printed at the end of a fable, such as the student's statement, "Virtue is its own reward." It is instead an *idea* running through an entire work that causes the work to form a cohesive unit in our minds. A theme is something readers make for themselves out of a literary work, when the work has gaps, puzzles, or open spaces that allow many views. It helps us put all the story pieces into place.

A theme might say something about what a character discovers in the course of the story, or it might say what the reader discovers. Another student's statement, "Sometimes the best reward is the less obvious one" (knowing you did a good deed) comes closer to a thematic statement and describes what the reader, rather than the character, may have learned. A theme may also be a question that readers ask themselves as they read, such as What do we do when an untrustworthy person asks for our help? What do you do in the face of trickery? Maybe the Crane was not gullible after all; maybe it simply could not say "no" to someone whose life was in jeopardy. Maybe the crane was a caring "person."

No *real* story ends at the ending; the ending is really the beginning of questions, of sorting out the dilemmas and choices humans face. When Peter suggests rewriting the story from the Wolf's point of view, he is thinking like a storyteller, and he is moving into **narrative reading.** In wondering about the Wolf's feelings, Peter notices a gap in the story and the way a teller or writer could fill such a gap. He either feels some empathy for the Wolf, some creative desire to build a defense for the Wolf's behavior, or both. (Writing from the Crane's point of view would, on the other hand, help readers see more about the feelings of those dealing with wily oppressors.)

Narrative reading is similar in some ways to **critical reading.** In narrative reading, readers function as storytellers, deciding how they feel about the characters and then asking themselves what story *they* would like to tell to fill in the gaps—or how they would rewrite the tale. In critical reading, readers think about how the author or storyteller feels about the world, the human condition, and these particular characters. They consider whether they, as critical readers, feel differently. They search for authorial signs or clues to meaning to make the comparison.

Lissa Paul (1998) suggests twelve questions we can ask ourselves as we read to dispel the unexamined cultural assumptions of both writers and readers: Whose story is this? Who is the reader? When and where was the reading produced? Who is named, and who is unnamed? Who is on top? Who is punished, and who is rewarded? Who speaks, and who is silenced? Who acts, and who is acted upon? Who owns property, and who is a dependent? Who looks, and who is observed? Who fights for honor, and who suffers? How are value systems determined? (page 16).

The language an author uses often reveals his or her social attitudes toward gender, class, and culture. (The author is a member of a particular social world; the author has likely absorbed the values of that world.) Imagining an opposing—or alternative—point of view, such as the Wolf's side of things, gives readers a chance to see how *individual* characters might think and feel, if they could break free of the author and the author's social values. In choosing to view things through a wolf's eyes, Peter can explore the stereotypical bad wolf and gain a better understanding of how humans pigeonhole other humans.

If we were to rewrite this fable from the Wolf's point of view, we might consider Charles Bennett's version, which adapts easily to a Marxist critical reading. Marxists take the position that capitalism forces people into oppressed social roles, thus producing an underclass of oppressed people and elitist views about this underclass. Elitism limits the potential of those born or thrown into disadvantaged economic circumstances. (Lissa Paul's questions are particularly relevant here.)

Charles Bennett's illustration for "The Wolf and the Crane" shows contrasts in the clothing each animal wears. The Crane has sleek leggings, a silk top hat, long coat, vest, and scarf. The wolf wears work boots, rumpled pants, a vest stretched to fit his burly chest, and a coat with a patched sleeve. The narrator's words about the wolf (previously quoted in Bennett's version of the fable) are even more telling. The wolf is "ragged-haired" (has no money for a haircut), is "sharp-fanged" (hungry), and has gorged himself on "honest men's property." Because others have him by the "throat," he has employed an expensive lawyer (a "clever Crane of the long-billed species"), who is charging a "considerable" amount. After the Crane lawyer saves him, this "knavish brute" refuses to pay.

The teller seems to be having some fun with both characters—the overpriced crane-lawyer and his ruffian client. But those reading from a Marxist perspective might see the Wolf as more an oppressed victim than a ruffian, or they might at least find ways to justify the Wolf's actions as he faces his predicament. As a member of the ragged underclass, what opportunity does he have for advancement other than by money-grubbing? It is easy to see that even in a supposedly simple story like a fable, we can find enough ambiguity that any number of interpretations are possible. The richer the story, the more varied and complex the dramatic roles, the actions, the motives of characters, and the possibilities for filling story gaps.

In longer, more complicated fiction, the characters may not make such clear-cut discoveries. The resolution might be hazy, puzzling, or even inconclusive. As we read and interpret novels, we can view them from many different perspectives, using any of the different ways of reading.

A Closer Look
Different Ways of Reading

In any story we are reading, we might be—consciously or unconsciously—asking ourselves many different questions, as we engage in different ways of reading:

GENERATIVE

How does the book begin? What do we notice first? What is happening? What kind of world are we stepping into? Who are the people in this world? What are they doing? What are they thinking and feeling? What are their hopes and dreams? What is helping or hampering them in reaching their goals? What conflicts do they face? What problems are arising for them? How do they deal with these problems?

PERSONAL/EMPATHETIC

What details do we notice and continue to think about? What connections do we find between the story and our own lives—our experiences, our interests, our understandings about the world? What characters do we find most interesting or most important to the story? What characters' feelings and attitudes are closest to our own? How would we feel or act in their situation? What choices would *we* make?

SOCIOCULTURAL

How do our experiences of the world help us to understand the story and to connect with the characters? How does the book connect us to the world—to social injustices, social challenges, puzzles about the world? What problems, questions, or issues does the book explore? What choices must the characters make? What actions do they take? What motivates their actions? (Why are they doing certain things or making certain choices?)

LITERARY

Who is the main character? (Whose fate is at stake? Whose needs are most pressing? Through whose eyes do we see the story?) What act sets the story in motion? What keeps the story going? What act pushes the story to a high point? How is the story resolved? What do the characters discover? How do characters change in the story—or do they change? What is the book, story, or poem about? What ideas run throughout the work to produce meaning? What is the author's vision of the world (of how things are or how they should be)? What dominant patterns run through the story? (What repeated details and ideas?)

NARRATIVE

What gaps or blank spaces does the author leave in characters and setting? What stories do we begin imagining to fill in these gaps? What choices does the author make in telling the story? What choices do we make as we "walk around" inside the author's story, telling stories of our own? What do the characters say? How do they act? What do they remember and talk about? What stories do they tell? Through whose voice do we tell our stories? How does the telling begin—in our stories and in the author's? What actions and events does the author repeat for emphasis? What words, images, and details are repeated? How do the characters solve their problems? What sense do we make of the ending? Does it tidily resolve the conflicts—or leave them open-ended?

CRITICAL

What knowledge, experiences, and values does the author bring to the story? What personal or cultural beliefs permeate the work? Is the narrator's view biased? Is it a neutral and tolerant one? Does one of the characters, or a group of characters, function as an ethical "center" of the work? Or are values left open? Does one character's viewpoint or view of the world influence the reader's feelings or ideas? Or does the author present multiple perspectives?

Authorial Signposts and Reader Response: Longer Fiction

Let's consider Peter's responses in his journal, then in small group discussion, and finally in another journal entry about Frances Hodgson Burnett's *A Little Princess* (Bantam, 1987; rpt. 1905). The first time he writes about this book, Peter engages in several different types of reading.

> *January 30*
> I wondered if he [Sara's father] was really rich. In today's time, military people aren't. **generative and sociocultural**
>
> Is she [Sara] pretty or not? She doesn't think she is. Others think she is. [In the book, Sara has black hair and green eyes, unlike her classmate Isobel, who has blond hair.] **generative**
>
> Is Sara supposed to be a princess because she's nice to everybody, like the fat girl who can't speak French? **generative**
>
> What's the point to the book, is my question for class. And what's wrong with green eyes? It reminds me of Hitler's ideas about everybody being Aryan [of Nordic ancestry]. **sociocultural**
>
> The doll is like a sidekick. The kids talk to the doll, and the doll helps the kids as much as it helps Sara. The way Sara uses the doll to tell the kids stories, maybe this is the only way female children can relate to themselves (through the doll). The doll is acceptable—it's blond and blue-eyed. A girl's ideas are accepted when an acceptable person is the one with the idea. [Female children see something acceptable in the doll; that "vision" gives them courage to say what they feel.] **sociocultural** and **critical**
>
> Sara supplies all that each one [each child in Miss Minchin's school] needs. She's the missing link, someone they can relate to. She accepted them. They needed that, especially Lottie and Ermengarde. **sociocultural**
>
> I've advanced to page 100, and I don't like that Miss Minchin. Sara reminds me of my cousin. I call her the Princess, from the Princess and the Pea story. **personal/empathetic**

In addition to **generative** and **personal/empathetic** reading, Peter engages in **sociocultural** reading when he thinks about the salaries of military people, when he connects the passage about Sara's green eyes to Hitler's beliefs about superior races and when he thinks about the doll's acceptability and female acceptability in society at the time. As a **critical** reader, he also tries to imagine what the doll means to the female children in the novel in an era (the Victorian period) when females were an underclass. He seems to sense the girls' lack of confidence in themselves as he tries to sort out what the doll signifies.

Peter continues his generative reading as he and his classmates discuss the book. They also move into **literary** reading as they evaluate the way the author crafts the story: they note foreshadowing, coincidence, emphasis or shaping patterns, and how the author brings characters to life.

February 5

Peter: My prediction is that she'll get the money back.

Lisa: Why?

Peter: When she's getting her ears boxed, she wonders if she is really a princess.

Kim: There's lots of foreshadowing. And then the Indian guy next door is looking for her.

Todd: Do you think he'll find her?

Kim: Yeah, why else would he be in there? It's too coincidental, though.

Peter: And I think the rat is taking over for the doll.

Lisa: The doll is not as much in the story now.

Peter: No. Well, it's there, but not as important. They're emphasizing the rat more now.

Todd: Was the doll all that important?

Kim: It showed her to be patient.

Todd: How?

Kim: By staring at her when she talked to it—and not answering.

In his second journal entry for this book, Peter moves among **personal/empathetic, narrative,** and **literary** readings. He relates the story to his own dreams and to his friend Eddie (personal/empathetic). He wonders if the entire book is a story (narrative). And he analyzes the function of stories in the book (literary). But Peter also continues to engage in **sociocultural** reading when he relates the story to the way the real world works and when he decides that fear is causing Lavinia to dislike Sara.

> *February 10*
> It's interesting how Lavinia was afraid of Sara and that's why she didn't like her. The people who didn't like her feared her because she was different. They don't understand her; she's not like them. **sociocultural**
>
> Sometimes even though she had a strong will, luck helped her [Sara]. When she was down the most, someone helped her. She needed a break once in a while. **sociocultural**
>
> Sara went through a big thing that she was afraid to open her eyes (it was like a dream when her room was transformed). That's interesting because you dream, and it's like that. **personal/empathetic**
>
> Stories helped out everybody. In the end, stories even helped with her and Mr. Carrisford, the Indian man. She told her side of the story and she wanted to hear his side of the story. Stories were an escape from reality that helped them get through things. But stories helped her more. If she didn't have an imagination, she'd be like anyone. Stories helped her fantasize, to get through it [her mistreatment by Miss Minchin]. Mr. M. [the rat that Sara names Melchisedec] turned out to be a friend. **literary**
>
> What if she never left India at all and the whole thing is a story she's telling her Dad? It would end up she fell asleep in her father' lap. [Sara's remark to Ermengarde at the end of Chapter 9 seems to have prompted Peter's response at this point. Sara says: "Everything's a story. You are a story—I am a story. Miss Minchin is a story." (page 89)] **narrative**

> "Spirit and will of any other child" (page 162) reminded me of my friend Eddie. Everyone wondered would he change when he went off to military school. Would he still be easygoing. He didn't and neither did Sara; she was always nice. [Peter is speaking of the passage in which Miss Minchin notes that any other child would have been broken by the changes in her life but that Sara seems as little changed as a princess.] **personal/empathetic**

> I thought about that I tell stories but not like that. She tells like someone who writes. Mine are fifteen-second stories. Hers are stories; mine are like television shows that go as far as I'm walking from one class to another. If I told [the stories to] someone, I'd have to elaborate, but I just picture it [to myself]. Mine are based on reality but contorted. Based on what I did. **narrative**

Peter's comparison of Sara's stories with his own stories reveals **narrative reading,** or more specifically, **narrative *literacy,*** because he compares both the reading and the writing—or composing—of stories. Peter notes that there is a difference between imagining stories as he walks through the day and writing stories down in some coherent, crafted way for others to read and understand. He compares his own inner storytelling to television shows; what he sees and hears in his mind as he walks includes scenes and dialogue similar to the scenes of a teleplay but different from those of a novel. Also, his stories are filled with breaks to go to class, similar to commercial breaks.

Peter is paying attention to the text and to his thoughts as he reads. In the process, he generates meaning about the story and thinks more about stories—how he feels about telling them and how they are told. His reading process is what theorists call "reciprocal," as we will see later on in this chapter.

INVESTIGATIONS: Ways of Reading

Read or reread a piece of literature—a fable, folk tale, picture book or novel—and consider what ways of reading you engage in:

Generative: Sorting out plot and character basics; building a framework for meaning-making.

Personal/empathetic: Developing feelings about characters and their actions.

Sociocultural: Interpreting characters' actions or behavior in terms of how the world works.

Literary: Thinking about what the story means and what themes it emphasizes.

Narrative: Filling in the gaps of the story with stories of one's own; thinking about how stories are told.

Critical: Investigating how the author or narrator really felt about events and people in the story—and in the world—and deciding if the authorial choices were balanced, objective, sensitive, and tolerant or conditioned by gender, class, or cultural circumstances.

In your journal, note your responses to the work as you read. Let your entries guide you to discover more about *how* you read. Notice whether your responses vary:

- Do you move beyond generative reading? Or do you always read simply to discover what happens?
- Do you see examples of all these ways of reading in your journal entries—or just one or two of them?
- Are there any ways of reading that you *never* seem to engage in?

Now read another piece of literature, and see if your ways of reading change. Continue investigating how you read with different literary works. Do you notice any patterns in your reading?

MEANING-MAKING PROCESSES: TEXTS VERSUS READERS

How do we make meaning of texts? Is meaning situated in the author's words or in the reader's reception of them? A story lies before us, and we are not merely deciphering the words; we are attempting to interpret them. Words have many different shades of meaning, even in stories as supposedly simple as fables. Whose interpretation counts more, the author's or the reader's? Because authors cannot always explain their work, and often do not wish to co-opt the reader's meaning-making process, the ball is nearly always in the reader's court—but *which* reader has the "correct" interpretation? Is it the one whose reading most closely matches the author's stated intention? Is it the one whose reading is the most sophisticated and complex? Or could it be anyone? Could it be a *child* reader? And who decides whose reading is "best" anyway? Politics, ideologies, cultural influences, and personal preferences affect the answer.

Ideas about reader response often fall into one of three categories—or somewhere along a continuum. At one end are those who say a story has only one valid interpretation. But this raises questions: When readers have different views about the "correct" interpretation (when they disagree about validity), whose view counts? Who has the greatest authority? Should that reader decide? And what gives a reader "authority"? Does majority rule decide? But what if the majority opinion is illogical, hastily conceived, biased, or self-serving?

At the other end of the continuum are readers who feel that words, phrases, passages, and entire works can mean any number of things; all textual meanings are unstable. Because interpretations arise from individual readers, all with their own prior experiences and unique views, the interpretive possibilities are limitless.

Between these two poles—those who believe the text contains one "correct" meaning and those who believe readers generate many valid meanings for themselves—we find "reciprocal" meaning making, which incorporates aspects of both. A look at all three categories, as they apply to children's books and child readers, will tell us more.

Text-Based Advocates

Text-based advocates believe that authors know exactly what they are trying to tell readers and that authorial signposts will emerge when readers engage in *close* readings of a work (picking apart the text to see what it *really* might be saying). They think that although different readers might find different meanings, some of the readings will be more nearly "correct" than others. In other words, some readers will come closer to what an author—conciously or unconciously—intended, than will others. Those who take this stance use biographical, autobiographical, and historical sources, as well as psychological theories, to uncover the meaning of a work.

The downside of this stance is that it can produce tunnel vision and passivity among readers. To search for and stop with one interpretation, even if that interpretation is supposedly the author's, limits one's perspectives—and the multiple insights that might rise from them. As we saw earlier, many authors want and expect readers to go beyond what they themselves have imagined. They welcome a variety of responses to their works, valuing the mind-stretching wealth of ideas—and the independent thinking—that can emerge.

Text-based reading can be active as well as passive, however. French literary theorist Roland Barthes believes that authors embed signs (symbols, metaphors, images, plot patterns, and details of words and pictures) within texts and that those signs produce "codes" for the reader's meaning making. (Readers "decode" these signs, and their decoding process produces meaning for them as they read.)

Literacy educator Margaret Meek (1988) has adopted many of Barthes's ideas in her own work in the field of children's literature and literacy. An advocate of teaching children to read with "real" books (developing literacy *through* literature), Meek sees a children's picture book as a sequence of images that signify meaning. The child must learn to read these "signs" in order to become a successful player of the reading "game," as Meek shows us with Ben, a child who had been making "slow progress with the phonics check list" (page 8).

As she and Ben begin reading a copy of Pat Hutchins's picture book *Rosie's Walk* (Puffin, 1970), they look first at the cover of the book and talk about the characters and the scene: a hen, a fox, some bees, and trees filled with apples and pears. Ben leads the discussion. He recognizes a hen coop, a windmill, and the farm buildings on the title page, and he adds his own comment: "There might be rain" (page 8).

Roland Barthes' Codes

Roland Barthes has discussed five "codes" that readers use to make meaning and that authors use to send meaning to readers.

The first is the **actions code,** which allows readers, to notice important actions, behaviors, conversations, and inner stories that characters or narrators tell. They notice the actions code as they trace the plot of a story. They ask, *What is happening here? What are the big scenes of the story? How do these scenes move the story along?*

With the **semic** or **semantic code,** readers notice small details about settings and characters that flicker through a story, poem, or pictures in order to transmit an idea. They ask *What threads of meaning are weaving through the story? What do we continue to notice? What is it adding up to?*

In using **cultural code,** they call upon unexamined assumptions about the world (the author's world or their own) in order to test the reality and authenticity of the work. These assumptions may relate to general knowledge about the world or to knowledge connected with a particular time or place. They ask, *What did we notice about the author's world—and about the author's ideas, values, and assumptions about this world? How do the author's ideas relate to our own?*

With the **enigma code** they try to solve various mysteries in the work. Gaps and blank spaces of meaning keep the work alive for them, from beginning to end. They ask, *What did we find puzzling? What do we continue to be curious about? What remains unanswered as we close the book? What truths does a puzzle conceal?*

With the **symbolic code** certain ideas emerge for readers, not necessarily from logic, reasoning, or experience, but arising, says Barthes, "like the logic of dreams" from "particles of meaning sprinkled all through the text." These ideas may cause readers to see larger patterns, make connections, and give pleasure in describing what they see or feel about a work. They ask, *What sense can we make of this work?*

Source: Roland Barthes, "On *S/Z* and *Empire of Signs,*" in *The Grain of the Voice. Interviews 1962–1980.* Translated by Linda Coverdale (Berkeley: University of California Press, 1985), pp. 74–75.

Meek is concerned about the stylized artwork. "There is no attempt at realism," she says about Hutchins's pictures. Will Ben be able to sort out the action? She is also concerned about Ben's ability to understand the story setting. His home is far from any farm. Yet to her surprise, Ben talks easily about Rosie "living" in the hen coop. "I doubt that he had ever seen a windmill and he had never encountered a fox," says Meek. "Yet he picked out the elements and seemed to anticipate something of what the story might be about" (page 8).

Meek then discusses the text of Hutchins's book. It is comprised of thirty-two words written all in one sentence that stretches out, phrase by phrase, over thirteen double page spreads: "Rosie the hen went for a walk across the year around the pond over the haycock past the mill through the fence under the beehives and got back in time for dinner . . ." How does Hutchins' "code" this story for children? Says Meek:

> Rosie's actual walk is described in the pictures in terms of the size of the trees, the nearness or distancing of the goat and the windmill. A rake, a pond, a haycock, a bag of flour hanging out of the mill, beehives and a group of carts become traps for Rosie's pursuer, the fox. The words to be read reflect a quiet stroll . . . Does she know he's there? That's a secret, but the reader decides. Rosie never looks behind, where all the action is. The fox, with his eyes constantly trained on Rosie, falls a victim to every hazard until he is stung by the bees into retreat. (page 11)

Ben liked the book so much that they read it together four more times. By the end of the day, he told Meek the story, nearly matching the words. He had learned "how a story goes in a book . . . Yet every reading yielded something more" (page 11).

Rosie's Walk has "clear antecedents" in Aesop, Meek tells us:

> But each double-page spread with its three words of text is full of possibilities. At 'over the haycock' there are terrified mice, a static tethered goat, the fox leaping so near to Rosie. (The reader has to 'read' [that] the scratch marks [diagonal lines] indicate jumping.) On the next page, the fox is buried in the hay; there's a different expression on the face of the goat; Rosie is walking on. This pattern comes four times. By the time the reader gets to 'through the fence,' he or she knows to look ahead to spot the next obstacle. But on this occasion, the author has changed the rules. The fox and the reader have ignored the empty cart, which the jumping fox tips so that it knocks over the beehives; not exactly what we expected, but there as a possibility from the very first picture . . . The reader has to learn which of the pictorial events carries the line of the story, while each rereading shows that other things can also be taken into account. (pages 12–13)

What is the essential lesson of the book—"Watch your back"? Perhaps, but Meek has a different view. The fox is in the pictures, but he is never mentioned in the words. *Yet child readers know there is no story without the fox.* Is this important? Yes, it means that children understand the major role pictures play in the **semic** code—or that they understand the semic code as an important tool for making meaning when they read. And what young children can learn to read well is pictures. "A page in a picture book," says Meek, "is an icon to be contemplated, narrated, explicated by the viewer. It holds the story until there is a telling" (page 12).

Meek's emphasis on the child's telling does not mean Ben is free to take just any path in his reading, however. In her view, Ben has to know which events carry the story line in order to be in the literary game, or at least to be a genuine "player" in it. He must distinguish the heroine from the villain (no easy task, as we have seen from examining fables), predict what will happen, feel the satisfaction of a happy ending, and evaluate the "rightness" of things (make meaning of text) in order to stay in the "game." How does he manage to do so?

Meek speculates that the rules of literary "play" match the rules of children's life play and risk taking. "In all children's stories," she says, "there are cultural features which locate them in a tradition" (page 13). Thus, Meek thinks that children's books themselves—or the author's coding strategies—*teach* children what they need to know in order to read these books. And the best books—the multilayered, multidimensional works—make the best reading teachers. Meek's way of reading might be called *sociotextual* (a combination of **sociocultural** and **literary**). The text teaches because it carries meanings that arise from cultural features of the child's life play.

Meek's stance is not psychological; she does not encourage Ben to shape the text to his own experiences, nor does she analyze how Ben's particular personality might be shaping his meaning-making. What Ben felt personally about the book, or how the book affected him, is less important to Meek than the way he responds to the literary and cultural coding.

Meaning resides first of all in the author's narrative choices, Meek would say. But what about readers and the different choices they make when they sort out

INVESTIGATIONS: How Texts Teach

Work with a child, eliciting and observing his or her responses to literature. Choose a picture book you think is particularly inventive—or one that the child chooses. Observe the way the child responds to authorial choices in words and pictures to make meaning. Observe how the child

- notices important actions, scenes, and conversations;
- notices small details about characters and setting that flicker through the story;
- steps into the author's world and tests the facts of it against his or her own life experiences;
- fills gaps in words or pictures in order to make broader and deeper meanings; and
- decides what the story is about, based on the patterns he or she is seeing.

Use the following suggestions for eliciting the child's responses:

1. If the child initiates a response at some point in the story, it usually indicates interest. To extend the response, pause and wait for the child to go on. Or ask, "What do you think about that?" or "How did you decide that?" Repeating the child's words also encourages expansion of an idea:

   CHILD: There might be rain.
   ADULT: There might be rain. (pause)
   [or]
   You think there might be rain. (pause)

2. If a child asks a question, try not to answer it quickly and directly. Encourage the child to think more and begin speculating about an answer; use the child's interest to stimulate him or her to think more. Ask, "What do *you* think will happen?" and "How did you know that?"
3. If the child does not initiate a response and you wonder what the child thinks, pause and say, "I wonder what's going to happen." Or ask, "What do you think is going to happen?" "Did you expect that?" or "What would you have done?" Do not push or probe at this point; the child's silence may indicate deep interest in the story line, so that the best thing to do is to push on; or it may indicate that the child is not ready to make a response.

words, pictures, and stories? Does meaning also reside within readers? Meek would agree that literature may serve as a shaping influence on children's personal lives, feelings, and ideas. But cultural influences also shape literature, she would say, and children make meaning based on their implicit knowledge of these influences, as they filter through a text.

What happens when theorists emphasize *readers* rather than texts?

Reader-Based Advocates

Stanley Fish was one of the first literary theorists to discuss the instability of texts and the indeterminate nature of words. What holds meaning firm, he asserts, is not a structure of conventions and codes, as Barthes or Meek would say, but the reader's own social setting. An individual's assumptions and ideas are not his or her own, Fish (1980) says. Ideas come from the reader's context, the "interpretive community" that shapes the reading activity. There is no set of literary "signs" present in a text; we simply pay a "certain kind of attention" to the text (page 326). This "attention" may result in a particular way of seeing or looking at the work, or in *many ways of seeing.* Interpretation is not a matter of uncovering an author's meaning; it is a matter of making meaning as we read. We *make* meaning rather than *find* it, Fish thinks.

Fish might look at Meek's story about Ben and say that Ben is already aware of the conventions that assisted him to make meaning of Hutchins's book. Ben sees with the eyes of a reader, he might say; readers sort out characters, plots, and ideas in stories; they predict; they notice literary conventions. Meek would agree, but she would add that some books, by the nature of their inventiveness—by their unconventionality—foster meaning-making more easily than others. Artfully crafted picture books evoke richly textured meaning-making, Meek would say.

Texts teach readers, Meek often says. Authors encode their texts with actions, semic details, cultural references, puzzles, and symbolic ideas; and ingenious texts produce good readers. Fish would say, by contrast, that readers make meaning of all kinds of texts—artistic or mediocre—and that this process of meaning-making is what produces good readers. (The more inventive the meaning-making, the better the reader).

For Fish, the meaning of a text resides neither in the author nor in the book; it rests instead in the readers and their interpretive communities—home, family, town, nation, or classroom. As Vivian Paley's work shows, children reading in an interpretive community see things differently: they are children (members of a child *culture*) and they are making meaning of a particular story at a particular moment *together.* Paley has produced nine books about her kindergarten students, their fantasy play, and their storytelling. Often she writes about their responses to literature.

First in *Wally's Stories* (1981) and more recently in *The Girl With the Brown Crayon* (1997), Paley has discussed children's responses to Leo Lionni's *Tico and the Golden Wings* (Pantheon, 1964), a story about a wingless blackbird, Tico, who wishes for golden wings. Tico gets his wish, but the golden wings anger the other birds, who accuse him of prideful thinking. So he gives the wings away—giving gold to the needy—and discovers that now he has an even better gift, black feathers like the others have. Now he has wings *and* friends.

They chirped with joy. "now you are just like us," They said.

We all huddled close together. But I was so happy and excited, I couldn't sleep. I rememberd the basket marker's son, the old woman, the puppeteer, and all the others I had helped with my feathers.

"Now my wings are black," I thought, "and yet I am not like my friends. We are all different. Each for his own memories, and his own inviible golden dreams."

From *Tico and the Golden Wings* (Pantheon, 1964)
by Leo Lionni.

Paley's discussion reveals her own take on the book. Applauding Tico as a nonconformist, she says it is not fair that he has to give up his golden wings. Paley's students, on the other hand, see Tico as his winged friends do—as too ambitious. Lionni's modern fables present the same bifocal conflicts as Aesop's do, thus lending themselves well to questions about human values, attitudes, and feelings. Readers can take Tico's side, as Paley does, or his friends' side.

What places Paley's approach firmly in the reader-based camp is her reaction to Tico's situation; she is more upset than Tico when he must give up his golden wings to make friends; but she does not think her interpretation is the most nearly correct nor the only possible reading. It is simply the one that stands out *for her*—at least, until the children cause her to see more. And herein lies the downside of reader-based thinking: It can produce tunnel vision for the reader, if the reader's own personal preoccupations crowd out the details of the text.

Paley isolates one aspect of the story: that Tico has to give up his wings. That is the primary meaning of the story for her. But the children do not see it her way. They see Tico through the eyes of the other birds. It *was* fair, they say.

Tico was "nice" when he did not have wings. When he had gold wings, he thought he was better than the other birds. They also see the story through Tico's eyes. They notice that once his friends fly away, Tico is lonely; he sees what needs to be done and he does it. "He *has* to decide to have black wings," says Wally, who creates a story in which Tico earns the gold wings through his own actions (Paley, 1981, page 26).

Wally's Tico kills a giant and receives golden wings because of his brave deed. In Lionni's story, Tico has not done anything to earn the wings when they first appear; thus, the other birds are jealous. To the children, their jealousy makes sense. Why doesn't it make sense to Paley? Why does her interpretation of the story differ so strikingly from theirs? Are the children simply paying attention to certain things that are especially important to children—friendship, jealousy, fairness? Or is Paley simply relating so strongly to Tico's nonconformity that it overshadows everything in the story for her?

Literary theorist Norman Holland (1975) says that every reader "will search out a unifying idea that matches his particular needs for sense and logic" (page 14). Writers "create by transferring unconscious wishes," says Holland, and readers do the same. The reader "transforms his own fantasies . . . into the conscious social, moral, and intellectual meanings he finds" in the work (page 16). Thus, readers read literature by focusing on whatever has significance for them. They transform it; they mold it to their own needs. From Holland's perspective, meaning resides in the reader, or more specifically, in the reader's personal identity construct, fused with certain constraints of text.

Is Tico's unconscious wish to fly with the eagles and be gloriously different a desire that matches Paley's personality construct? Is she transforming Lionni's story into a new work that meets her need for sense and logic (**personal/empathetic** and **narrative** reading combined)? Or does her own personal take on the story cause her to read across the grain of it, challenging the text, as she interprets it (**critical** reading)? In *The Girl with the Brown Crayon,* Paley has written more about this same story, expanding on her view of it:

> The behavior of Tico's friends has always been unacceptable to me . . . How harshly they deal with him. Their anger hurts me as much as it does Tico. This is unfair, I have argued over the years; and, to my dismay, each class has taken the flock's point of view. 'He made them jealous!' is the yearly refrain. 'He wanted to be too special, he didn't have to ask for *golden* wings.'

INVESTIGATIONS: Reading Against the Grain

Share a children's book with a group of children. As you begin, consider what you think the author intended the "big" idea of the story to be. Then try to read *across the grain* of the story to challenge this meaning (**critical** reading). Enter the discussion, telling the children what bothers you about the main character and what he or she must say or do to resolve the story conflict. Invite the children to express themselves freely and notice whether their responses

- are similar or different from yours;
- are similar or different from one another;
- help you get to know the children better;
- help you get to know the book—or yourself—better;
- help you to see whether the book elicits deep feelings and curiosities.

> Poor, undefended Tico. His so-called friends loved him when he was weak, but as soon as he develops in exceptional ways they abandon him. Only when he gives away his feathery splendor to a series of needy people and each golden feather is replaced by a black one do his friends glow with satisfaction and accept him back into the flock. ('Now you are just like us,' they said.) Tico is happy and the children are relieved, but I feel betrayed.
>
> Suddenly I must know how Reeny feels about Tico. Surely she, with her brown crayon and her eye for distinctiveness, will defend Tico's right to nurture a special, self-defining quality. (page 12)

At this point, Paley finds her worn copy of the book and calls the children to the rug, anticipating Reeny's response. Five-year-old Reeny—a child who impresses Paley because of her nonconformity—reveals another way to look at the reading and meaning-making process. This time, it is neither the text-based camp nor the reader-based advocates that prevail, but those who combine the two points of view.

Reciprocal Advocates

Paley gathers the children on the rug and begins reading. As they reach the scene where Tico's friends forsake him, she says, "Poor Tico. He could fly so high with his golden wings and see so many things he had never seen before" (page 12). Paley is not just filling in gaps of the story with her own strong feelings about conformity versus nonconformity. She is creating gaps where there may have been only the tiniest of openings in the story structure. But her reader-based inclinations do not limit the meanings the children are making for themselves. The rapport is strong between Paley and these children, and she is only one member of the interpretive community. The children simply integrate her feelings with their own.

It is Reeny's turn now. Paley has been awaiting her response, and she steps back as Reeny explains to them all that Tico *wanted* his friends, and he wanted them more than gold. "But see, he wasn't really thinking he's better. But *they* thinked he was . . . so he took all his gold to give to the poor people so they could have something and then he could have his friends back . . . Else he be too lonely" (page 13). As Paley now sees, listening to Reeny, Tico "must accommodate to their feelings. The choice is his to make: golden wings and loneliness or conformity and lots of friends. This," Paley adds, "from the girl who refuses to blend in, yet has everyone for a friend" (page 14).

Paley's teacher-journal entry for this day reveals that readers in an interpretive community can have different ideas about story meaning. It is not a matter of which idea is right, or even how many ideas can be right, but how rich the learning experience is when teachers encourage different ways of meaning-making to emerge and unfold:

> *Journal entry, October 15:* Reeny's social reality overwhelms mine. She takes the question of Tico's rights out of the narrow boundaries I've drawn and insists we consider, quite simply, *the way people are.* Some friends are generous to those who fly off in other directions and some feel deeply offended. On the other hand, certain individuals are more sensitive to the feelings of the group, finding ways to give away some of their golden feathers or perhaps to include their friends more often in their flights of fancy . . . (page 15)

Later that day, Paley walks home feeling she has sprouted golden wings, so delighted is she in what Reeny's response has taught her: "For her, Tico is not the martyr I have believed him to be. He is a perceptive friend who values the flock and empathizes with its feelings" (page 17). Reeny, Paley sees, has recognized Tico's empathetic gifts. In fact, she has been able to empathize with Tico so intensely that she has extended Paley's meaning-making. How was she able to do so?

According to literary theorist Wolfgang Iser, readers become so occupied by the text (the characters, the plot, the story structure) that their "individuality temporarily recedes into the background" (page 293) and different or alien thoughts—those of the author or the characters—move into the foreground of the reader's thinking. The reader sees the story's meaning as something outside the reader's earlier thoughts. How does this process work? Or why does it not work the same for all readers? Why doesn't Reeny's individuality temporarily press into the foreground, as Paley's does? How is Reeny able to think the thoughts of fictional "others," not only those of Tico but of his argumentative, jealous, fault-finding friends as well?

First of all, Reeny is a child, as Lionni's child characters are, and a "natural-born innovator" (page 4). In addition, she is an empathetic reader; she enters easily into a personality unlike her own. Perhaps of greatest importance, she knows that Paley values her responses. It is Reeny who has set Paley's study in motion with her strong response to another Lionni story, *Frederick* (Pantheon, 1967). Reeny's empathetic personality enables her to become deeply engaged with Lionni's books. But the question remains, is it something about the book that draws her in? Or is it something about her way of reading the book *in this particular setting*? We are back to square one: Where does meaning really reside, in texts or in readers? Could the answer be, in both?

As literary theorist Louise Rosenblatt (1994) explains, the reader uses the words of a book to select and organize a work of his or her own. In other words, the reader replays the author's creative role. During the actual reading event, the reader not only decodes "the images or concepts or assertions that the words point to, he also pays attention to the associations, feelings, attitudes, and ideas that these words and their referents arouse in him. 'Listening to' himself, he synthesizes these elements into a meaningful structure. *In aesthetic reading, the reader's attention is centered directly on what he is living through during his relationship with that particular text* " (page 25).

What is "lived-through," Rosenblatt adds, "is felt constantly to be linked with the words" (page 29). The text stimulates the reader's thoughts and feelings. Then, guided by those thoughts and feelings, the reader begins making meaning of the text. This aesthetic response, as Rosenblatt calls it, actually heightens the reader's "awareness of the words as signs" (page 29). Can children in an interpretive community respond in this aesthetic way? Do certain books—or certain ways of teaching—evoke **aesthetic** reading? If so, will we see the response in *all* children reading a book together, or will we see it only as an individual phenomenon? What can Paley's children show us this time?

When Reeny first encounters another Lionni mouse character, Frederick, she is "wide-eyed with wonder," says Paley: "That brown mouse seems to be just like me!" she exclaims. Why? "Because I'm always usually thinking 'bout colors and words the same like him" (page 5). Paley finds this response surprising. She hasn't seen Reeny in this way at all. Frederick, as Paley knows, is a field mouse who concentrates on his own ideas above anything else, which reminds Paley more of herself than of Reeny.

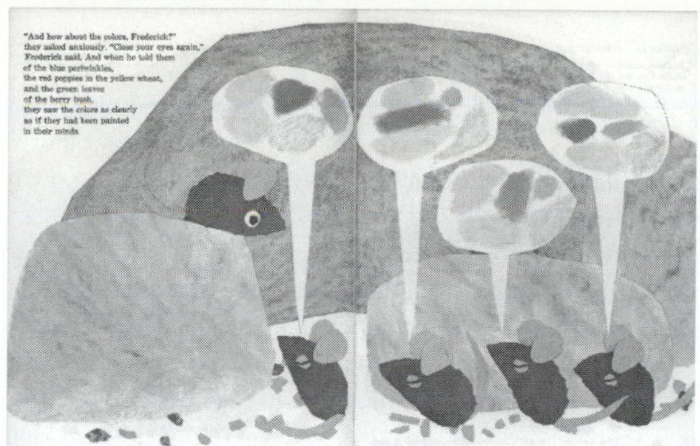

From *Frederick* (Pantheon, 1967) by Leo Lionni.

Because Frederick is an artist, thinking—or concentrating—is his work. By dreaming and imagining, he gathers words and colors for his stories and poems, rather than *doing* or gathering food like the other mice. With similar concentration, Reeny begins tracing the mice with her finger, drawing them with her brown crayon, taking the character into her very being, defending him when her classmate Cory says Frederick is mean: "He so quiet . . . You hasta be quiet for thinking" (pages 6–7).

As Reeny draws the mouse's eyes, she returns to the book to see how the mice look when they close their eyes. At this point, she asks to hear the book again, and as she listens, she rubs the colors, saying "My crayon is dreaming" (page 7). Then she holds up the book, crying out "Guess what, guess what! This is Leo Lionni we doing!" (page 8). Later she begins composing a song about the Leo Lionni mice, and the other children sing along with her.

Reeny pays attention to the text and to her own reception of it—her feelings, associations, attitudes. She also pays attention to the responses of others, like her classmate Cory. Listening to it all, she synthesizes these elements into a meaningful structure that she is creating alongside the author. She draws the mice; she closely observes the author's drawings to get her own picture just right, and she lets her crayon signify the artist in her. Just as both Frederick and Lionni are artists, so is she. Her comment that they are "doing" Leo Lionni reveals that she is able to pull back and watch herself and her classmates in their strong engagement with text and to describe it vividly—very much an aesthetic response. Literature has become a way of *knowing* for her.

Finally the children act out the story, and to Paley's surprise, Reeny decides to be one of Frederick's friends, rather than Frederick himself. As Reeny explains, it is not that she does not want to *be* Frederick, it is that the other mice "love him so much" (page 10), and she wants to be part of that group that feels so deeply about Frederick. She knows how it feels to be the artist—to be Lionni and to be Frederick. Now she wants to know how it feels to step back and be Frederick's audience as well. Reeny is testing out all the roles in order to submerge herself more deeply in this story, because it has become so meaningful to her. She can experience the story—or live through it more fully—if she becomes one of the mouse friends who loves Frederick.

Noticing that Lionni offers "a clear and consistent form of reference for our feelings and observations" (page 18), Paley suddenly decides to spend the year reading all of Leo Lionni's books in her classroom. They will study one book with great intensity and "dramatize, paint, and discuss its finer points, comparing new characters

INVESTIGATIONS: Aesthetic Reading

In Paley's discussion of Reeny's reading, we see **aesthetic** reading—deep, personal engagement with a book. Add aesthetic reading to the six ways of reading listed earlier and see if you ever read this way. When does it happen? What books cause you to become deeply engaged, living through the experience with the characters?

Now share some favorite children's books with a group of children. Invite them to express themselves freely and notice whether any story stimulates aesthetic reading among them. Notice also whether they

- make emotional connections between the text and their own personal lives;
- become absorbed in what they are thinking, feeling, seeing, and hearing as they *experience* the story, living through it with the characters;
- form mental images about plot, characters, and setting;
- become actively and personally involved in a search for meaning in the book;
- imagine, select, explore, connect, and create ideas; and
- reflect back on their own responses or feelings about the story.

to those [they] already [knew] and to those in other books as well" (page 49); then the characters will enter their stories, their play, and their conversations.

Art, music, games, math, science, and writing fill Paley's kindergarten curriculum, as do birthday and holiday celebrations, visitors, and picture books by other authors—including the children's own stories and the stories Paley creates for the children. All of these ideas and events produce new ways of seeing. "To invent is to come alive" (page 50), Paley says.

In the next two chapters, we will take a closer look at stories as one of the most important influences affecting children's growth into literacy.

INVESTIGATIONS: Transmission and Reception Theories—and You

We have examined transmission-reception theories in three categories: *text-based* (Barthes and Meek); *reader-based* (Fish, Holland, and Paley); and *reciprocal* (Rosenblatt, Iser, and Paley).

With the first category—text-based theories—meaning derives from the way a reader negotiates the conventions and gaps in texts to produce an interpretation of the story. *The text stimulates the meaning making.*

With the second category—reader-based theories—meaning derives from the way an interpretive community decides the meaning of a text or from a reader's personal identity construct as it meets the text. In either case, *the reader initiates the meaning-making.*

With the third category—reciprocal theories—meaning derives from the way a reader selects and organizes a text to evoke a new work. The reader reenacts the author's creative role. The *text stimulates the reader, who then initiates meaning-making in concert with the verbal and visual "signs" of the text.*

With these categories in mind, select a children's book and read to see how *you* derive meaning from the books. Afterward, read a different book and see whether your way of meaning-making changes. What—in your opinion—determines meaning? The reader? The text? Or some combination of the two?

Continue to observe yourself as a reader as you examine other books. See whether you can construct any reception theories of your own, based on your personal reading patterns.

PART THREE

Children and Adults: Learning and Teaching

Chapter 9

How Children Learn to Read and Write with Literature

Topics in This Chapter:

- Learning to read; reading to learn
- Guided versus individualized reading
- Literature-based approaches to reading and writing
- Literature-related approaches to reading and writing
- Language-based approaches to reading and writing
- Children and Storymaking

"And how many hours a day did you do lessons?" said Alice, in a hurry to change the subject.

"Ten hours the first day," said the Mock Turtle, "nine the next, and so on."

"What a curious plan!" exclaimed Alice.

"That's the reason they're called lessons," the Gryphon remarked, "because they lessen from day to day."

This was quite a new idea to Alice, and she thought it over a little before she made her next remark, "Then the eleventh day must have been a holiday?"

"Of course it was," said the Mock Turtle.

"And how did you manage on the twelfth?" Alice went on eagerly.

"That's enough about lessons," the Gryphon interrupted in a very decided tone. "Tell her something about the games now."

"The Mock Turtle's Story" in Alice's Adventures's in Wonderland, 1865
—Lewis Carroll

We have been talking about stories, how writers compose them, and how readers respond to them. Now we will turn to an exploration of how children learn to read and write with literature, and as we do so, we want to examine what writers for both adults and children have said about their early reading experiences. Their recollections tell us much about the importance of story. They also tell us a great deal about the often neglected category of **family literacy.** Children often begin the reading and writing process on the home front. They interact with literature in many different—and *pleasurable*—ways as

- adults tell stories,
- family members read aloud and children listen and chime in,
- adults and older siblings offer help in the decoding process,
- children and adults have leisurely conversations about books, and
- children have freedom to read any time, any place, any book.

LEARNING TO READ; READING TO LEARN

Young adult novelist and educator Aidan Chambers (1993a) says that, as a child, he stared at the pictures in a collection of Aesop's fables as his mother told him the stories, and the concept of reading fell into place. Yet he did not become a "proper" reader until age nine. Chambers remembers his passage into formal reading as he was recovering from an illness:

> I could read individual words, but the trick of making the words into sentences and the sentences into paragraphs evaded me. Until one evening just after my ninth birthday when I was looking at the pictures in a book I'd been made to bring home from school, and suddenly everything came together and I heard voices talking in my head. One voice was telling the story, the other voices were the people in the story talking to each other. I was almost frightened for a moment, certainly shocked, as well one might be when a book full of strangers suddenly inhabit your head all unannounced. I still remember the moment vividly, with as much excitement, as fresh, as immediate as ever. My parents were in the room at the time; my mother noticed that a change had come over me and realized what it meant. Which must have been a relief; worry about my backwardness had meant gloomy meetings at school. (page 14)

Still, Chambers remembers, he did not become an avid reader at that point. The reading habit took root simply by chance a year later. Suddenly, learning to read—or gaining **print literacy**—fused with his desire to learn more about other things, including:

- the story itself,
- a friend's response to a book,
- the subject of nature, which was of special interest to him,
- the genre of poetry,
- the world of books generally, and ultimately,
- the meaning of life.

When Chambers was recovering from a three-week hospital stay for scarlet fever, his grandmother presented him with a picture storybook called *Worzel*

Gummidge by Barbara Euphan Todd (Puffin, 1941). Aidan began "reading" it by looking carefully at the pictures (drawn by Elizabeth Alldridge) one by one, from the front to the back of the book. One picture in particular caught his attention:

> It is the full-page drawing of Susan sitting in the farmhouse kitchen eating with a large spoon from a pudding bowl. The wartime hospital food had been meagre, dull, and repetitive . . . so I was curious about what Susan was eating. And why out of a pudding bowl, something my mother would have thought 'not right'? . . . In the end there was only one way to find out. Read the story. I set to and the result was that for the first time I read a book from cover to cover without wanting to stop, and for the first time the words in print flowed so fluently that I didn't even notice them but was aware only of the theatre in my head playing out the story as it happened, it there in me, me there *in it.* A kind of paradise, a life fuller, livelier, richer than my own everyday life, and one replete with meaning: intuitively, I understood why it was as it was, why it was *just so.* (page 15).

Worzel Gummidge not only became the first book Chambers read "from cover to cover not wanting to stop (or the story ever to end)," it was also the first book he reread (thirteen times during the next two years). Chambers's family moved at about this time, and the boy across the road was just his age and a reader. They shared books, says Chambers, "and read bits to each other that then seemed more inordinately hilarious than they had done when we read them to ourselves. This was my introduction to the added pleasure of sharing enjoyment by talking about what one has read" (page 17).

Aidan's friend Alan encouraged him to join the town library and showed him how to use it. "The place scared me to death," says Chambers. "Had Alan not been with me, twisting my arm and blackmailing me, I'd never have gone inside. It seemed very large and dauntingly mysterious, sepulchrally hushed." They went every week to the library; it became a routine because Alan wanted to swap books so that they could read the same ones and then talk about them. The two boys always had one book in mind to search for and then went their separate ways to find something new. Books in this day, Chambers explains, had no illustrated covers and no jacket blurbs to tell about the story. Children had to depend on titles, authors, and what they found on the pages. Still, Chambers managed to discover many of the classics.

Between the ages of eleven and fourteen, Aidan wanted to read stories about the countryside or ships. Listening to a children's radio program called "Wandering with Nomad," he learned about nonfiction books that encouraged him to wander the countryside, keeping notes in a nature diary. Later he wrote to one of these authors, asking for advice in nature writing, and he received a reply.

At age thirteen, Chambers encountered a teacher, Jim Osborn, who became his mentor. Other teachers had read aloud in Chambers's classrooms, but Osborn managed to turn *pleasure* reading into *literary* reading:

> My first formal encounter involved *Kubla Khan.* Jim strode into the room . . . carrying a record player . . . said "Listen," and dropped the needle onto the record. . . . After four seconds of this, he lifted the needle, pointed to the nearest boy and said, "Repeat what you heard." The boy couldn't. Jim went round the class. No one could. . . . Jim gave out a set of books. A page number was rapped out. "Listen, again." . . . Jim read the poem to us himself. Made one or two of us have a go at the first lines. Played some more of it on the gramophone.

Asked us what we thought of it, if we liked anything about it, whether we knew anything about the author. Gave us the story in his own words. Made us listen to the way the sounds were orchestrated. No concessions. No attempt to ingratiate. An insistence on precision. Sweated work. And an assumption that we would discover in this something enjoyable and worth possessing.

I don't know about anyone else in the room that day, but I do know that when Jim swept out . . . the world for me had changed. Words had come to mean more than something. Language was a sacred river. Poetry was fertile ground. No book was ever the same again, never simply a means to a pastime activity that filled spare corners of my life. (pages 20–21)

By the time Chambers was fifteen, he was using half his spending money on what he felt were the best books—Penguins. There were still no cover illustrations nor blurbs in the early 1950s, but on the back cover, publishers often included a small photo of the author and a brief biography, and these were very influential for Chambers as he made his choices. Cycling home on Friday night, he would try the first few pages "to get myself used to how it was going to be" (page 25). Then, after the movies, he would read late into the night and up through the next Friday, entering the title, author, and a one-line comment in his notes. A favorite book, he discovered, was "quite as engaging as the effect of *Worzel Gummidge* five years earlier. . . . Books, literature, reading were about what happened to me, and what happened to me made a kind of sense, when discovered in writing, that it didn't otherwise" (page 26).

Finishing D. H. Lawrence's novel, *Sons and Lovers,* at about this time, Chambers knew he wanted to be a writer. First he felt an "I wish I had done that" feeling; then he thought, "Why shouldn't I?" The school librarian, Percy Moss, had invited Chambers to become a member of the school library staff and help build a school library. Aidan began purchasing books, unpacking them when they arrived, entering them in the classification system, and shelving them, responsibilities that resulted from inspired teaching on the librarian's part, he notes, since Percy Moss always discussed the list with him but never interfered with his choices.

Chambers went on to become an educator, editor, literary theorist, and, novelist—in other words, a lifelong reader and writer. His story illustrates four pathways into reading, each equally important to producing **lifelong literacy:** *personal* (his independent pleasure reading from *Worzel Gummidge,* at age ten, to *Sons and Lovers* at fifteen); *social* (his shared reading and discussions with a new friend, Alan); *specialized* (the lessons in particular subjects he had with Nomad and Jim Osborn); and *professional* (the selection process he undertook in his library job with Percy Moss). His story also teaches us that the process of learning to read does not begin and end with learning to decode print; it is a lifelong undertaking, and a reader's skills and competencies develop as the reader changes and grows.

In 1997, the Children's Book Council published a collection of stories by twenty-nine notable children's book writers, *Books Remembered: Nurturing the Budding Writer* (Lisa Mahmoud, editor). The writers tell about how they became readers and writers. Only a few of these writers—Joan Aiken, Katherine Paterson, and Laurence Yep—write about their actual entry into the decoding process. Each of these authors was an early reader, and each recalls how parents read aloud, stimulating the future author's later love of reading. Joan Aiken's memories are particularly instructive:

> Reading aloud was a daily habit in our family. My mother read aloud to me; she also read to my brother (twelve years older) and to my sister (seven years older). My brother read aloud to my sister; she read aloud to me. My stepfather and my mother read to each other. And I, as soon as I was old enough to do so, read aloud to anyone who would listen; my mother and I plugged our way steadily through the Bible, one of us reading and the other slicing beans (or whatever). . . . And, of course, we all read to my younger brother, who was seven years my junior.
>
> These various threads of reading-aloud made, I now see, a very interesting and comfortable series of extra connections throughout the family. It was as if we all met on a whole system of different interlocking levels: While I was having *Pinocchio* read as a bedtime treat, my elder brother and sister would come and curl up on the end of the bed to listen; and while they were having *The Cloister and the Hearth* [1861, by Charles Reade] after tea, I would be building with my bricks on the sitting room floor and listening to *that,* understanding, I suppose, less than half of what went on, but the half I did understand, wow! what a gripping story!—with its terrific adventures. When I was seven or eight I read it all over again to myself and enjoyed it even more . . .
>
> Looking back I now realize that my mother cunningly practiced the carrot-and-donkey technique in *her* choice of books to read aloud. She would never read us something that we were able to read ourselves. As soon as I had achieved the last page of *Peter Rabbit* and so was officially declared a reader, my mother read books that would still have been to difficult for me unaided. (1997, page 20)

Laurence Yep's parents read to him as far back as he can remember, mostly comic books. (His first real vocabulary word was "obnoxious" from *Little Lulu.*) "And when I was ready," he adds, "books were there" (1997, page 52). He found the Oz (by L. Frank Baum) books at the library, which opened a new world for him; so did the science fiction and historical fiction shelves; he would later write in both genres himself. "Though it started with something as simple as comic books, I had discovered the secret pleasure of reading—of projecting myself in my imagination through time as well as space" (page 54).

Katherine Paterson recalls reading on her own well before first grade, she had listened to so many stories read aloud. But she kept this skill a secret. Her first-grade teacher "was unhappy enough that a five-year-old had been placed in her class, so I stumbled through Dick and Jane with the rest of the slow readers" (1997, page 41). Paterson's comment might cause us to stop and reflect on how stories help produce successful readers. What opened the doors of reading for these writers? Many different features stand out, but the first one on the following list was nearly always the key:

INVESTIGATIONS: Learning to Read and Reading to Learn

You have been reading writers' stories about their early experiences with reading. Try to remember your own experiences as you entered the **print literacy** stage. What helped you to begin reading? Was it an experience in school or out of school? How did **family literacy** contribute to your learning to read—or did it? Which came first for you in your reading experiences—learning to read, or reading to learn more about something else? Share your story of learning to read—or reading to learn—with others.

1. A particular story or book engaged the child's interest.
2. The child had a thirst for knowledge.
3. The child began to recognize letters.
4. Interesting new words caught the child's attention.
5. A book or story connected to something positive the child had experienced—or to a special place the child knew.
6. The child heard a favorite story, book, or poem read many times.
7. A particularly engaging or mysterious character propelled the plot.
8. A parent or grandparent paid special attention to the child, or an illness brought special attention.
9. The child read series or comic books (the literature of popular culture).
10. An accessible library or book collection was available.
11. Engaging illustrations caught the child's interest.
12. The child became interested in captions for the illustrations.
13. A narrator's commentary or dialogue between characters created interest.
14. The child discovered the right book at the right time; something in the book connected to the child's curiosity or emotional needs.
15. The child met a friend who was an avid reader.
16. The child was fascinated with a special subject or pastime and wanted to learn more about it.
17. A teacher was passionate about literature.
18. The child had the chance to buy books for him or herself.
19. A teacher gave students responsibility for choosing classroom books.
20. The child's family had a rich collection of books.
21. The family was one in which members read aloud to one another.
22. The parents read what the children wanted to hear—comic books, series books, or classics.

Because none of these features are characteristic of synthetic "nonstories" like the Dick and Jane tales, we might wonder why so many schools—even today, years after Katherine Paterson suffered through them—still use schemed or basal approaches to teach reading. Have reading schemes become suddenly better, or are teachers and school systems simply bogged down in tradition? Because so many children's writers, like Paterson, learned to read at home, their stories have a great deal to tell us about natural approaches to reading acquisition. We will consider the contrasts between real and basalized stories as we examine the topic of learning to read with children's books.

First we will look at two very different approaches to classroom reading instruction that have been around for some time now: guided reading and individualized reading. Then we will look at three forms of literacy teaching: literature-based, literature-related, or language-based.

GUIDED VERSUS INDIVIDUALIZED READING

In the beginning, basal readers helped teachers and parents measure students' progress. Many school systems were hiring teachers who had taken far fewer teacher-training classes than colleges and universities require today. One way to ensure that all children covered the same territory and emerged with the same competencies was to use an approach in which children mastered skills and subskills sequentially (*guided*—or directed—reading). Teachers instructed children to identify letters, (alphabetic approach), sound out words (phonics), recognize particular words or sentences (the whole word/whole sentence method), understand particular words (vocabulary study), decide what the author was saying in a passage (comprehension), and become familiar with literary concepts such as setting, plot, and genre.

As time passed, an entire industry grew up around skills teaching. It began when textbook staffs created synthetic stories like the Dick and Jane stories that the Scott Foresman Company introduced in 1930. These stories provided teachers with controlled-vocabulary reading materials. Soon these little stories had elaborate instructions, workbooks, worksheets, and flash cards to accompany them.

Publishers marketed these materials as appropriate for all children in particular grade levels, and these little books—primers and preprimers, as they were called—probably did little to harm children like Katherine Paterson, who were able to survive their boredom. However, other children, unlike Paterson, did not have a well-stocked library at home, nor attentive, story-reading parents. Whether primers fostered a love of reading among these children is another matter.

By 1959, Jeannette Veatch had discovered that the one-size-fits-all approach to reading was not best or even necessary for most children. Veatch began to write about a new way to teach reading with children's books. Teachers continue to reinvent this method when they phase out basal readers and adopt literature-based approaches.

Individualized Reading

How to Teach Reading with Children's Books (1968) by Jeannette Veatch was a simple, twenty-five-page illustrated handbook that explained how teachers could create a classroom in which the pupils "cannot be stopped from reading." Veatch called the classroom teacher a "teacher-reader." In this format, teachers would reveal their own love of books as a model for students.

Veatch told teachers to get books of all kinds from librarians, PTAs, book clubs, and the attic, and to get lots of them—about a hundred, or three for each student. She also instructed them to find a good place for the books and place them face up, organized under general headings—animals, fun, science, poetry, sports, and adventure, for example. Next, the teachers were to find a place to sit where they could see all the students as they read and fix up a private place for conferencing. Finally, said Veatch, teachers should show children how to choose books wisely, selecting books they were sure to like. From that point on, students should simply read, getting help when they needed to from dictionaries, other books, the teacher, friends, the pictures, beginning sounds, and by guessing. All students should read individually, to themselves.

Veatch also believed children should write stories of their own after reading and share these stories with a friend. Other possible follow-up activities included a class newspaper, drama, letters, discussions, science experiments, research projects, crafts—and more reading. "WORKBOOKS—KEEP OUT!" Veatch concluded.

Individual conferences with students should take place twice a week for five to ten minutes. While others continued to read silently, an individual child would talk with the teacher about

- the book,
- the child's interest in the book,
- why the author might have written it, and
- what the book said about the child's world.

The child should also read a little of the book aloud, and the teacher should keep a record of the child's interests, reading progress, and reading difficulties. Later, the teacher should study all the children's records to find common problems and to plan group conferences for help in particular skills.

The value of using children's books or real literature, said Veatch, was that "creative artists" produced them, and they provided many choices. There was no one-size-fits-all book in the real world; there were as many books as there were readers. Therefore, no child had to read any one particular book. According to Veatch's plan, students could always stop reading a book they did not like and choose a new one. She was also an early proponent of **critical literacy:** "They [children's books] have a point of view—you can take it or leave it." When she encouraged children to give responses to their books and what they revealed about the world, she placed herself squarely in the reader-based camp.

Although more basal reader publishers are now incorporating children's literature in their textbooks, their teacher manuals keep children tied to a code-cracking model, finding one "intended" meaning for a passage. Child readers must derive the meaning that writers of the basal manuals decide is *there* in the text. Consider the basalization of a Leo Lionni story, *Alexander and the Wind-Up Mouse,* originally published as a trade book in 1969 (Pantheon), a Caldecott Honor book, and a popular story with six- and seven-year-olds.

The story, in its original form and format, shows Alexander, a lonely mouse, who meets Willy, a wind-up mouse and one of Annie's favorite toys. Soon Alexander and Willy are talking as human friends do. Willy understands Alexander's desire to be loved. He tells Alexander about a magic lizard in the garden who can change one animal into another. When Willy loses his place as favorite toy and is thrown away, Alexander, who dreams of becoming a favorite wind-up toy like Willy, has an even better idea. He asks the Wizard if Willy could be a real mouse—like he is. Running back in the dark, Alexander discovers the empty toy box; then, to his relief, he finds Willy—real and alive—in the mouse hole. The mice hug one another, run away, and dance until dawn.

Lionni dramatizes this mouse adventure with an intricate—and artistic—pattern of words and pictures, with every picture contributing to the overall effect, every word building to the dramatic conclusion, and every word feeding into—and fed by—the pictures. What happens when this book is basalized?

Guided or Basal Reading

Basal reading lessons usually have five general parts:

- Preparation (advance organizer)
- Silent reading

From *Alexander and the Wind-Up Mouse* (Pantheon, 1969) by Leo Lionni.

- Teacher questions to apply comprehension skills
- Workbook exercises to reinforce skills
- Extensions of the story

Preparation involves six steps. These steps include everything that the teacher must do before a child can open the book and begin trying to read:

- Build a background
- Establish motivation
- Set the purpose
- Introduce vocabulary
- Teach phonics skills
- Examine illustrations

The preparation stage is necessary because children are not working on materials they have chosen themselves. Nor are these materials familiar stories, songs, or poems that children might have memorized earlier. Familiar materials would produce a problem; teachers would not know if they had taught a new word or if children already knew or guessed it. To avoid this problem, Guided Reading introduces new materials. Thus, students (whether or not they have any interest in a story) must go through a long string of events—or an "advance organizer"—before beginning the book.

The basal manual or guide gives teachers a summary of the story that they can relay to children, letting the children know what the story is about generally in order to **build background.** (Book blurbs and movie ads do somewhat the same thing.) In this case, the story "Alexander and the Wind-Up Mouse" has been anthologized in a basal program. The program places the story into a thematic category of friendship and a subcategory of favorite toys "so special" that they are a child's friends (Lionni, 1989, page 205). The basal publisher directs teachers to ask if students have ever had a special toy and to discuss their answers in order to stimulate interest in the story; this builds **motivation.** The purpose for using this particular story in the textbook—according to the teacher's manual—is to teach the concept of fantasy: "Setting Purposes: Strategies for Reading Fantasy." So to **set the purpose,** students are asked to think about fantasy stories and "to use the term *fantasy* . . . That way they will know what to expect" when the mice talk and magical things happen (page 205).

Next, the basal writers list words from the story they think children might not understand: "quivering, broom, hungry, tears, adventures, cuddle, precious, dawn, thrown, purple, pebble, circles, mysteriously, blinding, and heart" (page 202). Teachers **introduce vocabulary** and **teach phonics skills** before the story begins—out of context or isolated from the story—so that children will be familiar with these words when they meet them. Thus, children at this point hear or see made-up sentences such as "The *quivering* mouse hid behind the large *broom*" (page 202).

If children were reading the story in the original trade book version, they would learn word meanings in natural ways, from the narrative context and the pictures. When they come to the word *broom,* they would find Lionni's picture of a broom and the words: "All Alexander wanted was a few crumbs and yet every time they saw him they would scream for help or chase him with a broom." For the word *quivering,* children would find the sentence, " 'Is it true that you could change me into a wind-up mouse?' asked Alexander in a quivering voice." Because they would be following the story line, they would know why Alexander was quivering—not in fright, but in anticipation and hope.

From *Alexander and the Wind-Up Mouse* (Pantheon, 1969) by Leo Lionni.

Children working with this basal series also receive a worksheet with a list of words like *broom* and the following directions: "Look at the underlined letter or letters in the sentence. Circle the word with the same vowel sound. The choices for answers are "a. nose; b. cross; c. school; d. hurts" (page 202). Then teachers take the practice sentence and discuss the underlined letters in relation to decoding skills and word meanings. For example, the basal manual instructs teachers to have children identify the initial consonant of *quivering* (kw/qu), and divide the word into syllables. Teachers explain that *quivering* means "shaking or trembling," and they ask why a mouse might quiver. They expect the supposedly "correct" answer: "Because it is afraid." Children are then asked to supply the correct answer for the use of a broom: "to sweep the floor" (page 203).

Basal manuals also instruct teachers to call attention to **illustrations** that accompany the stories—though they may be different from the original trade book illustrations. In this textbook version, a picture of the mice playing in a pair of shoes has been taken out of the original sequence to become the cover picture. The original cover of the mice playing in a Russian nesting doll has been discarded, possibly because the textbook writers thought that the shoes would be a more familiar object than the doll.

But the doll also carries meaning: Both Willy and the doll are toys, and the doll is a pull-apart toy with parts that fit tightly together to make a whole entity. The doll is thus a perfect symbol of friendship for this story about two mouse friends who each help the other to survive. In addition, none of the pictures in which Alexander is alone have been retained in the basal version, possibly because of space limitations and budget constraints. Thus, the impact of Alexander's loneliness and the tension between togetherness and isolation is lessened considerably.

In a guided lesson, children study the pictures and consider what kind of story they think this one will be. In this case, teachers encourage children to use terms such as *fantasy* and to see that in fantasies, events happen "that couldn't happen in real life" (page 205).

The **preparation** phase is now complete. After the children read the story to themselves—**silent reading**—teachers go through the story with the students. They ask **comprehension questions** that help them determine whether the children are understanding what they are reading—at least, according to what the publishers have decided they should understand—and to see whether children are able to decode the words. Most teachers have children read aloud at this time. Then they ask questions—those in the manual or questions of their own—to teach problem-solving strategies such as:

- Comparing/contrasting
- Drawing conclusions
- Interpreting
- Predicting outcomes
- Ordering events sequentially

At the first opening, the comprehension question checks to see if children are able to draw conclusions: "Why do you think Alexander wanted to find a few crumbs?" The book provides suggested answers. In this case, the answer is: "He was looking for something to eat. He was not a pet mouse who got fed regularly" (page 207).

Basal "kits" also supply teachers with **workbooks** and worksheets to reinforce skills and with activity pages—**extensions**—to teach skills in written expression or to foster creativity. In this program, one such page is a "Story Grammar" sheet filled with questions related to the setting, characters, characters' feelings at the beginning and the end of the story, the goal of the main character, and what the character learns. The purpose of the activity is to help students recognize the structural elements in a story: settings, characters, characters' feelings, characters' goals, and changes in characters' goals.

A workbook page, "Writing Activity: Story" (page 65) invites children to write a story about the story in the book. They plan their story on the chart, telling who will be in it, where it will take place, and what will happen, first, next, then, and last—making these decisions at a "prewriting stage". They then write sentences for the story, using three vocabulary words from Lionni's story—the "writing" stage. Finally, they read their story, checking it against the questions on the chart and checking the spelling, and then they make a neat copy—the "revision" stage (pages 65–66).

Individualized Reading versus Guided Reading

The strength of the individualized approach is that children work directly with real literature and have real purposes for reading it (children choose stories that match their interests and life experiences). Children and teachers are active, independent learners. From the beginning, everyone is a reader and everyone is reading together, although in different ways—as "real" readers do. Children might "read" pictures or tell stories to themselves as they linger over the pictures. Or they might work in pairs, helping one another identify words, as they talk about pictures and stories. Thus, everyone gains experience—and competency—in independent thinking.

When teachers must move from compartmentalized instruction to integrated, cross-curriculum, and *interdisciplinary teaching,* as school systems these days

INVESTIGATIONS: Individualized and Guided Reading

Examine basal readers for examples of anthologized trade books. Compare the anthologized stories with the original picture books to discover whether publishers:

- retained all the original pictures;
- retained the original artist;
- retained the original cover picture;
- positioned the words and pictures differently in the new version.

Then study the original book and think about how the author's choices might affect children's meaning-making. What is the importance of each picture? What would children lose if textbook publishers omitted any one of these pictures? What is the importance of the picture sequence as the author has arranged it? What would children lose if textbook publishers tampered with this sequence in some way, removing or rearranging scenes?

Finally, share the original trade book with a group of children. Invite the children to speculate about why the author might have made certain choices for the original book. Does the cover picture announce the book in a way that no other picture does? Do the original artist's choices concerning style, scene, mood, colors, and details contribute to the story meanings? Does the original artist's positioning of characters in scenes contribute to the story meanings? Would repositioning characters produce a loss of meaning for child readers?

often insist they do, those who have been working in individualized settings are less dependent on the authority figures in basal manuals telling them every step to take. They can adjust to new programs more easily. Not only are they more adaptable because they have had to do a great deal of creative thinking as they worked with individual children, but they are also more confident about their abilities to take on new tasks.

The strength of the basal approach is still accountability: Every child is learning the same skill at the same time, so teachers can check student competency in particular code-cracking skills. But a question arises—Do the strategies for developing comprehension skills apply equally to the reading of imaginative literature and the reading of nonfiction materials?

What Is Interdisciplinary Teaching?

Integrating the curriculum or the disciplines has become an increasingly desirable notion recently, but often educators use terms like *integrating* or *crossing the curriculum* and *interdisciplinary teaching* interchangeably, when these categories are really approaches that lie at different ends of a continuum.

At one end of this continuum is the thematic or topic-based unit. Teachers, or teachers and students, choose broad ideas, concepts, or subjects, such as Native American Legends, Saving Our Planet, Art as Social Action, or Strong Females, that could embrace, integrate, or "cross" many different curriculum areas, such as science, math, social studies, language arts, fine arts, and kinesthetic studies. For language arts, students might read, write, talk about, and view materials connected to the topic. They might integrate the language arts materials with a fine arts project, with kinesthetic studies, or with a social studies or science unit.

At the other end of the continuum is the inquiry—or problem-solving—project. In this type of project, teachers (or teachers and students) choose some question that arises out of a particular curriculum area or stands outside the curriculum as a real-life venture. For example, they might choose to ask:

- What was the most important invention of North American indigenous people?
- What was a day in the life of a North American Indian female like: hardships or rewards?
- Why do people tell stories?
- How do you make a movie?

Such an inquiry-based project requires students to synthesize ideas from many curriculum areas, rather than simply "covering," crossing, or integrating them. It works outside the bounds of compartmentalized thinking, causing students to generate new ways to think about knowledge or to study the world. It fosters interdisciplinary, rather than merely integrated study of a subject.

Between these two ends of the continuum are many different ways of breaking down existing boundaries or of studying the world in the usual ways. How—and why—shall we construct new knowledge? Those favoring interdisciplinary learning and teaching cite many advantages for students, according to Guice and Angelis (1998):

- Increased understanding of multiple perspectives concerning human values
- Increased use of critical and creative thinking
- Increased ability to synthesize knowledge and solve new problems
- Stronger concept of student as learner
- Stronger concept of student as member of social and cultural communities
- Increased motivation for learning

Teachers enjoy advantages also:

- Stronger relationships with students
- Increased flexibility in scheduling
- More ways of teaching new concepts
- More and better ways of working with colleagues
- Increased understanding of how curriculum areas connect with one another

Source: Sherry Guice and Janet Angelis, "Integrating Curriculum," *English Update* (University of Albany, The Center on English Learning & Achievement, Judith Langer, Director; Fall, 1998; pp. 4–5).

Because the anthologized materials in basals are predominantly fiction, folk tales, or poetry, textbook editors seem to believe that all reading is the same—fiction or nonfiction—and that we can teach all reading materials in the same way. But as we saw earlier, Louise Rosenblatt makes a distinction between fact-driven, information-based *efferent* reading—which is closely related to the purpose readers have for *nonfiction* reading, and feeling-driven, experiential-based *aesthetic* reading—which is closely related to the purpose readers have for engaging with *imaginative* literature.

Rosenblatt (1991) describes the two stances readers may take toward texts as operating on a continuum, depending on the reader's focus at the time. The person reading fiction for *pleasure* and simply absorbing information about the world as incidental learning would be at one end of the continuum. (She would call this side *aesthetic* reading.) The person reading nonfiction to glean *information* but deriving pleasure from exploring a favorite subject would be at the other end. (She would call this side *efferent* reading.)

Efferent reading can be pleasurable, if readers are reading nonfiction that interests them. Efferent reading can also lack pleasure. If children are reading a Lionni story in a basal textbook, they are focused on efferent reading (trying to find vocabulary words or answer a worksheet question), and the pleasure of reading to experience the story fades quickly. They are extracting information from the story, rather than living through the characters' experiences.

Of course, on many occasions children might be balancing a dual focus. If children in a basal classroom were listening and responding to a Lionni story during read-aloud story time, they would be experiencing aesthetic reading. If the children liked mice and wanted to read more about how mice live, and a nonfiction piece about mice turned up in their basal reader, they would be reading efferently and satisfying their curiosity—a pleasurable experience.

For the most part, however, basal instruction does not encourage children to participate *naturally* in literature experiences. They do not read simply to enjoy the story—to share the characters' experiences or to live through their experiences alongside them. They do not respond to the story naturally by telling or writing a story *in their own words for their own reasons.* Basal instruction is based on the principle that children need materials to practice with as they learn to decode words, to make meaning of printed passages, and to encode (write) messages—not on the idea that they will gain these skills naturally as they read for interest and pleasure.

Despite the fact that basal readers have been anthologizing more and more trade book stories, they have continued to emphasize convergent—one intended meaning or one "correct" meaning—over divergent—creative—thinking. Basal reading means learning problem-solving strategies in order to determine what someone—usually a basal editor—thinks a story selection *means.* A story is a comprehension test that the child must take every time he or she opens the textbook, rather than an *experience* to be shared with a character or other readers, and writing is an exercise in using words from the story to produce synthetic sentences.

According to this way of thinking, literacy means acquiring the skills to decode or encode the nonfictional print found in newspapers, workplace reports and memos, reference tools (dictionaries, encyclopedias, textbooks), letters, advertisements, signs, tickets, menus, and recipes. Reading to make one's way through the world we call **print** or **functional literacy.** But, as we have seen, many different literacies exist.

Print literacy might seem to be at the core of all the other literacies. Often, however, children learn to love literature—and to consume it avidly—by listening to stories, reading pictures, and recognizing familiar words long before they learn to decode. Print literacy is, at the same time, "survival" literacy. Though children might make their way through life without ever engaging in aesthetic literacy, who can imagine trying to negotiate the highway or an airport without print literacy skills? But reading instruction need not *exclude* the pleasure of imaginative literature to be effective.

It might, in fact, be easier for children to learn to decode print if they were to do so as natural readers, immersed in stories for pleasure rather than skills training. Then they would acquire many other literacies at the same time that they became *functionally* literate. They would learn to be critical thinkers; they would develop narrative and literary competencies; they would read in sociocultural, aesthetic, and empathetic ways, and they would read and write to generate learning about themselves, others, and the world, rather than simply to receive or send messages.

Functional or print literacy need not always serve as the first step in acquiring additional literacies. As writers like Aidan Chambers, Joan Aiken, Laurence Yep, and Katherine Paterson reveal, print literacy can intersect with other literacies from the beginning, if children are behaving as real readers and writers *before* they are actually able to read and write. In other words, children can think of reading and writing as ways to learn more about themselves, others, and the world, even as they are learning how to decode words. This happens when adults—parents, teachers, librarians, and authors—regard children as apprentices learning not just a set of skills, but a new craft.

LITERATURE-BASED APPROACHES TO READING AND WRITING

One of the simplest ways to teach reading is one that many parents and caretakers use naturally with children at home: They produce natural meaning-making experiences through *conversations* about reading and books. The child learns from the adult many techniques that good readers use. The adult leads the child to become a reader by talking about the book—and about life outside the book, as it relates to the story—and by inviting the child to ask questions about both. (The games begin, as Alice knew, when learning is fun.)

Bedtime Story Reading

Gordon Wells (1986) observed mother and child conversations during story reading and found, in the most productive situations, that the mother scaffolds the child's meaning making. She "leaves space for the child to offer comments and ask questions and her contributions build on his, extending his understanding" (page 152) of both the story and the world.

In one of the conversations he discusses, the mother shares a verse picture book with her son, age 3. The book is *The Giant Jam Sandwich* by John Vernon

Lord, who created the story and pictures, and Janet Burroway, who produced the verses (Houghton Mifflin 1987). The mother reads the first page, and David hears that millions of wasps descended one hot day on the little town of Itching Down. Then she asks David, "Who is this here on the first page?" (152)

When he replies "the wasps" (152), she gives no evaluation like "Right!: She simply proceeds with the reading after the child responds. "Here's some more [wasps], she says "Wow!" (152). David initiates a response of his own at this point. "I don't like wasps" (152). His mother asks why. He answers, "Because they sting me" (152). She offers some information, saying that wasps only sting if they are angry.

She continues to read and David learns that the wasps chased away the people who were picnicking and the farmers gathering hay. Then they stung Lord Swell, fat and bald, on his "pate" (meaning the very top of his head).

David joins in with the word "pate," and she responds with a question, to see if he knows that a pate is the top of a person's head. Mother and child take several conversational turns discussing the word "pate." He says "hair." She says, "Well—yes. It's where his hair *should* be. It's his head—look, His *bald* head. All his hair's gone" (page 153). Pointing to the bald-headed character, Lord Swell, she both leads him back into the story and defines further the word "pate."

The mother then asks David if he thinks wasps eat people. He answers no. She asks what wasps eat. He answers vegetables, and they both laugh. David asks about a detail in the picture, and his mother answers him directly. Several conversational turns occur. She then asks another question about a picture, and the reading proceeds in this manner—picture, question, response, picture—until she returns to the text. As the story ends, David participates as reader by filling in a rhyming word (page 153).

In conversational reading—or meaning-making—each participant asks questions out of curiosity, and each offers answers just as naturally. Here we see David, at different points in the reading, say that he does not like wasps because they sting, that wasps eat vegetables (a humorous hypothesis on his part), and that a fly swatter is a sign (a placard or poster) on a stick. His mother *explains* that wasps sting only when they are angry, *laughs* along with him about the vegetables, *asks* whether he knows what a *pate* is, *tries to discover* if he thinks wasps eat people, and *compares* a fly swatter to a plastic spatula in order to identify it as something used to hit a wasp (or to teach him what a swatter is, so that he makes better meaning of the story).

The adult reader is, as Wells says, helping the "child to explore his or her own world in the light of what happens in the story and to use the child's own experience to understand the significance of the events that are recounted" (page 152). As the child sees print and hears the flow of language, he joins in when picture clues enable him to predict text. Because he has heard the book before, he can remember certain words and phrases of text. Thus, he is actively engaged in the reading process long before he becomes an independent reader. Listening to the story, he begins to figure out how stories work: They have repeated structures; they have meaning; they have outcomes.

David hears repeated patterns and begins to predict words, word-arrangements, outcomes, and meanings of words. He does not recognize the fly swatter; perhaps the picture looks to him more like a sign. (The slots of the swatter could easily be taken as printed words, their legibility blurred by distance.) But from his mother's input, he can bring meaning to the text and obtain meaning from it; in other words he can behave like a reader.

Readers constantly sort out the meanings of texts by using context to push themselves on through the story. They classify naturally: A sign on a stick and a swatter each produce a shape that David knows, so he substitutes the word *sign* (an image he knows) for the word *swatter* (an image he doesn't know) as he views the pictures. Readers make discriminations and reason things out quickly in order to proceed with the story.

David's mother enables him to behave as a natural reader at this point. She values his meaning-making as *learning.* As Frank Smith (1978) defines learning, it is more than simply comprehending a text—more than simply relating new experiences to older, more familiar ones; it is building upon what we already know. It is changing the old or elaborating on it—very much a **generative literacy.**

David's "miscue" (Goodman, 1986, page 52), his "picture reading" of a swatter as a sign on a stick, takes him, for the moment, away from meaning. When he asks his mother what the sign on the stick says (when he asks her to read the sign to him), his mother simply begins to explain what a swatter is. Then David learns—through natural dialogue—more about the story. David's mother never makes him feel unsuccessful; his confidence remains high. He is "reading" because his mother treats him as a reader and invites him to participate in the reading process on his own terms. The parent provides a model of the way readers build a framework of meanings—again, generative literacy.

The parent provides a model of natural reading. She places a high priority on the story itself, on reading to learn what happens next—or on pushing forward to keep the momentum. An equally high priority for her is the child's participation in the storytelling process. She invites David to become a full reading partner when she pauses often to allow his meaning-making to unfold.

When children enter school, teachers take up where parents leave off, using literature-based approaches that are similar in many ways to bedtime story reading. Their apprenticeship approaches have been called reading with "real" books (Hart-Hewins and Wells, 1990; Meek, 1988), learning to read by reading (Meek, 1982), or "read with me" (Waterland, 1985, 1989). Teachers serve as active partners by reading *with* children and allowing them to decide what they will read—just as David is rereading a favorite book here.

Says Liz Waterland (1988), who has written extensively about her use of apprenticeship reading with six- and seven-year-olds: "We must accept that children are not 'cheating' if they read a text already known or if they ask the adult to read first and then follow; that the vital object of the exercise is not to see if the child can decode, build words, guess from context or exercise any other skill, but to get meaning and pleasure from the story" (page 25). How do teachers help children gain meaning and pleasure from stories?

INVESTIGATIONS: Meaning-Making Conversations

Share a book with a child, and encourage the child to make connections between the story world and the child's real world. Let the child join in to complete lines of text, to ask questions about the words and pictures as they relate to the child's own experiences, and to make meaning of the story and of the world generally. Offer responses of your own to encourage the child to talk. See if your shared reading produces shared (give-and-take) conversation.

They talk with children in *small groups.* They invite children to help one another sort out stories in *literature circles* and *peer partnerships.* They conduct *individual reading lessons and conferences* with students about their reading progress.

Small Group Teaching and Learning

Small group settings are important in fostering **generative** and **literary literacies.** Children might be simply learning to behave like readers—sorting out texts through picture reading and listening to stories read aloud. Or they might be learning to decode—or gaining **print literacy**—and learning better how to read literary patterns in words and pictures. In either case, the teacher can help them—as reading apprentices—learn the *craft* of reading. Educator Sonia Landes (1985) asks children two questions again and again: "What do you see?" and "What does the picture tell that the text does not?" (page 54). These open questions leave children free to voice their own thoughts. They also "send the children back and forth between picture and text, responding all the while to the wholeness of the story" (page 54).

Landes also recommends asking children in small groups what "pleases or frightens them in a picture and what makes them feel happy or sad, friendly, safe, or in danger." Then teachers "will have led them into reading and understanding ideas through symbols" (page 53). Landes discusses four ways that author-illustrators communicate ideas through symbols. The first occurs through the artists's *manipulation of size and perspective* so that the scene—and details of the scene—shape the meaning. The second occurs through the *size and shape of the entire scene.* "Open borders imply freedom and fantasy," says Landes (page 53). The third and fourth ways occur in the *cover picture(s)* and the *structural design* of the book.

The cover (back and front) functions as a "true wrapping around the book," Landes says (page 51). It serves to develop character, mood, and theme by setting the scene and luring the reader into the story. The structural design shapes the text, as when the ending of the book comes back full circle to the beginning. On a second reading of the book, Landes asks children to look at the first and last scenes of a book and to tell what they see. The same characters usually appear in these scenes, she says, but they are changed. Complication leads to resolution. She also asks children, as they look at the first and last scenes, whether they can make connections between the two. Examination of the cover is important at this time, too. Sometimes the first and last scenes are on the front and back covers.

Aidan Chambers (1993b) advocates helping children "tell each other what they know and what they have discovered" in their reading (page 58). He finds the question "How did you know that?" useful; it causes students to return to the text and to "their experience of reading it in order to discover the source of their knowing" (page 60). In his literature study groups, Chambers begins with a general question such as "What did you first notice about the book?" just as Landes begins by having children look at the cover picture and tell her what they see. He then moves on to questions such as "What parts [of the book, story, or poem] did you like? What parts puzzled you? Did you notice any patterns?" (page 98).

Educator and reader response researcher Don Fry (1985) reveals another way to interact with children in small group settings so that children see themselves as readers. In his work with young readers, Fry often begins with a very general question, "Why don't you tell me a little bit about the story?" (page 117). He might explain that he has only skimmed the book or that he does not know the story that well; he only discovered it the day before. In other words, Fry places the child in the role of the "expert"; thus, he removes any threat of right or wrong answers.

As he and the children read books to share impressions and compare responses, Fry always asks children to tell him more about their ideas, revealing his respect for the child's growing interpretation: "Tell me a bit more about______. Is he the main character in the story?" (page 120). His stance is that of the interested listener; thus he fosters **personal/empathetic literacy.** Eight-year-old Clayton discussed his favorite scenes from *The Snowman,* a wordless picture book by Raymond Briggs (Random House, 1978), with Don Fry:

CLAYTON: I like that best where he runs and flies. And this is my favorite, the sad part, where he melts at the end.
DF: Yes. Yes, it is a bit sad, isn't it?
CLAYTON: Yes. Usually when I do it I don't look at the end page.
DF: Why?
CLAYTON: It's so sad.
DF: When you read the book you don't look at the last page?
CLAYTON: No. I always turn it over to the white pages and then go back to the front cover. (page 119)

Literature Circles

Teacher educator Kathy Short and teacher Gloria Kauffman (1988) explain how the concept of "literature circles" in the reading workshop mirrors the concept of "author circles" in the writing workshop. In literature circles, children share a favorite book; in author circles, they share their own texts as part of the writing process. In either circle, they receive feedback on what they share.

Short and Kauffman begin with open-ended questions such as "What was this story about?" or "I wonder why [*x* did not see that *y* was . . .]" (pages 109–10). As Short (1995) says, "the primary focus of a literature circle is not on the reading process but on life and inquiry" (page xi). Short and Kauffman value open questions because they enable children to share reactions about what they find most interesting in a book.

The literature circle discussion takes off into the children's interests and into the "strengths of the particular book" (page 109). Open questions about these interests continue to drive the discussion. The children determine the direction of the talk at all times, although the adult may ask more specific questions to help children link the literature to their life experiences. The adult encourages children to "expand and support their comments" (page 109).

INVESTIGATIONS: Small Group Teaching and Learning

With a small group of children or with a group of your friends, study a book to deepen your understanding. Encourage participants to share their early impressions of a book—their questions, puzzles, and insights—and to develop their understandings as they share and hear additional interpretations.

Short and Kauffman see these circles—literature or author—as especially valuable for giving students a way to explore half-formed ideas with others" (page 107), giving them a **generative,** meaning-making capacity as well as a **sociocultural** one. As the two educators explain the origin of the circle concept, children had thirty minutes a day for individualized reading in Gloria Kauffman's first-grade classroom. She also read aloud several times a day and shared big books. They also had writing experiences to complete the authoring cycle: they wrote personal journals, letters, written stories and reports, and published books of their own. Yet something was still missing—"a way for children to explore intensively the meanings they were constructing during reading with other readers and to present these meanings publicly to others," as they did during their author's circle (page 106).

To deepen children's understandings about literature, Short and Kauffman created the now widely implemented concept of literature circles—a time for children to meet in small groups, explore newly formed ideas, and "revise their understandings of a piece of literature through hearing other readers' interpretations" (page 107). Writing process educator Lucy Calkins (1991) tells of a visit to Kauffman's classroom, which had by this time progressed to fourth grade. So impressed was Calkins with the students' work with text sets, she began incorporating this practice in her own writing process work:

> As part of her literature program, Gloria's children gather in small adhoc groups to read and discuss clusters of books. When I was in the classroom, Gloria's children were divided among five text sets, each text set loosely fitting under the umbrella of pioneer life. Several children were reading copies of Patricia MacLachlan's *Sarah Plain and Tall.* Another cluster of children was reading picture books about quilts, including Patricia Polacco's *The Keeping Quilt,* Tony Johnston's *The Quilt Story,* and Valerie Flournoy's *The Patchwork Quilt.* Still other clusters were reading about early immigration to this country, pioneer families, and family traditions. In each instance, the first task of the cluster was for each member to read all the books. Then the cluster members would gather to brainstorm all the ways they might talk about their shared texts. On huge sheets of newsprint or on the chalkboard, each group made itself a web of possible angles for discussion. One group, for example, decided they could compare the families in the different books, or discuss the various roles the quilt played in each of the stories, or look at the various techniques used by the illustrators, or discuss differences in authors' styles. (page 133)

Writing enters the literature circles through literature "logs" that children keep about their responses to the books. In these journals we find

- notes about characters (how they connect to readers' lives and why they act as they do);
- notes about what students liked or did not like about the story;
- predictions about the story and the characters;
- personal meaning-making;
- ideas linking books to life experiences; and
- notes about the author's crafting choices.

The logs help students "organize their thinking and think more deeply about the literature," say Short and Kauffman (page 112). They also open up discussion because students write about issues or questions raised in their group discussions as they share logs with one another.

Working as a classroom researcher with fifth graders, Shelley Harwayne (1992) took the literature log strategy a step further, inviting students to imagine what they might talk about with a friend concerning literature she had read aloud to them. Afterward, they opened their notebooks and wrote to probe their ideas further. Harwayne asked the students to write responses in a two-column format. On the left side, they wrote what the story was about; on the right side, they wrote what the story made them think about. Thus, students would shift from writing about literature to writing literature themselves. Ultimately, Harwayne saw phrases like "I wonder," "I realize," "I think," and "I notice." Thus these students moved beyond simply telling whether they liked or did not like a book. Harwayne's strategy shows us that literature logs are one of the best ways to help reader-writers bring meaning to a story or make meaning of it—**generative literacy.**

Peer Partnerships

Peer settings are important in fostering individual and collective meaning-making. With older children, adults step out of the picture and group members assume responsibility for their reading schedule, their selection of books, and their questions. With younger children, adults might place themselves nearby, listening in and chatting.

Teacher/researcher Barbara Kiefer (1983) watched first and second graders engaged in partnership reading. They selected several books and read to one another: One child read a page; then the other child read a page. Some children concentrated on words more than pictures, she noticed, unless the suspense built to the point that they needed to stop and examine the picture more carefully. Once the high point passed, they moved quickly to the end. Other children stopped more often to discover what they saw as they read. Often children expressed feelings, made predictions and inferences, questioned one another, and exchanged information about stories.

In small group settings, children set their own reading goals: what pages to read, what passages or pictures to share or discuss, what issues to resolve. Teachers might set aside time in the classroom schedule for book browsing and study groups (daily, twice weekly, or three times weekly) and then assume a more inactive, behind-the-scenes position. Penny Redman (1995), a fifth-grade teacher, describes taking notes for a "debriefing" at the end of a group meeting (page 64).

Teachers might also assume the role of co-researcher, as Elizabeth Close (1990), a seventh-grade teacher, reveals. Close asks students to jot down questions and responses they have to books as they read; then she selects certain questions as springboards for discussion. Students often work as partners, writing notes to

INVESTIGATIONS: Literature Circles

Create your own literature circle with a group of children or peers. Collect text sets of books—books that are connected in subject matter, genre, theme, setting, plot, or characters to some umbrella topic. Encourage group members to read the books and brainstorm ways to talk about them. Notice the learning taking place as children talk about books. Encourage members to also keep literature logs and to share their responses to literature.

one another, or in small groups of three to four students, talking together. Close joins in at intervals as a co-reader.

Another popular approach is to talk to students about books through teacher-student notes or letters, as Nancie Atwell has described in *In the Middle* (1987/1998). Atwell began by asking students to tell her what they thought and felt about certain books and authors—and why. She invited them to ask her questions and then to respond to her answers. In this dialogic format, Atwell's students developed strong opinions about authors and took greater satisfaction in their own writing, because they were reading as writers.

Individualized Reading Lessons

Liz Waterland describes her apprenticeship reading approach with beginning readers in *Read with Me: An Apprenticeship Approach to Reading* (1988) and *Apprenticeship in Action* (1989). Her children first listen to her read stories; then they begin to join in as she reads, as we saw David doing with his mother earlier. Next, the students begin to take over the reading as they learn more words from the context; finally, they begin to read independently. In this system, Waterland points out, teachers do not need graded texts or reading "levels." No book is too difficult for a child if the child shows interest in it, since the child is simply behaving like a reader while the adult does the actual reading or joins in when the child finds the book too difficult. With this approach, children take pleasure in a self-selected book and in making meaning of it **(generative literacy).**

Teachers utilizing an apprenticeship approach fill their classrooms with books that have natural language, rhythm and pattern, illustrations that support and enrich the text, humor, artistic quality, and emotional content. A particular book "speaks" to a particular child who is emotionally involved in the story **(aesthetic literacy).** Then the child is likely to work harder to read that particular book.

To encourage independent reading, the adult might begin reading the story, then invite the child to take on the larger burden of the reading. The adult watches carefully to see what strategies the child uses to make meaning. If the child pauses for some time, the adult might suggest that the child go back to the sentence beginning and read up to the puzzling word or that the child read on to the end of the sentence—back-tracking or running forward. The adult encourages the child to look for picture clues and also to guess. Waterland (1988) suggests two questions at this point: "What is this word likely to be?" and "Does the word begin with the letter or couple of letters that it should if [your guess] is right?" (pages 35–36).

For those using an apprenticeship approach, meaning-making about the story comes before the study of phonics or of letters in isolation. What gives a letter or sound meaning, says Waterland, "is its place in written text and its use as a small

INVESTIGATIONS: Writing to Children About Books

Encourage a small group of children to write to you, as Nancie Atwell's students did, telling you about the books they are reading. Then read these books yourself and write back to the children, telling them about your own feelings.

part of that text. The word 'well' has no meaning till we know if we are reading about hospitals or singing 'Ding, Dong, Bell' or if we are just exclaiming in surprise" (page 34). The child must be emotionally engaged in a story before the child learns how to use particular reading skills. Thus **generative, personal/empathetic,** and **aesthetic literacies** actually precede **print literacy** in this approach. Waterland quotes Margaret Meek's words in *Learning to Read* (1982): "The adult's job is to read with him what both can enjoy, to let him see how the story goes, to help him observe what is there to be read, and to tell him what he needs to know when he finds it difficult" (page 16).

The child moves from listening to a story, coming to know a variety of words, and telling various parts of the story, to approximating the text with greater and greater exactness **(print literacy)** and observing the way a story works in terms of narrative patterns **(literary literacy).** In Meek's words (1987), the text "teaches the reader how the book is to be read." The way the story is told "shapes the reader's understanding of it . . . the writer, or in most cases of early reading, the artist, is the real teacher" (page 1). The first episode in a story is often repeated, and then both episodes are related to what happens in the end. But certain words are all the while carrying what Meek calls the "narrative drift" (page 2), and children must sort out which words these are. Also, they are learning that "more is meant [in a text] than is said," or that "stories are hidden in stories, and the readers are expected to know the secrets of what is referred to" (page 4)—**narrative literacy.**

Readers must learn to make stories mean more than they actually say; at the same time, they must read closely the author's clues in words and pictures, maintaining a delicate balance of reading both the lines and "between the lines." The individualized reading lesson in an apprenticeship approach is therefore valuable for fostering **generative, literary, narrative** and **print literacies** *all at the same time.* The adult who works with the child as the child is coping with a challenging text has a good opportunity to help the child see the fine points of reading: nuances of style and genre, artistic puzzles, and sophisticated patterns in words and pictures.

Children with competence in interpreting texts, or in **literary literacy,** have the confidence to take on more challenging texts. As they do so, they become more skillful in reading these texts and more likely to continue reading others like them. Literary literacy is often the key to lifelong reading of nuanced texts or what we often call *quality literature.* Could narrative literacy be the key to lifelong writing?

The reading "lesson" can become a reading "conference" when the children are working in individualized settings and the teacher needs to check on progress. In a conference, teacher and student sit down together, usually at two-week intervals, and

INVESTIGATIONS: Reading with Real Books

Help a child learn to read a children's book. First let the child choose a favorite book to read with you. As you read the book aloud, invite the child to join in when he or she can. Then continue with apprenticeship reading strategies (see Liz Waterland's ideas). If the child is struggling with a book that is too difficult, let the child's interest be your guide. If the child continues to struggle, try to find a book that is a good match for the child's competencies (more pictures, fewer and simpler words and shorter phrases).

the child reads a favorite passage. The teacher notes on a running or continuous record the child's fluency, meaning-making strategies (word recognition and self-correction), intonation, and story interpretation. The teacher converses with the child about the book, the author, the connections the child is making between the book, his or her life experiences, and other books. The teacher might also ask what the child is reading at home. The teacher watches to see if the child takes pleasure in reading, and the teacher tries to stimulate the child's interest in literature in various ways: suggesting related books, sharing responses to the book, and inviting the child to engage in creative ventures with literature—writing, storymaking, artwork, and drama.

The reading conference might involve seven steps:

1. The teacher asks the child how she is getting along in her reading. The child reflects on what she is reading outside of school; the child might begin talking about a particular book, describing it, and telling what part of the book she is now reading; the teacher listens and elicits more responses.
2. The teacher asks about favorite books, authors, or characters the child has mentioned in previous conferences ("Do you like all the E. B. White books, or just *Charlotte's Web?*" "Did you like *Stuart Little?*" "What kinds of things did Stuart do?")
3. The teacher chimes in with his or her own responses to the child's favorite books, encouraging a conversation rather than a testing format.
4. The teacher mentions other books the child might enjoy; the child might tell about additional books she has read or about favorite parts of a book (the conversation keeps going).

The Running Record

The running record tracks the students reading progress. The record might include the teacher's notes about a student, in four categories: general response to the story, reading strategies, reading growth, and literacy progress both in and out of school.

The student's *general response* involves taking pleasure in the reading process. (Is the child selecting books easily and enthusiastically? Is the child seeing links between literature and life?)

Reading strategies involve fluency in oral and silent reading, intonation, prediction, and self-correction. (How easily and quickly does the child move through a passage? Does the child place emphasis on certain words or join certain words together to produce meaning for the listener? How does the child identify new words? How does the child make sense of the story? How does the child sort out passages, when what the child says makes no sense in terms of what went before or what comes after?)

Reading growth involves a comparison between the child's strategies now and at an earlier time. Again fluency, meaning-making strategies, word recognition, intonation, prediction, matching sound and sense, and self-correction play a role.

Literacy progress involves an overall look at the child in terms of the child's reading and writing strategies and activities. (Is writing lagging behind reading—or vice versa—or are they working in tandem? Does the child enjoy reading and writing equally? Does the child participate easily in both? Does the child read and write easily with others? Does the child expect to figure out words, passages, meaning of stories in both reading and writing activities? Is the child reading and writing in a variety of genres—reading fiction, nonfiction, and poetry, and writing stories, poems, informative reports, and scientific observations?

5. The teacher asks the child what she might do to extend her ideas about a book (the teacher encourages the child to engage in literacy events surrounding books). The child makes suggestions.
6. The teacher asks the child what she is reading in the classroom today. The child and the teacher discuss the book (cover, book blurbs, author/illustrator); the child reads a little, and the teacher notes the child's meaning-making attempts, word recognition, self-correction strategies. (If the child makes sense of the passage, the teacher does not intervene.)
7. The teacher asks about other stories or poems by the same author, asks what book the child is thinking of reading next, and asks what the child is writing about her reading at this time.

LITERATURE-RELATED APPROACHES TO READING AND WRITING

Apprenticeship approaches work well with most children in classroom settings; however, some children need extra help at the beginning, when they are first trying to read. When they do, teachers turn to various approaches for reading acquisition such as the Reading Recovery program that New Zealand educator Marie Clay first described in the early 1970's

Reading Recovery

Reading Recovery is a specialized program: Children are taken out of classrooms, given individual help for a span of time, then released back to the classroom when they reach the reading level of their classmates. But many of the methods and procedures this program uses are those that any teacher might use when special intervention is necessary.

As with the basal approach, Reading Recovery teachers begin by introducing the book to the children and familiarizing them with the plot, vocabulary, syntax, pictures, and style of writing. The more children know about the story, these teachers feel, the easire it is for them to decode it. Reading Recovery teachers use the text as a site for instruction in decoding, because, like basal teachers, they think the reader needs to unravel and comprehend the text.

Says Clay (1985): "When you read, you have to produce responses which are precisely the ones the author wrote. You have to match your thinking to the author's" (page 7). When Reading Recovery teachers talk about children making meaning, they mean that children are making the one meaning that they (the adults) have decided the author meant. Children must extract this as the "correct" (author-determined) meaning of the text. Reading Recovery therefore follows a text-based, code-cracking model.

Unlike the basal approach, however, in which teachers enact a set of step-by-step activities, Reading Recovery teachers observe children and analyze the strategies they are using and the help they need. The teachers then adjust their teaching to meet those needs. Reading Recovery teachers do not keep children in special instruction longer than necessary—a practice that produces boredom and frustration.

Neither do they neglect children who are not able to master what others in the group can do—a practice that produces frustration and humiliation. Rather, they use an individualized intervention program for first graders that begins where the child is, not where the textbook series is.

Reading Recovery practices arise from three assumptions:

- Children have "stores of knowledge and ways of processing information from the world and from language, and literacy instruction can build upon their prior knowledge" (Clay, 1991, page 56).
- The school experience can help children who have otherwise not been able to learn to read, even if they do not have high scores on intelligence or maturity tests or if they are second-language users.
- Children show us how to help them; therefore, close observation is the first step to teaching them.

The program emphasizes problem-solving strategies that teachers see children using, rather than teacher-directed activities. Children lead, and teachers follow their lead, monitoring and helping them to search for cues (aspects of the text that help readers see how the text is to be read) and asking questions to encourage the children's self-monitoring. For **semantic** (meaning) **cues,** Reading Recovery teachers ask, "Does that make sense?" For **syntactical** (grammatical) **cues,** they may ask: "Does that sound right?" or "Can we say it that way?" For **graphic** (letters) **cues,** the question might be: "Does it look right?" And for **letter-sound cues,** "What would you expect to see?" (Clay, 1985, pages 73–74).

With this approach, children use graded series of "little books" written especially for this program, similar to basal reader "stories." But these texts are written in natural language, as opposed to the controlled vocabulary format that basal readers often use. Children puzzle out the words and sentences in these texts, and the teacher records what the children say and do. The teacher's objective is to uncover the processes each child is using for responses and self-corrections. The teacher says, "I liked the way you worked that out. How did you do it?" or "How did you know that?" If the child hesitates, the teacher asks, "Why did you stop there? What did you notice?" or "What were you thinking about there?"

The teacher constantly observes what strategies the child is using and helps the child to implement additional strategies. The teacher also helps the child to understand the strategies he or she is using. If a child is using cues from the sentence structure, the teacher might say, "You found the hard part. Where was it?". If a child needed to use a meaning-making strategy, the teacher might ask, "What happened in this part of the story?" If the child needed to use a strategy for letter recognition, the teacher might ask, "What would you expect to see at the beginning? at the end? after the *M?*" (Clay, 1985, page 73). Observing the child's reading behavior is what this approach is all about (**generative** and **print literacies** combined).

As teachers observe the child's reading behaviors, they might detect difficulties such as

- word by word reading,
- inattention to meaning, or
- inattention to first-letter cues or endings of words.

Or they might see *strengths* such as

- reading fluently,
- enjoying the plot and character's actions,
- taking the initiative in working on words or reading strategies, and
- making associations between literature and life experiences.

Information about both difficulties and strengths finds its way into the running record, and the teacher also keeps a record of the child's growth in adopting new strategies. The running record is a continuous part of the ongoing teaching, as opposed to standardized tests that report group progress at periodic intervals. The teacher monitors the child's concepts about print as the child progresses through increasingly difficult texts such as the little books written especially for the Reading Recovery program, trade books, or children's dictated stories.

Reading Materials in Reading Recovery Programs

The little books made for Reading Recovery Programs are manufactured materials that use natural language. With these books, children can more easily make predictions in their own words and in the language people in real life use. As children progress through these little books, their words expand in natural ways; no child is ever held back or given a false sense of what literature is, based on a controlled vocabulary format.

Like basal readers, little books are not children's trade books in the commercial sense, but they are nevertheless actual stories. Teachers may also substitute trade books if they select familiar books that relate to individual children's personal experiences and their stages of reading development. Beginning teachers who are adopting Reading Recovery methods might find it difficult to select books to link with different stages of reading acquisition. A good resource for such a plan is *Real Books for Reading: Learning to Read with Children's Literature* by Linda Hart-Hewins and Jan Wells. Hart-Hewins and Wells (1990) identify five stages of reading development:

- Prereader (child chimes in as adult reads, or child "reads" pictures)
- Beginning Reader (pictures enable child to predict words)
- Emergent Reader (pictures help child predict and decode words)
- Developing Reader (pictures support child's meaning-making)
- Independent Reader (words, not pictures, carry the meaning)

Reading Recovery teachers also use simple stories that children have dictated to an adult scribe for student reading materials. As Clay (1985) explains her procedure for story dictation, the adult invites the child to tell a story—or to make a sentence. The story or sentence might be about the best part of the story the child just read or about some topic of interest to the child. The teacher first talks with the child about something the child has done or read, or about a TV show the child has seen, a subject that interests the child, or an experience the class has had. The child then draws a picture and tells a story about it.

The teacher encourages the child to write the words he or she might know, while the teacher writes difficult words or takes the story down as dictation. Phonics instruction becomes a part of the process at this point, but it differs from the phonics lessons in basal readers. In Reading Recovery, teachers do not emphasize words or sentences in isolation, as basal workbooks and worksheet exercises do; instead, children examine letter-sound correspondences in words *as the words appear in the story context.* Children also work with letters on a magnetic board to make words—an encoding exercise.

Story dictation in the Reading Recovery approach involves seven steps:

Five Stages of Reading Development

A closer look at the five stages of reading development reveals that in the **prereading** stage, children do not yet have any concept of print. The adult must do the reading, though the child may chime in from memory or "read" the pictures. Good books for this category include wordless picture books, patterned books in which only one word changes from page to page like Eric Carle's *Have You Seen My Cat?* (Picture Book Studio, 1987) and concept books like Tana Hoban produces and like Bill Martin and Eric Carle's *Brown Bear, Brown Bear, What Do You See?* (Holt, 1983).

In the **beginning reader** stage, children have some concept of print. They need books that will help them develop an awareness of the one-to-one correspondence of print to sound. Such books have a picture and a sentence on every page. They also have many repeated words and repeated sentence patterns so that children can easily chime in. The pictures must help predict the vocabulary, and the print should be large and well-spaced. John Burningham's little picture books like *The Rabbit* (Crowell, 1974) and *The Baby, The School, The Friend,* and *The Snow* fit this category.

In the **emergent reader** stage, children understand the concept of a word: They know that each word in a text is a separate unit and that it corresponds to one spoken word. They can find isolated words on a page; they can point to first letters of words, and they can follow print across the page. They are developing a small sight vocabulary. Children at this stage use picture clues and initial consonants to help decode unknown words. Books in this category tell a story and have well-spaced print. They usually include a picture on each page, and the pictures help children predict the words of the story. Only one or two sentences appear on a page, and these sentences are often patterned with strong rhythms or repetitions. The language structure is still close to the oral language patterns of young children. Many of Pat Hutchins' books fit this category, including *Rosie's Walk* (Puffin, 1970). Eric Carle's *The Hungry Caterpillar* (World, 1969) also fits here, as does Janet and Allan Ahlberg's *Each Peach Pear Plum* (Puffin, 1979).

In the **developing reader** stage, children use a combination of cues—semantic, syntactic, and phonic—to decode words. They have developed sight vocabularies, but they still need the support pictures provide, a clearly printed vocabulary, and familiar words and ideas. Books have more print on the pages now, and the print might be smaller or appear in more innovative formats. Sentences might also be more complex, and children need less patterning (less rhyme and repetition) now. Many of Ezra Jack Keats' picture books fit here, as does Maurice Sendak's *Where the Wild Things Are* (Harper, 1963). Arnold Lobel's Frog and Toad books (Harper) and Else Minarik's Little Bear books, illustrated by Maurice Sendak, (Harper) also work well for developing readers.

In the **independent reader** stage, children can read fluently, silently, and for longer periods. Pictures take a backseat to words, although they break up large blocks of text. The print is smaller now, and stories take on a literary style. Books include anything from Eric Carle's *The Grouchy Ladybug* (Harper, 1977) to Janet and Allan Ahlberg's *The Jolly Postman* (Little, Brown, 1986), picture storybooks by Shirley Hughes, Beatrix Potter, and William Steig, and novels by Roald Dahl, Beverly Cleary, and E. B. White.

Source: Linda Hart-Hewins and Jan Wells, *Real Books for Reading* (Portsmouth NH: Heinemann, 1990).

1. The adult engages the child in conversation.
2. The adult invites the child to tell something of interest (an experience, book, or TV show, for example).
3. The child draws a picture about the subject of interest.
4. The child tells a story about the picture.
5. The child writes familiar words; the teacher writes difficult words—or the teacher scribes the entire story.
6. The teacher and child study words in the story context, looking for sound/symbol relationships.
7. The child makes words from letters on a magnetic board.

The thirty-minute reading recovery lesson begins with the child rereading one or two familiar books—to build confidence and fluency. It continues with the child rereading the book he or she read the day before. The teacher keeps a running record of this book. Next, the child might identify and work with letters on a magnetic board or write a story. Then the teacher introduces a new book.

The teacher begins by discussing the subject of the book, one or two important new words, and the pictures, or the teacher might ask the child to look at all the pictures and tell something about the story. Then the child tries to read the story—or read as much as possible—with the teacher providing support when necessary. The child reads as independently as possible, while the teacher makes comments such as "I liked the way you tried to work that out" (Clay, 1985, page 73). Reading Recovery teachers encourage children to develop strategies they can apply to a variety of situations.

As the child rereads the new story to gain fluency, the teacher provides support by reading along with the child. But the teacher also allows the child to lead when he or she hits problem words, in order to monitor the child's mastery and to help the child see more than one way to decode a difficult word. The teacher asks questions like, "How did you know that the word was *house* and not *home?*" and "Is there any other way we would know that?" The new book then goes into the child's own box of books to be reread later. The lesson thus involves four readings or rereadings and a writing activity:

1. The child *rereads* a familiar book.
2. The child *rereads* yesterday's "new" book, as the teacher makes notes on the child's progress.
3. The child makes words or *writes* a story (see the story dictation procedure previously described).

INVESTIGATIONS: Story Dictation

Try letting a child dictate several stories to you about a life experience, a book, or a subject of interest. Then help the child read the story, using one of the approaches just described. Start with the apprenticeship approach and move on to Reading Recovery strategies, if you think the child needs extra help. Record what happens as you proceed, noting when the child's interest and engagement with the story seems strongest.

4. The teacher introduces today's new book; the child *reads* it with the teacher's support.
5. The child *rereads* the new book, with the teacher's assistance.

Eventually "new" books become "familiar" books that the child removes to make room for more new ones. Reading Recovery teachers prefer short books; they want children to read a new book in its entirety at a sitting. Getting caught up in the plot helps the child to predict words.

The strengths of the Reading Recovery approach for decoding or **print literacy** are its use of natural language (or the words and phrases familiar to the child, rather than the controlled vocabulary and phrasing of basal readers) and of the child's own natural strategies for decoding and meaning-making. The downside is that it separates children from their regular classrooms and peer groups. If more teachers were familiar with this approach and could use it in the classroom, children would not have to be segregated.

The concept of using natural language in children's early reading materials emerged in the work of New Zealand educators as early as the late 1930s. At that time, Sylvia Ashton-Warner was teaching Maori children to read with an approach she called "organic" reading and writing. Today we might call this **holistic literacy.**

LANGUAGE-BASED APPROACHES TO READING AND WRITING

In her isolated New Zealand setting, Sylvia Ashton-Warner had few text or trade books to use. Even if she had had access to the resources teachers use today, her students would not have comprehended them easily. What they could understand were their own words—their own adventures. They could easily tell about these experiences if they were encouraged to do so. Ashton-Warner decided to use these words to teach not only reading, but writing, too. At the heart of both processes was language—talk and stories.

Ashton-Warner's work is important, if not crucial, to an understanding of the way we think about reading instruction now. We simply do not divorce reading from writing anymore. We might begin by teaching children to read, but almost immediately we find ourselves thinking of reading and writing in tandem, or as mirror images of one another.

Organic Reading and Writing

"Organic reading is not new," Sylvia Ashton-Warner (1963) announced, as she began telling the story of her creative teaching in a small, rural New Zealand school and her approach to reading through "first words." Egyptian hieroglyphics, as she explained, were one-word sentences. (An eye, for example, represented divinity.) In New Zealand, said Ashton-Warner, "A boy's first drawing is anything that is mobile; trucks, trains and planes, if he lives in a populated area, and if he doesn't, it's horses" (page 28). The girls, she said, drew houses, mothers, and dolls. So she made a set of early readers based on these two gender-related themes. How could anyone take a child into the reading process with a generic, "arranged" (Dick and Jane) book? she wondered. "And how good is any child's book, anyway, compared with the ones they write themselves?" (page 28).

First words, said Ashton-Warner, meant first "wants"; thus, children should choose their own subjects to read and write about. "First words must have intense meaning for a child. They must be part of his being" (page 33). For her Maori students, words had intense meaning; finding that meaning evoked a love of reading. "The longer his reading is organic, the stronger it becomes," she said, "until by the time he arrives at the books of the new culture [for the Maori child, the new was the dominant—English-speaking—culture], he receives them as another joy rather than as a labour" (page 34).

Ashton-Warner dismissed the basal reader with its "preparation/motivation" step that caused children to "be led to feel that Janet and John are [their] friends" (page 33). Why would we lead a child to feel "that these strangers are friends?" she asked. "What about the passionate feeling he has already for his own friends? To me it is inorganic to overlook this step" (page 33).

"Out press these ["first"] words," she said, "grouping themselves in their own wild order. All boys wanting words of locomotion . . . and the girls the words of domesticity . . . Then the fear words, *ghost, tiger, . . . alligator, bulldog, wild piggy, police.* The sex words, *kiss, love, touch*" (page 39). She continued: "No time is too long spent talking to a child to find out his key words, the key that unlocks himself, for in them is the secret of reading, the realisation that words can have intense meaning. Words having no emotional significance to him, no instinctive meaning, could be an imposition, doing him more harm than not teaching him at all. They may teach him that words mean nothing and that reading is undesirable" (page 44).

Ashton-Warner began each morning by calling the children up, one at a time, and asking them what words they wanted to learn that day. She printed each word in black crayon on a strong, rectangular card, five by twelve inches, with the children's names written in the corner of their cards. The children watched and said the words as she printed them. She then showed them their words, engaging them in conversation so that they began to talk about what the word meant to them. The word became a story in itself. If the words had meaning to the children, they became "one-look" words—words that immediately became part of their sight vocabularies.

The children then took their word cards back to their mats and traced letters with their fingers, after which they placed their cards into a word container. The next morning, Ashton-Warner tipped the cards out of the container onto the mat, and the children found their cards. They chose partners and sat together to hear each other's words as she called them separately to select new words for this day. With this method, Ashton-Warner combined **personal/empathetic** and **print literacies.**

As the children came to her, they brought their old word cards and said their words, putting their cards back into the container. (Forgotten words she discarded as unimportant.) After the children had forty words in their Key Vocabularies, they progressed into Organic Writing time, during which they wrote sentences from their Key Words and kept writing books for their sentences.

As their word capacities increased, the children wrote first two sentences, then three, then half a page, and finally a page or more each day. Their stories were personal; therefore she left them unchanged. The children had freedom to say what they wished; she simply showed interest in what they wrote, and she elicited more ideas from them. As the children wrote, they conversed with others; Ashton-Warner also encouraged them to fill in story gaps to keep the story line flowing. Organic writing led naturally back to organic reading. What each child wrote became that child's reading materials.

For Organic Reading time, the children entered one to ten new words on the chalkboard. They read and spelled these words for ten to fifteen minutes, as Ashton-Warner circulated, asking each child to spell one of his or her words. The next day, new words went up. After chalkboard time each day, children went to a circle of chairs to read for fifteen minutes. First they read their own stories; then they exchanged and read one another's stories, helping each other identify words new to them. Children worked hard to produce legible and intelligible stories using appropriate grammar, punctuation, and clarity of phrasing, because they knew others would be reading their work. After reading their stories, children talked about them for fifteen minutes.

Writing and reading also grew out of a continuous activity that Ashton-Warner called her "Golden Section." During this time, she and the children went for walks, counting things, handling real objects in nature, studying natural movement and dance in nature, and writing with sticks in the soil. When they returned to the classroom, they drew and wrote about what they saw during their walks, and they imitated the movements of birds, leaves, and fish. Thus numbers, nature, and natural forms became linked in the children's minds. These regular walks also helped children notice changes in nature and to learn new words like *autumn.* In addition, they all brought animals and insects into the classroom as "visitors" and they collected songs, poems, and stories about natural things. Experiencing—and recording what they experienced—became important parts of the curriculum.

Ashton-Warner's work was particularly welcome to educators like Don Holdaway, who found himself working with Maori children a few decades later in New Zealand and who was also trying to create a more natural, child-centered curriculum. Ultimately, Holdaway (1979) devised a "shared-book experience" to teach these children to read with a language-based approach.

In a shared-book approach, teachers replicate the words of children's trade books—predictable, patterned books or familiar folk tales and songs are best—on large chart paper, with children producing their own illustrations. Then the teacher reads aloud from the "big book," and the children join in when they remember a familiar word or line. The teacher uses a pointer to show children what words he or she is reading aloud. Children then begin to see words in context and words as

INVESTIGATIONS: Reading and Writing with First Words

Elicit "first words" from a group of young children to see better what Sylvia Ashton-Warner was doing. Do you notice gender differences among children's key words? Encourage the children to draw and talk about their words so that you see the importance these words hold for them. Print the children's words on individual cards as the children talk and help them to trace the letters with their fingers. Let the children talk about their words with partners. Invite them to spin stories out of their favorite words.

parts of phrases. The pointer can also encourage children to guess; the teacher points, then listens as children respond independently.

The shared-book experience brings to the classroom the advantages of apprenticeship reading, as we saw in Gordon Wells's transcript of David and his mother reading *The Giant Jam Sandwich.* At home, the child is free to participate as he likes while the adult carries the story-reading load; at school, the child is free to participate as he or she likes while the entire class carries the load, along with the teacher. But a great deal more directive teaching goes on with shared-book experiences in the classroom because the teacher is pointing to words as children read along. The teacher also reveals concepts of print, methods for pronouncing and analyzing words, and even strategies for writing or composing in various genres, such as poetry, that children often explore more intensively in the upper elementary grades.

Genre-Based Writing

Teaching poetry, says Myra Livingston (1990), demands a commitment to eliciting children's feelings and experiences and then encouraging them to record their voices into some form of rhymed or free verse that "may approach, but not yet be, a poem" (page 36). The point of poetry, she emphasizes, is "to arrive at an experience—to feel, to bring our emotions and sensitivities into play" (page 23). Her own approach is to have children write in journals at home, on walks, and in the classroom as they observe nature and as they examine and think about objects of interest they have brought in with them. The children receive "praise for the good things, improvement for the bad, and most important, models of good poetry" that she reads at the beginning and end of a class (page 36).

"Praise for the good and improvement for the bad" describes exactly what happens when children work with Arnold Adoff in his poetry workshops. Adoff wants his poems to *sing,* as he tells students. He wants his work "to have rhythms and melodies the way much of music does" (Chapman, 1985, page 236). He wants his poetry to have story, description, images, word pictures, he adds—"to combine the saying and the singing," he adds. "I must do things in my poems to help you understand the meanings and feel the rhythms. And what I do then is to shape and space and control and polish and give my poems structure" (page 236).

In a workshop for fifth and sixth graders, he commends eleven-year-old Carrie for her poem "Chocolate Delight," inspired by his own collection, *Eats: Poems* (Lothrop, 1979). Revealing his own obvious delight in her very musical line, "that never-ending road to the chocolate delight," he says to Carrie, "You're saying something specific . . . vivid, immediate, and a picture flashes, and a feeling" (page 236).

For Bobby's poem "Tornado," inspired by Adoff's collection *Tornado!* (Delacorte, 1977), Adoff suggests more research to produce just the right word. But first there is praise: " 'Running the hard earth' is a terrific opening line, because I can *see* that twister running along!" (page 237). He doesn't like the word *swallowing* for what the tornado does to the trees, he adds; he would think about that.

He does not think a twister has a "long skinny tail," as Bobby has written. "You've got to do some research. Have you ever seen one? Not just a cartoon drawing. I don't know if the tail is skinny. There's got to be another word for what the tail of the twister looks like. You can go to the library and get books," he tells Bobby (pages 237–38). "You need unusual words to go with your unusual first line. They're okay if you want to leave them. They're good, but I think you can reach a little more" (page 238).

Bobby does a little reaching and revising, saying later: "Arnold said the tornado's tail didn't come down skinny, like a pencil, but it was wide first and then little. I looked in the encyclopedia and it had four different stages: first clouds; then it starts to form, and gets bigger, and then there's the final one. I saw that the tip of the tail come down on the ground, so I just wrote, 'the tip of the tail'" (page 238).

Adoff encourages Emily to use her imagination to add something unusual, something her own. He suggests altering the word *at* to *for* and wonders about the word *plucking* in her line, "plucking cautiously at the grain." Adoff says to her, "This is a beautiful poem. The first thing I saw was, 'The helpless crow drops down.' That's good, because there's the feeling of not gliding down, but klunk! 'Drops down.' Then I saw, 'plucking' at the ground that isn't there" (page 239). He wonders aloud what birds do when they go around? "Is it pecking, or is it picking, or is it plucking, or what is it?" (page 239). When Emily decides exactly what "plucking" is, he tells the children, "she will have continued to rewrite and make that poem better, because one of the reasons we rewrite is to make sure that every word is as perfectly correct as it possibly can be. End of lesson! Good poem." Says Emily later, "I had one word, and it didn't make sense, and we changed it, and it changed the whole poem!" (page 239). Now her bird is "pecking cautiously for the grain" (page 239).

With Eddie's poem, Adoff suggests playing with the spacing, which changes the rhythm: "What would happen if you opened it up . . . putting a little space in there?" Eddie takes the chance and reshapes his poem. "It really is like a great big breath," says Adoff. " 'I'm not saying that it's better. It's different . . . it adds a few sparkles to it. I like it!'" (page 241).

With Mary Lou's poem, he also suggests reshaping:

> It's a beautiful poem in what it says . . . But wouldn't it be nice to take this and to *play*—to take it apart the way you take apart a puzzle perhaps, after you've put it together? . . . The first thing to do with poetry after you're satisfied that you've written a poem that you like—if it were me or if you'd like to follow my advice—would be to then take that poem and to play with it some more, to break the first line as many ways as you possibly can do. If you have time, that's always a valuable way of learning to become a better writer and also to play, to

INVESTIGATIONS: Poetry Workshop

Form a poetry group with peers or children. Keep a journal in which you record your feelings, experiences, and ideas. Encourage group members to do the same. Choose one of your poems to share with others. Then encourage your listeners to share their poems and to make suggestions to strengthen the sound and sense patterns. Notice what the poetry writing causes members of the group to see, feel, or express about themselves and their worlds. What ideas emerge as important subjects to talk about?

> have fun with it. the number of letters and the number of words and the number of spaces in the title and first line of a poem are equal to how many different choices you have . . . You can take a whole week to do nothing but just the first line! (pages 241–42)

One important link between reading and writing is the fact that each process is *authored*—or "storied"—as Adoff's teaching shows us. Both the author and the reader of the author's work "compose." The author composes the initial document, story, or poem. The reader composes an interpretation of it—setting in motion **generative** and **literary literacies.** But author and reader are each composing something they want to remember, reexperience, or experience through another person's eyes—using **aesthetic literacy.** In each process, author and reader are

- making meanings that draw on their life experiences;
- engaging in reflective thinking and revising as they reread, rewrite, or retell,
- sharing their meaning-making with others;
- observing a symbolic system with print and literary conventions;
- engaging in a process they will repeat each time they return to the piece.

CHILDREN AND STORYMAKING

In his influential study *The Meaning Makers* (1986), Gordon Wells compared children's language experiences before and after they entered school. Wells believed this study would help educators think of better ways to support underachieving children. He recorded the family conversations of thirty-two male and female children in Bristol, England, then selected six of these children and followed their progress from fifteen months to five years of age. After they entered school, Wells continued to keep track of them. He discovered a strong match between the value parents placed on reading and writing and the achievement of literacy in school. Therefore, he advocated that educators place more emphasis on oral language activities in the classroom.

Exploratory Talk about Stories

Children need to hear and produce stories, says Wells. They also need to engage in exploratory talk or conversation about stories, as we saw earlier from Wells's transcript of David and his mother reading *The Giant Jam Sandwich.* Teachers need to draw on the "rich oral language resources that all children have by the time they come to school, whatever the class or ethnic group to which they belong" (page 146). If parents have not read aloud frequently to children or have not surrounded books with meaning-building conversation, teachers can fill the gap.

At its best, adult-child "collaborative talk" (page 152), in Wells's view, encourages children to make life and literature connections. Thus, it produces an expanded picture of both the story-world and the real world. The aim of this talk or conversation, says Wells, "is to make the *words fit the world*" (page 156). The child is building a framework of meaning about the world from stories and is gaining an understanding that language can create meaning for the story-world.

Children who had listened to many stories, Wells found, were better able to tell their own stories and better able to understand the talk and stories they heard at school. A "shared interpretation of experiences," says Wells, is "one of the most fundamental means of making meaning" (pages 194–95). When we share an interpretation, we make our own way of seeing things apparent to others, and they make their way of seeing evident to us. Then both—or many—pictures of the world come into sharper focus.

One story confirms, changes, modifies, shifts, extends, or elaborates on the other. We order and select experiences as we tell stories. We also reorganize and make connections between ideas. In addition, we explore our emotions, our value systems, our priorities, and our preoccupations. Making meaning about an experience, says Wells is "to a great extent being able to construct a plausible story about it" (page 196)—**narrative literacy** in the making.

Language and Literature Conversations

Echoing Shirley Brice Heath and Harry Rosen, whose ideas he cited in his study, Wells advocates giving stories a central place in the classroom, with teachers reading stories aloud, students reading alone and in small group settings, and most importantly, pupils writing and telling stories of their own.

Heath's purpose, as she stated in her influential study *Ways With Words* (1983), was similar to that of Wells. She wanted to "make accessible to teachers an understanding of the differences in language and culture their students bring to their classrooms" (page 256) and to indicate what teachers could do in the light of these findings. Heath observed three social groups of families in the Piedmont Carolinas:

- White mill workers living in a place she called "Roadville"
- Black mill workers and sharecroppers living nearby, in a place she called "Trackton"
- Townspeople—white or black—in what she called "Gateway," a town near both Roadville and Trackton

Heath discovered that parents in these different groups transmitted different strategies for meaning-making. She also found that the strategies Gateway families used insured the success of their children in school, in contrast to those that

INVESTIGATIONS: Exploratory Talk about Stories

Try engaging a small or large group of children in a meaning-making conversation similar to the one David and his mother had when they read *The Great Jam Sandwich.* Choose a popular picture book and share it with students, inviting them to chime in with their comments and questions as you read along. Encourage them to make life and literature connections and to sort out the story by stopping to explain words and pictures whenever the need arises. Ask the children questions when you want to broaden your own meaning-making experiences with their input. Make your story time a give-and-take dialogue in which you serve as a partner in thought—not simply a discussion leader or authority figure.

families in either of the outlying communities used. Stories and storymaking were evident in each group, but the Gateway parents' kind of talk about life and literature was influential in terms of school achievement.

Roadville parents did a great deal of directive teaching when they talked to children. They labeled items in life and books and asked many directive questions. They preferred children to stick to the facts when they talked or told stories. This also held true in conversations about stories; reading aloud meant asking children to name objects in their books and to answer questions about the factual content of stories.

Trackton parents had a different perspective. Life is filled with unpredictability and change, in their view. Children therefore tried different approaches; they were flexible, and they learned for themselves. Nobody could tell them about the world because of the world's instability—the instability of words, events, life itself. Thus their parents' "teaching" was much less directive, much more intuitive.

Trackton children grew up in large, extended families surrounded by wide circles of neighbors, and they were immersed in a flow of talk from birth on. The entire community took a hand in childcare. Adults listened to children's stories at times, but often children were sharing their stories with other children, who listened and extended the stories with verbal challenges, teasing, and stories of their own. But such free and sociable storytelling led to trouble later in school, Heath said, with teachers complaining that these children talked too much.

Gateway parents, in contrast to their counterparts in either Roadville or Trackton, surrounded their children with a great deal of descriptive talk, providing a running commentary about what their children were seeing, hearing, reading, writing, or experiencing. They questioned their children, as Heath explained in a later essay (1986), but they used their questions to "scaffold a narrative" (page 161). Thus, they drew children out to provide many details and much commentary about what they had seen or done. They invited their children to tell their experiences—and to clarify and explain these narratives—on a routine basis.

Heath's findings prompted her to initiate a program with local teachers in which children became researchers of their own family literacy. They talked to their parents about how they learned to talk and tell stories. They brought these stories about themselves into the classroom. Then teacher and students discussed them together. The emphasis throughout Heath's study was that classroom activities involving conversation, drama, storymaking, and oral history could help Roadville and Trackton children perform as successfully as Gateway children.

What has perhaps not been emphasized enough for those drawing on Heath's findings is that Trackton children have something valuable to offer Gateway and Roadville children, too. Because adults have not constantly interrupted their flow of thought, thus allowing them to become fluent storytellers outside the classroom, they provide a model of what storytelling is like in the "real" world. As experienced and proficient storytellers, they could become leaders in classroom storymaking activities, if teachers value their input and storytelling talents.

The Importance of Story

People generally tell stories, says cultural theorist Harry Rosen (1993), for five reasons:

1. "To command [the] full attention and interest" of others—or to entertain (page 135)
2. To reminisce with others about a shared experience
3. To respond to an invitation to tell about something that happened to them or others
4. To make a point in a discussion
5. To initiate a discussion

Children in Trackton families frequently tell stories in Category 1, entertaining and commanding attention. In Gateway families, they often tell stories in all the other categories. In Roadville families, they tell stories in Category 3, when they are encouraged to do so. But in Rosen's view, the more opportunities all children have to experience *all* of these ways of storytelling, the better. The classroom, because it brings together all of these different children, is a good place for children to try out many ways of telling.

Heath's research, says Rosen (1987) highlights the need for a "culture-sensitive curriculum" (page 443), or a deeper understanding among teachers of their students' cultures. The challenge is how to help Roadville and Trackton students "develop their own voices so that they can articulate a critical view of society and act more powerfully in it" (pages 451–52)? Rosen's view is that the teacher's role is not simply to help students get better at reading and writing, but to help them think more critically about what reading and writing can do to change their place in the social class structure. How could teachers help to empower children as critical learners?

As early as 1977, Rosen had stressed the value of home-school links, particularly in relation to working class families. If there is anything education gives us, he said, it is the belief that there is "nourishing resource and vigour in the pupil's homes and

INVESTIGATIONS: Language Learning and You

Become a researcher of your own literacy and language learning. Collect data from your parents about how you learned to talk and tell stories. See if the way you learned language correlates to any one of the three groups Heath describes: Roadville, Trackton, or Gateway.

INVESTIGATIONS: Storytelling and You

Consider Rosen's five reasons why people tell stories, and then try to determine why *you* usually tell stories. Notice yourself through a day's time as you interact with others. Notice whether you tell stories for any reasons Rosen does not mention. Notice whether you never tell stories for any of the reasons he mentions. If this is the case, try telling a story to broaden your opportunities for meaning-making and imaginative capability and for developing **narrative literacy.**

community and that we have much to learn from that community" (page 206). In other words, teachers could evoke and nurture those responses that grew out of the child's home place—and out of the cultural influences of parents, grandparents, and townspeople. Often children of "Gateway" cultures had silenced not only the stories of other cultures but also their ways of storytelling. Why are cultural stories so important?

First of all, narrative is a meaning-making strategy, as Rosen (1984) has asserted. Narrative is the way we structure our world and order our experiences, or the way we place our own value on what we see. Second, autobiographical storytelling—personal meaning-making—says Rosen, allows tellers to define themselves. It also allows all members of the teller's social and cultural community—all of those listening—to define themselves. Third, the construction of a social self establishes the worth of the teller's culture; it helps tellers to know who they are. Personal identity merges with social and cultural identity. Thus, intricate webs of stories and cultural meanings emerge, and we see storytelling as a social—and consequently a *human* experience.

Literacy for Critical Consciousness

Intersections of class, gender, race, ethnicity, and nationality—cultural connections, as Rosen discusses—cause us to see different purposes and approaches we can use to teach reading and writing. It is not enough, as literacy researcher Anne Dyson (1995) says, for children to be writing what they know or even what they want to figure out or reflect on. It is not enough for children to be able to make their intentions clear to others or to react to the clarity of one another's texts, as they are encouraged to do in writing-process classrooms. Now, says Dyson, children need to react "to the choices others [make] in representing these stories" (page 325).

Children who are continually crossing the borders of gender, class, and ethnicity, both inside and outside of the classroom, need to "learn to participate in and help build a fair world that can contain them all" (page 324). Thus, they need to help one another see how "fair" texts are—both their own texts and those of adult authors. No one is more responsible for this movement toward cultural and critical consciousness in the field of literacy than Paulo Friere, whose studies began appearing in English in the early 1970s and whose ideas then began filtering into classrooms.

In his work with adult literacy in Brazil, Friere (1973) became strongly committed to the idea that "men can intervene in reality in order to change it." When they do, they "enter into the domain which is theirs exclusively—that of History and of Culture" (page 4). *Integration* is a word he used to explain what is distinctively human—the ability not merely to adapt to the world, but to make choices and transform the world, the result of humanity's *critical capacity.* Such a capacity

INVESTIGATIONS: Storymaking and Family Literacy

Interview someone in your family or your extended family about one of your ancestors, your ancestral place of origin, or the details for a family tree. Listen to stories, record stories, compose stories, tell stories. Encourage parents and grandparents to tell you stories about their lives as children or about their memories of an earlier time in history. Let their stories become part of your own cultural identity.

means the ability to reflect on oneself, one's responsibilities, and one's role in the world, as well as on one's own power to reflect, because reflectivity produces "an increased capacity for choice" (page 16).

We might ask, what would either literature-based or literature-related reading and writing instruction look like if it arose from such a critical capacity? What would teachers be doing? What would children be doing? It would first of all be rooted in dialogue, Friere would say, since he felt the best way to stimulate critical consciousness or the human capacity to act creatively within one's environment was through talking together. Dialogue is, in turn, rooted in empathy between those of opposing forces "who are engaged in a joint search" (page 45).

What could link these opposing forces? Mutual trust, Friere explained, a critical attitude, humility, and love; in other words, *equals* talking together—as opposed to one person standing over others, issuing proclamations. If a powerful elite rules the passive and silent masses and the leaders never invite members of the underclass to confer cooperatively, never listen to their ideas, the masses remain backward, illiterate, and unprepared for critical thinking. And the same principle applies to either government or school situations.

"Acquiring literacy," Friere asserted, "does not involve memorizing sentences, words, or syllables—lifeless objects unconnected to an existential universe [one based on existence without meaning]—but rather [it involves] an attitude of creation and re-creation, a self-transformation" (page 48). Such an attitude results from taking action to change one's own setting. In Friere's view, we must see the choices we have and then act on them, and one of these choices is taking on literacy. Learning to read and write is not simply learning to master—or dominate—a text. It is not simply passing a test, being promoted to the next grade, reading the "right" books or the most books, writing an "A" paper, or getting into the "best" school. It is seeing real and necessary reasons for literacy: to acquire more human experience and to act creatively in our world for *everyone's* advancement.

In Friere's adult literacy program, the students examined a series of pictures depicting the way men and women make critical life choices; then they discussed the pictures in terms of their own lives. Later, they learned to read and write by

- generating words,
- combining and recombining these words into new and different words, and
- discussing what these words meant *to them* in their own cultural context.

We might compare the way Sylvia Ashton-Warner helped children learn to read. Friere's approach is, in many ways, an adult version of it.

The words students selected were those filled with the greatest meaning—or strongest emotional content—for them as individuals and as members of a cultural group. Friere's approach was rich in **personal/empathetic, sociocultural,** and **critical literacies.** In listening to his students discuss their words in terms of their worlds, Friere learned about their hopes, beliefs, frustrations, and knowledge—and their desire to learn to read and write, in order to change their worlds.

In the same way, Anne Dyson (1995) learned about the feelings of an urban, working-class, African-American third grader, Tina, and her world, as she observed Tina's encounters with peer stories, media stories (cartoons, movies, and videos), and the Greek myths her teacher was reading aloud. What are the possibilities of critical action in the classroom? Dyson asks. In what are they rooted? In dialogue, she answers, in children turning outward, listening to the voices around them and then "being moved to speak" (page 325).

In Tina's classroom, children performed their own stories in Author's Theater. Then they discussed their stories—as authors. They had choices about what characters to include, what qualities to give to characters, and what actions to place into the plot. Language was the medium through which these children were creating a child *self,* says Dyson, and the role of the child-as-author was to contribute to an ongoing dialogue in the classroom social community.

Tina and her classmates listened often to voices of the popular culture, and unfortunately, as Dyson explains, these voices were often filled with gender stereotypes, sexist attitudes, females in limited and limiting roles, and males in heroic positions. But, she adds, because children, both male and female, were so fascinated by these stories, they found ways to use them in their own stories to explore and express their identities. The children's stories therefore told her a great deal about their lives and about their meaning-making processes.

In Tina's classroom, the exclusion of females in media stories often led to spirited classroom discussions and theater presentations. Tina—tough-talking, loving, knowledgeable, and humorous—found a way to write her way out of the constricting roles placed on the females in media stories, and she did so in three stages. At the beginning of the year, Tina simply co-opted the strong male roles for her female characters. (Her female characters were able to do what the boys did.)

Later in the year, she reversed the world depicted in most media stories. Usually, the main character in these stories was a tough male; in Tina's story, the main character was a tough girl, but she had a nurturing mother who protected the children. Thus, Tina brought into play a relational role, which media stories so often ignore, as another kind of power source for her characters.

As the school year ended, Tina moved into a third stage. She wrote two long stories at home that were linked to classroom talk about gender roles. In one there was "marked equality of male and female action" (page 330) that offered "new visions of relational possibilities" (page 331). The other story emerged from a unit on Greek heroes and the teacher's reading aloud of Greek myths, and here Tina transformed Venus into a black goddess. First she and her friends redrew the book illustration of Venus as black, rather than as white and blonde. Then, in her story, she renamed the heroine for herself—Venus Tina.

Her heroine was a black female who rode a magical, flying, female horse and saved a girl and boy oppressed by two male terrorists. But Tina transformed (or converted) the terrorists, so that at the end of the story, life on earth was "fun"

INVESTIGATIONS: Storymaking and Critical Literacy

Consider how you might want to change the world in some small—or large—way. Then read stories to uncover more about the issue that is important to you. You might be reading a myth or folk tale which places females in limited roles. You might be reading a novel in which members of a particular ethnicity or class—or children—are silenced or oppressed. You might be reading a picture book in which males are the dominant characters or Eurocentric characters are the important ones. Rewrite the story—reading and writing across the grain of it to present your new "reading" of the world.

again. Thus in the second story, gender and race intersected, as Tina clearly reacted to both popular and traditional literature in which blonde females have limited—and limiting—roles. Tina wrote her own new "reading" of the world to change these roles. Responding to the choices authors make as they represent females and persons of color, she made textual choices to rewrite the story on her own terms. Such a stance, says Dyson, takes courage—and responsibility.

With Friere's ideas and Dyson's observations, we see educators focusing on **critical** and **sociocultural literacies** as the way children can learn—from the beginning—to read and write. What is the teacher's place in such a program?

The teacher's role is to *coordinate* rather than teach; says Friere, to create *dialogue* rather than deliver speeches; to invite group *participants,* instead of pupils; and to produce programs or *learning units,* rather than "alienating syllabi" or lesson outlines (page 42). We will keep these four defining terms—coordination, dialogue, participation, and learning units—in mind, as we continue to discuss classroom practices. Perhaps they can help us see more ways to foster courageous readers and writers—or students who would use language to *transform* reality, rather than adapt, silently and passively, to the powers that be.

As Tina replies when her friend Makeda says that people from Greece are not black, "Yes, they can be," says Tina. "Maybe Venus is White to you. But not to me" (page 331).

Chapter 10

Children Learning through Literature and Literacies

Topics in This Chapter:

- Literature for personal development
- Literature for curriculum needs
- Literature for literary learning
- Literature for cultural and multicultural learning

The Hatter opened his eyes very wide on hearing this; but all he said was, "Why is a raven like a writing-desk?"

"Come, we shall have some fun now!" thought Alice. "I'm glad they've begun asking riddles—I believe I can guess that," she added aloud.

"Do you mean that you think you can find out the answer to it?" said the March Hare.

"Exactly so," said Alice.

"Then you should say what you mean," the March Hare went on.

"I do," Alice hastily replied, "at least—at least I mean what I say—that's the same thing, you know."

"Not the same thing a bit!" said the Hatter . . .

The Dormouse shook its head impatiently . . .

"Have you guessed the riddle yet?" the Hatter said, turning to Alice again.

"No, I give it up," Alice replied. "What's the answer?"

"I haven't got the slightest idea," said the Hatter.

"Nor I," said the March Hare.

"A Mad Tea-Party," in Alice's Adventures in Wonderland, 1865
—Lewis Carroll

Reading *Alice's Adventures in Wonderland,* we see a great chasm between what adults perceive as important for educating children and what children themselves value. Adults want things explained. Forms, rank, order, and conventions are all-important to them. What Alice wants is fun and games—and riddles—and she goes running after the rabbit to find them. What she finds instead in her underground world is what children often find in school—a world where adult aims conflict with those of children, and riddles often have no answers.

Robert Protherough, an educational researcher in classroom literature programs, lists three types of goals teachers have for using literature in the classroom: personal, curricular, and literary. "At the simplest—personal—level," he says,

> . . . stories offer enjoyment, pleasure, relaxation; they develop positive attitudes towards reading. They develop, in some undefined sense, the imagination. Socially books can aid personal development and self-understanding by presenting situations and characters with which our own can be compared, and by giving the chance to test out motives and decisions. [In addition, they] extend experience and knowledge of life . . . by introducing us to other kinds of people, places, periods, situations. (page 7)

The curricular function, on the other hand, assumes that literature can produce learning about school subjects. Books, Protherough says, develop students' use of language, their vocabulary, and writing standards. When children study literature, they read and write more. Literature also carries over into the arts and humanities: music, painting, drama, and history, "helping to 'bring alive' the past or other countries, or presenting material for the discussion of moral and ethical values" (page 8).

The literary function is related to both the personal and the curricular. It involves a deeper, more *discriminating* use of language. If literature is part of the curriculum, then a literary function teaches students more about literature, literacy, and the language arts. If, on a personal level, students are also taking pleasure in literature, the literary function simply strengthens their interest in literature and in reading more. They are then able to take on more demanding works as they become more aware of literary forms, conventions, and genres.

Which one of these aims do teachers favor, or do teachers give equal attention to personal development, curriculum needs, and literary learning? Because children would very likely favor the personal function, we might also wonder if teachers bring the personal aim far enough into the foreground. Do they make school a *good* place to be, from the student's viewpoint?

Another question is whether any other aims besides these three are important for literature-based classrooms today. Certainly since 1983, when Protherough was conducting his research, multicultural literature has become an important social and curricular emphasis. So another important function of teaching literature might be to foster cultural learning.

In this chapter, we will examine these four aims for teaching literature—personal, curricular, literary, and cultural (the *why* of literature teaching). In the next chapter, we will examine the *how*—studying how to plan, teach, and assess in a literature-based classroom.

Before 1966, teaching literature to young children meant teaching reading, and for older students it meant teaching students to write essays about the artistic "elements" of literature (setting, theme, conflict, characterization). All this changed in a watershed year when English and American educators met at Dartmouth College to discuss how English, language arts, reading, and literature classes should be taught, and educators began to see other purposes for teaching literature. Children could study literature to learn more about themselves, others, the world, and the world of literature itself.

D. W. Harding, English educator and researcher in reader response, chaired the Dartmouth seminar in the mid 1960s. His report from the conference explains well the personal function of literary teaching. For far too long, Harding said literature teaching meant shutting off the inner person responding to the work. What was needed was more attention to the "moment-by-moment experiencing by one or several perceivers." Any work of art must be viewed as a "constantly growing and developing body of perceptions" (page 389). Like Rosenblatt, Harding said that the primary reason for reading was enjoyment. How could teachers help to bring this enjoyment about?

The teacher's role, said Harding, is to have a great many books on hand and to be well-acquainted with the books and the children; then the teacher can match child and story. Children read independently and in small and large groups. Children might also tell stories and engage in role play and related activities that elicit deeper responses to text. Teachers do a great deal of informal talking with children about books. They also share literature—reading aloud entire works, or just enough to get things started—and invite reader responses for the cross-pollination of ideas.

Consider the work of June McConaghy (1990), whose research and practices as a first-grade teacher exemplify the "growth" model Harding described. Literature teaching in McConaghy's classroom means seating children in a group on the floor and reading stories aloud at least four times a day: early in the morning, mid-morning, before noon, and as the afternoon begins. During these times, the children talk, ask questions, tell how stories make them feel, and share ideas about their lives and what puzzles them in their worlds (page 29). McConaghy describes her mid-morning story time, reading Eric Carle's *The Very Hungry Caterpillar* (World, 1969):

> As we read the book, I turned the pages slowly so children could notice its slightly different format, the colorful pictures, and the sequential order of the days of the week. We laughed at meeting a caterpillar who eats plums, strawberries, pickles, and ice cream. When we turned to the last page and saw in vivid color that the caterpillar had miraculously changed into a beautiful butterfly, we paused to talk about how this transformation had come about. One little girl wondered if the bright colors of the butterfly represented the colors of the food the caterpillar had eaten. She thought she too might turn orange if she ate too many oranges or carrots, or turn purple if she ate too many grapes.
>
> At this point I simply suggested they write their own stories about the very hungry caterpillar: 'If anyone is doing any writing today, you might like to think about this story when you are writing your own' . . . As a result of my suggestion,

a number of children created beautiful butterfly pictures. A few children made letters on their pictures and one little girl, Brenda, even printed out a complete story. (page 43)

Brenda's butterfly story reads: "Once upon a time I turned in to a butterfly. I was pink and blue and orange and green and purple and red I thought I was pretty. I flew away and I met a ladybug. It was a boy. I took him out for dinner" (page 44).

McConaghy uses an individualized reading approach, in which she incorporates:

- shared reading with big books,
- literature circles,
- partner reading,
- independent reading (quiet reading time), and
- a writing workshop.

In addition, she integrates different curriculum areas through thematic activities by using children's books. She chooses books that deal with specific concepts; she reads them aloud; then she integrates them into projects and activities to help children understand particular concepts, especially in math and science.

The important part of McConaghy's approach is that she chooses a book like *The Very Hungry Caterpillar* for story time reading rather than for concept teaching. What has concerned literary theorists over the years is that too often teachers choose a book and then design activities to "cover" various curriculum areas,

INVESTIGATIONS: Reading for Personal Development

Susan Cooper (1993) tells about what happened when a teacher in Kent, England began reading one of Cooper's books aloud to students. The teacher felt hesitant because the book—*The Dark Is Rising* (Simon & Schuster, 1973)—is a complex work, and this was a mixed-ability group of students. As the school librarian wrote to Cooper, "What pleased and surprised everyone was the way *The Dark Is Rising* became *their* book to that class, and their sheer enjoyment and enthusiasm spilled over into so many other things that they were doing in the class, in the school and at home" (page 163).

The teacher encouraged the children to create responses to the book. They made pictures and slides and posters, Cooper reports. They wrote poems and recorded them to jazz on cassettes, which spawned a book club. The librarian received questions about the book and the author when she visited the classroom. She told them about the sequels to this book and left them a copy of *Greenwitch* (Simon & Schuster, 1974), the next book in the series. Then, as she says, "I had one of the greatest compliments a librarian can have—seeing a hand reach out surreptitiously and take the book from the pile before I had finished speaking" (page 163).

The students sent letters to Cooper about their responses to the book. One child purchased a paperback copy of *The Dark Is Rising* for his father and told of his disappointment when Perry Wilson beat him to the copy of *Greenwitch.* As adults communicated enthusiasm for the book, they produced an enjoyable reading experience, understanding, and deep engagement in the story for these children. The teacher took a chance with the first book, and the librarian reached out to say, "Hey—try this. You might like it" (page 164).

Take a chance with children, as this teacher did. Choose a book that you especially like and read it to children or with children in a small group setting. Encourage the children to respond to the book in various creative activities of their own choosing. Introduce them to more books by the same author. Then step back to see what children do with the book in terms of their own personal development.

Source: Susan Cooper, *Dreams and Wishes* (New York: McElderry Books, 1996).

whether or not the book lends itself to concept teaching. Literature is a means to a conceptual end, rather than a pleasurable end in itself.

At first glance, *The Very Hungry Caterpillar* seems to lend itself well to many conceptual activities. A vibrantly colored worm eats its way through die-cut pages over the course of a week—Sunday to Sunday—consuming a variety of fruits—apples, pears, plums, strawberries, and oranges—arranged sequentially from one to five. Then on Saturday, the caterpillar gorges on a feast of ten items, arranged as one of each kind of delight, from one piece of chocolate cake to one slice of watermelon. The caterpillar develops a giant stomachache, cures itself by eating "one nice green leaf," retreats into its cocoon for two weeks, and emerges at last as a beautiful butterfly.

Is this a story? An informational book? If so, what does it inform children about? Science (metamorphosis)? Food groups? The days of the week? Numbers? Cause-and-effect relationships? Sequences? All of this and more? It is also a good example of a cumulative story—and good for children's storytelling experiences—and it invites painting and cut-paper explorations. It is surely an important interactive book as well. Says educator Bernice Cullinan (1989): "Books for very young children often make counting a game or invite the child to participate, the way Eric Carle does in *The Very Hungry Caterpillar* . . . The hungry caterpillar eats holes right through the pages, and the holes lure children to stick tiny fingers through them as they count" (page 113).

But even though Carle's book works well as a concept book that cuts across many curriculum areas—science, math, art, and the language arts (storytelling, writing, reading), it also is a story that young children relate to on a human level: They are growing quickly, like the caterpillar, and they need to consume large amounts of food. This is a book about doing the basic things young children do—waking, sleeping, eating—and the one thing they do most: change. It is a book about transformation and how it feels to be growing. Sometimes sudden growth is uncomfortable, as Carroll's Alice knew; sometimes it is puzzling; sometimes it makes no sense at all. Sometimes it seems impossible.

As four-year-old David said to educator Victor Watson (1992), as they came to the last page of this story: "That's silly! They don't do that" (page 12). David continued to return to the book and to reiterate his surprise. Watson's response was simply to say, yes, it did seem strange, but that he believed caterpillars did turn into butterflies. David did not need a science lesson, as Watson explains. It was less important for David to know how a butterfly develops than to know that he is allowed to be surprised, or even sceptical" (page 13).

From *The Very Hungry Caterpillar* (World, 1969) by Eric Carle.

When adult and child meet stories together, says Watson, "what should take place is a liberating of thought and response, the creation of *possibilities,*" and the best children's books, he adds, are "liberating texts" (page 12). But when we begin using such versatile books in the classroom, liberation can easily turn into curriculum strait-jacketing. Consider the many children's books that are *not*—in any way—concept books. Would we want to use *Charlotte's Web* to teach science lessons on spiders, or to use *Peter Rabbit* to teach facts about bunnies?

The nonfiction writer does not tell the reader "how it *feels* to have legs just right for jumping," says educator Terry Johnson. "But the author of [Robert Lawson] *Rabbit Hill* does" (page 37; Puffin, 1944). The "good writer of literature," he continues, "puts the reader inside the rabbit—or hobbit, or war orphan, or castaway, or delinquent. Other disciplines (e.g., science, history, geography, etc.) make the reader an observer of the phenomena discussed. Only fiction puts the reader within the situations presented. . . . Fiction offers myriad opportunities to gain insight into the human condition. . . . The teacher's role is to help children to develop a deeper insight into the stories that they encounter" (page 37).

LITERATURE FOR CURRICULUM NEEDS

Often the teacher walks a thin line between using literature for personal development and using literature for curricular needs. Thus the *art* of teaching literature, as Johnson says, at times requires one to decide if using the book will "send the reader-listener back into the story" (page 38), deepening the child's engagement with the book. Consider Anita Silvey's horror upon encountering a hundred-page, skills-in-isolation—or basalized—study guide for *The Very Hungry Caterpillar.* In an editorial in *The Horn Book,* she comments that the caterpillar "would have more than a stomachache if he could see" it (1989, page 549).

This is not to say that children's books are outside the bounds of *any* curriculum purpose. Children might be learning to read with patterned books like *The Very Hungry Caterpillar,* and they will, of course, be learning to count and learning about science concepts like metamorphosis, life cycles, and the concept of transformation as they read this book for pleasure. But almost any children's book is equally—or more—effective for simply helping children learn about themselves.

Integrating the Curriculum with Literature

"Probably the greatest value of using literature in the reading program," says Charlotte Huck (1977), "is that children experience joy in reading and become 'hooked on books.' Instead of reading 'bits and pieces' of a story, they have a chance to become engrossed in an entire book. They may reread favorite books if they so desire, or favorite parts of well-loved books. Students who experience this kind of pleasure in reading are well on their way to becoming lifetime readers" (page 365). Encountering a lonely or shy child in a story brings "a moment of sudden awareness of feeling what it would be like to be someone else" (365); thus they develop compassion. This is the *feeling* side, the humanizing side. But there is also a *knowing* side.

Consider the way June McConoghy read *The Very Hungry Caterpillar* at story time, and then invited her class to write about it when she noticed one child's question opening up imaginative possibilities. Literature, Huck (1977) says, helps to "stretch children's imagination and help them to see their world in a new way, or [to] entertain the possibilities of new worlds" (page 365). She elaborates on this point in a later essay (1982):

> Today, television has made everything so explicit that children are not developing their own interior landscapes. One of the qualities of a well-written book for me is whether I can see it in my mind's eye, for I mentally visualize every book and poem I read. The books of the well-known Scottish author, Mollie Hunter, are rich in a sense of place. I can see scenes from her suspenseful story, *A Stranger Came Ashore* (1975), as if I had visited the Shetland islands myself . . . All of Mollie Hunter's books have this power to make you see the setting—to help you *be* there. (page 317)

Literature, Huck adds, "can help the child to begin to develop a sense of wonder, an appreciation for the beautiful, and joy in living" (page 319). Biographies and nonfiction books about science "present the wonder, the excitement, the tragedy of man's discoveries and mistakes," says Huck. "Not to use them is to deny children their right to participate in the drama of the making of our civilization" (1977, page 368). As for history, Huck says: "Children need to know that such things as slavery, the Holocaust, and nuclear war can happen. The horrors of these atrocities can only be personalized in the particular. History books can tell us that 6 million Jews were killed in Germany, but books such as Siegal's *Upon the Head of a Goat* (1981) help the child to *be there,* to be part of a Jewish family growing up in Hungary and finally to board the train for the 'work camp' of Auschwitz" (1982, page 316).

Cross-curricular emphases emerge in thematic units that teachers and students create together, as Huck (1987) explains. She describes the classroom of first-grade teacher Kerstin Kerstetter. The heart of Kerstetter's unit-building process is a classroom collection of books (400 titles). Kerstetter has a $300 annual budget for purchasing books, and she uses the library to obtain 100 of her 400 titles. The children take part in selecting and classifying books. They make lists of special books and book subjects; then Kerstetter sets off for the library each month to find as many of the special books and subjects as possible. When she returns, they all examine the new books together, and they share favorite parts. Children organize their book collection by genre and author. At times they design their own special categories.

Kerstetter, like McConoghy, reads one to three stories twice or three times daily, and she rereads favorite stories twenty times a month. The children scrutinize some books for details. They use patterned books for shared reading. They look at different versions of a story to compare features. Kerstetter suggests ideas for reexperiencing books at center time. Often daily work arises from the study of a cluster of books with a similar focus, such as a particular story character like the giant.

Children help to plan a thematic unit on a subject such as *Giants* by brainstorming ideas that Kerstetter places on a "web" diagram. The threads spin out into four concepts and many ideas for studying them. *Size relationships*—in book illustrations, classmates' sizes, recipe ingredients, and legendary creatures that are big (giants) and small (elves and fairies)—is a math category. *Giants of the past*—dragons and dinosaurs—is a history category. *Giants today*—skyscrapers, stadiums, airplanes, machines—is a social studies category. *Giant stories*—books about Fin M'Coul, Paul Bunyan, the giant of "Jack and the Beanstalk"—is literature. See Figure 10.1.

Other web threads are activity-based. Under *telling giant stories,* Kerstetter can list things to do to find story ideas. Under *making giants,* she can list things to do to create giant figures—real and imaginary. Under *dramatize stories,* she lists stories the children can dramatize.

Kerstetter makes a flowchart to sequence these ideas and to decide on main activities for the class. Then she collects books to link with the various web strands or to support the theme (thirty of the best books she can find). She considers the order of the books for the activity and the unit itself and how the books and the characters in the books will be important for comparison. Daily work starts to flow out of the reading and the talk about giants. The children make "giant cake" and think about how much cake a giant could eat, then they write about their cooking activity; they also interview the school cook about the gigantic proportions needed to feed the entire school.

In this classroom, children visit other classes to share written stories; older students visit to read with them. Everyone in the school community works together to help children see that people read for pleasure on a daily basis. Evaluation focuses on determining whether children

- enjoy reading,
- choose to read at home,
- take on book knowledge and a sense of story, and
- integrate literature into their daily lives.

Classrooms like McConaghy's and Kerstetter's are literacy-centered, with centers and thematic units functioning together to instigate work across the curriculum. Literature helps children learn concepts in these areas and helps promote literacy, especially *lifelong* literacy. However, a teacher might reverse this emphasis. Classrooms might be topic-centered, with all of the work flowing out of the topic and literature supporting the topic work. In this method of teaching, literature is a resource for exploring a particular idea. The goal is to help students to see the world as fertile ground for research—or to promote investigation of the world for *lifelong learning.*

FIGURE 10.1. A "web" diagram.

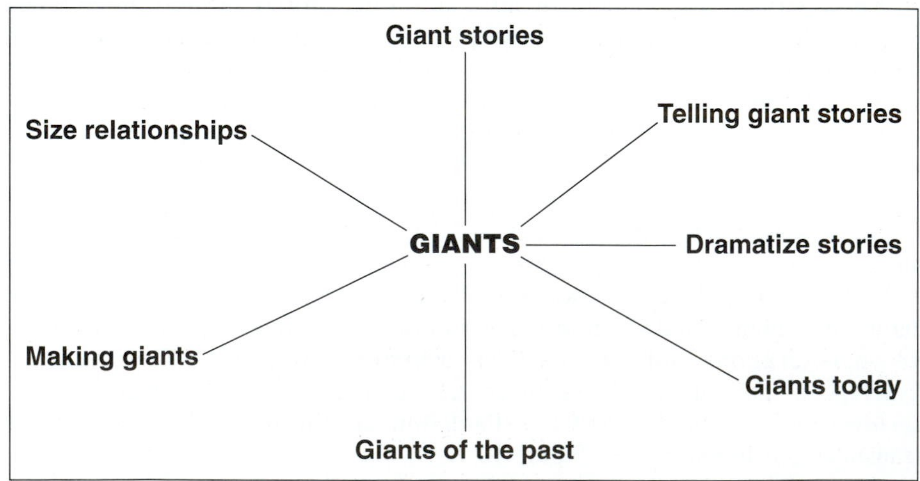

Exploring a Topic with Literature

When Mary Hilton embarked on a project for the topic "History Around Us" with her class of seven-year-olds in England, her hope was to give these students a sense of the past, or the idea of historical time as "an imaginative extension of meaning" (page 178). Says Hilton:

> Some of the most exciting recent history projects in primary schools have been oral history ones. Children have gone out into the community around them and talked to older people and have built up a picture of the past of their own locality. Because the children were so young I felt we had to go beyond living testimony further back in time to stories and old myths, to explore how history is built up from a vast range of voices and interpretations through the ages. This would give me more flexibility in tuning the topic work to the children's own writing voices. For I was anxious that the children should learn history through the process of writing it.
>
> I feel that *writing* history is the best way to be actively involved in building up an understanding of the past. . . . And after all, the professional historian's task is to capture the complexity and uniqueness of past events in prose. For me this means that children, however young, should be encouraged to develop their own writing voice and to approach historical ideas and evidence in their own creative autonomous way. Central to this is the respecting of their own memories. (page 179)

Literature in Hilton's unit fell into three categories: British history (narrative, legend, drama), oral history or living history (family stories, class trips to museums, marketplaces, map study), and the children's own writing, or as Hilton says, "their own preferred form of written expression—narrative" (page 179). Children would have an active involvement with the past in order to shape an understanding of it. (American teachers could emphasize American history instead, using the many children's books focused on historical figures such as Christopher Columbus, Pocahontas, Abraham Lincoln, or Martin Luther King.)

To shape her plan, Hilton began with a description of the purpose of the topic work: "To deepen the children's sense of historical time and place by looking at our environment, both natural and humanmade aspects of it . . . to build up bit by bit a rough picture of the medieval world in this region . . ." (page 180). Then she placed short lists of subject areas, activities, and resources that will serve as the structural "branches" of this growing topic. See Figure 10.2.

Hilton began one morning by setting the historical scene to discover what the children knew already about Britain at the time of William the Conqueror:

> As a class they were extremely hazy about the idea and very wary . . . Because I knew of their love of a story I pointed out that Britain was an island and that when the Romans had gone away England had been invaded several times. I quickly followed this up with the story of William the Conqueror and the Battle of Hastings. I showed them a map of England with the Norman Baronies marked in colour and I asked them to think how the Saxons must have felt when they lost their king and had been conquered. (page 181)

That afternoon, the children became more engaged as they retold the story she had told them of William and Harold, and she was surprised by "how their discourse and their appreciation of factual evidence became more sophisticated and assured once involved in narrative" (page 182). In fact, it was as if some of the children only "gathered factual material together within the coherence of a story" (page 182).

To build their concept of history, the children visited churches and graveyards. They sketched, noted dates, scraped off moss, and connected what they learned to famous people of the past they knew about. Then they went to museums, looked at books on towns that had grown up around markets and rivers, and actually traveled on these roads and rivers. Even the school building had a history—it had once gone through a fire—and one of the teachers remembered the event and told the children about it. Thus, the topic work wedded history to self-expression, and the stories linked teller and listeners to encourage the children's personal investment in the past. (It was *their* school.)

Since Hilton had chosen the topic herself, she watched the children as they were drawn into it, and discovered that oral history produced the strongest engagement. The children questioned their parents and grandparents about their school lives; the adults told and wrote stories for the children. Hilton encouraged the children to try to imagine what they would remember when they were older, like their parents, and their comments became the basis for a play about a class reunion years hence.

FIGURE 10.2. A Topic Plan.

Family History
Oral History
Talking to Older People

Work On Churches,
Markets, Villages,
Cathedrals, and
Monasteries
Transactional [nonfiction] Writing
Using Reference Material

History Of The School
Considering Firsthand Evidence
Finding Clues to the Past

HISTORY AROUND US...

Listening to Stories
of British History:
William I,
Considering Motives and
Context

Recording and Reenacting
Writing and Drama
Using Maps, Pictures, and Timelines

Field Trips
Looking at Landscape, Buildings, [& Plant Life]
Considering Roads and Rivers

At this point, Hilton asked a retired teacher—who was a good storyteller—to tape stories about her life at age seven. Once involved, the teacher-storyteller had an idea also: to invite the children to write to her about their own lives, as they saw links to her life—or differences between them. Thus, the children began to see themselves as participants of history. They wrote to her as those who already had memories themselves—and important memories, too, because someone wanted to hear about *them.* The storyteller wrote back to them, and the letters, filled with memory stories, flowed back and forth as meaningful dialogue.

The children spontaneously shaped their writing with care because they cared about what they were hearing and saying. They complimented Miss White, the storyteller, on her writing, too; she had become their friend. The children had begun to ask different questions about history, Hilton noticed, questions based on their own storytelling experiences, such as What happened? When? Why did it happen?

With an interdisciplinary focus like Hilton's, students explore various topics that embrace different curriculum areas. Teachers foster learning for real purposes in the real world. Educator Stephen Tchudi (1994) lists themes teachers could use in connection with various curriculum areas, as Hilton's topic was related to history. For science, a class might explore the topic "Patterns of Change"; for history, it might investigate "Effects of Imperialism on Families" or "Cultural Causes and Effects of War" (page 58). Such topics as these "cry out for the use of fiction, poetry, drama, and nonfiction" Tchudi adds (page 58).

A broad interdisciplinary curriculum is the best preparation for life, Tchudi argues, and literature and literacy educators have the best opportunity to bring such a curriculum to life because "language and literature encompass the full range of disciplinary interests and are enhanced by them" (page 60).

Teaching in Interdisciplinary Ways

Building interdisciplinary programs means reading, writing, and thinking in interdisciplinary ways. What would an **interdisciplinary literacy** look like? How would we teach with children's books keeping many curriculum needs in mind? Usually such a plan emerges in either of two ways. The first way is deceptively simple. We would take just one book and "map" the possibilities for its use in various centers or subjects.

INVESTIGATIONS: Literature for Curricular Needs

Read novels by Madeleine L'Engle, which often have a strong science component in the plot line; characters are often scientists, children of scientists, or fantasy science characters. A favorite genre of L'Engle is, in fact, science fantasy. See what topics you see emerging from her fiction.

Or read fiction by Mildred Taylor or Laurence Yep, which often has a strong history component in the plot line. They often set their stories in the past, and they create characters who face conflicts that actual people of African-American and Asian-American heritage faced in the eras depicted. See what topics you see emerging from their fiction.

Or read *Alice's Adventures in Wonderland* or *Alice Through the Looking Glass* by Lewis Carroll, a mathematics professor. Consider how this fantasy reveals mathematical tools such as exploration, logic, creative thinking, participation in society, problem solving, and building understanding.

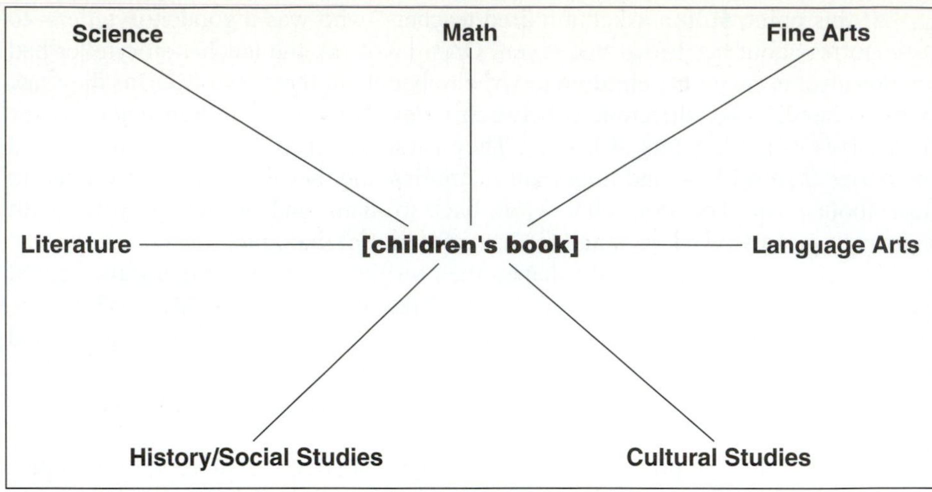

FIGURE 10.3. Mapping the possibilities of one book.

Mapping the Possibilities for a Book

Before we could create such a map, however, we would have to find a book that has major strengths in many areas—and few books do. *The Very Hungry Caterpillar* is such a book, and that is why teachers often use it for cross-curricular needs. But even with this very versatile book, it is still important to find the strengths that relate to this book on its own terms, and not just *use*—or *abuse*—the book for whatever teaching lesson we have scheduled for a particular day: teaching the /k/sound; baking cupcakes; writing a story using the word *hungry;* studying adverbs like "very." Instead, we would search the book to see what it has to offer for various curriculum areas:

- Math (counting activities)
- Science (study of life cycles, metamorphosis)
- Social studies (eating habits of humans and animals, days of the week)
- Literature (compare other stories with surprise endings; other patterned stories, other interactive books; other books by Eric Carle; other books that dramatize the idea of transformation; other stories that explore the theme of growth and change; other stories that offer a narrative experience in counting)
- Literacy (shared big book reading and writing; personal stories that flow out of children's responses to the book)
- Fine arts (finger painting activities; experimenting with vibrant colors)

Teachers need to share books with children on a regular basis and observe children's responses to books in order to better see the intrinsic strengths of a book, just as June McConoghy listened to her students as they revealed a good way to extend *The Very Hungry Caterpillar.* Trusting children to see important aspects of a book, as McConoghy did, is much wiser than stretching a book to a preconceived one-size-fits-all notion.

Discovering Thematic Connections Among Books

The second way to teach a book with an interdisciplinary plan is to take one book and link it to several others so that children learn more about an idea and more about different books. For *The Very Hungry Caterpillar,* one important

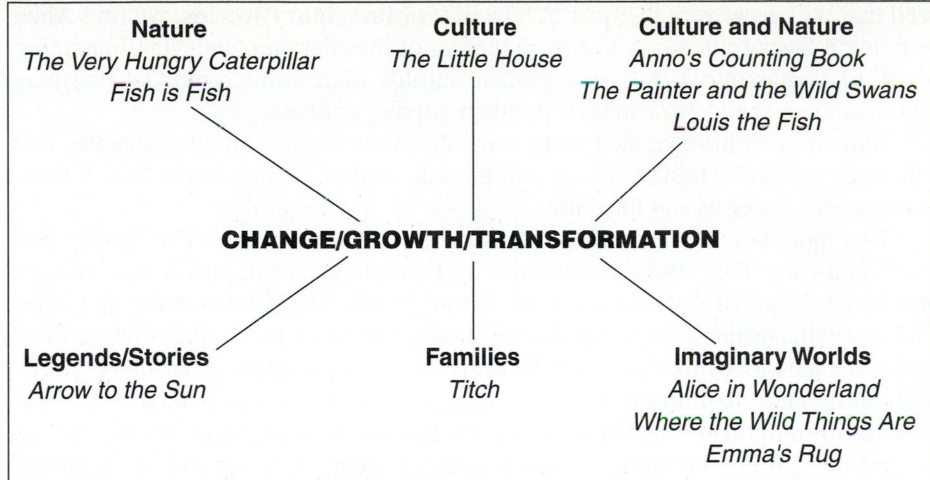

FIGURE 10.4. Finding thematic links among books.

theme is change and growth, or transformation. As this theme weaves through books, we see change and growth in:

- **Nature** (Leo Lionni's *Fish Is Fish,* Knopf, 1974)
- **Culture** (Virginia Burton's *The Little House,* Houghton Mifflin, 1942)
- **Nature and culture** (*Anno's Counting Book* by Mitsumasa Anno, Crowell, 1975 *The Painter and the Wild Swans* by Claude Clement, Dial, 1986; *Louis the Fish* by Arthur Yorinks and Richard Egielski, Farrar, 1980)
- **Legends** (*Arrow to the Sun* by Gerald McDermott, Viking, 1974)
- **Families** (Pat Hutchins's *Titch,* Puffin, 1974)
- **Imaginary worlds** (*Alice's Adventures in Wonderland* by Lewis Carroll; *Where the Wild Things Are* by Maurice Sendak, Harper, 1963; *Emma's Rug* by Allen Say, Houghton, 1996)

In relation to change and growth in **nature,** Lionni's *Fish Is Fish* shows us a tadpole and a minnow growing up together—and changing—so that one goes out to see the world and the other stays back imagining what the world looks like. For **culture,** we see in Burton's *The Little House* that time passes and life changes all around the Little House, once built in the country, now surrounded by city. Still, while architecture, means of transportation, and populations change, some things remain the same: memories handed down within a family and the children's caring spirit.

Anno's Counting Book embraces both **nature** and **culture** to show growth in many ways: As the years pass, as the seasons change, as the day turns into night, a village grows up from empty, snow-covered fields to a small Christmas village. Both a wordless picture book and a counting book, this story has number symbols on the church clock and on the pages themselves. The book begins with zero; we see a snowy patch of land, with a stream running through. Overleaf we see one house and the number one. For the number two, the church and the clock stand beside the one house, by the last page, the house is surrounded by nine more houses and a barn. The human characters in the scenes change and grow also—from no people to clusters in two, three, and so on.

Change and growth in **families** is related to both **nature** and **culture:** it bridges both. In *Titch,* the youngest and smallest member of the family plants a seed that will grow very big, just as he will. For **imaginary worlds,** we find Alice bringing a boring afternoon to life, dreaming of Wonderland, and Max imagining his Wild Things into a lively story—that unfolds right in his room. Titch, Alice, and Max change and grow in their problem-solving abilities.

Humans also have created many transformation stories—myths, legends, and folk tales—that emphasize change and growth, such as *Arrow to the Sun,* a book that connects **legends** and **families.**

Two more books link **nature** and **culture:** Claude Clement's *The Painter and the Wild Swans* (Dial, 1986; illustrations by Frederic Clement) and Arthur Yorinks and Richard Egielski's *Louis the Fish* (Farrar, 1980). The painter in the first story finds the wild swans so beautiful that he gives up painting and changes into a swan himself. Louis loves fish so much, he draws them and dreams about them and finally turns into one himself. Finally, Allen Say's *Emma's Rug* (Houghton, 1996) links **families, culture,** and **imaginary worlds.** In this story, a child-artist grows beyond her earlier imaginings about how she can create so easily and "magically."

Thinking about a Book in Interdisciplinary Ways

There is a third, less common way to engage in interdisciplinary thinking besides mapping topics from one book or making thematic connections among several books. This approach takes us back to one book, but this time we ask ourselves open-ended questions about a *familiar* book as it relates to a particular curriculum area. Students would then become even more deeply engaged with a well-liked story and with a curriculum area—or several curriculum areas—as they intersect. In relation to both science (the concept of variables) and math (subtraction and addition), for example, we might ask what would happen if one character or one action were taken away or added to the story? How would this change the story?

What if Eric Carle moved the setting of *The Very Hungry Caterpillar* to a busy city street? What if his caterpillar were old rather than young and liked caviar rather

From *Anno's Counting Book* (Crowell, 1977) by Mitsumasa Anno.

than chocolate cake? What if the caterpillar were a "she," not a "he"? What if the caterpillar woke up not hungry but lonely and went to look for a friend instead of food? What if the caterpillar turned into a little prince or princess at the end, released from some enchantment? What if Carle used a surrealistic art style to tell his story? Or what if he used pen-and-ink sketches, instead of vivid colors? What if he filled his backgrounds with colorful details instead of large blocks of white space? What if we heard the story from the caterpillar himself—*his* view, rather than a narrator's interpretation? What if Carle expanded this picture book into a fantasy novel?

In relation to math, we might ask, What about the use of numbers in a book? How many characters does the author (or illustrator) place in a scene? How does the author work—in twos, threes, some other multiples? How does the author's use of numbers affect the plot or the theme? (Why is the number one so important in *The Very Hungry Caterpillar?* Why is the number two so important in E. B. White's *Charlotte's Web* and in Lionni's *Alexander and the Wind-Up Mouse?* Why is the number three so important in Virginia Hamilton's *Cousins* and *Second Cousins?*)

In relation to literature and LITERACIES, we might ask, Does a particular character, action, scene, or theme remind us of another book by this author—or by another author? How do intertextual links among different books give us creative ideas for our own stories? (How is Lewis Carroll's caterpillar different from Carle's? How is Carle's caterpillar similar to or different from his busy spider, his quiet cricket, or his grouchy ladybug characters in other books?)

INVESTIGATIONS: Teaching in Interdisciplinary Ways

Imagine you are an elementary teacher gathering children's books for a lesson in each of the following areas:

- A science lesson on air
- A literature lesson on dreams and wishes
- A history/social studies lesson on cultural values and beliefs
- A language arts lesson on flying

You have a two-hour block of time for language arts, and you decide to combine all your lessons, if you can find some way to connect these areas. You begin by "mapping" the possibilities for the concept of flying. In Map I, you arrange the concept "flying" at the center of your map with paths leading to "air," "dreams and wishes", and "cultural values and beliefs."

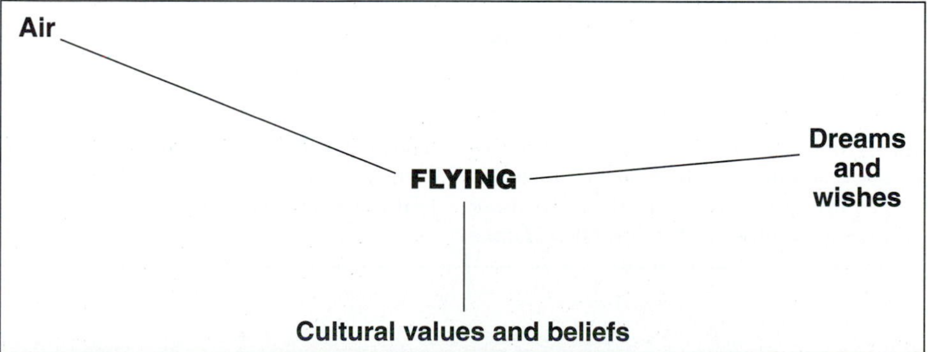

FIGURE 10.5. Mapping possibilities for the concept "flying."

(Continued)

INVESTIGATIONS: Teaching in Interdisciplinary Ways (Continued)

In Map II, you arrange the concept "flying" at the center and create branches of ideas and activities.

FLYING

History of flight

Explore principles of aerodynamics kites/hot air balloons/parachutes

Study folk tales for cultural values and beliefs about flying

- **Julius Lester's "People Who Could Fly" in** *Black Folktales* **(Grove, 1969)**
- **Virginia Hamilton's** *The People Could Fly* **(Knopf, 1985)**
- **Laurence Yep's "Dream Flyer" in** *The Rainbow People* **(Harper, 1989)**

Write a legend based on beliefs from your own cultural heritage and identity

Set *Brother to the Wind* **to music and perform it; making kites**

Compare male and female flyers

Write poetry/stories about wishes and dreams

Collect books/do research on hot air balloons

Invite hot air balloonist as guest speaker

Investigate flying dragons

Look at stories/books/poems about dreams/wishes for flying:

Myths/legends: Icarus

Stories/poems about angels and dragons

Picture books:

- *The Emperor and the Kite* **(fantasy) by Jane Yolen/Ed Young (Philomel, 1988); female flyer**
- *Tar Beach* **(fantasy) by Faith Ringgold (Crown, 1991); female flyer**
- *Brother to the Wind* **(fantasy) by Mildred Walter/Leo and Diane Dillon (Lothrop, 1985); male flyer**
- *The Glorious Flight* **(nonfiction) by Alice and Martin Provensen (Viking, 1983); male flyer**
- *I'll See You in My Dreams* **(realism) by Mavis Jukes/Stacey Schutt (Knopf, 1993); female flyer**
- *Isla* **(fantasy) by Arthur Dorris/Eliza Kleven (Dutton, 1995); female flyers**

Finally, you collect more children's books about flying and add them to the branches, then you create suggestions for activities related to these books. Maurice Sendak's *Outside Over There* (Harper, 1981) comes to mind, as does Claude Clements's *The Painter and the Wild Swans* (Dial, 1986). See how many more books you can find.

Or, we might ask, What in the story connects to our own lives or experiences? What does a particular scene, person, action, detail, or picture remind us of, or cause us to think about? How do *we* fit into this story? How does the story fit us? What is especially effective in the author's style and use of language? What could we learn to make our own writing better?

In relation to the *fine arts,* What do we notice in the book and what do we want to remember and translate into another art form? What story would we want to tell or show after hearing this one? What picture would we want to draw? What drama would we like to create? What music comes to mind as we read this book?

In relation to history, social studies and cultural studies, we might ask, How does this story connect to the larger world? What larger issues and ideas emerge for us? What does the story cause us to know more about? What does it cause us to *want* to know more about? What do we learn about a time in the past? What do we learn about another culture? What do we see now that we did not see before—about ourselves, others, or the world?

Of course, we would never use *all* of these questions with any one book or any one group of children at any one time. We would choose the questions we feel might help children see the story through a different "lens," or think in less compartmentalized ways.

Wherever we look in the real world, compartmentalized thinking abounds. Tchudi and Lafer (1997), writing recently about the traditional distinctions educators make between the arts (painting, sculpture, dance, music) and the humanities (philosophy, social sciences), ask where literature fits into the scheme? How should literature be taught—as an art or as a humanity? They opt for teaching it as a humanity, believing that the humanities path allows us to help students reflect upon the world at large (**sociocultural reading**), whereas literature as an art directs us to focus only on the literary object itself (**literary reading**). But to better understand the concept of literature as a humanity, we need to see clearly what happens when we study literature solely as an art.

LITERATURE FOR LITERACY LEARNING

In *Grand Conversations: Literature Groups in Action,* educators Ralph Peterson and Maryann Eeds (1990) discuss what literature teaching is from their perspective, a viewpoint that sees literature as an art.

Literary Elements

What enables readers to become imaginative readers, say Peterson and Eeds, is an "awareness of literary elements" (page 25). Readers gain this awareness more easily, recognizing plot, point of view, structure, tension, character, setting, and mood, when they study multilayered literature. "Multilayered books," say Peterson and Eeds, "contribute more dramatically to the feelings readers experience and the thoughts they create, and make the resolution of the central story conflict more compelling" (page 26). Whatever story design or structure the author chooses will create dramatic tension, and this tension stretches the readers' imagination. As excitement and suspense rise, readers speculate about how things will turn out for the characters.

Conflict increases the tension. Watching characters grow and change as they work through conflicts produces more tension, uncertainty, and speculation. A richly imaginative story setting contributes to this tension and to the reader's imaginative meaning-making. "Imaginary places created by authors are some of the best known places in the world," say Peterson and Eeds, citing examples of Alice's Wonderland, Narnia, the barn in *Charlotte's Web,* the garden of *The Secret Garden,* Bilbo's cozy underground home in *The Hobbit* and the home of the Wild Things. Often, they add, authors use a unique setting to show the passing of time, "as in the phrase 'In Max's room a forest grew . . . and grew . . . and GREW' " (page 37).

Authors can show time passing quickly in the story events or slow it down considerably inside characters' minds. In either case, the author is increasing the story tension to create a particular mood. "Mood," say Peterson and Eeds, "stimulates our imagination and calls on us to make personal connections" (page 42). Authors also use sounds and images to intensify perceptions and cause readers to read between the lines.

To stimulate literary literacy, teachers help students discover how a story elicits certain feelings and how one literary element affects another to produce new and different meanings as readers move through a text. Literacy theorist and educator Judith Langer takes us deeper into the literature-as-an-art perspective. At the same time, her work shows us the need to pay more attention to literature as a humanity when we teach.

Literary "Stances"

Langer (1995) describes the way readers move through texts as envisonment building. The reader's understanding of a story evolves within a framework of "stances," and she describes this framework as an "envisionment." "I use the word *envisionment,*" she says, "to refer to the world of understanding a person has at any point in time" (page 9). These understandings differ from reader to reader. The word *envisionment,* as Langer uses it, is similar to Rosenblatt's concept of a reader's "transactions" with text. Both concepts—envisionment and transaction—refer to stances or perspectives that readers develop as they wade more deeply into a story or as they reread and think more about the meanings they are making.

The difference between Langer and Rosenblatt's ideas is one of purpose. Why should readers build envisionments or make literary transactions in the first place? Rosenblatt wants readers to become more deeply engaged in the story in order to live through it and gain the understanding that comes from participating in a character's experience. Reading produces the *pleasure* of human response. Langer wants students "to think about ideas, consider alternative views . . . and build interpretations . . . to become more thoughtful readers" (page 20). Reading produces literary *competency,* in this view. Rosenblatt wants readers to become more involved emotionally in the story; Langer wants students to "think more clearly or effectively about the ideas they are considering" (page 20).

Langer identifies four stances that readers take as they engage with texts:

- Stepping into the work to sort it out (Stance 1)
- Moving through the work to understand it (Stance 2)
- Stepping out of the work and rethinking their lives as a result of their reading (Stance 3)
- Stepping out of the work but reflecting back on it to make more meaning of it (Stance 4)

These stances are not stages, Langer adds, although they might occur progressively. They might recur, or occur at the same time, or not occur at all. (Not every stance occurs for every reader at every reading.) Therefore, these stances should neither be formally taught nor tested. They simply give teachers a way to think about how students might be making meaning.

Readers "step in" to a text (Stance 1) "to gather enough ideas to gain a sense of what the work will be about" (page 16). This is similar to what we have previously described as **generative** reading. Stance 2 occurs as readers "become more immersed in developing understandings" . . . they "use personal knowledge, the text, and the context to furnish ideas and spark [their] thinking" . . . they "are caught up in the narrative of a story or the sense of feel of a poem" (page 17). They use "knowledge of the text, [them]selves, others, life, and the world to elaborate upon and make connections among [their] thoughts, move understandings along, and fill out [their] shifting sense of what the piece is about" (page 17). As they move into Stance 2, readers might engage in **personal/empathetic, sociocultural,** or **narrative literacy.**

Stance 3 moves from making sense of the text to making sense of the world as the text reveals it. Readers use their knowledge of the text world as raw data for understanding the real world; the text becomes another experience for knowledge building. Readers are thinking about what the story ideas mean for their lives. This stance resonates strongly with both **sociocultural** and **critical literacies.** It may not involve reading against the grain of a text, but it might initiate some social action.

Stance 4 moves back toward the text. In this stance, readers might be evaluating the work, comparing the author's vision of the world to their own. They might be thinking about authorial crafting choices. They might be analyzing literary elements by closely reading the text. Or they might be making new—and deeper—interpretations. This stance is similar to what we have previously described as **literary literacy.**

Stance 2 is the most popular with readers, says Langer; they can bring something of themselves to the text. Stance 3 is the one students use least because, as she explains, the work might not intersect with the readers' lives in any way they can see *at that moment.* The real reason we read—when no one is requiring us to read—is to make sense of life, she says, but we may not understand the impact of a work until much later.

INVESTIGATIONS: Envisionment Building

Select a children's book that you would like to read and record your responses throughout the reading. Notice if—and when—you take any of the four stances Langer describes. See if you:

- notice yourself stepping into the work to make preliminary sense of it (Stance 1);
- bring your experiences to bear upon the text to make deeper meaning of it (Stance 2);
- step out of the work to make meaning for your own life (Stance 3); or
- step out of the work but reflect on it to make more meaning of the story (Stance 4).

Consider which stance is the one you take most—or least—often. Consider which stance is the most pleasurable. Now reread the book and see if your stance changes—deepens, widens, narrows. Or read a different book and see what changes emerge in your envisionment process.

It is important for teachers to understand these stances, says Langer, because they reveal ways to talk with students about literature that will help them explore other types of meaning-making. Teachers can invite students into books (Stance 1) by encouraging them to search for clues to a story's meaning. Then if things become puzzling, they can invite students to try stepping into the piece again—to reread it. They can help students tap their personal experiences in order to bring richer meaning-making to the text (Stance 2). They can encourage students to "imagine alternative values, beliefs, and emotions" (page 18) in response to their own life questions and conflicts (Stance 3).

They can also encourage students to think as writers, in order to understand better authorial choices for their own writing (Stance 4). Says Langer, "The envisionment-building classroom is likely to include a great variety of different writing activities: freewriting, quickwriting, brainstorming, journal entries, reading logs, oral readings, role playing, written and oral conversations, small group and whole class presentations, portfolios, artwork, essays, computer graphics, and the like" (page 140).

Teachers can also "invite students to move in and out of the variety of stances as ways to consider and share their growing understandings" (page 22). The important thing, says Langer, is that these stances give teachers ways to talk with students about their literary understandings—or ways to open up *dialogue.*

Dialogic Teaching

In their study of literacy learning in elementary classrooms, teacher educators Carole Edelsky, Bess Altwerger, and Barbara Flores (1991) describe how fifth/sixth-grade teacher Karen Smith interacts with members of a literature study group. The students in this classroom are children whose first language is Spanish, and they have self-selected the books for the study groups. Today the group is discussing Esther Hautzig's fictional autobiography *The Endless Steppe* (Harper, 1987; rpt. 1968).

As the authors explain, Hautzig's books focuses on "Hautzig's family's exile to Siberia during World War II. It follows young Esther in a forced labor environment as she and her family struggled to stay alive. With exquisitely poignant details, Hautzig tells a story of a grandmother who refused to give in to despair and of the strength of this family that sustained them all through their terrible ordeal" (page 80).

During this first session with the book, the four group members—Lisa, Robert, Marcella, and Tere—meet for twenty-five minutes to talk about the parts of the book they considered important. In terms of Langer's envisionment stances, the students in the study group are in Stance 4—reflecting back on the story. Lisa says, "From the start I could see not only character change, but story change" (page 82). In her earlier independent reading, Lisa stepped into the book to sort it out (Stance 1). At this time, she is preparing to converse with others about ongoing classroom objectives: to study literary elements. She needs no prodding from the teacher; she is simply responding to the classroom format. She supports her remark about character and story changes: "It was like, at the start, she was a little girl. She knew she was rich but she wasn't that snobby. And at the end, she had to deal with a lot of things, but she started noticing that they had other needs, not just material; they needed love to get through the war" (page 82).

Robert jumps in at this time, adding a detail to support Lisa's interpretation, and the others chime in with their recollections. Tere enters the discussion, referring back to

Lisa's statement about character change: "I saw a big change of character 'cause in the beginning she [Esther] was rich and then when they took her to Siberia she didn't like it there and—" Robert interrupts: "—she started adapting" (pages 82–83). Tere adds more to this idea: "She got used to it and she *kind* of liked it because she had friends. It reminded me of *The Upstairs Room* 'cause she didn't have any friends at first" (page 83).

Over a fifteen-minute span of time, the students have woven a growing web of understanding. Their "envisionments," as Langer would say, are developing through the interaction of self and text. Now Karen Smith, the teacher, enters the conversation. The students are discussing a minor character—a beggar that Esther's mother treats kindly. Lisa says that Esther's mother's behavior made a big impression on Esther. Smith paraphrases and extends Lisa's comment: "She dignified him. She treated him as a human being, regardless of what he had on, and he seemed to respond to that" (page 83). Marcella in turn adds to Smith's comment, drawing on her own experiences as she moves into Stance 2: "She gave him confidence because, you know a person like that could be shy. I thought she gave him confidence that they wouldn't laugh at him" (page 83).

At this point, Smith unfolds her own envisionment. She is in Stance 4: Smith steps back from the work and reflects on the author's crafting choices to make meaning of it:

> It was interesting to me why they [Hautzig] even put that character in there. I thought—well, maybe because it was really true—but I couldn't figure out why they put that character, the bum, in the story. I didn't see where it added to it or enhanced the story in any way other than maybe what you're saying here. Maybe that was the point. I hadn't really thought about it that way. Maybe it just shows one more time the mother maintaining her values from Poland even though she had been transposed to a different place and conditions were poor. Maybe that's it. (page 83)

The informal phrasing of Smith's dialogue is important for keeping the discussion on an even keel. When she enters the conversation with a personal response, she does not offer her idea as the "correct" answer to any question; she is merely one of the group, thinking aloud to make sense of the book. Informal phrasing is important modeling. If students see adults wondering about books, working through their puzzlement ("But I couldn't figure out why . . . Maybe it just shows . . . Maybe that's it . . .), the students will feel more inclined to bring their own spontaneous and untested thoughts to light.

Similar to writing process classes in which children engage in writing to improve at writing, literature study groups engage children in reading to get better at reading—or at reading literature. In these classrooms, both literature and writing are taught as *art* forms, and the focus is on the writing or literature piece as an object for reflection and discussion. Readers converge on a story and create meanings for it, then reflect on how the story "works."

Those who teach literature as a *humanity,* on the other hand, focus on the world outside the text. They let the text lead them to reflect on their lives and on the world itself (Langer's Stance 3). In these classrooms, teachers would ask questions such as, What is this book making you think about? How is it affecting your life? What does it cause you to want to do? How is it changing you? How does it make you want to change the world?

Of course, children do need to study authorial choices if they are to read and write like writers. The better they get at reading and writing, the more they read and write, and the more they read and write, the better they get at reading and writing (the circle of literature and literacy). But if the value of literature is to help us understand our lives (Stance 3), as Langer asserts, and if sorting out our lives is, as she says, "a primary reason that we read and study literature" (page 18), then we need to find ways to develop this value—or stance—with students.

Do teachers bring to the foreground cultural—as opposed to literary—learning, as often as they might? Do they invite students to reflect on their lives—and on the state of the world—as they read literature? Or do they focus much more frequently on the text as an object to be sorted out, interpreted, and reflected on in terms of authorial crafting—treating literature as art?

What do educators do when they teach literature as a *humanity?* What do they show us about literature for cultural and multicultural learning? For the remainder of this chapter, we will examine six different possibilities for valuing literature in this way when we use it in the classroom.

LITERATURE FOR CULTURAL AND MULTICULTURAL LEARNING

Tchudi and Lafer (1997) say: "We've come to see the best English language arts teaching is 'experiential,' focusing on the ideas and experiences in the world around us rather than first and foremost on language" (page 26). To focus on literature as an art is to diminish "the potency of the experience" for the reader (page 22). When teachers focus on literature and life connections rather than on the story as an object, or when they teach literature as a *humanity* rather than an *art,* the classroom picture changes.

Literature as a Way of Knowing

Liz Waterland (1989), an English educator, kept one literature unit in motion for three years running. The children who participated were six to eight years old, and some children participated for the entire time. Her unit focused on "classics"—or, as she defined the term, books having

- literary language or distinctive literary style,
- depth of character,
- artistic integrity,
- multidimensional characters and ideas,
- popular acceptance over a long span of time, or at least over one generation, and
- longer length than most books in an era of television, fast foods, and computer technologies.

Waterland's unit springs out of a question she asked herself about children's classics: What happens when children encounter the popular version of a book rather than the "real thing?" Do they begin to see the Disney version as the "true" story—or the only one? After a while will they believe there is no original version? When so many parents are enchanted by the cuteness of a Disney movie, book, or video based loosely on the original, such as A. A. Milne's *Winnie-the-Pooh* (Dutton,1926; illustrations by Ernest Shepherd), will children lose all knowledge about the original text and illustrations?

Waterland's student Suzanne did have this knowledge. At home, she had her own copy of the original Pooh text, and she saw the Disney version as "not true." It was Suzanne who prompted Waterland to build a unit focusing on classics, flying in the face of popular notions that such books were too long and complex and too distant from today's child in setting and language to be meaningful.

Before the unit began, Waterland was reading aloud twice each day and listening to children's responses. At one session, she read modern picture books. At the other, longer session, she read a little each day from a children's novel, usually a chapter at a time, and it was into this session that she decided to plug her classics unit. She chose the books herself, using two basic criteria: whether *she* as a child had loved the book, and whether the book had now become a much-loved book in the broader culture. Her choices, she says, were fortunate: No child disliked any book she chose, and each child had at least one or two special favorites.

Waterland began her study with Milne's *Winnie-the-Pooh;* she followed it with Milne's sequel, *The House at Pooh Corner* (1928); Lewis Carroll's *Alice's Adventures in Wonderland* (1865), and Kenneth Grahames's *The Wind in the Willows* (1905). The second year, she read C. S. Lewis's *The Lion, the Witch, and the Wardrobe* (1950), Charles Dickens's *A Christmas Carol* (1843), Anna Sewell's *Black Beauty* (1877), and Lewis Caroll's *Through the Looking Glass* (1871). The third year, she read J. R. R. Tolkien's *The Hobbit* (1937) and Frances Hodgson Burnett's *The Secret Garden* (1909).

Literature as a tool for learning about life was the central value of Waterland's unit. When she asked at the end of a chapter of *Winnie-the-Pooh* in which Rabbit had played a trick on Kanga, "Why did Rabbit do that, do you think?", the discussion that followed touched on "the nature of power and authority, radial prejudice, the mother's role in children's lives, the use of talents to gain popularity, and the role of jealousy as a motivator" (pages 190–91). The children were discussing Milne's characters in terms of their own experience of what the world is like—demonstrating **sociocultural literacy:**

Steven: He was jealous of Kanga, I expect, because she was new and I expect Christopher Robin played with her more.

Me: [Waterland]: What's jealousy?

David: Like when someone's got something you haven't and you want it, and Rabbit thought Christopher Robin likes her more than him.

Rachel: Yes, and he thought she would go away if she was frightened. I think it wasn't very nice because she would think Roo had gone with a stranger or something . . . (page 190)

As the group heard *Alice's Adventures in Wonderland,* their discussions focused on why the Duchess was so angry at one point and so affable at another. The

INVESTIGATIONS: Reading Classics for Sociocultural Literacy

Consider reading a classic not on Liz Waterland's list to a group of children—a book such as *Little Women* (1868–69), *Hans Brinker and the Silver Skates* (1865), *Treasure Island* (1881), *Kidnapped* (1886), or *A Little Princess* (1905). Before you begin, think about how you might need to adapt certain aspects of the book, like length and old-fashioned language, for today's child readers. Then consider what information you might need to supply and what you might need to look up to prepare yourself for questions children might ask. Examine the books to see if gender bias, class distinctions, or ethnic stereotypes from an earlier time are present and decide how you might deal with this factor as you present the book. Finally, share the book with children, inviting them to discuss what the story makes them think about in terms of their own lives, their questions, puzzles, values, and beliefs. Note their responses, and see if you agree with Waterland that reading a classic is a valuable experience for children.

children also wondered what happened to the Dormouse after Alice left the party. Hearing Dickens's story, they wondered if Scrooge's ghosts were real or a dream. Hearing *The Hobbit,* they talked about what elves were really like. Reading *The Secret Garden,* they thought about why Colin was so disagreeable. They dramatized *The Hobbit* for parents and played through scenes from *Alice's Adventures in Wonderland* and *The Secret Garden* among themselves on the playground.

Waterland saw her role as that of an informant: When the children asked for information, she filled in gaps about old-fashioned words and concepts in the story. She was also a catalyst for discussion; her "why" questions helped children explore character motivation in light of their own experiences. At other times, she became an adapter of text, condensing long, adultlike passages in the books by Tolkien, Grahame, and Dickens.

The unit was valuable, says Waterland, for a number of reasons. First of all, the students were enthusiastic: Children looked forward to reading the books and hated stopping each time a session ended, and they continued reading these books—and other classics—at home. Second, the children expanded their understandings: "New worlds," says Waterland, "were opened for them" (page 193). Third, exposure to unfamiliar settings in the books helped to deepen the students' imaginative powers and enrich their language base.

A fourth reason the unit was successful was because communication within families expanded as a result of the reading. Parents had read many of the same books, so adults and children began talking about classics together. Fifth, intertextual activities emerged: Seeing videos and films of these classics led children to read the books in their original form; reading the books also led them to view media adaptations and to discuss the differences between the two forms. Finally, a sixth value of the unit was that children became confident that they could tackle literature of greater intellectual and emotional range.

Drama as a Sociocultural Experience

John Rainer and Paul Bunyan (1996), English drama in education specialists, have created a way to fuse history, role play, and children's picture books for personal, social, and cultural meaning-making. They begin with an activity involving quilt squares. Each participant picks up a square and begins imagining and telling a story behind that particular piece of fabric. When did this piece of fabric come into my life or into the life of someone in my family? the person might ask. How did it become a quilting square? How does it connect to *me*—then or now?

The cloth square is a catalyst for memories that tellers draw out of themselves in order to build a personal, social, cultural, and historical context for the larger drama to come. As the participants tell stories, they come to know one another empathetically as characters in the story. The story they are constructing comes from the common experience of picking up the squares and imagining stories about them. The principle is that people bring their different pasts to any collective social experience, and they can work through these different pasts to make meaning of the present.

From cloth squares and storymaking, participants go on to view a picture—or part of a picture—from a children's book, such as Valerie Flournoy's *The Patchwork Quilt* (Dial, 1985; illustrations by Jerry Pinkney). Rainer and Bunyan project part of a scene on a large screen and ask questions that help participants build a fiction—or make a drama for themselves—from just this glimpse of a person. The glimpse

From *The Patchwork Quilt* (Dial, 1985) by Valerie Flournoy, illustrated by Jerry Pinkney.

shows the grandmother seated in a chair with a patchwork quilt on her lap, looking up at her granddaughter. (They block out the child.)

Who is this woman? they ask. What is her personal history? What is she feeling at this moment? What might a caption for this picture be? What might the story text be? Is this woman alone in the scene—or in the world? Is she a stereotype—a collection of preset notions—of a lonely older person? Is she more than a media "image"? Who else might be in this picture? What is its cultural context? This woman is black, yes, but many different cultures could account for her history—African, West Indian, American, European, native, immigrant, emigrant, traveler, guest, homemaker, worker, professional.

What stories does she know? What stories has she told? What might she have written about in letters? What might she have told about in a diary? What music has she heard? What songs does she know? What has she seen? What has she done? What might she want to remember—or forget? Is she a victim of prejudice? Or is such an assumption just another stereotype? What cultural "baggage" do readers bring to literature?

Think of the voices in this woman's head, Rainer and Bunyan urge participants. Describe the voices as she might. Tell her story, walk back into her past. Build her memories. Become this woman. Try to remember her life, based on what you imagine. Try to forget something in her life based on what you have known.

Drama, art, music, reading, writing, language, talk, movement, filmmaking (flashbacks, fast forward, slow motion), photography (still image or freeze frame), history, geography, critical thinking, and risk taking all come together in this approach. Participants work together to build a social art form, one that enables them to make meaning of their cultural and personal experiences. This way of teaching is completely open-ended, once the drama begins. Participants interact to build scenes and imagine themselves in a story. The leader assumes the role of narrator-director, assisting the participants to speak, move about, gesture, stand, sit, laugh, cry, talk, gossip, tell stories, remember, think aloud, wonder, write, read, paint, draw, and make music.

The teacher, playing the dual role of narrator/director, orchestrates the casting and script creation by asking questions of participants (What are you seeing? What are you feeling? What are you remembering?). Participants arrange themselves around the grandmother, assuming various roles—friends, family members, strangers, adults, children—who see, feel, and remember something about this person's life as it connects to theirs.

Many participant roles emerge as the story evolves. Because only one person can physically be the grandmother, others must enter the story in other roles. They might be passengers on a boat or train, people in a marketplace, or children passing the woman's door. This story exploration is never scripted ahead of time; it is spontaneous. It evolves on the spot as participants transact—or envision—the story *together.*

Holocaust Literature in the Classroom

Vicki Zack (1992) writes about a unit on Holocaust books that she used in her fifth-grade classroom. In her literature-based classroom, children choose books to read from the books Zack selects, features, introduces, and displays in her classroom, and they respond to books in reading/writing logs and group discussions. The Holocaust as a subject for study arose in connection with a time fantasy movie that came to Zack's city of Montreal. She began featuring time-travel books, including Jane Yolen's *The Devil's Arithmetic* (Viking, 1988), a children's time-travel novel about the Holocaust.

Zack asked herself two questions as she deliberated including Yolen's book as one of the twelve time fantasies in her classroom display. Should children's authors write about the Holocaust? If they do, should these books become part of the classroom program? Just as Zack's parents had been fearful of her reaction in learning about her own cultural history (she was a child of Holocaust survivors), Zack worried about her students' reactions. Could they cope with such a horrifying subject?

In Zack's classroom, students can choose to stop reading at any point. When they do, she simply conferences with them, asking them to try to tell her why they stopped. She does not force any child to read—or finish—any book. In this case, some children did decide to switch to Lois Lowry's *Number the Stars* (Houghton, 1990), a book about Jewish people during the Nazi invasion of Denmark. Lowry's book does not focus on scenes of concentration camps, as Yolen's does. Lowry's book also has fewer characters and a less complex plot, which might also have

INVESTIGATIONS: Drama as a Sociocultural Experience

Think about other picture books that could be used as effectively as Valerie Flournoy's *The Patchwork Quilt*—other books about quilts, like Patricia Polacco's *The Keeping Quilt* (Simon & Schuster, 1988); other books about elderly people; other books about cross-cultural or multicultural characters; other books with illustrations that readers could use to to imagine mysteries or hidden stories waiting to be told. Then invite a group of children to work through a drama experience with you as the narrator/director.

been factors in the children's choices. Three children did want to know more about the Holocaust, or felt they should know, so they persisted.

As these three children continued reading Yolen's book, Zack noted questions they asked in their group discussions, comments they made, what troubled them about the subject, what puzzled them, and how they sorted out authorial strategies like the title. She discovered that their interpretations contributed to her own meaning-making:

> "One plus one plus one The Devil's arithmetic Gitl called I" [Zack was reading aloud from Yolen's book]. "Oh, that's why it's called *The Devil's Arithmetic,*" Harlie responded to my reading of this selection. . . . Shortly thereafter, Harlie added her own interpretation of the title ["It . . . could only be done by the . . . devil, someone really mean"]. As Harlie spoke, I thought of the diverse ways Yolen presents the fiendish arithmetic . . . numbers tattooed on arms, numbers replacing names and identities (page 46).

Zack ended the unit by telling her students something that was not in Yolen's book: that often the first ones to go to their deaths in the Nazi camps were children and the elderly—those too small or too weak to be used for labor. Was this fact too shocking for the children to hear? she wondered later. There were no easy answers for Zack, who described her students flinching. She continued to wonder whether teachers should study the Holocaust with children, but she remembered Yolen's words at the end of the book—that fiction can be a witness to memory and to the miracle of those who survived—and her answer seems to be "yes."

Six years after Zack questioned whether the Holocaust should be taught, Sandra Stotsky raised another question—should teachers reveal *so much* about the Holocaust? Stotsky explains that Biblical literature, which she feels is "the chief contribution of the Jewish people to history and world civilization" (page 52) is taking second place in the curriculum to Holocaust studies. In addition, she says, there is today" the almost complete absence of literature on the life of the Jewish people after the Holocaust, either in this country or elsewhere" (page 54). In anthologies, textbooks, and children's books generally, she says, we hear nothing about the *living* Jewish culture, and she places the blame on multicultural literature, because it focuses on people of color and excludes Euro-American ethnic groups.

Stotsky addresses racism and intolerance as a moral lesson or a social issue running through Holocaust literature that undercuts the very purpose it should serve—the miracle of survival. Yolen's choice of genre for *The Devil's Arithmetic*—historical time fantasy—helps us to see Stotsky's point. Yolen's modern Jewish child, Hannah, travels back in time to live through the Holocaust experience in order to understand, learn, and remember the horror. But what she finds there—the experience of the extermination camps—tends to overshadow the miracle of survival (the 1940s scenes squeeze out the scenes of modern day life). Thus, to the concern of educators like Stotsky, teachers continue to replay the historical horror story, to the exclusion of the more hopeful, modern story.

Avoidance of the modern scene, in Stotsky's opinion, is tied to politics. Writers want to avoid discussing Middle East complexities. Much learning, she adds, lies fallow as a result. We might be discussing literature that links the Holocaust to the *living* Jewish culture of Israel, Stotsky says, or that links it to contemporary anti-semitism. Instead we keep Nazi beliefs alive, she says, by teaching so much about them in schools today.

Multicultural Literature for Humanized Learning

For some time now, educators have used multicultural literature across the curriculum to foster humanistic learning, or as African-American educator Rudine

Bishop (1997) says, "to make visible underrepresented groups and to counter negative images and stereotypes" (page vii). As Bishop (1987) notes, many ethnic and cultural groups in the United States have never become assimilated, and although all Americans share "some common experiences, many of the diverse groups that make up the country maintain distinctive cultural traditions and experiences. It is a multicultural society" (page 60).

Literature, she says, could help children understand the common bonds and "celebrate the differences among us" (page 60). Literature could also help children understand the way social issues such as racism and poverty impact underrepresented people. If children of unassimilated groups find their life experiences mirrored in literature, they will feel that the dominant culture values—and authenticates—them. Bishop advocates that teachers

- integrate literature about various cultures into the curriculum areas;
- incorporate African-American history into units on U. S. history, rather than limiting the study of black literature to certain times, such as Black History month, or to classrooms that are predominately black, Asian, Hispanic, or Native American;

INVESTIGATIONS: Cultural/Multicultural Literature—Growing up Jewish-American

Consider Sandra Stotsky's idea that we often neglect the living Jewish culture in literature classes today. See how many books you can find for a unit focusing on *contemporary* Jewish children. See also if you encounter any problems in doing so. For example, Patricia Polacco's *The Keeping Quilt* (Simon & Schuster, 1988) seems to fit this category; yet the focus is actually balanced equally between past and present. The same is true of Kathryn Lasky's *The Night Journey* (Penguin, 1981), in which the past gains the edge; the historical survival story is simply more exciting in terms of plot and conflict.

Judy Blume's *Are You There God? It's Me, Margaret* (Bradbury, 1970) focuses on a child who is part Jewish, but the general focus on growing up—a young girl's coming to terms with puberty—soon crowds out everything else. Elaine Konigsberg and Lois Lowry have written books about contemporary children of Jewish heritage, but the families are often so assimilated that any living Jewish traditions are scarce or nonexistent.

Assimilation might more accurately account for the problem Stotsky notices. As Kathryn Lasky has written, "I am the daughter of midwestern Jews by way of Russia. I grew up in shopping malls and dreaming about rock and roll and Jack Kennedy and his New Frontier" (page 7). Twice, Lasky says, she has written about "Midwestern Jewish girls of Russian extraction," and by "the new rules of this multicultural game, I would be destined to keep writing about [them]" (page 5). But, she adds, "life is too short to tell the same story twice" (page 7), and she wants to move on to other subjects and to other ethnic groups for her characters. Sonia Levitin does the same in *The Golem and the Dragon Girl* (Dutton, 1993), a story of cross-cultural friendship between an Asian-American character and a Jewish-American friend.

Authors of various ethnicities may therefore choose not to focus on their personal heritage and identity, if they become so assimilated that their interests grow into other areas. The assimilationist tendency of twentieth-century Jewish-American families both before and after the Holocaust may prevent our finding many books for this category unless we look *outside* America. Esther Hautzig's *A Gift for Mama* (Viking, 1981) is the story of growing up Jewish in Poland a few years *before* the Holocaust. Nava Semel's *Becoming Gershona* (Viking, 1990; translated by Seymour Simckes) reveals a great deal about *living* Jewish traditions, or growing up Jewish in Israel.

Consider also interviewing Jewish members of your community to add more stories to your collection. And add a story of your own growing up experiences, if you are a member of this cultural group.

Source: Kathryn Lasky, "To Stingo with Love," *The New Advocate* 8 (Winter, 1996): 1–8.

- notice similarities among folk tales and share them with children to emphasize commonalities across cultures;
- encourage children to interview older members of their cultural communities and families about "special growing up memories" (page 64) after they read ethnic biographies like Eloise Greenfield's *Childtimes: A Three-Generation Memoir,* written with Lessie Jones Little, Greenfield's mother (Harper, 1979; drawings by Jerry Pinkney);
- read aloud realistic fiction by ethnic authors as students read along in individual copies, asking students questions such as, Why do you suppose the character responded as he or she did? How might the person have responded differently if the person had been a member of the dominant culture? (Mildred Taylor's fiction is especially applicable here); and
- attempt to find examples of poetry and fantasy by ethnic authors (less available than realistic fiction by ethnic authors) and share these works alongside works by writers of the dominant culture.

Educator Gillian Klein (1985) advocates, in addition, that teachers use children's literature to study racism and bias. Teachers can encourage students to challenge books—to read against the grain culturally as a way of "demystifying print" (page 112). It is far less threatening to study racism in books, she explains, than to point it out in people or confront people directly about their behavior. One strategy is to *look for the omission* of ethnic people or females or a for a preponderance of white people or males, she says.

Another strategy is to read books and *create role reversals* that will alert students to inequities in society. Asking Bishop's question about how characters might respond if they were members of the dominant culture—with more power and with more options for resisting unfair or unlawful behavior—is one way to invoke Klein's role-reversal strategy. Students must put themselves in the character's place in order to answer such a question. Students could also rewrite and act out scenes, replacing an ethnic character with a white character, to see what people of color face in conflicts of power.

Literature is able to take readers inside characters to feel their joy or pain. Thus, it extends readers' knowledge of the human condition. When literature has a multicultural emphasis, students learn more about what it feels like to be a victim of bias, prejudice, or oppression, and they learn more about their own social context, too. As a result, they can begin to consider how they might *take social action* regarding injustices related to housing, employment, education, print, or the media.

Klein also recommends holding discussions about what is a good author. The usual definitions about literary style, exciting story, and depth of character carry little weight if the book is sending negative messages. Klein suggests that students write protests to publishers. They might also write authors or committees that award biased books. However, students must first *read problematic books*—rather than shun them—and discuss them to uncover stereotypes and to learn how to negotiate literature that focuses on racial differences.

Negotiating Multicultural Texts

Educational researcher Patricia Encisco (1997) studied children's responses to Jerry Spinelli's *Maniac Magee* (Little, Brown, 1990). She read this book over a four-week span of time to fourteen children in a fourth/fifth grade classroom (five white males, five white females, one Asian male, two African-American males, and one child of mixed heritage—white, African American, and Hispanic).

Encisco's purpose was "to find out how they made sense of the themes, characters, and plot of the story" (page 15) and to help them read critically for multicultural meaning. Children's books that depict racial division can be problematic, Encisco says, because "images and ideology [of the author are] inscribed within it" (page 36). Even, as in this case, when it is the intent of the author to "construct a humanitarian, heroic white child [as protagonist] who is innocent of color" (page 21), problems can crop up.

The problem in *Maniac Magee* is that the author sets the main character, Maniac, in conflict with an angry black male, Mars Bar. If this were not enough, the white male, Maniac, a twelve-year-old "legend" for his magical feats in sports, searches for racial harmony in a black community where Mars Bar is a leader. Maniac's innocence—his color-blind condition—is a stretch, but his legendary sports abilities places the book in the tall tale genre. Maniac becomes a bigger-than-life character in contrast with the others. As Encisco says:

> Maniac's legendary persona is new and exciting to readers. However, his ability to be a better insider than the insiders is not unusual in popular, Hollywood portrayals of cross-cultural encounters. In *Dances with Wolves,* for example, Kevin Costner portrays a white soldier who learns the ways of the Lakota people and eventually leads them into battle. The portrayals of white outsiders' moves toward the inside appear to be sympathetic to the lifestyles and sensibilities of the "others." However, such sympathies can also be read as an appropriation of the "other" that inevitably limits and diminishes the self-determining potential of a people (page 21).

When the white author, as narrator, tells the story through the eyes of Maniac Magee, whiteness, says Encisco, becomes the "norm" for both white author and white readers (page 37). Teachers must therefore help children to see alternative norms. Encisco began by helping children to make sense of the book in terms of their own experiences. In the process, she uncovered several more problems.

First, the white children had very few resources beyond popular media images to fill in the large historical gaps in the story. They had little idea why there was so much anger or resentment between white and black neighborhoods in the story—or why racially divided neighborhoods exist in America. Thus, they resorted to stereotypes and oversimplified thinking to fill these gaps: Mars Bar, they told Encisco in discussions, acts tough to cover up his weakness; his name probably comes from stealing candy bars; the neighborhoods divisions are the way things were in the days when blacks and whites were "separated . . . [and they had separate] pencils . . . separate brands or something so they wouldn't even know it [that they had different school supplies]," and "they ride on the bus or something" (pages 31–32).

Second, the ethnic differences among members of this classroom played a part in their responses to the story. The white students preferred to deny the differences among the races, as Maniac Magee does in the story. The students of color recognized that there are differences—or at least *perceived* differences—in people's skin colors and that people often get hurt because of the color of their skin. To deny skin color differences perpetuates this hurtful situation, Encisco emphasizes. Thus, it was important that Marisa (of mixed heritage) and Richard (of African-American heritage) identified—at least in one way—with Mars Bar. As Richard said at one point, "Me and Mars Bar are black" (page 29).

A third problem arose because teachers stand as authority figures who hold the values of the dominant culture, especially, in Encisco's view, if they are white. Thus she decided to divulge and discuss her own Mexican-American heritage. (The children perceived Encisco as white until she began to talk about her identity.) At one point, Marisa interjected the comment that she had black relatives, after which Marisa and Richard began to talk about her family's ethnic ties. Encisco described her own ethnic background at this time, helping Marisa to address her mixed heritage rather than to suppress it among classmates of monocultural heritage, black or white. It is important for children to express their identities during literature discussions, says Encisco, so that the negotiations for meaning-making about cultural differences do not all fall to one cultural group alone. Then only one set of cultural references, one set of perspectives, and one set of values are visible.

A final problem, according to Encisco, is that the teacher's role is to "open up dialogues" (page 34) about cultural differences we all see and experience, but some books make such dialogue difficult. In *Maniac Magee,* she explains, the characters do not engage in dialogue about race, and the author says little about the history of race relations in America. Thus, class and race divisions that crop up in the novel are confusing. In addition, she says, the book is a Newbery winner (part of the official canon); thus, it imposes its own intimidating *social authority* on any teacher who works with it.

Encisco's intent is not to censor any work of literature, "but rather to initiate a more complex dialogue about its representations of difference" (page 37). Her discussion leaves teachers with several questions to ask themselves as they read multicultural literature with students:

- Who is the author's implied audience? Whose values is the author espousing? His or her own? Those of one cultural group? Does the work suffer from imbalances of ideology? What social imbalances or inequities could I assist students to consider? Encisco asked students questions such as, Is this something that you know about [in your own life]? (page 31).
- How can I encourage students to ask, Is that character like me? Is the person of color like me? Is the white character like me? Which story is *my* story? Whose experiences have *I* had? Whose experiences would I want to have? Encisco asked questions such as, What are you thinking, Marisa? (page 29).
- How can I help students to engage in discussions that make connections between life and literature? How can I help them to see that they can do something about racial divisions? Encisco asked questions such as, How do you think it [prejudice] happens? Do you think you have to be brave not to be prejudiced in this country? How can you not be prejudiced? (pages 34–35)
- What wider sociohistorical references will students need to consider as the reading evolves? Does the author provide any help in this area? Does the author mask, blur, or gloss over social issues or historical experiences that should be clarified or refuted?

Refuting a child's misinformation is an important task for any teacher. In this case, if Encisco had stopped the discussion for a history lesson on divided neighborhoods and segregated schools, she would have deviated from her own purpose—to see how the students made meaning of this book—and she might also have destroyed the trust she was trying to build. As a visiting teacher, she did not have the opportunity to follow up in other classroom activities during the day. If she had been the regular classroom teacher, what might she have done to help students build sociohistorical references for a work of literature?

One idea is fairly common: offer students more information when the opportunity arises. If students are writing journal entries, teachers can write back to them to supplement what they know—or build such explanations into a large group mini-lesson. Teachers can also suggest other books that focus on the subject in question. If students are reading a novel and they ask for information, teachers can suggest a research activity to explore the question in more depth.

Teachers can also orchestrate such an activity if they notice that students are misinformed about some aspect of a book. Was it really different *pencils* that African-American students had during segregation—or different *textbooks?* the teacher might ask. How would this affect their learning? The next session might begin with the teacher reading a little of Mildred Taylor's *Roll of Thunder, Hear My Cry* (Dial, 1976). Taylor, a black author, tells stories of her father's experiences growing up in rural Mississippi in the 1930s, and the first part of the book focuses on school—and textbook—segregation.

Some teachers would coordinate Taylor's books about the segregation experience with other history topics, such as the Reconstruction era or the segregated South from Reconstruction days to the Civil Rights era of the 1960s. Students might read Taylor's books in literature study groups and pursue additional research, or they might pursue history topics and read supplementary novels in connection with them.

The teacher might also prepare students to read multicultural fiction by first teaching them something about the social background, as Howard Miller (1997), a seventh-grade teacher, did when his class studied Taylor's books. He focused first on the Civil War, the Reconstruction era, and the 1896 Supreme Court case, *Plessy v. Ferguson,* that set institutionalized racism in motion. He continued by reading aloud Taylor's first book about the Logan family, picture storybook *Song of the Trees* (Dial, 1975), to prepare students for the much longer and more complex novel, *Roll of Thunder, Hear My Cry.*

As Miller read Taylor's novel, he peppered the class with open-ended questions: How are the two schools (the white and the black one in the Logan children's community) "separate but unequal"? What if the schools had been separate but really equal? How would *you* have felt about it? Is it right to institutionalize separation on the basis of skin color? After reading the books, students wrote about these topics, supporting their responses with "solid reasons and specific examples from their reading and our discussions," Miller says (page 89). Finally, he introduced his students to the case of *Brown v. Board of Education of Topeka, Kansas,* the 1954 Supreme Court Decision that ended segregated public schools by proclaiming them unconstitutional.

Multicultural and Postcolonial Readings

Another way to help students build sociohistorical references for a work of literature is to invite them to read with a multicultural perspective. "To read multiculturally," says educator Vivian Yenika-Agbaw (1997) "is to read against and around the text in order to uncover ideologies of domination and resistance" (page 450). Taylor's characters take action to change their lives. They constantly resist the dominant white social structure. In *Song of the Trees,* David Logan, the children's father, takes strong and courageous action against the white bigots who try to usurp his land—and he wins.

In *Roll of Thunder, Hear My Cry,* the Logan children exhibit fierce pride and strong self-respect. The youngest child refuses to accept the decrepit books given to black children in their segregated school. Cassie's brother plays a trick on the white bus driver, who always splashes mud on them as he roars past. (Members of the black community of this era are not allowed any transportation to school; one child walks more than three hours one way to earn an education.) Cassie and her brothers do not divulge information about their friend, T. J., when he becomes involved in a robbery and shooting. This resistance becomes more complex and life-threatening as the children grow older in later books of the series.

The wealth of resistance patterns we see in books by black authors lends support to those who say that insiders of particular ethnicities should tell their own stories. Because white writers have usually not experienced domination and oppression themselves, they might not realize the subtle strategies people of color adopt to resist domination and oppression. They may also have been socialized to believe that people of color are passive victims—or are contented with their lot. *Postcolonial* readings—readings that reflect on and challenge colonial racial views—are especially important at this point.

As Yenika-Agbaw explains, readers can challenge the colonizer's belief that the person of color is inferior—or passive, contented, unresisting, weak, gullible, groveling, unimaginative, or lacking in courage. Readers must examine texts for embedded signs that a society

- approves of inequality (accepts an uneven distribution of wealth, power, and justice);
- recognizes one language variety as supreme or "standard" in terms of upward social or economic mobility; or
- treats people of color as less intelligent, less capable, or less deserving as a natural state.

Readers ask questions like: Why are these people of color living in a segregated *setting?* Why are they doing different kinds of *jobs* (physical versus mental tasks)? Why is their *clothing* different (slaves in rags versus plantation owners in silk and satin)? What are the connections between a person's color and *positions* of power? What are the connections between power positions and *unlawful acts of oppression?*

It is interesting and enlightening for students to step out of the book and look at the text through the lens of a "colonizer"—a member of a dominant culture in which people of color are forced to remain in many ways unassimilated. At this point, students will notice feelings of either comfort or discomfort with the story. The Logan children are the major figures in Mildred Taylor's books, which means white readers will see the world through their eyes. But whether they accept this view easily is another matter.

Taylor's African-American characters constantly resist those who keep them oppressed. Thus, it is nearly impossible to think that the Logan children are inferior (passive, weak, gullible, unimaginative, or lacking in courage). However, a dominant culture may have socialized readers to feel superior to other groups. If readers have few cultural or historical references to help them feel empathy toward those resisting a power structure, their response to Taylor's books may be defensive—or even hostile.

The more discomfort white students feel with books like Taylor's, the greater the need for teachers to surround the text with a frame of historical references, or to help children undertake the postcolonial and multicultural readings that Yenika-Agbaw recommends. The important point is that teachers can incorporate strategies to help students negotiate multicultural literature.

We can define *multicultural literature* as stories or poems focused on children growing up in a culturally diverse world and seeing one another as human (cooperating for survival). By this definition, multicultural literature simply teaches children more about their own cultural background and/or the backgrounds of others.

We might also say that multicultural literature focuses on underrepresented, unassimilated ethnic or racial groups—or on any group that stands out as different from the dominant culture. By this definition, multicultural literature reveals members of various ethnicities interacting with the members of the dominant culture yet maintaining their cultural uniqueness.

Yet another definition of multicultural literature might be stories about members of an ethnic culture authored by insiders who present an authentic picture of that this group—its heritage, traditions, life patterns, language varieties, values, and history. Yet some multicultural literature is written by outsiders who want to tell stories about those in other groups.

Obviously, we can "paint" our definitions of multicultural literature with either broad or fine brush strokes. But it is important that we teach children to read against the grain of books that paint insider cultures with the broadest strokes, producing biased or stereotyped pictures. To do so means helping students learn to read in **critical** ways. It is also important that we teach children to read *with* the grain of books that paint insider stories of oppressed people resisting the dominant culture. To do so means helping them learn to read in **personal/empathetic** ways.

INVESTIGATIONS: Producing Multicultural and Postcolonial Readings

Read two books about children of color, one by an insider writer like Mildred Taylor, and one by an outsider writer like Jerry Spinelli. Then conduct a multicultural or postcolonial reading of each book. See if you can detect patterns of resistance the ethnic characters take in each book, along with patterns of oppression perpetuated by the members of the dominant culture in each book. How comfortable are you with each group—the colonizers and the colonized? How empathetic a reader are you? Do you find you are steeped in the unexamined assumptions of a dominant culture, or more familiar with the experiences of the resistant culture?

INVESTIGATIONS: Aims of a Literature-Based Classroom

You have examined four different reasons for teaching with children's books: fostering *personal development,* advancing *curriculum needs,* deepening *literary learning,* and producing *cultural and multicultural learning.*

Consider which of these aims you would foster in your own classroom. Does one aim seem more important than the others? If so, try to explain why. Then explain how you would focus on that aim in your teaching. Does one aim seem less important to you than the others? If so, explain why. Does more than one aim seem very important or even crucial to you? Explain your reasoning. Or do they all seem equally important? Support your case for this stance.

You have also examined two ways of defining literature teaching—as an *art* and as a *humanity.* Consider which appeals to you as a way of teaching literature and defend your position. Or do you see them as equally important? Why?

Chapter 11

Coordinating a Literature and Literacies Classroom

Topics in This Chapter:

- Collaborative planning and teaching
- Collaborative teaching and assessment
- Response journals, checklists, and portfolios

> *"Oh, I've had such a curious dream!" said Alice, and she told her sister, as well as she could remember them, all these strange Adventures of hers that you have just been reading about; and when she had finished, her sister kissed her, and said, "It was a curious dream, dear, certainly: but now run in to your tea; it's getting late." So Alice got up and ran off, thinking while she ran, as well she might, what a wonderful dream it had been.*
>
> ***"Alice's Evidence," in Alice's Adventures in Wonderland***
> **–Lewis Carroll**

We might wonder what made Alice's dream so wonderful, when at times her experiences became so confusing, the animals so insulting, the Queen so overbearing, that Wonderland must have seemed more like a nightmare than a dream. But the strange creatures—for all their shrieking, squeaking, sobbing, sneezing, and shrill voices—were never dull. Best of all, Alice could tell her sister all about her adventures when she woke up. And she was such a good storyteller, her sister could begin imagining the story for herself. In fact, all the creatures came to her so vividly she almost believed herself to be in Wonderland reliving Alice's adventures:

> The long grass rustled at her feet as the White rabbit hurried by—the frightened Mouse splashed his way through the neighbouring pool—she could hear the rattle of the teacups as the March Hare and his friends shared their never-ending meal,

> and the shrill voice of the Queen ordering off her unfortunate guests to execution—once more the pig-baby was sneezing on the Duchess's knee while plates and dishes crashed around it—once more the shriek of the Gryphon, the squeaking of the Lizard's slate-pencil, and the choking of the suppressed guinea-pigs, filled the air, mixed up with the distant sobs of the miserable Mock Turtle. (page 118)

Alice's telling of her dream—and her sister's daydreaming about Alice's story—produce a collaborative frame for the entire fantasy, and that frame is *re*-framed when the sister begins imagining Alice telling the story of Wonderland to more and more children in the future. On and on, frame within frame, the story would be retold, as it has been for years—in newly illustrated versions, condensed versions, Walt Disney films and books, stories adults have told about their encounter with the story, and children's own story recreations.

The collaborations of child and story go on, and collaboration is what we want to talk about in this last chapter, as we take a final glimpse at what happens when literature enters the classroom and teachers work with children to coordinate books, curriculum areas, literacy events, and children's interests. The hope of all good teachers is that even though things in the classroom might be confusing and strange at times, they will never be dull—and they might at some later time be remembered as wonderful. When children become full partners in the planning, teaching, and assessment processes, the chance that this will happen improves dramatically.

COLLABORATIVE PLANNING AND TEACHING

When Dawn first began teaching, she wanted to find a way to organize her first-grade reading program around children's books, but she had no idea how to begin. One day she brought a pile of bear books into her classroom, simply because she

Dawn's Notebook Entry

Children said:
"Bears eat a lot of food. They eat honey."
"Bears have fur on them. Some have bigger fur than others."
"They can stand on their feet like a person."
"They are brown and stubby."
"They are in zoos."
"They are in the circus."
"Some are stupid. Some are smart."
"They can kill people."
"I like them. Bears are terrific."
"They are funny. They have little black noses."
"They have fluffy tails. They are cute."
"They have to get put in cages sometimes."
"Some live in the woods."
"They don't go to school."

Children asked:
"Why do bears eat people?"
"Why do bears get so fat?
"Why do bears have to have claws and teeth? They could scratch me."
"Are bears afraid of bees if there are hundreds of bees? Do bears eat bees?
"Are bees afraid of bears?"
"Can bears see when they are born? My kitten could not see."
"How do bears get so stupid? Papa bear was stupid."
"Why are polar bears white?"
"Do bears eat other bears up?"
"Do baby bears drink milk?"
"Why do bears live in zoos? They live in the woods too, but why do they live in zoos?"

knew her students loved animal stories. She had never taught before and she had no idea what the children were thinking as they looked at the books. One day as they all sat together on the rug, each child "reading" a different book, Dawn turned on the tape recorder. Later in her notebook, she made two headings, "Children said" and "Children asked"; then she set down the responses as they occurred.

Collaborative Planning

Literature helped Dawn understand better what was meaningful in the children's lives. She could have used this knowledge in many different ways: to help develop their awareness of the animal world *(literature for curriculum needs),* of themselves *(literature for personal development),* of literature itself *(literature for literacy learning),* or of culture *(literature for cultural learning).* Which category did she decide was the best one for these particular responses? Dawn chose the first—**curriculum needs,** focusing on **science** and **social studies.** The children wanted to know more about bears, and she let their curiosities guide her planning. Her next task was to synthesize the children's responses into questions and her own preliminary answers (when she had answers). She wanted to help the children connect what was meaningful in their lives to their present awareness of the animal world:

- What does a bear look like? How can you tell a bear from other animals? What kinds of bears are there? *Brown, black, honey, sloth, polar, panda, grizzly, stuffed, wind-up*
- What does a bear eat? How does it find food? How do a bear's paws, claws and teeth help him?
- How does a bear store food? What does a bear do in the winter? Why does he hibernate?
- Where do we find bears? *Zoo, circus, forest, mountain, United States, China, North Pole, Australia, toy stores, books*
- How do bears arrive at the zoo or the circus? Why are they taken there?
- Where is the best place for a bear?

Structuring the children's responses as questions helped Dawn create a concept map about bears, or to start mapping this subject for a classroom unit on Bears.

FIGURE 11.1. Dawn's original concept map about bears.

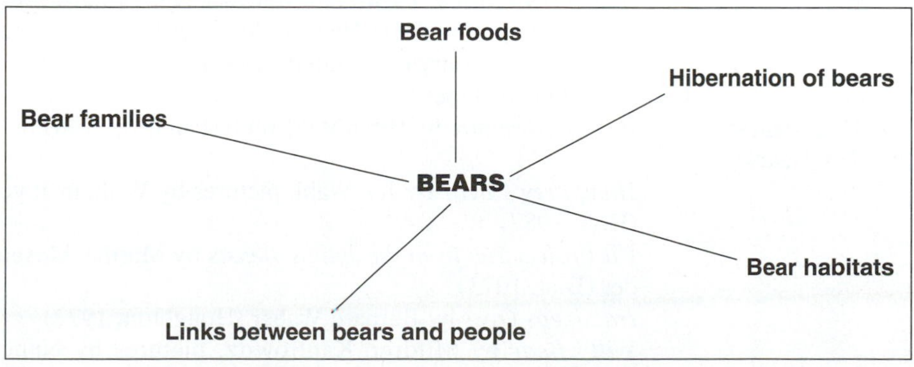

One category on Dawn's map—links between bears and people—spawned a second concept map.

FIGURE 11.2. Dawn's second concept map.

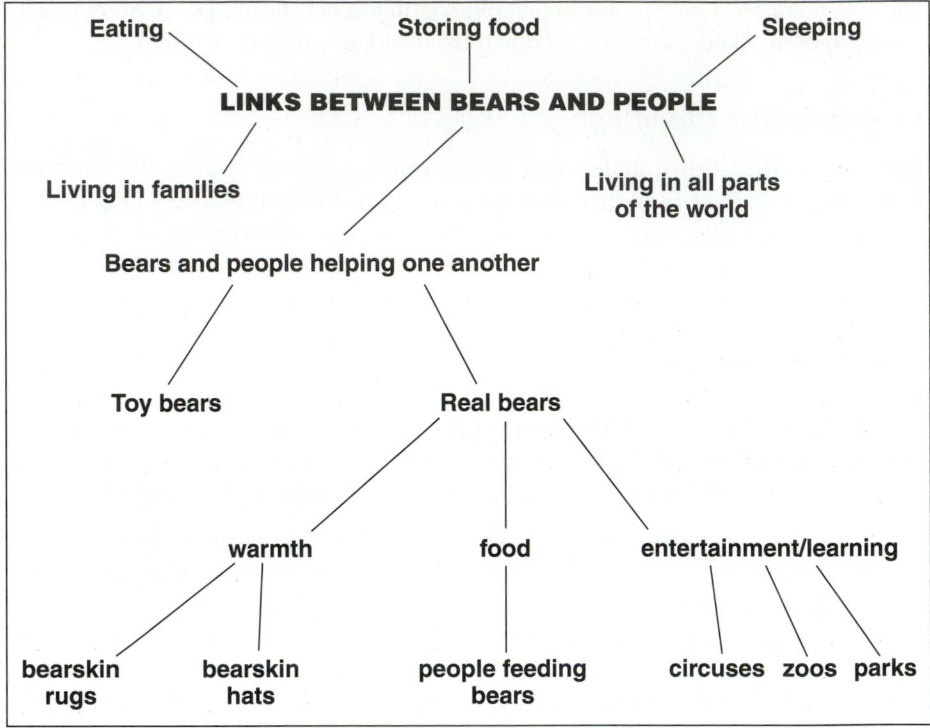

Dawn's next step was to find books to support the categories in her concept maps:

- **Bear Families:** *Panda* by Susan Bonners (Delacorte, 1978)
- **Bear Foods:** *Rumprump* by Ivan Gantschev (Picture Book Studio, 1984)
- **Bear Hibernation:** *The Happy Day* by Ruth Krauss; pictures by Marc Simont (Harper, 1949)
  Sleepy Bear by Lydia Dabcovich (Dutton, 1982)
- **Bear Habitats:** *The Biggest Bear* by Lynd Ward (Houghton Mifflin, 1952) *Eddie's Bear* by Miska Miles (Little, Brown, 1970)
- **Links Between Bears and People:**
  Eating: *Blueberries for Sal* by Robert McCloskey (Viking, 1948)
  Sleeping: *We're Going on a Bear Hunt* by Michael Rosen, pictures by Helen Oxenbury (Macmillan, 1989)
  Bears and People Helping One Another:
- **Real Bears:** *Bear's Adventure* by Brian Wildsmith (Pantheon, 1981)
- **Toy Bears:**
  Humphrey's Bear by Jan Wahl, pictures by William Joyce (Holt, 1987)
  I'll Protect You from the Jungle Beasts by Martha Alexander (Dial, 1973)
  Ira Sleeps Over by Bernard Waber (Houghton, 1972)
  Willy Bear by Mildred Kantrowitz, pictures by Nancy Parker (Parent's Magazine Press, 1976)

The Winter Bear by Ruth Craft, pictures by Erik Blegvad (Macmillan, 1974)

At the same time, Dawn was looking for a nonfiction book that would help her find answers to the children's questions, preferably a book simple enough for first graders to understand if she both read it aloud and told it. She found the book she wanted in Megan Stine's *Bears* (Trumpet Club, 1993), and she found pictures to supplement it in *Bears of the World* by Terry Domico (Facts on File, 1988), a reference book for much older students but one she could keep in her classroom for browsing.

After reading Stine's book, Dawn was able to explain to the children that bears are not stupid, that they are very intelligent and that is why they have so often been pursued, captured, and trained for circus work. The children wanted to hear more about circuses, so Dawn's next unit became "Bears in the Circus." This time, she sent the children to explore library shelves to uncover books about this special kind of bear.

Meanwhile, Dawn was using bear books to teach her first graders to read. She found that Bill Martin's *Brown Bear, Brown Bear, What Do You See?* (Holt, 1970; pictures by Eric Carle) was available in big book format, and it became an important book to add to her unit. She found she could also use Lydia Dabcovich's *Sleepy Bear* with children who were just beginning to read and *The Happy Day* by Ruth Krauss for children who had advanced a little beyond the beginners. She used books in the *Little Bear* series by Else Minarik and Maurice Sendak (Harper, 1957) for children ready for I-Can-Read books, and Ivan Gantschev's *Rumprump* for children who were reading independently.

Recently Dawn moved to a second-grade classroom, but she did not forget her bear books. In September during story time, she read *A Bear Called Paddington* by Michael Bond (Houghton, 1958). When the children showed great enthusiasm for the book, she decided to set up book circles for them to read, discuss, and write about bears. The first unit of the year became "Learning About Bears in Books." She and her students went to the library as literature-researchers to find bear books they could group together in various ways for their classroom book collection. They ended up with nine sets:

1. Books of the same *title,* four to five copies to a set for the entire group to read together. The children chose the Paddington book so that they could reread it for themselves.
2. Books by the same *author.* They chose A. A. Milne and his Pooh books and more Paddington books by Michael Bond.
3. Different *folk tale versions.* They discovered versions of "The Three Bears" by Jan Brett, Lorinda Bryan Cauley, Paul Galdone, Tony Ross, Brinton Turkle, and Bernadette Watts.
4. Different stories about a *folk tale character.* They discovered Julius Lester's and Barry Moser's retelling of the B'rer Rabbit tales, each containing several stories about B'rer Bear.
5. Different *folk stories* about bears. They chose *tall tales:* Anne Isaacs's *Swamp Angel* (Dutton, 1994) and Tomie de Paola's *The Cat on the Dovrefell* (Putnam, 1979).
6. *Joke/riddle/workplay* books about bears. They found Mort Gerberg's *Bear-ly Bear-able* (Scholastic, 1987) and Phyllis Demong's *Celebearties and Other Bears* (Avon, 1979).
7. *Realistic* stories about bears. They discovered Alvin Schwartz's *Fat Man in a Fur Coat and Other Bear Stories* (Farrar, 1984) and Walt Morey's *Gentle Ben* (Dutton, 1965).

8. *Nonfiction: Science and History* books about bears. Donna noticed Peter Bull's *A Hug of Teddy Bears* (Dutton, 1984) and Ada and Frank Graham's *Bears of the Wild* (Delacorte, 1981).
9. *Fantasy* stories about bears. They selected Jan Brett's *Berlioz the Bear* (Putnam, 1991), Anthony Browne's *Bear Hunt* (Scholastic, 1979), and David McPhail's *First Flight* (Little, Brown, 1987). Donna chose Michael Foreman's *Panda's Puzzle* (Bradbury, 1977).

Collaborative Teaching

For the next few months, Dawn shifted gears from a first-grade teacher helping children learn about life through literature to a second-grade teacher helping children learn about bears in books, and about literature—authors, illustrative styles, narrative choices, genres—as they read about bears. A book the children brought back from the library was one Dawn remembered one of her first graders looking at when she began her bear unit—Marjorie Weinman Sharmat's *I'm Terrific* (Holiday House, 1977). She remembered the book and his response: "I like them. Bears are terrific!"

The book gave Dawn an idea. She would ask her second graders what they *liked* about bears and what *worried* them about bears. Soon the second graders were talking excitedly to one another about their trips to the zoo and how they felt seeing bears in cages (not good).

That day, to lift the mood, Dawn chose a book with a bear in a happier state. She read aloud *Annie and the Wild Animals* by Jan Brett (Houghton, 1985). It was January and just right for the wintry setting of this story about a little girl whose cat suddenly disappears. When Annie places corn cakes at the edge of the wood, hoping that a small, furry animal will appear and she can tame it for a pet, wild animals come running for the corn cakes. The moose, wildcat, stag, and big, growling, grouchy bear who come roaring for their next meal nearly shake down her house,

From *Annie and the Wild Animals* (Houghton Mifflin, 1985) by Jan Brett.

but luckily spring arrives the next day. The wild animals return to the forest to find their food, and Annie's cat Taffy returns with three soft and friendly kittens.

As Dawn shared the book, she noticed that it caused the children to talk about their own pets. She suggested that the children bring favorite books to share the next day—about bears or animals generally, pets or wild creatures. Dawn was trying to decide where to go next with her unit. Would they do more with bears or move on to something else? Interest in bears was still strong, she noticed. Jeremy brought a book he found in the library that week, *Ahoy There, Little Polar Bear* by Hans de Beer (North South, 1988). This book was about a little polar bear that gets caught on a ship and finds his way back home with the help of the ship's cat, Nemo.

Ann brought in a book she had received for Christmas, Eric Rohmann's *The Cinder-Eyed Cats* (Crown, 1997). This story tells about a child who sails off to a faraway island where "twilight falls on fair and wind-swept days" and "Cats like velvet shadows move." Dawn especially liked the rhythmic language. This was a book she knew she would read over and over again, the children liked looking at the pictures so much.

Angela brought a book of Valentine poetry, Arnold Adoff's *Love Letters,* illustrated by Lisa Desimini (Scholastic, 1997). Adoff's poems focused on letters to school friends, siblings, parents, and pets. In honor of the cinder-eyed cats, the children wanted to hear the cat poem first: a valentine from "Sleepy Head Girl" to "Dear Old Cat."

Nicky also brought her Christmas present, a copy of Paul Zelinsky's *Rapunzel* (Dutton, 1997) with an announcement from her mom that her book was a Caldecott Award winner. Dawn read it at their last read-aloud time that afternoon, thinking that perhaps it would lead them all into a unit on folk tales. She noticed from the jacket information that Paul Zelinsky had illustrated other folk tales—*Hansel and Gretel, Rumpelstiltskin,* and *Swamp Angel.* Maybe the children could collect different versions of these old stories and compare them. But it was the cat the students noticed. They began to follow it through the pages of the story, although there was no mention of a cat in the story.

The cat was just a kitten as the story began. It must have belonged to the old lady who stole Rapunzel from her parents, or maybe the old woman gave it to Rapunzel for a friend, they reasoned. The cat follows along when the sorceress leads Rapunzel into the tower, and it stays with her in her tower home. It grows along with her, so that when she is older and the prince visits the tower, the cat is a big cat that sits watching over them. At this time, it goes with Rapunzel to watch over her when the sorceress banishes the girl from the tower, sending her into the wilderness. The cat is there, too, when Rapunzel and the Prince are reunited, and on the last page, the cat appears in the family portrait of the Prince, Rapunzel, and their two children. The cat has become the family cat now and the children's pet, Dawn's students decided.

That night, as Dawn began planning what she would do the next day, she thought about all of these books and the children's responses to them. Cats were everywhere, it seemed. Jessica and Todd had asked to hear *Annie and the Wild Animals* again. The day before, they had taken it into their literature circle and studied the border pictures of the behind-the-scenes-story of the cat when it disappeared to have kittens. Dawn remembered the children's talk about pets. She could see their values about pets as friends and the fun of taking care of their pets weaving through their talk and stories. Jan Brett's book was about friendship, Dawn recalled, as she thought about the ways Annie and Taffy played together and "talked" to one another before Taffy went away.

From *Rapunzel* (Dutton, 1997) by Paul Zelinsky.

She leafed through the book again, noticing that it was also about how children cope with loneliness and separation. Annie is lonely when Taffy leaves, but she sets out to solve her problem by feeding the wild animals, hoping to find another pet. The book was also about the storytelling process itself, Dawn saw, as she looked at the border pictures that told Taffy's story, the one Annie could not see. Dawn decided to set up a space in her classroom for children to extend literature with storytelling. She would allow time for activities to build on children's interest in behind-the-scenes stories like those in Jan Brett's border pictures and in Zelinsky's addition of the cat to the Rapunzel story. But which books would she use, and how would she choose these books? Dawn decided to let the children decide.

Collaborative Units

The next day Dawn called a class meeting and asked the children to design a questionnaire about pets. She needed to know the following:

1. What wild animals did they like to read about?
2. What other kinds of animals did they know of, and what kinds did they like to read about?
3. What animals were their favorite pets?
4. What would they like to know about their favorite pets?
5. What kinds of books would they like to read in connection with animals or pets? Real-life stories? Fantasies? Fact books? Rhymes or poems? Picture books?
6. What kinds of picture books did they want to read?

The children decided to do a survey instead of a questionnaire; three children volunteered to collect the information and report back at the afternoon story time. Dawn learned from her students that afternoon that she would need books of all types about cats and dogs. Cats were very popular because they included both pets and wild animals. But dogs were still a big favorite, and children volunteered to begin looking for cat and dog books at home, in the library, on the classroom shelves, and among the stories they themselves had written. Dawn would do the same. Meanwhile, at writing time, she invited children who were ready to start new stories to write about the animal they had chosen as a favorite pet.

During the next week, everyone brought books and worked on categorizing them as they chose books for read-aloud times and for literature circles. Dawn asked the children to think about how they would like to work—in pairs, in their small-group literature circles, or individually. The children began to find partners for particular kinds of books, according to their experiences with pets and their preferences for particular kinds of pets.

On the first day, Dawn explained the schedule. The children would have time to read books quietly at first, then time to talk about the books in a large group right after silent reading time. They would have time to share books in small groups, and time to listen to Dawn read aloud favorite books from the collection. Dawn learned what her students were discovering in the large group meeting when children told about the books they were reading. She also watched carefully what books children were choosing and talking about in small groups. Then at story time, she held up several books that she had noticed several children sharing. She described each book; then she asked the children to make one collective choice for read-aloud time.

"Help me decide," she said. "You'll be taking a vote right before story time this afternoon. Look at the cover and think about which one you would like: one about a real cat, Sid, living with six different families called *Six-Dinner Sid;* a fantasy book about cats dreaming called *When Cats Dream;* a wordless book called *Here Come the Cats!;* or a story of a cat that has an adventure called *The Patchwork Cat.* You will also have time during the day to look at the books and decide which one you want to hear."

The children voted to hear *When Cats Dream* by Dav Pilkey (Orchard, 1992). *The Patchwork Cat* by William Mayne (Puffin, 1984; illustrated by Nicola Bayley) came in second place, and Dawn promised to read it the next day. The children gathered on the rug for closer inspection of the pictures. They spent some time looking at the colorful cover. Then they noticed the colors disappearing as the book began. "Look what happened to the colors," Dawn said. "It makes it the real-life part" [the black and white scenes at the beginning], one child said. "When he dreams, it's color." It reminded another child of the way the movie *The Wizard of Oz* began and ended.

Dawn then read the words to emphasize the rhythm and the genre, saying, "It sounds like a poem." The book elicited many responses immediately: "The fish are screaming their lungs out!" "The cat's wearing a necklace—a girl cat!" "The house is upside down!" "Fish are flying!" "The cat is eating the stars!" "Is that a cow jumping over the moon?" "No, the cat is!" "The cat jumped over the moon!" "Cowboy boots. He's drunk!"

Dawn asked the children to help read the pages. One child stumbled on the word *stalking.* So Dawn paused to ask what the word *stalk* might mean. "Being quiet," said one child. "You're quietly following something, aren't you?" Dawn suggested.

From *When Cats Dream* (Orchard, 1992) by Dav Pilkey.

"The fish are still flying," one child noted next. "When are the cats going back to real life?" another child wondered. Dawn read on to the words, "Cats must go home. Running, running, running," and asked what they thought would happen now. They chorused, "Wake up!" Dawn said she was not sure the cats would wake up because the pictures were still in color. Then, turning the page, they saw that the colors really were fading. "He's waking," one child said. Seeing the cat asleep once more on the last page and hearing the words, "Cats go back to their dreaming," the children cried out, as they burst into applause.

"Why don't we take time now for you to draw or tell a story or write now or continue with a story you started before," Dawn suggested after story time. Five of the children drew scenes they remembered from the story, and she noticed that two of the children replicated, in line and color, the bold diagonal lines and bright colors that projected the feelings and the mood of the cats' dreams. Five children drew pictures of *their* dreams—or told "stories" in their pictures about wishes and dreams. Eight children continued with stories they had been working on the day of the survey, when they began focusing on stories about favorite animals.

In the drawings, Dawn saw the importance of art itself (color and design), of dreams, of pets. In the stories the children wrote, she saw the importance to them of:

- mothers (Sam)
- birthday celebrations (Gloria)
- writing stories (Denny)
- pet friendships and bravery (Todd)
- sharing as a basis for friendship (Teresa)
- love for elderly family members (Angela)
- safety for animals (Maggie)
- a good leader (Nicky)

Stories by Children in Dawn's Classroom

A bird was flying around and a man was shooting at birds and he and his mother was flying away the mother was flying and got shot the boy was sad the many was happy but the birds mother was ok he wa happy the man thought She had a family so he let her go (Sam)

A dog and it was his birthday he's going to be 7 years old and his whole family and every body he knows it's his birthday but they pretend like they don't know and he goes to the playground with his friends he has a great he tells them that it's some body's birthday but they just guess famous people when he gets home every body shouts Happy Birthday! (Gloria)

A smart dog. The dog would write stiry just like me. (Denny)

A little bunny was hopping cheerfully in the forest. He stoped to eat. He met up with a snake. He ran away. Years later when the bunny had fully grown up he met up with the same snacke. The snake crawled into a house. He saved a little boy. The little boy had the bunny for a pet. (Todd)

He will be in a race and he win's and get's a trofe and his friend is sad so he gives the trofe to his friend. (Teresa)

Once there was a snake named Sherri. She was an old snake she died a month ago. Her family was very, very, sad. (Angela)

A rabbit. I would like it to get home safely. (Maggie)

Once upon a time their was a mammoth named Ella and she was a star she was the one in the world she was nice too and when she saw someone in a fight she made them stop. (Nicky)

Dawn began sketching a plan of how her unit was taking shape, or the way three mini-units were coalescing around one another, as she studied the children's responses to literature. The children's talk about pets flowed out of and helped them connect to stories. Their responses to the author's words and pictures revealed their own personal, social, and cultural values, just as their own life-based stories did. She wanted to continue read-aloud sessions as well as small-group literature circles, writing time, and individual reading, with children responding to books through stories, pictures, and drama activities.

Dawn also wanted to think about how children—as authors—express their values naturally in their stories, just as adult authors do. All of the authors whose books she had been sharing had placed a value on friendship, on pet friendships, on helpfulness, bravery, sharing, and imaginative ventures, and she wanted to help children see the different ways these authors expressed their values through their characters actions, thoughts, and dreams. She was not sure how she would do this; she simply wanted to note it on her planning sketch. See Figure 11.3.

At this time, Dawn began to fill in another sheet, based on a chart she had found in a book by Australian educator Brian Cambourne. She had attended a whole language workshop that Cambourne presented, and in studying the workshop book, she became interested in a flowchart he had devised. Cambourne's flowchart could help teachers see a "network of relationships" (page 20) among the various learning activities they initiated with children. Dawn especially liked the fact that Cambourne began by inviting teachers to examine their own values.

FIGURE 11.3. Dawn's planning sketch.

Survey about pets	**Reading/Writing/Drawing/Drama**
Discussions about surveys	**individually**
Collecting Books	**in pairs**
Book Browsing	**in small groups**
	in large group

TALKING ABOUT PETS
CONNECTING TO STORIES
STUDYING STORIES AND ILLUSTRATIONS

Considering stories and illustrations:
How do authors express values through characters' actions, dreams and daydreams?

Lines, colors, objects in scenes: How do they express ideas, moods, feelings, values?

As she began her new unit, Dawn used his five categories—ideology of literacy, literacy goals/objectives/expectations, organizing time, ways of operating, and nature of the activities (page 20)—as a guide for her own five planning areas:

Teacher Values
Children are helpful in teacher planning.

Units flow out of children's choices in books, activities, subjects.

Teacher learns from children's responses.

Practices
Democratic

Turn taking

Participatory

Teacher and students are partners in learning.

Expectations
Children accept responsibility for learning. They:
- make decisions;
- consult a variety of resources;
- read and write daily;
- engage in art and drama;
- help one another;
- engage in reflective thinking; and
- take risks.

Procedures
Units flow out of children's responses.

Activities flow out of units as children respond to literature and teacher responds to their responses.

Activities tap children's potential for learning and independence by promoting:

Schedule
Read aloud story/conversation time (spontaneous responses and teacher feedback).

Individual and paired or small group reading time.

Sharing time (children reporting what they notice in a book; teacher interacting and reading another story).

Storytelling and story sharing time.
- invented spelling;
- self-selected books; and
- collaborative assessment.

INVESTIGATIONS: Collaborative Planning and Teaching

Think of *questions* children have asked or *interests* they have expressed, or think of a concept, subject, topic, theme, book, author, or issue you think children would want to explore and that you would want to explore with them. To get started, you might want to make a concept map. Place the title of your unit at the center of your map and place subcategories flowing out from this center. If possible, let children help you brainstorm these categories; you will discover more about their interests, curiosities, questions, and ideas. Then you can consider how you will build on what they already know and care about, as you consider the questions you would like to pursue and the schedule you want to keep.

Now consider the *books* you can use to tie together your central idea and its subcategories. If possible, encourage children to help collect the books, or invite them to bring books from home to supplement the classroom book collection.

Consider *activities* for the unit, including trips to the library. Also consider *resources* for the unit: interviews with people in the community and families of students, artifact collections, drama and role play activities, photography events, correspondence, discussions about various concepts, and stories to tell or write. Catalog your resources: books, films, objects, artwork, writing, tapes, maps, and field trips.

Construct a preliminary *schedule,* deciding which activities will take place on certain days and what you will need in the way of resources.

Write a brief introduction, setting forth your focus, the ideas to be explored, and what you feel may be the value of this focus for children's learning. Describe your first activity and some possibilities for closure as a frame of reference. You might also want to chart the classroom network of relationships with headings like *teacher values, expectations, schedule, practices,* and *procedures.*

Design an *inquiry-based* lesson plan for your first day. Consider the following five-step plan:

1. *Focus:* What do my students and I want to see, know, or discover? What are they curious about? What am I curious about?
2. *Intentions:* What do I plan to do in order to help students build on their curiosities or discover new curiosities? What do I hope to learn alongside them? What is my tentative schedule?
3. *Back-up plans, alternatives, additional possibilities:* If it rains, we can . . . . If the book I'm waiting for at the library does not materialize, I will use ______ instead. If the students need another day to write their stories, we will reschedule the next activity. If a student comes up with an important idea that takes us off track, then we can put the discussion about _____ on hold for a day or two.
4. *Wrap up:* How can I bring closure or partial closure to the work? If we're not ready for closure, what do I need to do to keep the unit going? What reminders do I need to provide? What future scheduling do I need to attend to?
5. *Self-evaluation:* How did it go? What did I discover? What do I think students discovered? How am I able to tell? What would I do differently if I repeated this unit? What do I want to do now? What am I still curious about? What are the students still curious about? Where am I going from here? What's happening next?

As you work through your unit, keep *records of children's responses* (note what is working, what is not working, what you are learning, what students appear to be learning). Share your questions and puzzles with students so that they can help you see more. You might want to keep a *diary/log/journal* of your thinking as the unit progresses. Note what's happening, what you see, what you are wondering about, what you are discovering, what you are having second thoughts about, where you seem to be heading, what's worth keeping, what needs to be discarded, what the children taught you, what you think you might have taught them. One month later, add to your journal, noting what you now find memorable about this unit.

What does *collaborative assessment* mean, in terms of the way Dawn uses it? How does she assess her students *collaboratively?* The answer depends on the type of reading children are doing, but it means essentially that Dawn resists using worksheets and tests, preferring instead to let student responses guide her assessment procedures. Her observations guide her teaching, which is itself collaborative, and her assessments—in turn—are based on what the children show and tell her. She wants to know whether they take pleasure in reading and writing at school or at home, whether they are developing knowledge about books, authors, genres, styles, and meanings, and whether literacy is becoming a natural part of their lives.

When children meet with Dawn individually for conferences (ten to fifteen minutes twice weekly at the beginning and twice monthly when they become fluent readers), she encourages them to discuss favorite passages and read them aloud. But she is not just concerned with *how* they read—or how they *behave* as readers—she is also interested in *why* they read. She might ask them questions like:

- What have they noticed about themselves as readers?
- When are they reading at home?
- What are they reading (both inside and outside school)?

Dawn's Observation Procedures

When children work independently, Dawn observes them to see if they

- choose books that produce strong engagement (Do children need help in book selection?)
- choose writing topics that produce strong engagement (Do children need help getting started?)
- sustain a regular span of time for quiet reading or writing (Do they need help getting started?)

When children work in small group settings—either reading and writing—Dawn observes to see if they

- tell and retell stories easily, confidently, and enthusiastically (How strong is their narrative literacy?)
- participate in groups easily, confidently, and enthusiastically (Do children share ideas readily?)
- exhibit independent thinking in a group setting (Do they value many ways of seeing?)
- exhibit knowledge of a variety of books, authors, and genres (Are they reading widely?)
- compare authors and books from a variety of perspectives (Do children notice links among books?)
- engage in responses to literature in a variety of modes (by talking, drawing, writing, storytelling)

When children listen to stories read aloud, Dawn observes to see if they

- can sustain the session (How developed are their attention spans?)
- show interest in a variety of genres (Do they need more variety in their reading experiences?)
- recommend books for large group sharing (Do they have favorite authors and subjects?)
- respond easily to books read aloud (Do they predict, chime in, react, notice, observe?)

When children talk to her about their reading and writing, Dawn observes to see if they

- behave like enthusiastic and confident readers at various stages in their development
- share their feelings and thoughts about books, stories, and poems
- respond to the author's craft
- self-correct for miscues and use prior experiences to figure out new words
- browse, skim, and read closely
- make connections with their life experiences

- Why are they reading (at home or at school)?
- Do they ever notice characters in their books reading? Why are these characters reading and writing?)

After Dawn shared Arnold Adoff's poetry picture book, *Love Letters,* in a read-aloud session, she asked about Adoff's child character, who is composing the Valentine letters and poems of the book. *Why* did the students think the child liked writing poetry? Dawn routinely asks children how they choose books and why they choose the ones they are now reading. They may tell her they like the pictures or the cover picture. They might like the first page and continue reading. She asks them if they ever choose a book and discover they do not like it, and they talk about books that did not "work" for them. They might tell her that one of their favorite authors has produced a disappointing book, one they expected to be funny or mysterious or scary—but it was not. They might tell her that they choose books their friends like and recommend. Peer opinions count, Dawn has discovered. Her students like to talk and compare notes about books with friends.

Dawn also encourages parents, grandparents, and other caretakers to send notes regularly about children's home reading: what they read, how they share books, when they share books and with whom (life and story connections), how they choose books, and how they talk about books with siblings and others in the home setting. This information adds to Dawn's knowledge about the child. Dawn wants to know how the child behaves as a reader both at school and at home. (Does the child value reading? Does the child enjoy reading? What help does the child still need on the journey to lifelong reading—and learning?)

Record keeping is especially important if teachers decide to assess student learning through observation and conferencing. Dawn keeps a small notebook in her pocket. Every day at odd moments—while events are still fresh in her mind—she makes notes about student responses, participation, and progress. After individual reading conferences, she writes a paragraph describing the individual student in a larger loose-leaf notebook. In these notes, she focuses on:

1. What the student reports about his or her reading at this time
2. What he or she is currently reading both at school and at home, and why
3. What the child likes or dislikes about the book
4. What the child may be finding puzzling or memorable about the book
5. What passage the child chose to share, and why
6. How the child read the passage aloud

In her notebook, Dawn describes a recent conference with a second-grade student, Angela, who had discovered another cat book, *Fred*:

> Angela felt good about her reading progress today. Reading Posy Simmonds' *Fred* [Puffin, 1989] at school and taking it home tonight to share with her little sister. Likes it (cartoon book) and can read more words than she could last week with *Cross-Country Cat* [by Mary Calhoun, illustrated by Erick Ingraham; Morrow, 1979]. Favorite part today was funeral scene; she *sang* the words. Puzzled over "caterwauley" but laughed when she noticed the way the word "cat" is part of the word. Shared the book with her group afterward. She is writing about *Fred*—making her own picture book sequel.

Many teachers also encourage children to keep response journals, checklists, and portfolios in order to bring themselves into the assessment process as full partners.

RESPONSE JOURNALS, CHECKLISTS, AND PORTFOLIOS

Response Journals

When students keep journals, recording their responses to literature, teachers can examine the journals to see how students are progressing in areas such as story interpretation (meaning-making strategies), decoding and encoding skills, knowledge of literary elements, aesthetic pleasure in reading, and life and literature links. Julie Wollman-Bonilla (1991) has written about the value of response journals for assessment purposes. If a student injects a personal opinion into a journal entry, she says, this demonstrates an interest in or deeper understanding of the characters' situation. If teachers pay close attention to students' opinions and follow up on them in small group discussions as they circulate among literature circles, they will learn a great deal about how students are making meaning of stories.

Because students know journal entries are freely written passages—no one is grading them or worrying about spelling or punctuation—students do not fear taking risks. Thus, their journals often include more expressive and creative ventures than a student's formal writing would reveal. They also show the teacher what skills the student still needs to learn. The important thing is that the teacher use the journal to provide help for the student rather than to punish the student for what he or she has still not learned. Although journals are not graded, the student might later take material from a journal entry and expand it into an assignment—a story, poem, or report that could be submitted for assessment.

Journal entries can help teachers see how students understand literary elements like mood, characterization, and the impact of setting on other story aspects. Teachers can use these entries to see what they need to emphasize in class discussions. They can also encourage students to share entries that might help other students to see literary elements more clearly. Or they can encourage students to write to one another in response to a question such as, What did you notice in this story—about people, places, mood?

Drawing from her own classroom experiences, Wollman-Bonilla helps teachers recognize journal entries that indicate strong involvement in a story. Children's questions, she says, are especially important. If a student asks a question while writing about or reflecting on a story, it indicates interest. Positive—and negative—remarks are also important, although teachers might tire quickly of the students raging against stories that they find too demanding or too unrelated to their own lives. Life and literature connections, she adds, are also important for signaling engagement with texts. If we want students to love literature, we must take comfort that they care enough about a text to puzzle over it, to reject it, to step out of it to remember events in their own lives, or to say what the author *should* have done. All of these responses indicate strong engagement.

Students can also tell us directly about their engagement with literature if we allow them to assess their own journal writing. Students could assess their journals for categories such as quantity (number of journal entries), quality (depth of discussion), and personal meaning-making (the value of journal writing for *them*).

For *quantity,* students could consider questions like, How much did you write, how often, and when (in what settings did you find yourself writing most easily)? For *quality,* they might consider questions like, What pieces of literature did you write about (or what pieces did you write the most about)? What kinds of writing did you do in response to that literature: expressive (informal, impressionistic, free writes), critical (formal, analytical, interpretive), or creative (fiction, poetry, plays, folk tales)? What kind of writing did you do most often (what kind did you like doing the most)? For *personal meaning–making* students might consider questions like, What pieces of literature deepened your thinking the most? (What pieces caused you to write more often about them or to return to the piece to reread it—and then to write more about it?) What entry would you want to add to now? Is there any one work you would want to write more about?

Checklists

The most common way of bringing students into the evaluation process is to give them responsibility for monitoring their classroom activities with questions or checklists. What if children in literature groups could take over part of this record keeping? Teacher educator Bonnie Hill (1995) adapts checklists so that children in the primary grades draw smiling, neutral, or frowning face symbols for the categories "I did my best," "I did ok," and "Not this time" to indicate whether they completed reading and writing tasks, participated in discussions, and listened well (page 180).

In another assessment form, "Literature Circle Debriefing" (page 184), Hill adds four more categories for children to consider, with space below each heading for children to write. The categories include:

- Important contributions you made in the discussion
- Important ideas someone else in the group expressed
- Strategies the group members used:
  - participating
  - staying on topic
  - contributing appropriate information
  - encouraging others to contribute
  - listening carefully
  - making good eye contact
  - being considerate of others' opinions
  - asking for clarification
- Suggestions for the next group meeting

Literature study groups often produce projects or make group presentations as they complete work with a book, author, or text set. Bonnie Hill describes a "Response Project Form" (page 194) that teachers devised for upper elementary students. The students filled up a blank page describing:

INVESTIGATIONS: Designing a Response Form for Self-Assessment

Consider making a self-assessment form for one of the **Investigations** you made as you journeyed through this book. How might you want to assess yourself for growth and discovery? How would you describe the process you went through? How would you explain the importance of the investigation? Would you want to determine criteria for the quality of your work? For your effort? What personal comments, feelings, or reflections would you want to make about your creation?

- the process they went through as they created the project;
- how the project related to the literature;
- how the projects showed *quality* and *effort* (definitions of these terms differed); and
- personal "comments, feelings, or reflections" about the project (page 194).

Portfolios

The concept of portfolio assessment for literacy classrooms arises from the concept of an artist's portfolio. Artists choose the best representative examples of their work and place them in portfolios in order to gain the attention of potential employers. When writing teachers adopted the portfolio concept—or borrowed it from the art model—they were focusing on literature as an art rather than as a humanity. The focus was on the writing piece itself—as an object of art—rather than on the writer interacting with the world *outside* the art form. Thus, the emphasis was on getting better *at* writing rather than learning about oneself, others, or the world *through* writing.

The studio artist preparing a portfolio looks at the work of art as *object* and assesses it for:

- *Technical expertise or craft* (skill in using tools, materials, and media),
- *Design* (organizing two- and three-dimensional forms: line, shape, color, texture, space),
- *Drawing* (the ability to integrate line, texture, and color or tone for various styles and effects: realism, naturalism, surrealism, modernism, cartooning),
- *Ideas* (personal meanings of the artist combined with social and cultural meanings), and
- *Creativity* (innovative, inventive approaches to any—or all—of the other areas).

The student writer compiling a portfolio for use in the classroom looks at various writing pieces and assesses them in five comparable areas:

- *Technical expertise or craft* (skill in using words, language, and writing style—selection and arrangement of words for maximum effect),
- *Design* (shaping the piece in terms of more important or less important ideas or to create the most dramatic tension),
- *Development* (the ability to integrate images, ideas, details, or information to produce the "texture" of the piece—the breadth and depth of it),
- *Meanings* (subject matter and purpose as they produce insight and involvement for both writer and readers), and
- *Authenticity* (individuality and inventiveness that makes the work unique).

In traditional art or writing classrooms, students might use the same self-assessment score sheet, one that emphasizes expertise. But teachers might be emphasizing something other than expertise. Says eight-grade teacher Linda Rief (1992): "We can introduce the concept of portfolios as places where students collect evidence of who they are" (page 59). She suggests three categories students can focus on to learn more about themselves. In the first category, students are *readers and writers* collecting their best examples of writing, lists of what they have read, and their best responses to literature. In the second category, they are *learners,* attaching early drafts of their writing to finished pieces to see how their ideas evolved. In the third category, they are *reflective learners,* producing self-evaluations in which they tell what they have learned—and how.

In classrooms like Rief's, where the emphasis is on growth rather than expertise, students might use a very different self-assessment form.

The expertise model asks, Where do I stand at this time in relation to others? The growth model asks, What am I like as a writer, how am I growing as a learner, and what do I need to do to make this piece stronger? A student could use either form to make choices about what to submit in a portfolio. A portfolio that emphasized expertise would include only the best pieces to demonstrate final quality. A portfolio that emphasized growth would include the entire spectrum of a student's work, including work-in-progress, to demonstrate effort and growth in quality over time and drafts. Thus, the *growth portfolio* would include self-reflective responses that document the growth process. Bonnie Hill (1995) recommends using a form

Categories for Assessment in Writing

CRAFTING

Does every word mean just exactly what I want it to mean? Does every sentence read just the way I want it to read? Do the sentences flow smoothly, with every word in place, no wasted words or sentences, no unnecessary repetitions? Do I have a balance of long and short sentences? Have I placed words and sentences strategically to emphasize my meaning? Have I left out any words, sentences, or ideas that I need to add for clarity? Do I need to rearrange parts of my sentences or paragraphs for greater flow, clarity, or emphasis? Have I proofread the piece carefully? Have I observed conventions in spelling, punctuation, grammar, or usage? How is the style memorable?

DESIGN

Does the piece have a recognizable shape or pattern? Does it move from one idea, place, position, time, situation, incident, or event to another? Does it produce some visual and memorable picture? Are the parts connected to one another and to some overriding idea in the whole work? Is the focus clear? Where is the concentration of details, the big moment? Where is the build-up? Where is the fade-out? How will readers feel at the end? What is the impact? Where is the power in the piece? What makes the shape memorable?

DEVELOPMENT

Did I produce the *picture* of the idea, the scene, the situation, the incident—or did I simply trail around the edges of it? Did I bring to light details, qualities, and images so that readers knew the character, saw the scene, participated in the experience, or grasped the idea as I did? Did I make the argument, the story, or the report convincing? Is the piece rich enough in background material to be memorable?

MEANINGS

Did I produce greater insight for readers and for myself through writing this piece? What did I learn or discover in writing it that I shared with others? Did I stretch anyone's mind or imagination in creating this piece—or did I simply confirm what readers already knew? Did I produce something new and memorable? Where would I go with this idea if I decided to write more about it—or more deeply into it? How could I extend this piece to make it more interesting, or to extend myself as I write more about it?

AUTHENTICITY

Did I write about something that was really important to me? Do I have firm convictions about this idea or vivid memories of this event? Do I have a strong urgency to be heard about this issue or great curiosity to explore some facet of this experience? Did I delve deeply enough into this subject that I could speak with authority about it? Or did I merely tread lightly over the surface of it? What tone does the piece project? What makes this piece one of a kind? What makes it memorable?

in which students tell about their selection of portfolio entries, or why they chose certain pieces for inclusion:

- What is the importance of the piece to them?
- What did they learn in creating it?
- What was their creation process like?
- What influenced them to create the piece at the beginning?
- What are they wondering now about the piece?
- What would they change next time? (page 197)

In using either kind of portfolio—*growth* (process-based) or *expertise* (product-based), the students in literature and literacy classrooms will be including a variety of "student-generated" (page 22), "multidimensional" (page 16) works, as teacher educator Allan De Fina (1992) notes. Pieces that reveal the student's competencies and growth will be among the possible selections; these may be creative writing, essays, reports, letters, response logs, journal entries, interviews, artistic work (illustrations, drawings, photography, comic strips, maps), collaborative works, surveys, reading lists (books read according to type, author, or number), tape or videotape recordings, self-assessment checklists and responses, teacher checklists and comments, peer reviews, parental responses, literacy activities from both home and school, multiple drafts of written stories, poems, problem-solving activities, and research projects.

PORTFOLIO REVIEW: EXPERTISE

Name______________________________ **Date**____________________

Artistic or Writing Areas	**Highly Superior 5**	**Superior 4**	**Average 3**	**Weak 2**	**Poor 1**
CRAFT/CRAFTING					
DESIGN					
DRAWING/DEVELOPMENT					
CONCEPTS/MEANINGS					
CREATIVITY/AUTHENTICITY					

Total:

Comments:

Evaluation scale:

Highly superior	25–21
Superior	20–17
Average	16–13
Weak	12–9
Poor	8–5

When portfolios become a significant part of the teacher's assessment process, these collections will be ongoing, creative student works. The teacher will examine them frequently. De Fina recommends that teachers look at two to three portfolios a day in order to keep up with workload demands, and that "every student's portfolio [should receive evaluation] at least once during the month" (pages 42–43).

The weight of the portfolio in relation to other assessment instruments varies from teacher to teacher. The portfolio might count as the entire grade. A teacher who wished to give no tests could turn the entire evaluation process into a student-centered project, with reports, activities, written work, projects, and creative ventures all included in the portfolio as evidence of the student's progress. Or the portfolio might count as only part of the grade, with tests, quizzes, projects, and daily work (participation) counting separately.

In either case, the portfolio is an important resource for collaborative assessment. Teachers set the process in motion at the beginning with a few simple guidelines and then give students the responsibility for the development of the portfolio. At regular intervals, the teacher meets with students to examine the portfolio selections, to arrive at interim conclusions about progress and best works, and to set new goals. The final stage occurs at the end of a marking period or term, with teacher and students drawing

PORTFOLIO REVIEW: GROWTH

Name ______________________________ **Date** ____________________

Artistic or Writing Areas	**Not Yet Visible** -	**Not Clearly Visible** ~	**Visible** +	**Strongly Visible** ++	**Memorable** *
CRAFT/CRAFTING					
DESIGN					
DRAWING/DEVELOPMENT					
CONCEPTS/MEANINGS					
CREATIVITY/AUTHENTICITY					

Comments:

conclusions together about competencies attained, goals reached, and evaluative marks. (See Appendix V for a look at how portfolio assessment works in the college-level literacy and literature classroom.)

Questions teachers and students might consider are:

- What are some of your favorite pieces and why do you like them?
- What do they tell or show about you?
- What do they cause you to learn about yourself as a reader and writer?
- What do you want others to notice in your work at this time?
- What do you want others to see about you as a reader and writer?
- What are some things you haven't done yet that you still want to try?

Teachers can, of course, bring along their own portfolios to these collaborative portfolio conferences. Says Linda Rief, "I keep a portfolio also. If I don't value what I ask the students to do, they seldom value it either" (page 46). Her portfolio is filled with a variety of different kinds of writing she has produced: an article about teaching, a poem, a letter, and a personal narrative. She also keeps a writer's/reader's notebook, in which she records the titles of books she is reading or has read with students, and she shares her responses to literature with her students. Her portfolio is important for building trust in her own lifelong learning, she explains.

INVESTIGATIONS: The Humanities Portfolio

Most portfolios in literature and literacy classrooms are based on either the expertise or the growth model. In either case, teachers are usually focusing on reading and writing as an *art.* Students focus on a written work (adult- or student-authored) rather than on the world beyond the words and pictures of the work. But suppose it were otherwise. Suppose teachers explored literature in the classroom to question how things work in the world, to make connections between literature and life experiences and to ask questions like Why are there social inequities? What can I—or others—do to change things? What *matters* in the world? Should we be reading and writing to explore how injustice affects some people's lives on an everyday basis? Should our portfolios explore ways to rid the world of social injustice (what we might call **ethical literacy**)? What if we saw reading and writing not as ends in themselves—to help us get better at reading and writing—but as a means to an end—to help us change the world? What would a *cultural*—or a *humanities*—portfolio look like? What record of literacy events would we see? What would students be reading, writing, and talking about? What would they be doing? How would they be changing—or working to change—the world?

Appendix 1
Multicultural Children's Books

A SURVEY OF MULTICULTURAL THEMES

Growing Up in a Parallel Culture in North America

African-American Picture Books/Illustrated Works

CARTER, DOROTHY *Bye, Mis'Lela.* New York: Farrar, Straus and Giroux, 1998 (realism).

CREWS, DONALD. *Bigmama's.* New York: Greenwillow, 1991 (realism; historical memoir).

FEELINGS, TOM. *Soul Looks Back in Wonder.* New York: Dial, 1993 (edited poetry collection).

GREENFIELD, ELOISE. *Grandpa's Face.* Illustrated by Floyd Cooper. New York: Philomel, 1988 (realism).

———. *Nathaniel Talking.* Illustrated by Jan Spivey Gilchrist. New York: Dial, 1988 (urban setting; poetry).

GRIMES, NIKKI. *Meet Danitra Brown.* Illustrated by Floyd Cooper. New York: Lothrop, 1994 (urban setting; realism; poetry).

JOHNSON, ANGELA. *Tell Me A Story, Mama.* Illustrated by David Soman. New York: Orchard Books, 1989 (realism).

POMERANTZ, CHARLOTTE. *The Chalk Doll.* Illustrated by Franc Lessac. New York: Lippincott, 1989 (African-Caribbean Culture, Jamaica; realism).

RINGGOLD, FAITH. *Tar Beach.* New York: Crown, 1991 (New York City, Harlem; realism/magic realism).

TARPLEY, NATASHA. *I Love My Hair!* Boston: Little Brown, 1998 (realism).

THOMAS, JOYCE CAROL. *Brown Honey in Broomwheat Tea.* Illustrated by Floyd Cooper. New York: HarperCollins, 1993 (poetry).

———. *Gingerbread Days.* Illustrated by Floyd Cooper. New York: HarperCollins, 1995 (poetry).

WATTS, JERI HANEL. *Keepers.* Illustrated by Felicia Marshall. New York: Lee and Low, 1997 (realism).

WYETH, SHARON DENNIS. *Something Beautiful.* Illustrated by Chris Soenpiet. New York: Bantam Doubleday Dell, 1998 (autobiography).

YARBROUGH, CAMILLE. *Cornrows.* Illustrated by Carole Byard. New York: Coward, 1979 (realism).

African-American Fiction (Realistic)

FENNER, CAROL. *Yolanda's Genius.* New York: Scholastic, 1995 (set in Chicago).

GREENFIELD, ELOISE. *Koya DeLancy and the Good Girl Blues.* New York: Scholastic, 1992.

HAMILTON, VIRGINIA. *Cousins.* New York: Philomel, 1990 (small-town Ohio).

———. *Plain City.* New York: Scholastic, 1993 (rural Midwest).

———. *Willie Bea and the Time the Martians Landed.* New York: Greenwillow, 1983 (rural Midwest).

HANSEN, JOYCE. *The Gift-Giver.* New York: Clarion, 1980 (New York City, the Bronx).

MYERS, WALTER DEAN. *Scorpions.* New York: Harper, 1988.

———. *Somewhere in the Darkness.* New York: Scholastic, 1992 (New York/Chicago).

TATE, ELEANORA. *A Blessing in Disguise.* New York: Delacorte, 1995 (South Carolina).

———. *Just An Overnight Guest.* East Orange, NJ: Just Us Books, 1997.

———. *The Secret of Gumbo Grove.* New York: Franklin Watts, 1988 (South Carolina).

———. *Thank You, Dr. Martin Luther King, Jr!* New York: Franklin Watts, 1990 (South Carolina).

WILLIAMS-GARCIA, RITA. *Blue Tights.* New York: Dutton, 1988 (New York City).

YARBROUGH CAMILLE. *The Shimmershine Queens.* New York: Putnam's, 1989.

African-American Poetry

JOHNSON, ANGELA. *The Other Side: Shorter Poems.* New York: Orchard, 1998.

STEPTOE, JAVAKA, COMPILER. *In Daddy's Arms I Am Tall; African Americans Celebrating Fathers.* Illustrated by Javaka Steptoe. New York: Lee and Low, 1997.

THOMAS, JOYCE CAROL. *Brown Honey in Broomwheat Tea.* Illustrated by Floyd Cooper. New York: HarperCollins, 1993.

Amish Fiction (Realistic)

AYRES, KATHERINE. *Family Tree.* New York: Delacorte, 1996 (Ohio).

BORNTRAGER, MARY CHRISTINE. *Ellie.* Scottdale, PA: Herald Press, 1988 (Ohio).

———. *Daniel.* Scottdale, PA: Herald Press, 1991 (Ohio).

———. *Rachel.* Scottdale, PA: Herald Press, 1990 (Ohio).

———. *Rebecca.* Scottdale, PA: Herald Press, 1989 (Ohio).

SMUCKER, BARBARA. *Amish Adventure.* New York: Viking Penguin, 1984 (Ontario).

YODER, JOSEPH. *Rosanna of the Amish.* Scottdale, PA: Herald Press, 1973 (Pennsylvania).

Appalachian Literature

HAMILTON, VIRGINIA. *M. C. Higgins the Great.* New York: Macmillan, 1974 (Kentucky; realistic fiction).

RYLANT, CYNTHIA. *Missing May.* New York: Orchard, 1992 (West Virginia; realistic fiction).

———. *When I Was Young in the Mountains.* Illustrated by Diane Goode. New York: E. P. Dutton, 1982 (Cool Ridge, West Virginia; realistic picture book).

Asian-American Literature

CHOI, SOOK NYUL. *The Best Older Sister.* Illustrated by Cornelious Van Wright. New York: Bantam/Doubleday, 1997 (Korean American; picture storybook; realism).

———. *Halmoni and the Picnic.* Illustrated by Karen Dugan. Boston: Houghton Mifflin, 1993 (Korean American; picture book; realism).

COUTANT, HELEN. *First Snow.* Illustrated by Vo-Dinh. New York: Knopf, 1974 (Viet Nam/New England; picture storybook; realism).

LEE, MARIE. *If It Hadn't Been for Yoon Jun.* Boston: Houghton Mifflin, 1993 (Korean American; Minnesota; realism).

TAN, AMY. *The Moon Lady.* Illustrated by Gretchen Schields. New York: Macmillan, 1992 (Chinese American; picture book; realism).

YEP, LAURENCE. *The Cook's Family.* New York: Putnam's, 1998 (Chinese American; realism).

———. *Ribbons.* New York: Putnam's, 1996 (Chinese American; realism).

———. *Thief of Hearts.* New York: HarperCollins, 1995 (Chinese American; realism).

Hispanic/Latino Literature

AUGENBRAUM, HAROLD, AND STAVANS, ILAN. *Growing Up Latino: Memoirs and Stories.* Boston: Houghton Mifflin, 1993 (story collection).

GARZA, CARMEN LOMAS. *Family Pictures/Cuadros de familia.* San Francisco: Children's Book Press, 1990 (Mexican American; picture book; realism).

———. *Magic Windows: Ventanas Magicas.* San Francisco: Children's Book Press, 1999 (Mexican American; picture book; realism).

MOHR, NICHOLASA. *Felita.* Illustrated by Ray Cruz. New York: Dial, 1979 (Puerto Rican New York; the Bronx; realism).

MORA, PAT. *A Birthday Basket for Tia.* Illustrated by Cecily Lang. New York: Simon and Schuster, 1992 (Mexican American; picture book; realism)

———. *Pablo's Tree.* Illustrated by Cecily Lang. New York: Simon & Schuster, 1994 (Mexican American; picture book; realism).

———. *Tomas and the Library Lady.* Illustrated by Raul Colon. New York: Knopf, 1997 (Mexican American; picture book; realism).

SÁENZ, BENJAMIN ALIRE. A *Gift from Papá Diego: Un regalo de Papá Diego.* El Paso, Texas: Cinco Puntos Press, 1998 (Mexican American; picture book; blending of realism and fantasy).

SOTO, GARY. *Cat's Meow.* New York: Little Apple, 1997 (Mexican American; picture book, magical realism)

SOTO, GARY. *Fire in My Hands.* New York: Scholastic, 1990 (Mexican American; poems).

———. *Living Up the Street.* New York: Bantam, 1985 (Mexican American; realism).

———. *Local News.* New York: Harcourt, 1993 (Mexican American; realism).

———. *The Skirt.* Illustrated by Eric Velasquez. New York: Delacorte, 1992 (Mexican American; realism).

———. *Small Faces.* New York: Bantam, 1986 (Mexican American; realism).

———. *Taking Sides.* New York: Harcourt, 1991 (Mexican American; realism).

———. *Too Many Tamales.* Illustrated by Ed Martinez. New York: Putnam's, 1993 (Mexican American; realistic picture book).

Inuit Literature

ANDREWS, JAN. *Very Last First Time.* Illustrated by Ian Wallace. Toronto: Douglas & McIntyre, 1985 (Northern Canada; Inuit; realistic picture book).

PAULSEN, GARY. *Dogsong.* New York: Bradbury Press, 1985 (realistic novel).

Jewish-American Literature

BLUME, JUDY. *Are You There, God? It's Me, Margaret.* Englewood Cliffs, NJ: Bradbury Press, 1970 (realistic novel).

———. *Starring Sally J. Freedman as Herself.* New York: Bradbury Press, 1977 (realistic novel).

COHEN, BARBARA. *King of the Seventh Grade.* New York: Lothrop, 1983 (realistic novel).

GLASER, LINDA. *The Borrowed Hanukkah Latkes.* Illustrated by Nancy Cote. Morton Grove, Ill.: Albert Whitman, 1997 (picture book: realism).

HURWITZ, JOHANNA. *Hurray for Ali Baba Bernstein.* New York: Scholastic, 1985 (realistic novel).

KONIGSBURG, E. L. *About the B'nai Bagels.* New York: Atheneum, 1969 (realistic novel).

———. *The View from Saturday.* New York: Atheneum, 1996 (realistic novel).

LAMSTEIN, SARAH. *Annie's Shabbat* Illustrated by Cecily Lang. Morton Grove, Ill.: Albert Whitman, 1997 (picture book: realism).

LASKY, KATHRYN. *The Night Journey.* New York: Frederick Warne, 1981 (realistic novel).

LEVITIN, SONIA. *The Golem and the Dragon Girl.* New York: Dutton, 1993 (realistic novel).

———. *The Singing Mountains.* New York: Simon, 1998 (realistic novel).

LOWRY, LOIS. *Anastasia Krupnik.* Boston: Houghton Mifflin, 1979 (realistic novel).

Native American

BEGAY, SHONTO. *Navajo: Visions and Voices Across the Mesa.* New York: Scholastic, 1995 (illustrated book).

BRUCHAC, JOSEPH. *Fox Song.* Illustrated by Paul Morin. New York: Philomel, 1993 (Abenaki; picture book).

HIRSCHFELDER, ARLENE, AND SINGER, BEVERLY. *Rising Voices: Writings of Young Native Americans.* New York: Ballantine, 1992 (story and poetry collection).

KEEGAN, MARCIA. *Pueblo Boy.* New York: Cobblehill, 1991 (picture book).

MOMADAY, NATACHEE SCOTT. *Owl in the Cedar Tree.* Lincoln: University of Nebraska Press, 1975 (Navajo; realistic novel).

Growing Up in Parallel Cultures Worldwide

Picture Books and Poetry Collections

APPELBAUN, DIANA. *Cocoa Ice.* Illustrated by Holly Meade. New York: Orchard, 1997 (Santa Domingo and Maine; realism; information).

CASTANEDA, OMAR. *Abuela's Weave.* Illustrated by Enrique Sanchez. New York: Lee & Low, 1993 (Guatemala; realism).

DALY, NIKI, *Jamela's Dress.* New York: Farrar Straus and Giroux, 1999.

FLEMING, CANDACE. *Gabriella's Song.* Illustrated by Giselle Potter. New York: Atheneum, 1997 (Venice; picture book; whimsical realism).

GRIFALCONI, ANN. *The Village of Round and Square Houses.* Boston: Little, Brown, 1986 (Africa: Camaroons, Central Africa, village of Tos; realism/legend, framed story).

KROLL, VIRGINIA. *Masai and I.* Illustrated by Nancy Carpenter. New York: Four Winds, 1992 (America and East Africa; realism).

MITCHELL, RITA PHILLIPS. *Hue Boy.* Illustrated by Caroline Binch. London: Victor Gollancz, 1992 (Caribbean Islands; realism).

NYE, NAOMI SHIHAB, EDITOR. *The Space Between Our Footsteps. Poems and Paintings from the Middle East.* New York: Simon and Schuster, 1998 (Middle East and North Africa; poetry).

———. *This Same Sky; A Collection of Poems from around the World.* New York: Simon and Schuster, 1992.

SAY, ALLEN. *The Bicycle Man.* Boston: Houghton Mifflin, 1982 (Japan; realism).

WALSH, JILL PATON. *Babylon.* Illustrated by Jennifer Northway. London: Andre Deutsch, 1982 (England; children of immigrant background from Jamaica, Africa; realism).

WALTER, MILDRED PITTS. *Brother to the Wind.* New York: Lothrop: 1985 (Africa; fantasy; folk tales).

Novels

CHOI, SOOK NYUL. *Echoes of the White Giraffe.* Boston: Houghton Mifflin, 1993 (Korea; realism).

———. *Year of Impossible Goodbyes.* Boston: Houghton Mifflin, 1991 (Korea; realism).

HAUTZIG, ESTHER. *A Gift for Mama.* Illustrated by Donna Diamond. New York: Viking, 1981 (Poland; realism).

HICYILMAZ, GAYE. *Against the Storm.* Boston: Little, Brown, 1993 (Turkey; realism).

MAHY, MARGARET. *Aliens in the Family.* New York: Scholastic, 1985 (New Zealand; fantasy/science fiction/legend).

NAIDOO, BEVERLEY. *Journey to Jo'burg.* New York: Lippincott, 1986 (South Africa; realism).

ORLEV, URI. *The Island on Bird Street.* Translated from the Hebrew by Hillel Halkin. Boston: Houghton Mifflin, 1984; Jerusalem: Keter, 1981 (Poland; 1940s; realism).

PROCHAZKOVA, IVA. *The Season of Secret Wishes.* Translated by Elizabeth Crawford. New York: Lothrop, 1989 (Czech Republic; realism).

SAY, ALLEN. *The Ink-Keeper's Apprentice.* New York: Harper, 1979 (Japan; realism).

SCHAMI, RAFIK. *A Hand Full of Stars.* Translated from the German by Rika Lesser. New York: Dutton, 1990 (Syria; realism).

SEMEL, NAVA. *Becoming Gershona.* Translated by Seymour Simckes. New York: Viking Penguin, 1990 (Israel; realism).

STAPLES, SUZANNE FISHER. *Shabanu, Daughter of the Wind.* New York: Random House, 1989 (Pakistan; realism).

YUMOTO, KAZUMI. *The Friends.* Translated by Cathy Hirano. New York: Farrar, Straus, and Giroux, 1996.

ZHELEZNIKOV, VLADIMIR. *Scarecrow.* Translated by Antonina Bouis. New York: Harper, 1990 (Russia; realism).

Parallel Worlds: Growing Up "Between" Cultures (coming to terms with two facets of heritage—children of immigrants or of cross-cultural or bi-cultural marriages)

CHOI, SOOK NYUL. *Halmoni and the Picnic.* Illustrated by Karen M. Dugan. Boston: Houghton Mifflin, 1993 (Korean/Korean American; picture book; realism).

———. *A Gathering of Pearls.* Boston: Houghton Mifflin, 1994 (Korean/Korean American; realistic novel; female coming-of-age book).

FRITZ, JEAN. *Homesick, My Own Story.* Illustrated by Margot Tomes. New York: Putnam's, 1982 (autobiographical novel).

———. *The Double Life of Pocahontas.* New York: Viking Penguin, 1983 (Native American/English; nonfiction; biography).

GAVIN, JAMILA. *The Wheel of Surya.* London: Methuen, 1992 (East Indian/English; contemporary fiction; realism).

GEORGE, JEAN CRAIGHEAD. *Water Sky.* New York: Harper, 1987 (North American (Eskimo) Indians; Alaska; American/Ologak ancestry; realistic novel).

GUY, ROSA. *The Friends.* New York: Holt, 1973 (East Indian/American Harlem; contemporary fiction, realism).

HAMILTON, VIRGINIA. *Arilla Sun Down.* New York: Greenwillow, 1976 (African-American, Native American; American Midwest; realistic novel).

———. *Junius Over Far.* New York: Harper, 1985 (Caribbean/American experiences; realistic novel).

HICYILMAZ, GAYE. *Coming Home.* New York: Farrar, Straus, and Giroux, 1999 (English/Turkish; contemporary fiction, realism).

HUNTER, LATOYA. *The Diary of Latoya Hunter.* New York: Crown, 1992 (Jamaican heritage; life in New York City; nonfiction; autobiographical diary).

KAYE, GERALDINE. *Comfort Herself.* London: Andre Deutsch, 1984 (England/Ghana; realistic novel).

———. *Great Comfort.* London: Andre Deutsch, 1988 (England/Ghana; realistic novel).

LEVITIN, SONIA. *The Golem and the Dragon Girl.* New York: Fawcett, 1993 (children of Chinese and Jewish heritage, realistic novel).

LINGARD, JOAN. *Between Two Worlds.* New York: Penguin, 1993 (Europe/Canada; realistic novel).

PERKINS, MITALI. *The Sunita Experiment.* Boston: Little, Brown, 1993 (Calcutta, India/California; realistic novel).

RINGGOLD, FAITH. *Bonjour, Lonnie.* New York: Hyperion, 1996 (France/America; picture book).

SAY, ALLEN. *Allison.* New York: Houghton Mifflin, 1997 (Japan/America; picture book).

———. *Grandfather's Journey.* Boston: Houghton Mifflin, 1994 (Japan/America; picture book; realism).

———. *Tea With Milk.* Boston: Houghton Mifflin, 1999 (American/Japan; picture book; realism).

WYETH, SHARON DENNIS. *Ginger Brown: The Nobody Boy.* Illustrated by Cornelius Van Wright and Ying-Hwa Hu. New York: Random House, 1997 (bi-racial, black/white, family; contemporary realistic fiction).

———. *Ginger Brown: Too Many Houses.* Illustrated by Cornelius Van Wright. New York: Random House, 1996 (bi-racial, black/white, family; contemporary realistic fiction).

———. *The World of Daughter McGuire.* New York: Delacorte, 1994 (bi-racial, black/white, family; contemporary realistic fiction).

YEP, LAURENCE. *Child of the Owl.* New York: Harper, 1977 (Chinese Americans in San Francisco; realistic fiction set in 1960s).

———. *The Star Fisher.* New York: Penguin, 1991 (Chinese Americans in West Virginia; historical fiction).

———. *Thief of Hearts.* New York: HarperCollins, 1995 (Chinese Americans in San Francisco; contemporary realistic fiction).

———. *The Cook's Family.* New York: Putnam's, 1998 (Chinese Americans in San Francisco; contemporary realistic fiction).

Crossing Cultures: Immigrant/Emigrant/Refugee Experiences

ALIKI [BRANDENBERG]. *Painted Words; Spoken Memories.* New York: Greenwillow, 1998 (Greece to America; picture storybook; autobiographical fiction)

BAWDEN, NINA. *Princess Alice.* Illustrated by Phillida Gili. London: Andre Deutsch, 1985 (Africa to England; picture book; realistic fiction).

BUNTING, EVA. *How Many Days to America?* Illustrated by Beth Peck. New York: Clarion Books, 1988 (Central America to the United States; picture book; realistic fiction).

BUSS, FRAN LEEPER. *Journey of the Sparrows.* New York: Dell, 1993 (Mexico to Chicago; realistic novel).

CHOI, SOOK NYUL. *Echoes of the White Giraffe.* Boston: Houghton Mifflin, 1993 (North to South Korea; realistic novel).

———. *Year of Impossible Goodbyes.* Boston: Houghton Mifflin, 1992 (North Korea during Japanese invasion; escape to South Korea; realistic novel).

COHEN, BARBARA. *Molly's Pilgrim.* Illustrated by Michael Deraney. New York: William Morrow, 1983 (Russia to America in early 1900s; picture storybook; realism).

GAVIN, JAMILA. *The Wheel of Surya.* London: Methuen, 1992 (India to England; realistic novel).

HANSEN, JOYCE. *Home Boy.* New York: Clarion, 1982 (Caribbean Islands to the Bronx; realistic novel).

HARVEY, BRETT. *Immigrant Girl, Becky of Eldridge Street.* Illustrated by Deborah Kogan Ray. New York: Holiday House, 1987 (Russia to New York City in 1910; historical fiction).

HAUTZIG, ESTHER. *The Endless Steppe.* New York: Crowell, 1968 (Poland to Siberia; Jewish family is arrested by the Russians; autobiographical novel).

HESSE, KAREN. *Letters from Rifka.* New York: Holt, 1992 (Russia to America; realistic novel).

HEST, AMY. *When Jessie Came Across the Sea.* Illustrated by P. J. Lynch. Cambridge, MA: Candlewick, 1997 (Europe to America, picture book; realistic fiction).

HICYILMAZ, GAYE. *The Frozen Waterfall.* New York: Farrar, Straus, and Giroux, 1994 (From Turkey to Switzerland; realistic novel.)

HOLM, ANNE. *I Am David.* London: Methuen, 1965 (Italy to Denmark; realistic novel).

LASKY, KATHRYN. *The Night Journey.* Illustrated by Trina Hyman. New York: Warne, 1981 (Russia to America in early 1900s; realistic novel).

LEVINSON, RIKI. *Watch the Stars Come Out.* Illustrated by Diane Goode. New York: Dutton, 1985 (Boat trip from Europe to America; picture book; realism).

LEVITIN, SONIA. *Journey to America.* New York: Atheneum, 1970 (Germany to America; Jewish family in 1938; realistic novel).

———. *The Return.* New York: Atheneum, 1987 (Ethiopa to Israel; realistic novel).

LINGARD, JOAN. *Between Two Worlds.* London: Hamish Hamilton, 1991 (Europe to Quebec, Canada; family of displaced persons in 1948; realistic novel; sequel to *Tug of War*).

———. *Tug of War.* London: Hamish Hamilton, 1989 (Escape from Latvia during Russian invasion in 1944; realistic novel).

LITTLE, JEAN. *Listen for the Singing.* New York: Dutton, 1977 (German family in Canada in 1940s; realistic novel).

LORD, BETTE BAO. *In the Year of the Boar and Jackie Robinson.* New York: Harper, 1984 (Asian-American immigrant experiences; realistic novel).

MEIR, MIRA. *Alina: A Russian Girl Comes to Israel.* Translated by Zeva Shapiro. Philadelphia: Jewish Publication Society of America, 1982 (Russia to Israel; realistic photo-story).

NYE, NAOMI SHIHAB. *Habibi.* Illustrated by Raul Colon. New York: Simon & Schuster, 1997 (St. Louis to Jerusalem; realistic fiction; autobiographical novel).

SMUCKER, BARBARA. *Days of Terror.* Toronto: Clarke, Irwin, 1979 (exodus of Mennonites to North America in 1917; realistic novel).

SURAT, MICHELE MARIA. *Angel Child, Dragon Child.* Illustrated by Vo-Dinh Mai. New York: Scholastic, 1989 (Vietnamese child in America; picture book; realism).

TANAKA, SHELLEY. *Michi's New Year.* Illustrated by Ron Berg. Toronto: Peter Martin, 1980 (Japan to Vancouver in 1912; picture book; historical fiction).

TAYLOR, SYDNEY. *A Papa Like Everyone Else.* New York: Doubleday, 1966 (historical fiction).

WINTER, JEANETTE. *Klara's New World.* New York: Knopf, 1992 (Sweden to America in the late 1860s; picture book; historical fiction).

YEP, LAURENCE. *Dragon's Gate.* New York: HarperCollins, 1993 (China to California in early 1900s; historical fiction).

———. *Dragonwings.* New York: Harper, 1975 (China to San Francisco in 1903; historical fiction).

ZHANG, SONG NAN. *A Little Tiger in the Chinese Night: An Autobiography in Art.* Plattsburgh, NY: Tundra Books, 1995 (China to Canada in 1989; autobiography)

Crossing Cultures: Travelers' Experiences

Picture Books

ANNO. *Anno's Britain.* New York: Philomel, 1982 (Japan to Britain; wordless).

BEMELMANS, LUDWIG. *Madeline in London.* New York: Viking, 1961 (Paris to London; realism/humor/verse).

BOND, NANCY. *The Love of Friends.* New York: Simon & Schuster/Margaret McElderry, 1997 (America to London and Scotland; novel).

BURNINGHAM, JOHN. *Around the World in Eighty Days.* London: Jonathan Cape, 1972 (London to Nairobi, Calcutta, Tokyo, Sydney, Fiji, Mexico, Toronto, New York; realism; autobiography; travel book).

CESERANI, GIAN PAOLO. *Marco Polo.* Illustrated by Piero Ventura. New York: Putnam, 1977 (Venice to China; nonfiction; history, geography, biography).

CHOI, SOOK NYUL. *Yunmi, and Halmoni's Trip.* Illustrated by Karen Dugan. Boston: Houghton Mifflin, 1997 (New York to Korea; realistic picture book).

DE BRUNHOFF, JEAN. *The Story of Babar.* London: Metheun, 1934 (Algeria to Paris; animal fantasy).

DORRIS, ARTHUR. *Isla.* Illustrated by Elisa Klenen. New York: Dutton, 1995 (New York City to the Caribbean; fantasy).

FOREMAN, MICHAEL. *Panda's Puzzle and His Voyage of Discovery.* Scarsdale, NY: Bradbury Press, 1977 (Asia to America; animal fantasy).

GREENFIELD, ELOISE. *Africa Dream.* Illustrated by Carole Byard. New York: John Day, 1977 (America to Africa; fantasy).

HOFFMAN, MARY. *Boundless Grace.* Illustrated by Caroline Binch. New York: Dial, 1995 (America to Gambia; realism).

KREIKEMEIER, GREGORY. *Come with Me to Africa: A Photographic Journey.* Racine, WI: Western Publishing Company, 1993 (Spain to Africa to London; nonfiction).

NYE, NAOMI SHIHAB. *Sitti's Secrets.* Illustrated by Nancy Carpenter. New York: Simon & Schuster, 1994 (America to Palestine; realistic fiction).

RINGGOLD, FAITH. *Aunt Harriet's Underground Railroad.* New York: Crown, 1992 (time travel: present to Civil War days; African-American ethnicity).

SIS, PETER. *The Three Golden Keys.* New York: Doubleday, 1994 (America to Prague; fantasy/framed story).

———. *Tibet: Through the Red Box.* New York: Farrar, 1998. (Czechoslovakia to Tibet; picture book; nonfiction: diary).

TURNER, ANN. *Nettie's Trip South.* Illustrated by Ronald Himler. New York: Scholastic, 1987 (Northern to Southern United States; historical fiction; Civil War era).

ZHANG, SONG NAN. *The Children of China: An Artist's Journey.* Plattsburg, NY: Tundra Books, 1998 (journeys across China; visual observations of nomadic minority peoples; nonfiction; art).

Novels

BAWDEN, NINA. *On the Run.* New York: Penguin, 1967 (East Africa to England; realistic novel).

BOND, NANCY. *A String in the Harp.* New York: Atheneum, 1976 (New England to Wales; realistic fiction that encases mythic/legendary time-slip fantasy).

CASEY, MAUDE. *Over the Water.* London: The Woman's Press, 1987 (England to Ireland; realistic novel).

FOX, PAULA. *Lily and the Lost Boy.* New York: Franklin Watts, 1987 (America to Greece; realistic novel).

GEORGE, JEAN CRAIGHEAD. *Water Sky.* New York: Harper and Row, 1987 (Boston to Alaska; realistic novel).

HAMILTON, VIRGINIA. *Junius Over Far.* New York: Harper, 1987 (New York to the Caribbean; realistic novel).

———. *The Magical Adventures of Pretty Pearl.* New York: Harper, 1981 (Kenya to America; folk fantasy that embraces historical time-slip fantasy).

HESSE, KAREN. *Letters from Rifka.* New York: Holt, 1992 (Russia to Belgium to America; realistic novel).

HUNTER, LATOYA. *The Diary of Latoya Hunter.* New York: Crown, 1992 (Jamaica to New York; nonfiction).

KAYE, GERALDINE. *Comfort Herself.* London: Andre Deutsch, 1984 (London to Ghana; realistic novel).

———. *Great Comfort.* London: Andre Deutsch, 1988 (London to Ghana; realistic novel).

PATERSON, KATHERINE. *Park's Quest.* New York: Dutton, 1988 (Washington, D. C. to farm in Virginia and discovery of Vietnamese half-sister; realistic novel).

SMITH, JOAN. *The Russian Doll.* Illustrated by George Buchanan. London: Julia MacRae, 1989 (England to Russia; realistic novel).

SMUCKER, BARBARA. *Amish Adventure.* New York: Viking Penguin, 1983 (Chicago to Ontario; realistic novel).

SOTO, GARY. *Pacific Crossing.* New York: Harcourt Brace, 1992 (California to Japan; realistic novel).

History and Culture: African-American Experiences

ADOFF, ARNOLD. *Malcolm X.* Illustrated by John Wilson. New York: Harper, 1970 (nonfiction; biography).

BURNS, BREE. *Harriet Tubman and the Fight Against Slavery.* New York: Chelsea House, 1992 (nonfiction; biography).

CURTIS, CHRISTOPHER PAUL. *The Watsons Go to Birmington—1963.* New York: Delacorte, 1995 (realistic fiction).

EVERETT, GWEN. *Li'l Sis and Uncle Willie.* Illustrated by William H. Johnson. New York: Hyperion, 1994 (genre blend: art, biography, history, fiction).

GREENFIELD, ELOISE, AND LITTLE, LESSIE JONES. *Childtimes: A Three-Generation Memoir.* New York: HarperCollins, 1979 (nonfiction; autobiography).

HAMILTON, VIRGINIA. *Anthony Burns.* New York: Knopf, 1988 (fictionalized biography; historical fiction).

———. *The House of Dies Drear.* New York: Macmillan, 1968 (realistic fiction).

———. *The Magical Adventures of Pretty Pearl.* New York: Harper, 1981 (historical folk fiction).

———. *Many Thousand Gone: African Americans from Slavery to Freedom.* Illustrated by Leo and Diane Dillon. New York: Knopf, 1993 (nonfiction; biography, history).

———. *The People Could Fly: American Black Folktales.* Illustrated by Leo and Diane Dillon. New York: Knopf, 1985 (folklore; story collection).

———. *Second Cousins.* New York: Scholastic, 1998 (realistic fiction).

HANSEN, JOYCE. *The Captive.* New York: Scholastic, 1994 (historical fiction).

———. *I Thought My Soul Would Rise and Fly: The Reconstruction Era Diary of Patsy.* New York: Scholastic, 1997 (historical novel).

———. *Out From This Place.* New York: Walker, 1988 (historical novel).

HASKINS, JAMES, AND BENSON, KATHLEEN. *African Beginnings.* Illustrated by Floyd Cooper. New York: Lothrop, 1998 (nonfiction: history).

HOWARD, ELIZABETH FITZGERALD. *Chita's Christmas Tree.* Illustrated by Floyd Cooper. New York: Macmillan, 1989 (picture book).

IGUS, TOYOMI. *I See the Rhythm.* Illustrated by Michele Wood. San Francisco: Children's Book Press, 1988. (picturebook, nonfiction: history of African-American music).

JOHNSON, TONY. *The Wagon.* Illustrated by James Ransome. New York: Tambourine, 1996 (picture book).

KING, MARTIN LUTHER. *I Have A Dream.* Illustrated by Fifteen Coretta Scott King Award and Honor Book Artists. New York, Scholastic, 1997 (picture book; nonfiction: history).

LESTER, JULIUS. *This Strange New Feeling.* New York: Dial, 1982 (realistic novel).

———. *To Be a Slave.* Illustrated by Tom Feelings. New York: Dial, 1968 (nonfiction; autobiography).

LYONS, MARY. *Letters from a Slave Girl: The Story of Harriet Jacobs.* New York: Simon & Schuster, 1992 (historical novel).

MCKISSACK, PATRICIA. *A Picture of Freedom: The Diary of Clotee, a Slave Girl: Belmont Plantation, Virginia 1859.* New York: Scholastic, 1997 (historical fiction).

———. *The Dark Thirty: Southern Tales of the Supernatural.* Illustrated by Brian Pinkney. New York: Knopf, 1992 (folklore; story collection).

MELTZER, MILTON. *The Black Americans: A History in Their Own Words 1619–1983.* New York: Crowell, 1984 (nonfiction; history).

MILLER, WILLIAM. *Richard Wright and The Library Card.* Illustrated by Gregory Christie. New York: Scholastic, 1997 (biographical picture book).

MYERS, WALTER DEAN. *At Her Majesty's Request; An African Princess in Victorian Enland.* New York: Scholastic, 1999 (nonfiction; biography).

———. *Harlem.* Illustrated by Christopher Myers. New York: Scholastic, 1997 (poetry picture book).

NICKEUS, BESSIE. *Walking the Log; Memories of a Southern Childhood.* New York: Rizzole, 1994 (autobiographical picture book).

PINKNEY, ANDREA DAVIS. *Duke Ellingston: The Piano Prince and His Orchestra.* Illustrated by Brian Pinkney. New York: Scholastic, 1998 (picture book biography).

RINGGOLD, FAITH. *Aunt Harriet's Underground Railroad in the Sky.* New York: Crown, 1992 (fantasy, time travel, picture book).

———. *Dinner at Aunt Connie's House.* New York: Hyperion, 1993 (fantasy picture book filled with biographical/historical portraits of famous African-American women).

———. *Tar Beach.* New York: Crown, 1991 (genre blend: picture book, realism, dream/daydream fantasy, history, autobiography, art).

ROBINET, HARRIETTE GILLEM. *Washington City Is Burning.* New York: Atheneum, 1996 (historical novel).

ROCHELLE, BELINDA. *Jewels.* Illustrated by Cornelius Van Wright and Ying-Hwa Hu. New York: Dutton/Lodestor, 1998 (picture book).

SHERROW, VICTORIA. *Phillis Wheatley, Poet.* New York: Chelsea House, 1992 (nonfiction; biography).

STRICKLAND, DOROTHY, EDITOR. *Listen Children: An Anthology of Black Literature.* Illustrated by Leo and Diane Dillon. New York. Yearling Books, 1999 (collection fiction, nonfiction, poetry, play).

SULLIVAN, CHARLES. *Children of Promise: African-American Literature and Art for Young People.* New York: Abrams, 1991 (nonfiction; history).

THOMAS, JOYCE CAROL. *I Have Heard of a Land.* Illustrated by Floyd Cooper. New York: HarperCollins, 1998 (historical fiction, picture book).

History and Culture: Asian-American Experiences

CHOI, SOOK NYUL. *Year of Impossible Goodbyes.* Boston: Houghton Mifflin, 1991 (Korea; historical and autobiographical fiction).

CHIN, CHARLIE. *China's Bravest Girl: The Legend of Hau Mu Lan.* Illustrated by Tomie Arai. San Francisco, CA: Childrens Book Press, 1997 (Chinese legend, folk poem, picture book).

JIANG, JI LI. *Red Scarf Girl; A Memoir of the Cultural Revolution.* New York: Scholastic, 1997 (nonfiction: autobiography).

LEE, JEANNE. *The Song of Mu Lan.* Arden, NC: Front Street Press, 1995 (Chinese legend, folks poem picturebook).

SAN SOUCI, ROBERT D. *Fa Mu lan; The Story of a Woman Warrior.* Illustrated by Jean and Mou-sien Tseng. New York: Hyperion Books, 1998 (picturebook; Chinese legend).

TAN, AMY. *The Moon Lady.* Illustrated by Gretchen Schields. New York: Macmillan, 1992 (China; picture book; realism/framed story).

YEE, PAUL. *Roses Sing on a New Snow: A Delicious Tale.* Illustrated by Harvey Chan. New York: Macmillan, 1991 (picture book; folk tale).

———. *Tales from Gold Mountain: Stories of the Chinese in the New World.* Illustrated by Simon Ng. New York: Simon & Schuster, 1990 (Chinese immigrants in Canada; fiction; folk fantasy).

YEP, LAURENCE. *The City of Dragons.* Illustrated by Jean and Mou-Sien Tseng. New York: Scholastic, 1995 (picture book; folk fantasy).
———. *Dragon's Gate.* New York: HarperCollins, 1993 (China; historical fiction).
———. *Dragonwings.* New York: Harper and Row, 1975 (China; historical fiction).
———. *The Rainbow People.* Illustrated by David Wiesner. New York: HarperCollins, 1991 (Chinese folk tales).
YOUNG, ED. *Mouse Match.* New York: Harcourt Brace, 1997 (picture book; folk fantasy).
———. *Seven Blind Mice.* New York; Philomel, 1992 (picture book; folk fantasy).
ZHANG, SONG NAN. The *Ballad of Mulan.* Union City, CA: Pan Asian Publications, 1998 (picture book, Chinese legend).
ZHANG, SONG NAN. *The Children of China: An Artist's Journey.* Plattsburgh, NY: Tundra Books, 1998 (illustrated-nonfiction).

History and Culture: Hispanic-American Experiences

ANCONA, GEORGE. Barrio: *Jose's Neighborhood.* Photography by George Ancona. New York: Harcourt Brace, 1998 (nonfiction).
HAYES, J. *The Day It Snowed Tortillas: Tales From Spanish New Mexico.* Santa Fe, NM: Mariposa Publishing, 1982 (stories).
LOMAS, GARZA. *Family Pictures.* San Francisco: Children's Book Press, 1990 (picture book).
MELTZER, MILTON. *The Hispanic Americans.* New York: Crowell, 1982 (nonfiction).
MOHR, NICHOLASA. *Old Lativia and the Mountain of Sorrows.* Illustrated by Rudy Gutierrez. New York: Viking, 1996 (picture book).
———. *Songs of El Coqui and Other Tales of Puerto Rico.* New York: Penguin, 1995 (stories).
MORA, PAT. *Confetti: Poems for Children.* Illustrated by Enrique Sanchez. New York: Lee & Low, 1996 (picture book; poetry).
———. *The Race of Toad and Deer.* Illustrated by Maya Itzna Brooks. New York: Orchard, 1995 (picture book; folk tale).
———. *Tomas and the Library Lady.* Illustrated by Raul Colon. New York: Knopf 1997 (picture book).
MOREY, J. *Famous Mexican Americans.* New York: Dutton, 1989 (nonfiction).
NYE, NAOMI, EDITOR. *The Tree is Older than You Are: A Bilingual Gathering of Poems and Stories from Mexico with Paintings by Mexican Artists.* New York: Simon & Schuster, 1995.
PENA, S., EDITOR. *Tun-ta-ca-tun: More Stories and Poems in English and Spanish for Children.* Houston, TX: Arte Publico Press, 1986 (stories).
PINCHOT, J. *The Mexicans in America.* Minneapolis, MN: Lerner Publications, 1989 (nonfiction).

History and Culture: Jewish-American Experiences

COHEN, BARBARA. *Molly's Pilgrim.* New York: William Morrow, 1983 (historical fiction).
GILMAN, PHOEBE. *Something for Nothing.* New York: Scholastic, 1993 (folklore).
GOLDIN, BARBARA DIAMOND. *Cakes and Miracles: A Purim Tale.* Illustrated by Erika Weihs. New York: Viking, 1991 (picture storybook).
HESSE, KAREN. *Letters from Rifka.* New York: Holt, 1992 (historical fiction).
HEST, AMY. *When Jesse Came Across the Sea.* Illustrated by P. J. Lynch. Cambridge, MA Candlewick, 1997 (picture book).
LEVITIN, SONIA. *Journey to America.* New York: Atheneum, 1970 (historical fiction).
LOBEL, ANITA. *No Pretty Pictures: A Child of War.* New York: Greenwillow, 1998 (memoir; history).
SCHWARTZ, HOWARD, EDITOR. *The Diamond Tree.* Illustrated by Uri Shulevitz. New York: HarperCollins, 1991 (Jewish tales from the Middle East, Africa, and Eastern Europe).
SHULEVITZ, URI. *The Treasure.* New York: Farrar, 1978 (Jewish folk tale).

SIEGAL, ARANKA. *Upon the Head of the Goat: A Childhood in Hungary, 1939–1944.* New York: Farrar, 1981 (autobiography).

SILVERMAN, ERICA. *Raisel's Riddle.* Illustrated by Susan Gaber. New York: Farrar, Straus and Giroux, 1999.

SINGER, I. B. *The Golem.* New York: Sunburst, 1996 (Prague; Jewish legend).

TAYLOR, SYDNEY. *All-of-a-Kind Family.* Chicago: Follett, 1951 (historical fiction).

———. *A Papa Like Everyone Else.* New York: Doubleday, 1966 (historical fiction).

YOLEN, JANE. *The Devil's Arithmetic.* New York: Viking, 1988 (historical fiction, time fantasy).

ZYSKIND, SARA. *Stolen Years.* Minneapolis: Lerner Publications, 1981 (autobiography).

History and Culture: Native American Experiences

BAYLOR, BYRD. *And It is Still That Way; Legends Told by Arizona Indian Children.* El Paso, Texas: Cinco Puntos Press, 1998 (Legends).

BEGAY, SHONTO. *Ma'ii and Cousin Horned Toad: A Traditional Navajo Story.* New York: Scholastic, 1992 (song/story picture book).

———. *The Mud Pony: A Traditional Skidi Pawnee Tale.* Retold by Caron Lee Cohen. New York: Scholastic, 1988 (picture book; folk tale).

BIERHORST, JOHN. *Doctor Coyote: A Native American Aesop's Fables.* New York: Macmillan, 1987 (folklore).

BRUCHAC, JOSEPH. *A Boy Called Slow.* Illustrated by Rocco Baviera. New York: Philomel, 1994 (biography).

———. *The Boy Who Lived with Bears and Other Iroquois Stories.* Illustrated by Murv Jacob. New York: HarperCollins, 1995 (illustrated folk tales).

———. *The Earth Under Sky Bear's Feet* (poetry).

——— *Flying with the Eagle, Racing the Great Bear: Stories from Native North America.* New York: Bridgewater Books, 1993 (folklore; folk tales/legends).

———. *On the Road of Stars: Native American Night Poems and Sleep Chants.* New York: Macmillan, 1994 (poetry).

———. *Tell Me a Tale; A Book About Storytelling.* New York: Harcourt Brace, 1997 (nonfiction; stories).

BRUCHAC, JOSEPH, AND LONDON, JONATHAN. *Thirteen Moons on Turtle's Back: A Native American Year of Moons.* Illustrated by Thomas Locker. New York: Philomel, 1992 (genre blend: poetry, folklore, legend, art).

BRUCHAC, JOSEPH, AND ROSS, GAYLE. *The Girl Who Married the Moon.* New York: Bridgewater Books, 1994 (folklore; folk tales/legends).

DORRIS, MICHAEL. *Guests.* New York: Hyperion, 1994 (historical fiction).

———. *Morning Girl.* New York: Hyperion, 1992 (historical fiction).

——— *Sees Behind Trees.* New York: Hyperion, 1996 (historical fiction).

GOBLE, PAUL. *Iktomi and the Ducks: A Plains Indian Story.* New York: Orchard, 1990 (picture book; folk story). See other titles also by Goble for this category.

HALEY, GAIL. *Two Bad Boys; A Very Old Cherokee Tale.* New York: Dutton Books, 1996 (picture book; Cherokee legend).

HIRSCHFELDER, ARLENE, AND BEVERLY SINGER. *Rising Voices: Writings of Young Native Americans.* New York: Ivy Books, 1992 (genre blend: poetry, history, autobiography).

LEVINE, ELLEN. *If You Lived with the Iroquois.* Illustrated by Shelly Hehenberger. New York: Scholastic, 1998 (nonfiction; history; illustrated information book).

MOMADAY, N. SCOTT. *Owl in the Cedar Tree.* Illustrated by Don Perceval. Lincoln: University of Nebraska Press, 1975 (novel).

SNEVE, VIRGINIA DRIVING HAWK. *The Cherokees.* New York: Holiday, 1996 (picture book; nonfiction; history).

WOOD, NANCY, EDITOR. *The Serpent's Tongue: Prose, Poetry, and Art of the New Mexico Pueblos.* New York: Dutton, 1997 (illustrated anthology).

ADOFF, ARNOLD. *Black is brown is tan.* Illustrated by Emily Arnold McCully. New York: HarperCollins, 1973 (African-American; picture book; realism/poetry).

BATESON-HILL, MARGARET. *Shotu and the Star Quilt.* Illustrated by Christine LaKota; Fowler. New York. Zero to Ten Limited, 1998 (contemporary realistic fiction).

CASTANEDA, OMAR S. *Abuela's Weave.* Illustrated by Enrique O. Sanchez. New York: Lee and Low, 1993 (Guatemala; picture book; realism).

COUTANT, HELEN. *First Snow.* Pictures by Vo-Dinh Mai. New York: Knopf, 1974 (Viet Nam; picture book; realism).

CREWS, DONALD. *Bigmama's.* New York: Greenwillow, 1991 (African-American; picture book; realism).

ERDRICH, LOUISE. *The Birchbark House.* New York: Hyperion, 1999 (Native American; Ojibwa; historical fiction).

FLOURNOY, VALERIE. *The Patchwork Quilt.* Illustrated by Jerry Pinkney. New York: Viking Penguin, 1985 (African-American; picture book; realism).

GARLAND, SHERRY. *The Lotus Seed.* Illustrated by Tatsuro Kiuchi. New York: Harcourt Brace, 1993 (Viet Nam; picture book; realism).

GARZA, CARMEN LOMAS. *Family Pictures/Cuadros de familia.* San Francisco: Children's Book Press, 1990 (Mexican-American; picture book; realism; autobiography).

GREENFIELD, ELOISE. *Africa Dream.* Illustrated by Carole Byard. New York: John Day, 1977 (Africa and America; picture book; fantasy).

GRIFALCONI, ANN. *The Village of Round and Square Houses.* Boston: Little, Brown, 1986 (Tos; the Cameroons; Central Africa; picture book; realism; legend/framed story).

HAMILTON, VIRGINIA. *Arilla Sun Down.* New York: Greenwillow, 1976 (Native Americans and African-Americans in the American Midwest; realistic novel).

———. *The House of Dies Drear.* New York: Macmillan, 1968 (African-Americans in the American Midwest; realistic novel).

———. *M. C. Higgins the Great.* New York: Macmillan, 1974 (African-Americans in the American Midwest; realistic novel).

———. *The Magical Adventures of Pretty Pearl.* New York: Harper, 1981 (African-Americans in the American Midwest; historical folk fantasy).

———. *Second Cousins.* New York: Scholastic. 1998.

HICKMAN, JANET. *Susannah.* New York: Greenwillow, 1998 (Shaker community in Ohio in early 1800s; realistic novel; historical fiction).

KROLL, VIRGINIA. *Masai and I.* Illustrations by Nancy Carpenter. New York: Four Winds, 1992 (East Africa and America; genre blend: history, geography, fiction, picture book).

LASKY, KATHRYN. *The Night Journey.* New York: Warne, 1981 (Russian Jewish/American; realistic novel; historical fiction).

MATHIS, SHARON BELL. *The Hundred Penny Box.* Illustrated by Leo and Diane Dillon. New York: Viking Penguin, 1975 (African-American; long picture book; realism).

MOMADAY, NATACHEE SCOTT. *Owl in the Cedar Tree.* Lincoln: University of Nebraska Press, 1975 (Native American; Navajo; realistic novel).

PAULSEN, GARY. *Dogsong.* New York: Bradbury Press, 1985 (Inuit; Canadian; realistic novel).

POLACCO, PATRICIA. *The Keeping Quilt.* New York: Simon & Schuster, 1988 (Jewish-American family immigrating from Russia; genre blend: autobiographical fiction, picture book).

RINGGOLD, FAITH. *Aunt Harriet's Underground Railroad in the Sky.* New York: Crown, 1992 (African-American; historical time fantasy; picture book).

———. *Dinner at Aunt Connie's House.* New York: Hyperion, 1993 (African-American; genre blend: biography, fiction, fantasy, picture book).

SIS, PETER. *The Three Golden Keys.* New York: Doubleday, 1994 (Czech immigrant returns to Prague; surrealistic picture book).

TAN, AMY. *The Moon Lady.* New York: Macmillan, 1992 (Asian-American; picture book; realism; frame story).

WALLACE, IAN. *Chin Chiang and the Dragon's Dance.* Toronto: Douglas & McIntyre, 1984 (Chinese family living in Canada; picture book; realism).

YARBROUGH, CAMILLE. *Cornrows.* Illustrated by Carole Byard. New York: Coward, Mc-Cann & Goeghegan, 1979 (Africa and America; picture book: realism).

YEP, LAURENCE. *Child of the Owl.* New York: Harper, 1977 (Asian-American, realistic novel).

———. *The Cook's Family.* New York: Putnam's, 1998 (Asian-American, contemporary realistic fiction).

———. *Dragonwings.* New York: Harper and Row, 1975 (Asian-American; historical novel; realistic fiction).

———. *The Star Fisher.* New York: Penguin, 1991 (Asian-American, historical novel; realistic fiction).

BLACK HISTORY MONTH

Nonfiction

The Best of the Brownies' Book, edited by Dianne Johnson-Feelings (Oxford, 1996). Collection of literature published in the 1920s as a monthly magazine for children. W. E. B. DuBois, a member of the Harlem Renaissance and editor of the magazine, was committed to giving African-American children a way to learn more about their history and culture as it was being depicted by an array of talented writers and artists. (history, art, biography, autobiography, fiction, and poetry).

Children of Promise: African-American Literature and Art for Young People, edited by Charles Sullivan (Abrams, 1991). Anthology filled with art, poetry, short literary pieces and historical photographs, all of which trace the African-American experience in America as it evolved from slavery (history and art).

Childtimes, by Eloise Greenfield and Lessie Jones Little (Scholastic, 1979). Three-generation memoir of family life in North Carolina and Washington, D.C. (autobiography, history).

The Great Migration: An American Story. Illustrated by Jacob Lawrence (Harper, 1992). Pictures drawn by the artist tell about the movement of African-Americans from the South to the industrial North from 1917 to 1940 (narrative art).

Harriet Tubman: Conductor on the Underground Railroad by Ann Perry (Harper, 1955). Tubman's life story, blended with historical narrative about American history (biography, historical fiction, history).

I Have a Dream by Martin Luther King, Jr.; illustrated by fifteen Coretta Scott King Award and Honor Book Artists. New York: Scholastic, 1997. King's famous speech delivered on August 28, 1963 for the March on Washington, with a Forward by Coretta Scott King.

In Praise of Our Fathers and Our Mothers: A Black Family Treasury by Outstanding Authors and Artists compiled by Wade Hudson and Cheryl Willis Hudson (Just Us Books, 1997). Poems, essays, pictures, photos, interviews, and true stories of forty-eight African-American writers and artists who honor their families in this collection (autobiography, history, art).

Li'l Sis and Uncle Willie by Gwen Everett (Hyperion, 1994). Picture storybook based on the life of African-American artist William Johnson (1901–1970). Illustrated by Everett's paintings (art, biography).

Minty by Alan Schroeder and Jerry Pinkney (Dial, 1996). Account of Harriet Tubman's life presented in illustrated storybook format (history, historical fiction, biography, picture book).

To Be A Slave by Julius Lester (Dial, 1968). Slaves' stories as recorded by members of Federal Writers' Project; selected and introduced by Lester (history).

Historical Fiction

The Captive by Joyce Hansen (Scholastic, 1994). Survival story of an African boy, Kofi, captured in 1788 and brought to America as a slave.

Letters from a Slave Girl: The Story of Harriet Jacobs by Mary Lyons (Simon & Schuster, 1992). Based on Harriet Jacobs's autobiography, this book takes readers into Harriet's mind through letters that Harriet might have written to her deceased parents, uncle, aunt, lost boyfriend, and brother.

Out From This Place by Joyce Hansen (Walker, 1988). A story based on incidents in post-Civil War days in the Sea Islands off the coast of South Carolina when freed slaves were displaced from their land.

The Watsons Go to Birmingham—1963 by Christopher Paul Curtis (Delacorte, 1955). Story of an African-American family in Michigan who traveled to Alabama for a family visit during the Civil Rights Movement of the 1960s.

Picture Books

Cornrows by Camille Yarbrough; illustrated by Carole Byard (Coward, 1979). Fictional storybook in which an African-American girl, Sister, learns about her heritage and the African clan symbol embedded in braiding patterns from her mother and great-grandmother's storytelling.

Dinner at Aunt Connie's House by Faith Ringgold (Hyperion, 1993). Melody and Lonnie learn about their heritage from paintings of famous African-American women who come to life to tell about themselves one day when the children visit Aunt Connie's attic.

Folk Tales

Black Folktales by Julius Lester, illustrated by Tom Feelings (Grove, 1969). Retellings of African and African-American stories from various eras and regions of America.

The Dark-Thirty by Patricia McKissack, illustrated by Brian Pinkney (Knopf, 1992). Original stories based on African-American history and oral stories with informative introductions.

Her Stories by Virginia Hamilton, illustrated by Leo and Diane Dillon (Scholastic, 1995). Tellings of folk tales, legends, trickster tales, and magical stories about African-American women characters.

Poetry

Brown Honey in Broomwheat Tea by Joyce Carol Thomas, illustrated by Floyd Cooper (Harper, 1993). Female child explores her African-American identity in twelve poems.

Children of Long Ago by Lessie Jones Little, illustrated by Jan Spivey Gilchrist (Philomel, 1988). Born in 1906, the author remembers her own childhood in the rural South—from paper dolls to Sunday school.

The Dream Keeper and Other Poems by Langston Hughes, illustrated by Brian Pinkney (Knopf, 1994). From their first appearance in 1932 during the Harlem Renaissance to this newly illustrated edition of sixty-five poems, Hughes's poetry has inspired African-American readers to dream their own American dreams.

Families Poems Celebrating the African American Experience by Dorothy S. Strickland and Michael R. Strickland, illustrated by John Ward (Honesdate PA: Boyds Mills Press, 1996). Anthology of poetry—works by Langston Hughes, Nikki Giovanni, Lucille Clifton, Gwendolyn Brooks, Eloise Greenfield and others—celebrating African-American family life.

Gingerbread Days by Joyce Carol Thomas, illustrated by Floyd Cooper (Harper, 1995). In poems for each month of the year, an African-American boy celebrates family life and African-American identity.

Shimmy Shimmy Shimmy Like My Sister Kate by Nikki Giovanni (Holt, 1996). The author selects, introduces, and interprets twenty-three poets from the Harlem Renaissance to the present day to produce a rich tapestry of African-American history.

MULTICULTURAL LITERATURE AND THE ARTS

(Discovering Oneself as an Artist, Art and Life, Art and Life Stories, Learning about Art and Artists, Art as a Way of Knowing, Art as Life/Life as Art, Art as Social Action/ Cultural Survival, Art as Storytelling, Storytelling as Art, Artists' Journeys).

Realistic Fiction (Contemporary)

Picture Books

ALIKI [BRANDENBERG]. *Painted Words; Spoken Memories.* New York: Greenwillow, 1998 (art as storytelling; artist's journey; child is Greek American).

FLEMING, CANDACE. *Gabriella's Song.* Illustrated by Giselle Potter. New York: Atheneum, 1997 (art and life; the power of music as it becomes art; Italy).

FLOURNOY, VALERIE. *The Patchwork Quilt.* Illustrated by Jerry Pinkney. New York: Dutton, 1985 (art and life; African-American family).

ISADORA, RACHEL. *Willaby.* New York: Macmillan, 1977 (discovering oneself as an artist; art as a way of knowing; child pictured is African-American).

MILES, MISKA. *Annie and the Old One.* Illustrations by Peter Parnall. Boston: Little, Brown, 1971 (art and life; art and life stories; art as a way of knowing; Navajo family).

SAY, ALLEN. *Emma's Rug.* Boston: Houghton Mifflin, 1996 (art as life, life as art; art as a way of knowing; family is Japanese American).

WILLIAMS, VERA. *Cherries and Cherry Pits.* New York: Greenwillow, 1986 (art and life stories; art as a way of knowing; child pictured is African-American).

Novels

MOMADAY, NATACHEE SCOTT. *Owl in the Cedar Tree.* Lincoln: University of Nebraska Press, 1975 (art and life stories; finding yourself as an artist; art and Native American life).

PATERSON, KATHERINE. *Bridge to Terabithia.* New York: Crowell, 1977 (art as life; life as art; rural Maryland).

Historical Fiction

COONEY, BARBARA. *Hattie and the Wild Waves.* New York: Viking Penguin, 1990 (discovering oneself as an artist; German-American immigrants; picture book).

HOPKINSON, DEBORAH. *Sweet Clara and the Freedom Quilt.* Illustrated by James Ransome. New York: Knopf, 1993 (art as social action/cultural survival; picture book; African Americans).

YARBROUGH, CAMILLE. *Cornrows.* Illustrations by Carole Byard. New York: Coward, 1979 (art and life; picture book; African Americans).

Fantasy

AGEE, JON. *The Incredible Painting of Felix Clousseau.* New York: Farrar, 1988 (human fantasy picture book; art as life/life as art; art as social action; life in France).

BANG, MOLLY GARRETT. *Tye May and the Magic Brush.* New York: Greenwillow, 1981 (art as social action/cultural survival; adaptation of a Chinese tale).

CLEMENT, CLAUDE. *The Painter and the Wild Swans.* Illustrated by Frederic Clement. New York: Dial, 1986 (picture book; Japanese setting; art as life/life as art).

HAMILTON, VIRGINIA. *The Magical Adventures of Pretty Pearl.* New York: Harper and Row, 1983 (historical folk fantasy novel; art and life; art and life stories; discovering oneself as an artist; art as social action/cultural survival; storytelling as art; African Americans).

Folklore

DEPAOLA, TOMIE. *The Legend of the Indian Paintbrush.* New York: Putnam, 1988 (retelling of a Great Plains legend; art as social action/cultural survival; art as life/life as art).

LEVINE, ARTHUR. *The Boy Who Drew Cats.* New York: Dial, 1993 (retelling of a Japanese legend; art as a way of knowing; art and life).

Poetry

BEGAY, SHONTO. *Navajo: Visions and Voices Across the Mesa.* New York: Scholastic, 1995 (poems and paintings by the author about growing up Native American.)

FEELINGS, TOM. *Soul Looks Back in Wonder.* New York: Dial, 1993 (thirteen African-American poets focus on cultural heritage and creativity, with paintings by Tom Feelings; art and life; art as life/life as art; art as social action/cultural heritage).

Nonfiction

History

SULLIVAN, CHARLES. *Children of Promise: African-American Literature and Art for Young People.* New York: Abrams, 1991 (illustrated reference book on African-American art and literature; learning about art and artists).

ZHANG, SONG NAN. *The Children of China: An Artist's Journey.* Plattsburg, NY; Tundra Books, 1998 (nonfiction illustrated book; artist's journey).

Biography

BJORK, CHRISTINA. *Linnea in Monet's Garden.* Translated by Joan Sandin; Illustrated by Lena Anderson. New York: Farrar, Straus, and Giroux, 1987 (learning and art and artists; France).

EVERETT, GWEN. *Li'l Sis and Uncle Willie.* Illustrated by William H. Johnson. New York: Hyperion, 1991 (fictionalized story based on life of African-American artist William Johnson, illustrated with his art; learning about art and artists; art and life stories).

PREISS, BYRON, EDITOR. *Art of Leo and Diane Dillon.* New York: Ballantine Books, 1981 (critical biography of these picture book artists and illustrators for cover art; learning about art and artists; Leo Dillon is African-American).

RINGGOLD, FAITH. *Aunt Harriet's Underground Railroad in the Sky.* New York: Crown, 1992 (time-slip historical fantasy in which contemporary children encounter African-American heroine Harriet Tubman; learning about art and artists; art and life; art and life stories; art as social action/cultural survival).

———. *Dinner at Aunt Connie's House.* New York: Hyperion, 1993 (biographical fantasy; African-American history/culture; learning about art and artists; art and life stories; art for social action/cultural survival).

WINTER, JEANETTE. *Diego.* Text by Jonah Winter. English and Spanish. Translated from the English by Amy Prince. New York: Knopf, 1991 (picture book biography; learning about art and artists; art and life; art and life stories; art as social action; Diego is Mexican.)

Autobiography

GARZA, CARMEN LOMAS. *Family Pictures/Cuadros de familia.* San Francisco: Children's Book Press, 1990 (picture book; author's family story; Mexican-American ethnicity; art and life; art and life stories; art as life/life as art; discovering oneself as an artist).

IGUS, TOYONI. *Going Back Home: An Artist Returns from the South.* Emeryville, CA: Children's Book Press, 1996 (African-American artist tells her story through paintings; illustrated book; art and life stories; discovering oneself as an artist; artist's journey; art as storytelling).

POLACCO, PATRICIA. *The Keeping Quilt.* New York: Simon & Schuster, 1988 (picture book; author's family story; Jewish-American ethnicity; art and life; art and life stories; art as life/life as art; art as storytelling).

RINGGOLD, FAITH. *Tar Beach.* New York: Crown, 1991 (genre blend: picture book, fiction, dream/daydream fantasy, autobiography, African-American history, art; reproduction of a story quilt made by the author/artist; art and life stories; art as life/life as art; art and life; art as storytelling).

SAY, ALLEN. *The Ink-Keeper's Apprentice.* New York: Harper, 1979 (author's story of growing up in Japan as a young artist; art and life stories; art and life).

ZHANG, SONG NAN. *A Little Tiger in the Chinese Night: An Autobiography in Art.* Plattsburgh NY: Tundra Books, 1995 (authors story of growing up in China as a young artist; art and life stories; art and life).

MULTICULTURAL LITERATURE AND CRAFTS

Quilting, Sewing, Weaving, Wood Sculpture, Stylized Writing

BATESON-HILL, MARGARET. *Shota and the Star Quilt.* Illustrated by Christine Fowler. New York: Zero to Ten Limited, 1998 (contemporary realistic fiction, quilting for Lakota Community Cohesion).

CASTANEDA, OMAR. *Abuela's Weave.* Illustrated by Enrique Sanchez. New York: Lee & Low, 1993 (picture storybook; weaving as valued artifact of Guatemalan culture).

FLOURNOY, VALERIE. *The Patchwork Quilt.* Illustrated by Jerry Pinkney. New York: Dial, 1985 (picture storybook, quilting for transmission of African-American family stories and family cohesion).

GILMAN, PHOEBE. *Something from Nothing.* New York: Scholastic, 1992 (picture book; adaptation of traditional Jewish folk tale, sewing to make family gifts and garments).

HAMILTON, VIRGINIA. *The House of Dies Drear.* New York: Macmillan, 1968 (novel; whittling and wood carving as a way of knowing and telling a story; African-American).

HOPKINSON, DEBORAH. *Sweet Clara and the Freedom Quilt.* Illustrated by James Ransome. New York: Knopf, 1993 (sewing and quilting for transmission of coded messages for Underground Railroad movement; African-American).

IVES, PENNY. *Granny's Quilt.* New York: Penguin, 1993 (quilting for transmission of family stories; English picture book).

JOHNSON, TONY. *The Quilt Story.* Illustrated by Tomie DePaola. New York: Putnam, 1985 (picture storybook; quilt as family artifact).

KINSEY-WARNOCK, NATALIE. *The Canada Geese Quilt.* Illustrated by Leslie Bowman. New York: Dutton, 1989 (picture storybook; quilting for family cohesion and intergenerational connections).

KONIGSBURG, E. L. *The View from Saturday.* New York: Atheneum, 1996 (novel; calligraphy; the pride of creating beautiful writing and of learning and teaching a craft; Jewish-American).

LYONS, MARY. *Stitching Stars: The Story Quilts of Harriet Powers.* New York: Scribners, 1993 (quilting as a way for slaves to "speak"; the narrative power of art).

MILES, MISKA. *Annie and the Old One.* Illustrated by Peter Parnall. Boston: Little, Brown, 1971 (picture storybook; weaving as metaphor of the life cycle in the Navajo world).

NYE, NAOMI SHIHB. *Sitti's Secrets.* Illustrated by Nancy Carpenter. New York: Simon & Schuster, 1994 (picture book; sewing to make family gifts; Palestinian grandmother).

POLACCO, PATRICIA. *The Keeping Quilt.* New York: Simon & Schuster, 1988 (picture book autobiography of four-generation Jewish immigrant family in America).

RINGGOLD, FAITH; FREEMAN, LINDA; AND ROUCHER, NANCY. *Talking to Faith Ringgold.* New York: Crown, 1996 (interactive biography of African-American Ringgold's life, work, ideas, art, and storytelling processes; includes invitations for reader participation in biographical writing).

RINGGOLD, FAITH. *Aunt Harriet's Underground Railroad in the Sky.* New York: Crown, 1992 (picture book; quilting for transmission of coded messages of the Underground Railroad movement).

———. *Tar Beach.* New York: Crown, 1991 (picture book replica of the artist's soft sculpture quilt telling this same story; the quilt as cultural artifact).

TURNER, ROBYN. *Faith Ringgold.* Boston: Little, Brown, 1993 (picture book biography of Ringgold as a female African-American artist for children).

WALTER, MILDRED PITTS. *Trouble's Child.* New York: Lothrop, 1985 (novel; quilting for transmission of African-American premarriage ritual).

Appendix 2
Awards in Children's Literature

American Library Association
Caldecott Award (Picture Books)
Newbery Award (Literature)
Coretta Scott King Award (African-American Authors and Illustrators)
Pura Belpre Award (Latino Writers and Illustrators)
Laura Ingalls Wilder Award (Author Whose Work Has Produced Lasting Contribution)
Andrew Carnegie Medal for Excellence in Children's Video

Canadian Library Association
CLA Book of the Year Award

British Library Association
Kate Greenaway Award (Picture Books)
Carnegie Award (Fiction)

International Board of Books for Young People
Hans Christian Andersen Award (Author and Illustrator's Entire Collection of Literature)

Children's Literature Association
Phoenix Award (Overlooked Books of the Past)

AMERICAN LIBRARY ASSOCIATION

Caldecott and Newbery Medals

Given annually since 1938 (Caldecott) and 1922 (Newbery) by the Association for Library Service to Children (ALSC) of the American Library Association (50 Huron Street, Chicago, IL, 60611), these awards go to the illustrator (Caldecott) and author (Newbery) who have made the most distinguished contribution to American children's literature in books published the previous year. Two or more Honor Book Awards are also given. Honor Books appear just after the winners for each year in the list that follows. (Get to know as many of these books as you can to understand what jurists have designated as "distinguished," what cultural values prevailed in various eras, and what at least one important selective "canon" of American children's books looks like.)

Caldecott Awards

Caldecott winners (artists' names) and titles are printed in boldface. Honor Books follow, with illustrators' names in boldface, also.

1938 ***Animals of the Bible, a Picture Book*** by Helen Dean Fish and **Dorothy Lathrop**
Seven Simeons, A Russian Tale by **Boris Artzbasheff**
Four and Twenty Blackbirds by Helen Dean Fish and **Robert Lawson**

1939 ***Mei Li*** by **Thomas Handforth**
The Forest Pool by **Laura Adams Armer**
Wee Gillis by Munro Leaf and **Robert Lawson**
Snow White and the Seven Dwarfs by **Wanda Gag**
Barkis by **Claire Newberry**
Andy and the Lion by **James Daugherty**

1940 ***Abraham Lincoln*** by **Ingri and Edgar D'Aulaire**
Cock-a-Doodle-Doo by **Berta and Elmer Hader**
Madeline by **Ludwig Bemelmans**
The Ageless Story by **Lauren Ford**

1941 ***They Were Strong and Good*** by **Robert Lawson**
April's Kitten by **Clare Newberry**

1942 ***Make Way for Ducklings*** by **Robert McCloskey**
An American ABC by **Maud and Miska Petersham**
In My Mother's House by Ann Nolan Clark and **Velino Herrara**
Paddle-to-the-Sea by **Holling Clancy Holling**
Nothing At All by **Wanda Gag**

1943 ***The Little House*** by **Virginia Burton**
Dash and Dart by **Mary and Conrad Buff**
Marshmallow by **Clare Newbery**

1944 ***Many Moons*** by James Thurber and **Louis Slobodkin**
Small Rain; Verses from the Bible by Jessie Jones and **Elizabeth Jones**
Pierre Pigeon by Lee Kingman and **Arnold Bare**
The Mighty Hunter by **Berta and Elmer Hader**
A Child's Good Night Book by Margaret Wise Brown and **Jean Charlot**
Good Luck Horse by Chin-Yi Chan and **Plato Chan**

1945 ***Prayer for a Child*** by Rachel Field and **Elizabeth Jones**
Mother Goose by **Tasha Tudor**
In the Forest by **Marie Hall Ets**
Yonie Wondernose by **Marguerite de Angeli**
The Christmas Anna Angel by Ruth Sawyer and **Kate Seredy**

1946 ***The Rooster Crows*** by **Maud and Miska Petersham**
Little Lost Lamb by Golden MacDonald and **Leonard Weisgard**
Sing Mother Goose by Opal Wheeler and **Marjorie Torrey**
My Mother Is the Most Beautiful Women in the World by Becky Reyher and **Ruth Gannett**
You Can Write Chinese by **Kurt Wiese**

1947 ***The Little Island*** by Golden MacDonald and **Leonard Weisgard**
Rain Drop Splash by Alvin Tresselt and **Leonard Weisgard**
Boats on the River by Marjorie Flack and **Jay Barnum**
Timothy Turtle by Al Graham and **Tony Palazzo**
Pedro, the Angel of Olvera Street by **Leo Politi**
Sing in Praise by Opal Wheeler and **Marjorie Torrey**

1948 ***White Snow, Bright Snow*** by Alvin Tresselt and **Roger Duvoisin**
Stone Soup by **Marcia Brown**
McElligot's Pool by **Dr. Seuss**
Bambino the Clown by **George Schreiber**
Roger and the Fox by Lavinia Davis and **Hildegard Woodward**
Song of Robin Hood by Anne Malcolmson and **Virginia Burton**

1949 ***The Big Snow*** by **Berta and Elmer Hader**
Blueberries for Sal by **Robert McCloskey**
All Around Town by Phyllis McGinley and **Helen Stone**
Juanita by **Leo Politi**
Fish in the Air by **Kurt Wiese**

1950 ***Song of the Swallows*** by **Leo Politi**
America's Ethan Allen by Stewart Holbrook and **Lynd Ward**
The Wild Birthday Cake by Lavinia Davis and **Hildegard Woodward**
The Happy Day by Ruth Krauss and **Marc Simont**
Henry-Fisherman by **Marcia Brown**
Bartholomew and the Oobleck by **Dr. Seuss**

1951 ***The Egg Tree*** by **Katherine Milhous**
Dick Whittington and His Cat by **Marcia Brown**
The Two Reds by William Lipkind and **Nicholas Mordvinoff**
If I Ran the Zoo by **Dr. Seuss**
T-Bone the Baby Sitter by **Clare Newberry**
The Most Wonderful Doll in the World by Phyllis McGinley and **Helen Stone**

1952 ***Finders Keepers*** by William Lipkind and **Nicholas Mordvinoff**
Mr. T. W. Anthony Woo by **Marie Hall Ets**
Skipper John's Cook by **Marcia Brown**
All Falling Down by Gene Zion and **Margaret Graham**
Bear Party by **William Pene Du Bois**
Feather Mountain by **Elizabeth Olds**

1953 ***The Biggest Bear*** by **Lynd Ward**
Puss in Boots by **Marcia Brown**
One Morning in Maine by **Robert McCloskey**
Ape in a Cape by **Fritz Eichenberg**
The Storm Book by Charlotte Zolotow and **Margaret Graham**
Five Little Monkeys by **Juliet Kepes**

1954 ***Madeline's Rescue*** by **Ludwig Bemelmans**
Journey Cake, Ho! by Ruth Sawyer and **Robert McCloskey**
When Will the World Be Mine? By Miriam Schlein and **Jean Charlot**
The Steadfast Tin Soldier (Hans Christian Andersen) by M. R. James and **Marcia Brown**
A Very Special House by Ruth Krauss and **Maurice Sendak**
Green Eyes by **Abe Birnbaum**

1955 ***Cinderella*** (Charles Perrault) by **Marcia Brown**
Book of Nursery and Mother Goose Rhymes by **Marguerite de Angeli**
Wheel on the Chimney by Margaret Wise Brown and **Tibor Gergely**
The Thanksgiving Story by Alice Dalgliesh and **Helen Sewell**

1956 ***Frog Went A-Courtin'*** by John Langstaff and **Feodor Rojankovsky**
Play With Me by **Marie Hall Ets**
Crow Boy by **Taro Yashima**

1957 ***A Tree Is Nice*** by Janice May Udry and **Marc Simont**
Mr. Penny's Race Horse by **Marie Hall Ets**
1 Is One by **Tasha Tudor**

Anatole by Eve Titus and **Paul Galdone**
Gillespie and the Guards by Benjamin Elkin and **James Daugherty**
Lion by **William Pene Du Bois**
1958 ***Time of Wonder*** by **Robert McCloskey**
Fly High, Fly Low by **Don Freeman**
Anatole and the Cat by Eve Titus and **Paul Galdone**
1959 ***Chanticleer and the Fox*** (Chaucer) by **Barbara Cooney**
The House That Jack Built by **Antonio Frasconi**
What Do You Say, Dear? By Sesyle Joslin and **Maurice Sendak**
Umbrella by **Taro Yashima**
1960 ***Nine Days to Christmas*** by **Marie Hall Ets** and Aurora Labastida
Houses by the Sea by Alice Goudey and **Adrienne Adams**
The Moon Jumpers by Janice May Udry and **Maurice Sendak**
1961 ***Baboushka and the Three Kings*** by Ruth Robbins and **Nicolas Sidjakov**
Inch by Inch by **Leo Lionni**
1962 ***Once A Mouse*** by **Marcia Brown**
The Fox Went Out on a Chilly Night by **Peter Spier**
Little Bear's Visit by Else Minarik and **Maurice Sendak**
The Day We Saw the Sun Come Up by Alice Goudey and **Adrienne Adams**
1963 ***The Snowy Day*** by **Ezra Jack Keats**
The Sun Is a Golden Earring by Natalia Belting and **Bernarda Bryson**
Mr. Rabbit and the Lovely Present by Charlotte Zolotow and **Maurice Sendak**
1964 ***Where the Wild Things Are*** by **Maurice Sendak**
Swimmy by **Leo Lionni**
All in the Morning Early by Sorche Nic Leodhas and **Evaline Ness**
Mother Goose and Nursery Rhymes by **Philip Reed**
1965 ***May I Bring a Friend?*** by Beatrice Schenk de Regniers and **Beni Montresor**
Rain Makes Applesauce by Julian Scheer and **Marvin Bileck**
The Wave by Margaret Hodges and **Blair Lent**
A Pocketful of Cricket by Rebecca Caudill and **Evaline Ness**
1966 ***Always Room for One More*** by Sorche Nic Leodhas and **Nonny Hogrogian**
Hide and Seek Fog by Alvin Tresselt and **Roger Duvoisin**
Just Me by **Marie Hall Ets**
Tom Tit Tot (Joseph Jacobs) by **Evaline Ness**
1967 ***Sam, Bangs and Moonshine*** by **Evaline Ness**
One Wide River to Cross by Barbara Emberley and **Ed Emberley**
1968 ***Drummer Hoff*** by Barbara Emberley and **Ed Emberley**
Frederick by **Leo Lionni**
Seashore Story by **Taro Yashima**
The Emperor and the Kite by Jane Yolen and **Ed Young**
1969 ***The Fool of the World and the Flying Ship*** (Arthur Ransome) by **Uri Shulevitz**
Why the Sun and the Moon Live in the Sky by Elphinstone Dayrell and **Blair Lent**
1970 ***Sylvester and the Magic Pebble*** by **William Steig**
Goggles! by **Ezra Jack Keats**
Alexander and the Wind-Up Mouse by **Leo Lionni**
Pop Corn and Ma Goodness by Edna Mitchell Preston and **Robert Andrew Parker**
Thy Friend, Obadiah by **Brinton Turkle**
The Judge by Harve Zemach and **Margot Zemach**
1971 ***A Story, A Story*** by **Gail Haley**
The Angry Moon by William Sleator and **Blair Lent**

Frog and Toad Are Friends by **Arnold Lobel**
In the Night Kitchen by **Maurice Sendak**

1972 ***One Fine Day*** by **Nonny Hogrogian**
If All the Seas Were One Sea by **Janina Domanska**
Mojo Means One: Swahili Counting Book by Muriel Feelings and **Tom Feelings**
Hildilid's Night by Cheli Ryan and **Arnold Lobel**

1973 ***The Funny Little Woman*** by Arlene Mosel and **Blair Lent**
Hosie's Alphabet by Hosea, Tobias, and Lisa Baskin and **Leonard Baskin**
When Clay Sings by Byrd Baylor and **Tom Bahti**
Snow-White and the Seven Dwarfs (Grimm Brothers) by **Nancy Ekholm Burkert**
Anansi the Spider by **Gerald McDermott**

1974 ***Duffy and the Devil*** by Harve Zemach and **Margot Zemach**
Three Jovial Huntsmen by **Susan Jeffers**
Cathedral by **David Macaulay**

1975 ***Arrow to the Sun*** by **Gerald McDermott**
Jambo Means Hello: Swahili Alphabet Book by Muriel Feelings and **Tom Feelings**

1976 ***Why Mosquitoes Buzz in People's Ears*** by Verna Aardema and **Leo and Diane Dillon**
The Dessert Is Theirs by Byrd Baylor and **Peter Parnall**
Strega Nona by **Tomie De Paola**

1977 ***Ashanti to Zulu: African Traditions*** by Margaret Musgrove and **Leo and Diane Dillon**
The Amazing Bone by **William Steig**
The Contest by **Nonny Hogrogian**
Fish for Supper by **M. B. Goffstein**
The Golem by **Beverly Brodsky McDermott**
Hawk, I'm Your Brother by Byrd Baylor and **Peter Parnall**

1978 ***Noah's Ark*** by **Peter Speir**
Castle by **David Macaulay**
It Could Always Be Worse by **Margot Zemach**

1979 ***The Girl Who Loved Wild Horses*** by **Paul Goble**
Freight Train by **Donald Crews**
The Way to Start a Day by Byrd Baylor and **Peter Parnall**

1980 ***Ox-Cart Man*** by Donald Hall and **Barbara Cooney**
Ben's Trumpet by **Rachel Isadora**
The Treasure by **Uri Shulevitz**
The Garden of Abdul Gasazi by **Chris Van Allsburg**

1981 ***Fables*** by **Arnold Lobel**
The Bremen-Town Musicians by **Ilse Plume**
The Grey Lady and the Strawberry Snatcher by **Molly Bang**
Mice Twice by **Joseph Low**
Truck by **Donald Crews**

1982 ***Jumanji*** by **Chris Van Allsburg**
A Visit to William Blake's Inn by Nancy Willard and **Alice and Martin Provensen**
Where the Buffaloes Begin by Olaf Baker and **Stephen Gammell**
On Market Street by Arnold Lobel and **Anita Lobel**
Outside Over There by **Maurice Sendak**

1983 ***Shadow*** by Blaise Cendars and **Marcia Brown**
When I Was Young in the Mountains by Cynthia Rylant and **Diane Goode**
A Chair for My Mother by **Vera Williams**

1984 ***The Glorious Flight*** by **Alice and Martin Provensen**
Ten, Nine, Eight by **Molly Bang**
Little Red Riding Hood by **Trina Schart Hyman**

1985 ***Saint George and the Dragon*** by Margaret Hodges and **Trina Schart Hyman**
Hansel and Gretel (Grimm Brothers) by Rika Lesser and **Paul Zelinsky**
The Story of Jumping Mouse by **John Steptoe**
Have You Seen My Duckling? By **Nancy Tafuri**

1986 ***The Polar Express*** by **Chris Van Allsburg**
The Relatives Came by Cynthia Rylant and **Stephen Gammell**
King Bidgood's in the Bathtub by Audrey Wood and **Don Wood**

1987 ***Hey, Al!*** by Arthur Yorinks and **Richard Egielski**
The Village of Round and Square Houses by **Ann Grifalconi**
Alphabatics by **Suse MacDonald**
Rumpelstiltskin (Grimm Brothers) by **Paul Zelinsky**

1988 ***Owl Moon*** by Jane Yolen and **John Schoenherr**
Mufaro's Beautiful Daughters by **John Steptoe**

1989 ***Song and Dance Man*** by Karen Ackerman and **Stephen Gammell**
Free Fall by **David Wiesner**
Goldilocks and the Three Bears by **James Marshall**
Mirandy and Brother Wind by Patricia McKissack and **Jerry Pinkney**
The Boy and the Three-Year Nap by Diane Snyder and **Allen Say**

1990 ***Lon Po Po: A Red-Riding Hood Story from China*** by **Ed Young**
Hershel and the Hanukkah Goblins by Eric Kimmel and **Trina Schart Hyman**
The Talking Eggs by Robert San Souci and **Jerry Pinkney**
Bill Peet: An Autobiography by **Bill Peet**
Color Zoo by **Lois Ehlert**

1991 ***Black and White*** by **David Macaulay**
Puss 'n Boots (Charles Perrault) by **Fred Marcellino**
"More, More, More," Said the Baby by **Vera Williams**

1992 ***Tuesday*** by **David Wiesner**
Tar Beach by **Faith Ringgold**

1993 ***Mirette on the High Wire*** by **Emily McCully**
Seven Blind Mice by **Ed Young**
The Stinky Cheese Man & Other Fairly Stupid Tales by Jon Scieszka and **Lane Smith**
Working Cotton by Sherley Anne Williams and **Carole Bayard**

1994 ***Grandfather's Journey*** by **Allen Say**
Peppe the Lamplighter by Elisa Bartone and **Ted Lewin**
In the Small, Small Pond by **Denise Fleming**
Owen by **Kevin Henkes**
Raven: A Trickster Tale from the Pacific Northwest by **Gerald McDermott**
Yo! Yes? By **Chris Raschka**

1995 ***Smoky Night*** by Eve Bunting and **David Diaz**
Swamp Angel by Anne Issacs and **Paul Zelinksy**
John Henry by Julius Lester and **Jerry Pinkney**
Time Flies by **Eric Rohmann**

1996 ***Officer Buckle and Gloria*** by **Peggy Rathman**
Alphabet City by **Stephen Johnson**
Zin! Zin! Zin! A Violin by Lloyd Moss and **Marjorie Priceman**

1997 ***Golem*** by **David Wisniewski**
Hush! A Thai Lullaby by Minfong Ho and **Holly Meade**
The Graphic Alphabet by Neal Porter and **David Pelletier**
The Paperboy by **Dav Pilkey**
Starry Messenger by **Peter Sis**

1998 ***Rapunzel*** (Grimm Brothers and Italian and French sources) by **Paul Zelinsky**
The Gardener by Sarah Stewart and **David Small**

There Was an Old Lady Who Swallowed a Fly by **Simms Taback**
Harlem: A Poem by Walter Dean Myers and **Christopher Myers**

1999 ***Snowflake Bentley*** by Jacqueline Briggs Martin and **Mary Azarian**
Duke Ellington. The Piano Prince and His Orchestra by Andrea Davis Pinkney and **Brian Pinkney**
No, David! by **David Shannon**
Snow by **Uri Shulevitz**
Tibet Through the Red Box by **Peter Sis**

Newbery Awards

Winning titles and authors appear in boldface; Honor Books follow.

1922 ***The Story of Mankind*** by **Hendrik Van Loon**
The Great Quest by Charles Hawes
Cedric the Forester by Bernard Marshall
The Old Tobacco Shop by William Bowen
The Golden Fleece by Padraic Colum
Windy Hill by Cornelia Meigs

1923 ***The Voyages of Doctor Dolittle*** by **Hugh Lofting**

1924 ***The Dark Frigate*** by **Charles Hawes**

1925 ***Tales from Silver Lands*** by **Charles Finger**
Nicholas by Anne Carroll Moore
Dream Coach by Anne and Dillwyn Parrish

1926 ***Shen of the Sea*** by **Arthur Chrisman**
The Voyagers by Padraic Colum

1927 ***Smokey, the Cowhorse*** by **Will James**

1928 ***Gay-Neck, The Story of a Pigeon*** by **Dhan Mukerji**
The Wonder Smith and His Sons by Ella Young
Downright Dencey by Caroline Dale Snedeker

1929 ***The Trumpeter of Krakow*** by **Eric Kelly**
The Pigtail of Ah Lee Ben Loo by John Bennett
Millions of Cats by Wanda Gäg
The Boy Who Was by Grace Hallock
Clearing Weather by Cornelia Meigs
The Runaway Papoose by Grace Moon
Tod of the Fens by Eleanor Whitney

1930 ***Hitty: Her First Hundred Years*** by **Rachel Field**
The Tangle-Coated Horse and Other Tales by Ella Young
Vaino: A Boy of New Finland by Julia Adams
Pran of Albania by Elizabeth Miller
The Jumping-Off Place by Marian McNeely
A Daughter of the Seine by Jeanette Eaton
Little Blacknose by Hildegarde Swift

1931 ***The Cat Who Went to Heaven*** by **Elizabeth Coatsworth**
Floating Island by Anne Parrish
The Dark Star of Itza by Alida Malkus
Queer Person by Ralph Hubbard
Mountains Are Free by Julia Adams
Spice and the Devil's Cave by Agnes Hewes
Meggy McIntosh by Elizabeth Gray
Garram the Hunter by Herbert Best
Ood-Le-Uk, The Wanderer by Alice Lide and Margaret Johansen

1932 ***Waterless Mountain*** **by Laura Armer**
The Fairy Circus by Dorothy Lathrop
Calico Bush by Rachel Field
Boy of the South Seas by Eunice Tietjens
Out of the Flame by Eloise Lownsbery
Jane's Island by Marjorie Hill Alee
The Truce of the Wolf and Other Tales of Old Italy by Mary Gould Davis

1933 ***Young Fu of the Upper Yangtze*** **by Elizabeth Foreman**
Swift Rivers by Cornelia Meigs
The Railroad to Freedom by Hildegarde Swift
Children of the Soil by Nora Burglon

1934 ***Invincible Louisa*** **by Cornelia Meigs**
The Forgotten Daughter by Caroline Snedeker
Swords of Steel by Elsie Singmaster
ABC Bunny by Wanda Gäg
Winged Girl of Knossos by Erick Berry
New Land by Sara Schmidt
The Apprentice of Florence by Anne Kyle
The Big Tree of Bunlahy by Padraic Colum
Glory of the Seas by Agnes Hewes

1935 ***Dobry*** **by Monica Shannon**
The Pageant of Chinese History by Elizabeth Seeger
Davy Crockett by Constance Rourke
A Day on Skates by Hilda Van Stockum

1936 ***Caddie Woodlawn*** **by Carol Ryrie Brink**
Honk the Moose by Phil Strong
The Good Master by Kate Seredy
Young Walter Scott by Elizabeth Janet Gray
All Sail Set by Armstrong Sperry

1937 ***Roller Skates*** **by Ruth Sawyer**
Phoebe Fairchild by Lois Lenski
Whistler's Van by Idwal Jones
The Golden Basket by Ludwig Bemelmans
Winterbound by Margery Bianco
Audubon by Constance Rourke
The Codfish Musket by Agnes Hewes

1938 ***The White Stag*** **by Kate Seredy**
Bright Island by Mabel Robinson
Pecos Bill by James Bowman
On the Banks of Plum Creek by Laura Ingalls Wilder

1939 ***Thimble Summer*** **by Elizabeth Enright**
Leader by Destiny: George Washington by Jeanette Eaton
Penn by Elizabeth Janet Gray
Nino by Valenti Angelo
"Hello, the Boat!" by Phyllis Crawford
Mr. Popper's Penguins by Richard and Florence Atwater

1940 ***Daniel Boone by James Daugherty***
The Singing Tree by Kate Seredy
Runner of the Mountain Tops by Mabel Robinson
By the Shores of Silver Lake by Laura Ingalls Wilder
Boy with a Pack by Stephen Meader

1941 ***Call It Courage*** **by Armstrong Sperry**
Blue Willow by Doris Gates

Young Mac of Fort Vancouver by Mary Jane Carr
The Long Winter by Laura Ingalls Wilder
Nansen by Anna Gertrude Hall

1942 ***The Matchlock Gun*** by **Walter Edmunds**
Little Town on the Prairie by Laura Ingalls Wilder
George Washington's World by Genevieve Foster
Indian Captive by Lois Lenski
Down Ryton Water by Eva Gaggin

1943 ***Adam of the Road*** by **Elizabeth Janet Gray**
The Middle Moffat by Eleanor Estes
"Have You Seen Tom Thumb?" by Mabel Leigh Hunt

1944 ***Johnny Tremain*** by **Esther Forbes**
These Happy Golden Years by Laura Ingalls Wilder
Fog Magic by Julia Sauer
Rufus M. by Eleanor Estes
Mountain Born by Elizabeth Yates

1945 ***Rabbit Hill*** by **Robert Lawson**
The Hundred Dresses by Eleanor Estes
The Silver Pencil by Alice Dalgliesh
Abraham Lincoln's World by Genevieve Foster
Lone Journey: The Life of Roger Williams by Jeanette Eaton

1946 ***Strawberry Hill*** by **Lois Lenski**
Justin Morgan Had a Horse by Marguerite Henry
The Moved-Outers by Florence Crannell Means
Bhimsa, the Dancing Bear by Christine Weston
New Found World by Katherine Shippen

1947 ***Miss Hickory*** by **Carolyn Sherwin Bailey**
The Wonderful Year by Nancy Barnes
The Big Tree by Mary and Conrad Buff
The Heavenly Tenants by William Maxwell
The Avion My Uncle Flew by Cyrus Fisher
The Hidden Treasure of Glaston by Eleanore Jewett

1948 ***The Twenty-One Balloons*** by **William Pene Du Bois**
Pancakes-Paris by Claire Huchet Bishop
Li Lun, Lad of Courage by Carolyn Treffinger
The Quaint and Curious Quest of Johnny Longfoot by Catherine Besterman
The Cow-Tail Switch and Other West African Stories by Harold Courlander and George Herzog
Misty of Chincoteague by Marguerite Henry

1949 ***King of the Wind*** by **Marguerite Henry**
Seabird by Holling Clancy Holling
Daughter of the Mountains by Louise Rankin
My Father's Dragon by Ruth Gannett
Story of the Negro by Arna Bontemps

1950 ***The Door in the Wall*** by **Marguerite de Angeli**
Tree of Freedom by Rebecca Caudill
The Blue Cat of Castle Town by Catherine Coblentz
Kildee House by Rutherford Montgomery
George Washington by Genevieve Foster
Song of the Pines by Walter and Marion Havighurst

1951 ***Amos Fortune, Free Man*** by **Elizabeth Yates**
Better Known as Johnny Appleseed by Mabel Leigh

Gandhi, Fighter Without a Sword by Jeanette Eaton
Abraham Lincoln, Friend of the People by Clara Judson
The Story of Appleby Capple by Anne Parrish

1952 ***Ginger Pye*** by **Eleanor Estes**
Americans Before Columbus by Elizabeth Chesley Baity
Minn of the Mississippi by Holling Clancy Holling
The Defender by Nicholas Kalashnikoff
The Light at Tern Rock by Julia Sauer
The Apple and the Arrow by Mary and Conrad Buff

1953 ***Secret of the Andes*** by **Ann Nolan Clark**
Charlotte's Web by E. B. White
Moccasin Trail by Eloise J. McGraw
Red Sails to Capri by Ann Weil
The Bears on Hemlock Mountain by Alice Dalgliesh
Birthdays of Freedom by Genevieve Foster

1954 ***And Now, Miguel*** by **Joseph Krumgold**
All Alone by Claire Huchet Bishop
Shadrach by Meindert DeJong
Hurry Home, Candy by Meindert DeJong
Theodore Roosevelt, Fighting Patriot by Clara Judson
Magic Maize by Mary and Conrad Buff

1955 ***The Wheel on the School*** by **Meindert Dejong**
The Courage of Sarah Noble by Alice Dalgliesh
Banner in the Sky by James Ullman

1956 ***Carry On, Mr. Bowditch*** by **Jean Lee Latham**
The Golden Name Day by Jennie Lindquist
The Secret River by Marjorie Kinnan Rawlings
Men, Microscopes and Living Things by Katherine Shippen

1957 ***Miracles on Maple Hill*** by **Virginia Sorensen**
Old Yeller by Fred Gipson
The House of Sixty Fathers by Meindert DeJong
Mr. Justice Holmes by Clara Judson
The Corn Grows Ripe by Dorothy Rhoads
The Black Fox of Lorne by Marguerite de Angeli

1958 ***Rifles for Watie*** by Harold Keith
The Horsecatcher by Mari Sandoz
Gone-Away Lake by Elizabeth Enright
The Great Wheel by Robert Lawson
Tom Paine, Freedom's Apostle by Leo Gurko

1959 ***The Witch of Blackbird Pond*** by **Elizabeth George Speare**
The Family Under the Bridge by Natalie Carlson
Along Came a Dog by Meindert DeJong
Chucaro; Wild Pony of the Pampa by Francis Kalnay
The Perilous Road by William O. Steele

1960 ***Onion John*** by **Joseph Krumgold**
My Side of the Mountain by Jean Craighead George
America Is Born by Gerald Johnson
The Gammage Cup by Carol Kendall

1961 ***Island of the Blue Dolphins*** by **Scott O'Dell**
America Moves Forward by Gerald Johnson
Old Ramon by Jack Schaefer
The Cricket in Times Square by Elizabeth George Speare

1962 ***The Bronze Bow*** by **Elizabeth George Speare**
Frontier Living by Edwin Tunis
The Golden Goblet by Eloise J. McGraw
Belling the Tiger by Mary Stolz
1963 ***A Wrinkle in Time*** by **Madeleine L'Engle**
Thistle and Thyme by Sorche Nic Leodhas
Men of Athens by Olivia Coolidge
1964 ***It's Like This, Cat*** by **Emily Neville**
Rascal by Sterling North
The Loner by Esther Wier
1965 ***Shadow of a Bull*** by **Maia Wojciechowska**
Across Five Aprils by Irene Hunt
1966 ***I, Juan de Pareja*** by **Elizabeth Borton de Trevino**
The Black Caldron by Lloyd Alexander
The Animal Family by Randall Jarrell
The Noonday Friends by Mary Stolz
1967 ***Up the Road Slowly*** by **Irene Hunt**
The King's Fifth by Scott O'Dell
Zlateh the Goat and Other Stories by Isaac Bashevis Singer
The Jazz Man by Mark H. Weik
1968 ***From the Mixed-Up Files of Mrs. Basil E. Frankweiler*** by **E. L. Konigsburg**
Jennifer, Hecate, Macbeth, William McKinley, and Me, Elizabeth by E. L. Konigsburg
The Black Pearl by Scott O'Dell
The Fearsome Inn by Isaac Bashevis Singer
The Egypt Game by Zilpha Keatley Snyder
1969 ***The High King*** by **Lloyd Alexander**
To Be A Slave by Julius Lester
When Shlemiel Went to Warsaw and Other Stories by Isaac Bashevis Singer
1970 ***Sounder*** by **William Armstrong**
Our Eddie by Sulamith Ish-Kishor
The Many Ways of Seeing by Janet Gaylord Moore
Journey Outside by Mary Steele
1971 ***Summer of the Swans*** by **Betsy Byars**
Kneeknock Rise by Natalie Babbitt
Enchantress from the Stars by Sylvia Engdahl
Sing Down the Moon by Scott O'Dell
1972 ***Mrs. Frisby and the Rats of NIMH*** by **Robert O'Brien**
Incident at Hawk's Hill by Allen Eckert
The Planet of Junior Brown by Virginia Hamilton
The Tombs of Atuan by Ursala LeGuin
Annie and the Old One by Miska Miles
The Headless Cupid by Zilpha Keatley Snyder
1973 ***Julie of the Wolves*** by **Jean Craighead George**
Frog and Toad Together by Arnold Lobel
The Upstairs Room by Johanna Reiss
The Witches of Worm by Zilpha Keatley Snyder
1974 ***The Slave Dancer*** by **Paula Fox**
The Dark is Rising by Susan Cooper
1975 ***M. C. Higgins the Great*** by **Virginia Hamilton**
Figgs & Phantoms by Ellen Raskin
My Brother Sam is Dead by James Lincoln Collier and Christopher Collier

	The Perilous Guard by Elizabeth Marie Pope
	Philip Hall Likes Me, I Reckon Maybe by Bette Greene
1976	***The Grey King*** by **Susan Cooper**
	The Hundred Penny Box by Sharon Bell Mathis
	Dragonwings by Laurence Yep
1977	***Roll of Thunder, Hear My Cry*** by **Mildred Taylor**
	Abel's Island by William Steig
	A String in the Harp by Nancy Bond
1978	***Bridge to Terabithia*** by **Katherine Paterson**
	Anpao: An American Indian Odyssey by Jamake Highwater
	Ramona and Her Father by Beverly Cleary
1979	***The Westing Game*** by **Ellen Raskin**
	The Great Gilly Hopkins by Katerine Paterson
1980	***A Gathering of Days: A New England Girl's Journal, 1830–32*** by **Joan Blos**
	The Road from Home by David Kherdian
1981	***Jacob Have I Loved*** by **Katherine Paterson**
	The Fledgling by Jane Langton
	A Ring of Endless Light by Madeleine L'Engle
1982	***A Visit to William Blake's Inn*** by **Nancy Willard**
	Ramona Quimby, Age 8 by Beverly Cleary
	Upon the Head of a Goat: A Childhood in Hungary, 1939–1944 by Aranka Siegal
1983	***Dicey's Song*** by **Cynthia Voight**
	The Blue Sword by Robin McKinley
	Dr. DeSoto by William Steig
	Graven Images by Paul Fleischman
	Homesick: My Own Story by Jean Fritz
	Sweet Whispers, Brother Rush by Virginia Hamilton
1984	***Dear Mr. Henshaw*** by **Beverly Cleary**
	The Sign of the Beaver by Elizabeth George Speare
	A Solitary Blue by Cynthia Voight
	Sugaring Time by Kathryn Lasky
	The Wish Giver by Bill Brittain
1985	***The Hero and the Crown*** by **Robin McKinley**
	Like Jake and Me by Mavis Jukes
	The Moves Make the Man by Bruce Brooks
	One-Eyed Cat by Paula Fox
1986	***Sarah, Plain and Tall*** by **Patricia MacLachlan**
	Commodore Perry in the Land of Shogun by Rhonda Blumberg
	Dogsong by Gary Paulsen
1987	***The Whipping Boy*** by Sid Fleischman
	On My Honor by Marion Dane Bauer
	Volcano by Patricia Lauber
	A Fine White Dust by Cynthia Rylant
1988	***Lincoln: A Photobiography*** by **Russell Freedman**
	After the Rain by Norma Fox Mazer
	Hatchet by Gary Paulsen
1989	***Joyful Noise*** by **Paul Fleischman**
	In the Beginning: Creation Stories from Around the World by Virginia Hamilton
	Scorpions by Walter Dean Myers
1990	***Number the Stars*** by **Lois Lowry**
	Afternoon of the Elves by Janet Taylor Kisle

Shabanu, Daughter of the Wind by Suzanne Fisher Staples
The Winter Room by Gary Paulsen

1991 ***Maniac Magee*** by **Jerry Spinelli**
The True Confessions of Charlotte Doyle by Avi

1992 ***Shiloh*** by **Phyllis Naylor**
Nothing But the Truth by Avi
The Wright Brothers by Russell Freedman

1993 ***Missing May*** by **Cynthia Rylant**
The Dark Thirty: Southern Tales of the Supernatural by Patricia McKissack
Somewhere in the Darkness by Walter Dean Myers
What Hearts by Bruce Brooks

1994 ***The Giver*** by **Lois Lowry**
Crazy Lady by Jane Leslie Conly
Dragon's Gate by Laurence Yep
Eleanor Roosevelt by Russell Freedman

1995 ***Walk Two Moons*** by **Sharon Creech**
Catherine, Called Birdy by Karen Cushman
The Ear, the Eye and the Arm by Nancy Farmer

1996 ***The Midwife's Apprentice*** by **Karen Cushman**
What Jamie Saw by Carolyn Coman
The Watsons Go to Birmingham—1963 by Christopher Paul Curtis
Yolanda's Genius by Carol Fenner
The Great Fire by Jim Murphy

1997 ***The View from Saturday*** by **E. L. Konigsburg**
A Girl Named Disaster by Nancy Farmer
Moorchild by Eloise McGraw
The Thief by Megan Whalen Turner
Belle Prater's Boy by Ruth White

1998 ***Out of the Dust*** by **Karen Hesse**
Lily's Crossing by Patricia Reilly Giff
Ella Enchanted by Gail Carson Levine
Wringer by Jerry Spinelli

1999 ***Holes*** by Louis Sachar
A *Long Way from Chicago* by Richard Peck

Coretta Scott King Award

This award is given annually since 1970 (to writers) and 1974 (to illustrators) to the outstanding African-American writer and illustrator producing books for children published during the preceding year. Award-winning illustrators are listed directly beneath the author awards for each year beginning in 1974. Examine Henrietta Smith's *The Coretta Scott King Awards Book* (ALA, 1994), which contains photographs of award-winning authors and illustrators and artwork and quoted passages from many of these books. Then read some of the books themselves to gain a better understanding of African-American children's literature.

1970 *Martin Luther King, Jr: Man of Peace* by Lillie Patterson
1971 *Black Troubador: Langston Hughes* by Charlemae Rollins
1972 *Seventeen Black Artists* by Elton Fax
1973 *I Never Had It Made* by Jackie Robinson (as told to Alfred Duckett)
1974 *Ray Charles* by Sharon Bell Mathis
Ray Charles, illustrated by George Ford

1975 *The Legend of Africana* by Dorothy Robinson
The Legend of Africana, illustrated by Herbert Temple
1976 *Duey's Tale* by Pearl Bailey
1977 *The Story of Stevie Wonder* by James Haskins
1978 *Africa Dream* by Eloise Greenfield
Africa Dream, illustrated by Carole Bayard
1979 *Escape to Freedom* by Ossie Davis
Something on My Mind (by Nikki Grimes), illustrated by Tom Feelings
1980 *The Young Landlords* by Walter Dean Myers
Cornrows by Camille Yarbrough, illustrated by Carole Bayard
1981 *This Life* by Sidney Poitier
Beat the Story-Drum, Pum-Pum by Ashley Bryan
1982 *Let the Circle Be Unbroken* by Mildred Taylor
Mother Crocodile by Rosa Guy, illustrated by John Steptoe
1983 *Sweet Whispers, Brother Rush* by Virginia Hamilton
Black Child by Peter Mugabane
1984 *Everett Anderson's Good-Bye* by Lucille Clifton
My Mama Needs Me by Mildred Pitts Walter, illustrated by Pat Cummings
1985 *Motown and Didi* by Walter Dean Myers
1986 *The People Could Fly* by Virginia Hamilton
Patchwork Quilt by Valerie Flournoy, illustrated by Jerry Pinkney
1987 *Justin and the Best Biscuits in the World* by Mildred Pitts Walter
Half Moon and One Whole Star by Crescent Dragonwagon, illustrated by Jerry Pinkney
1988 *The Friendship* by Mildred Taylor
Mufaro's Beautiful Daughters by Jerry Pinkney
1989 *Fallen Angels* by Walter Dean Myers
Mirandy and Brother Wind by Patricia McKissack, illustrated by Jerry Pinkney
1990 *A Long Hard Journey* by Patricia and Fredrick McKissack
Nathaniel Talking by Eloise Greenfield, illustrated by Jan Spivey Gilchrist
1991 *The Road to Memphis* by Mildred Taylor
Aida by Leontyne Price, illustrated by Leo and Diane Dillon
1992 *Now Is Your Time!* by Walter Dean Myers
Tar Beach by Faith Ringgold
1993 *The Dark-Thirty: Southern Tales of the Supernatural* by Patricia McKissack
Origins of Life on Earth by David Anderson, illustrated by Kathleen Atkins Smith
1994 *Toning the Sweep* by Angela Johnson
Soul Looks Back in Wonder by Tom Feelings
1995 *Christmas in the Big House* by Patricia and Frederick McKissack
The Creation by James Weldon Johnson, illustrated by James Ransome
1996 *Her Stories* by Virginia Hamilton
The Middle Passage by Tom Feelings
1997 *Slam!* By Walter Dean Myers
Minty: A Story of Young Harriet Tubman by Alan Schroeder, illustrated by Jerry Pinkney
1998 *Forged by Fire* by Sharon Draper
In Daddy's Arms I Am Tall by John Steptoe
1999 *Heaven* by Angela Johnson
I see the rhythm by Toyomi Igus, illustrated by Michele Wood

Pura Belpre Award

Administered by the Association for Library Service to Children and the National Association to Promote Library Services to the Spanish-Speaking, this award is given every other year to Latino writers and illustrators whose books, published in the preceding year, celebrate the cultural experiences of children of Spanish-speaking descent. This award was established in 1996. Begin reading books in this category to learn more about the many varieties of books for children of Spanish descent.

1996	Author Award:	An Island Like You: Stories of the Barrio by Judith Ortiz Coffer
	Honor Awards:	*Baseball in April and Other Stories* by Gary Soto
		The Bossy Gallito/El Gallo de Bodas; A Traditional Cuban Folktale by Lucia Gonzalez; illustrated by Lulu Delacre
	Illustrator Award:	*Chatto's Kitchen* by Gary Soto; illustrated by Susan Guevara
	Honor Awards:	*The Bossy Gallito,* illustrated by Lulu Delacre
		Family Pictures/Cuadro de Familia, illustrated by Carmen Lomas Garza
		Pablo Remembers: The Fiesta of the Day of the Dead, photographs and text by George Ancona *(Pablo Requerda: La Fiesta de el Dia de los Muertos)*
1997	Author Award:	*Parrot in the Oven; Mi Vida; A Novel* by Victor Martinez
	Honor Awards:	*Spirits of the High Mesa* by Floyd Martinez
		Laughing Tomatoes and Other Spring Poems by Francisco Alarcon, illustrated by Maya Christina Gonzalez
	Illustrator Award:	*Snapshots of the Wedding* by Gary Soto, illustrated by Stephanie Garcia
	Honor Awards:	*The Golden Flower* by Nina Jaffe, illustrated by Enrique Sanchez
		My Family by Carmen Lomas Garza
		Gathering the Sun: An Alphabet in Spanish and English by Alma Flor Ada, illustrated by Simon Silva

Laura Ingalls Wilder Award

Established in 1954, this award goes to an author or illustrator whose books, published in the United States, have made a lasting contribution to the field of children's literature. Before 1983, the award was given by the Association of Library Service to Children (ALSC) every five years; since that time, it has been awarded every three years. Read works by these authors and try to decide what influenced the jurists' choices. Was it the number of major awards an author had won? Children's interest in the author's books? The author's treatment of American history or culture? Humor? Artistic talent? Storytelling talent?

1954	Laura Ingalls Wilder
1960	Clara Ingram Judson
1965	Ruth Sawyer
1970	E. B. White
1975	Beverly Cleary
1980	Dr. Seuss
1983	Maurice Sendak
1986	Jean Fritz
1989	Elizabeth George Speare
1992	Marcia Brown

1995 Virginia Hamilton
1998 Russell Freedman

Andrew Carnegie Medal for Excellence in Children's Video

Established in 1991, this award, given by the Notable Films and Videos Committee of the Association for Library Service to Children, honors outstanding video productions released during the preceding year in the United States by an American producer or company. The video must respect children's intelligence, imagination, and interests. Adapted works must maintain the spirit of the original and use the special techniques of the film medium: visuals, voices, music, language, and sound effects. Read *The Antic Art* (Highsmith Press, 1993; edited by Lucy Rollin), a collection of essays about films and videos for children, to learn more about how these films and videos intersect with children's literature, as well as what film and video makers say about their creative processes and products. Then view as many of these winners as you can.

1991 *Ralph S. Mouse* by George McQuilkin and John Matthews, based on the book by Beverly Cleary
1992 *Harry Comes Home* by Peter Matularich
1993 *The Pool Party* by John Kelly and Gary Soto
1994 *Eric Carle: Picture Writer* by Rawn Fulton
1995 *Whitewash* by Michael Sporn
1996 *Owen* by Paul Gagne, based on the book by Kevin Henkes
1997 *Notes Alive! On the Day You Were Born* by Tacy Mangan, based on the book by Debra Frasier
1998 *Willa: An American Snow White* by Tom Davenport, based on the Grimm Brothers story
1999 *The First Christmas* by Frank Moynihan

CANADIAN LIBRARY ASSOCIATION

CLA Book of the Year

Established in 1947 by the Canadian Library Association (200 Elgin Street, Suite 602, Ottawa, Ontario, Canada K2P 1L5), this medal honors the best children's book published in Canada during the preceding year by a Canadian citizen or resident. In 1949, 1951, 1953–55, and 1962, no award was given. In 1966, two books were awarded. Choose one of the authors from the following list who has won several times (Doyle, Harris, Houston, Lunn, Lee, or Pearson) and read more books by this author. Try to determine what Canadians jurists value about this author, what makes the books popular with child—and adult—readers, and what particular historical and cultural features of Canada the books illustrate.

1947 *Starbuck Valley Winter* by Roderick Haig-Brown
1948 *Kristli's Trees* by Mabel Dunham
1950 *Franklin of the Arctic* by Richard Lambert
1952 *The Sun Horse* by Catherine Anthony Clark
1956 *Train for Tiger Lily* by Louise Riley
1957 *Glooscap's Country and Other Indian Tales* by Cyrus MacMillan
1958 *Lost in the Barrens* by Farley Mowat
1959 *The Dangerous Cove* by John Hayes

1960 *The Golden Phoenix and Other Fairy Tales from Quebec* by Maruis Barbeau and Michael Hornyansky
1961 *The St. Lawrence* by William Toye
1963 *The Incredible Journey* by Sheila Burnford
1964 *The Whale People* by Roderick Haig-Brown
1965 *Tales of Nanabozho* by Dorothy Reid
1966 *The Double Knights: More Tales from Round the World* by James McNeill
Tikta'liktak: An Eskimo Legend by James Houston
1967 *Raven's Cry* by Christie Harris
1968 *The White Archer: An Eskimo Legend* by James Houston
1969 *And Tomorrow the Stars* by Kay Hill
1970 *Sally Go Round the Sun* by Edith Fowke
1971 *Cartier Discovers the St. Lawrence* by William Toye
1972 *Mary of Mile 18* by Ann Blades
1973 *The Marrow of the World* by Ruth Nichols
1974 *The Miraculous Hind* by Elizabeth Cleaver
1975 *Alligator Pie* by Dennis Lee
1976 *Jacob Two-Two Meets the Hooded Fang* by Mordecai Richler
1977 *Mouse Woman and the Vanished Princesses* by Christie Harris
1978 *Garbage Delight* by Dennis Lee
1979 *Hold Fast* by Kevin Major
1980 *River Runners* by James Huston
1981 *The Violin-Maker's Gift* by Donn Kushner
1982 *The Root Cellar* by Janet Lunn
1983 *Up to Low* by Brian Doyle
1984 *Sweetgrass* by Jan Hudson
1985 *Mama's Going to Buy You a Mockingbird* by Jean Little
1986 *Julie* by Cora Taylor
1987 *Shadow in Hawthorn Bay* by Janet Lunn
1988 *A Handful of Time* by Kit Pearson
1989 *Easy Avenue* by Brian Doyle
1990 *The Sky is Falling* by Kit Pearson
1991 *Redwork* by Michael Bedard
1992 *Eating Between the Lines* by Kevin Major
1993 *Ticket to Curlew* by Celia Barker Lottridge
1994 *Some of the Kinder Planets* by Tim Synne-Jones
1995 *Summer of the Mad Monk* by Cora Taylor
1996 *The Tiny Kite of Eddie Wing* by Maxine Trottier
1997 *Uncle Ronald* by Brian Doyle

BRITISH LIBRARY ASSOCIATION

Kate Greenaway and Carnegie Awards

Established in 1955 (Greenaway) and 1937 (Carnegie) by the Youth Libraries Group of the British Library Association (Information Services; The Library Association; 7 Ridgmount Street; London 7Ae WC1E); these awards are given annually for the best books published in the United Kingdom during the preceding year. The Kate Greenaway Medal, named after the famous nineteenth-century illustrator, is presented for the most distinguished illustrations in books for children. The Carnegie, named for the Scottish-born benefactor who created many public libraries in the United States, is presented to an outstanding book for children. The nominees and winners are not required to be English or Scottish writers; the books are eligible if they are published in the United Kingdom prior to export—and written in English. A shortlist of books is published each year on May 1. The winners are announced later that month or in early June and presented during the summer. See how many of these winners you can find in your library; some may have "crossed over" more—or less—easily into the American culture than others (because of British words, cultural and historical references, English places). Read to discover which ones appeal most to you—and why.

Kate Greenaway Award

1956 No award given.
1957 *Tim All Alone* by Edward Ardizzone
1958 *Mrs. Easter and the Storks* by V. H. Drummond
1959 No award given.
1960 *Kashtanka* (Anton Chekov) by William Stobbs
A Bundle of Ballads by Ruth Manning-Sanders
1961 *Old Winkle and the Seagulls* by Elizabeth Rose, illustrated by Gerald Rose
1962 *Mrs. Cockle's Cat* by Philippa Pearce, illustrated by Anthony Maitland
1963 *Brian Wildsmith's ABC* by Brian Wildsmith
1964 *Borka: The Adventures of a Goose With No Feathers* by John Burningham
1965 *Shakespeare's Theatre* by C. Walter Hodges
1966 *Three Poor Tailors* by Victor Ambrus
1967 *Mother Goose Treasury* by Raymond Briggs
1968 *Charley, Charlotte and the Golden Canary* by Charles Keeping
1969 *A Dictionary of Chivalry* by Grant Uden, illustrated by Pauline Baynes
1970 *The Quangle-Wangle's Hat* by Edward Lear, illustrated by Helen Oxenbury
1971 *Mr. Gumpy's Outing* by John Burningham
1972 *The Kingdom Under the Sea* by Jan Pienkowski
1973 *The Woodcutter's Duck* by Krystyna Turska
1974 *Father Christmas* by Raymond Briggs
1975 *The Wind Blew* by Pat Hutchins
1976 *Horses in Battle* and *Mishka* by Victor Ambrus
1977 *The Post Office Cat* by Gail Haley
1978 *Dogger* by Shirley Hughes
1979 *Each Peach Pear Plum* by Allan Ahlberg, illustrated by Janet Ahlberg
1980 *The Haunted House* by Jan Pienkowski
1981 *Mr. Magnolila* by Quentin Blake
1982 *The Highwayman* by Alfred Noyes, illustrated by Charles Keeping
1983 *Long Neck and Thunder Foot* by Helen Piers, illustrated by Michael Foreman
Sleeping Beauty and Other Favorite Fairy Tales, complied by Angela Carter, illustrated by Michael Foreman
1984 *Gorilla* by Anthony Browne
1985 *Hiawatha's Childhood* by Errol LeCain
1986 *Sir Gawain and the Loathly Lady* by Selina Hastings, illustrated by Juan Wijngaard
1987 *Snow White in New York* by Fiona French
1988 *Crafty Chameleon* by Mwenye Hadithi, illustrated by Adrienne Kennaway
1989 *Can't You Sleep, Little Bear?* by Martin Waddell, illustrated by Barbara Firth
1990 *War Boy; A Country Childhood* by Michael Foreman
1991 *The Whales' Song* by Dyan Sheldon, illustrated by Gary Blythe
1992 *The Jolly Christmas Postman,* by Allan Ahlberg, illustrated by Janet Ahlberg
1993 *Zoo* by Anthony Browne
1994 *Black Ships Before Troy* by Rosemary Sutcliff, illustrated by Alan Lee
1995 *The Way Home* by Libby Hathorn, illustrated by Gregory Rogers

1996 *The Christmas Miracle of Jonathan Toomey* by Susan Wojciechowski, illustrated by P. J. Lynch
1997 *The Baby Who Wouldn't Go To Bed* by Helen Cooper
1998 *When Jessie Came Across the Sea* by P. J. Lynch by Amy Hest, illustrated by P. J. Lynch
Ginger by Charlotte Voake

Carnegie Award

1937 *Pigeon Post* by Arthur Ransome
1938 *The Family from One End Street* by Eve Garnett
1939 *The Circus Is Coming* by Noel Streatfield
1940 *Radium Woman* by Eleanor Doorly
1941 *Visitors From London* by Kitty Barne
1942 *We Couldn't Leave Dinah* by Mary Threadgold
1943 *The Little Grey Men* by Denys Watkins-Pitchford
1944 No award given.
1945 *The Wind on the Moon* by Eric Linklater
1946 No award given.
1947 *The Little White Horse* by Elizabeth Goudge
1948 *Collected Stories for Children* by Walter de la Mare
1949 *Sea Change* by Richard Armstrong
1950 *The Story of Your Home* by Agnes Allen
1951 *The Lark on the Wing* by Elfrida Vipont Foulds
1952 *Nicholas and the Wool-Pack* by Cynthia Harnett
1953 *The Borrowers* by Mary Norton
1954 *A Valley Grows Up* by Edward Osmond
1955 *Knight Crusader* by Ronald Welch
1956 *The Little Bookroom* by Eleanor Farjeon
1957 *The Last Battle* by C. S. Lewis
1958 *A Grass Rope* by William Mayne
1959 *Tom's Midnight Garden* by Philippa Pearce
1960 *The Lantern Bearers* by Rosemary Sutcliff
1961 *The Making of Man* by I. W. Cornwall
1962 *A Stranger at Green Knowe* by Lucy Boston
1963 *The Twelve and the Genii* by Pauline Clarke (U.S. title: *The Return of the Twelve).*
1964 *Time of Trial* by Hester Burton
1965 *Nordy Bank* by Sheena Porter
1966 *The Grange at High Force* by Philip Turner
1967 No award given.
1968 *The Owl Service* by Alan Garner
1969 *The Moon in the Cloud* by Rosemary Harris
1970 *The Edge of the Cloud* by K. M. Peyton
1971 *The God Beneath the Sea* by Leon Garfield and Edward Blishen
1972 *Josh* by Ivan Southall
1973 *Watership Down* by Richard Adams
1974 *The Ghost of Thomas Kempe* by Penelope Lively
1975 *The Stronghold* by Mollie Hunter
1976 *The Machine-Gunners* by Robert Westall
1977 *Thunder and Lightnings* by Jan Mark
1978 *The Turbulent Term of Tyke Tyler* by Gene Kemp

1979 *The Exeter Blitz* by David Rees
1980 *Tulku* by Peter Dickinson
1981 *City of Gold* by Peter Dickinson
1982 *The Scarecrows* by Robert Westall
1983 *The Haunting* by Margaret Mahy
1984 *Handles* by Jan Mark
1985 *The Changeover* by Margaret Mahy
1986 *Storm* by Kevin Crossley-Holland
1987 *Granny Was A Buffer Girl* by Berlie Doherty
1988 *The Ghost Dream* by Susan Price
1989 *Pack of Lies* by Geraldine McCaughrean
1990 *My War With Goggle Eyes* by Anne Fine
1991 *Wolf* by Gillian Cross
1992 *Dear Nobody* by Berlie Doherty
1993 *Flour Babies* by Anne Fine
1994 *Stone Cold* by Robert Swindells
1995 *Whispers in the Graveyard* by Theresa Breslin
1996 *Northern Lights* by Philip Pullman (U.S. title: *The Golden Compass*)
1997 *Junk* by Melvin Burgess
1998 *River Boy* by Tim Bowler

INTERNATIONAL BOARD OF BOOKS FOR YOUNG PEOPLE

Hans Christian Andersen Award

Established in 1956, this international award is given by the IBBY (USBBY, P. O. 8139, Newark, DE 19714) every two years to an author (and, since 1966, to an illustrator) whose entire body of work is celebrated for distinguished contribution to the world of children's literature. Explore in your library to see how many books by foreign writers and artists listed here have found a home in America. If you cannot find a particular author's work, write to the USBBY address above and request any materials available that would introduce this person's words or pictures to you. Examine the American authors' works to see what might have appealed to jurists from around the world. (What makes an *international* children's author?)

1956 Eleanor Farjeon (Great Britain)
1958 Astrid Lindgren (Sweden)
1960 Erick Kastner (West Germany)
1962 Meindert DeJong (USA)
1964 Rene Guillot (France)
1966 Tove Jansson (Finland; author)
Alois Carigiet (Switzerland; illustrator)
1968 James Kruss (West Germany; author)
Jose Maria Sanchez-Silva (Spain; author)
Jiri Trnka (Czechoslovakia; illustrator)
1970 Gianni Rodari (Italy; author)
Maurice Sendak (USA; illustrator)
1972 Scott O'Dell (USA, author)
Ib Spang Olsen (Denmark, illustrator)
1974 Maria Gripe (Sweden, author)
Farshid Mesghali (Iran, illustrator)

1976 Cecil Bodker (Denmark, author)
Tatjana Mawrina (Russia, illustrator)
1978 Paula Fox (USA, author)
Svend Otto (Denmark, illustrator)
1980 Bohumil Riha (Czechoslovakia, author)
Suekichi Akaba (Japan, illustrator)
1982 Lygia Bojunga Nunes (Brazil, author)
Zbigniew Rychlicki (Poland, illustrator)
1984 Christine Mostlinger (Austria, author)
Mitsumasa Anno (Japan, illustrator)
1986 Patricia Wrightson (Australia, author)
Robert Ingpen (Australia, illustrator)
1988 Annie Schmidt (Netherlands, author)
Dusan Kallay (Czechoslovakia, illustrator)
1990 Tormod Haugen (Norway, author)
Lisbeth Zwerger (Austria, illustrator)
1992 Virginia Hamilton (USA, author)
Kveta Pacovska (Czechoslovakia, illustrator)
1994 Michio Mado (Japan, author)
Jorg Muller (Switzerland, illustrator)
1996 Uri Orlev (Israel, author)
Klaus Ensikat (Germany, illustrator)
1998 Katherine Paterson (USA, author)
Tomi Ungerer (USA, illustrator)

CHILDREN'S LITERATURE ASSOCIATION

Phoenix Award

Established in 1985, this award given by the Children's Literature Association (P. O. 138, Battle Creek, MI 49016) is given to books published in English twenty years earlier that received no major award at that time. Honor books, when they were awarded, are listed after the winners' names. Examine as many of these older works as you can to see what critics today value in them (what they feel was overlooked in the past and deserves a second look now).

1985 ***The Mark of the Horse Lord*** by Rosemary Sutcliff
1986 ***Queeny Peavy*** by Robert Burch
1987 ***Smith*** by Leon Garfield
1988 ***The River and His Horse*** by Erik Christian Haugaard
1989 ***The Night-Watchmen*** by Helen Cresswell
Brother, Can You Spare A Dime? by Milton Meltzer
Pistol by Adrienne Richard
1990 ***Enchantress from the Stars*** by Sylvia Louise Engdahl
Ravensgill by William Mayne
Sing Down the Moon by Scott O'Dell
1991 ***A Long Way From Verona*** by Jane Gardam
A Game of Dark by William Mayne
The Tombs of Atuan by Ursula Leguin
1992 ***A Sound of Chariots*** by Mollie Hunter
1993 ***Carrie's War*** by Nina Bawden
A Proud Taste for Scarlet and Miniver by E. L. Konigsburg
1994 ***Of Nightingales that Weep*** by Katherine Paterson

	My Brother Sam is Dead by James Lincoln Collier and Christopher Collier
	Listen for the Fig Tree by Sharon Bell Mathis
1995	***Dragonwings*** by Laurence Yep
	Tuck Everlasting by Natalie Babbitt
1996	***The Stone Book*** by Alan Garner
	Abel's Island by William Steig
1997	***I Am the Cheese*** by Robert Cormier
1998	***A Chance Child*** by Jill Paton Walsh
	Beauty by Robin McKinley
	The Devil in Vienna by Doris Orgel
1999	***Throwing Shadows*** by E. L. Konigsburg

Appendix 3
Resources in Children's Literature

ORGANIZATIONS

Professional organizations related to children's literature and literacy provide information for teachers about current educational goals, teaching strategies, and literary materials. They also provide ways for educators to meet and share ideas during annual conferences and conventions. Dues vary between $20 and $100, but often student memberships (or new members) receive bargain rates. Goals and emphases of the organization also vary. Some focus on the needs of language arts or reading teachers; others on the needs of librarians, booksellers, storytellers, reviewers, researchers, or some combination of these. Write to the organizations in the list that follows, or check their internet web sites, and request information about the goals, services, and publications of these groups to see which one might be most applicable to your professional needs.

American Library Association. Association for Library Service to Children (ALSC). 50 East Huron Street, Chicago, IL 60611. Founded in 1900, the children's wing of this organization is best known for its children's book awards services and ceremonies: Caldecott, Newbery, Laura Ingalls Wilder, and Coretta Scott King. It publishes the *Journal of Youth Services in Libraries* and holds conventions in January and July. *http://www.ala.org*

Children's Book Council. 568 Broadway, New York, NY 10012. Founded in 1945 by a group of children's trade book publishers, this organization is best known for sponsoring annual Children's Book Week activities in mid-November. It also publishes a newsletter, *CBC Features,* and produces a catalog of educational materials—posters, bookmarks, streamers, booklets—for teachers and librarians. *http://www.cbcbooks.org*

Children's Literature Association. P. O. Box 138, Battle Creek, MI 49016. Since 1973, this organization has been fostering research in children's literature. It holds a yearly conference in the late spring and publishes *Children's Literature Association Quarterly* and *Children's Literature.* The summer issue of the *Quarterly* contains a bibliography of scholarly, critical, biographical, historical, and educational books and articles in children's literature.

International Board of Books for Young People. United States Board of Books for Young People. P. O. Box 8139, Newark, DE 19714. Founded in 1984, the American branch of the parent organization teams with offices of the International Reading Association to foster the dissemination of information about children's books worldwide. This organization has sixty-four national sections; it encourages developing nations to build children's book collections and all nations to establish national and international libraries of children's literature. It publishes a journal, *Bookbird,* and administers the Hans Christian Andersen awards every other year at a conference held in various countries around the globe. *http://www.usbby.org/member.htm*

International Reading Association. 800 Barksdale Road, P. O. Box 8139, Newark, DE 19714. Founded in 1956, this organization is best known for its interest in promoting literacy worldwide. It publishes *The Reading Teacher* and holds regional, national, and international conventions. Its primary audience is educators in the area of literacy. *http://www.reading.org/publications/journals/journals.htm*

Multicultural Publishing and Education Council. 2280 Grass Valley Highway, #181; Auburn, CA 95603. Founded in 1994, this organization promotes the publishing of books and media by and about people of color. Its primary audience includes publishers, booksellers, writers, illustrators, educators, libraries, and professionals concerned with new ethnic/multicultural works. The MPEC Newsletter comes with membership (resource materials, marketing tips for writers/illustrators, book and video reviews). *http://www.quiknet.com/mpt/mpec/mpec.html* and *http://www.quicknet.com/ammg/mpec/mpec.html*

National Council of Teachers of English. 1111 W. Kenyon Road, Urbana, IL 61801. Since the 1970s, the Children's Literature Assembly of NCTE has been providing teachers and librarians with educational materials and participating in the fall and spring conventions of the parent organization. It publishes *Language Arts, English Journal,* and the *Journal of Children's Literature* and presents the NCTE Award for Excellence in Poetry for Children, established in 1977, and the Orbis Pictus Award for Outstanding Nonfiction for Children, established in 1990. *http://www.ncte.org/profdevel*

PUBLICATIONS

Book Clubs

Book Clubs allow teachers (and pupils) to purchase children's books at lower prices than bookstores offer, and they enable potential purchasers to choose from among many varieties of paperbacks and some hardcover editions of current books. Teachers can build text sets around many topics, including Caldecott and Newbery winners, and purchase class sets at discount prices. They order through catalogs that appear on a monthly basis, and their orders earn bonus points that count toward free purchases.

Carnival Book Club, Box 6035, Columbia, MO 65205
Golden Book Club, P. O. Box 475, Ramsey, NJ 07446
Puffin Book Club, Bath Road, Harmondsworth, Middlesex, England UB7 0DA
Scholastic Book Clubs, P. O. Box 7503; Jefferson City, MO 65102
Troll Book Club, Troll Associates, 100 Corporate Drive, Mahwah, NJ 07430
The Trumpet Club, P. O. Box 6003, Columbia, MO 65205

Book Publishers

Children's books are published by various "imprints" within larger parent companies—and by the larger companies themselves. One of the largest is Simon & Schuster, which owns many imprints, including Alladin, Atheneum, Bradbury Press, Four Winds Press, Green Tiger, Margaret McElderry Books, Macmillan Reference Books, and Charles Scribner's Sons.

Other large companies are HarperCollins and its imprints of Thomas Y. Crowell, Harper Trophy, and Lippincott Junior Books, and Penguin with imprints of Dutton Children's Books, Puffin Books, Viking, and Frederick Warne.

An important Grolier imprint is Orchard Books (95 Madison Avenue, New York, NY 10016), which has received many awards in the last decade. Philomel is also an important imprint of G. P. Putnam's Sons. Candlewick Press (2067 Massachusetts Ave., Cambridge, MA 02140) is a relatively new company that is producing high-quality picture books (output: 120 per year). Greenwillow Books (1350 Avenue of the Americas, New York, NY 10019), which publishes 50 picture books yearly, is headed by the long-established editor Susan Hirschman.

Several smaller independent presses focus on multicultural books:
African-American: Just Us Books, 356 Glenwood Avenue, Orange, NJ 07050
Black Butterfly Children's Books, Writers and Readers Publishing, 625 Broadway, New York, NY 10012
Asian-American: China Books, 2929 24th Street, San Francisco, CA 94110
Hispanic-American: Arte Publico, University of Houston, 4800 Calhoun, Houston, TX 77204
Hispanic-American and Native American: Children's Book Press, 246 First Street, #101, San Francisco, CA 94105

The companies publishing the largest number of children's books, based on net sales during the mid-1990s, were:
Western Publishing, 850 Third Ave., New York, NY 10022
Random House, 201 E. 50th Street, New York, NY 10022
Simon & Schuster Books for Young Readers, 1230 Avenue of the Americas, New York, NY 10020
HarperCollins, 10 East 53rd Street, New York, NY 10022
Puffin Books, 375 Hudson Street, New York, NY 10014
Bantam Doubleday Dell, 1540 Broadway, New York, NY 10036
G. P. Putnam's Sons/Penguin Putnam, 200 Madison Ave., New York, NY 10016
Scholastic, 555 Broadway, New York, NY 10012
William Morrow, 1350 Avenue of the Americas, New York, NY 10019
Little, Brown, 34 Beacon Street, Boston, MA 021087
Viking Children's Books, 375 Huron Street, New York, NY 10014

Write for a current sales catalog; you will discover more about new books and authors and the kinds of books that different companies accept for publication.

Journals

Many journals focusing on children's literature are now available to those working in this field. Check library shelves to see which ones fit your own particular needs, or write directly to the following addresses for information about a particular journal or to request a sample copy.

The following journals often publish *general articles of interest* about

a. Children's books (historical features, publishing trends, controversial issues, censorship, international publishing)
b. Children's book writers and illustrators
c. The literature and literacy process for child readers
d. The use of children's books in the classroom
e. Book reviews

Subscriptions range in price from $20 to $40.

Bookbird, The International Board of Books for Young People, P. O. Box 807, Highland Park, IL 60035 (International emphasis; a, b, e)

Book Links, 434 W. Downer, Aurora, IL 60506 (Emphasis on teaching guides for children's books; a, b, d, e)

Children's Literature in Education, Human Sciences Press, 233 Spring Street, New York, NY 10013 (Equal emphasis on British and North American books/authors; a, b, c, d)

English Journal, National Council of Teachers of English, 1111 W. Kenyon Road, Urbana, IL 61801 (Secondary emphasis, but often publishes materials on middle school readers; b, c, d)

The Five Owls, Hamline University, St. Paul, MN 55104 (a, b, e)

Horn Book Magazine, 11 Beacon Street, Boston, MA 02108 (a, b, e)

Journal of Children's Literature, Children's Literature Assembly, National Council of Teachers of English, 1111 W. Kenyon Road, Urbana, ILL 61801 (a, b, c, d, e)

Journal of Youth Services in Libraries, American Library Association, 50 E. Huron Street, Chicago, IL 60611 (a, b)

Language Arts, National Council of Teachers of English, 1111 W. Kenyon Road, Urbana, IL 61801 (b, c, d, e)

New Advocate, Christopher-Gordon Publishers, 480 Washington Street, Norwood, MA 02062 (a, b, c, d, e)

Reading Teacher, International Reading Association, 800 Barksdale Road, Box 8139, Newark, DE 19714 (c, d)

School Library Journal, P. O. Box 57559, Boulder, CO 80322 (a, b, e)

Signal, The Thimble Press, Lockwood, Station Road; Woodchester, Stroud; Glos., England, UK GL5 5EQ (a, b, c)

Teaching and Learning Literature, Essmont Publishing, P. O. Box 180; Brandon, VT 05733 (a, d)

The following journals are known for *scholarly research* in the area of children's literature:

Canadian Children's Literature, P. O. Box 335, Guelph, Ontario, Canada NIG 2W1 (Canadian emphasis)

Children's Literature, Yale University Press, P. O. Box 209040, New Haven, CT 06520 (annual publication; international emphasis)

Children's Literature Association Quarterly, Children's Literature Association, P. O. Box 138, Battle Creek, MI 49016 (Summer issue contains a comprehensive bibliography of articles and books about children's literature published three to four years earlier.)

Children's Literature in Education, Human Sciences Press, 233 Spring Street, New York, NY 10013 (English and North American emphases).

Lion and the Unicorn, Johns Hopkins University Press, 2715 N. Charles Street, Baltimore, MD 21218

Marvels & Tales: Journal of Fairy-Tale Studies, Wayne State University Press, Department of German and Slavic Studies, 906 W. Warren Ave., 443 Manoogian Hall, Detroit, MI 48202

Signal, The Thimble Press, Lockwood, Station Road; Woodchester, Stroud; Glos., England, UK GL5 5EQ (British emphasis)

The following journals are known for their comprehensive *reviews* of children's books (subscription price range: $30 to $60).

Booklist, American Library Association, 50 E. Huron Street, Chicago, IL 60611

The Bulletin of the Center for Children's Books, University of Illinois Press, 51 E. Armory, Champaign, IL 61820

Horn Book Magazine, 11 Beacon Street, Boston, MA 02108

Publishers Weekly, R. R. Bowker, 245 W. 17th Street; New York, NY 10011 (Two issues during the year, spring and fall, focus on children's books in order to advertise new titles.)

School Library Journal, P. O. Box 57559, Boulder, CO 80322

Wilson Library Bulletin, The H. W. Wilson Company, 950 University Ave., Bronx, NY 10452 (Monthly column on children's books)

Library Collections

You can visit libraries across the nation (and around the world) to see special collections of children's books. The most famous in the United States is the Children's Literature Center of the **Library of Congress** (101 Independence Ave., S. E., Washington, DC 20540), with nearly 200,000 books. In Canada, the **Toronto Public Library** is important for its Osborne Collection of children's books, dating from the fourteenth century. It also encompasses the Lillian Smith Collection, to which fantasy novelist Susan Cooper has donated her manuscripts.

Other notable collections include the **Baldwin Library** of Historical Children's Books (George Smathers Libraries, University of Florida, Gainesville, FL 32611) with nearly 100,000 books; the **Center for the Study of Books in Spanish** for Children and Adolescents at California State University, established by Isabel Schon, San Marcos, CA 92096, with 50,000 books; the **Cooperative Children's Book Center** (4290 Helen White Hall, University of Wisconsin-Madison, Madison, WI 53706) with over 35,000 books; the **De Grummond Children's Literature Collection** (McCain Library, University of Southern Mississippi, Hattiesburg, MS 39406) with over 40,000 books; the **Jordan Collection** of the Boston Public Library (Boston Public Library, Copley Square, Boston, MA 02117) with over 157,000 books; the **Kerlan Collection** (109 Walter Library, 117 Pleasant St., University of Minnesota, Minneapolis, MN 55455), a large holding of original manuscripts, artwork, galleys, and color proofs for over 8,500 children's books of the past eight decades, as well as over 70,000 books; and **Morgan Library's Early Children's Books Collection** (The Pierpont Morgan Library, 28 Easts 36th Street, New York, NY 10016), with over 10,000 books.

To examine one of these large library collections, choose a collection near you and browse through the holdings. If you are visiting the Library of Congress, you should go with a special, hard-to-find book in mind; the books are placed in many different locations, rather than centrally located.

Or you might choose one of the libraries listed above for its special strength, and travel there to study a particular writer, illustrator, genre, or historical era. The Baldwin Library specializes in books published before 1800. The Schon Collection has a large accumulation of books in Spanish. The Cooperative Children's Book Center specializes in multicultural books. The De Grummond Collection has rich holdings in fables and classic picture books. The Jordan Collection specializes in international children's books, and the Kerlan Collection has accumulated many original authors' drafts (write Karen Hoyle, Curator, for a listing of these authors). The Pierpont Morgan Library has many French children's books, as well as works by Randolph Caldecott.

Media

Films and Videos

Film companies often adapt children's books for television series like PBS's Wonderworks and Reading Rainbow (GPN/Nebraska ETV Network, P. O. 80669, Lincoln, NE 68501–0669; WNED-TV, Buffalo, NY) and for general sales to libraries, schools, and individuals. Reading Rainbow offers a web site: *http://gpn.unl.edu/index.htm* and a catalog listing over eighty programs available on video for purchase. Each video features a different children's book and activities emerging from the reading event, including three to four reviews of related books.

Companies such as the National Film Board of Canada (1251 Avenue of the Americas, New York, NY 10020), SRA-McGraw Hill (155 N. Wacker Drive; Chicago, IL 60606), and Weston Woods (P. O. 2193, Norwalk, CT 06850) produce catalog listings of films, filmstrips, and tape-recorded adaptations of children's books.

Weston Woods, now associated with Scholastic Books, specializes in audiovisual adaptations of outstanding children's books (videos, filmstrips, 16mm films, audiocassettes, and the accompanying books). Their Story Hour collection contains books themed around animals, fairytales, family life, fantasy, feelings, friendship, folk tales, growth and change, humor, music, multicultural, school, and seasons and nature. Other collections include Holiday Titles, Spanish Materials, and Favorite Author Documentaries.

Book publishers also offer films and videos featuring popular children's book authors and illustrators: Philomel (Patricia Polacco), Dutton Penguin (Lloyd Alexander), and Dial Puffin (Jerry Pinkney and Rosemary Wells).

The Trumpet Club also offers tape-recorded interviews with many children's authors and films about authors such as Donald Crews, Mem Fox, and Gary Paulsen.

Tim Podell Productions (Box 244, Scarborough, NY 10510) offers author talks with Natalie Babbitt, Betsy Byars, E. L. Konigsburg, Robin McKinley, Patricia and Fred McKissack, Jerry Spinelli, Nancy Willard, and Jean Craighead George.

CD-ROM

The Horn Book Guide, Interactive is a database composed of over 29,000 brief, critical reviews of children's books. Books are rated on a scale of 1 to 6 for strengths and weaknesses and are organized by author, title, subject, grade level, genre, publishing data, and rating. Individual teachers building classroom libraries and matching books and readers can purchase the program for $35 from Heinemann, 88 Post Road West, P. O. Box 5007, Westport, CT 06881.

Newsletters

CBC Features. Semiannual publication of the Children's Book Council, 568 Broadway, New York, NY 10012. Lifetime subscription, $60. Includes articles by children's book authors/illustrators, editors, and educators on themed subjects such as picture books, multicultural books, international books, children's books in the classroom, the environment, remembered books from childhood.

English Update. Center on English Learning & Achievement (CELA), University at Albany, State University of New York, 1400 Washington Ave., Albany, NY 12222. Reports on studies that researchers are conducting in literacy; literacy often intersects with literature in these studies. Directors of the Center are Judith Langer and Arthur Applebee.

Kerlan Collection. Published three times yearly by Children's Literature Research Collections, Kerlan Library University of Minnesota, 117 Pleasant St., University of Minnesota, Minneapolis, MN 55455. Reports on recent acquisitions, book awards in the field, events at the library, exhibits, and research produced from collection holdings ($6 annual membership).

Newspapers

Many metropolitan newspapers run weekly columns in which they review recently published children's books. *The New York Times* and *The Washington Post* are perhaps the best known in the East. The *Post* also runs features on children's authors. The *Times* publishes a bimonthly Sunday column of children's book reviews and a twice yearly feature on children's literature (November and May). The November issue often includes a colorful spread on the ten Best Illustrated Books of the Year. The May issue often includes a "Children's Best Sellers" list (the top picture and story books, chapter books, series books, activity books, and poetry books, as reflected by sales for six weeks prior to publication at over three thousand general interest bookstores and reports from over two hundred children's bookstores, geographically distributed).

Many newspapers also publish a syndicated column for child readers by Betty Debnam, "The Mini Page," which often focuses on children's literature, children's authors, book awards, and holidays. Columns include topics such as "The Magic of Myth" (March 30, 1998), "Meet Rosemary Wells/Celebrate Children's Book Week" (November 17, 1997), "Meet the Author/Illustrator: Newbery Winner E. L. Konigsburg," "Meet Caldecott Winner David Wisniewski," "Coretta Scott King Winners" (April 14, 1997), "A Victorian Christmas" (December 15, 1997), and "Summer is Reading Time" (May 24, 1999).

Reference Works

Indexes

Books in Print and *Children's Books in Print.* R. R. Bowker Publishers, 245 W. 17th Street, New York, NY 10011. Author, subject, and title volumes.

Annotated Bibliographies

Adventuring with Books: A Booklist for Pre-K-Grade 6. National Council of Teachers of English, 1111 Kenyon Road, Urbana, IL 61601.

Childrens Books from Other Countries, edited by Carl M. Tomlinson. Metuchen NJ: Scare Crow Press, 1998.

Children's Catalog. H. W. Wilson Company, 950 University Avenue, Bronx, NY 10452.

Children's Writer's & Illustrator's Market 1998, edited by Alice Buening. Writer's Digest Books, 1507 Dana Avenue, Cincinnati, OH 45207.

Everyone's Guide to Children's Literature by Mark West. Fort Atkinson, WI: Highsmith Press, 1997.

The Horn Book Guide to Children's and Young Adult Books. Horn Book, 11 Beacon Street, Boston, MA 02108.

Oxford Companion to Children's Literature by Humphrey Carpenter and Mari Prichard. New York: Oxford University Press, 1984. Entries on authors, books, characters.

Biographies and Literary Criticism: Individual Authors

Black Authors and Illustrators of Children's Books, edited by Barbara Rollock. New York: Garland Publishing, 1992.

Something About the Author; Something About the Author, Autobiography Series; Children's Literature Review; and *Dictionary of Literary Biography.* Detroit: Gale Research. Many volumes published from 1971 to the present in which biographers or the authors themselves record details of the authors' lives and commentaries about their books.

Children's Books and Their Creators, edited by Anita Silvey. Boston: Houghton Mifflin, 1995. Features information about authors, inserts written by authors themselves, and entries on general topics, such as genre (fantasy, poetry), multicultural emphases (African-American books for children), and awards.

United States Authors Series, edited by Ruth K. MacDonald. Twayne Publishers, Macmillan Reference, 1633 Broadway, New York, NY 10019. Includes volumes on Arnold Adoff, Louisa May Alcott, Lloyd Alexander, Natalie Babbit, Beverly Cleary, Susan Cooper, Louise Fitzhugh, Wanda Gäg, Nikki Giovanni, Virginia Hamilton, E. L. Konigsburg, Astrid Lindgrin, Arnold Lobel, Robert McCloskey, Katherine Paterson, Ellen Raskin, Maurice Sendak, Dr. Seuss, Shel Silverstein, Elizabeth George Speare, and Laura Ingalls Wilder.

Twayne's *Young Adult Authors Series,* edited by Patty Campbell, includes volumes on Judy Blume, Madeleine L'Engle, Walter Dean Myers, and Laurence Yep, among others.

Twayne's *English Authors Series* includes volumes, edited by Lois Kuznets, on Lewis Carroll, Roald Dahl, Charles Dickens, Kenneth Grahame, Ted Hughes, Rudyard Kipling, C. S. Lewis, Penelope Lively, Hugh Lofting, Mary Norton, Beatrix Potter, Arthur Ransome, Robert Louis Stevenson, Noel Streatfield, Jonathan Swift, J. R. R. Tolkien, and P. L. Travers.

Twayne's *Masterwork Studies,* edited by Robert Lecker, include volumes on *Alice's Adventures in Wonderland* and *Through the Looking Glass, Charlotte's Web, The Chronicles of Narnia,* and *The Wind in the Willows.* (These volumes provide biographical information on Lewis Carroll, E. B. White, C. S. Lewis, and Kenneth Grahame.)

Writers for Young Adults, edited by Ted Hipple. New York: Simon & Schuster, 1997. Three-volume set focusing on writers of young adult literature and their work. Includes the work of such authors as Louisa May Alcott, Judy Blume, Eve Bunting, Betsy Byars, Paula Fox, Anne Frank, Virginia Hamilton, Kathryn Lasky, Madeleine L'Engle, C. S. Lewis, Lois Lowry, Nicholasa Mohr, Katherine Paterson, Gary Soto, Jerry Spinelli, Rosemary Sutcliff, Mildred Taylor, Joyce Carol Thomas, J. R. R. Tolkien, Laura Ingalls Wilder, Laurence Yep, and Jane Yolen.

Histories

AVERY, GILLIAN. *Behold the Child: American Children and Their Books, 1621–1922.* Baltimore, MD: Johns Hopkins, 1995. Children's books in America through the eyes of a British writer.

AVERY, GILLIAN, AND BRIGGS, JULIA, EDITORS. *Children and Their Books.* Oxford, England: Clarendon Press, 1989.

BADER, BARBARA. *American Picturebooks from Noah's Ark to the Beast Within.* New York: Macmillan, 1976.

HUNT, PETER. *An Introduction to Children's Literature.* New York: Oxford University Press, 1994. British emphasis.

HUNT, PETER, EDITOR. *Children's Literature: An Illustrated History.* New York: Oxford University Press, 1995. British emphasis.

HURLIMANN, BETTINA. *Three Centuries of Children's Books in Europe.* New York: World, 1968.

MEYER, SUSAN. *A Treasury of the Great Children's Book Illustrators.* New York: Harry Abrams, 1983.

TOWNSEND, JOHN ROWE. *Written for Children.* New York: Harper, 1992. British emphasis.

Topics in Children's Literature and Literacies: General

After Alice: Exploring Children's Literature, edited by Morag Styles, Eve Bearne, and Victor Watson. New York: Cassell, 1992.

Children and Books, 9th edition, by Zena Sutherland. Reading, MA: Addison-Wesley, 1996.

Celebrating Children's Books, edited by Betsy Hearne and Marilyn Kaye. New York: Lothrop, 1981.

Celebrating Children's Literature in Education, edited by Geoff Fox. New York: Teachers College Press, 1995

The Child and the Book: A Psychological and Literary Exploration by Nicholas Tucker. New York: Cambridge University Press; Canto edition, 1990.

The Children's Bookroom; Reading and the Use of Books, edited by Dorothy Atkinson. Stoke-on-Trent, England: Trentham Books, 1989.

Children's Literature in the 1890s and the 1990s by Kimberley Reynolds. Plymouth, England: Northcote House, 1994.

The Cool Web: The Pattern of Children's Reading, edited by Margaret Meek and others. London: Bodley Head, 1977.

Don't Tell The Grown-Ups by Alison Lurie. Boston: Little, Brown, 1990.

Great Expectations, edited by Eve Bearne. New York: Cassell, 1995.

Only Connect: Readings on Children's Literature, edited by Sheila Egoff. New York: Oxford University Press, 1996.

The Prose and the Passion: Children and Their Reading, edited by Morag Styles, Eve Bearne, and Victor Watson. New York: Cassell, 1994.

Signs of Childness in Children's Books, by Peter Hollindale. South Woodchester, England: Thimble Press, 1997.

Understanding Children's Literature, edited by Peter Hunt. New York: Routledge, 1999.

The Voice of the Narrator in Children's Literature, edited by Charlotte Otten and Gary Schmidt. New York: Greenwood Press, 1989.

Specialized Topics in Children's Literature: Specialized

Awards

The Coretta Scott King Awards, edited by Henrietta Smith. Chicago: American Library Association, 1994.

Newbery Medal Books: 1922–1955, edited by Bertha Mahoney Miller. Boston: Horn Book, 1955. Information about authors and trends in the voting decisions; texts of acceptance talks.

Caldecott Medal Books: 1938–1957, edited by Bertha Mahoney Miller. Boston: Horn Book, 1957.

A Caldecott Celebration: Six Artists and Their Paths to the Caldecott Medal by Leonard Marcus. New York: Walker, 1998. Studies the Caldecott books of Robert McCloskey, Marcia Brown, Maurice Sendak, William Steig, Chris Van Allsburg, and David Wiesner on the Sixtieth Anniversary of the Caldecott Medal.

Newbery and Caldecott Medal Books: 1956–1965, edited by Lee Kingman. Boston: Horn Book, 1965.

Newbery and Caldecott Medal Books: 1966–1975, edited by Lee Kingman. Boston: Horn Book, 1975.

Newbery and Caldecott Medal Books: 1976–1985, edited by Lee Kingman. Boston: Horn Book, 1985.

Cultural and Multicultural Emphases

African-American Review, 32 (Spring, 1998), edited by Dianne Feelings-Johnson and Catherine Lewis. Terre Haute, IN: Indiana State University. Issue focused entirely on African-American children's literature.

The All White World of Children; Books and African-American Children's Literature. edited by Osayim Wense Osa. Trenton, NJ: Africa World Press, 1995.

Art and Story: The Role of Illustrations in Multicultural Literature for Youth, edited by Anthony Manna and Carolyn Brodie. Fort Atkinson, WI: Highsmith Press, 1997.

Battling Dragons: Issues and Controversy in Children's Literature, edited by Susan Lehr. Portsmouth NH: Heinemann, 1995.

Black Books Galore; Guide to Great African-American Children's Books by Donna Rand, Joni Parker, and Shiela Foster. New York: John Wiley and Sons, 1998.

Breaking the Magic Spell: Radical Theories of Folk and Fairy Tales by Jack Zipes. Austin: University of Texas Press, 1979.

Many Faces, Many Voices: Multicultural Literary Experiences for Youth, edited by Anthony Manna and Carolyn Brodie. Fort Atkinson, WI: Highsmith Press, 1992.

The Need for Story: Cultural Diversity in Classroom and Community, edited by Anne Haas Dyson and Celia Genishi. Urbana, IL: National Council of Teachers of English, 1994.

Paradoxa, 2 (Numbers 3–4, 1996), edited by Alleen Pace Nilsen. Box 2237, Vashon Island, WA 98070. Issue focused entirely on Censorship in Children's Literature.

Reading Across Cultures: Teaching Literature in a Diverse Society, edited by Theresa Rogers and Anna Soter. New York: Teachers College Press, 1997.

Reading Otherwise by Lissa Paul. South Woodchester, England: The Thimble Press, 1998.

Teaching Multicultural Literature, edited by Violet Harris. Norwood, MA: Christopher-Gorden, 1993 (2nd edition, 1997). Essays on African-American, Asian-American, Latino, and Native American books for children and strategies for classroom use of multicultural literature.

Telling Tales: The Pedagogy and Promise of African-American Writers, 1968–1993: A Critical and Annotated Guide by Dianne Johnson. Westport, CT: Greenwood, 1996.

Waking Sleeping Beauty: Feminist Voices in Children's Novels by Roberta Trites. Iowa City: University of Iowa Press, 1997.

Genres: Fairy Tales and Fiction

EGOFF, SHEILA. *Worlds Within: Children's Fantasy from the Middle Ages to Today.* Chicago: American Library Association, 1988.

OPIE, IONA, AND OPIE, PETER. *The Classic Fairy Tales.* New York: Oxford University Press, 1974.

REES, DAVID. *Painted Desert, Green Shade.* Boston: Horn Book, 1984.

SALE, ROGER. *Fairy Tales and After.* Cambridge, MA: Harvard University Press, 1978.

Genres: Picture Books

CIANCIOLO, PATRICIA. *Picture Books for Children.* Chicago: American Library Association, 1990.

CONSIDINE, DAVID; HALEY, GAIL E;, AND LACY, LYN. *Imagine That: Developing Critical Viewing and Thinking Through Children's Literature.* Englewood, Colorado. Libraries Unlimited, 1994.

DOONAN, JANE. *Looking At Pictures in Picture Books.* South Woodchester, England: Thimble Press, 1993.

GRAHAM, JUDITH. *Pictures on the Page.* Sheffield, England: National Association of Teachers of English, 1990.

KEIFER, BARBARA. *The Potential of Picture Books.* Columbus, OH: Merrill, 1995.

NODELMAN, PERRY. *Words About Pictures.* Athens, GA: University of Georgia Press, 1988.

SHULEVITZ, URI. *Writing with Pictures.* New York: Watson-Guptill, 1985.

SPITZ, ELLEN HANDLER. *Inside Picture Books.* New Haven, CT: Yale University Press, 1999.

WATSON, VICTOR, AND STYLES, MORAG. *Talking Pictures.* London: Hodder and Stoughton, 1996.

Learning and Teaching

CHAMBERS, AIDAN. *Tell Me: Children Reading and Talk.* South Woodchester, England: Thimble Press, 1993.

CONSIDINE, DAVID; HALEY, GAIL E. *Visual Messages; Integrating Imagery into Instruction.* Englewood, Colorado: Teacher Ideas Press, 1999.

CULLINAN, BEATRICE. *Literature and the Child,* 3rd edition. San Diego, CA: Harcourt Brace, 1994.

GILLARD, MARNI. *Storyteller, Storyteacher.* York, ME: Stenhouse, 1996.

HILL, BONNIE; JOHNSON, NANCY; AND NOE, KATHERINE, EDITORS. *Literature Circles and Response.* Norwood, MA: Christopher-Gordon, 1995.

HUCK, CHARLOTTE, AND OTHERS. *Children's Literature in the Elementary School.* Madison, WI: Brown & Benchmark/McGraw-Hill, 1997.

LANGER, JUDITH. *Envisioning Literature.* New York: Teachers College Press, 1995.

MAY, JILL. *Children's Literature and Critical Theory.* New York: Oxford University Press, 1995.

MEEK, MARGARET. *Information and Book Learning.* South Woodchester, England: Thimble Press, 1996.

———. *On Being Literate.* London: The Bodley Head, 1991.

MINNS, HILARY. *Language, Literacy & Gender.* London: Hodder & Stoughton, 1991.

NODELMAN, PERRY. *The Pleasures of Children's Literature.* New York: Longman, 1995.

NORTON, DONNA. *Through the Eyes of a Child: An Introduction to Children's Literature,* 5th edition. New York: Prentice Hall, 1998.

UNSWORTH, LEN, EDITOR. *Literacy Learning and Teaching.* South Melbourne, Australia: Macmillan Education, 1993.

Literary Criticism: Individual Titles

Beauty and the Beast, edited by Betsy Hearne. Chicago: University of Chicago Press, 1989. History and interpretation of this literary fairy tale.

The Cinderella Story, edited by Neil Philip. New York: Penguin, 1989. Retellings of 24 versions of this long-lived folk tale, framed by history and interpretation.

Touchstones: Reflections on the Best in Children's Literature, edited by Perry Nodelman. West Layfayette, IN: Children's Literature Association, 1985. Literary analysis in a three-volume set (fiction; folklore/poetry; and picture books) focusing on classics of children's literature. Volume One has essays on *Little Women, Alice's Adventures in Wonderland, The Adventures of Pinocchio, The Wind in the Willows, Anne of Green Gables, Heidi, Treasure Island, The Hobbit,* and *Charlotte's Web.* Volume Two includes essays on Aesop's *Fables,* Richard Chase's *The Jack Tales,* Joel Chandler Harris's *Tales of Uncle Remus,* Andrew Lang's *The Blue Fairy Book,* Edward Lear's *The Book of Nonsense,* and collections by Hans Christian Andersen, Padraic Collum, the Grimm Brothers, Joseph Jacobs, and Charles Perrault. Volume Three has essays on Leslie Brooke's *Johnny Crow's Garden,* Virginia Burton's *The Little House,* Wanda Gäg's *Millions of Cats,* Ezra Jack Keats's *The Snowy Day,* Robert Lawson's *The Story of Ferdinand,* Leo Lionni's *Swimmy,* Robert McCloskey's *Make Way for Ducklings,* Beatrix Potter's *The Tale of Peter Rabbit,* Maurice Sendak's *Where the Wild Things Are,* and books by Randolph Caldecott, Walter Crane, Kate Greenaway, Arthur Rackham, and Dr. Seuss.

The Wizard of Oz by L. Frank Baum, edited by Michael Patrick Hearn. New York: Schocken Books, 1983. Collected essays focused on this American fairy tale.

Literary Memoirs

Caldecott & Co.: Notes on Books and Pictures. New York: Farrar, 1988.

Dreams and Wishes: Essays on Writing for Children by Susan Cooper. New York: McElderry Books, 1996.

TalkTalk: A Children's Book Author Speaks to Grown-Ups by E. L. Konigsburg. New York: Atheneum, 1995.

Worlds of Childhood: The Art and Craft of Writing for Children, edited by William Zinsser. Boston: Houghton Mifflin, 1990. (Essays by children authors Jean Fritz, Maurice Sendak, Jill Krementz, Jack Prelutsky, Rosemary Wells, and Katherine Paterson).

The Zena Sutherland Lectures, 1983–1992, edited by Betsy Hearne. New York: Clarion Books, 1993. (Essays by children's authors Maurice Sendak, Lloyd Alexander, Katherine Paterson, Virginia Hamilton, Robert Corner, Paula Fox, David Macaulay, Jean Fritz, Trina Hyman, and Betsy Byars).

WEB SITES

Amazon Books *http://www.amazon.com*
Search by title or browse by subject through a 2.5-million-title catalog. You can also order directly, read author interviews, and learn about new books. Click onto "Children's Books" (categories include ages 0–3, 4–8, and 9–12; animals; audio books; history and historical fiction; literature; people and places; science; nature; series books; sports) and "Children's Books Essential Bookshelf" (categories include bestsellers; new in paperback; classics by age; award winners; hot off the press; and ages 4–8 and 9–10).

Barnes and Noble Bookstores *http://www.barnes*
Includes Children's and Young Adult Bookshelf organized by topics (animals, biography, classics, history); and Points of Interest (Top Ten, New Releases, New in Paperback, Books about Sibling Rivalry, and Author Chat Transcripts).

Black History *http:www.netnoir.com/spotlight/bhm98/index.stm*
Many sites focusing on black history: Black Facts online, African-American perspectives, Rapsodies in Black, plus information for children about black history and Black History Month (which was initiated in 1916 as Negro History Week to hand down information about African-Americans that had been changed, erased, or misrepresented).

Children's Book Council *http://www.cbcbooks.org*
Explore five major categories: Publishers; Teachers and Librarians; Booksellers; Parents; and Authors and Illustrators. Each category includes general information about CBC materials, resources, publications, bibliographies, What's New (recently published books), Meet the Author (talks for children), Online Showcases (short descriptions of books organized thematically: Historical Fiction, Holiday Titles, the African-American Experience, Books on Friendship, Summertime Reading, Nature and Science, My First Book, Fantasy/Science Fiction, Paper-Engineered Books). The Publishers category includes a listing of all publishers who are members; many of them have web site addresses that provide information about newly released and forthcoming children's books; some, like Bantam, provide resources for teachers:

Atheneum, Simon & Schuster: *http://www.simonsays.com*
Bantam Doubleday Dell *http://www.bdd.com*
Beech Tree Books, Lothrop, Lee & Shepard, Morrow Junior Books, Mulberry Books (William Morrow) *http://www.williammorrow.com*
Crown *http://www.randomhouse.com*

Dial, Dutton, Puffin, G. P. Putnam's Sons, Viking Children's Books, Frederick Warne (Penguin Putnam) *http://www.penguinputnam.com*
Harper Trophy *http://www.harpercollins.com*
HarperCollins *http://www.harperchildrens.com*
Houghton Mifflin *http://www.hmco.com*
Hyperion *http://www.disney.com/Disney*
Jewish Lights *http://www.jewishlights.com*
Alfred Knopf, Random House *http://www.randomhouse.com*
Lee & Low *http://www.leeandlow.com*
Little, Brown *http://www.littlebrown.com*
Orchard Books *http://www.grolier.com*
Scholastic *http://www.scholastic.com*

Children's Literature Web Guide *http://www.ucalgary.ca/~dkbrown*
David K. Brown of the Doucette Library of Teaching Resources, University of Calgary, Calgary, Alberta, Canada T2N 1N4, maintains this important web site. Explore the main categories:

Features. Quick Reference, and **More Links.**
Features leads to:
What's New, Newbery & Caldecott Winners, Best Books of 1997, Notable Videos, and Web-Traveller's Toolkit: Essential Kid Lit Web sites.
The Web-Traveller's Toolkit subcategory leads to:
Authors (Information about individual children's authors and their books, different types of books, "Ask the Author"—readers' questions answered by authors)
Publishers (Web sites and home pages of children's book publishers, which leads to the authors and illustrators these companies publish and stories about how they create children's books, with photos of the authors)
Carol Hurst's Children's Literature Web Site (Reviews, teaching ideas, children's books grouped thematically)
The Purple Crayon (Tips for writers; publishing trends)
Kay Vandergrift's Special Interest Page (Resources in children's literature of all types; explore the category "Children's Literature," which leads to various genres such as "Biography," which in turn leads to "Biography of Authors"—author and illustrator web sites and home pages, sites that individual authors design in which they list their books, inform readers about new books, describe their writing processes, where they live, and where they are giving talks around the country—and "Videos of Authors"—information about producers and distributors of videos)
Fairosa Cyber Library (Information and cross-references on authors and illustrators; leads to web site on the de Grummond Collection)
Online Library Catalogs (The Bank Street College Library, New York City; The Internet Public Library)
Travel Around the World (Library of Congress, The National Library of Canada)
Resources for Writers
A Guide to Books (The BookWire Index)

Quick Reference (Children's Book Awards, Children's Bestsellers, Teaching Ideas)
More Links (Authors' web sites and home pages; recommended books, journals, teacher resources, storytelling resources, children's publishers and booksellers)
Links to listserver for KIDLIT-L AND CHILD_LIT:

KIDLIT-L is a discussion group for teachers, librarians, and students; to join, e-mail to: *listerv@bingvmb.cc.binghamton.edu.*

CHILD_LIT is a discussion group for academics interested in critical analysis of children's books; to join, e-mail to: *listserv@email.rutgers.edu.*

Cooperative Children's Book Center *http://www.soemadison.wisc.edu/ccbc/index.htm*
Located at the School of Education, University of Wisconsin-Madison; 600 N. Park Street, Madison, WI 53706, the CCBC offers many resources in the field, including online bibliographies of children's books and book discussions among CCBC staff members. For a sample discussion of Karen Cushman's *The Midwife's Apprentice* during November 1995, immediately preceding the Newbery balloting, and information about how jurists select Newbery books, see: *http://www.soemadison.wisc.edu/ccbc/midwife.htm.*

De Grummond Collection *http://www.lil.usm.edu/~degrum*
Explore highlights of this collection (Ezra Jack Keats, Kate Greenaway, Randolph Caldecott) at the University of Southern Mississippi. This site also leads to other children's literature special collections on the web, such as the Baldwin Library (University of Florida), the CCBC (University of Wisconsin-Madison), and the Osborne Collection (Toronto Public Library), among others.

Doubleday Dell *http://www.bdd.com/teachers*
This publisher's web site offers many resources for teachers. Browse through author biographies and autobiographies, new releases of children's books, ideas for teaching award-winning books, authors' talks about their writing processes, and teacher guides for individual titles.

Heinemann Publishers, United Kingdom *http://www.heinemann.co.uk*
Explore the largest educational publisher in Great Britain, noting in particular its Educational Resources. Sunshine Online *http://www.sunshine.co.uk* has many teacher resources and features on literature and literacy. Heinemann's magazine about children's books, *New Windmills, http://www.heinemann.co.uk/windmill* includes author visits, information about new releases, and extracts of books.

Native American Sources *http://www.hanksville.org/NAresources*
Provides many links to information about Native American education, art, social programs.

Simon & Schuster *http://www.simonsays.com*
Discover more author autobiographies and teacher guides for books published by this large company.

Appendix 4: Interview with a Classroom Teacher

The author of this text, Nina Mikkelsen, had the opportunity to interview a teacher in a literature-based classroom. Here is a transcript of that interview.

NM: How did literature-based teaching begin for you? Did you always use children's books in the classroom?

SARA: When I began teaching, I taught all subjects every day, with a set time allotted for each subject. Reading was one of these subjects; I taught a structured basal approach with separate classes in spelling and language arts (creative writing, book reports, poetry). I read books like *Heidi* aloud, chapter by chapter, each day. Then came what I call the era of Jim Trelease [author of *The Read-Aloud Handbook,* Penguin, 1984]. Workshop leaders were visiting our in-service programs and talking about read-aloud approaches and whole language ideas. Teachers were getting in touch with children's books again. Our school system decided to tread into the waters of children's books, too. We decided to set aside one month each year as Author Month. Children would become familiar with as many books of that author as possible. Teachers were slowly getting back in touch this way, too. There were lots of authors that weren't in the basal. We had a lot to learn about!

NM: Who were some of these authors for your second graders?

SARA: Stephen Kellogg, Bill Peet, Leo Lionni, Jan Brett. Actually, I was teaching first grade at that time. I remember when my first graders were working with Leo Lionni's books, I had my first glimpse of how children could be exposed to literature outside the basal program.

NM: Do you mean how you could teach with children's books?

SARA: I mean I discovered, reading a Leo Lionni story, that children—these very young children—were capable of expressing very adult concepts just from hearing and talking about a story. This incident is as vivid today as it was over ten years ago! We had been reading and discussing *Frederick* in terms of the story and artwork. Even though Lionni presents this story in a straightforward way for children, there is an underlying universal idea that "Man does not live by bread alone." My students were typical first graders, of mixed ability, in the second semester of the year. I asked a "thinking" question for the entire class: "Since it was late winter and all the mice were slowly starving," I said to them, "why do you think the mice asked Frederick for help when they knew he had no food to give them?"

NM: Wow! That's some big question for first graders? How did they handle it?

SARA: Well, maybe I said it a little differently, but it was essentially that question. I gave them a little quiet time afterward to think about it, and I remember one child's answer: "Frederick could *say* good pictures for them to think about, and besides, food isn't the only thing that makes us happy." I was truly stunned at her remark!

NM: She said that Frederick could "say" good pictures. That meant she knew the mice knew what Frederick's special talent was?

SARA: Yes, and that was Frederick's way of helping. The other mice asked Frederick for help of a different kind; they knew he had no food [no real food], but he had a different kind of "food"—another something to give and this was something they all needed to be happy.

NM: Or to be more *completely* happy?

SARA: Yes! She understood that really difficult concept—that there are both physical and emotional needs we all have, if we are going to be happy in a deeper way.

NM: So this child made you feel that you could trust the author's story to teach itself, if you asked the right questions. And that gave you the confidence to use more literature in your reading classes? To pull a little away from the basal?

SARA: Yes, I began to incorporate more and more literature selections into the daily plan of the basal program. I expected my students to be able to read a wider variety of stories, to compare and contrast selections, and *stretch* their minds. The stretching part was what I liked best. It made me feel I was really teaching or teaching something besides just words and sounds of words.

NM: And the children—were they happier, too? Did they feel they were really learning now or learning more? Or could you tell?

SARA: Well, it took a little time for this intellectual freedom to sink in. But as I kept going with it, they began to lose their fears of expressing themselves [in case their ideas were not the "right" answers]. Later when I was teaching second and third graders, I found it took even longer for them to express their own opinions. But that was the best thing to watch—these expanding horizons.

NM: This was the 1980s, you're saying. So what's been happening since? Have things continued in your school, your classroom, in the same vein mostly?

SARA: Oh no, there have been so many more changes; this was just the beginning.

NM: For you, in your own professional growth? Or in the entire school, or the system itself?.

SARA: The entire system. Around this time, the early 1990s, we all became involved in the national reading encouragement program, Read Aloud. Today every classroom teacher has at least one trained parent volunteer reading to the children on a weekly basis. Since each volunteer brings at least three books for each visit, the children are constantly introduced to more literature. At the same time, the administrators were encouraging us to attend workshops and discussion groups, on a school-by-school basis, to investigate alternative approaches to the basal and to decide how they would use the adopted basals already in place.

NM: So you had choices.

SARA: Oh, yes. We could decide to do a total literature-based approach or stay with the structured basal approach as we worked with the newly adopted textbook series, or we could use a combination of these [a modified plan]. We had three choices.

NM: So what did you do?

SARA: After much soul searching, I decided to keep what I considered to be the strong points of the basal, while using the newer literature-based program. In other words, since the State Department of Education gives us certain goals and objectives that we must meet, I decided on the modified plan, and I've been using it for the last eight years.

NM: And you're happy with your decision?

SARA: Very happy, and I feel that my method has been very successful in teaching reading.

NM: Tell me about your method.

SARA: Part of each day, I use the basal—or different basals. Even when my county drops a certain series, I keep copies of it around and use different textbooks with different children, depending on what learning experiences a child needs. That gives me a wider variety of literature selections. I don't always feel that the basal story that the county has adopted meets the objective that I have at that time, so I find another story from all the books I have in my room. This way I can pick and choose. Later in the day, I use the thematic units that a committee of teachers in our county developed for different grade levels.

NM: So the thematic units approach is what you mean by your "literature-based program."

SARA: Yes, each teacher in our county receives a large notebook to work from. The notebooks are composed of many thematic units for classroom use. Each unit includes whole language background materials, reading [literature] lists, daily plans, activities, samples of parent letters, sample evaluations, and ways to correlate activities with other subject areas. When our county adopted the thematic unit approach, it purchased small sets (six books to a set) of children's books and individual copies of books that were necessary for teaching the units.

NM: Is this all of the children's books that you need? All that you have?

SARA: We can obtain additional copies of books—or more books—if we want them.

NM: How do you pay for them?

SARA: I have $200 each year, of state money, to purchase books. Also I can save bonus points from the different book club companies like Troll, Scholastic, Cardnial, Golden, and Trumpet. I have now built up a classroom library that works well for me. The children don't have individual copies of all books; sometimes they sit in pairs. I use single copies of books from the library; I order from interlibrary loan at other times [to obtain books to share with the entire class]. The children can order books of their own, too, through the different book clubs.

NM: How does that work?

SARA: Books clubs—Trumpet, Carnival, Golden Book, Scholastic, and Troll—send teachers monthly catalogs with duplicated pages that I pass out to students. They choose books to purchase and bring in the money to give to me for the classroom order. I send the total order on to the company. With the bonus points, I can purchase books for the classroom library. If a book turns out to be too difficult for a second-grade room, I donate it to the school library.

NM: What are some of the activities you use with a literature-based approach?

SARA: Journal writing, response logs, story writing, semantic webbing, oral and silent reading, sustained silent reading. Grammar is still a separate class, but the thematic notebooks show us how to correlate it with the literature teaching. My weekly spelling list (twenty words) comes from high-frequency words, words from the basal and thematic unit stories for the week, and words from other subject areas—math, social studies, science.

NM: How does SSR [sustained silent reading] work for you?

SARA: The children choose a book when they come in that morning. It should last that day or into the next day if necessary. By mid-year, the majority of my students can sustain twenty-five to thirty minutes of quiet, personal reading. Many children actually lose themselves in their books and are surprised that the time has passed so quickly!

NM: What about media events, use of the library, computers? (Things outside literature—and yet related to it?) How do these events work with your approach?

SARA: I frequently use the Reading Rainbow series on Public Television with my students. The varied subject matter and book choices are well presented, and the children are always thrilled to see books that they have read or seen in the school library. We have computer programs in reading and math for reinforcing skills and typing skills. Internet access is available. The librarian visits us and we visit the library regularly. Our school librarian is my best partner for teaching with children's books. She is always willing to take my input for organizing sets or groups of books to complement a thematic unit and for ordering additional books for the units. She organizes Book Fairs for fundraising activities. Teachers browse at these Fairs and suggest books to add to our thematic units; then she buys the books for us, as long as her funding permits.

NM: What are some of the themes for these thematic units?

SARA: It might be an individual author (like Leo Lionni) or a subject like "Ancestors" or a genre like "Tall Tales." When we started our use of thematic units several years ago, I found we had a lack of tall tales with female characters. It has taken some time, but we have now located and purchased books to give us a more balanced selection for this theme. A theme might also be focusing on a place. Since the school librarian and I share a common interest in Alaska, we have worked together to find stories about the Iditerod [the premier dog sled race in Alaska]. The new Scholastic Basal series we are using also has a story of Balto, the dog that saved Nome, so my modified plan [combined use of the basal and of children's books] works well for the thematic approach. Our computer teacher helps children locate web sites on the Internet to go with the thematic units. With this unit, "Alaska," we were able to follow the progress of the race and even enter an art contest about it! And this year we have internet pen pals in Anchorage, Alaska.

NM: So sometimes children are participating in literature activities that range beyond the units of thematic study—or the thematic units take the children out into the real world.

SARA: Yes, in March we participated in a National Reading Council activity to celebrate the birthday of Dr. Seuss. The children brought their own favorite rhyme books to share. Then we read and discussed several of the harder stories that focus on social issues and ecology concerns.

NM: Are there times when you leave the school for outside events—things related to literature like plays, movies, art exhibits?

SARA: Twice a year we take our students to live theater productions. This year, "Cinderella" was one of the productions. To prepare for the trip, I used a multicultural approach to this story. I read different versions of the story aloud: French [Susan Jeffers's *Cinderella*], African [John Steptoe's *Mufaro's Beautiful Daughters*], Egyptian [Shirley Climo's *The Egyptian Cinderella*], and Native American [Rafe Martin's *The Rough-Face Girl*]. The children then compared and contrasted the stories through discussion and artwork.

NM: Were all of these books already in your classroom library? If they hadn't been there, how would you have obtained them? How do teachers collect books for classroom use? Is it a big, time-consuming, horrible job? Or do you—or could you—just ask the librarian to collect the books for you?

SARA: I could ask her to help out and I have asked her, when I was really busy and needed something quickly. I don't know if she would have time to collect books for every teacher every day. We probably wouldn't put that much of a burden on her. But I love browsing in bookstores, so it's not ever a horrible job for me. I don't mind that it's time-consuming; it's something I like to spend my time doing. I often stop in the public library, Waldenbooks, or B. Dalton Books, after school or on Saturday, to look for new books to add to special topic areas. Only two hours away there is a larger chain, Josephy-Beth Bookstore, a real treat! Familiar authors, illustrators, and topics catch my attention. Summers I have even more time for browsing. This past summer I found several books to ask the librarian to order.

NM: Tell about those.

Sara: I found two books for our November unit on "Ancestors." They each focus on the idea of records that families keep for making cloth designs. (One is about a family from Asia; the other is about an African family.) Another book is *Cross-Country Cat* by Mary Calhoun [Morrow, 1979; illustrated by Erick Ingraham]. *Hot-Air Henry* [also by Calhoun; Morrow, 1981] is a favorite story of my students; they have seen it on Reading Rainbow. So I suggested she buy two more books about Henry, the "high-flying cat." I also found an excellent book on multicultural holidays—*Celebrations* [by Barnabas and Anabel Kindersley; photographs by Barnabas Kindersley; Dorling-Kindersley Limited, 1997] and another book for our teacher bookshelf about multicultural "etiquette" [Norine Dresser's *Multicultural Manners,* John Wiley and Sons, 1996].

NM: And did you purchase books this summer too, using funds from your teacher budget?

Sara: Yes, every summer I keep my eye out for books and purchase them when I find the ones I need.

NM: How many do you usually buy?

Sara: Over the past two summers I have purchased about twenty books.

NM: What kinds of books did you choose?

Sara: One was a story about the Vietnam Veterans Memorial for social studies; one was a story about wagon trains, also for social studies. One was a story of Hercules. Another was a story of Chinese "lucky money" for social studies. Then there was a story about school celebrations (for math) and two books for science (a book about planting a garden and a story about the life cycle of a harp seal). [Sara's annotated list of these books follows.]

- *The Wall of Names* by Judy Donnelly (Random House Step Into Reading Series, 1991; photographs). This is the story of the Vietnam Veterans Memorial; I can use it when teaching a unit on Washington, D. C. and on Memorial Day.
- *Wagon Train* by Sydelle Kramer; illustrated by Deborah Ray (Grosset & Dunlap All Aboard Reading Books, 1997). This book will be good for Social Studies and SSR.
- *The Twelve Labors of Hercules* by Marc Cerasini; illustrated by Isidre Mones (Random House Step Into Reading Series, 1997). This book works well with our thematic unit, "Treasured Tales."
- *Sam and the Lucky Money* by Karen Chinn; illustrated by Cornelious Van Wright and Ying-Hwa Hu (Troll, 1995). I will use this multicultural book when I am teaching a unit on the Chinese New Year.
- *The 100th Day of School* by Angela Medearis; illustrated by Joan Holub (Scholastic, 1996). I will use this book with math; it shows celebrations for 100 different school days. (On the hundredth day, we have a party and each child makes a project at home, showing 100 in groups of 10.)
- *Your First Garden Book* by Marc Brown (Trumpet, 1981). This book will be good for science (ecology).
- *Little Harp Seal* by Karen Young; illustrated by Brian Shaw (Soundprints, 1996; Smithsonian Oceanic Collection). Good for science; ecology.

NM: And the others?

SARA: The others are also useful for thematic units and various subject areas. I'm particularly interested in science, and I like integrating the different subject areas. [Sara's annotated list of these books follows.]

- *Clouds of Terror* by Catherine Welch; illustrated by Laurie Johnson (Carolrhoda Books, 1994). Good for both science and SSR; this is the story of a grasshopper plague on the Western plains.
- *The Greedy Man in the Moon* by Rick Rossiter; illustrated by Dick Smolinski (Riverbank Press, 1994). A Chinese folk tale; this book works with the thematic unit, "Treasured Tales."
- *Three Billy Goats Gruff* by Ted Dewan (Scholastic, 1994). A funny rhyme book; this is a playful version of a familiar folk tale.
- *The Day of Ahmed's Secret* by Florence Heide and Judith Gilliland; illustrated by Ted Lewin (Scholastic, 1990). A multicultural book; an Egyptian child is learning to write his name.
- *Legend of the Milky Way* by Jeanne M. Lee (Holt, 1982). A Reading Rainbow book; a Chinese folk tale that is useful for the thematic unit, "Sunshine and Shadows" (about the solar system and the stars).
- *Heart of a Tiger* by Marsha Arnold; illustrated by Jamichael Henterly (Dial, 1995). Useful for the "Ancestors" unit; it shows the importance of your name. I can do a research project for the children to find out about their own names.
- *Kwanzaa* by Sharon Gayle (Watermill, 1994). Multicultural book/history. I can do a special project for this African-American holiday.
- *The Floating House* by Scott Sanders; illustrated by Helen Cogancherry (Macmillan, 1995). A good book for social studies; focuses on traveling by flatboat on the Ohio River, the children's own geographical area.
- *Gorillas* by Joyce Milton; illustrated by Bryn Barnard (Random House; Step Into Reading Book, 1997). Good for science/ecology.
- *Gold Fever* by Catherine McMorrow; illustrated by Michael Eagle (Random House, 1996). About the Gold Rush in the United States; good for SSR.
- *The Bracelet* by Yoshiko Uchida; illustrated by Joanna Yardley (Philomel, 1993). Multicultural book; story of Japanese-Americans being detained during WW II. I can use this one to teach history, especially the importance of trust and understanding.
- *Raven* by Gerald McDermott (Scholastic, 1993). A multicultural, trickster tale (from the Pacific Northwest Indians). I can use this one in the unit, "Treasured Tales."
- *Barbara Fritchie* by John G. Whittier; illustrated by Nancy Parker (Greenwillow, 1992). A good book for teaching courage as part of strong character (history).
- *Keelboat Annie* by Janet Johnson; illustrated by Charles Reasoner (Troll, 1998). This one is an African-American legend and a female tall tale; important for multicultural themes.
- *Birdie's Lighthouse* by Deborah Hopkinson; illustrated by Kimberly Root (Atheneum, 1997). A Reading Rainbow book; I'll use this one for a unit on lighthouses.
- *Something from Nothing* by Phoebe Gilman (Scholastic, 1992). Multicultural (a Jewish folk tale); I will use this book to teach family values and ecology (recycling fabric/sewing).

NM: You also choose many multicultural books.

SARA: Every year, I have students from many different cultures in my classroom. I want to provide literature for them—and not just for them, but for all the children to see customs and beliefs of different people around the world. In February, our school participates in a multicultural program—The National African-American Read-In Chain, a special program of the National Council of Teachers of English (NCTE). The children always enjoy the Anansi tales and modern black history stories. So I'm always on the lookout for new authors and stories that we can use.

NM: Would you say these books you purchased for your classroom are what other teachers would have purchased? If I were to go into different second-grade classrooms around the country, for example, would I be likely to see these same books?

SARA: Well, I guess you would see some similarities in the reading and comprehension levels or what children this age would understand. Other than that, I don't think you could expect to see these very same books in any one classroom, even here in this county where we are all using many of these same themes like "Ancestors." Remember, I was choosing them, according to my own interests and ideas about the themes, although at meetings we always share ideas about books that work well with the units. So if teachers liked my discovery, they could borrow this same book from the library or order a copy of their own.

NM: So there isn't a certain "list" of books that teachers anywhere will tend to have in their classrooms when they use a literature-based approach.

SARA: Do you mean a required list?

NM: Required or maybe even preferred, something you could describe as "typical": a typical second-grade classroom (a well-stocked classroom) would have these fifty books in common?

SARA: No, and I wouldn't want it that way. I mean, you're going to have some books in common simply because teachers get together and share ideas and word gets around quickly that one book reads well aloud and another book is great for the Ancestors unit and another book is just one that kids love. That's going to happen naturally. But it would take the fun out of it for me to be told here's $200; now buy these fifty books, and you won't ever have to look for anything else this year or next year—or maybe even the next!

NM: I guess I'm thinking about beginning teachers who say they might feel more willing to try a literature-based approach, if they could start out with some kind of list in hand. Suppose they didn't know a lot about what went over well with second graders, or if they didn't know the best books for a unit on "Sunshine and Shadows"?

SARA: I think the teachers working on our thematic units committee prepared well for that possibility when they suggested certain books to use with the units. It isn't a huge list of books for each one, just a few. That gives beginning teachers a little notion of how to get started, and if they never used any other books than a few the first time around, they could still proceed. But if we all used the same few books forever, things would get awfully dull for us and for the children. What happens is that teachers start sharing ideas about books. New teachers would also be talking to seasoned teachers and the librarian. And children start noticing books at home or in the library and they bring them in. Pretty soon, even new teachers know a whole lot more than they knew a few days or weeks ago.

NM: So you don't see any need for some kind of proclamation: "Here's what you should have in your classroom bookcase." Or "Here's what the well-equipped second-grade classroom will have: five copies of *Charlotte's Web,* five copies of *Mufaro's Beautiful Daughters,* five copies of *Hot-Air Henry,* twenty-five copies of *Frederick,* one copy of *Celebrations,*" and so on.

SARA: Well, you could have this, of course. But who would do the deciding? Wouldn't we be back to basal textbook teaching? In a basal series, you might have twenty-five students reading a selection from each of the books you just mentioned. And the teacher wouldn't have to do anything but open the book and start doing what the textbook says to do that day with that selection. But most of the teachers in my county like the way that we now have some say in choosing what we'll do every day. It gives more variety and more ideas. It gives you a way to connect different subjects. We make our own list for our own classroom, and then change it when we need to do so. We add or drop books from it. We revise it—and share it.

NM: So the basal gives a sort of "list" of what might "typically" be in a classroom? Is that why so many systems have opted for a basal plan over the years?

Sara: A basal tells you what a particular textbook company might think is typical. But "typical" is anybody's guess, isn't it? If we had some preferred list, we wouldn't need but one publishing company for children's books. All the others could just go out of business. I think the professionalism would go out the window, too, the feeling that you are the one with the knowledge of what works best for this group of children and this set of teaching goals. Plus there's the fun of choosing the books *you* want to work into your plan for that week or that unit, the fun of just looking at new books and talking to the librarian and other teachers about them—and of trying them out.

NM: How do you know how to choose—or if you're making *good* choices?

Sara: In college, I took a children's literature course and learned a lot about a lot of different children's books. Then I started teaching with the basal and I sort of lost touch with children's books, all the new ones that were coming out all the time. When our literature-based plan arose, I had to get back in touch with children's literature—and I did—and I love being in touch with it. How do I know if I'm making the best choices? Well, I watch the children—how they make connections and see new things from the books I choose. I talk to other teachers, see how their students are responding to the books they're choosing. I talk to the librarian and listen to her ideas about new books. I talk to parents and listen to their ideas and I learn from them too. I don't want to be hemmed in with a list of books now that would mean losing touch again with books or other people. I don't see any professionalism in that. Of course, it might make it easier when parents complain about a certain book I have chosen. If I hadn't done any choosing, they'd merely be arguing with the "list"—like arguing with the wall—and I wouldn't have to worry about anything!

NM: Let's talk about that. Is censorship a big worry for you? For other teachers? Do you get a lot of parent complaints about books you've chosen? Do other teachers in your system?

Sara: Our county is probably famous for the book protests of the 1970s. Since then, there have been scattered incidents. I remember the parent who complained about a basal story of "Red Riding Hood" and the picture that she thought showed teeth that were too sharp.

NM: How would you have responded to that comment?

Sara: I probably would have told her that no wolf would last very long on this earth if its teeth weren't sharp!

NM: And maybe humor is a good way of dealing with censorship at times. But what about those times when it wouldn't work?

Sara: Our school has a committee consisting of parents, our principal, and the librarian. The committee deals with any problems that occur. Two years ago, I had to deal with two complaints from a parent, concerning two books in my room, but it never went to the committee stage.

NM: That was the situation with *Chester's Way* and the Annie Oakley biography, right?

SARA: Yes, in the Henkes book, there are two male mice and a female mouse that are friends. The story is about making new friends and solving problems. The parent's objection was that the two male mice friends were "too close," and the three mice friends had a sleepover. Then she objected to her daughter choosing a Step Reading book about Annie Oakley (*Little Sure Shot: The Story of Annie Oakley*).

NM: I find the first complaint humorous; I think you're saying she thought the mice were gay.

SARA: Yes, as I recall, she actually did say that—more or less. She thought the two male mice friends were too chummy, too close, even for best friends. She felt it was sending an "unhealthy message."

NM: About the other book, I don't understand what was bothering her about the guns. She objected to having her daughter read about people using guns? Or did she not want her daughter to see a woman using firearms?

SARA: She objected to the guns in the story. But how do you tell this story without the guns? She thought firearms were emphasized too much in the story. And she felt it was not a "ladylike" role model that she wanted for her daughter, because Annie Oakley made her living shooting guns. "Guns are not for my daughter," was the way she put it.

NM: So she didn't want to think a girl could have a gun. How did you respond?

SARA: My response in both cases was polite, understanding, but firm, but it was never a verbal fight. This parent was not a loud, angry person when she came in. In both these instances, she was simply concerned and firm about her feelings; she was never rude or loud. She was a parent tutor. She sat and listened to two or three children read a selection that I, or the children, chose. The Annie Oakley book was a student-level biography in a group of books about famous people that the children could choose for Sustained Silent Reading time. This day they were to read their choice to her.

NM: And that's when she encountered the book.

SARA: Yes, as they read orally, she realized that she didn't like the story and she came to tell me that she didn't want her daughter to continue reading about Annie Oakley. Since I had chosen the biographies for free reading time and it was not required reading for a grade, I told her that her daughter would not be required to read any more of the book, but that I would not remove the book from the room. It would remain as a choice in the "biography basket" because I had read the book and found no problems with the language or content.

NM: How was the Henkes book used in your classroom?

SARA: *Chester's Way* is part of the supplementary sets of books that the county had purchased from Scholastic for all second graders. I had already read it aloud to the class, and because we had only six copies, three children were taking turns reading it to her when she first encountered the book and spoke to me about it. I explained that the book was not required reading. Her daughter would not have to practice oral peer reading with it or read it in a small group setting again. Again, I said I would not remove the book from the room but I would excuse her daughter from any more contact with the story. I said I didn't feel there was any "wrong" message in the story. Since the theme of the story was friendship and sharing, I was emphasizing accepting new friends into old circles of friends—looking for talents that would add to your group.

NM: Then what happened?

SARA: In both cases, I spoke to my principal and the school librarian about the objections. They reviewed the books and agreed with my decisions. The parent was apparently satisfied with my solution; she made no further complaints.

NM: How did you choose these books—or why?

SARA: I purchased the Oakley book at Waldenbooks with my own money allotment. There were two copies in the room already. Children of this age are very interested in famous people and in what they have done with their lives. It isn't easy to find interesting biographies on a second- or third-grade level. When I find any, especially female personalities, I usually try to buy them that minute. I read this book standing there in the store before I bought the first two copies. It was just a straightforward, interesting account of Annie Oakley's life, with illustrations. Since I feel that my training and experience qualify me to choose the children's books, I felt—and still feel—there is no problem with the books. After using *Chester's Way* with so many different children over the last two years—and seeing how much they liked it—I ordered another book by Henkes, *Lilly's Purple Plastic Purse* [Greenwillow, 1996], when I saw it in the Troll catalog. I constantly browse in catalogs and bookstores for books that I feel will appeal to children. Henkes never fails to appeal. Well, almost never!

NM: What if you wanted a book and couldn't find it anywhere—in catalogs, bookstores, libraries? Could that ever happen?

SARA: It really did happen. I often use these literature-based activity books for math, geography, science, and I saw an ecology unit on a book called *I Am the Ocean.* I wanted to use it with our thematic unit, "Sharing Our Land." So I went to the bookstore but it was an out-of-stock or out-of-print book. The library didn't have it, but the librarian suggested interlibrary loan. I ordered it, and it arrived in time for me to use it with my ocean unit.

NM: What if a book from another country were not available in America? Maybe it was mentioned in an English magazine or journal and you wanted to get it for your class. Would it be impossible?

SARA: A parent came back from England with several books to share. The next year I wanted to read them aloud again, so I ordered two of them through interlibrary loan, at the public library, and they arrived from Canada two weeks later!

NM: So any book a teacher decides to work into her teaching, she could somehow obtain it? Any book—in print, out of print, American, foreign, expensive, moderately priced—could turn up in her classroom, if you she wanted it there? In other words, even though that book was not in the "typical" classroom and she wanted it, she could get it?

SARA: There is no typical classroom. There are just classrooms with children and books and teachers trying to find the right books for all these different children. That takes lots of different books and lots of ways of finding them. I've had wonderful experience with librarians. If you want to find a hard-to-find book, they help you find that book. It might take a little while, but eventually it turns up. The important thing is to keep thinking about what you want children to learn about or read about or see in books and then to enjoy finding and sharing these books!

Appendix 5
A Literature and Literacies Portfolio

David, Tara, Sandy, Amy, and Vinny are students in children's literature classes in which portfolio assessment accounts for 60 percent of the entire grade. The remaining portion comes from essay questions on material in their textbooks and from class participation. The semester begins with the instructor explaining the procedure. The students have midterm and end-of-term essay questions which reveal their growth in literature and literacy learning during the semester. Following are same examples of the types of questions students answer:

- Discuss the social relevance of *Alice's Adventures in Wonderland* for us today. Why is it still an important work of children's literature?
- Choose a favorite children's poem and tell why you like it. What makes it a *good* poem for you or for children?
- If you added a character or a scene to Susan Cooper's *Greenwitch,* who or what would it be? If you deleted a character or a scene to this book, who or what would it be? Explain your choice.
- Defend—or attack—the choices of a particular picture book artist who has recently won an important award, such as the Caldecott or Kate Greenaway. Explain what you would have done had you been a selector on the awards committee.

Literature cannot be tested, explains the instructor; it can only be *experienced.* There are no right or wrong answers to literature (or to the essay questions), only individual responses. Literature is one of the humanities *and* one of the arts; it is not an exact science.

Students in the class have books to read, journal entries to write, projects to pursue, and reflective responses to write. They meet in literature study groups and writing circles throughout the semester as they read and talk about children's books, record responses to the books in journal entries, build individual classroom book collections, and engage in project work, or what we have been calling "Investigations." All of these activities will eventually feed into the portfolio collection.

The emphasis is on cooperation and collaboration, not on competition and "correct" answers. All the work involves collaborative assessment. Students read and write and then evaluate their own work; the instructor observes and confirms the completeness of the work. Incomplete work may be completed and then reevaluated by student and instructor. The instructor's own criteria serve as a guide for the student self-evaluation procedures.

The criterion for **essay questions** is development. Students must unfold their thoughts clearly and fully enough for others to understand what they are thinking, and they must support their assertions.

The criteria for **class participation** include attending class, working as an active partner in literature study groups, keeping up with reading assignments, rereading when necessary, and exploring library stacks to find additional books for classroom examination.

The contents of the **portfolio** fall into four categories:

- Response journals
- Descriptive report of books read
- Annotated list of books
- Investigative projects.

Criteria for the **response journals** are a wide variety of books read, including the textbook; in-depth reading and exploratory writing about the readings; and discussions about the books both inside and outside the classroom.

Criteria for the **annotated list of books** are balance, diversity, development, appropriateness for age level, and variety.

The criterion for **investigative work** is growth in learning and writing. Students must focus their work, organize their findings, provide detailed and supported statements or detailed scene building, produce insight for writer and readers, write clearly, and proofread carefully. Students thus assess their growth and build on their strengths in these six areas: *focus, organization, detail, insight, clarity of writing style,* and *proofreading.*

The criterion for assessment of the **portfolio** is reflective thinking about growth. Students produce descriptive reports of their "journey" through the class, and they select examples of their best work—but "best" is a relative term. Students define this word according to their own reasoning and then unfold their reasoning for others to see. The portfolio includes what students choose to include—plus the following:

- Their five "best" *journal entries* developed and polished for clarity of phrasing
- A *descriptive report* of what children's books they read and reread—and why
- An *annotated list of children's books* for a classroom library collection (primary or upper elementary)—at least ten books and at least one paragraph describing each book and its importance to such a collection
- A report or description of *completed investigative projects* that the student turned in during the semester for a mark of "complete" or "incomplete" (those receiving a mark of "incomplete" were either reworked—and completed—or left incomplete and submitted as *work in progress*)
- A discussion of what each student thinks is his or her best project—and why.

BEST JOURNAL ENTRIES

As students read and respond to their reading in journals, they note passages that puzzle or intrigue them or insights they gain as they read. What makes an entry "good" or "the best" varies. Sometimes students choose long entries. They write more because they begin thinking of more things to say as they continue writing and thinking about the book. Journal writing is exploratory, expressive, and informal in tone. As they write, they think more and discover more or make more connections. Learning more becomes the criterion.

Sometimes students choose as best an entry that others in their response group liked (they often share entries during class). Peer approval validates the response as worthwhile.

Sometimes students simply enjoy reading, thinking, and writing about particular books and about the ideas that grow out of them; their enjoyment marks that entry as best. Taking pleasure in literacy becomes the criterion.

David's response to *Alice's Adventures in Wonderland* in the next several paragraphs is discovery writing: He learns more as he unfolds his thoughts. When he shared his story with peers, they enjoyed it. He also seems to have enjoyed sharing the book with his younger brother. Thus, his choice of this journal entry as a good one fits all three criteria categories: learning more, demonstrating audience appeal, and taking pleasure in the literacy process:

> I decided to read *Alice's Adventures in Wonderland* to my brothers partly because I enjoyed it myself when I read it in class and felt bad that I hadn't been exposed to it as a child, and partly because I had already read it for class and was thus already familiar with the story line. I didn't read the whole book to them at one time; I only read them the first two chapters and promised to read them two chapters every time I came home. Andrew is in third grade and Ethan just had his fourth birthday in January.
>
> I remember in class that there were questions as to why this book was considered a children's classic because no one ever saw children reading the book. After reading to my brothers, I think I have discovered part of the answer. They loved the story, although they didn't say too much while I was reading. But every once in a while when I would take a pause, I looked at their faces. Both had wide grins. They laughed and giggled several times, especially at the beginning of Chapter Two when Alice has grown and is thinking about having to send presents to her feet. In fact now that I think about it, the vast majority of times when they laughed was when Alice was talking to herself and getting things all jumbled up. I thought then that maybe Andrew was laughing because he knew better than Alice did, and Ethan, of course, I concluded, was just laughing because Andrew was laughing. Ethan, though, was enjoying the story in his own right. I remember somewhere in the course of the story, for whatever reason, he got the notion into his head that Alice had gotten mouthwash in her shoe. I was going to correct him, but changed my mind. With all the other wildly improbable things happening in this story, why bother if it gave him such enjoyment to think so.
>
> This brings me to another point that was brought up in the class discussion—if the book were too scary for young children. Watching my brothers as I read the story, I would have to say no. I think that sometimes, when we grow older, we tend to underestimate a child's intellect. As I said before, Andrew knew better, and that's why he was laughing.
>
> To return to my original question as to why children aren't seen reading this book, I would conclude that it is because of its length. That in itself can be very intimidating for an average young reader. As I said, my brothers immensely enjoyed the story as I read it to them, but I don't think that either one of them would actually try to read it themselves, simply because it looked too difficult for them to read. I think perhaps that this book, along with *The Wind in the Willows,* has been "upshifted" in the levels of literature, and is perhaps no longer considered by uninformed children (uninformed, I mean, about the individual books) to be written for children, when in fact it is. (David)

DESCRIPTIVE REPORT OF THE READING PROCESS

As students write the story of their reading, they talk about their reading process (how they read and reread and what caused them to do so); their response to the books now, in childhood, or in some comparison of the two times; and their reactions to books—favorable or unfavorable. The more favorable the response, the greater the likelihood the student will revisit the book, as Tara shows us in the next passage. The descriptive report arises from the students' journal entries. To write it, students dip into their journals and pull out responses they wrote as they were reading their way through the course; then they weave these responses into a descriptive account of their reading in its entirety.

> I really enjoyed reading *Alice's Adventures in Wonderland* again. When I was a little girl, my mother read it to me dozens of times. I can still remember what my mother's copy of the book looked like. It was a red hardcover book with a Wiliamsburg blue binder. The words *Alice's Adventures in Wonderland* were written in cursive on a black label in gold ink. I don't even know if my mother still has the book. It may have fallen apart after all these years.
>
> The only part of the book that I remembered from my childhood was the section when Alice went down the rabbit's hole. I remember being fascinated by her growing and shrinking, depending on whether she ate the cake or drank the potion. Maybe this fascinated me so much because I was always very small for my age. I was always the shortest child in the class in elementary school. I guess the idea of eating or drinking something to make me tall really appealed to me. If foods and drinks like those that Alice found existed in real life, I could have been the tallest person in my class.
>
> Another thing that I remember from my youth about *Alice's Adventures in Wonderland* is the pictures. Before I could actually read, I used to look through the book myself and pretend to read it. I imagine that I used the pictures of the book to assist me in retelling the story myself. Two pictures of the book stand out for me. I remember these two pictures vividly from my childhood. One is the picture of Alice looking at the bottle which said "Drink me." I don't know why these two pictures have stayed with me through all of these years, but they have. Thinking back to this reading of the book, I honestly cannot remember more than two pictures other than these two. I can think of no reason for this. Maybe my initial reactions to "Alice" are so strong that they interfere with my ability to create new reactions to the book.
>
> Many students commented in class that they disliked the book. I, on the other hand, enjoyed it. Perhaps this is due to an early exposure to the book. I can honestly say that this book has as much appeal to me today as it had for me eighteen years ago. (Tara)

ANNOTATED LIST OF CHILDREN'S BOOKS

As students produce an annotated list of books for a classroom collection, they may reveal ideas or understandings about books that they discovered simply from reading the books. They might interview classroom teachers. They might try them out with children, as David read *Alice's Adventures in Wonderland* to his young brothers. They might remember the book from childhood as Tara did. They might have ideas about how they would use the book in their own classroom teaching. They might write only a paragraph with some books and go into much greater detail with others. The important thing is that they tell something about why the book would be a good addition to a classroom collection. (Why is this book too good for children to miss? Why do I want this book in my collection?)

INVESTIGATIVE PROJECTS

As students write up a report of their project work, they respond—either within the report itself or on a Project Self-Assessment Form—to four questions:

1. What did you do? (What were you curious about as you began your study or as things progressed?)
2. How did you go about finding an answer?
3. What answer, conclusion, insight, or understanding did you finally come up with?
4. What do you want to know about now? (What would you do to extend this project, in order to learn more?)

Before submitting their work, students evaluate it in six categories: **focus, organization, details, insight, clarity of writing style,** and **proofreading,** giving themselves either a check, a check minus, or a check plus for each of the categories.

The way students check off these categories tells the instructor and peers where the writer feels uneasy—and, therefore, where the writer wants or needs feedback. "*Seems* to be working ok" says "I'm not really sure; what do *you* think?" Usually writers' instincts are good; they simply need a way to risk asking for input. When everything is working—or working well—the student is ready to place that project into the portfolio. Projects need to have all categories marked as either "check" or "check plus" to be considered *completed*

PROJECT SELF-ASSESSMENT FORM

1. **Question or Idea:**
2. **Procedure or Process:**
3. **Discoveries:**
4. **New Question or New Idea:**

Category	**check minus (needs more work)**	**check (seems to be working ok)**	**check plus (working well)**
Focus:			
Organization:			
Details:			
Insight:			
Clarity of Writing:			
Proofreading:			

Comments:

projects. Students receive guidelines about what these categories mean to help them determine whether they have earned a check or check plus.

We will look at Sandy's study of a preschooler's responses to Margaret Wise Brown's *Goodnight Moon* (Harper, 1947) as she and five-year-old Melissa read this picture book together. Then we will see Amy studying her own and her father's responses to E. B. White's *Charlotte's Web* (Harper, 1952) in a collaborative rereading of this novel. Sandy answers the four questions— what she did, how she proceeded, what she discovered, and what she would do next—within her report; Amy answers the questions on a self-assessment form.

Sandy's Investigation

While I was visiting the Head Start Center, I observed Melissa, age five. The following is an account of our conversation as I transcribed it:

Sandy: I thought it might be more fun for you to show me your favorite book at school. Is there a book you really like?

Melissa: Saying Goodnight to the Moon.

Sandy: Is this the book?

Melissa: That's it! That's it! Can I hold the book? I know when to turn the pages. Wait till you see the pictures. They're beautiful. (She turns to the next page.) See his [the bunny's] beautiful room. There's the red balloon. My mom got me one just like that at the store with hearts on it. I keep it on my doll bed. Start reading!

Sandy: "In the great green room there was a telephone and a red balloon."

Melissa: "And a picture of the cow jumping over the moon. And there were three little bears sitting on chairs."

Sandy: "And two little kittens and a pair of mittens."

Melissa: "Pair of mittens."

Sandy: "And a comb and a brush and a bowl full of mush."

PROJECT ASSESSMENT CATEGORIES

Focus: The reader needs to know what the project is all about. What were you doing? What one idea were you exploring? What questions were you trying to answer? What answer did you find?

Organization: The project, as it is written up, needs to move forward easily in some clear ordering of ideas. First this happened . . . then . . . finally.

Details: The piece needs to be filled out so that readers see just exactly what you thought, felt, saw, discovered—or exactly what happened. Check to see if you have left gaps or blank spaces that need to be filled in. If you are writing a fiction story as your project, you may want to leave gaps to stimulate the reader's imagination. Still, you will need background details to fill in the story "picture." If you are writing a nonfiction report, you will want to fill in as many gaps as possible.

Insight: Readers want to learn something from what you have written. The more they can learn, the better. You will be pursuing your inquiry as far as you can to get some results, to come to some conclusions, or to help readers see something more clearly.

Clarity of writing: Sentences should make sense. Try to rid your work of ambiguities, unclear and awkward phrasing, and repetitions.

Proofreading: Check for errors in spelling, punctuation, legibility, and typos.

Melissa: "A bowl full of mush."

Sandy: "And a quiet old lady whispering hush."

Melissa: (points to picture and puts finger over her lip and whispers) Hush, wush, hush, brush. (turns page)

Sandy: "Goodnight room; Goodnight moon."

Melissa: "Goodnight moon, goodnight stars, goodnight window."

Sandy: "Goodnight cow jumping over the moon" . . . (reads to "And goodnight to the old lady whispering hush" with Melissa reading along).

Melissa: See how dark it's getting, he's going to sleep. Wait till the book's real dark and he'll go to sleep. The only light is the fire. I have a Mickey Mouse light that is on when I sleep. He doesn't. He has a fire. I don't want a fire at my house. It hurts. But it's ok, his mommy is watching him" (turns page)

Sandy: "Goodnight stars."

In unison: "Goodnight air."

Melissa: "Goodnight stars."

In unison: "Goodnight air."

Melissa: (turns page) See how dark it is, he's sleeping. Hush. His mommy stopped sewing and went to bed, too.

Sandy: "Goodnight noises everywhere."

Melissa: "Goodnight noises everywhere." Goodnight books, goodnight moon, goodnight stars, stars are so beautiful, goodnight air, goodnight house, goodnight sheets and goodnight, goodnight. Shhh, he's sleeping.

According to her teacher, Melissa was a girl who enjoyed all types of books. I was interested in analyzing why this one book attracted her more than others. After completing the story, I talked with Melissa for a few minutes. She said her favorite part of the story was the bowl full of mush. "It's yucky. It's silly. Everything's silly—the house and the mouse—the house, goodnight comb and goodnight brush." I asked Melissa what she says before she goes to sleep. She told me she says her prayers and says goodnight to the moon, stars, sheets, and air. Then her mom reads her a story.

The language style provided Melissa with a fun-filled game of words. The rhyming words made it easy for her to predict what would be next. She enjoyed pointing to the objects mentioned in the story. These were familiar items in her own life. She thought the pictures were beautiful with bright, bold colors. The alternating black and white drawings were just as acceptable to her. Since the book was first published, many styles have changed. But this was the only book Melissa noticed or mentioned. Art style, language or word sounds, setting, theme of saying goodnight, and characters (humanized rabbits—mother and child) were important for creating her enthusiasm. It was a joy to see Melissa excited about this book. I want to repeat this same activity with her to see if she makes the same kind of responses, and I want to talk to her mother to learn more about her interest in this book.

Amy's Investigation

Amy decided to correspond with her father and compare his responses to one of her favorite children's books with her own responses. Her self-assessment form gives us an advance organizer for her study, which is composed of an introduction and the letters themselves.

Excerpts from Amy's letters:

And a quiet old lady who was whispering "hush"

From *Goodnight Moon* (Harper, 1947) by Margaret Wise Brown.

Dear Dad,

. . . I recently finished *Charlotte's Web.* My reaction—I love it! What is your opinion? Why do you think this book has attracted so many readers throughout time? I think E. B. White gives each character a heart and soul, and no one can help being touched by these characters. Of course, my favorite character was Wilbur because of his simple, modest nature. The poor thing had to suffer the humiliation of being dressed up—bonnet included. Who was your favorite character?

I can remember my first experience with *Charlotte's Web.* I believe you read the story to me long before I ever could have done so on my own. I loved the book then, and I love the book now. As a child I took the story line literally . . . placing myself in Fern's position of raising and falling in love with a pet . . . Now I look at the story line from a much different perspective. I still see myself as Fern, but I see you and Mom as Wilbur, too. During my younger years we spent endless hours together, like Fern and Wilbur did. Now that I have "grown up" I have distanced myself from home. I know that the love and caring still exists, but I have moved toward friends and sorority, just as Fern found her love at the fair and seemed to somehow forget Wilbur.

Love,
Amy

Dear Amy,

. . . I, too, recently finished reading *Charlotte's Web* for my umpteenth time. I've read it to my class or showed the video so many times I've lost count, but each year the reaction of my students is quite predictable. They laugh, they cry, they sit in silence. The reason I feel that this book has attracted so many for so long is that

AMY'S PROJECT SELF-ASSESSMENT FORM

1. Question (What did you want to know?)

I wanted to study a favorite book from childhood. I reread *Charlotte's Web* and asked my father to do the same. We then began corresponding about the book, and through a series of letters, discovered why we enjoyed the book so much. My main question was what makes *Charlotte's Web* such a loved book and why did I love it as a child, compared to why I love the book now.

2. Procedure (How did you go about finding an answer?)

I started the project by writing a letter to my father. In the first letter I gave suggestions about why I might have loved the book so much as a child. I asked for my father's reactions to my thoughts. He then wrote back to me and together we attempted to find the answer. We wrote to each other a few more times. I feel that with each letter we made more progress toward the answer.

3. Discovery (What did you finally come up with as an answer?)

Together we decided that my love for the book as a child probably resulted from a relation to some character within the story. I think that as an adult I like the book for the same reason, but now I relate to a different character.

4. New Question (What do you want to know more about now?)

I wonder if all of E. B. White's books have a similar effect on children and adults. I realize that *Charlotte's Web* is the most popular, but does *Stuart Little* intrigue people as much as *Charlotte's Web?* To extend the project further, I could have children read the E. B. White collection and see their reactions to the less popular books. I could again correspond with my father on this aspect. He could use the books in his classroom.

	check minus (needs more work)	**check (working)**	**check plus (working well)**
Focus			+
Organization			+
Details			+
Insight			+
Clarity			+
Proofreading			+

Comments:

For this project I decided to reread one of my favorite childhood books, *Charlotte's Web,* and have my father do the same. We then planned on corresponding about what attracted us to the book. I chose my father for this project because he is an elementary teacher and has used *Charlotte's Web* many times in his classroom. Because he has read the book so many times, I assumed that he would be able to think about intriguing aspects of the book. I wrote the first letter. I asked many questions and gave my opinions. Anxiously awaiting a reply, I wondered how my father's opinions would differ or agree with my own. I could not wait to hear his own insight. I was quite happy as I wrote and as I received two letters. My father really put himself into the project, and I was extremely pleased with the outcome. We ended up discussing specifics of the story and how to incorporate the book into the classroom too. I think this will benefit me in the future. I cannot thank my father enough for his help.

the innocence and gentle love personifies everyone's dream. Also, each person reading it can identify with Wilbur or Fern or some character in the story.

You asked what difference do I see in you loving the book as a child and now. As with all great literature, each time you read it a new and wonderful message comes across. Perhaps it depends upon a present life situation or some past memory or a futuristic dream. Now you have grown into a well-rounded person with enough experiences to relate to the story from your past, your present, and your future dreams.

You mentioned that now, grown up, you have distanced yourself from home as Fern did. . . . I'm sure Fern would always love and care for Wilbur, but Wilbur's becoming the loving adopted father of Charlotte's children and able to take care of himself and others is the goal that Fern unconsciously wanted to accomplish when she first stopped her father from doing away with Wilbur.

Love ya,
Dad

Dear Dad,

. . . You mentioned that you've shown the video and read the book numerous times in your classroom. One new question that pops into my mind after reading your letter is as a teacher. Which do you feel children enjoy more? Do you ever use a combination of the two? I feel that children probably enjoy seeing the animator's version of the characters and visualizing the facial expressions. . . . By reading the book after viewing the video, they would understand more of Templeton's sarcasm.

. . . I decided that perhaps you and Mom could relate even better to Charlotte than Wilbur. Charlotte was such an ego-booster for Wilbur. I have received much of my self-confidence from you. In many ways you both have spun TERRIFIC in your web and made me feel I actually was special . . .

Love,
Amy

Dear Amy,

You asked about the children's reaction to hearing and seeing *Charlotte's Web.* Well, each group of children you have in a class develops its own personality. When watching the video, some groups—well, perhaps all groups—are reacting to being entertained, whereas when I read the story, usually a chapter per day, I can see some in-depth thinking. I prefer to read it in my class. I've never tried the combination of both, but perhaps one of these years, I will do that.

You brought up an interesting idea when you suggested that Mom and I might relate to Charlotte more than Wilbur . . . Remember Charlotte watched Wilbur try to spin a web even though she knew he might fail. Charlotte was very lucky in that the lessons she taught Wilbur, he learned and remembered. . . . In time Charlotte's little insignificant cocoon became the center of Wilbur's life . . . and his true joy was caring for and nurturing the needs of others.

I'm looking forward to the future knowing that you, too, will be a great Wilbur because you and your brother are our "Magnum Opus."

Love ya,
Dad

It is not surprising that Amy submitted her collaborative study of *Charlotte's Web* in the "Best Project" category. Together, she and her father attempted to find the answer to her question—and they discovered so much else in the process, as they continued to exchange ideas about the book.

Another collaboration arose in the children's book that Vinny wrote for his younger brother during the Thanksgiving holidays when he was recovering from the extraction of his wisdom teeth. Vinny saw the book as his "best project" because the book was special: His brother, Mark, gave him the idea for the story, and he, in turn, gave the story to his brother as a Christmas present a few weeks later. Vinny's response partners received a sneak preview of the book just before the holidays. As they listened, Vinny told the story-behind-the-story of his project. In doing so, he responded to the four questions student writers ask themselves, or one another, when they have chosen to create a children's book of their own:

1. How did the idea first come to you?
2. What was your creative process? (How did you proceed?)
3. What ideas were you exploring and discovering?
4. If you did more with this work, what would you do?

Here is Vinny's story:

My brother called me "Fat Fox" (my cheeks were all swollen up after having my wisdom teeth out). I couldn't go out; couldn't leave the house. I was lying around the house, eating too much ice cream. Soon I wouldn't be able to fit through the door. So I wrote a story about a character called "Fat Fox." It reads like this *[he reads aloud and shows the pictures]:*

Fat Fox (Illustration 1: Cover Picture)

by Vincent Mikkelsen II

One day, Fox and a few friends decided to go for a picnic. (Illustration 2) Fox brought his lunch bag. Big Bear brought a crock of honey. Fred the Frog brought his jar of flies. Rabbit brought fine vegetables, and Beaver brought some of his tastiest fish. (Illustration 3) Just as Bear began to taste his honey, Fox exclaimed, "Not until we say grace!" Then while everyone prayed, Fox grabbed the food and ran. "Sorry to dine and dash, but see ya later!" explained Fox. (Illustrations 4 and 5)

When Fox got home, he ate everything, even Fred's flies. (Illustration 6) Of course, as you would expect, his friends were furious. They went to Fox's den and told him never to come out. Their friendship was over! (Illustration 7) Little did they know, but their wish was already granted. Fox was so fat he couldn't fit through the hole to his den. (Illustration 8) So for weeks, all Fox did was watch TV and sleep.

Eventually, Bear and Beaver came to Fox's den to tell him he was forgiven. They felt really bad making him stay indoors all through the fall. Now winter had come and Bear couldn't even sleep, he was so down in the dumps. (Illustration 9) What the animals didn't know was that Fox would have come out months ago. He just couldn't fit! But now FAT fox had an incentive.

He exercised with vigor. Running, jumping rope, sit-ups, you name it, Fox did it. (Illustration 10) Eventually Fat Fox was thin again and went to visit his friends. (Illustration 11) Although his friends were glad to see him, they laughed at his situation. "Why didn't you just ask me to get you out?" the Beaver asked. "I got Rabbit out of his burrow once when he ate too much." (Illustration 12) Fox felt so stupid. He had put himself to so much trouble. But he was glad to be on good terms with all of his friends. And all was well once again. (Illustration 13)

From *Fat Fox* by Vincent Mikkelsen.

To get started, I drew 7 to 8 different characters. I knew I could draw a frog, so I drew a frog first. I said, Fat Fox ate the frog's flies, and that's how I worked the frog in. I just used the animal with the corresponding food. Just as a frog eats flies, a bear eats honey. I start out drawing the characters and worked them into the story, so the pictures came first. The story grew out of the pictures.

There are two ideas in the story. There is gluttony and stealing—or maybe three—Fox thought he didn't need anyone. He stole his friend's food and ate too much. When he couldn't get back out the door, he realized he needed his friends' help, but he had lost the friends. I suppose on some unconscious level, I was remembering Winnie-the-Pooh. (Pooh gets wedged in his door and can't get out.) Or there might be four ideas. He needed his friends, but he never really lost his autonomy; he had to rely on himself to lose the weight. I wanted him to have some autonomy. He needed his friends' help, but he needed to help himself, too.

If I worked on it more, I might try writing a new story, something that doesn't have any connection to the Pooh story—nothing about weight gain, no problem getting out of a door. And I'd make the pictures better—take more time to develop them. I'm making them darker now. I'd say it's working well at this point. The important thing for me is if the person you write it for likes it—if it works for them—once you get it to work the way you want it to work. With something like this, you either like it or you don't; it works or it doesn't. If I didn't like it, I wouldn't give it as a gift. You can't rate something you make one to ten, good or not good. It depends on *you* and how you feel about what you've done.

INVESTIGATIONS: Making A Literature and Literacies Portfolio

Consider making your own portfolio. Decide what you will place into it. You might have been keeping a journal, jotting down responses to the children's books you were reading. You might want to write a report describing the journey of your reading. You might also want to produce an annotated list of books you would want for your classroom collection someday. And you might have been working on projects—investigations such as those that appear in the chapters, or some you have designed for yourself. If you have completed some projects, you might want to choose one that you think is your best, deciding what *your* criteria are for making that choice.

You might have been working on only one or two long-term projects or three to five short-term investigative projects. In either case, you will probably want to let others know, either in a question-answer form or within the discussion itself:

- What were you curious about? How did your idea come to you?
- How did you go about finding an answer to your questions? What was your creative process?
- What did you finally come up with as an answer or insight? What ideas were you exploring?
- What do you want to know about—or do—now as follow-up? What are you curious about *now*?

You might also want to include some form of self-assessment so that you are part of the evaluation process. How do you feel the project is working at this point? How can you tell if it is working? What would need to happen for you to feel that the project is complete—and working well?

You might place into your portfolio anything else that you choose. What are some possible portfolio entries you would add? What would indicate to others—or to you, someday looking back at these artifacts—how you are growing in your literature and literacies process?

Consider how you might want to assess your portfolio when you have completed it. What will your criteria for assessment be? What percentage of your grade will the portfolio comprise?

References

Adoff, Arnold. 1986. "Politics, Poetry, and Teaching Children: A Personal Journey." *Lion and the Unicorn* 10: 9–14.

———. 1992. Visit to East Pike Elementary School; videotape of the Author's Workshop; 21 April.

Aiken, Joan. 1997. "Joan Aiken." *Books Remembered: Nurturing the Budding Writer.* Lisa Mahmoud, editor. New York: Children's Book Council, pp. 18–22.

Alderson, Brian. 1975. "Postscript to the 1975 Edition." *The Blue Fairy Book.* Andrew Lang, author; Brian Alderson, editor. New York: Penguin, pp. 359–63.

Aoki, Elaine. 1993. "Turning the Page: Asian Pacific American Children's Literature." *Teaching Multicultural Literature in Grades K–8.* Violet Harris, editor. Norwood, MA: Christopher-Gordon, pp. 109–35.

Aries, Philippe. 1960. *Centuries of Childhood.* New York: Penguin.

Aronson, Marc. 1993. "Letters to the Editor." *Horn Book* (July/August): 390–91.

Ashton-Warner, Sylvia. 1963. *Teacher.* New York: Simon & Schuster.

Atwell, Nancie. 1998. *In the Middle.* Portsmouth, NH: Heinemann, (rpt. 1987).

———. 1984. "Writing and Reading Literature from the Inside Out." *Language Arts* 61 (March): 240–53.

Bader, Barbara. 1976. *American Picturebooks from Noah's Ark to the Beast Within.* New York: Macmillan.

———. 1997. "Only the Best." *Horn Book* (September/October): 520–28.

Baring-Gould, William, and Baring-Gould, Ceil. 1962. *The Annotated Mother Goose.* New York: Bramhall House.

Barrera, R. 1993. "Ideas a Literature Can Grow On: Key Insights for Enriching and Expanding Children's Literature about the Mexican-American Experience." *Teaching Multicultural Literature in Grades K–8.* Violet Harris, editor. Norwood, MA: Christopher-Gordon, pp. 203–41.

Barthes, Roland. 1974. *S/Z: An Essay.* Translated by Richard Miller. New York: Farrar.

———. 1985. "On *S/Z* and *Empire of Signs.*" *The Grain of the Voice: Interviews 1962–1980.* Berkeley: University of California Press.

Bawden, Nina. 1976. "A Dead Pig and My Father." *Writers, Critics, and Children.* Geoff Fox, editor. London: Heinemann, pp. 3–14.

———. 1991. "The Outside Child." *Horn Book* (November/December): 688–94.

Bennett, Charles. 1986 (rpt.) *Aesop's Fables.* London: Bracken Books.

Bishop, Rudine. 1987. "Extending Multicultural Understanding Through Children's Books." *Children's Literature in the Reading Program.* Bernice Cullinan, editor. Newark, DE: International Reading Association, pp. 60–67.

———. 1997. "Foreward." *Reading Across Cultures: Teaching Literature in a Diverse Society.* Theresa Rogers and Anna Soter, editors. New York: Teachers College Press, pp. vii–x.

Blake, William. 1946. *The Portable Blake.* New York: Viking.

Bond, Nancy. 1984. "Conflict in Children's Fiction." *Horn Book* (June): 297–306.

Bosmajian, Hamida. 1996. "Children's Literature and Censorship." *Paradoxa* 2: 313–17.

Briggs, Julia. 1995. "Transitions (1890–1914)." *Children's Literature: An Illustrated History.* Peter Hunt, editor. New York: Oxford University Press, pp. 167–91.

Briggs, Katharine. 1970. *British Folktales.* New York: Pantheon.

Brown, Sterling. 1933. "Negro Character as Seen by White Authors." *Journal of Negro Education* 2: 179–203.

Bruchac, Joseph. 1995. "All Our Relations." *Horn Book* (November/December): 158–62.

———. 1997. *Bowman's Store: A Journey to Myself.* New York: Dial.

Burnett, Frances Hodgson. 1987. *A Little Princess* (rpt. 1905). New York: Bantam.

Cai, Mingshui. 1997. "Reader-Response Theory and the Politics of Multicultural Literature." *Reading Across Cultures.* Theresa Rogers and Anna Soter, editors. New York: Teachers College Press, pp. 199–212.

Cai, Mingshui, and Sims, Rudine. 1994. "Multicultural Literature for Children: Towards a Clarification of the Concept." *The Need for Story.* Anne Haas Dyson and Celia Genishi, editors. Urbana, IL: National Council of Teachers of English, pp. 57–72.

Calkins, Lucy. 1983. *Lessons from a Child.* Portsmouth, NH: Heinemann.

———. 1991. *Living Between the Lines.* Portsmouth, NH: Heinemann.

Calvino, Italo. 1986. *The Uses of Literature.* Patrick Creagh, translator. San Diego: Harcourt Brace.

Cambourne, Brian. 1992. *Whole Language Strategies That Build Student Literacy.* Torrance, CA: The Education Centre.

Campbell, Patty. 1997. "Review: Brock Cole." *Horn Book* (November/December): 678–79.

Carpenter, Humphrey. 1989. "Excessively Impertinent Bunnies: The Subversive Element in Beatrix Potter." *Children and Their Books.* Gillian Avery and Julia Briggs, editors. Oxford, England: Clarendon Press, pp. 271–98.

Carroll, Lewis. 1981. *Alice's Adventures in Wonderland* and *Through the Looking-Glass* (rpt. 1865–66). New York: Bantam Books.

———. 1988. *Alice's Adventures in Wonderland* (rpt. 1896). Illustrated by Anthony Brown. New York: Knopf.

Chambers, Aidan. 1993a. "Pick Up A Penguin." *Signal 70* (January): 13–27.

———. 1993b. *Tell Me.* South Woodchester, England: Thimble Press.

Chapman, Diane. 1985. "Poet to Poet: An Author Responds to Child-Writers." *Language Arts* 62 (March): 235–43.

Cianciolo, Patricia. 1983. "A Look at the Illustrations in Children's Favorite Picture Books." *Children's Choices: Teaching with Books Children Like.* Nancy Roser and Margaret Frith, editors. Newark, DE: International Reading Association, pp. 27–38.

Clay, Marie. 1985. *The Early Detection of Reading Difficulties,* 3d edition. Auckland, New Zealand: Heinemann.

———. 1991. "Reading Recovery Surprises." *Bridges to Literacy.* Diane DeFord, Carol Lyons, and Gay Su Pinnell, editors. Portsmouth, NH: Heinemann, pp. 55–76.

Cleary, Beverly. 1982. "The Laughter of Children." *Horn Book* (October): 555–64.

———. 1975. "Laura Ingalls Wilder Award Acceptance." *Horn Book* (August): 361–64.

———. 1995. *My Own Two Feet: A Memoir.* New York: Morrow.

Close, Elizabeth. 1990. "Seventh Graders Sharing Literature." *Language Arts* 67 (December): 817–23.

COOPER, SUSAN. 1976. "Address Delivered at the Children's Round Table Breakfast." *Texas Library Journal* (May): 52–54.

———. 1996. *Dreams and Wishes: Essays on Writing for Children.* New York: McElderry Books.

COTT, JONATHAN. 1983. *Pipers at the Gates of Dawn.* New York: Random House.

COX, SUSAN. 1989. "A Word or Two with Eve Merriam: Talking About Poetry." *New Advocate* (Summer): 139–50.

CULLINAN, BERNICE. 1989. *Literature and the Child,* 2d edition. San Diego: Harcourt Brace.

CUNDALL, THOMAS. 1970. "The Three Bears" (rpt. 1856). *British Folktales.* Katharine Briggs, editor. New York: Pantheon, pp. 108–10.

CURTIS, CHRISTOPHER PAUL. 1997. "Children's Books." *New York Times Book Review* (22 June): 22.

DASENBROCK, REED WAY. 1987. "Intelligibility and Meaningfulness in Multicultural Literature in English." *Publications of the Modern Language Association* 102 (January): 10–19.

DE FINA, ALLAN. 1992. *Portfolio Assessment.* New York: Scholastic.

DENNISTON, ROBIN. 1993. "A Children's Book Publisher of the Fifties." *Signal* 70 (January): 46–52.

DILLON, DAVID. 1988. "Dear Readers." *Language Arts* 65 (October): 535–36.

DOONAN, JANE. 1994. "Into the Dangerous World." *Signal* 75 (September): 155–71.

———. 1993. *Looking at Pictures in Picture Books.* South Woodchester, England: Thimble Press.

DORRIS, MICHAEL. 1995. "Waiting to Listen." *Horn Book* (November/December): 698–703.

DYSON, ANNE. 1995. "The Courage to Write: Child Meaning-Making in a Contested World." *Language Arts* 72 (September): 324–33.

EDELSKY, CAROLE; ALTWERGER, BESS; AND FLORES, BARBARA. 1991. *Whole Language: What's the Difference?* Portsmouth, NH: Heinemann.

EGAN, TIMOTHY. 1998. "An Indian Without Reservations." *New York Times Magazine* (18 January): 16–19.

EGOFF, SHEILA. 1979. "Beyond the Garden Wall: Some Observations on Current Trends in Children's Literature." May Hill Arbuthnot Honor Lecture. Chicago: American Library Association.

ENCISCO, PATRICIA. 1997. "Negotiating the Meaning of Difference: Talking Back to Multicultural Literature." *Reading Across Cultures.* Theresa Rogers and Anna Soter, editors. New York: Teachers College Press, pp. 13–41.

ERNST, SHIRLEY. 1995. "Gender Issues in Books for Children and Young Adults." *Battling Dragons: Issues and Controversy in Children's Literature.* Susan Lehr, editor. Portsmouth NH: Heinemann, pp. 66–78.

FEELINGS, TOM. 1985. "The Artist At Work: Technique and the Artist's Vision." *Horn Book* (November/December): 685–95.

FISH, STANLEY. 1980. *Is There a Text in This Class?* Cambridge, MA: Harvard University Press.

FISHER, MARGERY. 1986. *Classics for Children and Young People.* Stroud, England: Thimble Press.

———. 1992. "Stories from a Victorian Nursery." *Signal* 69 (September): 176–89.

FOX, MEM. 1992. *Dear Mem Fox.* San Diego: Harcourt.

FRANK, ANNE. 1967. *Anne Frank: The Diary of a Young Girl.* B. M. Mooyaart, translator. New York: Doubleday.

———. 1983. *Anne Frank's Tales from the Secret Annex.* New York: Doubleday.

FREEDMAN, RUSSELL. 1995. "Eleanor Roosevelt." *Horn Book* (January/February): 33–36.

———. 1992. "Why I Voted for Lincoln and Roosevelt." *Horn Book* (November/December): 688–93.

FRIERE, PAULO. 1973. *Education for Critical Consciousness.* New York: Continuum.

Fry, Don. 1985. *Children Talk About Books: Seeing Themselves as Readers.* Philadelphia: Open University Press.

Gherman, Beverly. 1992. *E. B. White: Some Writer.* New York: Atheneum.

Goodman, Kenneth. 1969. "Analysis of Oral Reading Miscues: Applied Psycholinguistics." *Reading Research Quarterly* 5: 9–30.

———. 1986. *What's Whole in Whole Language?* Portsmouth, NH: Heinemann.

Graham, Judith. 1990. *Pictures on the Page.* Sheffield, England: National Association of Teaching of English.

Graves, Donald, and Sunstein, Bonnie. 1992. *Portfolio Portraits.* Portsmouth, NH: Heinemann.

Graves, Donald. 1989. *Experiment with Fiction.* Portsmouth, NH: Heinemann.

———. 1989. *Investigate Nonfiction.* Portsmouth, NH: Heinemann.

Griffith, John. 1993. *Charlotte's Web: A Pig's Salvation.* New York: Twayne.

Guice, Sherry and Angelis, Janet. 1998. "Integrating Curriculum: Review of the Literature." *English Update.* The Center on English Learning & Achievement, Judith Langer, director. University of Albany (Fall): 4–5.

Haley, Gail. 1982. "Everyman Jack and the Green Man." *Proceedings of the Ninth Annual Conference of the Children's Literature Association.* University of Florida (March): 1–19.

———. 1986. "From the Ananse Stories to the Jack Tales: My Work with Folktales." *Children's Literature Association Quarterly* 11 (Fall): 118–21.

———. 1990. "Of Mermaids, Myths, and Meaning: A Sea Tale." *New Advocate* (Winter): 1–12.

Hamilton, Virginia. 1992. "A Toiler, A Teller." *Many Faces, Many Voices: Multicultural Literary Experiences for Youth: The Virginia Hamilton Conference.* Anthony Manna and Carolyn Brodie, editors. Fort Atkinson, WI: Highsmith Press, pp. 1–8.

———. 1984. "Boston Globe-Horn Book Award Acceptance." *Horn Book* (February): 24–28.

———. 1993. "May Hill Arbuthnot Honor Lecture: Everything of Value—Moral Realism in Literature for Children." *Journal of Youth Services in Libraries.* 6 (Summer): 363–78.

———. 1986. "On Being a Black Writer in America." *Lion and the Unicorn* 10: 15–17.

Hampl, Patricia. 1994. "Once Upon a Time in Prague." *New York Times Book Review* (13 November): 34.

Hanford, S. A., translator. 1954. *Fables of Aesop.* New York: Penguin.

Harding, D. W. 1977. "Ways Forward for the Teacher: Making Way for the Child's Own Feeling Comprehension.' " *The Cool Web.* Margaret Meek, Aiden Warlow, Griselda Barton, editors. London: The Bodley Head, pp. 379–92.

Harris, Violet. 1993. "Contemporary Griots: African-American Writers of Children's Literature." *Teaching Multicultural Literature in Grades K–8.* Violet Harris, editor. Norwood, MA: Christopher-Gordon, pp. 55–108.

Harris, Wendell. 1991. "Canonicity." *Publications of the Modern Language Association* 106 (January):110–21.

Hart-Hewins, Linda, and Wells, Jan. 1990. *Real Books for Reading: Learning to Read with Children's Literature.* Portsmouth, NH: Heinemann.

———. 1992. *Read It in the Classroom! Organizing an Interactive Language Arts Program, Grades 4–9.* Portsmouth, NH: Heinemann.

Harste, Jerome, and Short, Kathy. 1988. *Creating Classrooms for Authors.* Portsmouth, NH: Heinemann.

Harwayne, Shelley. 1992. *Lasting Impressions.* Portsmouth, NH: Heinemann.

Haugen, Tormod. 1990. "Acceptance Speech." *Proceedings: Literacy Through Literature: Children's Books Make a Difference.* Williamsburg, VA: International Board on Books for Young People, pp. 70–73.

Heath, Shirley Brice. 1986. "Separating 'Things of the Imagination' from Life: Learning to Read and Write." *Emergent Literacy: Writing and Reading.* William Teale, Elizabeth Sulzby, editors. Norwood, NJ: Ablex.

———. 1983. *Ways with Words.* New York: Cambridge University Press.

HEINS, PAUL. 1976. "Children's Classics; Recommended Editions." *Children's Classics.* Alice Jordan, author. Boston: Horn Book.

HELLER, PHILIP. 1992. "Allen Say: A Scholastic Author Tape." New York: Scholastic.

HENDRY, DIANA, BICKNELL, STEPHEN, AND WILSON, JENNIFER. "The Signal Poetry Award." *Signal* 71 (May): 71–93.

HENKES, KEVIN. 1992. "The Artist at Work." *Horn Book* (January/February): 38–47.

HICKMAN, JANET. 1996. "The Long Road to Jericho." *Horn Book* (January/February): 50–57.

HILL, BONNIE. 1995. "Literature Circles: Assessment and Evaluation." *Literature Circles and Response.* Bonnie Hill, Nancy Johnson, Katherine Noe, editors. Norwood, MA: Christopher-Gorden, pp. 167–98.

HILTON, MARY. 1989. "Stories and Remembering." *Collaboration and Writing.* Morag Styles, editor. Philadelphia: Open University Press, pp. 178–92.

HOFFMAN, HEINRICH. 1987. "Struwwelpeter" (rpt.1845). *A Children's Garden of Delights.* The New York Public Library and Bernard McTigue, editors. New York: Harry Abrams, 1987.

HOLDAWAY, DON. 1979. *The Foundations of Literacy.* New York: Ashton Scholastic.

HOLQUIST, MICHAEL. 1994. "Introduction. Corrupt Originals: The Pardox of Censorship." *Publications of the Modern Language Association* 109 (January): 14–25.

HOLLAND, NORMAN. 1975. *Five Readers Reading.* New Haven, CT: Yale University Press.

HOLLINDALE, PETER. 1988. "Ideology and the Children's Book." *Signal* 55 (January): 3–22.

HUCK, CHARLOTTE. 1982. "I Give You the End of a Golden String." *Theory Into Practice* 21 (Autumn): 315–21.

———. 1977. "Literature as the Content of Reading." *Theory Into Practice.* 16 (December): 363–71.

HUCK, CHARLOTTE AND KERSTETTER, KERSTIN. 1987. "Developing Readers." *Children's Literature in the Reading Program.* Bernice Cullinan, editor. Newark, DE: International Reading Association, pp. 30–40.

HUCK, CHARLOTTE, HEPLER, SUSAN, HICKMAN, JANET, AND KIEFER, BARBARA. *Children's Literature in the Elementary School.* Sixth Edition. Madison, WI: Brown & Benchmark, 1997.

HUNT, PETER. 1995. *Children's Literature: An Illustrated History.* New York: Oxford University Press.

INGLIS, FRED. 1981. *The Promise of Happiness: Value and Meaning in Children's Fiction.* New York: Cambridge University Press.

ISER, WOLFGANG. 1978. *The Act of Reading: A Theory of Aesthetic Response.* Baltimore: Johns Hopkins University Press.

———. 1974. *The Implied Reader.* Baltimore: Johns Hopkins University Press.

JAMES, CARYN. 1994. " 'Little Women' and the Cult of Jo." *New York Times Book Review* (25 December): 3, 17.

JENSEN, JULIE, AND HAWKINS, ROBERT. 1983. "Writing by Children for Children." *Children's Choices: Teaching with Books Children Like.* Nancy Roser and Margaret Frith, editors. Newark, DE: International Reading Association, pp. 12–26.

JOHNSON, GEORGIA. 1995. "One Sings . . . The Other Doesn't: The Role of Ritual in Stories About Native Americans." *New Advocate* 8 (Spring): 99–108.

JOHNSON, TERRY. 1979. "Presenting Literature to Children." *Children's Literature in Education* (Winter): 35–43.

JONES, LINDA. 1986. "Profile: Elaine Konigsburg." *Language Arts* 63 (February): 177–84.

JORDAN, ALICE. 1947. *Children's Classics:* Boston: The Horn Book.

KAY, JACKIE. 1992. *Two's Company.* Shirley Tourret, illustrator. London: Blackie.

KIEFER, BARBARA. 1983. "The Responses of Children in a Combination First- Second-Grade Classroom to Picture Books in a Variety of Artistic Styles." *Journal of Research and Development in Education* 16 (Spring): 14–20.

Klein, Gillian. 1985. *Reading Into Racism: Bias in Children's Literature and Learning Materials.* London: Routledge.

Konigsburg, Elaine. 1995. *Talk-Talk.* New York: Atheneum.

La Fontaine, Jean de. 1984. *La Fontaine's Fables.* London: Andre Deutsch.

Lamott, Anne. 1994. *Bird by Bird.* New York: Doubleday.

Landes, Sonia. 1985. "Picture Books as Literature." *Children's Literature Association Quarterly* 10 (Summer): 51–54.

Lanes, Selma. 1980. *The Art of Maurice Sendak.* New York: Abrams.

Langer, Judith. 1995. *Envisioning Literature.* New York: Teachers College Press.

———. 1990. "Understanding Literature." *Language Arts* 67 (December): 812–16.

Larrick, Nancy. 1965. "The All White World of Children's Books." *Saturday Review* 48: 63–65; 84–85.

Lasky, Kathryn. 1996. "To Stingo With Love: An Author's Perspective on Writing." *New Advocate* 9 (Winter): 1–8.

Lehr, Susan. 1995. "Wise Women and Warriors." *Battling Dragons.* Susan Lehr, editor. Portsmouth NH: Heinemann, pp. 194–211.

L'Engle, Madeleine. 1987. "Introduction." *A Little Princess* (rpt. 1905). Frances Hodgson Burnett, author. New York: Bantam, pp. v–xii.

Lewis, C. S. 1988. *Letters to Children.* Lyle Dorsett and Marjorie Lamp Mead, editors. New York: Macmillan.

Lewis, David. 1995. "The Jolly Postman's Long Ride, or, Sketching a Picture-Book History." *Signal* 78 (September): 178–92.

Lewis, Naomi. 1981. *Hans Andersen's Fairy Tales.* Naomi Lewis, translator. New York: Puffin.

Lionni, Leo. 1989. "Alexander and the Wind-Up Mouse." *Friends Aloft.* Virginia Arnold and Carl Smith, editors. (Unit I, Caring; 2–2; Reader/Level 7.) New York: Macmillan.

———. 1984. "Before Images" *Horn Book* (November/December): 727–734.

Lind, Michael. 1998. "The Beige and the Black." *The New York Times Magazine* (16 August): 38–39.

Livingston, Myra Cohn. 1990. *Climb into the Bell Tower.* New York: Harper.

MacCann, Donna. 1993. "Native Americans in Books for the Young." *Teaching Multicultural Literature in Grades K–8.* Violet Harris, editor. Norwood, MA: Christopher-Gordon, pp. 137–69.

Machado, Ana Maria. 1990. "Presentation Speech." *Proceedings: Literacy Through Literature: Children's Books Make a Difference.* Williamsburg, VA: International Board on Books for Young People, pp. 62–69.

Mahmoud, Lisa, editor. 1997. *Books Remembered: Nurturing the Budding Writer.* New York: Children's Book Council.

Marcus, Leonard. 1991. "Rearrangement of Memory: An Interview with Allen Say." *Horn Book* (May/June): 295–303.

———. 1994. *75 Years of Children's Book Week Posters.* New York: Knopf.

McConaghy, June. 1990. *Children Learning Through Literature.* Portsmouth, NH: Heinemann.

McDowell, Myles. 1976. "Fiction for Children and Adults: Some Essential Differences." *Writers, Critics, and Children.* Geoff Fox, editor. London: Heinemann, pp. 140–56.

McTigue, Bernard. 1987. *A Child's Garden of Delights.* Bernard McTigue, compiler. New York: Harry Abrams.

Meek, Margaret. 1996. "The Constructedness of Critics." *Signal* 81 (September): 171–88.

———. 1988. *How Texts Teach What Readers Learn.* South Woodchester, England: Thimble Press.

———. 1997. "In Two Minds: Topics and Themes in 'The Natural History of Make-Believe.' " *Signal* 83 (May): 101–14.

———. 1982. *Learning to Read.* London: The Bodley Head.

———. 1987. "Playing the Texts." *Language Matters* 1:1–5.

MEEK, MARGARET; WARLOW, AIDAN; AND BARTON, GRISELDA, EDITORS. 1977. *The Cool Web: The Pattern of Children's Reading.* London: The Bodley Head.

MELTZER, MILTON. 1986. "Notes on Biography." *Children's Literature Association Quarterly* 10 (Winter): 172–74.

MEYER, SUSAN. 1983. *A Treasury of the Great Children's Book Illustrators.* New York: Abrams.

MIKKELSEN, NINA. 1994. "A Conversation with Virginia Hamilton." *Journal of Youth Services in Libraries* 7 (Summer): 392–405.

———. 1995. "Virginia Hamilton: Continuing the Conversation." *New Advocate* 8 (Spring): 67–82.

MILLER, HOWARD. 1997. "Beyond 'Multicultural Moments.' " *English Journal* 86 (September): 88–90.

MOSS, ELAINE. 1977. "The 'Peppermint' Lesson." *The Cool Web: The Pattern of Children's Reading.* Margaret Meek, Aidan Warlow, and Griselda Barton, editors. London: The Bodley Head, pp. 140–42.

MOSS, GEOFF. 1992. "Metafiction, Illustration, and the Poetics." *Literature for Children: Contemporary Criticism.* Peter Hunt, editor. London: Routledge.

MUIR, PERCY. 1954. *English Children's Books, 1600 to 1900.* London: B. T. Batsford.

MYERS, WALTER DEAN. 1986. "I Actually Thought We Would Revolutionize the Industry." *New York Times Book Review,* 9 November: 50.

NAYLOR, PHYLLIS. 1987. *How I Came to be a Writer.* New York: Macmillan.

NIETO, SONIA. 1993. "We Have Stories to Tell: A Case Study of Puerto Ricans in Children's Books." *Teaching Multicultural Literature in Grades K–8.* Violet Harris, editor. Norwood, MA: Christopher Gordon, pp. 171–202.

NILSEN, ALLEEN PACE. 1996. "Focus on Censorship." *Paradoxa* 2: 307–12.

NEUMEYER, PETER. 1982. The Creation of *Charlotte's Web,* Part I." *Horn Book* (October): 489–97.

OPIE, IONA, AND OPIE, PETER. 1974. *The Classic Fairy Tales.* New York: Oxford University Press.

———. 1955. *The Oxford Nursery Rhyme Book.* London: Oxford University Press.

OTTEN, CHARLOTTE. 1992. "An Interview with Maurice Sendak." *Signal* 68 (May): 110–27.

PALEY, VIVIAN. 1990. *The Boy Who Would Be A Helicopter: The Uses of Storytelling in the Classroom.* Cambridge, MA: Harvard University Press.

———. 1997. *The Girl with the Brown Crayon.* Cambridge, MA: Harvard University Press.

———. 1995. *Kwanzaa and Me.* Cambridge, MA: Harvard University Press.

———. 1986. *Mollie is Three.* Chicago: University of Chicago Press, 1986.

———. 1994. "Princess Annabella and the Black Girls." *The Need for Story.* Anne Haas Dyson and Celia Genishi, editors. Urbana, IL: National Council of Teachers of English, pp. 145–54.

———. 1981. *Wally's Stories.* Cambridge, MA: Harvard University Press.

———. 1992. *You Can't Say You Can't Play.* Cambridge, MA: Harvard University Press.

PATERSON, KATHERINE. 1981. *Gates of Excellence.* New York: Dutton.

———. 1997. "Katherine Paterson." *Books Remembered.* Lisa Mahmoud, editor. New York: Children's Book Council, pp. 40–43.

———. 1991. "Living in a Peaceful World." *Horn Book* (January/February): 32–38.

———. 1989a. *The Spying Heart.* New York: Dutton.

———. 1989b. "Tale of a Reluctant Dragon." *New Advocate* 2 (Winter): 1–8.

PAUL, LISSA. 1998. *Reading Other Ways.* South Woodchester, England: Thimble Press.

PETERSON, RALPH, AND EEDS, MARYANN. 1990. *Grand Conversations: Literature Groups in Action.* New York: Scholastic.

PINKNEY, JERRY. 1991. "The Artist at Work: Characters Interacting with the Viewer." *Horn Book* (March/April): 171–79.

PRELUTSKY, JACK. 1990. "In Search of the Addle-pated Paddlepuss." *The Art and Craft of Writing for Children.* William Zinsser, editor. Boston: Houghton Mifflin, pp. 97–120.

PROTHEROUGH, ROBERT. 1983. *Developing Response to Fiction.* Philadelphia: Open University Press.

QUINDLEN, ANNA. 1993. "Introduction." *Mad About Madeline: The Complete Tales of Ludwig Bemelmans.* New York: Viking.

RAINER, JOHN, AND BUNYAN, PAUL. 1996. *The Patchwork Quilt.* Sheffield, England: National Association of Teachers of English.

REDMAN, PENNY. 1995. "Finding A Balance." *Literature Circles and Response.* Bonnie Hill, Nancy Johnson, and Katherine Noe, editors. Norwood, MA: Christopher-Gordon, pp. 55–70

REIF, LINDA. 1992. "Eighth Grade: Finding the Value in Evaluation." *Portfolio Portraits.* Donald Graves and Bonnie Sunstein, editors. Portsmouth, NH: Heinemann.

ROCHMAN, HAZEL. 1995. "Against Borders." *Horn Book* (March/April): 144–57.

———. 1998. "Children's Books: *The Tulip Touch.*" *New York Times Book Review* (15 February): 26.

ROSCOE, WILLIAM. 1987. "The Butterfly's Ball and the Grasshopper's Feast" (rpt. 1807). *A Child's Garden of Delights,* Bernard McTigue, compiler. New York: Harry Abrams.

ROOSEVELT, ELEANOR. 1952. "Introduction." *Anne Frank: The Diary of a Young Girl.* Anne Frank, author; B. M. Mooyaart, translator. New York: Doubleday.

ROSEN, HAROLD. 1977. *The Politics of Literacy.* Martin Hoyles, editor. London: Writers and Readers Publishing.

———. 1984. *Stories and Meanings.* Sheffield, England: National Association of Teachers of English.

———. 1993. *Troublesome Boy.* London: English and Media Centre.

———. 1987. "The Voice of Communities." *Teaching and Teacher Education.* Margo Okazawa-Rey, James Anderson, and Rob Traver, editors. Cambridge, MA: Harvard Educational Review.

ROSENBLATT, LOUISE. 1982. "The Literary Transaction: Evocation and Response." *Theory Into Practice* 212: 268–277.

———. 1983. *Literature as Exploration.* 4th ed. New York: Modern Language Association.

———. 1991. "Literature-S.O.S.!" *Language Arts* 68: 444–48.

———. 1994. *The Reader, the Text, the Poem.* Carbondale: Southern Illinois University Press.

ROSSUCK, JENNIFER. 1997. "Banned Books: A Study of Censorship." *English Journal* 86 (February): 67–70.

SALE, ROGER. 1978. *Fairy Tales and After.* Cambridge, MA: Harvard University Press.

SAXBY, MAURICE. 1988. "At Mrs. Tucker's House." *Horn Book* (March/April): 180–85.

SAY, ALLEN. 1995. "Grandfather's Journey." *Horn Book* (January/February): 30–32.

SCHWARTZ, LYNNE SHARON. 1990. "Afterword." *A Little Princess.* Frances Hodgson Burnett, author. New York: Signet, pp. 223–35.

SENDAK, MAURICE. 1988a. "An Informal Talk": 207–214 *Caldecott & Co.* New York: Farrar.

———. 1988. "Randolph Caldecott"; 21–37. *Caldecott & Co.; Notes on Books & Pictures.* New York: Farrar.

———. 1988b. "Caldecott Medal Acceptance"; 145–156. *Caldecott & Co.* New York: Farrar,

———. 1990. "Visitors From My Boyhood." *The Art and Craft of Writing for Children.* William Zinsser, editor. Boston: Houghton Mifflin; 47–70.

SHANNON, PATRICK. 1989. "Overt and Covert Censorship of Children's Books." *New Advocate* 2 (Spring): 97–104.

SHORT, KATHY. 1995. "Foreward." *Literature Circles and Response.* Bonnie Hill, N. Johnson, and Katherine Noe, editors. Norwood, MA: Christpher-Gordon, pp. ix–xii.

SHORT, KATHY AND KAUFMAN, GLORIA. 1988. "Reading as a Process of Authority." *Creating Classrooms for Authors.* Jerome Harste and Kathy Short, authors. Portsmouth, NH: Heinemann, pp. 105–15.

SILVEY, ANITA. 1989. "The Basalization of Trade Books." *Horn Book* (September/October): 549–50.

———. 1995. *Children's Books and Their Creators.* Boston: Houghton Mifflin.

———. 1993. "Varied Carols." *Horn Book* (March/April): 132–33.

SMITH, FRANK. 1975. *Comprehension and Learning.* New York: Holt.

———. 1978. *Understanding Reading.* New York: Holt.

SMITH, LANE. 1993. "The Artist at Work." *Horn Book* (January/February): 64–70.

SOTO, GARY. 1997. "Dressing Like A Poet." *Children's Book Council Features* 50 (Spring).

———. 1990. "Foreward." *A Fire in My Hands: A Book of Poems.* New York: Scholastic, pp. 5–7.

———. 1995. "Voices of the Creators." *Children's Books and Their Creators.* Anita Silvey, editor. Boston: Houghton Mifflin, p. 614.

SOUTHEY, ROBERT. 1974. "The Story of the Three Bears" (rpt. 1837). *The Classic Fairy Tales.* Iona and Peter Opie, editors. New York: Oxford University Press, pp. 264–69.

SPEARE, ELIZABETH GEORGE. 1989. "Laura Ingalls Wilder Award Acceptance." *Horn Book* (July/August): 460–64.

———. 1995. "Voices of the Creators." *Children's Books and Their Creators.* Anita Silvey, editor. Boston: Houghton Mifflin, p. 616.

STAPLES, BRENT. 1998. "The Shifting Meanings of 'Black' and 'White.' " *New York Times* (15 November): 4, 14.

STEVENSON, DEBORAH. 1997. "Rewriting the Rules: Girls and Books." *Horn Book* (November/December): 654–59.

STOLTZ, MARY. 1993. "Letters to the Editor." *Horn Book* (September/October): 516.

STOTSKY, SANDRA. 1996. "Is the Holocaust the Chief Contribution of the Jewish People to World Civilization and History? A Survey of Leading Literature Anthologies and Reading Instructional Textbooks." *English Journal* 85 (February): 52–59.

STYLES, MORAG. 1996. "Inside the Tunnel: A Radical Kind of Reading—Picture Books, Pupils, and Post-Modernism." *Talking Pictures: Pictorial Texts and Young Readers.* Victor Watson and Morag Styles, editors. London: Hodder & Stoughton, pp. 23–47.

SUMARA, DENNIS; DAVIS, BRENT; AND VAN DER WEY, DOLORES. 1998. "The Pleasure of Thinking." *Language Arts* 76 (November): 135–43.

TAYLOR, MILDRED. 1977. "Newbery Award Acceptance." *Horn Book* (August): 401–9.

TCHUDI, STEPHEN. 1994. "Interdisciplinary English and Reforming the Schools." *English Journal* 83 (November): 54–61.

TCHUDI, STEPHEN, AND LAFER, STEPHEN. 1997. "Interdisciplinary English and the Contributions of English to an Interdisciplinary Curriculum." *English Journal* 86 (November): 21–29.

THOMAS, KEITH. 1989. "Children in Early Modern England." *Children and Their Books.* Gillian Avery and Julia Briggs, editors. Oxford, England: Clarendon Press, pp. 45–78.

TOLKIEN, J. R. R. 1965. *Tree and Leaf.* Boston: Houghton Mifflin.

TOWNSEND, JOHN ROWE. 1992. *Written for Children.* New York: Harper.

TYLER, ANNE. 1986. "Why I Still Treasure ' The Little House.' " *New York Times Book Review* (9 November): 56.

VARDELL, SYLVIA. 1991. "An Interview with Jack Prelutsky." *New Advocate.* (Spring): 101–12.

VEATCH, JEANNETTE. 1968. *How to Teach Reading with Children's Books.* New York: Richard Owen.

WALLACE, IAN. 1989. "The Emotional Link." *New Advocate* (Spring): 75–82.

WARNER, MARINA. 1994. *From the Beast to the Blonde: On Fairy Tales and Their Tellers.* New York: Farrar.

WATERLAND, LIZ. 1989. *Apprenticeship in Action: Teachers Write About Read With Me.* Liz Waterland, editor. South Woodchestser, England: Thimble Press.
———. 1989. "Reading Classics with Young Children." *Signal* 60 (September): 187–94.
———. 1988. *Read with Me: An Apprenticeship Approach to Reading.* South Woodchester, England: Thimble Press.
WATSON, VICTOR. 1992. "The Possibilities of Children's Fiction." *After Alice; Exploring Children's Literature.* Morag Styles, Eve Bearne, and Victor Watson, editors. New York: Cassell, pp. 11–24.
WEBBER, ANDREW LLOYD. 1994. *Andrew Lloyd Webber's Sunset Blvd.* American Premiere Recording. Hollywood, CA: The Really Useful Group, Ltd.
WELLS, GORDON. 1986. *The Meaning Makers.* Portsmouth, NH: Heinemann.
WELLS, ROSEMARY. "The Well-Tempered Children's Book." *The Art and Craft of Writing for Children.* Ed. William Zinsser; 123–143. Boston: Houghton Mifflin, 1990.
WHITE, E. B. 1947. "Death of a Pig" in *Essays of E. B. White.* New York: Harper and Row (reprint, 1999; Harper Collins).
WHITE, MARY LOU. 1988. "Profile: Arnold Adoff." *Language Arts* 65 (October): 584–91.
WILLIAMS, GARTH. 1987. Quoted in "Introduction." *The Horn Book's Laura Ingalls Wilder.* William Anderson, editor. Boston: Horn Book, pp. 3–7.
WINTER, MILO. 1919. *The Aesop for Children.* New York: Checkerboard Press.
WOLLMAN-BONILLA, JULIE. 1991. *Response Journals.* New York: Scholastic.
WOODSON, CARTER G. 1933. *The Mis-education of the Negro.* Washington, DC: Africa World Press.
WRIGHTSON, PATRICIA. 1986. "The Geranium Leaf." *Horn Book* (March/April): 176–85.
YENIKA-AGBAW, VIVIAN. 1997. "Taking Children's Literature Seriously: Reading for Pleasure and Social Change." *Language Arts* 74 (October): 446–53.
YEP, LAURENCE. 1997. "Laurence Yep." *Books Remembered.* Lisa Mahmoud, editor. New York: Children's Book Council, pp. 52–55.
———. 1991. *The Lost Garden.* New York: Julian Messner.
ZACK, VICKI. 1992. "It Was the Worst of Times: Learning About the Holocaust Through Literature." *Language Arts* 68 (January): 42–48.
ZELINSKY, PAUL. O. 1998. "Caldecott Medal Acceptance." *Horn Book* (July/August): 433–41.
ZIPES, JACK. 1981. *Breaking the Magic Spell.* New York: Routledge.
———. 1985. *Don't Bet on the Prince.* New York: Routledge.
———. 1985. *Fairy Tales and the Art of Subversion.* New York: Routledge.
———, TRANSLATOR. 1987. *The Complete Fairy Tales of the Brothers Grimm.* Jacob and Wilhelm Grimm, authors. New York: Bantam.
———. 1989. "The Origins of the Fairy Tale for Children." *Children and Their Books.* Gillian Avery and Julia Briggs, editors. Oxford, England: Clarendon Press: pp. 119–34.
———. 1994. "Power Rangers of Yore." *New York Times Book Review* (13 November): 30.
———. 1993. *The Trials and Tribulations of Little Red Riding Hood.* New York: Routledge.

Index